D1596707

*ONE STEP BACKWARDS*
*TWO STEPS FORWARD*

# ONE STEP BACKWARDS
# TWO STEPS FORWARD

## Soviet Society and Politics
## in the New Economic Policy

ROGER PETHYBRIDGE

CLARENDON PRESS · OXFORD
1990

Oxford University Press, Walton Street, Oxford OX2 6DP
Oxford New York Toronto
Delhi Bombay Calcutta Madras Karachi
Petaling Jaya Singapore Hong Kong Tokyo
Nairobi Dar es Salaam Cape Town
Melbourne Auckland
and associated companies in
Berlin Ibadan

Oxford is a trade mark of Oxford University Press

Published in the United States
by Oxford University Press, New York

British Library Cataloguing in Publication Data
Pethybridge, Roger
One step backwards, two steps forward: Soviet society and
politics under the New Economic Policy.
1. Soviet Union. Society, 1917–1953. Political aspects
I. Title  947.084
ISBN 0–19–821927–X

Library of Congress Cataloging in Publication Data
Pethybridge, Roger William, 1934–
One step backwards, two steps forward : Soviet society and
politics in the New Economic Policy / Roger Pethybridge.
p.    cm.
Includes bibliographical references.
1. Soviet Union—Politics and government—1917–1936.   2. Soviet
Union—Economic policy—1917–1928.   I. Title.
DK266.5.P32  1990
947.084—dc20      90–35280
ISBN 0–19–821927–X


Typeset by Latimer Trend & Company Ltd, Plymouth
Printed and bound in
Great Britain by Bookcraft Ltd.
Midsomer Norton, Bath

# *Acknowledgements*

In the preparation of this book I was helped immensely by three institutions which gave me the time and resources to pursue my research. They are the Australian National University, Canberra, the Kennan Institute, Washington, and the Economic and Social Research Council, London.

I also wish to thank Mrs Pat Yates for her long-term secretarial assistance. Amongst a plethora of other duties, she found time to type this book.

R.P.

# Contents

# *Chronology*

THIS chronology is intentionally idiosyncratic, in order to reflect the overall aim of the book, which is to recapture the general *Zeitgeist* of NEP. Events are put into a context in which the political personalities of Lenin, Stalin, and others recede.

1921

| | |
|---|---|
| February | Demobilization returned about 3 million men to civilian life. |
| | Gosplan is set up. |
| | Rebellion in Tambov guberniia begins. |
| March | Birth of NEP. |
| | Tax in kind introduced. |
| | Legalization of private trade. |
| | Kronstadt Rebellion. |
| | Tenth Party Congress. |
| | 'Resolution on Unity' condemns factional groupings within the Communist Party. |
| May | Revocation of decree nationalizing all small-scale industry. |
| | Between May and late August, no rain fell in the central and eastern Ukraine, the Middle Volga, and the steppes north of the Caucasus. |
| September | Grain harvest only 43 per cent of pre-war average overall. |
| November | Rationing abolished. |
| | Commercial accounting (*khozraschet*) introduced. |
| December | Eleventh Party Conference. |

1922

| | |
|---|---|
| February | Government decree on the collection of church valuables to aid the famine. |

| | |
|---|---|
| March | The creation of the GPU announced at the Eleventh Party Congress. |
| | All local control organs brought under the direct control of the Central Control Commission. |
| April | Stalin becomes General Secretary of the Communist Party. |
| | House arrest of Patriarch Tikhon. |
| May | The government guarantees peasants freedom of choice of land tenure. |
| | Establishment of the Soviet Procuracy. |
| | Lenin's first stroke (returns to work, October). |
| July | A new currency unit, the *chernovets*, created, and backed by gold. |
| September | Controversy starts over Georgia and the nationality question. |
| October | One pre-war kopeck equals about 100,000 nominal roubles. |
| December | Union of Soviet Socialist Republics is established. |
| | Agrarian Code issued, stimulating individual-istic tendencies. |
| | By the end of 1922 one-third of government revenue came from the food tax, one-third from direct money taxes, and one-third from the issuance of bank notes. |
| | Lenin's second stroke. |
| | Lenin's 'Testament' (postscript 4 January 1926). |
| | USSR established. |

## 1923

In 1923–4 rail transport carried 54 per cent of its 1913 traffic. In the financial year 1923–4 the budget is balanced (with a surplus in 1924–5). In the same period industrial selling-prices fell by 23.3 per cent. The Nepman was almost the sole caller in many rural areas in 1923.

| | |
|---|---|
| January/March | Lenin's last articles. Controversy over party reform. |
| March | Lenin's break with Stalin. |
| | Lenin's third stroke. |
| April | Twelfth Party Congress. |
| July | USSR Constitution published. |
| October | The 'scissors crisis' reaches its peak. |
| December | Resolution of the Politburo on Workers' Democracy. |
| | Trotsky's New Course letter. |
| | Campaign against the Opposition begins. |

## 1924

In 1924–5 only 1.82 per cent of large-scale industry was private. From about 17 or 18 million family peasant-holdings before 1917, the number rose to 23 million on comparable territory by 1924.

| | |
|---|---|
| January | Unemployment reaches 1.24 million (falling to 950,000 by 1925) out of 8½ million classified as 'workers' or 'employees' in the USSR. |
| | Death of Lenin. |
| | Thirteenth Party Conference. Opposition condemned. |
| February | Devalued roubles are converted into new roubles. |
| | 'Lenin Enrolment'. |
| May | A new drought begins, though less severe than in 1921. |
| | Lenin's will is read out to the Central Committee. |
| | Thirteenth Party Congress. |
| October | Trotsky's '*Lessons of October*' published. Anti-Trotsky campaign (to December). |
| December | Stalin proposes theory of 'Socialism in one country'. |

## 1925

The whole of the Soviet Union contains 7,448 cars, 5,500 lorries, and 263 buses.

Both wholesale and retail trade rose by about 50 per cent in 1925–6. The government bought 75 per cent of marketed grain over this period.

Over 90 per cent of all peasants belonged to village communities in this year.

NEP reaches the height of its prosperity in 1925.

By 1925 Moscow reached its pre-war population level.

There were 26 serious work accidents per 1,000 workers in Moscow. 200,000 peasants, barely 40 per cent of the number in 1907, emigrate eastwards.

| | |
|---|---|
| January | Trotsky dismissed as War Commissar. |
| April | Fourteenth Party Conference. High point of NEP. |
| | Bukharin launches the slogan 'Get Rich' to the peasants. |
| | The doctrine of 'Socialism in one country' is accepted. |
| December | Fourteenth Party Congress. Defeat of Zinoviev Opposition. |

1926

Thirty-one cities had over 100,000 inhabitants.
In 1926 rail transport surpassed the traffic levels of 1913.
In 1926–7 the general level of state procurement prices fell by about 6 per cent compared with 1925–6.
The death-rate fell to 21.4 per thousand. The number of smallpox deaths was one-fifth that in 1913.

| | |
|---|---|
| February | Zinovievists removed from leadership of the Leningrad party organization. |
| April | Plenum of the Central Committee stresses the need for capital accumulation and the strengthening of state planning. |
| | United Opposition formed by Trotsky–Zinoviev coalition. |
| July | Reduction by 10 per cent of retail prices of goods in short supply made by state industry. |
| | Removal of Zinoviev from Politburo. |
| October | Trotsky expelled from the Politburo. |
| December | The population of the USSR was 147 million, according to the census; 120 million were peasants. |
| | Two million minors were abandoned between 1920 and 1927. |
| | As late as 1927 98.3 per cent of sown areas were run by individual peasants. |
| | Sixty to seventy million were regular church-goers into 1927. |

After 1926

By 1928 there were 4 million officials, as against 600,000 in 1897.
Schooling for children aged 8 to 12 became universal after 1930.
In 1928 only 8,000 engineers and technicians of all kinds were produced by the educational system.
The party was only 20 per cent peasant in 1927.

Map of European Russia. The five guberniia capitals referred to in the text are in bold type.

# Introduction

I HAVE had the notion of trying to examine two separate years of early Soviet history. I fell upon this idea because I think it may have certain methodological advantages (as well as some disadvantages) in the treatment of Soviet politics and history. When I came to look at other historians and other countries and periods I could find very few scholars who had in fact chosen single unimportant years of past time and studied them in any detail. It has been undertaken in studies of 1848 in Western Europe, but of course 1848 was a very significant revolutionary year. In this book I take two apparently insignificant years, 1922 and 1926, and examine and compare them. I wish later to explain in some detail why I thought of taking up this approach.

Let us look first of all at contemporary observers of the year 1922 and then turn to look at how the period is treated in present-day studies. Inside the Soviet Union around the year 1922, it is true that there were a few historians, some of them professional, who were sympathetic enough to the Bolshevik cause to write about it. Unfortunately, they were so preoccupied with the struggle of living that they had little time to comment on passing events. After 1917 Professor Pokrovsky could only take off half an evening a week for historical research. He devoted most of his energies to the organization of elementary education. In any case, Pokrovsky and others urged that the study of history should be replaced by the study of what they called 'socio-economic formations'. Russian history was not taught for some years during this period in Russian schools. A very small number of active politicians turned their minds to general surveys. One of these was Zinoviev, who wrote his lectures on the history of the Communist Party in

1922, and published them in the following year.[1] Unfortunately, his work and that of others has been rather neglected by both Bolshevik and Western historians. It was censored in the Stalinist period.

If we turn to look at subsequent Soviet histories which included a discussion of the early years of the New Economic Policy (NEP), we discover a pattern that is so well known that it hardly needs elaborating upon. The historian in Russia came to be seen as a fighter, an official whose views were subject to swift change due to pressures from the ruling élite and from the censor. This was Whig history with a vengeance. Pokrovsky had once written that history was the most political of all the sciences, and so indeed it became in the Soviet Union. At least more than a science, it was a kind of scripture. Later waves of Soviet history writing overwhelmed in their bulk and their propaganda the small amount of serious contemporary material. The Marxist view of history has coloured all Soviet writings. This implies—at least for non-Marxists—that there is a certain heavy teleological and quasi-determinist influence at work. These trends, if allowed for, of course add to the swell of the Whig interpretation of history. Thus Leninism as a doctrine appeared only after Lenin had died and Lenin's contemporaries had disappeared. Even Pokrovsky had to admit in 1924 that he was not familiar with Lenin's writings on history. Lenin's name hardly appeared in 1922, or indeed in any other year between 1917 and 1924 in the party theoretical journals.

Were contemporary Western observers of early NEP any more perspicacious than the Russians? This is doubtful. Unlike the French Revolution, the Russian Revolution did not take place at the centre of European culture in close proximity to understanding nations. The Russian language was little known abroad in 1917. The Allied missions withdrew all their personnel during the autumn of 1918 and the blockade of Soviet-controlled territory severed most of the means of communication. Foreign correspondents were relegated to Baltic listening posts like Riga, Reval, and Helsingfors. There were a few small delegations from the West, but very few of them wrote much of lasting value apart from Bertrand Russell,

[1]  G. Zinoviev, *History of the Bolshevik Party—A Popular Outline* (Moscow, 1923).

H. G. Wells, and Arthur Ransome. Given the controversial nature of the Revolution, there was an unfortunate trend of political opinion towards opposite extremes outside Russia. Serious writers took up maximalist and non-serious positions which have subsequently seemed to have been rather laughable. If one looks at *The Times* for the year 1922, and therefore one is looking at the serious press, the impression is rather a poor one. Even Bernard Pares, the outstanding expert on Soviet Russia, wrote on 5 January 1922 that Bolshevism was dead. He called for Britain to help in the capitalist reconstruction of Russia and he warned that the Germans should be kept out of business dealings with the Russians. Most of the articles in *The Times* for that year completely missed the important events and dwelt on superficial matters like the Moscow races, the reopening of the Nizhnii Novgorod fair, the selling off of the Tsar's wine-cellar abroad, and the refusal on the part of the New York customs authorities to allow Isadora Duncan into the USA. It was obviously very difficult to find serious items to write up for the press. One correspondent even maintained that as it was completely impossible to take photographs, so paintings were run off and smuggled out in order to portray what Russia looked like at the time.

It is natural that contemporary observers were subject to acute myopia in their examination of early Soviet history. But is the situation any better when that same year is examined from our own Olympian heights in 1990? The perspective has widened, but the prejudices and lack of judgement remain. The Whig interpretation of history, as Herbert Butterfield aptly named it, is also rampant in Western studies of Soviet history. The past is far too much evaluated in terms of the present. This is a universal pitfall to which all historians are subject, but I think that it is particularly applicable to the Soviet scene. The Revolution of 1917 succeeded in making conservative Western historians even more hidebound and converted many of those in the centre and even on the moderate left wing into pseudo-conservatives. I am thinking of Western historians who were writing on Russia in the 1920s and 1930s. Horrified views of this kind had two main biases. The first one was, in the words of an article in *The Nation* published in London on 18 October 1920, 'They chose to picture Bolshevism as a fabulous monster; to exaggerate its vices, or to invent them ... to present its work as a carnival of human malice and corruption.' The second main bias was, in good conservative tradition, to see continuity on every point between Soviet reality and the Tsarist past. After the nervous honeymoon of the Second World War period, a new genera- tion of historians coupled up with the previous one and only served to add to the Whig interpretation. These were the manipulators of the totalitarian model, which certainly had its uses, but it tended to see Stalinism as the apogee of a creeping authoritarianism which by the 1930s was converted into a full- blooded totalitarian system. A kind of teleological determinism also invaded most studies of the near-static evolution of totalitarianism. The model was conceived of in a kind of Darwinian way as an inevitable evolutionary growth like a slowly spreading fungus. Senior Western historians would object now to being labelled conservatives, and indeed with some justice the majority of them might better be classified as political liberals, but all the same it appears that they have a sort of vested interest in their interpretation of Soviet history. In their turn they wish to label Stalinism and its antecedents as conservative in the sense of being restrictive. It is interesting to speculate whether they will turn tail if the thaw in domestic Soviet policies continues.

Recently there have been various attempts to counteract this teleological determinism. It has come on two fronts. The first is the Trotskyist front. Backed by strong ideological motives, this group tries to see a complete hiatus between Leninist and Stalinist methods. The second and more scholarly approach deserves more serious consideration. Historians of this group too claim, and with some justice, that the continuity effect has been exaggerated. Unfortunately they fall into the counter- trap of trying to prove that there is no continuity whatsoever between Leninism and Stalinism and between the 1920s and the 1930s. I agree with some of their arguments, but not with all of them. They, and others too, argue against the idea that Bolshevik ideology can be seen as an element of continuity. In the first place it is not as monolithic as has been made out. Secondly, ideology can influence events in many diverse ways, and in the other direction events can often influence ideology. I have tried to show in my book *The Social Prelude to Stalinism* how the military culture of the Civil War infused many new minor patterns into Bolshevik ideological thought. In the third place ideology could and did change radically as the Soviet period progressed. These assertions may sound too obvious, but perhaps they need to be repeated. Another weapon of the traditionalists is that of the central party organization as outlined in Lenin's *What Is To Be Done?* There are two major snags with this rather overdone interpretation of *Chto delat'*. Some scholars have shown the main aim of *What Is To Be Done?* was not to lay down a centralized party organization for all time. The second snag is that party organization did change enormously over the years after 1903. Another charge on the part of the anti-continuity group to which I also subscribe is that NEP was so pluralist in its activities that it cannot be seen as leading in an almost deterministic manner to what happened in the 1930s. To take only one example, the great economic debate was conducted on a knife-edge, and the argument might have gone in many different ways. However, like all crusaders, the anti-continuity group goes too far in its condemnation of the Whig interpretation. I have been taken to task by one member of this group in his review of my book, *The Social Prelude to Stalinism*. Despite the fact that I myself warned against the dangers of Whig history on two occasions in that book, I am interpreted as seeing Stalinism as the necessary and inexorable outcome of Bolshevism in power. Now I admit that the word 'Prelude' in the title does assume a certain amount of teleological methodology, but I maintained in that book, which after all was devoted mainly to the social background to political events from the Revolution until the final rise of Stalin, that it is impossible to ignore the enormous weight of Russian social backwardness which impinged on the 1930s as well as on the 1920s, and which was by no means swept aside before the rise of Stalin. When one deals with political and economic events, it is possible to notice turning-points of some precision and changes of great import. The *social* interpretation of history must always be evolutionary in nature to make any sense, and one cannot divide Leninism from Stalinism into watertight compartments so far as social considerations are concerned. Of course the amalgam of political, economic, and social developments can never be dissolved. Only for the purposes of scholarly examination can a temporary dissection be made before the animal is put together again.

It may be thought that so great and idiosyncratic a historian as E. H. Carr might stand apart from both camps in this debate, but in my personal opinion this is not the case. If one wants to get to the heart of Carr's view of history, one has to look at his work *What Is History?* Listen to this quotation from it, keeping in mind the probable fact that Carr believed that the Bolshevik model was for the most part rational and also fruitful.

We distinguish between rational and accidental causes. The former since they are potentially applicable to other countries, other periods and other conditions, lead to fruitful generalisations and lessons can be learned from them; they serve the end of broadening and deepening our understanding . . . it is precisely this notion of an end in view which provides the key to our treatment of causation in history; and this necessarily involves value judgements . . . only the future can provide the key to the interpretation of the past . . . the historian's judgement cannot rest on some fixed and immovable standard of judgement existing here and now, but only on the standard which is laid up in the future and is evolved as the course of history advances. History acquires meaning and objectivity only when it establishes a coherent relation between past and future.[2]

Carr undoubtedly admired the Bolshevik model as it was around the year 1917. Since that model was not merely political, but also social and economic in its scope, given its Marxist basis, it was able to cover all aspects of a given society. Carr sees that model as fact, cause, and discoverer of history. As discoverer of history, the Bolshevik model selects, partly embodies, and also in particular limits the reportable causes of only as much of political, economic and social structure and change as are specified within itself. So at this point a deterministic element creeps in. Since neither certainly Nepmen nor until a very late stage the *kustari* were specified within that model, the Bolshevik programme largely ignored them. Carr also did the same in his turn, and indeed many subsequent historians have also done so. We still need a complete detailed history of both these social and economic phenomena.

[2] E. H. Carr, *What is History?* (London, 1961), pp. 101, 117, 124.

However, some critics have been unfair in claiming that Carr is uncritical of the Bolshevik model. One only has to read his brilliant chapter on class and party in order to deny this accusation. But what is true is the fact that in concentrating so much on the Bolshevik model, Carr excludes many other major and minor models, and here again determinism creeps in. He has often been accused, and rightly in my opinion, of neglecting the political aspirations of the Social Revolutionaries and the Mensheviks. Carr does offer us one major alternative to Stalinism, but this is a very significant alternative in its choice. He worries about the fate of Russia and whether Russia would follow that of France by getting involved in a Thermidor. This is in a sense hardly a real model, since Carr throws it up as a bogey which he subsequently knocks down. He knocks it down by alluding to what he calls the Bolsheviks' inventiveness for future progress and their ability to prevent the Soviet Union from settling back into bourgeois capitalism. He goes on to assert that without Stalin's revolution from above, 'Lenin's revolution would have run out in the sand. In this sense Stalin continued and fulfilled Leninism . . .' Here we are back fairly and squarely in the continuity camp. Another difficulty with Carr's interpretation at this point is that what he calls Bolshevik inventiveness can also be construed as fantasy. At various stages and on various subjects after 1917 the Bolsheviks soon diverged from their close approximation to reality as of the revolutionary year. If one looks at the course of Soviet history from the stance of post-1928, one might as easily take the long-standing model of Russian tyranny instead. This was indeed the model generally adopted by both conservatives and liberals from that time on. Carr's position was rather like that of someone who excused the short-term consequences of the early surgeons' bloody assaults on their patients, since the experiments were to lead to brilliant advances for the whole of mankind. This is a very reasonable position to have adopted if one had lived in the years shortly after 1917, and indeed into the 1930s, through lack of close knowledge of what was happening at that time in the USSR. But since the surgeons' bloody assaults continued into the 1950s, the model adopted by Carr seemed to have less persuasiveness. Unlike de Tocqueville, Carr did not seem to be able to bring himself to condemn the fact of the Revolution, given his sincere admiration of the force of values behind it.

It is necessary to try to pin-point the defects in Carr's approach to the study of Soviet history, since his grasp of detail is so great that he is apt to mesmerize us into accepting his hidden iceberg theories. I am quite sure from my perusal of the years 1922 and 1926, that alone of all historians, Carr has a grasp of the detailed events of those years, and particularly of the relationship between events.

Let us return to the Soviet treatment of NEP. Earlier Soviet histories can still be of use if they are based on a general concept of laws and are not entirely bound by the necessity to produce specific political results at any given time. The long discussions about the so-called Asian mode of production could be mentioned as an instance in this context. But the combination of the later censorship of early histories and their great paucity combined with the enormous and heavily prejudiced weight of later histories meant that the latter-day historians have prevailed in the Soviet Union. If it can be maintained that Soviet historians have seen the detailed development of the early Soviet period through a glass darkly, then one can hardly expect the Bolsheviks themselves—I mean the politicians rather than the intellectuals and historians—to have had a better grasp of what was really going on in their country. I am not here merely expressing my own personal prejudice as a political historian against the pragmatic politician. I think that there were many well-known reasons why leading Bolsheviks were to a great extent incapable of taking a broad and detached view of the events taking place around them in the 1920s. Not only were they extremely busy men and too fanatical to consider alternatives; they were in fact ignorant in several ways of aspects of life in their own country. Many Bolsheviks had lived abroad for years before 1917 and particularly through the crucial years 1914–17 when Russia changed so fast. When they did return to Russia, the Bolsheviks could not rely on statistics of any scholarly value right through the 1920s. The upheaval of the Revolution and the backwardness of the country saw to that. Living in the largest country in the world with all its variety, the Bolsheviks could not rely on statistics of any scholarly value right through the 1920s. The upheaval of the Revolution and the backwardness of the country saw to that. Living in the largest country in the world with all its variety, the Bolsheviks were townsmen in a sea of peasants who considered them almost like Martians, as men 'from the centre'. The isolation of the Bolsheviks became worse as the Revolution progressed. It is well known that the links between the *apparat* and the proletariat weakened substantially soon after 1917. Military recruitment, disease, and lack of employment and food in the cities caused urban depopulation on a vast scale. Most of the men lost by the Red Army were workers. The Bolshevik élite was even isolated further from the pre-revolutionary intelligentsia, out of which many members of the Bolshevik party had emerged. After the October Revolution the intelligentsia was deprived of many of its more brilliant representatives, who now found themselves too far to the right to stay in Russia. The middle and the left in the guise of the fellow-travellers and *Proletkul't* both caused embarrassment to the Bolshevik leaders. By the 1920s the old Bolshevik intellectuals were in some ways more rather than less culturally isolated than they had been prior to 1917. Psychological motives were also at work. Even if in some ways the actual state of affairs could be properly examined in NEP, it was often neglected in favour of a study of the future or of the foreign situation. Looking at the future is a typical pastime of the young, and the Bolshevik Party was very young shortly after the Revolution. Another pressing reason was that the existing state of society seemed such a rebuttal of Bolshevik aspirations that it was more comforting to neglect it by looking to the future. Abortive, short-term practical experiments like workers' control in the years prior to NEP had taught the Bolshevik policy-makers to divorce their theoretical ideals more and more from the recalcitrant nature of society and to plan optimistically for the future on more abstract lines. In doing this they were only reverting to what they had been used to doing during the long years out of power before 1917. In the realm of imagination, Maiakovsky reflected this impatience of the Bolsheviks with menial, customary daily life (*byt*). In the first version of *Mystery-Bouffe*, completed in September 1918, Maiakovsky combined a brief account of the Revolution with a vision of an imminent Utopia on earth. It is significant that the second version of the play, dating from 1920, revealed a considerable decline of Maiakovsky's hopes for social revolution.

Maiakovsky committed suicide, but the party had to go on. The Bolshevik politicians produced far more than contemporary Soviet historians did. They gave endless speeches to the public and at conferences, and wrote a great number of ephemeral articles. For all the reasons listed above they tended to play down or even ignore those aspects of Soviet life of which they remained in partial ignorance. The result led to a reification of many aspects of reality. The most famous example by the early 1920s was the continuing belief on the part of the Bolshevik Party that it consisted of as well as represented the proletariat. If one looks at Zinoviev's lectures which I have already mentioned and which were published in 1923, one can see quite clearly how he is worried by the growing divergence between reality and theory on the question of the proletariat's relationship to the Party. Thus he comforts himself by saying at the outset that 'it is a simple concept that our party is a part of the working class ... forged over decades of theoretical and practical struggle'.[3] His own words belie his position. The integration of the proletariat in the Bolshevik Party remained at the level of a concept which had been forged over decades of theoretical struggle. Later in the same lecture Zinoviev gives us a subheading entitled 'The pre-history of the Russian proletariat'.[4] Here is an excellent example of the Whig interpretation of history. The Ur-proletariat is said to have arisen in a disturbance dating from 1796 among Kazan' factory workers. The same sort of optimistic theorizing is clearly evident with regard to the peasantry at the same time. When Lenin at the introduction of NEP looked for a new and closer relationship between the Party, the working class and the peasantry on a political as well as an economic basis, he made out a case in 1921 that 'statistics show quite definitely that there has been a levelling out, an equalisation, in the village ... the peasantry in general has acquired the status of the middle peasant'.[5] This was to prove to be a very bad case of the

[3] Zinoviev, op. cit., p. 7.
[4] Ibid., p. 18.
[5] V. I. Lenin, *Collected Works*, vol. 32 (Moscow, 1965), p. 216.

Emperor's clothes, as subsequent writers like T. Shanin have
shown in his description of the cyclical mobility of the peasantry throughout the 1920s.[6] Another theoretical concept,
that of *smychka*, was now proclaimed to be the hinge which
would link the middle peasant to the proletariat embedded in
the Bolshevik Party. The theory was only too often accepted as
reality, although the small number of party agents that were at
the grass-roots level knew that this was not the case. Not only
was it virtually impossible for the Party itself to establish
relationships at the local level; even peasant teachers and ex-
Red-Army peasants were ostracized because of their intellectual and administrative contacts respectively with 'the Centre'.

Let us turn to another abstract generalization which has
been much used and abused in this century in the description
of social and political situations. I mean the concept of
bureaucracy. Here again we find the Bolsheviks relying on it
heavily as a useful abstraction. Because Lenin and other
Bolsheviks found it so difficult to diagnose the social reasons for
slow political progress, bureaucracy could be used as a kind of
self-causing evil at which to launch perpetual attacks. Now
even in the 1990s sociologists find it hard to pin down a proper
definition of the word 'bureaucracy'. I have spent the greater
part of one chapter in my book *The Social Prelude to Stalinism*
trying to describe the struggle for a definition of bureaucracy
both inside and outside the Soviet Union. It can hardly be
expected of Lenin and his colleagues in the early 1920s to have
had the sociological expertise that is now available to us. They
had little leisure to read Weber and Durkheim. However, we
should not exaggerate the speed with which the Party always
ran to generalized reifications. Their vision of international
revolution is interesting in this respect, since they registered a
gradual retreat from abstractions into detailed realities. It is
interesting to note all the same that the concept of 'Socialism
in one country' did not arise as a fully fledged generalization
until 1924: it took several years of gradually accumulating
facts from the international situation to push the Party in
general and Stalin in particular into dropping one concept but

[6] T. Shanin, *The Awkward Class: Political Sociology of Peasantry in a Developing Society:
Russia 1910–1925* (Oxford, 1972).

unfortunately adopting this new one which contained its own reified notions, though perhaps to a rather less extreme degree.

We have now briefly surveyed some Soviet and Western distortions, both at the time and subsequently, of the early development of Russia after the 1917 Revolution. If even only one-quarter of my criticisms are valid concerning their defects then much remains to be done by those of us living now and working on the Soviet period. How are we to set about it? Perhaps one way of digging away and uncovering the obliterating sands of time and determinist prejudice might be to take a very short period of Soviet history, preferably one that has not been studied *per se* before, and look at it in detail. Let us take the years 1922 and 1926 as an example. This might at least liberate us more easily from preconceptions. If one takes the years 1917, 1921, or 1928, then one is surrounded by so many well-worn arguments that it is difficult to clear one's head. What are the possible advantages of confining oneself to the interpretation of two years of early Soviet history? I think that the chief advantage would be the leisure to look at in descriptive and analytical terms the complex connections between economic, social, and cultural history in order to see them in the round. It would help us to rebel against the traditional dominance of political and economic history in the interpretation of Soviet Russia. I believe also that one would have the time to learn something from geographers, sociologists, linguists, and even psychologists. Such a method which is taken in part from that of the *Annales*, has been applied to non-Russian history, chiefly by French historians, but the only thoroughgoing example I can think of in the Soviet context is the volume by Marc Ferro on the 1917 Revolution.[7] In Britain and in the USA, in my view, there are still considerable 'tunnels' at work in the sense that J. H. Hexter refers to them. Great barriers are thrown up between different disciplines. In Britain in particular there is a broad rift between social history and intellectual history. If one took a single year in early Soviet history, it would not be in the interests of a mere gimmick or of trying to find a short cut. In fact the opposite would be the case. It would be an attempt to achieve a more total and more

[7] *La Révolution de 1917: Octobre* (Paris, 1977).

human kind of history. The older school of political and constitutional history was unsatisfactory not necessarily because it was laborious and painstaking, but often because it lacked these qualities and was too prone to over-simplify conclusions.

Since I seem to be indulging myself in abstractions, I had better give illustrations of what I would like to do myself. One particular ambition, though perhaps a difficult one, would be to try to give a much wider local and national minority coverage. Many writers on Soviet history, including myself, have paid lip-service to the many divergencies from Great-Russian and Moscow- and Leningrad-based norms, but unless historians have been writing explicitly on the nationalities, the peasantry, or the federal system of the Soviet Union, they have in fact virtually concentrated on the old Great Russian heartland. So many works on Soviet history remind one of what Michelet wrote in the preface to his *Histoire de France*, in 1869. 'Without a geographical basis, the people, the makers of history, seem to be walking on air, as in those Chinese pictures where the ground is wanting. The soil, too, must not be looked upon only as a scene of action. Its influence appears in a hundred ways, such as food, climate, etc.' In the past there have always been two staple objections to such a project. In the first place it has often been averred that there simply are not sufficient local sources available. In the second place, scholars like Carr have stressed that it is no use relying on one local source, say the Smolensk Archives, because one only receives a highly atypical picture. It may be difficult to get round these objections, but with reference to the years 1922 and 1926 it may not be entirely impossible. For instance, besides the Smolensk Archives for 1922, we have two most full and reliable surveys in great detail done by Yakovlev for the peasantry of the Russian Central Agricultural Region and also for the Poltava guberniia in the Ukraine.[8]

Another area that might be well deserving of further investigation is that of law. By this I do not mean the retailing of higher political and economic degrees, nor even the publication of laws on social and criminal behaviour, but rather on the

---

[8] I. Iakovlev, *Derevnia kak ona est* (Moscow, 1923).

practical effect of those laws. John Hazard has written a most interesting book in this vein, *Settling Disputes in Soviet Society*, but this covers a large period of time. It would be interesting to delve into the day-by-day reverberations of legislation for the year 1922. In the study of a revolutionary society, it is of little use to record legislation without going on to see to what extent it was enacted. This was notoriously the error made by the Webbs in the 1930s, but it had already been made by Kerensky when he edited those two large volumes of documents, most of them of a legislative nature, on the Revolution of 1917. As Professor Mosse noted in a review of these documents,[9] Kerensky made the typical lawyer's mistake compounded with that of the optimistic politician who happened to be in partial control for much of 1917. He neglected to see whether the legislation enacted was ever carried through. Of course it was not. This kind of error has often been made in subsequent Soviet and Western histories, right up until the present day.

Devotion to one particular year in Soviet history could afford leisure in other ways than geographical, periodical, and social coverage. One could also apply a wider variety of source materials. For example, more use could be made than is normally the case of *belles-lettres*. I cannot go here into the advantages and disadvantages of the use of *belles-lettres* for the illustration of history, but I could refer to the interesting comments of Gerschenkron and Koutaissova on this subject.[10]

The study of two single years might be advantageous in another way. Connections between men, ideas, and events might be noticed that have been passed over in more general histories of entire periods. It might be easier to detect how far political moves in 1922 were polarized round political events and ideas, and to that extent insulated from social development and from the masses. To come back to the particular again, it seems to me useful to undertake a study of the collected works of leading Bolsheviks over a single year's span. In my view serious distortions have been made in the inter-

[9] W. E. Mosse, 'The Russian Provisional Government of 1917', in *Soviet Studies* (Apr. 1964).

[10] The best of these two is A. Gerschenkron, 'A Neglected Source of Economic Information on Soviet Russia', in *American Slavic and East European Review*, 9 (1950), pp. 1–19.

pretation of Soviet history through examining the whole of the collected works of, say, Lenin, and thereby crediting him with too much coherence and also, incidentally, with the memory of an elephant. But at least this pitfall would not be a danger if one took a single year. And indeed, when one examines Lenin's writings for the year 1922, new connections seem to come to light. For instance, his antipathy to what he conceived of as large-scale, central bureaucracy is set in direct contrast to his advocation of peasant co-operation, which he took up at this time. For the future at least he was looking for small-scale administration at the grass roots which would eventually fit into an efficient large-scale administrative network. Even if a genius remains coherent within the theoretical scope of a year's writings, it is not wise to conclude with the historian's natural logic that Lenin's actions also reflected the same coherence. In May 1922 Lenin incorporated discretionary repressive acts into the whole of the Soviet legal system, just at the time when he was worrying most in his writings about centralization and its authoritative overtones.

Interesting relationships between other sets of events need to be explored for this period. One example is the question of migration of the Russian population in 1922 and in the neighbouring years. By migration I mean not only internal migration due to famine, the results of the Civil War, the search for employment, etc., but also the diaspora of the Russian nation throughout Europe. The comings and goings of the temporary exiles, the fellow-travellers, and the like, set up a whole network of political, social, and cultural problems that need closer examination. Apart from this instance of grand connections there are coincidences on a much smaller scale which may be of some interest. For example, it is widely known that in the year in which Lenin suffered his first stroke there were many other leading Bolsheviks who were almost as ill. Zinoviev was ordered to take a rest by his doctors. Lunacharsky was seriously ill with heart trouble. Rykov was worn out with his work as Lenin's substitute on the Council of Labour and Defence. Leaders of Russia, like society at large, were all slowly convalescing from the crisis of the Civil War.

Another advantage of tackling two single years might be that through thoroughly immersing oneself in as many subjects and types of sources as possible, one might emerge with a more sensitive feeling of what has been called 'the inner life of the Revolution'.[11] It is notoriously difficult to grasp such a fragile plant as this and to keep it alive for one's readers without it becoming a pressed flower, a cardboard image. Yet it is worth trying to search for this. Psychological phenomena are so fleeting that they escape at once through the gaps of time, leaving small trace in history. As for all of medieval history, so in Soviet history, we have been left with what Southern has called 'bad' and 'good' kings. There are many aspects of the psychology of Lenin or Stalin which we have lost for ever, but some may still be gleaned. When we turn to the study of the society as a whole and its mentality, the difficulties loom even larger. It is never easy to trace the *Zeitgeist*, but it is even harder in the case of Russia, since the *Zeitgeist* as of 1922 can only refer to a minute élite isolated above the submerged dark people. We are in acute danger of falling into facile descriptions and even reverting to those first students of Russia like Mérimée, with their vague allusions to the 'Slav soul'. Nevertheless, it is something that should be attempted, and although there are obvious disadvantages in the idea of a single historian trying to cover so many different aspects of one year, yet on this topic it may be less of a hindrance, since in order to have the feel of the year in a psychological sense, it is better for one observer to be submitted to nuances from all quarters of society.

In the study of history, the mental climate of an age has often been attached too artificially to the psychological make-up of the leading figure of that age. For want of sufficient materials, this has sometimes happened with regard to the history of the Soviet Union. Perhaps Isaac Deutscher is some-what at fault here. His biography of Trotsky is far more subtle in this way than his treatment of Stalin. Deutscher wrote of Stalin that 'two years after the end of the Civil War Russian society already lived under Stalin's virtual rule'.[12] As a devoted student of Marxism, Deutscher should have remembered the

[11] A. Berkman, *The Bolshevik Myth: Diary 1920–1922* (New York, 1925), p. vii. He wrote that most treatments deal with 'the fall and rise of institutions, of the new State and its structure, of constitutions and laws—of the exclusively *external* manifestations, which nearly make me forget the living millions who continue to exist, to be, under all changing conditions.'

[12] I. Deutscher, *Stalin—A Political Biography* (London, 1949), p. 228.

remark by Plekhanov that 'our imagination becomes confused and it seems to us that without Napoleon [Stalin] the social movements upon which his power and influence were based could not have taken place.'[13] In this statement Deutscher is not only subsuming far too much of Russian society and politics in the name of Stalin; he is also indulging in a prime example of the Whig interpretation of history. By concentrating on isolated periods in Soviet history, it might be easier to avoid such a mistake. In the same year to which Deutscher's quotation about Stalin refers, a highly intelligent member of the intelligentsia living in Moscow tells us that 'the only time I remember hearing [Stalin's name] was when Varvara Mikailovna told me with some pride that she was making a dress for Allilueva, and that the person was the wife of Stalin— "someone very senior in the Kremlin".'[14]

To sum up therefore, the study of two short periods may help us to examine critically the many ready-made generalizations which we have borrowed, knowingly or not, from historians of the Soviet period. Many writers do not realize that they are borrowing generalizations and even deny that they are making any new ones. This is probably nonsense. Every scholar borrows from works of the past. It is better to realize what generalizations he has received and to try and examine them critically as I have tried to do in the first half of this introduction. Our job should be to refine these borrowed generalizations by any means—definition, qualification, reservation, conformity to known facts, psychology, statistics, matched comparisons, etc. In the end we might even originate and advance some restricted, tentatively acceptable generalizations of our own. We should have the humility to realize that they are generalizations and that they will include new distortions, even if they get rid of some of the old ones.

Now I have explained my method, I should also mention why I have chosen the years 1922 and 1926 for my research. I have already said that I am looking for apparently less significant years than those that have been mulled over many times before. A second reason is that the year 1922 seems to be,

---

[13] G. V. Plekhanov, *The Role of the Individual in History* (London, 1940), p. 50.
[14] E. Fen, *Remember Russia 1915–1925* (London, 1973), p. 286.

as far as I can see at present, a kind of breathing-space between revolution and civil war on the one hand and the development of NEP on the other. The relative positions of the Bolshevik leaders were all in a fluid state; Lenin in decline, Stalin on the ascent, Trotsky duck-shooting in the provinces, and dreaming intellectual dreams. Articulate figures were reflecting both on the past and on the future. We have seen how Zinoviev was composing one of the earliest histories of the Party. Lenin was recapitulating the recent past and worrying about the growing danger of what he called bureaucracy. Stalin was making more mundane administrative plans for his personal future. Many developments of great moment passed through the year, but few reached a cumulative point. Of course the appointment of Stalin as General Secretary, although it did not seem important at the time, was crucial. But there are few other turning-points on which one can suitably fix. The vestiges of pre-1917 society still hung heavily over the scene in many ways.

Like 1922, 1926 was a Janus-headed year, looking anxiously backwards and forwards whilst representing within itself a state of flux exceptional even by the standards of early Soviet history. The year 1925 was the economic apex of NEP, though this moderate summit of achievement was to have no lasting stability. In 1926 the Party decided to embark on a grandiose scheme of industrialization. The way in which this was to be achieved was not settled finally during the year. Stalin's sole ascendancy was still not clear. The Bolshevik leaders continued to be at loggerheads with one another in a shifting series of personal coalitions that had been changing in rapid succession since 1922. Trotsky's star was on the wane, but the comparative roles of the proletariat and the peasantry in the coming industrial campaign had still not been sorted out. As in 1922, no developments on any political, social, or economic front reached a cumulative point. Only at its very outset and in its final moments should NEP be conceived of on a narrow corridor with determined aims leading in a clear direction from one political and economic mould to another. For the rest of the time it was as unstable as an ocean of mercury which might flow quickly in any number of ways as a result of political fiats from above and socio-economic pressures from below.

The following chapters attempt to juxtapose these two

gigantic pressures and to show how they interacted, or often ignored each other. I may well be accused of formlessness, but I am merely trying to give a reflection of the huge, unstable variety of Russia in the 1920s. For too long scholars have tried to impose over-logical *Ordnung* on the near-chaos that was NEP. In doing this they have merely repeated the errors of the brilliant Bolshevik intellectual leaders who were compelled to do the same in order to stop the regime and the country from falling apart. At least they had a vital practical motive for over-generalizing. Armchair academics have no such excuse. We should remember Wittgenstein's dictum: 'A clear picture of a fuzzy object is a fuzzy picture.'

This book reverses the normal method of starting at the top of the body politic. Chapters 1 to 3 proceed from the local geography, economy, and society of three provincial areas of Russia in 1922 to political consequences and actions. Chapters 4 and 5 deal respectively with aspects of communications and control mechanisms between the localities and the nation's twin centres, Petrograd and Moscow, whose conditions and presiding thinkers are looked at in Chapters 6, 7, and 8. Chapter 7 serves also as a bridge in time between 1922 and 1926. Chapter 9 examines linking institutions and agents between the hub and the periphery in 1926. Chapters 10, 11, and 12 look at life in three provincial areas in 1926. Thus one of many possible trajectories of NEP is mapped out. No conceivable trajectory could either be called typical or atypical, since there was nothing at all typical about NEP, apart from its flimsy economic foundations and premises as formulated hastily in 1921. A trajectory is a curve described by a body under the action of many complex forces. This book is no more than a shooting star set in a vast canopy that remains dark to the observer. There is still so much work waiting to be done on early Soviet history.

I have chosen this particular trajectory because it starts from the social bedrock and ends there. On its solid but very varied basis were built all those Soviet control systems that are treated in Chapters 4, 5, and 9. The central Chapters 6, 7, and 8 form the highest points, in cultural, political, and social terms respectively. They were the moving forces set above provincial society and brooding over it. Perhaps the main contention of this book is that the edges both affected and evaded the thoughts and the actions of the centre more than has been realized or studied so far. I have not always adhered strictly to the years 1922 and 1926, sometimes in order to paint in significant backgrounds, at other times to dwell on the significant retrospections and predictions of Bolshevik leaders. Chapter 7 deals in particular with thoughts of this kind.

Rarely are the prophecies that I examine compared with what actually happened after 1926. This is done on purpose so as to avoid the Whig interpretation of history. For the same reason I do not discuss a number of articles that have appeared recently in the Soviet press on NEP's place in Soviet historiography. Almost without exception, these articles obfuscate more than they enlighten, since they set out to try to prove that the reforms of the Gorbachev era have a close relationship to those of NEP and to the ideas of Bukharin in particular. This is yet another example of hopeful Whig interpretation and vast over-simplification, not to talk of anachronism. Indeed, one of the aims of writing this book is to try to present an unvarnished view of NEP, based on contemporary sources, untinged by all later manipulations. This is all the more important to do at a time when Gorbachev and the Chinese are resurrecting NEP in a reified form as a myth for our time. I cite China, since in 1982 I was invited to lecture at the Chinese Academy in Peking on the subject of NEP, just at the moment when the Party there was using NEP as a reason or excuse for retreating into semi-capitalism, before the Russians did likewise. I was struck by the way in which Chinese scholars and politicians in 1982 were not interested in the enormous complexities of NEP, but only in its facile and distorted message for them. Something similar to this is happening in the USSR today.

In a previous book, *The Social Prelude to Stalinism*, I adopted quite a different approach to NEP, treating it in the light of what was to follow in the political sense. In this work I concentrate on society rather than on politics, and examine the periphery more than the centre.

I think I should conclude by pointing out some of the disadvantages of the method I have chosen. It is true that I will not have to represent the past in terms of movement through time as is usually the case. I will have less difficulty in achieving the usual balance between narrative and analysis, between a chronological approach and an approach by topic, that is the bane of most historians. But on the other hand I will probably forfeit the fundamental historical essence of showing change through time. Continuity after all is the historian's stock-in-trade. Scientific experiments can be isolated, but history is often seen as a seamless web. Given my method, I will also probably find myself over-accommodating to what is unique and contingent and prone to play down the method of the social sciences. Social scientists nowadays look for recurrent patterns which can be examined quantitatively. It would be hard to find a model or models of this kind for a single year of history. The closer one draws to one's subject, the more confusing and multiform it will probably seem. But I could counteract some of the disadvantages by comparing 1922 with 1926 as barometers of NEP. I may therefore also tend to exaggerate that aspect that I have called the inner life of the Revolution. Thus I may avoid the frying-pan of Whig teleology only to fall into the fire of discontinuous chaos. That is why I shall spend a good deal of time exploring prophecies, retrodictions, and speculations in general about the past and future indulged in by political leaders and, wherever I can find them, by representatives of the common Russian people. This should help to relieve the myopia a little.

# 1. *The West*

THE Western borderlands of Soviet Russia were the nearest to
Moscow of all frontier regions, yet they were relatively neglected by historians and travellers alike.[1] Even by 1926 party
contacts between the capital and Smolensk were to remain
mostly at the written rather than at the human level. Arnold
Toynbee once argued that it is the 'barbaric' vital periphery
that finally topples a declining civilization, but this maxim
does not hold for the Russian Revolution. The political
centre suffered a series of heart attacks from 1905 onwards, of
which the body of society as a whole was only to become fully
aware after 1928. Despite Lenin's theory of national self-
determination, the new Soviet Union still embraced the great
bulk of the old imperial domains, including minorities like the
Georgians and the Ukrainians who had been civilized for
centuries before the denizens of what was to become Muscovy.
After the Civil War Bolshevik control expanded easily from its
bastion which had been reduced to the size of medieval
Muscovy. The Tambov revolt and other peasant disturbances
were soon contained and squashed.

This does not mean that the vast provinces of Russia should
be ignored, although they usually are. The idea of centre is
deeply rooted in the human mind. The concept of a national
centre has been a hierarchical mental device used by historians
since the Reformation to over-simplify the chaos of diverse local
stimuli. In primitive societies with small, self-sufficient units
there was no differentiation between centre and periphery, and
it could be argued that many peasants in Russia remained at

---

[1] It is odd but none the less true that in the Tsarist period travellers from Western
Europe hardly even turned their attention to this area. See R. W. Pethybridge, 'The
Merits of Victorian Travel Accounts as Source Materials in Russia', *Jahrbücher für
Geschichte Osteuropas* (March, 1972), pp. 10–23.

this level of perception during NEP. Yet urban, industrial polarization had already developed to a considerable degree before 1917, creating awareness of the political centre among the more sophisticated peasant strata such as village teachers, zemstvo clerks, bookkeepers, doctors' and veterinarians' assistants. E. D. Vinogradoff has shown how local agrarian social and economic conditions shaped the collective political behaviour of peasants elected to the Fourth State Duma.[2] This was clearly the case in the Central Agricultural Region, which we shall consider in Chapter 2. The difficulty is that its traditional features—communal tenure, a three-field system, and growing land pressure—have often served as all-Russian criteria, but they did not apply to the West. Prior to 1917 most Belorussian peasant farms had belonged to individual families and had averaged less than 20 acres. The small upper class—mainly Polish and Russian—had owned most of the land.[3] When this class disappeared in the Revolution, the peasants increased their landownership to 28 per cent more than they had before 1917.[4] Pressure was reduced further by state funds applied in 1922 to the improvement of the large marshy areas.[5] The Central Region also lacked those national and religious minorities whose commonly held views in some borderlands had bridged the psychological gap between town and country and had led to the formation of political parties after 1905.[6]

Agrarian, ethnic, and religious influences will be examined here, but in the post-revolutionary situation they all had negative rather than active political influence on the conduct of high politics. That an atheist regime was likely to take scant notice of advice based on religious preference is self-evident. Less obvious is the indifference to ethnic variations, despite the fact that Belorussian nationalism was itself weak. Moscow also neglected agrarian provincial variations even in the liberal conditions of early NEP. Yet negative influences, so long as they were sufficiently weighty and cumulative, could have

---

[2] E. D. Vinogradoff, 'The Russian Peasantry and the Elections to the Fourth State Duma', in L. H. Haimson, *The Politics of Rural Russia 1905–1914* (Bloomington, 1979), pp. 219–60.

[3] See I. S. Lubachko, *Belorussia under Soviet Rule 1917–1957* (Lexington, 1972), p. 38.

[4] L. S. Abetsedarskii (ed.), *Istoriia BSSR*, vol. 2 (Minsk, 1961), p. 187.

[5] *Istoriia gosudarstvo i prava BSSR 1917–36 gg.*, vol. 1 (Minsk, 1970), p. 204.

[6] Ibid., p. 289 and n. 18.

enormous effects on the formulation of all-Russian policies. This proved to be the case by the end of NEP. The only positive line of local–central political communication was the Bolshevik Party network. We shall see how much or how little of local nuances it succeeded in conveying to the top authorities.

Let us begin at the roots of this multifarious society. In January 1922 79.29 per cent of the entire population of the ex-Empire, estimated at 133,890,100, lived in European Russia; 77.3 per cent of all inhabitants lived in the countryside.[7] Thus it is clear that our typical inhabitant is a peasant living in European Russia.

In a village somewhere in the *uezd* of Roslavl' in the south-west of the Smolensk *guberniia*[8] a peasant mother rises at dawn in the spring of 1922 on hearing the passing herdsman drum on his *barabanka*, a cast-iron drum. She has slept in her clothes as usual, so she reaches at once for her birch-bark pail (*podoinik*) with its removable lid and spout for pouring out the milk once she has returned from milking her cow, or two cows if she is rich. It has been calculated that in 1922 an average of 38 minutes would be spent on going to work and coming back, with a working day of between 14 and 15 hours in the warmer months.[9] The second job of the day is to light the stove, a monument in itself, taking up a quarter of the thatched hut with its various extensions—a sill (*pod*) with an area for keeping dishes warm (*chestok*), niches (*pechurki*) for small objects and matches, holes on the side for drying out leg and foot wrappings (for lack of shoes), holes near the summit for reviving chilled hens in winter, and on the triumphal summit worn clothing on which to stretch out and sleep in the delicious warmth—'*U kholodnoi pechi ne sogreesh'sia*' ('You can't heat yourself at a cold stove'). Diagonally opposite the stove is the icon corner, although for a Belorussian peasant the most sacred spot is the stove column, where the souls of predecessors reside. Together with the first harvest sheaf hanging beside the icon

[7] E. Z. Volkov, *Dinamika narodnonaseleniia SSSR za 18 let* (Moscow, 1930), pp. 183, 204, 270.

[8] See the map on p. xiii.

[9] S. G. Strumilin, *Problemy ekonomiki truda* (Moscow, 1964), pp. 168–71. The author acknowledges the help of the staff of the State Museum for the Ethnography of the Peoples of the USSR, Leningrad, in this description of Belorussian peasant life.

for its protective magic, these are reminders that our peasant lives in several cultural times simultaneously, one of them embedded deep in the pagan past, another in the religious present, a third focused on the trip she is about to take to the town of Roslavl'. And away and above her imagination lie the remote worlds of elegant Petrograd, and of Moscow, the city of the Communist future as well as of her inherited religious past.

After making first animal feed (*korm*) and only later cabbage soup (*shchi*) for the family, she may finally turn to the work that occupies the womenfolk from November until Lent—spinning flax from that blue-flowered, frail-leaved plant plucked by the root in handfuls in the August of 1921. The thread is spooled on an enormous reeling-machine (*nituchka*) before being woven on a primitive loom into mens' shirts and trousers, household linen and curtains (*pologa*) to protect the sleeper from the mosquitoes that are so prevalent in the marshes of the western plains.[10] When the women gossip at their looms, they do not speak Tolstoy's pure peasant Russian, but a dialect that differs from one village to the next. Here in Struga they speak what they call '*struskii*', a hotchpotch of Belorussian, Russian, and Ukrainian.[11] It would be mental laziness to assume that each national minority was more of a unity than the ex-empire as a whole. Innumerable subcultures split up by language, region, class, religion, generation, type of work, and sex existed within Belorussia alone. Women lived a different cultural, economic, and political life from men in the 1920s, as will be seen in more detail when we return to this area and topic in 1926.

Our peasant is starting off today to Roslavl', 55 miles away, in order to see her soldier son who has been away in the Civil War, and is passing with his peacetime unit by train tomorrow from Briansk further south to the city of Smolensk with an hour's stop in Roslavl'. She knots up some girdle-cakes

[10] After 1917 the cultivation of flax, one of the main occupations here, declined sharply. Population pressure and the increasing needs of home consumption led to a considerable shift to grain, potatoes, and fodder crops. See also n. 35 below. In Petrograd the situation was worse. In April 1922 there was a female unemployment rate of 85% in textiles. See *Trud*, 22 Apr. 1922.

[11] Even in 1980 the older generation had a different dialect in every village in these parts. See G. Szczebiot, 'Belusha and Struga in Belorussia', in *Newsletter* 14 of the Welsh Branch of the Great Britain–USSR Association, Nov. 1980, p. 8.

(*lepëshki*) in a kerchief and plunges through the thick spring mud of the village track to the river Iput' near by where she catches one of several small boats plying to Volga, a market town on the way to Roslavl'.[12] The next day she transfers to the much slower cart (*telega*) which arrives in the late afternoon in Roslavl', a bustling railway-town. She buys some soap and ribbons in the market, where she notes the huge rise in prices since her last visit.[13] The gossip flows in, as at all meeting-places in a largely illiterate environment. She gathers that she has been lucky on her journey to avoid the widespread banditry, carried out more often than not by deserters from the army.[14] Her son had better stay within the ranks, she thinks. Another danger she must avoid is the typhus still raging in the town.[15] She hurries to the railway station. Near chaos prevails here. A group of people have just been arrested by the railway Cheka for trying to travel without tickets,[16] yet our peasant notes how the wife of a Roslavl' party member flourishes an authorization for a free pass typed out on a Tsarist form.[17] It is clear to her that the old ropes are still being pulled by the new masters. She wonders if she will in fact see her son, since a tender has come off the track down the line. She knows from home that many trains do not run because thousands of peasants have not been paid for hauling wood to the engine fuel-dumps for the whole of 1920–1, and so have refused to carry on.[18]

In fact the son's military train, despite the fact that it has priority (a hangover from the days of the armoured trains), only passes through on the following day, when his mother has left. On the platform he picks up the local rumours. The

[12] This would probably be a boat run by a small private enterprise. In 1922 many river services in this area went over from state to private ownership. See F. S. Martin-kevich and V. I. Drits, *Razvitie ekonomiki Belorussii v 1921–27 gg.* (Minsk, 1973), p. 43.

[13] Smolensk Archive, file WKP 273/32 comments on this.

[14] Ibid.

[15] Ibid. There were 16 cases in Roslavl' hospital in the second half of March. Some railway-workers had also been suffering from typhus in January.

[16] Ibid. 74 persons were arrested for this between 15 March and 1 April in Roslavl'.

[17] Ibid.

[18] Ibid. There was also 'massive' pilfering of wood from the dumps (report for the period 15 March–1 April). The situation in the whole of the area had been so bad at the end of February that it 'threatens the economic revival of the Republic'. There was a shortage of coke and anthracite in the Roslavl' railway workshops, so that casting was delayed. An acute shortage of nails meant that it was virtually impossible to repair wagons.

Roslavl' party cell is thinking of recruiting up to seventy-five soldiers from the town garrison in order to collect potatoes from the area as a tax in kind. He is glad that at least he will not be pitted against his own class in this way.[19] His pay is appallingly low and one month in arrears,[20] and yet he hears that the local party is about to mobilize by force peasants aged between 20 and 40 for the army.[21] He fears a further decline in peasant confidence in the Bolsheviks. In the voting for the Constituent Assembly during the winter of 1917 his vote, together with that of many thousands of other ex-front soldiers and their wives and neighbours, had given the Bolsheviks healthy rural support.[22]

On arrival at Smolensk, our peasant soldier discovers that all the equipment of his unit has been embezzled or stolen from the luggage-van.[23] To make matters worse, he finds that his unit has been brought to Smolensk in order to organize the procurement and protection of wood at local timber yards and fuel dumps. All recalcitrant peasants are to be arrested, and the Presidium of the Smolensk *gubispolkom* (the party executive committee) has put the campaign 'on wartime footing'.[24] Shades of Trotsky's labour armies, he and his comrades murmur between themselves when the political commissar leaves them.

In 1922 the capital of the guberniia could hardly be called a bastion of the proletariat. The nearest useful census is for 1923, when the total population of Smolensk was only 63,669 of which a mere 15.1 per cent were workers. Like the population of all the cities of European Russia, it suffered a decline (from 72,559 in 1917 to 56,826 in 1920).[25] This was far less dramatic

---

[19] Ibid.

[20] Smolensk Archive, file WKP 125, T87/16.

[21] Ibid., WKP 273/32. This was said by the Roslavl' town party-cell to be an anti-Soviet rumour, and not based on fact

[22] See O. H. Radkey, *The Election to the Russian Constituent Assembly of 1917* (Cambridge, Mass., 1950), pp. 73 etc. Over half of able-bodied male Belorussian peasants had been enlisted in the First World War, and the area had been overrun by the military in 1917. The civilian population of Minsk was 110,000 plus an extra military establishment of 150,000. I. S. Lubachko, *Belorussia under Soviet rule 1917–1957* (Lexington, 1972), p. 11.

[23] Smolensk Archive, WKP 273/32.

[24] Ibid., WKP 125 T87/16.

[25] *Goroda SSSR* (Moscow, 1927), p. 53.

than in a much larger city like Petrograd.[26] At the turn of the century industrial production in Belorussia had been half that of the average for Russia as a whole.[27] The area was thus unusually weighted towards agriculture, but it was only an exaggeration of the normal situation in all provincial regions. Throughout NEP Russia remained plunged in a largely pre-industrial society, conditioned far more by its natural environment (of marshes, flax, large forests in Belorussia) than by its few industrial cities. By the end of 1923 only 12,323 persons were engaged in all of Soviet Belorussian industry, compared with 23,438 railway-workers.[28] Belorussian industrial capacity had been split in half by the World War and its consequences. Western Belorussia still lay under Polish control, with its heavier concentrations of textile-workers. In 1922 10,000 textile-operatives in the Belostok region of Western Belorussia struck under the influence of the Polish Communist Party. Ironically, and not for the last time in history, the Communist-inspired proletariat had more clout outside the Soviet borders than within.[29]

Given Russia's high latitudinal position, her short farming season, low productivity, absence of markets, and scant incentives for yield improvement in the late Tsarist period and until the advent of NEP, the natural result was a strong peasant urge to supplement agricultural income by *promysly* (craft industries), one of which was the production and working up of flax for the *kustarnyi* industry. The latter was defined by Soviet terminology in the 1920s as all establishments producing goods for more than one household but employing thirty wage-earners or less; or if motive power was used, fifteen wage-earners or less.[30] The accent on rural industry had actually increased heavily over the years prior to 1922. The chaotic transport situation did not harm it, since it had access to local raw materials and fuel. The clothing industry, including flax, had flourished because it supplied both the Tsarist and the Red

[26] See p. 189 below.
[27] *Bol'shaia sovetskaia entsiklopediia*, vol. 4 (2nd edn.), p. 483.
[28] Martinkevich and Drits, op. cit., p. 143.
[29] *Khronika vazhneishikh sobytii istorii kommunisticheskoi partii Belorussia, 1919g–1941g.*, pt. 2 (Minsk, 1970), p. 43 ff.
[30] For the late Tsarist background to the kustarnyi industries, see R. W. Pethybridge, *The Social Prelude to Stalinism* (London, 1974), pp. 229–31.

Armies which trampled through Belorussia. There were also other reasons for the growing importance of small-scale industry during the Civil War and NEP. The famine of 1919–21 forced industrial workers back to the countryside, where they proceeded to apply their skills, encouraged by the local peasantry, thwarted by the lack of industrial consumer goods from the towns. The loss of the Polish and Baltic provinces, which had supplied the Russian market with a large quantity of consumer goods, also served to increase the dependence of the Soviet population on the kustari, particularly in the west. The 1897 census had listed 20,000 kustari for the six Belorussian provinces of that period. By the end of 1922 the number rose to 33,800 for Soviet Belorussia, a smaller area. This figure was 2.7 times higher than for employees in large-scale industry. Their volume of production was one and a half times greater, and they were engaged chiefly in clothing, woodwork, skins, and agricultural repairs.[31]

During the war years 480 large and small-scale industrial enterprises had been knocked out in Belorussia.[32] A further huge reduction of about 80 per cent in the labour force had taken place since the introduction of *khozraschet* at the start of NEP.[33] Throughout Russia heavy industry suffered the most. Whereas the national monthly output of iron-ore had sunk from 45.87 million *pudy* in 1913 to 0.98 by September 1922, and cast-iron from 21.43 to 0.94, flax yarn had only sunk from 0.236 to 0.104.[34] This set-back meant that flax prices went up steeply in 1922 to meet demand, and sowing increased sharply in the autumn, bringing quick prosperity to parts of Belorussia.[35] Another consumer industry of prime importance to this area, paper, recovered very rapidly during 1922, in the effort to supply the hungry central bureaucracies and cultural institutions which had been sorely deprived.[36] Yet until 1923

---

[31] Martinkevich and Drits, op. cit., p. 48.

[32] Narodnoe khoziaistvo *BSSR za 40 let* (Minsk, 1957), p. 26.

[33] Martinkevich and Drits, op. cit., p. 28.

[34] *Ekonomicheskii biuleten' koniunkturnogo instituta*, 7–8 (1923), p. 8.

[35] By July 1923 the price of flax was 83% higher than it had been on the eve of the First World War. See *Na novykh putiakh*, vol. 3 (Moscow, 1923), p. 29. On flax-sowing in 1922, see N. P. Oganovsky in *Narodnoe khoziaistvo SSSR 1923–24 gg.* (Moscow, 1925), pp. 7–8.

[36] See Martinkevich and Drits, op. cit., pp. 39–44. On the hunger of the central paper consumers, see Ch. 6, p. 214.

much pulp had to be imported from abroad in view of the atrocious transport situation in Belorussia and the chaotic state of the timber industry.

Capital investment in Belorussian industry, centred on Smolensk, was only 485,000 roubles in 1922, but this was stepped up by 271 per cent in 1923. On average workers' pay in Belorussia had dropped by 1922 to 73.5 per cent of the 1913 level, but in 1923 it was to rise to 112.5 per cent. In the first half of 1921 nearly all workers and state employees had been paid almost entirely in kind but by June 1922 66 per cent came in the form of cash. The best-paid workers in Belorussia were in the bristle industry. Metal-workers, the vanguard of the 1917 proletarian revolution in Petrograd, here received two-thirds less than bristle-workers, and flax-workers, most of them unqualified and women, earned four-fifths less.[37] Private firms paid up to 28 per cent of wages towards social insurance for their workers, whereas state concerns contributed between 15 and 19.5 per cent. By the end of 1922 many relatives of war casualties began to receive small social-welfare payments. Yet. in all Belorussia there were only 1,669 hospital beds.[38]

Such was the frail nature of the Belorussian working class, cut off from its metropolitan Russian brothers by a broad sea of peasants. Now it is time to consider the area's ethnic relationship as a whole to the Great-Russian heartland. Subsequently, three themes of great concern both to the local population and to the political authorities in Smolensk and Moscow will be treated—taxation, religion, and cultural and political education. In the course of this book we shall come across other national minorities: the Ukrainians and the Kazakhs in our tour of the provinces, and the Georgian question at the more theoretical level of high politics.

At the outset it may prove useful, if only to discover differences rather than similarities, to contrast Great-Russian nationalism with French. Both nations were highly centralized, and both underwent fundamental revolutions, but their geographical scale and relationship to national minorities were

[37] Martinkevich and Drits, op. cit., pp. 71, 82, 301, 304.

[38] Ibid., pp. 263–4, 317. For a contemporary discussion of social and medical insurance in particular, see *Trud*, 4 Jan. and 2 Mar. 1922. See also I. I. Bykhovsky, *Chto daet rabochemu sotsial'noe strakhovanie* (Moscow, 1922), pp. 1–3.

very different. After 1789 politicians were the main architects of French nationalism, but in Russia at the start of NEP Marxist internationalism and Trotsky's theory of permanent revolution still imbued most leading Bolsheviks, with the significant exception of Stalin, whose treatment of Georgia in 1922 was to shock Lenin. French patriotism had been whipped up through the antics of her revolutionary armies abroad, but the Russian Civil War had no effect of this kind. For the most part Great Russians were fighting Great Russians, and in the process trampled over the lands of peasants, whether Russian, Belorussian, Ukrainian, etc., none of whom was more inclined thereafter to feel particularly attracted to Muscovite patriotism. Moreover Lenin held the view from Babeuf via Marx that regular armies should be abolished, thus reducing the danger of the nationalistic Bonapartism that overcame France.

The second chief instrument of French post-revolutionary nationalism was her culture as disseminated through her educational institutions. In the early Soviet period, until well after Stalin's introduction of the notion of 'Socialism in one country', state education was rigorously infused with those same ideas of proletarian internationalism that influenced military circles. Much of Russia's traditional culture was still rejected in early NEP. What little remained of it had never rejoiced in the calm self-assurance of the French, who had equated their race with civilization. Paris was the world's cultural capital in their eyes, but Russia suffered alternately from a deep-rooted inferiority complex, saddled with two cultural capitals looking away from each other towards Asia and Europe; or from an unstable Messianic superiority complex, derived from Byzantium via Dostoevsky and now resurrected phoenix-like by the Bolsheviks under a new guise.

The results of this brief comparison may surprise those Whig interpreters of Soviet history who read back into it before its time the dominant Great-Russian nationalism of the 1930s. The only glimmer of it in early NEP was, ironically, the attitude of one Georgian, Stalin, towards his own national birthplace. Nothing had changed radically between shortly before 1917 and 1922 to cause any further deterioration in non-Russian–Russian relationships. As before 1917, so by 1922 the central political authority still mingled quite closely, at least in the European provinces, on territorial and cultural grounds with the minorities, whether in Belorussia or the Ukraine. Indeed the three languages were very close to each other. The Bolsheviks proved in the Civil War that they could defend the minorities just as well, or indeed better than the Tsarist regime had done in the Great War. One type of authoritarian rule had been followed by another, not allowing for that kind of unsettling liberalization which is so conducive to uprisings among minorities. The Bolsheviks at least promised to tackle regional socio-economic backwardness, and their bureaucratic intervention in the localities was at first less oppressive in some ways than in the Tsarist past simply for lack of personnel.

The relatively relaxed stance of most of the leading Bol-sheviks, many of whom in any case were themselves not Great Russians, was met at least half-way by the malleable reactions of the Belorussians. A leading Western authority on the reincorporation of the nationalities into the Soviet Union opined that of all the minorities the Belorussians had the weakest urge to set themselves apart.[39] In purely practical terms the largest population in Belorussia after the indigenous inhabitants remained from the 1897 to the 1926 census the Jews and not the Russians.[40] Prior to the Revolution there was scant institutional evidence of deep-rooted nationalist senti-ment. There were no institutions of higher learning except for an obscure agricultural college in Mogilev province. The very few secondary schools and the rare rural schools gave lessons in Russian only, on general Russian lines. Belorussia had the lowest literacy rate among all the peoples of European Russia.

Without going into the intricacies of Belorussia's fate between 1917 and 1921 (she was occupied in turn by Germans, Poles, and Russians, and there were three successive Soviet governments), a few salient points may serve to show the indifference of all the four nationalities involved to Belorussian national claims. In 1917 the Belorussian National Committee,

---

[39] See R. Pipes, *The Formation of the Soviet Union: Communism and Nationalism 1917–1923* (Cambridge, Mass., 1964), p. 150.

[40] By 1926 the Jews still made up 8.19% of the total population of the Belorussian Republic, as against 7.7% Russians and 80.62% Belorussians. See *Prakticheskoe razreshenie natsional'nogo voprosa v BSSR*, vol. 2 (Minsk, 1927), p. 12.

a hotchpotch of indecisive and divided intellectuals, eventually mustered sufficient unity to send demands to Petrograd, only to be nullified by the differing views of the Petrograd- and Moscow-based Belorussian groups (intimations of those wider cultural and political differences between the twin capitals which are taken up in a later chapter). Abstract theorizing continued in Moscow and Petrograd, unrelated to the practical needs and wishes of the ordinary Belorussian back at home. As a result, in the first free elections in the spring of 1917 to the *zemstvo* and municipal Belorussian governments, not a single nationalist representative won any popular support. If this tendency to ratiocinate in central isolation was already rife by 1917 in the microcosmic situation of the Belorussians, how much greater were the potential dangers for the future of the Bolsheviks' wider theories as applied to the all-Russian macrocosm. At least, after the outcome of the Civil War and the suppression of all other parties, the Bolsheviks no longer feared non-election.

When the Germans invaded Belorussia in February 1918, they paid no attention to nationalist aspirations. After the Polish invasion of April 1919, Belorussia was said to be historically an inalienable part of the Polish Commonwealth. The local landowners were reinstated and Polish introduced as the official language.[41] At the end of 1919 Lenin showed Russian indifference by offering virtually all of Belorussia to Poland in order to stave off a Polish offensive, but the most telling instance of Russia's attitude had already occurred after the German withdrawal in December 1918, when the North-western Regional Committee of the *Russian* Communist Party held a conference at Smolensk. It blithely renamed itself the Belorussian Party. When even Belorussian Communists complained, they were told that 'the majority could not form a faction'. The majority cited was not in fact the Belorussian Communists, since Russians predominated: the reference was to the Belorussian ethnic majority in the republic's population.[42] The final Russian snub, though it does not appear to have been taken as such by the Belorussians, came in January

---

[41] V. K. Shcharbakou, *Kastrychnitskaia revoliutsyia na Belarusi i belapol'skaia okupatsyia* (Minsk, 1930), pp. 100–1.

[42] See Lubachko, op. cit., p. 28.

1921 when the Belorussian SSR was constituted. It was confined to a small border strip of 20,000 square miles and
1,500,000 inhabitants, encompassing Roslavl' and Smolensk,
but excluding important districts centred on Vitebsk, Gomel,
and Mogilev which were incorporated into the RSFSR.

Over the last two centuries minority unrest has often
stemmed from a thwarted intelligentsia impatient for power
and capable of perceiving its nationality's relative backwardness. However energetic such a group may be, it has to draw on
popular ethnic support. Its traditional ally, newly settled city-
dwellers, were almost completely lacking in Belorussia, as we
have seen. The peasant grass-roots culture that has been
examined briefly here was too local in scope, too illiterate, to
line up strongly with the intelligentsia. Two authorities on this
question disagree with each other, the one claiming little or no
contact, the other maintaining that some Belorussian intellectuals appealed to the peasant masses throughout the 1920s by
proclaiming the *Bezburzhuaznost'* (the non-existence of a bourgeoisie) of the whole nation.[43] On the positive side one could
cite the wider political knowledge acquired by a territory
invaded on all sides during 1917–21, so that at least the many
peasants, caught up in military life, like our travelling soldier,
might acquire broader interests. On the negative side it should
be recalled that many Belorussian nationalists were more pro-
Western than specifically Belorussian in their emphasis, while
many others became so identified with the Bolshevik Party that
they shed earlier inclinations. On balance Voltaire's maxim
that the poor could have no *patrie* probably still held sound for
the vast majority of Belorussian peasants in early NEP. Their
main foe, irrespective of his nationality, was the tax-collector,
and their main ally, if only they knew it, the educator,
irrespective of whether he spoke Russian or Belorussian. The
only widespread bond that clearly separated some of them
from Russians was their Catholicism, but it also separated
them from fellow Belorussians.

We shall turn to these three themes shortly, but finally the
relatively smooth course of Russian–Belorussian collaboration

[43] The two authors respectively are N. P. Vakar, *Belorussia: The Making of a Nation*
(Cambridge, Mass., 1956), p. 97, and W. Kolarz, *Russia and her Colonies* (New York,
1967), p. 155.

during NEP should be underlined. One of the liberalizing facets of NEP was the effort to reconcile the Bolsheviks and local nationalists, and even Stalin endorsed it.[44] This era of mild concessions to Belorussian culture impressed Belorussians amongst the diaspora abroad who continued to believe that a truly democratic system might yet emerge.[45] Only towards the end of the 1920s did the central regime start to suppress Belorussian cultural institutions, and it was not until 1933 that general persecution of nationalism became prevalent in the area.

Religious rather than political beliefs permeated the everyday lives of both Russian and national minority peasants. These beliefs were rooted far deeper in the past than attitudes to taxation or to education, and they were to remain tenacious into late NEP despite mounting persecution, as will be seen when this same area is re-examined later. There have been many Western and Soviet studies of religious belief *per se*, and of the interaction in Soviet history between an atheist regime and a highly religious peasantry, but scant reference is made to socio-economic views and actions derived from religion that had ultimate political repercussions. Emphasis is laid on them here, since they coincide with the line of approach adapted for other themes.

Merle Fainsod once wrote 'The vantage point which the Smolensk Archive affords for a study of religious activity in the area is a peculiarly distorted one'.[46] This is because we can read only of anti-religious work as described in party documents and, from 1925 onwards, in the reports of the local League of the Godless. In order to circumvent this bias to some extent, let us first burrow beneath this middle level to look at grass-roots religious sentiment which for the most part in 1922 escaped party supervision, since the latter was restricted geographically to the larger centres of habitation and their immediate hinterland.

The arrival of the atheist Bolsheviks as the new élite merely

---

[44] J. Stalin, *Sochineniia*, vol. 5 (1st edn., Moscow, 1952), p. 294.

[45] See V. I. Seduro, 'Belorussian Culture and Totalitarianism', *Proceedings of the Conference of the Institute for the Study of the History and Culture of the USSR* (New York, 1953), p. 85.

[46] M. Fainsod, *Smolensk under Soviet Rule* (New York, 1963), p. 430.

accentuated the cultural schism between the peasantry and the
ruling strata that had existed since Peter the Great's reign.
Whereas the peasants continued to be edified through oral
accounts of the lives of the Saints and of holy pilgrims, and
occasionally learnt to read the alphabet through the Psalter,
the upper classes had paid lip-service to the state religion whilst
immersing themselves in rationalist Western thought. Towards
the end of the Tsarist period the Slavophils, Dostoevsky,
Tolstoy, and others tried to bridge this gulf. The last Empress,
a German, was more Russian than peasant Russians in her
devotion to Orthodox religion and to unorthodox holy men.
Yet all these trends were eccentric, neither pulling the bulk of
the intelligentsia with them, nor penetrating to the heart of
peasant psychology. This was hardly surprising, given that
earthy pagan beliefs mingled in the peasant mind with Christian tenets, creating a 'double faith' (*dvoeverie*), the icon and the
wheatsheaf together. Before confessing to a priest, most peasants would ask the earth for forgiveness. The passionate faith
in the deep influence of the soil on man might at first sight
appear to be an idea which a Marxist regime could easily
harness to its own ideology, as was the Russian peasant's deeply
ingrained sense of co-operative toil on the land, a notion
likewise derived from his dvoeverie.[47] In accounts of religious
opposition to the Bolsheviks, these possible points of conver-
gence have always been overlooked. That they never bore fruit
was due as much to Bolshevik neglect of them as to the eventual
insistence from above on the abolition of the private farms.

Another trait stemming from religious inspiration was the
passive humility of the peasants. Quite apart from educational
and other handicaps, this was one reason why they and even
their social betters took so little part in government, leaving it
so often to Balts or Germans before 1917, and to other non-
Russians after that date. When they did bestir themselves on
rare occasions, as in 1917, but more slowly than any other
group, they could read plainly Christian meanings into Bolshevik slogans such as 'universal peace' and 'if any would not
work, neither should he eat'. When their typically apocalyptic

[47] For more thoughts on peasant agricultural co-operation and Bolshevik intervention, see Ch. 10.

vision of a new world faded, they retreated for the most part into traditional humility.

In their rural isolation Belorussian peasants were at first little affected by anti-religious campaigns and actions emanating from the towns, even if priests disappeared and churches were commandeered. Before 1917, as in most other parts of the Empire, one wooden church served for up to forty or fifty scattered villages. There was no feeling, as there was among Catholics, that priests were indispensable: heads of families could and did conduct simplified forms of service in front of their domestic icons. Increasingly some peasants realized the truth of the proverb '*Dlia popa temnota naroda—istochnik dokhoda*' ('For the priest the unenlightened people is a source of income').[48] Yet for lack of personnel, funds, and initiative, Bolshevik Party members were not making sufficient capital out of the situation. As a peasant from the Kursk guberniia put it in 1922: 'We are not for priests nor for the church, but if only the Comrades would give us a little of what they promise: they promise a school and Socialism, but our hands are still as empty as ever.'[49] Certainly it would be wrong to associate anti-Bolshevik sentiment with religious persecution in too many cases. Priests in the Tambov area, the centre of peasant revolt in 1921, reported in 1922 that church attendance had dropped by more than half as compared with pre-1914.[50]

The extent and depth of religious belief is notoriously difficult to estimate at any time in any country, but a few general statistics can be applied reliably to the peasantry of 1922 in areas like Belorussia, Kursk, and Tambov. Older people were more religious than the young, women more than men, and above all, the rural areas more than the urban workers, as S. G. Strumilin discovered in 1922 (Table 1).

That anyone could dream up the notion of quantifying time spent on prayers was indicative of the 'scientific' attitude of the central authorities, to whose actions in 1922 we now turn

---

[48] Priests' fees in this region and in the Kursk and Tambov regions remained roughly the same from 1919 to 1924—1 pud of grain for a baptism or a child's burial, 2 to 3 for an adult burial. See Ia. Yakovlev, *Nasha derevnia* (Moscow, 1924), p. 127, and I. Lin, 'Popy na khozraschete', *Izvestiia VTsIK*, 16 Oct. 1923.

[49] Yakovlev, *Derevnia kak ona est'* (Moscow, 1923), p. 89.

[50] Yakovlev, *Nasha derevnia*, p. 127.

TABLE I.    *Time spent in hours per year on reading and on religion (daily prayers and Sunday church visits in the towns and the countryside)* [51]

|  | Workers | | Peasants | |
| --- | --- | --- | --- | --- |
|  | Male | Female | Male | Female |
| Reading | 294 | 270 | 35 | 15 |
| Religion | 18 | 44 | 121 | 173 |

briefly before considering the middle level of the local party men in Smolensk. At the close of 1921 the Soviet government ordered a survey of church valuables, and in a decree of 16 February 1922 commanded that they should be collected and sold for the benefit of those suffering from the Famine. When a further instruction stated that vessels used in services were not exempt,[52] the Patriarch Tikhon told the faithful to resist. Although similar requisitions were carried out on treasures in museums, it did seem that the state had finally decided to test the power of the Orthodox Church on a socially explosive question. The government had also noted the proliferation of schismatic religious movements over the previous few years.[53] When Tikhon was placed under house arrest in June 1922, one of these movements, the Living Church, was given numerous concessions by the regime, and at first looked set to take over the role and some of the property of the Orthodox. Trotsky went so far as to call the agreement 'an ecclesiastical NEP',[54] implying a similar tolerance to that meted out to '*kulaks*' or to Nepmen, but this was a superficial and short-sighted judgement redolent with propaganda. The year 1922 in fact marked the start of the regime's long-term siege of the Church. In the spring a weekly journal, *Bezbozhnik*, was set up to conduct a popular anti-religious campaign.[55] The rise of the Living Church, which itself soon split into various groups, allowed the

[51] Strumilin, *Biudzhet vremeni russkogo rabochego i krest'ianina v 1922–23 godu* (Moscow, 1924), pp. 120–1; for statistics by age and sex, see pp. 68–71, 74.
[52] *Sobranie Uzakonenii*, 19 (1922), arts. 217, 218.
[53] For an account of these religious movements, see W. C. Fletcher, *The Russian Orthodox Church Underground, 1917–1970* (London, 1971), pp. 28–32.
[54] L. Trotsky, *Literatura i revoliutsiia* (1923), p. 29.
[55] *Izvestiia*, 5 Aug. 1922.

party to divide and rule; at no point did it commit itself unconditionally to any sect. The Living Church owed its popularity to the parish priests, the oppressed 'white' clergy whom it supported, rather than to any enthusiasm amongst the masses. Like all cultural movements during NEP, its influence did not extend far beyond the towns. Both Soviet and hostile critics observed subsequently that in the eyes of the people Living Church members often looked like Soviet agents and opportunists.[56]

In the light of high political intent and peasant sentiment, let us now return to the market town of Roslavl' and examine Party and urban reactions there in 1922. It is interesting to note that the local Party cell's initial report for January, that is, prior to the central decree of 16 February on church valuables, already concentrates on two things—possible rifts within the Church, and the flow of ecclesiastical monies. A very large amount had already been collected on a voluntary basis by religious groups for the Famine, making it seem almost superfluous or extortionate to do more. Party spies had been assigned to people sending sums through the post for the personal use of the bishop.[57] The February decree was only implemented in Roslavl' one month late, on 15 March. This may have been due to a reluctance to suck more money out of a generous population, or to the usual delays in carrying out orders from Moscow. On 15 March Party officials took gold objects from the main church, despite protests outside from a large crowd including factory workers. When the clergy tried to calm them, the crowd declared that the valuables belonged to the people, not to the church, so that priests could not give them away. Further Party raids were carried out into April. On one occasion the church bell was rung to summon protesters. Troops were called in (as they had been to protect fueldumps). There was some shooting and a number of people lay dead on the church steps. Others were arrested.[58]

The Roslavl' Party also reported on events in Smolensk,

---

[56] For a Soviet view, see M. M. Sheinman, *Religion and the Church in the USSR* (Moscow, 1933), pp. 48–9, and for an exile's opinion, V. Alekseev, *Russian Orthodox Bishops in the Soviet Union, 1941–1953* (New York, 1954), p. 79.
[57] Smolensk Archive, file WKP 273.
[58] Ibid.

where shots were fired on 28 March when factory workers downed tools to protect churches. From Vitebsk it was heard that a railway-wagon workshop meeting convened on 30 March with the aim of helping in the requisition of church valuables broke up because of the 'thunderous outcries of believers'. Others in Vitebsk suspected that gold seized would not go to the Volga famine relief but into the Bolsheviks' pockets or their mouths in the shape of much-fancied gold teeth.[59] One workers' meeting had even suggested that it would be better to shoot Lenin or Trotsky rather than Patriarch Tikhon. In the same period Trotsky was suggesting from his ivory tower in the capital that in order to avoid saints' names, children should be called Ninel (Lenin backwards) or simply Rem (the initials for revolution, electrification, and peace).[60]

The remarkable features of this struggle were the extent of violence, the number of urban workers involved, and the outspoken nature of their protests. Undoubtedly much of the anger was directed at further extortions of any kind, whether anti-religious or not. In April the Smolensk Party advised the Roslavl' cell that contributions to the Famine were tailing off in the Roslavl' area, so two new directives were issued: first, to collect another famine tax, with every twenty town-workers or employees supporting one hungry child, and every five peasant households contributing for one hungry adult; second, to hold agitational meetings in all trade-union branches and at village *skhod* meetings.[61] In view of the vastness of Russia and the striking parochialism of the localities, it must have been hard to whip up yet more sympathy and funds for remote peasants in the Lower Volga. Yet as we shall see, the Famine did produce considerable horizontal side-effects between one province and another. As a general principle it should not be imagined that all economic, social, and above all political repercussions were of a vertical central–local nature or vice versa. Horizontal influences have been virtually ignored in Soviet and Western historiography alike. Here we have stumbled on the first of many.

Another feature of Party activity in Roslavl' and Smolensk

[59] Smolensk Archive, file WKP 273.
[60] Trotsky, *Voprosy Byta* (Moscow, 1922), p. 64.
[61] Smolensk Archive, file WKP 124 787/16.

reflected in microcosm top-level efforts in Moscow to divide
and rule by setting the Living Church and other sects against
the official Orthodox Church. A January Party report in
Roslavl' noted with glee that the local clergy were divided,
even before the February decree.[62] By May the Smolensk
authorities were writing that the 'black' Bishop Philip in the
city still opposed the collection of church valuables, whereas
the rural 'white' clergy assented to it. The latter were to be
encouraged by Party propaganda at the uezd level to send in
supportive letters to the press.[63] Other religious scapegoats were
not hard to find, especially in Belorussia with its preponderance
of urban Jews and large Catholic minority. In Roslavl' during
March and April it was frequently noted that the public
believed that ecclesiastical gold was to be handed over to the
Jews. In June town employees were angered because they had
to pay six million roubles commission to Jews in order to
exchange a hundred million given to them in the form of bonds
for their pay. The Smolensk open-air market was flooded in
April with leaflets declaiming 'Down with the Yids—save
Russia!' On 13 May three Jews were robbed and killed 10
versts from the village of Liozno, and the perpetrators were
allowed to get away.[64] At least a portion of the Jewish
population was saving its skin by allying with the Party, for in
April we discover 400 Jewish delegates in Minsk speeding up
the fight against Zionism and proposing the closure of their
religious schools in Belorussia,[65] a notion which had become a
reality by September according to the central press.[66] No doubt
the local Party authorities were helped in their divide-and-rule
policy by Orthodox allegations that the Living Church had
arisen due to 'Jewish agitators'.[67]

Although Catholics are not cited in the Smolensk Archive
with reference to the taking of church valuables, their activity
can be traced from other sources. At the time of the last and
only census of 1897, there were more of them in the Vitebsk
area than in any other part of the Empire except for Kovno,

[62] Ibid., file WKP 273.
[63] Ibid. The 'black' clergy comprised the higher categories of unmarried priests.
[64] Ibid.
[65] *Zhizn' natsional'nostei*, 10 (1922), p. 10.
[66] *Pravda*, 3 Sep. 1922.
[67] See *Orientalia Christiana* (Rome), 4 (1923), pp. 214–17.

Vilno, and Grodno. As with the Orthodox Church, so with the Catholics it was the February decree that precipitated the crisis in relations with the Soviet government. Catholic churches in Smolensk were heavily plundered. Like Patriarch Tikhon, but rather later, the Catholic Archbishop Cieplak was called to trial for 17 November 1922.[68] Here too the Party could fend off opposition by a policy of divide and rule. When an agreement was drawn up in 1922 between the Vatican and the Soviet government for a Catholic famine relief mission,[69] some Orthodox leaders in Western Russia declared that the Communists hoped that Catholic propaganda would bring about the downfall of the whole Orthodox Church.[70] This was clearly a wild exaggeration, but it showed, at least as far as the large Catholic minority of Belorussia was concerned, that any attempt to base nationalism on Catholic separatism would be doomed to failure.

Despite the considerable pressures on the churches at the central and top provincial levels in 1922, sparse reverberations as yet reached that grass-roots base which was considered earlier. On 2 February 1922, a reporter in *Izvestiia* enthused,

It is a great rarity in the countryside to find a Communist who does not have an icon hung up at home. Religion and Communism make an excellent household together. Here are the facts. A Communist gets married in a village. All the wedding procession goes to church. In front, the red flag with the inscription, 'Workers of the world, unite!' Next come the icons, and then the bridegroom, with a red sash on his chest. Such marriages are frequent in the villages. In his fashion the peasant understands Communism and Soviet power.

Although the rustic idyll was no doubt the result of wishful thinking, it may have approximated to the real situation in some localities.

No such co-operation was possible in the sphere of taxation, but then it never had been under the Tsars, so Bolshevik extortion seemed hardly more arbitrary than previous methods. There was no volte-face here as there had been on religion.

[68] See F. McCullagh, *The Bolshevik Persecution of Christianity* (New York, 1924), pp. 111–13, and the Cieplak Archive, Chicago.
[69] *Osservatore Romano* (Rome), 16–17 May 1922.
[70] National Archives, Document Division, Russian Section, Washington, DC, file no. 861.404/49, 5 June 1922.

Requisition of grain at the point of a gun during War Communism had proved a novel experience for the peasantry, but by 1922 that had been replaced by slightly more civilized methods.

The lack of administrative control from the centre during the Civil War together with a rapidly depreciating currency meant that taxation became a dwindling resource after 1917. In theoretical terms, however, Lenin had made it quite clear, when local Soviets advocated independent local finances in 1918, that 'democratic centralism' would be vigorously enforced.[71] Over the first nine months of 1922 money taxes reached on average a mere 3 per cent of the pre-war level in real terms. Two-thirds of this was raised through excises, which had been the most common method in the late Tsarist period. Despite the need to return to a monetary economy under the liberal market conditions of NEP, by the end of 1922 over one-third of total revenue still came in the form of taxes in kind.[72] A special series of graded poll-taxes towards famine relief began in February 1922.

Since national expenditure reached 14 per cent of the pre-war level in the first three-quarters of 1922,[73] huge currency issues had to be made to bridge the gap between income and expenditure. The rate for the pound sterling was 1,650,000 roubles in January 1922 and 71,730,000 by October. Internally the value of the rouble decreased seventy-two times with regard to goods during 1922.[74] Only at the end of November did the State Bank introduce a new denomination of notes equal to the gold content of the pre-war ten-rouble coin. By the end of the year there were at least five methods of conducting business, starting at the centre and moving towards the periphery. Moscow traders kept cash balances in gold or foreign valuta. The more sophisticated provincial dealers tried to acquire the new denomination at the end of the year as a means of hoarding. Meanwhile they and nearly all other levels below them in geographical terms were condemned to use the

[71] V. I. Lenin, *Sochineniia*, vol. 23 (Moscow, 1966), pp. 18–19.

[72] *Desiatyi Vserossiiskii S'ezd Sovetov* (1923), p. 138.

[73] R. W. Davies, *The Development of the Soviet Budgetary System* (Cambridge, England, 1958), p. 52.

[74] S. S. Katzenellenbaum, *Russian Currency and Banking, 1914–1924* (New York, 1925), pp. 90, 155.

rapidly inflating old notes. In the sluggish provinces, as in some towns, double-headed-eagle notes from the old regime over-stamped with Bolshevik signs continued to circulate for lack of anything else. Below all these strata lay the immemorial peasant base of straight barter and the still-important tax in kind.[75] Thus NEP as a monetary phenomenon took time to seep slowly through the various levels of society, just as pistoles and *écus* had competed with the franc in the French provinces after that other great revolution.

The same was true of NEP as a fiscal reform. The revival of trade between town and country was crucial to the NEP system, but it could clearly be conducted only in money. Yet heavy taxes in kind continued until after the end of 1922. The central authorities had great difficulty from the start of NEP in collecting taxes of any sort. Confused data on peasant land-ownership and family size made it virtually impossible to make accurate assessments, so that for many provinces only half of the taxable land per head was in fact recorded in the tax lists.[76] This was exactly the proportion of the tax in kind collected in the Roslavl' area up to November 1921. Since October 1921 military detachments had been sent out to the local villages to billet in them and to insist on the tax in kind[77] (shades of expropriation by force in the period of War Communism). Another throw-back to the past was reported by the Roslavl' Party cell in January: at a *volost'*[78] meeting an ex-member of the Kadet Party had spoken up against taxation. In the same period a peasant group calling itself the Union of the True was also advocating opposition to taxes.[79]

Resistance of this kind was to keep the authorities extremely nervous throughout 1922, and one has the sense from the enormous detail of the Smolensk Archive that fear of outright revolt and even counter-revolution was ever present in the local Party's thoughts. Roslavl' officials would have lain quieter in

[75] This general schema is derived from M. Dobb, *Russian Economic Development since the Revolution* (London, 1928), p. 225; Katzenellenbaum, op. cit., p. 86; and an unpublished talk by Professor R. McNeal on early Soviet currencies and inflation, University College, Swansea, February 1981.

[76] A. Sviderskii, 'Nado iskat' propavshuu pashniu', *Pravda*, 5 Nov. 1921.

[77] Smolensk Archive, file WKP 273.

[78] The volost' was a small administrative unit comprising a small cluster of villages.

[79] Smolensk Archive, file WKP 273/32.

their beds at night if they had bothered to read Maxim Gorky's book *On the Russian Peasantry* published that same year. He pointed out that peasant opposition to government did exist, but on account of Russia's huge distances it expressed itself more by evasion than through open fighting. This psychology naturally lingered on into the supposedly liberal atmosphere of NEP in the form of the utopian hope that obligations imposed 'from the Centre', as the peasants put it, could be avoided, whilst retaining economic rights.[80] At the end of the winter of 1921–2 a cautious directive went out from Roslavl' Party headquarters to all local head collectors of the tax in kind. They were not to put undue pressure on the peasants themselves, but only on their fellow subordinate collectors. Non-paying peasants were to be arrested in minimal numbers, and only millers were to be imprisoned. They were to be very 'diplomatic' with recalcitrant poor peasants, and on no account were they to take to court more than a small minority in any one area, even if a majority were guilty. Memories obviously lingered of the War Communism strategy of trying to divide richer from poorer peasants. Above all head collectors were ordered to omit from court lists of non-payers all persons in positions of authority, and particularly Party members.[81] The Roslavl' Party report for 15 March hinted at the reason for this order when it revealed that peasants were of the view that the volost' authorities were imbued with self-seeking (*shkurnichestvo*); Soviet Russia was turning into a 'purely bourgeois republic'. The peasants could not muster enough cash, on account of galloping inflation, to pay the excise duties. The rumour was going round that a new tax on cattle and horse-ownership was to be introduced. This was not true, but in a largely illiterate society the snowball effect of malicious rumours worried the Bolsheviks, as it had the Tsarist officials before them. The last we hear from Roslavl' on taxes is in May, when fifty-eight of the seventy-eight soldiers requested from the town garrison were sent out to collect the potato tax in kind. This failed in the main, not because of violent peasant resistance, but because they were simply too poor to give up

[80] M. Gorky, *O russkom krest'ianstve* (Berlin, 1922), p. 7.
[81] Smolensk Archive, file WKP 273.

any of their potatoes. The local Cheka quoted ominous peasant complaints against the government: 'They aren't planning freedom for us, but serfdom. The time of Godunov has already begun, when the peasants were attached to the landowners. Now we are attached to the Jewish bourgeoisie like Modkowski, Aronson, etc.'[82] This reminds us again of the anti-Semitism prevalent in Belorussia. State investment, rare enough in itself, was earmarked for industry (in the 1923 national budget less than 5 per cent was to be allocated to agriculture). The peasants had to rely on themselves, which meant recourse from 1922 onwards to private lenders—local Jews in this area. It is interesting to observe that private capital was more significant both in absolute terms and in relative importance at these provincial levels than in the great urban centres in 1922.[83] Thus although the political initiative for the start of NEP came from the top, the economic life-blood at first began to flow from the bottom upwards.

The Roslavl' authorities were besieged by continual instructions on taxation from the Smolensk guberniia Party committee. They were told in May to avoid making errors in assessments, and to stop peasants concealing the extent of their property.[84] This was not the only class at fault in this respect. A female landowner of substance induced a handsome peasant to live with her in her mansion; the estate was cunningly converted into a collective farm, but the local peasantry frowned on this breakdown of the old class barriers.[85] A telegram from Smolensk on 1 June urged that the peasants be better informed on tax matters. The wording of the telegram was badly misspelt[86] and like some local banknotes was stamped with the Imperial eagle. As was to be the case with far more important orders to the peasantry from the very highest level at the start of collectivization after NEP, bureaucratic delays and excessive central demands soon resulted in comparable excess of zeal at local levels. By October we find Smolensk party officials

[82] Smolensk Archive, file WKP 273.
[83] See S. L. Fridman, *Chastnyi kapital na denezhnom rynke* (Moscow, 1925), p. 25.
[84] Smolensk Archive, file WKP 124, T87/16.
[85] E. Fen, *Remember Russia 1915–1925* (London, 1973), pp. 246–8.
[86] This instance of semi-literacy in elements of the population which, given their status, should have been better educated reminds one of the telegraph official in M. Zoshchenko's story *Rachis* who could not decipher the capital of France.

annulling a delayed payment of 425 pudy of rye still being demanded by one local authority (some taxes in kind had been reduced from March onwards to a single uniform tax calculated in terms of rye).[87] In November the Smolensk guberniia executive committee is being rebuked in turn by no less a person than V. Molotov, Secretary of the Central Committee in Moscow, for allowing subordinates to impose taxes beyond those laid down in the All-Union list.[88]

The years 1921–2 did in fact cover one of the worst periods in the economic fortunes of the Smolensk guberniia. By 1923 the area sown for food crops had increased by 14.8 per cent compared with 1920, making for improved incomes, more cash, and so more taxes in this area; but viewed from the middle of 1922, there was little prospect of such a happy outcome. Over the whole of Russia there was a dearth of agricultural goods caused mainly by the Famine, and a comparative glut of industrial products from the towns. This was the start of the famous 'scissors crisis'. The terms of exchange between manufacturers and agricultural produce moved swiftly to the disadvantage of the towns; a pair of boots which in 1913 had been worth 283 lb. of rye flour was worth as little as 133 lb. by May 1922.[89] Central reforms were eventually to adjust such discrepancies, but as with the tax changes, they turned out to be blunt bureaucratic instruments not sufficiently finely tuned to local needs. By 1923 the scissors had opened too widely in the opposite direction, this time in favour of the towns.

In fact the whole financial framework of NEP was shaky, and much of it was brought in piecemeal on *ad hoc* lines, as was the case with the vital currency reforms. The introduction of the profit notion through khozraschet looked promising on paper, but in reality at the start of 1922 there was no definition, even in the highest economic organs, of what was meant by 'profit'.[90] As late as 1923 there were still many

---

[87] Smolensk Archive, file WKP 125. For details of the uniform tax in kind calculated in terms of rye, see *Sobranie Uzakonenii*, 2 (1922), art. 233.

[88] Smolensk Archive, file WKP 125.

[89] I. S. Rozenfeld, *Promyshlennaia politika SSSR* (Moscow, 1926), p. 428.

[90] *Finansovaia politika za period s dekiabria 1920 g. po dekabr' 1921 g: otchet k IX vserossiiskomu s'ezdu sovetov* (1921), pp. 60–1.

different ways of assessing production costs and profits.[91] Similar discrepancies opened up in the agricultural sphere. The Agrarian Code of 1922 strictly forbade the sale of land and the granting of mortgages. Yet poorer peasants in their thousands in this year were turning to private, mainly peasant, lenders, though many Jews were also involved in Belorussia, as we have seen. Many soon found themselves in long-term debt to richer peasants, particularly in the Famine areas. This phenomenon was noted in the central press, where the lenders were often referred to as 'beglye' (unstable):[92] however the shaky nature of their new-found prosperity, like the uncertain fits and starts of NEP in economic terms, was soon to turn into solid gains which looked like becoming permanent. The 'beglye' became '*kulaks*' when many poor peasants were unable to liquidate their debts despite the better harvests of 1922 and 1923.

Thus the very foundations of NEP were steeped in economic obscurities, loose interpretations, and plain evasion of coded principles. In this sense as a system it was a house built of sand which could scarcely have lasted as long as Bukharin and others wished it to. It seemed a near miracle that it got off to a relatively smooth start, politically speaking, in 1921–2. Although these years witnessed a very low tide of economic activity including the horrors of widespread famine and even peasant revolts in some areas like Tambov, problems concerning religious belief and taxation never led to large-scale uprisings in the Smolensk guberniia (nor indeed anywhere else in Russia). After all, the Civil War was over in most areas, so the peasants' best chance of retaliation, by linking up with local White armies, was lost. Again, Lenin's promise that the main aim of NEP was to restore peasant fortunes did begin to bear real fruit before the end of 1922.

Yet through most of the year many government promises remained on paper. The Bolshevik Party was therefore especially eager to win over minds by means of cultural and ideological propaganda and education. Let us follow the method already adopted in an examination of religion and taxes, looking briefly at central political attitudes and then

---

[91]   *Na novykh putiakh*, vol. 3 (1923), pp. 133–7.
[92]   *Trud*, 16 Feb. 1922.

observing their impact at middle and local levels in the Smolensk guberniia.

The general situation had been most unsatisfactory right from the start in 1917, even amongst the proletariat of Petrograd, the core of Bolshevik support. In her capacity as a pedagogue, Krupskaia discovered a high proportion of illiterates among the factory workers of the Vyborg *raion*.[93] At many cultural levels the old Petersburg continued to prevail for a while over Moscow in many informal, non-governmental ways, as will be noted in a later chapter. Its slightly more liberal ethos seemed to affect Krupskaia, for when she first went to work in the People's Commissariat of Education (*Narkompros*) after the revolution, she stressed the need for independence from central management by intellectuals.[94] Yet by 1920 she was already submitting to governmental pressures in her Moscow office. She acknowledged that 'cultural work must be closely combined with political tasks', and went on to prove it by signing three directives on the censorship of libraries between 1920 and 1924.[95]

The tighter political hold was in part a reaction to the worsening economic and organizational situation in cultural affairs. Whereas 10.4 per cent of the central budget was allocated to Narkompros in 1920, this was reduced to 4.2 per cent for 1922. A substantial proportion of educational costs was transferred to local authorities at the end of 1921; although the latter had neither sufficient financial nor administrative means to carry out their new assignments.[96] The result was an alarming drop in resources—3,684 public libraries in 1922 as opposed to 14,800 in 1920; 1,126 'illiteracy liquidation points' as against 17,462 before NEP. Only 38 per cent of children attended elementary schools at the close of 1922, compared with roughly 48 per cent in pre-revolutionary Russia. A. Lunacharsky underlined the growing rift between

---

[93] N. Krupskaia, *Pedagogicheskie sochineniia*, vol. 1 (Moscow, 1957–1960), pp. 436, 438.
[94] See R. McNeal, *Bride of the Revolution: Krupskaia and Lenin* (London, 1973), pp. 193–4.
[95] See R. Pethybridge, 'Spontaneity and Illiteracy in 1917', in R. C. Elwood (ed.), *Reconsiderations of the Russian Revolution* (Cambridge, Mass., 1976), pp. 93–4.
[96] See *Izvestiia VTsIK*, 16 and 18 Dec. 1921.

the educational health of the larger towns and the benighted countryside, but to no avail.[97]

As was so often the case in central–local relationships, poor distribution was often to blame. The nation-wide state publishing organization, *Gosizdat*, was responsible for the dissemination of official literature of all kinds, but the flow of materials to the provinces remained very weak even as late as 1923. Only seven of the fifteen large bookstores in Moscow took the trouble to send anything out to provincial peasant reading-centres. None of them made a special selection of materials suitable for the peasantry, so the few books that were dispatched were often too dry or too expensive. Credit for this trade was hard to get, since publishers argued over terms with distributors. In March 1922 a monopoly was granted to a new state advisory body on the publication of textbooks, but through the rest of 1922 it was powerless to stem the growing tide of texts from private publishers which threatened to drown official party ideology in educational affairs.[98] The precarious hold of the party over cultural ideology will be examined in greater detail in Chapter 6.

Turning now to middle levels of cultural control, in this case to the Smolensk guberniia offices and then to Roslavl', our chosen locality, it is clear that fresh unorthodoxies were apt to creep in below and beyond those emanating from private central sources. It should not be imagined that the tiny Party élite at either of these provincial levels could maintain a tight hold. By the end of 1922 the size of the guberniia Party organization totalled 5,925,[99] compared with, for instance, 3,286 local officials of the Commissariat for agriculture, most of whom were not Party members, but who, by the very nature of their work as surveyors, land-reclaimers, timber and livestock experts, were scattered more widely round the rural areas than were Party workers.[100] As late as 1 April 1924, 3,704 out of the 5,416 Party members were concentrated in the towns.[101]

[97]  *X and XI vserossiiskii s'ezd sovetov* (Moscow, 1923), pp. 76 and 179–80 respectively. The statistics recorded by the Menshevik-inspired journal *Nasha zhizn'* for Nov. 1922 actually gave a slightly less gloomy picture than official Bolshevik figures.

[98]  *Bolezni nashego pechatnogo dela* (Moscow, 1924), pp. 13–26.

[99]  *Izvestiia TsK*, 3 (1923), pp. 162–4.

[100]  *Materialy mestnykh soveschanii oblastnykh konferentsii narodnogo kommissariata zemledeliia o vesennei kampanii 1922 goda* (Moscow, 1922), p. 28.

[101]  *Izvestiia Tsk*.

Thus there was obviously scope for the propagation of non-party unorthodoxies at the grass-roots level.

The traditional sowers of culture at middle provincial levels were the schoolteachers. They had far wider influence over the peasants than was indicated by their formal school syllabuses. In the Smolensk area as elsewhere, they linked up with agricultural advisers in the effort to make the peasants realize that subsistence farming was a form of self-exploitation, since their energies were dissipated in a multitude of tiring undertakings. It was the teachers too who taught the metric system as against the local weights and measures, thus slowly inculcating a sense of wider, national unity. Yet as of 1922 the political reliability of the teachers was notoriously low: large numbers of them were remnants from the old regime. Their pay in paper money was so bad and came so late that unless they had peasant relatives who could supply food, they were reduced to making shoes, singing psalms in church, or hiring themselves out as labourers to peasants. When schools shut for lack of fuel in the winter, they gave private lessons to the richer peasants' children. Thus their dubious loyalty to the new regime was eroded even further.[102]

The inculcation of political orthodoxy and instruction of a more coercive nature was left strictly in the hands of the Party. A reading of the directives of the Smolensk guberniia committee to all executive committees at lower levels for 1922 reveals centrally isolated bureaucrats surrounded by a swamp of unreliable social elements. On the occasion of the first All-Russian Congress of the peasant committees of mutual social aid, a directive exhorted all local branches to interest the peasantry in the workings of central management. Wherever possible, Red Army men were to be installed on the committees. As we have seen, they were amongst the staunchest Bolshevik supporters in the voting for the Constituent Assembly, and in Belorussia they were more than usually numerous and influential due to the fact that this territory had lain directly in the path of invading and retreating forces in the Civil War. Administrative help from Smolensk brought with it obligations, such as 'compulsory self-taxation' (*samooblozhenie*)

---

[102] *Trud*, 13 Feb. 1923; P. Ya. Lezhnev-Finkovsky, *Kak zhivet derevniia* (Moscow, 1925), pp. 31–2.

for the peasant committees. Within a mere three weeks the Smolensk Party authorities also required all uezd executive committees to collate, check, and comment to them on the minutes of every single peasant meeting on mutual aid.[103]

When we shift our attention away from sources emanating from Smolensk city to Party archives based on Roslavl', we recapture through official documents that feeling of social, economic, and possibly political unrest sensed more informally by our peasant-woman visitor and her soldier son. Even at the height of NEP prosperity in 1926, considerable resistance to central patterns and instructions was to linger on the further one got away from Moscow down through all the provincial levels, but in 1922 strong fears of such resistance provoked a siege psychology among those party officials located nearest to the grass roots. They juggled nervously in Roslavl' with the various leading local social and power groups.

The agitation section of the town's Communist Party committee decided, or rather passed on a directive probably originating in Moscow, that the Paris Commune of 1871 should be celebrated on 18 March. In particular all local factories and the military were ordered to rejoice. Lectures and concerts were to be given, for which topics of current interest should be very carefully chosen, and which had to be free for all comers.[104] Throughout the year the anxieties of the Party were focused on local workers and soldiers rather than on the surrounding sea of peasants. Great concern was often expressed about lack of military interest in political affairs. At a meeting of the commissars of the Roslavl' garrison the military commander of the town hospital admitted that the political cell in his institution did not really exist, although there were occasional discussions of newspaper articles. The automobile workshop, likewise under tight military control, had a cell with ten members, but the commander reported that few attended its *Marsiksii* (*sic*) circle. At a level where either the commander concerned or the typist could not render 'Marxist' correctly in Russian, it seems doubtful whether rejoicing for the Paris Commune would be very well informed or sincere. The deputy

---

[103] Smolensk Archive, file WKP 124 T87/16. The directive was issued on 11 Nov. 1922. Replies had to be in by 2 Dec. 1922.
[104] Ibid.

commander of the first artillery battalion reported that all its cell members had been so busily engaged on operations amongst the civilian population that there had been no meeting for over a month (they were probably occupied in some of the unsavoury tasks noted earlier by our peasant soldier and his mother). The only optimistic statement came from the third cadre of military transport, which had recently held two cell meetings. Thirteen per cent of the cadre were illiterate, so political and cultural training was being concentrated on this sector. Work had begun on equipping a club.[105]

The Roslavl' party committee expended most energy of all on plans for the commemoration of the fifth anniversary of the October Revolution. Again, workers and soldiers were subjected to especially close scrutiny and control. The four local factories were told in no uncertain terms that they had to celebrate. Gifts were to be handed out to all soldiers, and their food rations were to be improved between 6 and 8 November. In return the garrison was to decorate the main square with red materials as issued. Military units were to stage a show depicting victories over counter-revolutionaries for the benefit of invited workers. On the following day, 7 November, there would be a joint parade by trade-union representatives and their military comrades. In the evening soldiers were detailed off to perform folk-dances in the primitive town theatre. On 8 November they would continue to sing for their suppers by reading out newspapers to the less literate and explaining the significance of the Third International.[106] This could be a formidable task in a society where even widely travelled soldiers firmly believed that Thomas Cook's wagon-lits were the spearheads of the Third International since the latter word could be read in Cyrillic on the side of carriages.[107] The majority of local Roslavl' workers would undoubtedly be railway rather than factory personnel. The main event on 7 November after the parade was to be a 'spectacle' in the railway club. The town Soviet was also to hold discussions with representatives from the factories and the women's section.

[105] Ibid. These reports on the military data from the middle of Oct. 1922.
[106] Ibid.
[107] See P. A. Polovtsov, *Glory and Downfall: Reminiscences of a Russian Staff Officer* (London, 1935), p. 206.

The sole reference to the peasantry in these laborious instructions was an order to open all rural reading-rooms in the surrounding volosti on 7 November. The meaning of the October Revolution was then to be explained to anyone who bothered to turn up.[108]

Given the importance of this area of Russia in the Civil War and the Polish campaign, the Party's care for and vigilance over the army does not come as a surprise; nor does the considerable military presence in 1922 in civilian organizations like the hospital and the automobile workshop. The Party's obvious nervousness about railway and other workers and relative neglect of the rural hinterland needs a little more explanation. As the year went by the economic sops to the peasantry provided by NEP began to have a relaxing effect on this class, but industrial unrest throughout Russia continued to rise. The level of productivity went up slowly, but employment prospects did not. Provincial market towns, in 1922 as throughout the Soviet period, collected the first rural tide of those looking for work—peasant vagrants, demobilized soldiers, and in the case of the Smolensk area, flax-workers out of a job as their industry began to decline after the boom of the war years. It also proved difficult at the start of NEP to gear local manufacturing industries to peasant demands. These are some of the reasons why the Party devoted so much care to its favourite but weakling class in provincial Russia. We shall come across this concern again in 1922 when we travel through the much stronger industrial nexus of Kharkov.[109]

The peasants in the Roslavl' region did come in for some attention during 1922, though supervision was at best paternalistic, sporadic, and myopic. In January 1922 the town Party committee observed that there was no anti-Bolshevik agitation amongst the local clergy, the main focus of possible rural discontent. It was noted however that what was contemptuously called the 'village intelligentsia' still maintained a hostile attitude to the Party and the Red Army. At the end of February news filtered in that no peasants were willing to join the military ranks, and there were quite a few desertions. The

[108] Smolensk Archive, file WKP 124 T87/16.
[109] See pp. 81–82 below.

greater part of the required *prodnalog* (tax in kind) had been collected, but several villages were fractious due to silly actions by some officials.[110]

Most of the Party's agitational work was devoted to the very small number of local *kolkhozy*, as if, like Catherine the Great, it sought to derive comfort from over-concentrating on its equivalents of Potemkin's model villages. The nation-wide number of these paragons for the Marxist future was a mere 8,641 even by 1924.[111] However, there was one big kolkhoz consisting of 150 households only 20 versts from Roslavl' that was said to be too well satisfied with itself, and so did not welcome visits from the town.[112] The party wished to introduce the *shefstvo* system in its relations with the *kolkhozy*. A *shef* organization from the towns such as an individual factory would take on the role of cultural and political mentor to some rural group. Shefstvo was intended to be a nation-wide movement, the concrete expression of the more abstract notion of smychka, the theory of town and country alliance as expounded originally by Marx.[113] The ideal was very far from being a reality in 1922, or indeed throughout NEP. A kolkhoz to the east of Smolensk city in the Dorogobuzhskii raion complained that in 1921 its two shefi, a nearby hospital, and a regiment, had helped with the harvest, but no one had visited it in 1922. Sometimes the tie was purely economic in rationale. One kolkhoz further to the north-east of Smolensk exchanged potatoes for farm machinery, whilst another shef factory that manufactured spare parts for linen plants gave iron to a local kolkhoz on its visits. It insisted on calling a separate meeting for the kolkhoz women, so as to persuade them of their independence from their menfolk.[114]

An undated set of questionnaires in the 1922 file for the Roslavl' area reveals the prickly atmosphere that prevailed between the busybodies from the towns, as the rustics perceived them, and the primitive mores of the rustics themselves. When asked if their shefi acted in too authoritarian a manner, some kolkhozniki at first said it was very rare, but then in peasant

[110] Smolensk Archive, file WKP 273/32.
[111] This was the figure given by *Narkomfin*. For 1924 it gave the number as 9,718. See M. Lewin, *Russian Peasants and Soviet Power* (London, 1968), p. 108.
[112] Smolensk Archive, file WKP 273/22.
[113] For more information on smychka at work in rural practice, see Ch. 2.
[114] Smolensk Archive, file WKP 273/22.

fashion slowly warmed up to the fact that they had been very angered by some young students who had written in *Rabochii put'* that their horses were badly fed and cleaned, and that they had not sown enough crops. The arrogance of Bolshevik-inspired youth towards the patriarchal rural community also transpires from other criticisms directed against younger visitors. But peasants also complained when what they called 'doctors' came out to inspect their cattle and sanitary arrangements, or when two peasants who had murdered their wives had to be handed over to a visiting 'social court' (*obshchestvennyi sud*) set up by a shefstvo team.[115] The party's myopic concentration on the kind of agricultural organizations it wished to nurture for the future is also shown in the frequent reports for 1922 on the fragile co-operative network.[116] These efforts proved to be in vain for the most part. By the middle of 1924 the Agitprop section of the *Smolgubkom* was openly declaring that both shefstvo and smychka were a farce in actuality because they had deteriorated into mass weekend outings to the countryside in search of illicit stills. This led to the usual 'drinking bout . . . This kind of smychka produces nothing but harm.'[117]

Three documents dealing with political culture at the Smolensk and Roslavl' levels convey several general impressions. Party officials full of earnest endeavour were passing down all-Russian directives from Moscow in rather a wooden manner. There were too many organizational structures with too few members and even less real action. Above all, local educational standards were as yet not up to the demands put upon them by 'the Centre'. In 1922 even the Moscow intelligentsia continued to confuse Old and New Style dates.[118] There was little hope for political enlightenment in the provinces at a time when the number of literary centres and of those attending them fell to one-tenth of what they had risen to in 1921.[119] This was largely the result of the application of khozraschet and the transference of funds for adult education to local budgets. Menshevik

[115] Smolensk Archive, file WKP 273/22.
[116] For an example see ibid., file WKP 125.
[117] Ibid., file WKP 277 for July 1924.
[118] N. Mandelshtam, *Hope Abandoned* (Oxford, 1975), p. 75.
[119] See *Pedagogicheskaia entsiklopediia*, vol. 3 (Moscow), pp. 355 ff.

critics of the regime claimed that compared with the pre-revolutionary period Russia in 1922 had 30 per cent fewer schools overall and that 70 per cent of all children between 8 and 11 years of age were illiterates.[120] When it is also remembered that Belorussia had the lowest literacy rate of all European Russia, the sluggish response of the denizens of the Roslavl' area comes as no surprise.

Local involvement in nation-wide politics does not just depend on intellectual evolution, however, but on the strong conviction that national affairs affect one's life and so need to be considered. After all, hundreds of fundamental revolutions involving the whole and almost completely illiterate populace of countries have taken place in the history of civilization. As late as the end of the nineteenth century in some Western European states local politics retained their dominance over central concerns, until markets, jobs, and communications like the railways became part of a national whole. Until such a time peasants in a country like France were really only interested in a few restricted matters like land, taxes, and the threat of military service. These remained the concerns of Belorussian peasants in the 1920s, but unlike French peasants there were no small-scale politics for them to latch on to in order to climb slowly out of their deep provincialism. For lack of alternative parties or serious candidates with known individual characters to vote for, a gulf opened up between the isolated villagers on the one hand and the Roslavl' or Smolensk Party men on the other, intent on modelling themselves strictly on Smolensk or Moscow prototypes and on Moscow's instructions.

When we read in the Roslavl' files that twenty-three agitator brigades were dispatched to villages in order to celebrate international Women's Day,[121] it is hard to imagine that they ever came across our peasant woman from Struga, and even more difficult to believe that they would have much impact on her ways of thinking even if they did. She would probably conform to the type of village heroine K. Fedin described in his story *Tishina* (Stillness) which depicts the depths of Smolensk guberniia in 1922–3, where Fedin was to spend several summers during NEP. In his notes Fedin writes of his heroine: 'She

[120] *Nasha zhizn'*, Nov. 1922.
[121] Smolensk Archive, file WKP 273/32.

is somehow reconciled, and of course she would never go off anywhere for good. She lives in stillness. There is no world for her outside this stillness ... the world ends somewhere beyond Kaluga' (a nearby provincial centre).[122]

The economic provisions of NEP were soon to act as a slow salve on the material well-being of the peasantry, but even before NEP had begun all political bridges between the centre and a free-thinking periphery had been burnt with the establishment of a one-party system and the elimination of any traces of local independence in the party hierarchy. This lack of initiative in the hierarchy will be examined at the middle (Moscow–Smolensk) levels in the chapter on Bolshevik controls. As good Marxists the Bolshevik leaders tended to believe that following on the eventual restoration and 'correct' development of favourable economic conditions, 'correct' social and political attitudes would also come about at all levels. This view seems to have rubbed off on foreign, non-Marxist interpreters of the passage of NEP, who as a whole are inclined to think that a cultural policy of *laissez-faire* was pursued throughout NEP. In fact this was not so right from the start, even at the sophisticated intellectual heights of Petrograd, as will be seen when we approach that city. If at the beginning of NEP local party attitudes appeared to contain an element of *laissez-faire*, this was only because very little in fact could be achieved for lack of human and other resources. Certainly in the Smolensk and Kursk gubernii the will was there from the outset to mould and to control. The strict pedagogic methods and moral precepts being worked out in 1922 by A. Makarenko at a microcosmic level near Poltava[123] were to be taken over and applied wholesale to Stalin's Russia in the 1930s. Even Krupskaia at the hub of power quickly modified her earlier liberal views concerning the inculcation of political culture. In the early 1920s she published a series of three guide-lines for the removal of what she termed as 'counter-revolutionary' literature from local libraries. The volume issued in the early spring of 1923 applied above all to village libraries. She took a no-nonsense approach. Although she held that both abstract and concrete points of view were valuable, she labelled all

---

[122] K. Fedin, *Sobranie sochinenii*, vol. 2 (Moscow, 1970), p. 543.
[123] See Ch. 2, pp. 83 ff.

Russian peasants as practically inclined. She therefore proscribed all religious, philosophical, or psychological books for
village libraries. Tracts were to be chosen solely for their
propaganda value and for their capacity to instil a Communist
'world' view.[124] The ex-peasant Maxim Gorky threatened to
renounce his Soviet citizenship on discovering 'this intellectual
vampirism', as he called it,[125] but Krupskaia's directives were
allowed to pursue their philistine course. If minds of the calibre
of Krupskaia were so firmly closed so soon, there was little hope
that her pedagogic instructions would serve to open the minds
of the *temnye liudi* in the Smolensk or any other guberniia.

[124] Krupskaia, op. cit., vol. 3, p. 139.
[125] See Gorky's letter to the poet Khodasevich of 8 Nov. 1923, in *Harvard Slavic Studies*, 1 (Cambridge, Mass., 1953), pp. 306–7.

## 2. *The Centre*

As the crow flies, or rather those rooks in A. K. Savrasov's famous painting, the distance south-east from Smolensk to Kursk is 480 km., which is a fraction more than the distance due north from Kursk to Moscow, and 80 km. deeper into the provinces than Smolensk from the capital. Like Smolensk, Kursk was a guberniia administrative centre in 1922 and also lay in a river-valley (the Seim) amongst low hills. However surrounding agricultural conditions were very different. We shall not linger in Kursk itself but wander gently down a side road through this part of the Central Agricultural Region until we reach the Nikol'skaia volost' (cluster of villages) roughly 40 km. to the south-east (Roslavl' lay 110 km. from Smolensk). Here relationships between the local inhabitants and party members and agents will be examined without reference to Kursk, let alone to Moscow. Then we shall head due south again on the same road, passing into the Ukraine and out of the hills. The first large and industrial city we reach is Kharkov. After a brief stay there, we move south-west into the ubiquitous rural ocean until we arrive at a remarkable experimental settlement just off the main road between Kharkov and Poltava. This is the colony for young vagrants and orphans recently established by Anton Makarenko. In order to make some local comparisons with Nikol'skaia, ties between the fifty-nine party cells and the people in Poltava guberniia will be looked at in passing. Again no reference will be made to party authorities in the guberniia capital, since this has already been done for Smolensk. In Chapter 3 the focus will be directed instead on those contacts between the guberniia centres of Saratov and Samara and Moscow which were crucial for the alleviation of the famine conditions.

Kursk guberniia was in the famous central Black-Earth area

which also covered all, or most of Tambov, Orlov, and Voronezh gubernii, with the southern uezdy of Tula and Riazan' gubernii. The fertile soil made it a grain-surplus area, in contrast to Belorussia and the north-west in general. However market relations were much less developed in the Kursk guberniia than in the productive Ukraine and Volga areas. This was partly due to the weak local transport system and remoteness from urban influences. The most striking difference from Smolensk lay in the large numbers of peasant communes: before 1917 most Belorussian farms had belonged to individual families. They had averaged less than 20 acres, whereas in Kursk guberniia heavily populated and extensive communes prevailed.[1] This system led to many problems. Plot sizes were very small and the distance between them large. Each household worked up to forty separate strips.[2] If a family held a small amount of land and was in a village with a large number of households, its strips could be so small and scattered that too much time was spent in travelling between strips. Some of these would therefore lie fallow. The overall result before and after the 1917 Revolution was pressure on land and frequent redistribution. In this Kursk guberniia was quite unlike Western Russia and also Siberia, which had never experienced strip-farming and redistribution.

What broad effects did these diverse economic and social conditions have on nascent political behaviour? Given the enormous upheavals in all areas from 1917 onwards and the consequent stirring up and obscuring of peasant reactions, the clearest historical clues on this question may be gleaned from peasant elections and behaviour in the quieter period of the State Dumas. Socio-economic problems remained largely the same in 1905–14 and 1922 in Kursk guberniia (though not of course in the Lower Volga area on account of the Famine).

Peasant representatives for the Black-Earth Region in the Dumas had shown no interest in any political problem apart from the land issue. On this question all social grades had taken the same line—the need to seize local gentry estates. Yet despite

---

[1] In the Black-Earth region as a whole, the commune comprised on average 400–500 households. See I. Oganovsky, *Obshchina i zemel'noe tovarishchestvo* (Moscow, 1923), p. 8.

[2] See V. P. Danilov, 'Zemel'nye otnosheniia v sovetskoi dokolkhoznoi derevne', *Istoriia SSSR*, 3 (Moscow, 1958).

this unanimous view, the peasants of the Central Agricultural Region were completely incapable of uniting amongst themselves or of taking any joint action. Instead of linking up with political parties, they relied on official helpers or on individual members of the gentry, who were normally their main opponents on the land question. This lack of sophistication and coordination was in marked contrast to the behaviour of the Siberian peasant representatives in the Dumas. They were active on a large number of political, economic, and cultural issues, and their views closely reflected their varying socioeconomic positions.

The fact that Siberia had never undergone strip-farming and redistribution, and was underpopulated, begins to account for this discrepancy. Most Siberian peasants also farmed the complex multifield rotational system. They could earn a return on a considerable number of different investments. They had to take many economic decisions in the course of each annual cycle, and according to their status and wealth they made different decisions from one another in various places and over the year. In all these ways they were more akin to urban dwellers, and felt they had some independent choices to make in order to improve their lives.

The lot of the Kursk peasant, in 1922 as shortly before 1917, was far more narrow. In his three-field system only investment in land really counted, and the commune, not the individual, controlled most forms of capital. Each annual cycle entailed the repetition of well-tried methods which had to be taken in common. A mentality of servile subordination interspersed by ineffective *jacqueries* tended to arise from such conditions. Furthermore there were minimal chances for urban or industrial employment in the vicinity. Worst of all there was very little interlocking between separate communes, a circumstance which was reflected in these peasants' lack of political cohesiveness in the Dumas.[3]

When we come to look in detail at the Nikol'skaia peasantry

[3] This comparison of differing political behaviour arising from varying socioeconomic conditions in Siberia and the Central Agricultural Region is based on an illuminating article by E. D. Vinogradoff, 'The Russian Peasantry and the Elections to the Fourth State Duma', in L. H. Haimson (ed.), *The Politics of Rural Russia 1905–1914* (Bloomington, 1979), pp. 219–60.

in 1922, many of these inhibiting features will become more evident. Yet the influence of the socio-economic background alone should not be exaggerated. Note should be taken of the political electoral system under which peasants had to vote, both in the Duma and the early Soviet period. The peasants of the Nikol'skaia volost', in the Duma elections as in 1922, did what all others did throughout Russia. The most enterprising and literate, those few who had travelled, in the army or otherwise, and the thin cream of village *intelligenty* (agronomists and the like) everywhere rose to the top in order to represent their less sophisticated brethren.

When a great political crisis arose, however, there was little to distinguish the political reactions of the Siberian from the Kursk peasantry. When the Constituent Assembly was dissolved after the 1917 Revolution, and the Bolsheviks' Land Decree had stolen the main plank of the Socialist Revolutionaries' platform, Siberian and Black-Earth peasants alike failed to give any further support to their still loyal party, despite the fact that for a period an SR-dominated Directory prevailed in eastern Russia. The vote for the SRs had been strong in the Kursk and Poltava gubernii.

Further non-economic influences that cannot be ignored are ethnic and religious differences. These do not concern us for Kursk guberniia, which was almost exclusively Great Russian and Orthodox, but the traditional independence of the Old Believer elements in the Siberian peasantry must not be forgotten. Kursk differed radically in this way from Poltava, which lay in the Ukraine. It was seen in the last chapter how minority ethnic and religious strands in the Smolensk guberniia presented a potential, though not an actual, source of unified protest against the central Great-Russian regime. Significantly, the European areas of the ex-Empire that had been more pronounced than Belorussia in their ethnic and/or religious divergence from the Great-Russian norm had either broken away from Bolshevik Russia (the Baltic littoral and Finland) or else created serious difficulties for the Bolsheviks (Georgia in 1922).

The various provinces of Russia were too many and too mixed to allow of any division into two or a few camps, irrespective of whether socio-economic conditions, nationality, religion, or politics are concerned. Thus in religious and ethnic matters, Smolensk stood somewhere between safer Kursk and insecure Finland, but numerous other areas were scattered along this spectrum between Finland and Smolensk, and between Smolensk and Kursk. In the present state of our knowledge of provincial life during the late Tsarist and early Soviet periods, no precise scale can as yet be drawn up on any single topic, let alone a general model that encompasses and balances all factors.

In 1917 Kursk guberniia was amongst the worst twelve Russian provinces affected by disorganized rural unrest. Four others also fell within the Central Agricultural Region. They all had a long tradition of agrarian troubles, and all suffered from overpopulation and land scarcity. Peasant rental of non-peasant lands was most widespread here and in the Middle Volga regions.[4] Violence was more widespread than in Smolensk and other gubernii near the fronts, despite the fact that the latter were more subject to disturbances caused by soldiers, according to militia reports.[5] The height of peasant unrest in the Central Agricultural Region was reached in early September 1917; the epicentre was the Koslov uezd of the Tambov guberniia, from where the killing of landowners and sacking of estates spread rapidly to Kursk and other neighbouring gubernii.[6]

Conditions in Kursk town seemed propitious for an anti-Bolshevik armed peasant uprising in October. Power lay in the hands of a Committee of Public Safety, which represented *all* local parties and institutions.[7] By the end of November the Kursk Soviet had cast aside this committee and set up its own provincial executive in which the Left Socialist Revolutionaries were the largest group. Rural representatives nearly outnumbered urban ones. Anarchists and SRs continued to wield considerable influence into the spring of 1918.[8]

In the middle of October 1917 peasants in the guberniia had carried out particularly aggressive seizures of land and timber.

[4] See A. Shestakov, 'Iiul'skie dni v derevne', *Proletarskaia revoliutsiia*, 5 (Moscow, 1927), p. 97.

[5] See G. Gill, *Peasants and Government in the Russian Revolution* (London, 1979), p. 167.

[6] *Delo naroda*, 15 Sept. 1917, p. 4.

[7] *Novaia zhizn'*, 11 Nov. 1917.

[8] I. Kolichevsky, 'Literatura ob oktiabr'skoi revoliutsii', *Proletarskaia revoliutsiia*, 37 (1924), p. 222.

According to the Bolsheviks' own admission, the local militia was incapacitated. The diminutive local garrison was ineffectual and demanded more pay. Peasants from nearby gubernii were coming in and exporting wheat. The local railway administrators were terrorized into collaborating.[9] Such tales of peasants stealing grain from one area to take elsewhere, or of refusals to supply it to hungry neighbours, were very common throughout all rural areas in 1917–18. Acts like these provide the superficial evidence for the failure, in Kursk as elsewhere, to keep Bolshevik encroachment at bay. The deeper reasons have been cited already. The peasants had little notion of belonging to any wider grouping than their own volost', like Nikol'skaia, or even sometimes, and depending on the subject, than their own village. If students in the 1990s have difficulty in distinguishing all the political parties and coalitions that sprang up in Petrograd after the February Revolution, how could a peasant in 1917 be expected to assimilate them in the place of the Tsar, who at least represented a more easily understood form of political authority? Peasant comprehension was low, but far from lacking altogether. It was clear to them in 1917 that if they smashed the local power structure, they were at least achieving some short-term practical aims, such as grabbing woods, estates, and livestock. They realized dimly that, for the moment at least, the Bolsheviks seemed even keener than the SRs to provoke similar disorder at all levels: and their Land Decree seemed indistinguishable from the old SR demands on behalf of the peasantry.

An outstanding example of peasant political particularism had occurred in 1921 in the Tambov guberniia bordering on Kursk. This was the best-known and recorded peasant revolt in Soviet history, yet its practical achievements were nil. As in Kursk, so in Tambov the potential had been there. In Tambov town there were reported to be as few as three Bolsheviks on the very eve of the October Revolution. The local Soviet was under the firm control of the SRs.[10] Yet at the height of the Tambov revolt in 1921 only three south-eastern uezdy of the twelve comprising the guberniia were engulfed by

[9] *Iz istorii kurskogo kraia. Sbornik dokumentov i materialov* (Voronezh, 1965), p. 407.
[10] Kolichevsky, op. cit., p. 223.

disturbances.[11] Even here the peasantry was soon split as a result of Communist organization and the creation of a privileged group of peasant soldiers whose better food and clothes cut them off from their fellows. More striking still was the failure of the Green movement to link up with Kursk or any other neighbouring area. The Bolsheviks clung to Tambov town and prevented any contact with Makhno to the south in the Ukraine, or with Sapozhkov, another peasant rebel, on the Volga. Antonov, the Tambov leader, probably never realized anyway the strength of his neighbours in a period of chaotic means of communication. Yet it is hardly likely that even if links had been made a ramshackle group of peasant armies using antiquated military techniques could have stood out for long against the Red Army.

The effect of the Famine in 1921–2 was far more crippling in the Volga provinces than in Tambov guberniia, so that one can argue either way as to whether it had a stimulating or depressing effect on the mettle of the Tambov Greens; certainly in Samara and Saratov its vehemence blew out all hope of resistance. More telling were the concessions ceded by NEP. When Antonov was finally caught and killed on 24 June 1922, his slayers were warmly greeted by peasants as the corpse was taken into Tambov. We know this from Soviet accounts, but there is little reason to doubt them. They chime too well with human and especially Russian peasant nature. What can be discounted as nonsense on the other hand is the conclusion drawn by a Soviet historian with regard to the Tambov revolt: 'In that period the kulaks' political banditry became the most important means of struggle by international imperialism.'[12] Antonov could not even make contact with subversive elements in Kursk guberniia, let alone London.

A closer look at relationships between the party and the people in the Kursk area may be obtained by accompanying Ia. Yakovlev, nine statisticians, and four peasant communists on horseback along the road from Kursk to Nikol'skaia volost' at the end of 1922. Yakovlev at this time was head of the

---

[11] See O. Radkey, *The Unknown Civil War in Soviet Russia: A Study of the Green Movement in the Tambov Region 1920–1921* (Stanford, 1976), p. 385.

[12] I. Ia. Trifonov, *Klassy i klassovaia bor'ba v SSSR v nachale NEPa* (Leningrad, 1964), p. 77.

Agitation and Propaganda Section of the Communist Party. His aim was to assess local reactions to Bolshevik rule in 775 peasant households. By travelling with him we are reversing the process adopted with our peasant woman in the Smolensk guberniia. Here the rulers are going to the ruled and examining them from their point of view.

The first change they noticed as a result of the Revolution was the indiscriminate and wasteful hacking down of the woods by the peasants: large trees had merely been deprived of their thinner branches. Schoolhouses were soon easy to spot by their lack of doors and window frames and dilapidated thatched roofs. They had been abandoned and pillaged. In many ways, however, the old customs continued. Although younger peasants stared with curiosity at the little band of visitors, the old ones made deep bows—'the legacy of the age of serfdom', as Yakovlev commented. The best-kept huts were still those of the village priests. They were the only ones with glass windows and metal roofs. Outside one church the crowd of peasants young and old was so large that it was reminiscent of Repin's famous painting of 1882 of a church procession in this pious guberniia. On asking the reason for such an assembly, Yakovlev was told that the local priest had refused to marry any couples unless the community attended services.[13] Here there was not the slightest evidence of 'religion and Communism making an excellent household together', as *Izvestiia* now reported.[14]

Another sign of the past was carefully concealed from passing strangers, but Yakovlev's interest was aroused by the frequent sight of windowless huts with smoke pouring out from all sides of their thatched roofs. On entering one, he discovered a home-brew still which the owners broke up in a trice, handing the retort to Yakovlev 'as a trophy'. This practice was very widespread in Kursk as opposed to the Smolensk guberniia. It was a prime grain-producing area with poor access to markets. A barter economy still prevailed widely in 1922, so that alcohol was a money substitute that kept and travelled better than grain. As one peasant put it to Yakovlev on a later

---

[13] The sights seen by the Bolshevik inspectors are recorded in Ia. Yakovlev, *Derevnia kak ona est': ocherki Nikol'skoi volosti* (Moscow, 1923), pp. 5–7.

[14] See ch. 2 above, p. 42.

occasion: 'No one will help you for cash, but everyone will for home-brew.' A local priest was even so bold as to call the system 'a home-brew democracy. ... In the towns they drink wine and liqueurs, but we can't do that in the villages ... the result is that the gents can drink, but it's forbidden to the lower classes.'[15]

Another difference between Nikol'skaia and Roslavl' was the obvious greater isolation of the former, although it was nearer to the guberniia capital. That did not mean much, since Kursk was itself a drowsy centre with almost no factories and only the main railway line from Moscow to enliven it. As late as 1926 90.9 per cent of all inhabitants in the guberniia were in rural locations, one of the highest percentages for European Russia.[16] Nikol'skaia volost' had actually become even more cut off since 1917. Whereas only 146 households out of 775 had lacked any horses, the number had risen to 175 by 1922. Virtually all local trading was transacted in grain rather than in cash, thus limiting peasants' ability to travel far with their heavy 'money' loads. Prior to 1917 there had been two annual fairs (*iarmarki*) in the area, but only one of them had been revived in 1921, with a quarter of its previous turnover. In the past some craft-trading had been carried on beyond the vicinity, but this and nearly all other economic ties with the Ukraine to the south and their fellow Great Russians to the north had stopped.[17] The picture was even worse with regard to information from outside. Out of the 775 households in five villages, only one, headed by an ex-merchant, subscribed to a newspaper of any kind. Even Ivanovka, the only village not far from the Moscow railway line, had received its last single copy of a newspaper some months prior to Yakovlev's visit.[18] A striking example of the area's isolation occurred when Yakovlev and his thirteen men arrived at the end of their horse-ride in the village of Nikol'sk. Since 1917 the locals had never seen such a large group of visitors. As a result the peasant gathering (skhod) which happened to be scheduled then assembled an unusually high number of villagers. All they could imagine was that some

---

[15] Yakovlev, op. cit., pp. 7, 107, 111.
[16] *Predvaritel'nye itogi perepisi po Kurskoi gubernii* (Kursk, 1927), p. 16.
[17] Yakovlev, op. cit., pp. 30, 34, 42–3.
[18] Ibid., pp. 86–7.

new sort of tax was to be imposed on them. They were relieved to find that this was not just another 'Communist trick'.[19]

How was the common lot of this audience changing in 1922? The number of working hands had risen in the volost' from 577 in 1917 to 872 now. This was mainly due to demobilization, but others may have been attracted to the region due to the fact that through the expropriation of landowners, the area held by peasants had gone up by 65 per cent since 1917.[20] This huge increase should have allayed the peasants' suspicions of the new regime, but this was not the case. By 1922 only 232 households owned a plough, whilst 278 lacked even a primitive wooden plough with which to turn over their new earth, if indeed they possessed any. In 1917 a mere fifty-three households had been able to sell off excess grain. In 1920 this figure dropped to twelve, despite the fact that this area suffered less in the Civil War than Smolensk guberniia. By the end of 1922 the figure had jumped to a remarkable 155, showing that recovery was on the way and economic activity increasing. Another sign of security was the rising number of households which did not need to buy seeds, but planted their own—634 in the autumn of 1922, as against 554 in 1920.[21] The other side of the coin was the increasing subjection in 1922 of the poor peasants to those better off. Yakovlev may have exaggerated this shift, given the abstract Marxist tenets on class struggle that he came equipped with from Moscow, but there was already some objective evidence of this right at the start of NEP. Peasants told his collaborators that under NEP conditions not even the poorest received financial help and advice on sowing and agricultural methods from the local Soviets, as they had done previously, during the period of War Communism. When the cutting of timber free of charge was prohibited, it affected the poor peasants most severely. They could not afford to buy a horse, and although the richer peasants were more heavily taxed, this did not compensate for the wide difference in equipment, which was not taxed. As there were up to sixteen different taxes, the more ignorant, who were usually also the poorest, were compelled to run to their more fortunate fellows for

---

[19] Ibid., pp. 9–10.
[20] Ibid., pp. 26–7.
[21] Ibid., pp. 26–32.

advice on how to calculate, time, and pay (or avoid paying) these complex dues.[22]

Another kind of hazard was already looming on the horizon for the weaker peasant elements. As trade slowly picked up, so did the number of non-peasant traders. They were later to acquire the vague title of 'Nepmen', but in 1922 they were not so clear-cut a phenomenon, and even by the end of NEP it was not possible, despite all Bolshevik propaganda efforts, to lump their origins and subsequent characteristics into the same abstract pigeon-hole. Their diverse origins can be seen in the microcosm of Nikol'skaia volost' alone. Most scholars, both Soviet and Western, have thought that Nepmen sprang up from nowhere like mushrooms under the gentle economic rain of NEP. In fact many of them were pre-1917 private traders who surfaced again after 1921.

The richest local personality was Dmitrii Alekseevich D'iakov. After twenty years of trading in the volost' and in Kursk town he came to own by 1914 eight houses (four of them in Kursk) and had a turnover of a million roubles. In 1918 his stock was confiscated, but he became chairman of the co-operative to which it was assigned. By 1919 he was also heading a government grain-collecting centre. When this job terminated at the start of NEP, he became the State Bank's Kursk agent for purchasing grain. In December 1922 he resigned graciously to return to his large goods store which had already started up in June. Here Yakovlev met him surrounded by packed shelves and metals acquired with two months' credit from the Tartar Republic. He confessed that everyone trusted him now, as they had done in the old days.[23] Three other local traders from pre-war times had also acted as careful vicars of Bray until 1922. All had served for state organizations during the period 1917–21. One had served as chairman of a local Soviet through these years, with a canny transformation into *starosta* (village elder) when the White Army appeared briefly. Another had kept a continual eye on the grain trade by serving in a Red Army supply regiment and then managing a state grain-collecting centre.[24]

Of the new 'Nepmen', two were Jews who had come in from

---

[22] Yakolev, op. cit., pp. 37–9.     [23] Ibid., pp. 44–7.     [24] Ibid., pp. 47–9.

some other guberniia, and the other three all had military experience but little capital in goods or cash. Nevertheless they were to flourish. From a monthly turnover of 400 roubles at the end of December 1922, one of them was to rise to a turnover of 2,000 by March 1923. At the time of Yakovlev's visit, the state-controlled grain organizations still controlled 45 per cent of all trading turnover in goods and cash, as opposed to 12 per cent through private hands, but Yakovlev realized that the balance was changing quickly in favour of the Nepmen.[25]

Thus not long after the start of NEP, in a province as sleepy as Kursk, we find already the seeds of socio-economic decay, from a Marxist point of view (Yakovlev's), leading to possible political difficulties for the centre. The irony was that many Nepmen had in fact been nurtured by the state during the harsh economic stringencies of War Communism. Here, as so often when one penetrates to particulars, the rigid historio-graphical divisions (War Communism, NEP, the Five-Year Plan years) crumble. In our survey of the financial arrange-ments of NEP as they applied to the Smolensk guberniia, it was noted how they were unstable and poorly defined from the outset, leading to economic and social tensions at the lower levels.[26] Right from its inception NEP carried within itself the germs of its own fatal illness, whether one looks at its fiscal organization or the economic persona (like these Nepmen) which it soon evoked, or in many cases re-awakened.

It is true that high-level Bolshevik theorists in Moscow and Petrograd tended to select, filter, and interpret evidence from the localities in the light of their prevailing general beliefs, so that their conclusions had little foundation in hard evidence. Yet although Yakovlev was one of their kind, his factual findings show little sign of conscious or unconscious censorship or exclusion. What we do find, as with the few collective farms in Roslavl', is an obsession with possible growth-points admired by the Bolsheviks. Yakovlev devotes loving attention to the single, insignificant *sovkhoz* (state farm) in the whole area, although it only employed eleven people. If only more leading Bolsheviks had left their ivory tower in the Kremlin in early NEP in order to examine Russia at first hand, as Yakovlev did,

---

[25] Ibid., pp. 49–53.     [26] See above, p. 47.

the reifications that poured out from their pens and mouths might not have succeeded in obscuring the realities of actual life in the 1920s.

On reaching the rarefied heights of Moscow politics, more attention will be paid to the ideas of Lenin and others on smychka, the Marxist-Leninist theory of town and country alliance. At this point of our journey attempts at smychka in practice between the more sophisticated and politically orthodox in and out of the party, and the Nikol'skaia peasantry, can be considered. The volost' party cell and its activities are taken first, before moving to less politically secure organs like the local village Soviets and the Komsomol (Young Communist League). Then other potentially useful agents, the ex-military, and teachers, will be examined.

At first sight the very core of party support appeared to be rotten. The party cell contained several dubious characters. Only three of the eleven members were peasants. Two of the others, including the chairman, were using their positions to feather their own nests. The cell secretary told Yakovlev that 'for one named Kochergin and for the chairman of the cell they [the peasants] have stabbing eyes.'[27] Kochergin was the son of a merchant, from the same type of background as D'iakov. The cell members said that four of them read papers regularly (that is, once a week), four read them seldom, and the rest very rarely. One member shone out from this picture of lethargy and petty corruption. He was a former horse-vet who provided the teachers with food when it was short, criticized the priests, and guarded the local fire-carts. This latter task was not as trivial as may be supposed in a society where wood and straw huts burnt down regularly.

There were no cell meetings open to the public. The cell failed to send anyone to take part in the few educational courses available, such as those arranged by the agricultural station. Its total energy seemed to be expended on the collection of taxes, and like Yakovlev himself, it had no interest in the mainsprings of peasant culture. It comes as no surprise to discover from another source that in 1921 the Kursk guberniia party committee had tried to deal with these problems;

---

[27] Yakovlev, op. cit., p. 66.

'the purge of the party was the first basic step towards the strengthening of the personnel of the party and yielded enormous results.' This declaration proved to be premature, although a recommendation that there should be a longer term for the candidate stage towards full party membership must have provided a useful mechanism for sifting the wheat from the chaff.[28]

The reasons for the centre's need for taxes like the prodnalog and many others had not been made clear to the villagers by the party cell. The peasants saw the cell as just one more town agency that confined itself to tax gathering, as all other organizations from the centre had done in history. Indeed since eight of the eleven cell members were not peasants, they probably fell easily into this view of their own roles. When an anti-tubercular campaign was initiated by the cell, the peasants called it the 'tubercular tax', because money gathering methods were applied. The party cell was afraid to have open meetings mainly because it feared criticism from what it called the '*kulaks*'.[29] Yakovlev acquiesced in this polemical and unfounded notion. In actuality it was the poorer peasants who grumbled louder and suffered more from taxation, as Yakovlev was to discover for himself a year later in Tambov guberniia. He at least, unlike his superiors in ideology in Moscow had the courage to revise his stereotyped class views in a second book he published in 1924.[30] He found that a poor Tambov peasant who harvested 35 pudy of grain from one desiatin of land had to pay 15 pudy of it for the hire of a plough, 7 pudy for having the grain carted off in a richer man's wagon, and to top it all 7 pudy in tax. This left a mere 6 pudy for his family's consumption and to provide seed. The crux of the problem lay in the lack of equipment. In 1922 on average throughout European Russia and Siberia the percentage of peasant households without a plough was about 33 per cent.[31] In the Revolution landowners had disposed of large quantities of farm equipment to those who could afford it.[32] Subsequently only the latter

[28] *Znamiia kommunizma: organ Kurskogo gubkoma RKP(b)*, 4–5 (1922), p. 33.
[29] Yakovlev, op. cit., p. 65.
[30] Yakovlev, *Nasha derevnia. Novoe v starom i staroe v novom* (Moscow, 1924), pp. 24–5.
[31] A. Gaister, *Rassloenie sovetskoi derevni* (Moscow, 1928), pp. 70–1.
[32] See M. Kubanin, 'K istorii oktiabr'ia v derevne', *Istorik Marksist*, 7 (Moscow, 1928), pp. 18–35. It is interesting to note that in some radical Black-Earth regions the

could pay to have complicated machinery repaired. None of the sixteen taxes endured by the Nikol'skaia peasants was aimed at capital held in the form of equipment.

Despite the trials of many peasants in 1922, the Nikol'skaia villagers tolerated the party cell although they disliked some individuals within it. Cell members themselves seemed to be much more impervious to the danger of possible political attacks on them than their nervous counterparts in Smolensk guberniia. This difference appears to be a clear reflection of the traditional lack of political sophistication amongst Black-Earth peasants. The quiet but bitter resignation of the vast majority was expressed to Yakovlev by one of them in this way: 'A peasant is a sheep, and whoever wants his wool fleeces him. The Tsar, the landowner, Denikin's troops, and your Comrades all fleeced him. But now they'll have to spare his wool, or they'll rip off his hide and then there'll be no wool left to fleece.'[33]

Even at the level of the Nikol'sk village Soviet a high proportion of time was spent on tax problems. *Rabkrin* (the Central Workers' and Peasants' Inspectorate) calculated that at the start of 1923 from 20 to 26 per cent of all village Soviet business lay in this sphere, whereas cultural and commune activities took up only 5 to 10 per cent of their time.[34] In the village Soviets of the Nikol'skaia volost' 162 out of the 775 households had served since 1917 in some capacity. This very high participation rate was due to the fast turnover in membership, especially of the chairmen, who were very poorly paid in a time of rapid inflation.[35] Two criteria had governed their election. The leading one was that there were sufficient other able-bodied persons in the household to enable one of them to be freed for Soviet work. The other indicator was political. When the Soviets were first set up, richer peasants had become chairmen, but soon and throughout the period of War Communism poor peasants had replaced them. Now, in 1922, some

local peasants managed to prevent this flow of capital wealth to the richer peasant element. For Tambov guberniia, see *Velikaia oktiab'rskaia sotsialisticheskaia revoliutsiia, dokumenty i materialy, mai-iun'* (Moscow, 1957), doc. 350.

[33] Yakovlev, *Derevnia kak ona est'*, p. 40.
[34] *Vlast' sovetov*, 2 (1924), p. 50.
[35] See M. Boldyrev, *Sel'skoe khoziaistvo na putiakh vosstanovleniia* (Moscow, 1925), pp. 769–823.

of the same rich peasants were making a reappearance together with newly prosperous ones.[36]

Relations between the village Soviets and the peasants varied according to local socio-economic conditions, not only from one region of Russia to another, but even between Nikol'sk and Ivanovka, roughly 75 km. apart. The Nikol'sk Soviet was dominated by an ex-merchant, who was chairman. He could compensate for his low official pay by means of the strings he could pull in conjunction with the other few rich peasants in the commune. Most of the other peasants were poor, but almost as deferential to the Soviet as the old men who bowed to Yakovlev along the road. They described their prosperous neighbours on the Soviet as 'very wise and under-standing', not only because they had proved it by accumulat-ing a little property, but above all because they were *pismennye*, or literate.[37] They had also survived what was referred to locally as the 'Old Economic Policy', or War Communism, which was universally disliked, even by the poorest. As one of them related to Yakovlev, he had tried to get straw from his brother in a nearby village when he ran out of lighting-fuel, but officials had stopped him, since he was stealing 'from the poor . . . there's sucilizm (*sic*) for you'.[38] Ivanovka Soviet on the other hand was managed by no obvious clique, and the very few rich peasants had no general influence in the village, which contained no poor households but a lot of middling ones. Yakovlev found this contrast with Nikol'sk bizarre and inex-plicable,[39] but he should not have done. The combination of deference to prosperity and literacy from one side, and the manipulation of equipment, local goods stores, and the like on the other easily created a vicious circle in Nikol'sk which could not be repeated in Ivanovka.

One of the prime aims of the system of Soviets was being thwarted in this region, and in many others throughout Russia. This was to draw the 'poor' and 'middle' peasants away from the private trade of the 'rich' and to turn them eventually towards an alliance (smychka) with urban inhabitants.

---

[36] Yakovlev, *Derevnia kak ona est'*, pp. 112, 116.
[37] Ibid., pp. 114–16.
[38] Ibid., p. 119.
[39] Ibid., p. 113.

Another important purpose was to use the village Soviets as
gates through which peasants would enter into wider administrative experience and escape from the stifling parochialism of
the mir and the skhod. This goal too appeared to be self-
defeating in the Nikol'skaia volost'. It was true that there were
now 'whole chanceries' of paperwork in the offices of village-
Soviet secretaries, but most of the secretaries had worked for
the volost' in the Tsarist regime and were somewhat suspect.
Other local agencies seemed to be flourishing. There were now
13 militiamen as against 6 in the old regime; 7 secretaries in the
medical centre as against 2; 72 administrators in the uezd-level
agricultural centre as against 16. The trouble was that their
general educational standard was much lower than in the past.
In 1922 11.6 per cent of all village Soviet officials were
illiterate.[40] Also there was a marked tendency for all efficient
personnel, especially Communists, to move quickly up the
hierarchy from the villages to the guberniia centres.[41] At the
highest levels by 1922 there was an almost complete overlap of
personnel between party and Soviet committees.[42] This meant
that the localities were overstaffed with poorly paid semi-
literates at the receiving end of an ever-growing mountain of
paperwork from the hyperactive guberniia towns and from
Moscow. The result, at least in Nikol'skaia volost', was that the
few literates from the old regime were starting to occupy the
best bureaucratic jobs and to run parish-pump economics and
politics in ways barely supervised from above and in fact quite
inimical to the aspirations of the guberniia officials. Yakovlev
realized this, and recommended that party men be sent out in
large numbers from Moscow and the guberniia towns. Not
only should they fill posts in the lower Soviets—they should
grasp the core of the political problem, which was cultural in
essence: they would have to run the literary points, the schools,
and the agricultural centres themselves in order to push the
peasantry into the twentieth century and towards socialism.[43]
It was the age-old problem that had not been solved since the
Populists first went to the people in the 1870s.

[40]   *Vlast' sovetov*, 1 (1924), p. 72.
[41]   Ibid., pp. 114, 120–1.
[42]   *Pravda*, 14 Jan. 1922.
[43]   Yakovlev, *Derevnia kak ona est'*, pp. 122–5.

For lack of sufficient members in the countryside, the party had to rely on the most lively agents to effect smychka between itself and the masses. Although the Komsomol in 1922 only enveloped 0.8 per cent of all peasant youth,[44] there did exist a cell in the Nikol'skaia volost', and seven of its twelve members were peasants. Unfortunately their crude tactics, due to a very low educational level, made them better counter-agents than agents for the Bolsheviks. They had not seen the party programme and regulations, nor any copy of their own journal *Young Guard*. They tried to drive the adult peasants into paying their taxes, instead of coaxing them. They spread round vicious tales about the priests, yet they had read nothing (those that could read) on religion. A local priest told Yakovlev that the Komsomols were the most eager and confirmed 'Communists', but then he had met no real ones to judge them by. The Komsomols themselves knew they did not understand the instructions they got from the party cell, and said so, but received no advice as a result.[45]

Yakovlev himself dismissed the Komsomols as 'scamps', and turned to demobilized Red Army men as another feasible link between party and people. This category was now proving vital to Bolshevik organization in the Roslavl' uezd, even if much of its work was more like security and espionage rather than positive encouragement to the peasantry to collaborate with the party. In the five villages of the Nikol'skaia volost' there were no less than twenty to twenty-five ex-servicemen in each. Their political knowledge surpassed that of the members of the party cell. They were more articulate, had seen something of the wider world, retained a thirst for knowledge, and were sceptical towards the Church. Yet this apparently admirable material proved to be of almost no use to the party. They feared that if they refused to marry or baptize their children in church, they would be ostracized in a particularly religiously minded part of Russia. They were sharp enough to realize that if they joined the party cell, they would likewise be cut off from their fellows for other reasons. In their view the older generation could never be persuaded of the value of a proletarian ideology. So they gave excuses of shortage of time or

[44] 'O sostave RKSM', in *Statisticheskii sbornik*, vol. 1 (Moscow, 1924), p. 10.
[45] Yakovlev, *Derevnia kak ona est'*, pp. 13, 68–70.

involvement in other activities to explain why they did not register for the rural party cell. One soldier even hid from Yakovlev the fact that he was a party member.[46]

It may be imagined that the village schoolteachers could establish cultural ties between party and peasant, but some of the weaknesses of these agents have already been revealed in the Smolensk guberniia.[47] Those that had not fled out of fear, political animosity to the Bolsheviks, or for lack of food and pay, were apt to be shackled as much by their own situation as by peasant recalcitrance to learn. Since the start of NEP schoolteachers had had to rely on the local mir, skhod, or Soviet for their pay. Any attempt on their part in, say, Nikol'sk village, to undermine the new controlling clique of richer peasants and nascent Nepmen through Communist-inspired teaching on class structure in the local school would result in their immediate loss of livelihood. Many peasants, particularly the less well off, still preferred the priest as a source of education. As one told Yakovlev: 'the priest is well taught, you can't chuck him out. We don't want any new religion: a new religion means new churches. We'd have to pay out more money, so let's stick to the old one.'[48] The schoolhouses had been left empty in the Revolution, and then ransacked by peasants, as the Bolshevik investigators had noticed on their way to Nikol'skaia. When questioned about this, one peasant retorted 'From where else are we to take thatch, there's nothing left on which to feed the livestock.'[49] An exception proved the rule. One peasant walked 15 versts to get Yakovlev to act on a building designated for a school that was still occupied by an influential peasant. He was granted his request, but he walked another 40 versts to the uezd party committee to see that the promise was kept. If necessary he would walk to Lenin himself in Moscow.[50] In this 'Leninist', as he was dubbed, still shone that naïve peasant trust in the very highest authority that had

---

[46] *Derevnia kak ona est'*, pp. 66–7, 70–3.

[47] Above, p. 51. The fact that by 1914 most rural teachers were women from urban backgrounds added two more reasons for the lack of respect towards them. See B. Eklof, 'The Village and the Outsider: The Rural Teacher in Russia, 1864–1914', in *Slavic and European Education Review*, 1 (1979), pp. 1–19.

[48] Yakovlev, *Derevnia kak ona est'*, p. 89.

[49] Ibid., p. 88.

[50] Ibid., pp. 94–5.

kept the Romanovs secure for so long. This anonymous peasant sensed intuitively the lack of communication between the centre and the grass roots, and was prepared to overcome it through personal effort. In any backward society the role of sympathetic intermediary agents and interpreters between high and rural politics is crucial. They have to ensure the concrete yet flexible transmission of written, central theories to illiterates by means of patient speech and demonstration. Their kind was sadly lacking in Nikol'skaia volost' in 1922. The plight of the teachers became even worse in 1923. The central authorities, late as usual, grasped this detail of local life by 1924, when Krupskaia at the Thirteenth Party Congress noted that due to the tightening of the economic 'scissors', the higher bread prices could no longer be afforded by starving village-teachers.[51]

For lack of sympathetic agents, the peasants were often left to their own devices in matters of general and even political culture. Yakovlev observed that state publications for 1922 from Gosizdat and Krasnaia Nov' included nothing on agricultural and rural affairs.[52] How could the undiluted works of Kautsky and Engels appeal to this audience at a time when even party members at lower levels rarely understood the meaning of such concrete words as 'official', 'categorical', 'Plenum', 'memorandum', or 'territory'?[53] Only five peasants in the whole of Nikol'skaia volost' had read any political or agricultural texts. The minds of the other literate villagers were dissipated on what they could pick up in a random manner: most of it naturally consisted of religious tracts, the traditional fodder left over from the past.[54]

To sum up, in 1922 the Soviet government found itself in a situation similar to that of the late Tsarist regime, which in its final years had grasped the connection between literacy and modernization and between formal schoolwork and social control. Neither political system could rely with confidence on those to whom it entrusted the task of educating the peasants.

---

[51] *Stenographic report of the Thirteenth Party Congress*, May 1924, pp. 480, 481–2.

[52] Yakovlev, *Derevnia kak ona est'*, pp. 98–100.

[53] See Ia. Shafir, *Gazeta i derevnia* (Moscow, 1924), *passim*. These were all words of foreign derivation. Even city-workers had difficulty in understanding acronyms. See Shafir, p. 69.

[54] Yakovlev, *Derevnia kak ona est'*, pp. 96–8.

Yakovlev's group understood this perfectly well. They advocated the promotion of party schools at the guberniia level to
speed up the educational attainments of local leaders so that
they really could set the tone in political culture in sufficient
numbers without having to depend so much on shaky agents.
Yakovlev wanted to see eight to ten thousand new cultural
workers sent to the villages over the next two to three years.
This large number would still provide just one per volost' in the
largest of all countries.[55]

The gulf between peasant and party which Yakovlev noticed
in the Kursk guberniia was typical of all rural localities in early
NEP, despite their enormous local differences from each other
in every other way. It was the case in Smolensk, and the
position was very similar in Poltava, the guberniia to the south-
west which we shall be visiting shortly. During this same period
a far wider survey had been undertaken of all the fifty-nine
party cells in the Poltava guberniia. It was found that scant
attention had been paid to raising the cultural level of party
members. As to the wider dissemination of culture, the few cells
that had been active in this respect seemed to equate success
with the regular dispatch of newspapers and made no personal
contacts to follow this up.[56]

In other spheres the results of the Poltava survey were closely
reminiscent of the Nikol'skaia findings. There were no discussions at all on the improvement of the peasant economy,
despite the fact that they would have reaped quick propaganda
rewards for the Bolshevik Party. This was the earth of which
Aleksei Tolstoy wrote: 'Know ye the land where all breathes
plenty and content, where rivers flow as silver clear.' It
comprised some of the very best of the Black-Earth belt, but
after the Revolution it had been trampled over first by the Red
Army advancing on Kiev from Kharkov, then by the German
20th Army Corps, and later by ruthless and bloodthirsty
'Green' armies. The worst peasant uprisings in the Civil War
had been against German expeditions in search of food supplies.[57] If there had to be a foreign, non-Ukrainian government

[55] *Derevnia kak ona est'*, p. 105. (Part of the preceding section was published as an
article in *The Slavonic and East European Review*, July 1985.)

[56] Ibid., pp. 80–2.

[57] See W. E. D. Allen, *The Ukraine: A History* (New York, 1963), pp. 282–3, 289, 297,
314.

in Poltava, then for the local peasantry Great Russians were preferable to Germans. Yet the Bolsheviks made no political capital out of the recent past. As in Nikol'skaia volost', all fifty-nine Poltava cells spent nearly all their time and energy on tax-collecting and expediting administrative directives from higher authorities.[58]

Let us now leave the Great Russians of the Kursk guberniia and move out of the hills to the south of Nikol'skaia volost'. Eventually the plains of the eastern Ukraine are reached, and the city of Kharkov. It was atypical of most provincial towns in that it had been a thriving industrial centre for some time, and was taking off again after the disruption caused by the Civil War. We would be imitating the Bolsheviks' own rose-tinted over-concentration on their favourite study topics (like the proletariat state and collective farms) if we lingered here too long. On the other hand any balanced survey of early Soviet society cannot ignore the presence in certain pockets of strong working-class forces. The proletariat of the guberniia capital of Tver and Moscow city will be studied in more detail in 1926. The special case of a disseminated labour force, the railway and other communications workers, will be looked at for 1922. In 1917 roughly one million had been employed on the Russian railway network.

The town census of 1923 gave the population of Kharkov as 324,500. Like its larger industrial brothers, Petrograd and Moscow, it had declined fast between 1917 and 1920 (the number of inhabitants fell by a quarter). Yet by the end of 1926 its strength would rise to 417,300, of whom 28.8 per cent were industrial workers, and 13.5 per cent independent traders, including kustary.[59] In 1926 38.3 per cent of the population were Ukrainian as against 37.9 at the time of the 1923 census.[60] Kharkov was a major centre for metallurgy, chemical, and machine-building plants. By 1924, when these industries had re-established themselves, one-fifth of all factory workers in the Ukraine were concentrated in the Kharkov and Ekaterina

---

[58] Yakovlev, *Derevnia kak ona est'*, pp. 78–84.

[59] M. V. Kurman and I. V. Lebensinsky, *Naselenie bol'shogo sotsialisticheskogo goroda* (Moscow, 1968), pp. 20–1, 122, 188.

[60] S. Kossior, *Die Ergebnisse und die nächsten Aufgaben der Nationalitätenpolitik in der Ukraine* (Moscow, 1934), pp. 17–18.

gubernii.[61] The kustar' system, which recovered much faster than heavy industry, had 122 *arteli* in the city in 1922. They organized a craft exhibition in January that attracted interest from abroad. The more isolated character of Kursk guberniia may be illustrated by the fact that the whole province contained only 595 arteli.[62] Although most of the new recruits to Kharkov's metallurgical plants in 1914–17 had been ex-peasants from western Ukraine, there was no danger of nationalist sentiment ousting the Bolsheviks from the city. They had wrested factory management from the hands of the very right-wing Congress of Mining Industrialists which had disallowed even neutral forms of workers' control in 1917.[63] For part of the Civil War Kharkov rather than Kiev became the temporary capital of the Ukraine, and a Bolshevik military stronghold. Its civilian upper echelons remained predominantly Great Russian into the 1920s.

As we travel south-west along the main road to Poltava, the feeling of being under secure Bolshevik rule recedes. In this rural area there had been no fewer than nineteen peasant uprisings in 1919.[64] It was clear from the reports on fifty-nine cells in this guberniia that collaboration between the party and the people was minimal. The density of population in this finest of all Black-Earth regions rose to 60–70 per sq. km. There were scarcely any towns of significance near Poltava. As in Kursk guberniia, the classical three-field system prevailed, but there was more variety. The lucrative sugar-beet industry had led to the buying up of large tracts of land before the World War. The production of vegetable oil, especially sunflower seed, was also important. The climate becomes more benign as we move nearer to the Black Sea. Male peasants in the fields wear their distinctive broad-brimmed straw hats, with their coats hanging loosely over their shoulders.[65]

---

[61] *Trud v SSSR: statistiko-ekonomicheskii obzor, oktiabr' 1922 do marta 1924* (Moscow, 1925), pp. 21–2.

[62] D. A. Kaplan, *Kustarnaia promyshlennost' Ukrainy* (Kharkov, 1922), pp. 15, 20, 22.

[63] The author is indebted to Dr Paul Flenley for the information on metal workers in Kharkov.

[64] A. G. Shlikhter, 'Bor'ba za khleb na Ukraine v 1919 godu', in *Litopys revoliutsii*, 2 (1928), p. 106.

[65] See the figures of Poltava peasants from the past in the State Ethnographical Museum of the Peoples of the USSR in Leningrad.

Six kilometres short of Poltava we turn aside from the highway into a colony for homeless vagabond children run by Anton Makarenko. He had come here in the autumn of 1920. Born in 1888 of working-class parents in Belopole, a small Ukrainian town, he had graduated from the Poltava Teachers' Institute in 1917 with a gold medal. He then taught in a higher elementary school, but became critical of the local Bolsheviks' lack of progress in educational and social affairs. As a challenge the chief of the Poltava guberniia Department of Education offered him the directorship of this residential school for war-orphans.

The human contents of the colony were symptomatic of the general state of Russia in 1922. The Civil War was over, but the social repercussions of external and internal war and revolution flowed on right through the 1920s. Young victims from all over the Ukraine and far beyond came in and out of Makarenko's institution. There are social phenomena that are specific to confined areas: that is why any survey of Soviet politics and society must refer to discrete geographical local-ities. Yet even in a country so vast and diverse as the ex-Empire, there were some features that affected most parts, and set up their own horizontal influences at all lower levels of society irrespective of any vertical political pressures acting from a single centre. The orphans were one of these pheno-mena, as was the great Famine of 1921–2. So that although reference is made here to a remote children's colony, its social significance had much wider reverberations, as indeed did the pedagogical theories worked out by Makarenko.

At the end of NEP the author of an article in the *Bolshevik Encyclopaedia* claimed that Russian orphanages were 'the result of capitalist exploitation of the masses'.[66] Krupskaia admitted more truthfully that at least three-quarters of their inmates were the result of contemporary conditions, not of past suffer-ings.[67] Since 1914 millions of Russians had been on the move— four to five million away from the advancing armies of the Central Powers; at least twelve million fleeing into exile during and after the Revolution; the largest land army in the world

---

[66] Article by A. B. Zalkind in *Bol'shaia sovetskaia entsiklopediia*, vol. 5 (Moscow, 1927), pp. 783–90.
[67] *Pravda*, 2 Dec. 1925.

manœuvring, dying, and deserting from the longest front-line in history—to give the major examples alone, with very approximate numbers. The Famine affected many more millions further east. Parents left children in food asylums by the thousands. The traditional founts of charity, the church and the local gentry, had dried up. Jobs were unavailable in the towns to which the hordes of young found their way. Overnight the new Soviet government, with plans for social welfare that on paper went far beyond those of Scandinavia or Britain in 1945, had to take over. It set up a succession of bodies to deal with the problem, but in 1922 it actually cut back expenditure, already insufficient, in this sphere.[68] Krupskaia reported in early 1923 that seven million *bezprizornye* (neglected ones) were registered; Lunacharsky later put the early NEP figure at nine million.[69] The pressure was still so great by 1924 that 40 per cent of all urban youths under the age of 18 were unemployed.[70] In 1920 the government discussed the idea of placing the bezprizornye in Red Army units.[71]

At the end of the Civil War roughly one-quarter of a million roved around the Ukraine,[72] a region that had suffered greatly from the hostilities. These orphans and vagabonds were just one group among many that were virtually lawless in the disturbed countryside. Leaving the reasonably safe confines of Kharkov town was like quitting E. Zamiatin's proletarian city for the rough no man's land of instinctive outsiders as described in his famous anti-Utopian novel *My*. The workings of the legal system in 1922 will be examined in a later chapter as one aspect of Bolshevik control over society, and the general extent of crime will be noted. In the daily life of Makarenko's colony crime can be observed in microcosm. For a long time after his arrival there, armed groups of various kinds continued to be chased through the nearby woods by Red Army units. Every evening throughout 1922 a band of youths from the colony volunteered to guard the local stretch of the main road into Poltava. This was to prevent attacks by bandits on

[68] V. Zenzinov, *Les enfants abandonnés en Russie soviétique* (Paris, 1929), p. 92.

[69] *Izvestiia*, 26 Feb. 1928.

[70] G. Shvartz and V. Zaitsev, *Molodezh' SSSR v tsifrakh* (Moscow, 1924), p. 7.

[71] Zenzinov, op. cit., p. 186.

[72] Ibid., p. 73.

travellers whose cries floated nightly over the fields to the colony.[73] Another youth patrol fended off neighbouring peasants who constantly tried to fell trees belonging to the colony (shades of Nikol'skaia volost'). They had already carefully taken away the entire orchard, roots and all, and the glass and window frames from the hostel buildings.[74]

Makarenko was thus driven to take the law into his own hands in order to survive, but his pupils needed no encouragement in this respect, since they themselves were the product of a disturbed society. Makarenko describes them in this way:

During those early years of the colony's existence we received very few of the homeless children who had grown accustomed to street wandering. The majority of the colonists had only recently lost contact with their families. During the war and the revolution many old criminal families, living on the outskirts of the town or in bandit villages, left their influence behind even after they had been broken up. The weakening of family ties during the war—through death, evacuation, and executions—led to many youngsters becoming accustomed to wandering as regimental camp-followers in Tsarist, White, Red, or guerrilla bands. These lads were adventurers who had acquired the habit of applying a simplified anarchistic logic to life, involving contempt for all property, contempt for life and human personality, contempt for cleanliness, order, and so on. But they were not used to wandering by themselves, in the manner of the later homeless children.[75]

Bands of boys and girls from the colony made illegal forays that were countenanced by Makarenko just in order to live. Their thefts of milk, honey, and melons from local household plots he ironically termed as acts of smychka. They also smashed up the peasants' illicit vodka stills.

More striking examples of lawlessness took place in Makarenko's dealings with several local authorities. They are indicative of the government's shaky hold over grass-roots politics. In 1922 Makarenko acquired the nearby estate of Trepke as a more suitable future home for his colony. The local village Soviet, whose members Makarenko referred to as 'a lot of parasites', declared that the Trepke cistern was state property.

[73] A. Makarenko, *The Road to Life* (London, 1936), p. 19.
[74] Ibid., pp. 46, 13.
[75] Ibid., pp. 68–9.

The issue was solved, not by due legal process, but by a brawl between the colonists and the village lads, who were chased back into the Soviet building which was later smashed up.[76] Nevertheless the official surveyors who came to map the Trepke boundaries remained too afraid to go into the fields of the estate.[77] When the Soviet sent the militia to the colony in order to accuse the inmates of robbing peasants, Makarenko sent even it packing.[78]

He showed the same scant respect for other agents of central power. His opinion of the local Komsomol was no doubt coloured by the fact that his own colony was a kind of rival organization, but his view broadly reflects that of Yakovlev on the Nikol'skaia Komsomol; Yakovlev was a more disinterested outsider. Makarenko wrote: 'The local Young Communists were very weak in both number and quality. They were far too interested in girls and vodka, and they had a rather negative influence on the colonists.'[79] Soviet historians have subsequently tried to cover over this situation. They have written that 'It is well known that the great Soviet pedagogue, A. S. Makarenko, succeeded in forming a genuine Soviet collective of charges only after a Komsomol organization was established in his colony.'[80] In reality, a Komsomol political instructor (with a criminal record) entered the colony in 1925, well after Makarenko had established discipline. This Komsomol representation apparently played no role in the subsequent administration of the colony.

Makarenko also dealt summarily with the Poltava educational authorities who had appointed him in the first place. He made fun of the pseudo-learned, bureaucratic speech of an inspector which began like this:

The localized system of medico-pedagogical influence on a child, in so far as it is differentiated in an institution for social education, ought to prevail to the extent that it is in accordance with the natural needs of the child and to the extent that it opens creative prospects for

---

[76] Makarenko, *The Road to Life* pp. 77, 170.
[77] Ibid., pp. 54, 133, 106–7.
[78] Ibid., pp. 173–4.
[79] Ibid., p. 264.
[80] I. T. Ogorodnikov and P. N. Shimbirev, *Lehrbuch der Pädagogik* (Berlin, 1953), p. 245; Makarenko, *Gesammelte Werke*, vol. 1 (Ravensburg, 1976), p. 110.

the development of the given structure—biological, social, and economic. Arising out of this, we consider ...[81]

This reads just like the conversational style of the Soviet satirist of NEP, M. Zoshchenko. It was used in a similar way by the newly literate or semi-literate Bolsheviks at the higher levels of the Smolensk and Kursk guberniia party organizations, as can be seen from even a cursory reading of their minutes. This style also reflects the attempt by the political élite in Moscow to hand down to the provinces general directives which were as sophisticated as possible and based on Marxist tenets in so far as they could be understood at lower levels. Zoshchenko could caricature them in the 1920s, but by the 1930s it became too dangerous to ridicule what had solidified into a standardized bureaucratic mode of oppression.

Makarenko went further than making fun of educational inspectors. When they tried to stop him from taking into the colony a youth from the Political Special Section of the Army First Reserves, he appealed over their heads to the Workers' and Peasants' Inspectorate (*Rabkrin*), which came down on his side.[82] This is not the first time nor the last that we encounter this influential organization. It was one of the more effective Bolshevik controls as early as 1922, and not only in negative ways. When the colony ran short of horses, the manager of the Economic Section of Rabkrin offered to lend some in exchange for wheels and wheat. He drew up an agreement in two copies, setting out the terms in ponderous detail: '. . . referred to henceforth as "the colony" . . . which wheels shall be considered as handed over to the Economic Section of the Provincial Workers' and Peasants' Inspection after their reception by a special commission and the signing of the corresponding protocol.'[83]

During his inspection of Nikol'skaia volost', Yakovlev prided himself on his objectivity in criticizing local party activities, given that he was a highly orthodox representative of the central apparatus with a broad knowledge of all-Russian affairs. In sharp contrast Makarenko was a deep provincial who had an independent, determined mind. He was never to become a party member, and was not conversant with Marxist

[81] Makarenko, *The Road to Life*, pp. 162–4.   [82] Ibid., p. 187.
[83] Ibid., pp. 230–1.

ideas in 1922. In any case Marxism was broad enough to lend itself to different educational interpretations. Makarenko made the important deduction that as the theories discarded at the Revolution had not been replaced by precise new ones, the abstract and muddled notions of officials like the education inspector were no substitute for practical self-help. This colony was virtually self-subsistent, in management methods as in food. Its solidarity was achieved by its sense of being a small-scale unit isolated from the rest of society, and frequently preying on it in 1922. There was a moral dilemma here, since what was good for the survival of the colony was harmful for others in a society which Makarenko wished to see participating in group ownership on collective lines. Education and socialization were almost synonymous in his view. He wanted to incorporate the individual into the collective in a way that he believed himself to belong to it—freely and without compulsion.

This noble idea was all very well in the relatively lax atmosphere and control of early NEP, with only one unique educational experiment involved. Yet even at this time many members of industrial trade unions realized fully that they were no longer free agents in a wider collective, but increasingly regimented subjects of the Party. The aim of creating a sense of prime loyalty among members of the colony, which was small enough for them to know each other, did not constitute any kind of a threat to central authorities in 1922, but it would not have been tolerated in the 1930s, when family members were encouraged to spy on one another in the state interest. Yet paradoxically Makarenko's educational theories were to be taken up, approved, and widely publicized in the Stalinist period. Why was this so?

One way of answering the question might be that Stalin was as unorthodox a Marxist as Makarenko, but this avoids the crucial problem of political control. The real answer lies elsewhere. A military career had fascinated the young Makarenko, though he disliked it and had to be discharged on account of poor eyesight. As if to compensate for this, he applied military techniques in the colony.

Without thinking twice about it, and without a single shudder, I began to drill the boys in military exercises and manœuvres. They were delighted, and gladly followed my lead. After the day's work we had all the colony drilling for an hour or two in the yard, which formed a spacious square. As we added to our knowledge we extended the field of our activities. By the winter our squads were carrying out very interesting and involved military manœuvres throughout the area covered by our group of villages. Soon afterwards we were able to use real rifles, for the authorities made us members of the 'Universal Training' organization, our criminal past being deliberately overlooked. I soon noticed the influence of military training. The change of behaviour in the boys was very marked. Their faces took on a different expression; they grew more spruce and upright of bearing, ceased to loll about on the tables or against the walls, and held themselves up.[84]

Makarenko had better relations with the local secret police than with any other official authority. They found many candidates for admission to the colony, and in 1922 Makarenko wrote of them:

Among the Cheka people high intellectual standards combined with education and culture had not assumed the outward expression which I had found to be so hateful among the former Russian intellectuals. . . . The Cheka people are devoted to principle . . . [they have an] all-pervading good humour, terseness of speech, a dislike of ready-made formulae.[85]

Makarenko was not alone in the disorderly climate of 1922 in thinking on these lines. Yakovlev was worried by the way in which teachers were being turned into what he called 'the slaves of the kulaks' through their financial dependence on richer peasants in the Kursk guberniia. He recommended that Red Army youths become village teachers to counteract this trend.[86] The shadow of long-term violence since 1914 hung over many aspects of Russian society. External and internal war produced their victims, of whom Makarenko's stray youths were but one example. Military violence had led to civil coercion in many forms, of which the Secret police in peacetime was the most notorious example. It had also led to

---

[84] Makarenko, *The Road to Life*, p. 240.
[85] Ibid., pp. 381–2.
[86] Yakovlev, *Derevnia kak ona est'*, p. 102.

the adoption of military influences in Bolshevik governmental organization and propaganda jargon which did not disappear at the end of the Civil War. Trotsky's idea of converting whole regiments into Labour Armies had failed, but it was symptomatic of the time.[87] Makarenko revived the military model in microcosm, and his strict pedagogical methods were adopted on a vast scale in the 1930s by Stalin, who reawakened many other lingering aspects of military-inspired government. Often in NEP when thoughtful leaders at many levels became exasperated by the seemingly chaotic situations they saw about them, they dreamt of, and sometimes put through, as in Makarenko's case, schemes which looked forward to the methods of the 1930s. Stalin was by no means alone. We find Makarenko by the 1930s writing, 'How is it that the resistance of materials is studied in all higher technical institutes, while in the pedagogical institutes no study is made of the resistance of personalities to educational measures?'.[88] Humans had become mere technical grist to the mill like any base metal. The position eventually taken up by Makarenko was one where the ultimate criteria of truth and morality had to reside in the centralized state. From there they would flow outwards to the masses through all state agencies, which by the 1930s included even the family. He failed to show how from the other direction values could arise from the people and become incorporated in the state ideology.

[87] For a fuller treatment of the encroachment of wartime methods and parlance on civil government, see R. Pethybridge, *The Social Prelude to Stalinism* (London, 1974), ch. 3, pp. 73–131.

[88] Makarenko, *The Road to Life*, vol. 3 (Moscow, 1951), p. 268.

# 3. *The South-East*

EASTWARDS from Poltava lay the gubernii of Tsaritsyn, Saratov, and Samara (now Kuibyshev) on the Volga.

In 1922 they were the hub of the maelstrom that was the great famine of 1921–2. The whole of Russia was affected by its repercussions.

Many historians maintain that they are concerned, not with human actions of all kinds, but only with those that are reflective, arising from a purpose pursued. They rarely study natural events, and only in so far as they impinge on the human world. In the Soviet context an inordinate amount of attention has been paid to the willed aims of Bolshevik leaders. On the other hand, since nearly 80 per cent of the nation were illiterate in early NEP, consisting of a disorganized and fragmented peasantry, it has often been assumed that the actions of this class have been both unreflective and ineffective. Illiterates leave no written record of their views, but they nevertheless reflect and act accordingly. Peasants caught up in the Tambov and other revolts did just this, although they remained politically ineffective for lack of large-scale organization. We have noted how the peasantry of the Black-Earth region was palpably influenced in its social and political manners by its traditional natural background. In the case of the famine of 1921–2, a sudden alteration in the agricultural setting deeply affected, not just the local peasantry, but all the other provinces of European Russia and the very basis of the economic and political calculations that had led to the introduction of the NEP in the first place. No such claim could possibly be made for the Smolensk, Kursk, or Poltava gubernii. They deviated from central expectations and in many ways escaped from rigid control from above, but their local eccentricities did not upset Moscow's broad calculations in the short term. Neither

Belorussian nationalists nor Catholics, nor the proximity of the
Tambov revolt to Kursk guberniia, set any major political fires
alight. In the longer term the accumulation of social and
economic deviations in all areas of Russia would indeed have
profound effects on Bolshevik plans for the future. This was
already clear by 1926, and could even have been in 1922, if
only the central authorities had kept a closer watch on the pulse
of rural life.

Any study of the Lower Volga in 1922 differs from investigations of other localities in another respect. Since foreign aid
from many countries poured into the famine area, a wide
variety of non-Russian accounts can be consulted. Not a single
articulate foreigner penetrated the Smolensk or Kursk gubernii
to leave a record behind. It is true that the Smolensk archives
dropped uncensored into German hands in the Second World
War, and that Yakovlev is remarkably self-critical of his own
party; but only Makarenko stands outside the Bolshevik view
of things. Yet we cannot take foreign accounts at their face
value either. Political propaganda on the part of the American
Relief Administration, by far the longest foreign source of aid,
warped its judgement at the time, and the subsequent polarization of Russian–American relations has not improved the
objectivity of later scholarly accounts of the Famine as seen
through American eyes.[1] Even F. Nansen, the esteemed Nor-
wegian co-ordinator of many other foreign relief organizations, could on occasion be carried away by his emotions and
give a semi-fictional account of conditions in the Volga provinces.[2] Calm assessments were hard to come by in the shadow
of a tragedy of such proportions. A native Russian of genius,
L. Tolstoy, had been blinded by his feelings in the famine of

---

[1] See H. H. Fisher, *The Famine in Soviet Russia 1919–1923: The Operations of the
American Relief Administration* (New York, 1927); C. M. Edmondson, 'Soviet Famine
Relief Measures 1921–1923', unpublished doctoral thesis of the Florida State Univer-
sity, 1970; B. M. Weissman, *Herbert Hoover and Famine Relief to Soviet Russia: 1921–1923*
(Stanford, 1974). These authors had close ties with the Hoover Institution on War,
Revolution and Peace. They provide well-documented accounts, but the Famine is
interpreted from the American point of view, and the contemporary background in
Russia is somewhat neglected.

[2] See League of Nations, *Records of the Third Assembly, Plenary Meetings*, III (Geneva,
1922), p. 59.

1891–2 when he made mildly inaccurate statements about the Tsarist relief administration.[3]

Most students of the 1921–2 Famine have concentrated on foreign aid, the causes of the Famine, statistical evidence on mortality and disease rates, and the extent of crop failures.[4] The aim here is to look at its political and social repercussions and to set it in the wider context of central–local administrative relations. Another interesting aspect that has been almost entirely neglected concerns horizontal influences in near and distant gubernii. But first the causes of the Famine should be given in order to put it in perspective.

The Middle Volga region, like the Nikol'skaia volost' in Kursk guberniia, was an area of good *chernozem* soils and so predominantly grain-producing. Unlike the Central Agricultural Region, the grain here was partly produced for market and transported on the Volga. The pressure on land was also less severe here. The number of strips held by households were larger and fewer than around Kursk, but distances between houses and plots were even larger, since peasants lived alongside the water-courses away from their land. Water shortage was often acute, especially in the Lower Volga area.[5] In general, conditions of land tenure, communal arrangements, and cultural traditions differed considerably in the Volga provinces from those in the West and the centre of European Russia. For instance, members of Volga communes were apt to be more outward-looking than those in Kursk guberniia because of their wider market ties and better transport facilities. This was one of the reasons why they were more prepared than many sedentary peasants to escape over huge distances in the Famine, though of course hunger was the main spur.

In August 1921 the Commissariat of Foreign Affairs stated that the Famine covered Ufa and Viatka and the Volga

---

[3] See M. Simpson, 'L. N. Tolstoy and the Famine of 1891–2', *Melbourne Slavonic Studies*, 15 (1981), p. 41.

[4] For statistical evidence see two papers by S. G. Wheatcroft, 'The Significance of Climatic and Weather Change on Soviet Agriculture', and 'Famine and Factors affecting Mortality in the USSR: The Demographic Crises of 1914–1922 and 1930–1933', in the *Soviet Industrialization Project Series*, 11, 20, and 21 (Centre for Russian and East European Studies, University of Birmingham 1977, 1981, and 1982).

[5] *Povol'zhe, ekonomichesko-geograficheskaia kharakteristika* (Moscow, 1957), pp. 43, 105, 108–10.

gubernii of Astrakhan, Tsaritsyn, Saratov, Samara, Simbirsk, and the German Volga Commune. Foreign sources added several other provinces: Tambov, Voronezh, Tula, Riazan', and the Ukrainian gubernii of Kherson and the Crimea.[6] The widespread implications of the Famine were already coming to the surface. Both Soviet and foreign estimates of the numbers threatened with starvation and death over the period 1921–2 varied enormously, and no amount of detailed research is ever likely to come up with reliable figures. By the early autumn of 1922 the Soviet government put the number at 22 million,[7] or about one-third of the population of the RSFSR. Nansen's estimates fluctuated between 20 and 30 million in September 1921 to 50 million twelve months later.[8]

For the long-term causes of the Famine we have to delve deep behind the flat time-dimension of 1922. Famines had been a cyclical phenomenon in the Volga region, as they had been in Asia, for centuries. Poor irrigation, transport, education, and medicine multiplied the chances of disaster, together with the fact that even in good years many peasants hardly existed above subsistence level. The organizational defects of the commune system were another barrier, as elsewhere in Russia. The short-term cause of overriding local significance were the droughts and crop failures in 1920 and 1921. Due to wartime conditions the peasantry got the same amount of agricultural machinery over the years 1915–21 that they had been able to buy in a single year prior to the World War.[9] They had suffered in the Civil War from requisitioning by Red, White, and Green armies, and to some extent from the Bol-shevik-inspired *kombedy* (committees of poor peasants). As the Famine grew, poor co-operation between the Soviet authorities and foreign relief groups, and amongst the foreign organiza-tions themselves, exacerbated the situation. The worst aspects

---

[6] C. E. Bechhofer, *Through Starving Russia: Being the Record of a Journey to Moscow and the Volga Provinces in August and September, 1921* (London, 1921), pp. 61–21; Comité des organisations russes réunies pour le secours aux affamés, *Mémoire relatif à la famine en Russie* (Brussels, 1921), p. 6.

[7] *Izvestiia*, 16 Sept. 1922.

[8] League of Nations, *Records of the Second Assembly, Plenary Meetings*, II (Geneva, 1921), p. 545; and ibid., *Records of the Third Assembly, Plenary Meetings*, III (1922) p. 59.

[9] *Snabzhenie krestianskogo naseleniia sel'skokhoziaistvennymi mashinami i orudiiami* (Moscow, 1925), p. 32.

of co-ordination, however, were central–local relations within the Soviet hierarchy. We will return to this later, but at this point the course of the Famine needs to be related very briefly.

Between early May and late August 1921, no rain had fallen in the Middle Volga, central and eastern Ukraine, and the steppes north of the Caucasus. Taken together, these areas supplied three-fifths of Russia's grain. The steppes were the first to be affected, so that in June alone over a million peasants left them for the Volga. Thousands died in transit. Since the total grain harvest proved to be a mere 52 per cent of what it had been in 1913, even the least affected areas had barely enough. Livestock was slaughtered in the worst-hit areas on the Volga, thus rendering any movement and the basis for any future recovery even more precarious. Epidemics spread with the diaspora. The winter of 1921–2 was bitterly cold. Grain-importing regions now suffered, beginning with the Donbas and then the Moscow region. It was only after the reasonable harvest of 1922 that the spectre of nation-wide starvation receded.

Since the accent in this study lies on 1922, a report in *The Times* for 6 January may suffice as an eye-witness account of conditions in Saratov and Samara gubernii. The author was an Englishman, Dr Farrar, who had just died from typhus. He can still be seen on film in November 1921 in Saratov surrounded by hungry children.[10]

It would need the pen of a Zola to do justice to the reality and appalling intensity of the famine in these parts (Saratov and Samara). It is getting steadily worse and is moving westward with the stream of refugees, who, having eaten their last stores and sold everything that would buy a morsel of bread, are wandering they know not whither.

To give an idea of the desolation of some of the villages (in the Saratov area) I may mention that the village of Kano, in the Markstadt district, which has a normal population of over 3,000, has now only 1,100 inhabitants left, and remember the winter is only just beginning.

One of the worst features is the number of *enfants trouvés*—orphans or children abandoned by their parents, who are found in the streets.

---

[10] The film was made by the UK branch of Save the Children International Fund Union. It was unearthed and shown recently by S. G. Wheatcroft (see n. 4 above).

The ghastly emaciation of these children is horrible. I saw yesterday in Markstadt a shelter which has beds for 100 of these children; 42 children had died in the last 24 hours, but these places had been filled up. I saw the corpses of eight, photographed some of them. More than 50 per cent of these *enfants trouvés* perish in spite of the care that is given them. But if the children come under the care of the relief agencies, little ones, who were emaciated, hollow-eyed, and listless, become after about a fortnight's feeding quite plump again and begin to laugh and sing.

Since beginning this letter I have been with Nansen in the Samara district, where the conditions are even worse than in Saratov, in spite of the very good work done by the ARA in Samara and by the Friends in Bouzoulouk.

We saw awful conditions in Bouzoulouk, where, out of a population of 35,000 they are dying at the rate of 100 a day. Corpses are found lying almost every day, and murders are frequent. We saw in the cemetery a pile of about 60–70 corpses, two days' accumulation (not reckoning the private burials), waiting to be tumbled into a pit, and also a pit full of other corpses. We saw in the main street the corpse of a woman already gnawed by dogs (people are beginning to be afraid of dogs). Copeman, of the Friends, told us that he seldom went out without seeing corpses lying about. There are whispered stories of cannibalism.

Conditions in the guberniia capitals were dire, but they were even worse in the rural hinterland. It was still possible in early 1922 to buy foodstuffs in the city markets if one had the money. Soviet and foreign relief organizations had installed themselves with efficiency and were giving out free food. The villages on the other hand were quite desolate. Up to half of the houses were boarded up in areas that were starving. Village clerks could not keep a proper record of deaths, since they were so frequent.[11] This was the source of the central authorities' difficulty in making adequate assessments. A member of the Indian Civil Service who visited Samara guberniia in January 1922 noted how the whole of the rural population in the famine region proper was absolutely starved. In Indian famines of which he had long experience, only landless labourers and smaller cultivators—'the submerged tenth'—needed relief.[12] Local agronomists from the Commissariat of

[11] Fisher, op. cit., p. 96.
[12] *The Times*, 13 Feb. 1922.

Agriculture discovered in the Samara guberniia that 40 per cent of the machinery that had been hired out was unusable, and virtually all the rest was in need of repairs. There was neither time nor money to deal with agricultural pests. The agronomists' reports on the spring-sowing campaign reveal a long list of mainly unfulfilled bureaucratic resolutions passed down from Moscow.[13]

In Saratov guberniia the reduction in livestock between the springs of 1920 and 1922 was found to have been 94.6 per cent in pigs, 68.7 in sheep, 61.3 in horned cattle, and 59 in horses. When agronomists held courses for peasants, they fretted that on average only 150 turned up, as compared with attendances of 4000 at a single conference in Smolensk guberniia.[14] Given their atrocious living conditions, it is a tribute to the tenacity of the Saratov peasantry that even this number appeared. The effects of rural famine took their toll on city-workers in due course. The sewing industry in Saratov reported that its factories were closing in January through lack of demand for its products. Another plant which made military uniforms was on the verge of closure for lack of orders from Moscow. This was due to the impossibility of conveying such goods between the two cities at a time when the railways could not cope with grain supplies coming into Saratov.[15]

Agronomists were much in evidence in the localities in the spring of 1922. This was not the case for those other connecting agents between town and country that have been studied in Smolensk and Kursk gubernii. Rural teachers melted away into the towns as their schools closed down for lack of pupils and funds. By February only forty-three of the 394 schools in Samara guberniia remained on the official food supply list.[16] All local funds, which had been cut as a result of the introduction of NEP, were poured into famine relief. There was even less money available for education after September, when many new famine duties and financial burdens were shifted from Moscow on to local authorities.[17]

---

[13] *Materialy mestnykh soveshchanii oblastnykh konferentsii narodnogo kommissariata zemledeliia o vesennei kampanii 1922 goda* (Moscow, 1922), pp. 236–7.

[14] Ibid., pp. 233, 229.

[15] *Trud*, 10 Jan. 1922.

[16] Ibid., 17 Feb. 1922.

[17] See p. 116 below.

There is little evidence of either the presence or practical aid of Russian priests in the afflicted rural areas, though a considerable number of West European churchmen came in with relief organizations.[18] Churches, like the schools, were abandoned. The government's anti-religious campaign in connection with the Church's alleged refusal to donate money and valuables for the Famine crippled the reputation of church aid and made some priests unwilling to become entangled in relief work. Others saved their own skins and left the worst-hit areas. At high and local levels the government intervened to stop what active church help there was. On 22 April the American Relief Administration wanted to clear a shipment to Patriarch Tikhon for him to distribute at his discretion. An earlier load had been passed on to him, but this was no longer permitted. Tikhon was arrested at the end of April and charged with advocating resistance to the confiscation of church treasures.[19] When ARA village committees wished to elect Russian priests as members, back came the objection, phrased in the usual official provincial style: 'according to the laws of our constitution, the said element (ecclesiastical) is harmful to the younger generation, and by the principles of the Soviet government this element is deprived of all active or passive participation in our work.'[20]

Another unwelcome element in Soviet eyes was lacking altogether. Whereas Nepmen were already flourishing in Kursk guberniia, they could not yet arise here in an area where as the Indian civil servant observed, rich and poor peasants alike were afflicted. The only conceivable opening for venality was in the private shipment of food supplies for profit. Traffic of this kind had occurred on a large scale in the period following on the October Revolution, but if there had been any 'bagmen' left by 1921–2 in the Middle Volga region, they would have been ruthlessly stamped out. It was lucky for the Bolshevik government, though not accidental, that two of its most suspected categories in local society were powerless in the Famine areas.

---

[18] Local American Relief Administration committees employed a number of Russian priests. See W. Duranty, *I Write as I Please* (New York, 1935), p. 133.

[19] Weissman, op. cit., pp. 120–1.

[20] Fisher, op. cit., p. 93.

On the other hand, neither did the faithful military figure so much here as it did in the political activities of the Smolensk party organization. During 1922 soldiers were used almost exclusively in civilian affairs for guarding the train-loads of grain entering the Famine region, and for monitoring the distribution of food. The rations of the Red Army were assiduously protected. In March food supplies purchased by the Commissariat of War for the Red Army were given priority in evacuation at the Black Sea port of Novorossiisk over ARA famine stocks. It was different for the rank and file at the receiving end. The officials who sent them off from the ports with the loaded railway-wagons gave them rations for the number of days which the grain would in normal times take to its destination. Due to the enormous delays, soldiers arrived in the Volga cities nearly dead for lack of food.[21]

It has been argued that the Famine led to a long-term levelling process amongst the afflicted peasantry,[22] thus keeping the '*kulak*' at bay in the stricken areas. This was indeed the immediate consequence, but only until the middle of 1922. In 1921, there was a huge increase in the emigration and physical extinction of households. A big drop took place in rates of partitioning. The poorest households suffered the most, and this led temporarily to both a levelling and an aggregate move downwards in Volga peasant society. Yet by the summer of 1922, when recovery was in sight, the slightest advantage of one peasant over another could be manipulated to gain quick and large profits. Meagre amounts of food were bartered by the less unfortunate to the starving in return for land and equipment. Between June and September 18,000 bargains of this kind in Samara guberniia were annulled by the government, which declared them to be invalid, but thousands more went undiscovered.[23] Twenty pounds of butter was enough for the lease of two and a half desiatiny of land for five years.[24] Five pudy of linseed cake were exchanged for the approaching

[21] Ibid., pp. 181, 191.
[22] T. Shanin, *The Awkward Class: Political Sociology of Peasantry in a Developing Society: Russia 1910–1925* (Oxford, 1972), p. 129.
[23] *Istoricheskii arkhiv*, 29 (1949), p. 29.
[24] A. Azizhan and I. Velikevich, *Arendnye otnosheniia v sovetskoi derevne* (Moscow, 1928), pp. 111 ff.

harvest of a desiatin of wheat.[25] Machinery was much scarcer than land, as has been seen. In 1922 the percentage of households without even a plough was 32.7 in the Central Industrial Region, 33.6 in the Siberian guberniia of Omsk, and 55.8 in the guberniia of Tsaritsyn, to the south of Saratov.[26] Peasants with a minimal surplus of food could barter it for vital equipment. In the spring of 1922 only those households in the Famine area which possessed the necessary machinery and livestock were given grain to sow for the next season. By the mid-1920s the universal result of the earlier shortage of equipment had become clear: 75 per cent of all cases of letting out land were due to lack of adequate tools.[27]

It was difficult for the authorities to detect this cumulative process at work. Richer and poorer peasants connived to hide the indebtedness of the latter, who were often described in the tax returns as relatives or voluntary helpers of the farmer.[28] As always, the better-off peasants were more successful than others in avoiding taxation. The new tax in kind fell on all areas of Russia and on all types of peasant in 1922 except for the completely destitute. A progressive tax on the more productive regions and peasants might have been more just and welcome from the political point of view, but it was not applied for fear of removing the incentive to sow from the better-placed peasants. Even the famine area was made to pay one-half of the supplemental tax levied for famine relief.[29] This had a crippling effect on the worse off at a crucial stage of recovery from the Famine. To this extent the region was actually encouraging the formation of richer peasant strata at the expense of the poorer.

At this point we can embark on an investigation of the spatial or 'horizontal' effects of the Famine in 1922. Internal movement within the worst-affected areas should be looked at first. Those peasants who continued to own draught animals had lent them to relief organizations at the height of the

[25] *Izvestiia VTsIK*, 6 July 1922.

[26] A. Gaister, *Rassloenie sovetskoi derevni* (Moscow, 1928), p. 72.

[27] Azizhan and Velikevich, op. cit., pp. 46, 53, 55, 90. Another source referring to 1926, gives the percentage as 72.4, for lack of both tools and draught animals. See *Sel'skokhoziaistvennaia gazeta*, 8 June 1929.

[28] L. Kritsman, *Klassovoe rassloenie sovetskoi derevni* (Moscow, 1926), p. 96.

[29] *Izvestiia*, 5 Oct. 1922.

Famine, but by the spring of 1922 they refused to do this any longer, since they now found many profitable uses for them. Owners of draught animals had a virtual monopoly on the transport of grain to the miller, the market, and the local collection-point for the tax in kind.[30] If the tax was paid promptly, a discount was given.[31] They could carry goods for local co-operatives and state authorities. Their cultural as well as their economic life could be broadened: in the winter of 1922–3 it was found that more peasant children from families owning draught animals attended school regularly than those without any.[32]

Less fortunate children still converged on the village relief-kitchens to which food and other supplies for a month or two months were brought in peasant carts over long distances from railheads and steamer-landings. In the more remote localities Bolshevik officials, desperate for transport facilities, 'ignored NEP and all its works, and commandeered right and left as if military Communism [War Communism] was still pure and undefiled',[33] yet another indication that military methods did not go completely out of fashion with the advent of NEP.

Communications did not improve away from the grass roots. For Saratov guberniia the main supply-base was at Pokrovsk, on the east side of the Volga, directly opposite the city of Saratov. From Pokrovsk railway lines ran in three directions through famine areas, but in January 1922 there was only one locomotive in the yards, and that took up to seventeen days to cover less than 150 miles. Camels were used for moving railway-trucks round the Pokrovsk yards.[34] The spring of 1922 was the crucial period, when the unmetalled roads began to break up into mud and the rivers had not yet melted. By the time grain had arrived from the Black Sea to an area north of Samara, only one in ten of the available sledges could get through to rural areas, so that instead of 48,750 pudy of corn, a mere 1,500 were delivered.[35] The ice disappeared from the

[30] Kritsman, op. cit., p. 164; A. M. Bol'shakov, *Sovetskaia derevnia* (Leningrad, 1925), pp. 99–106.
[31] *Izvestiia VTsIK*, 19 Sept. 1922.
[32] Ia. Yakovlev, *Nasha derevnia. Novoe v starom i staroe v novom* ((Moscow, 1924), p. 114.
[33] Fisher, op. cit., p. 118.
[34] Ibid., p. 215.
[35] Ibid., p. 220.

Volga in the last days of April, when steamers, tugs, and barges converged at Tsaritsyn on the warmer Lower Volga to transport supplies up the river and its tributaries. There were six village landing-points in the Samara guberniia and eight to the north and south of Saratov. This campaign suffered from the reduction of the river fleet from four to two thousand steamers between 1917 and 1921. Barges had been destroyed for fuel or left by their previous owners to be broken up by ice or swept downstream by the spring floods.[36]

Grain converging on the Middle Volga from other parts of Russia and from abroad was subject to similar near-chaotic conditions. Massive bottle-necks built up in the early spring on the railway network, at Koslov, west of Saratov on the route to Moscow and particularly at Balashov, between Saratov and Tsaritsyn on the west side of the Volga. On 21 March there were forty-two trains there, each with about thirty trucks. The leader of the American Relief Administration agreed with A. Eiduk, his Soviet counterpart, that 1,100 trucks should be unloaded temporarily into warehouses.[37] Coal specially imported from England to Baltic seaports was still stuck there, so that most engines were fuelled with 'nothing but logs . . . in most cases wet and covered with ice and snow . . . giving no heat. . . . The gratings are ruined and finally the engines have to be taken out of service . . .'[38]

The number of ARA truck-loads failing to reach their destination had accelerated, from 11 per cent in October 1921 to 35 per cent by the end of January 1922. The position began to improve in spring. Later figures showed that for the whole of 1922 over twice as much grain was transported by rail and waterways as in 1921.[39]

The Famine in the south-east of Russia even affected international relations in the far north-west. The ARA used its good offices to speed up railway agreements between Latvia and Poland on the one hand, and Russia on the other, so that relief supplies could flow in more easily from Western Eur-

[36] S. Brooks, *America and Germany* (New York, 1925), p. 74.

[37] Fisher, op. cit., pp. 193–4.

[38] *Ekonomicheskaia zhizn'*, 3 Mar. 1922.

[39] 513,900,000 pudy for 1922 as against 227,200,000 for 1921. See *Trudy Zemplany*, vol. 1 (Moscow, 1924), p. 101.

ope.[40] Goods trains coming from the Baltic to Moscow took between one and four weeks, a distance that was covered in fourteen hours by passenger trains. The first goods train from Novorossiisk, a vital grain port in the north-east corner of the Black Sea, wandered over much of European Russia before arriving at Ufa.[41] Novorossiisk like most other ports had suffered from the Revolution and Civil War. Scuttled ships lay in the bay and only two quays were fit for use. Bottle-necks were not restricted to the railways; at the end of March twenty-five ships lay in Reval harbour waiting for berths. At Theodosia in the Crimea dockers struck for better wages and rations. In good capitalist fashion local officials recruited Tartar shepherds and quarrymen from the hills to act as temporary stevedores and strike-breakers.[42]

Drastic action was indeed necessary to keep transport cogwheels turning all over Russia to supply the Volga provinces. Vital grain supplies due in from Siberia were so badly held up that in January 1922 the national Council of Labour and Defence sent there Felix Dzerzhinsky, the head of the secret police, and since April 1921 Commissar for Transport. With forty picked men he was given special powers; 228 wagons were needed, but only thirty had been sent to Siberia. Dzerzhinsky found explosives in many of the railway workshops. They had suffered from twenty cases of arson in the last two months of 1921, which he ascribed to White supporters of Kolchak. He proceeded to declare a state of military alert in nineteen railway stations. The trucks slowly began to roll.[43] ARA officials met Dzerzhinsky on 12 April to complain about the requisitioning of their supplies. By 27 April the problem was solved, to the surprise of the Americans. Thereafter they learnt to invoke the name of the head of the secret police when dealing with obdurate local officials.[44]

Central intervention was successful to a certain degree where means of communication were concerned, especially those between Moscow and the provinces. They will be examined in

[40] Fisher, op. cit., pp. 176-7.
[41] Ibid., p. 187.
[42] Ibid., p. 182.
[43] N. Zubov, *F. E. Dzerzhinsky: biografiia* (Moscow, 1965), pp. 296-9.
[44] Weissman, op. cit., pp. 115-16.

more detail when we quit regional life and approach the political capital. Traditionally Tsarist as well as Soviet local government was conducted on a strictly bilateral basis between the centre and each separate guberniia. Independent lateral contacts at provincial levels were discouraged. So that when vast numbers of non-directed peasants began to spill out of the disaster areas in the early summer of 1921, the Central Committee of the Communist Party ordered its guberniia counterparts to put a stop to migration 'since the flight of the peasants . . . will ruin entirely our economic life'.[45] Fears for the political stability of the area, once the bastion of the Socialist Revolutionaries and bordering on Tambov guberniia, were also rising, though not expressed publicly.

Refugee movements were very complex throughout 1921–2, but the main tides swept in a south-westerly direction from Saratov and Tsaritsyn gubernii towards the Ukraine or westwards from Samara, Simbirsk, Ufa, and Kazan' towards Moscow and beyond.[46] In one sense international or even civil war had less disturbing effects on central administration, since they had more clearly defined fronts than those of the Famine. Troop numbers and locations were also much more precise. It is impossible to give even approximate figures for the diaspora. One careful observer, a British Quaker, gave a figure of 800,000 for the period between 1 July 1921 and April 1922.[47] The fact that Omsk railway station on the less-frequented eastern escape route was sometimes deluged with up to 20,000 refugees a day gives some idea of the scale of migration.[48]

Another reason for our inability to give accurate figures is due to the prevalence of several other types of population movement, some of them on a huge scale, although extended over a longer period. In the winter of 1921–2 an American relief organizer discovered several thousand Polish war refugees huddled in railway trucks at Orenburg, waiting to be repatriated.[49] The dislocations caused by the World War and the Civil War were immense in terms of human lives. The

[45] US National Archives, *Records of the Department of State Relating to the Internal Affairs of Russia and the Soviet Union: 1910–29*, file no. 861.48/1562.

[46] For more detail see the map of refugee movements in Fisher, op. cit., p. 107.

[47] M. Asquith, *Famine Quaker Work in Russia 1921–3* (London, 1943), p. 8 ff.

[48] *Itogi posledgol s 15.10 1922 g.–1.8.1923 g.* (Moscow, 1923), pp. 114–15.

[49] Fisher, op. cit., p. 106.

White emigration added at least another twelve million. Then there were the mass flights from the industrial cities of European Russia after 1917,[50] besides many regional movements too numerous to mention. Given this situation, which persisted into 1922 and beyond, what hope was there for Gosplan to construct a carefully planned economy and society under any kind of political conditions, whether those of War Communism, NEP, or the Five-Year plans of the future? The future was indeed at stake, since official Soviet figures put the number of starving children in the famine areas at 7,246,317.[51] By 1920 the government had already been giving public support to 7,667,769 children in need.[52] These colossal numbers diminished very slowly through NEP. Makarenko's colony near Poltava was a drop in the ocean at a time when 200 children a day were abandoned in Samara.[53] Renewed commitment to child welfare had the initial effect of inducing parents to desert their offspring at an even faster rate.

The incidence of the Famine was in fact worse for those peasants who wandered into the nearby Volga cities or travelled much further afield. Cut off from regular feeding-points, subjected to atrocious public transport conditions, and more prone to the cold and disease, up to half of the migrants died in transit on the railways.[54] A minority were more fortunate, if one can take as reasonably accurate the report by the Commissariat of Agriculture that 109,705 peasants were taken out of the famine zone and settled on farming land in Siberia, the Ukraine, the Caucasus, and elsewhere.[55] The results were beneficent, but less well handled were the reverse migration procedures ordered by *Pomgol* on 15 March 1922. They appear to have been premature. For example 1,530 persons were re-evacuated to the Saratov guberniia in early June, despite the fact that the Central Evacuation Department had taken 2,151 refugees away from there in late May.[56] More ominous for the

[50] See Ch. 6, p. 189.

[51] Glavnyi politiko-prosvetitel'nyi komitet, *Chto govoriat tsifry o golode* (Moscow, 1922), p. 4.

[52] Narodnogo komissariata po prodovol'stviiu, *Tri goda bor'by s golodom* (Moscow, 1920), p. 84.

[53] *Pravda*, 14 Sept. 1921.

[54] Edmondson, op. cit., p. 174.

[55] *Itogi bor'by s golodom* (Moscow, 1922), p. 89.

[56] Ibid., pp. 116–18.

future was the fact that the central authorities were learning how to control and transport huge numbers of peasants. The great bulk of population movement occurred independently of Moscow in the years 1917–22, but after the end of NEP it was to be strictly enforced, and took place on a vast scale again.

Another horizontal effect of the Famine that was also hard to check was the spread of disease, carried above all by refugees. Those fugitives who congregated on the Omsk railway passed on spotted typhus to 60 per cent of the regional railway workers.[57] Through Samara passed the chief railway lines from Siberia and Central Asia, bringing in diseases of all kinds from the east. The ARA dispensary at the station filled out 75,000 prescriptions for arriving passengers and inspected 868 trains.[58] At the receiving end of refugees from the Middle Volga, Rostov-on-Don was the prime source of cholera outbreaks. They occurred from 1920 onwards, but 1921 and 1922 were the peak years. Rostov stood at the crossroads of another traffic stream, from north-west Russia to the northern Caucasus by train and boat.[59] At the hub of the crisis, hospital conditions in Samara and Saratov were atrocious. Patients suffered from frost-bite in bed. Thermometers were lacking completely.[60] It has been estimated that in a narrow clinical sense the Famine probably accounted for under 15 per cent of the extra mortality recorded at the height of the disaster in Saratov in 1921–2: but in a broader sense, including deaths due to severe malnutrition and other causes, the Famine contributed to most of the rise in mortality that took place before the 1922 harvest.[61] After that point, the recovery from widespread disease and the high death-rate was dramatic. By the end of 1923 levels were down to the best pre-1921 records for Saratov.[62]

For lack of funds, equipment, and means of control, central

---

[57] Zubov, op. cit., p. 297.

[58] Fisher, op. cit., p. 441.

[59] V. Baukin and H. Cazeneuve, *Le foyer endémique de choléra de Rostov-sur-le-Don* (Geneva, 1925), pp. 27–8.

[60] For medical conditions in these cities, see H. Beeuwkes, 'American Medical and Sanitary Relief in the Russian Famine 1921–1923', in the *ARA Bulletin*, series 2, vol. 45 (1922).

[61] See Wheatcroft, 'Famine and Factors affecting Mortality', p. 17.

[62] *Ocherki po demografii Saratova* (Saratov, 1928), p. 6.

government and famine-free areas had to stand by passively to some extent as disease-ridden migrants besieged them. In other ways positive help could be given by more fortunate regions. Indeed M. I. Kalinin, the nominal head of famine relief, claimed that 70 to 80 per cent of the adult population of Russia was active on the 'hunger front'.[63] Party, Soviet, co-operative, military, educational, and trade-union organizations were involved. The latter designated special weeks for the production or collection of goods to be contributed to the aid programme.[64] By February 1922 trade-union lotteries were being held in forty-eight gubernii.[65] For lack of sufficient central funds the rudimentary basis of a welfare state was being set up through contributions from the workers' own meagre wages. In Saratov itself it was suggested that there should be a 2 per cent deduction from water-workers' pay in order to improve cultural facilities.[66] The national union of workers in education and the arts gave 5 per cent of their pay for famine relief.[67] The prestigious university of Petrograd, whose affairs will be reviewed later in another context, set up a famine commission and sent an expedition to afflicted areas.[68]

On 2 January 1922 a decree issued by VTsIK (the All-Union Central Executive Committee of the Communist Party) arranged for the requisitioning of valuable articles from museums, and this was followed on 16 February by the more controversial decree on the seizure of Church treasures.[69] The violent repercussions of the second decree have been examined in the case-study of Roslavl' in the Smolensk guberniia. Citizens died on the church steps in their attempt to prevent altar-pieces being taken away. If tension was so high in an area not stricken by famine, it may be assumed that as much or more violence occurred in regions like the Ukraine and Tambov guberniia, which were nearly as badly off as the Volga. Every twenty Roslavl' inhabitants had also to contribute to the support of one hungry child in the distant south-east, whilst

---

[63] *Itogi bor'by s golodom*, p. 3.
[64] *Trud*, 25 Aug. 1921.
[65] Ibid., 23 Feb. 1922.
[66] *Gudok*, 27 Aug. 1922.
[67] *Izvestiia VTsIK*, 6 Jan. 1922.
[68] *Istoriia Leningradskogo universiteta* (Leningrad, 1969), pp. 250–1.
[69] *Itogi bor'by s golodom*, pp. 418–19.

every five peasant households had to help one hungry adult. In
addition a special series of graded poll-taxes for famine relief
began in February 1922.[70] By 11 October we find local party
authorities demanding from peasants the delayed payment of
425 pudy of rye for maintaining ten children on the Volga.
This order was annulled on 26 October by the Smolensk
guberniia party committee for being excessive and too late to
be of any use. On 9 November a Moscow circular from
Secretary V. Molotov himself forbade somewhat belatedly the
imposition of any local taxes not laid down in the list issued by
VTsIK.[71] This move can be interpreted either as yet another
instance of poor central–local ties or as deliberate slowness so as
to let more money flow into public funds. In contrast local
military authorities would brook no delay. The commander of
the Western Front virtually ordered the *Smolgubispolkom* to eject
school number 9 out of what was now a Volga orphans' home
run by a 'revolutionary military committee'.[72]

The effects of the Volga famine were more disruptive and
politically dangerous in another national minority area that
had more ethnic pretensions, and above all suffered nearly as
much from famine as the Great-Russian Volga provinces. On
the day of the Kronstadt uprising, 23 February 1921, Lenin
appealed to the Ukraine to step up its aid, in the form of
foodstuffs to the workers of Petrograd and Moscow.[73] The
proclamation of NEP did not apply to the Ukraine, where the
punitive requisitioning methods of War Communism were
officially extended until the autumn of 1921.[74] In the Civil War
the Red Army had blocked off the northern part of the
Ukraine from the hungry south and commandeered the crops
from the north for Great-Russian cities.[75]

When the 'official' Famine struck the Volga, the Soviet press
made no mention of the position in the Ukraine. Only later did
occasional references appear on inner pages devoted to food
collection there. It was poor propaganda for the outside world
to know that the granary of Europe was suffering from famine

[70] See Ch. 1, pp. 39–40.
[71] Smolensk Archive, file WKP 125.
[72] Ibid.
[73] V. I. Lenin, *Polnoe sobranie sochinenii*, vol. 42 (Moscow, 1963), pp. 591–2.
[74] K. K. Dubyna (ed.), *Istoriia Ukrains'koi RSR*, vol. 2 (Kiev, 1967), p. 178.
[75] *Die Hungersnot in der Ukraine* (Berlin, 1923), p. 15.

conditions. In fact it soon found out, since by the end of July 1922 the ARA was having to feed 822,000 children and over a million adults in the Ukraine.[76] When the starvation rate accelerated in the southern provinces, and no help was available from outside, peasant refugees from the west added to the flood from the east converging on the less afflicted Ukrainian gubernii of Chernihiv and Poltava. It was not at all surprising that the main road to Poltava town near Makarenko's colony was full of travellers and plagued by bandits. Ukrainian sources claimed that ninety-two wagons of grain were collected from starving Ukrainian gubernii, of which thirty-six were sent off to feed the hungry in the Volga–Ural area.[77] So-called food gifts arriving in Saratov were forced out of Ukrainian peasants by the food-collecting army (*Prodovol'stvennaia armiia*), although they were still paying agricultural taxes which had been waived in the Volga provinces.

Central policy seemed to be so prejudiced against the Ukraine that it evoked the suspicion in several foreign observers that this particular national minority was being deliberately neglected as a punishment for its hostility to Russian rule in the Civil War.[78] In the religious sphere the government was quite clearly using the Famine as a political weapon with which to subdue the Orthodox Church. Certainly in 1922 Ukrainians came to envy and hate the preferential treatment given to their eastern neighbours on the Volga, thus falling prey to the methods of divide and rule which the Bolsheviks inherited from their imperial predecessors. In terms of the survival of the regime, such a policy may have been deemed necessary. The peasant revolt that broke out in February 1921 in the Tambov guberniia threatened to cut off rail connections between Moscow and the Volga region, since hungry peasants held up wheat trains and ransacked them. Bolshevik sources reveal that about half the population of the guberniia did not have enough to eat by then, and the position was no better by spring

[76] Fisher, op. cit., p. 270.
[77] See I. Harasymovych, 'Holod na Ukraini', *Ukrainskoe Slovo* (Berlin, 1922), p. 201. I am indebted to Dr W. Veryha for information on the situation in the Ukraine in 1922.
[78] See e.g. Fisher, op. cit., p. 266.

of 1922.[79] The revolt was squashed, but Tambov peasants in
1922 were still compelled to pay a levy on the acorns they
picked to eat as a substitute for bread.[80] The economic plight of
the Volga peasantry was even more crippling than that of the
Tambov or Ukrainian population. There was no fear of revolt
in the countryside on the Volga, due to sheer exhaustion.
Consequently no clearly visible political strings were attached
to relief operations there. This does not mean that they were
entirely lacking, as will be seen later. The main problems in the
Volga region, however, lay more in the administrative than in
the political domain. Most of them arose as a result of an all-
Russian phenomenon in 1922—the lack of co-ordination and
exchange of information between the centre and the localities,
together with nonchalant neglect of provincial problems so
long as they did not affect central political issues.

These attitudes were reflected in the arrangements for
famine relief in Tsaritsyn guberniia, to which we will now turn,
since our attention has been directed so far on Saratov and
Samara gubernii to the north of it. Organization at the grass-
roots level was clearly the most urgent need in order to reach
remote starving villages, yet in Tsaritsyn as in other gubernii
no local relief committees were set up at the uezd and volost'
levels until October 1921, that is, over two months after the
formation of the guberniia committee.[81] This was due to the
lethargy of the central and guberniia authorities who
appointed local committee members. Uezd and volost' organs
were required to report twice a month only to the guberniia,
which sent a monthly summary to Moscow.[82] The local committees varied greatly in their composition and operating
procedures, some of which were highly unusual. Between
January and May 1922 no money from any central agency was
given to them, so they had to depend on the surplus of local

[79] For 1921 see V. A. Antonov-Ovseenko, 'O banditskom dvizhenii v Tambovskoi
gubernii', T-686 in the Trotsky Archive, Harvard University, p. 4. For 1922 see I. Ia.
Trifonov, *Klassy i klassovaia bor'ba v SSSR v nachale NEPa (1921–1923)* (Leningrad,
1964), p. 120.
[80] O. H. Radkey, *The Unknown Civil War in Soviet Russia: A Study of the Green Movement
in the Tambov Region 1920–1921* (Stanford, 1976), p. 385.
[81] B. de Tef'e (ed.), *Chernaia godina i sbornik o golode v Tsaritsynskoi gubernii i obzor
deiatel'nosti gubkompomgola za 1921–1922 god* (Tsaritsyn, 1922), p. 15.
[82] Glavnyi politiko-prosvetitel'nyi komitet, *Nakaz mestnym komissiam pomoshchi golodaiushchim* (Moscow, 1922), p. 1.

revenues and gifts after the guberniia relief committee had made its own collections.[83]

These local committees were supplemented in the autumn of 1921 by the newly formed peasant Committees of Self-Help. They had been suggested as early as 3 August by VTsIK, but typically no action was taken until the Communist Party had time to look into the question.[84] Village as well as volost', uezd, and guberniia peasant committees were established in Tsaritsyn and other gubernii. At the lower levels their aim was to promote aid from less unfortunate households to the poor and the starving. They also collected seed grain for the 1922 sowing campaign.[85] Neither they nor the local relief committees were given any remit whatsoever with regard to how food should be dispensed or who was eligible to receive it. The contrast between this complete lack of instructions and the highly detailed directives from the centre to, say, the Roslavl' uezd or the Nikol'skaia volost' party committees on political matters is striking. The results were often counter-productive. In the villages the peasant committees consisted entirely of local peasants. Some of them were ex-members of the committees of poor peasants (kombedy) that had requisitioned in military style during War Communism, a style that lingered on. There were many cases of theft, misappropriation, and favouritism which tended to destroy confidence in officialdom in general.[86] Since peasants who still possessed any seed reserves or livestock were excluded from relief, they were compelled to sell them off in some cases in order to survive. This depleted the famine areas further, and sparked off new hatred amongst the peasants. In the subsequent scramble for survival and enrichment which mounted towards the end of 1922, it was not surprising that those who were slightly better off often took a kind of revenge in driving hard bargains with their poorer neighbours, as has been noted earlier.

The intermediary between local bodies and Moscow were the guberniia Commissions for the Relief of the Starving. The

---

[83] De Tef'e, op. cit., pp. 18–19.

[84] *Itogi bor'by s golodom*, p. 14.

[85] *Na bor'by s golodom, sbornik statei i materialov* (Petrograd, 1921), p. 112.

[86] See R. W. Fox, *People of the Steppes* (New York, 1925), pp. 182–3; Asquith, op. cit., p. 49.

Tsaritsyn Commission was set up on 8 August 1921, and like its counterparts in other gubernii, were very closely modelled on Pomgol, the all-Russian organ in Moscow. It had no special apparatus, but consisted of thirty-one members chosen from nearly every branch of local government. Its working methods were almost a caricature of those prevailing in high political bodies in Moscow. Plenary sessions were held once a month only, even at the height of the Famine, and merely ratified previous decisions of the two-man presidium. Five subsections were supervised by eight 'technical staff', whose title by implication precluded them from taking political decisions. The sections were for agitation, public works, public feeding, the investigation and procurement of resources, and after February 1922, a special section for the removal of church treasures.[87]

The Tsaritsyn gubpomgol was similar in structure and operation to other gubpomgoly. Like them it relied heavily for income on local sources such as gifts, taxes, profits from licences, lotteries, etc. They yielded over 68 million roubles by December 1921. By that date Moscow had provided a mere three and a half million roubles, and one million had come in from other gubernii.[88] Each guberniia that was officially designated as lying within the famine area was linked up with supposedly 'rich' gubernii which had to provide supplies. Tsaritsyn was linked with Kursk and Voronezh, Saratov with Kursk and Voronezh again, and also with Tambov and Orël, while Samara was allied with no less than five other gubernii.[89] Given that co-operation and consultation in more normal times was virtually unknown on this lateral basis, inexperience led to many defects. There were no specifications as to what type or quantity of goods should be sent. Poor control over shipments led to theft and other misdemeanours. Despite internal and foreign suggestions as to how to improve horizontal co-operation, the central authorities took no action throughout 1922.[90]

[87] De Tef'e, op. cit., p. 15.

[88] Ibid., p. 18.

[89] Russian Trade Delegation, *The Famine in Russia: Documents and Statistics presented to the Brussels Conference on Famine Relief* (London, 1921), p. 47.

[90] 'Resolutions of the All-Russian Conference of Representatives of Famine Relief Commissions', ARA Russian Relief, Box 106, Folder no. 1. We know that guberniia co-operation was still poor in Apr. 1922 from the reports of Rabkrin. In Ivanovo-

At both guberniia and central levels the Soviet government established a liaison system between their own plenipotentiaries and all foreign relief organizations. It was headed by Alexander Eiduk, a pugnacious character who was a member of the GPU collegium. Foreign organizers soon discovered that the system seemed to be modelled on Trotsky's military commissars. Co-operation was often subordinated to the more important task of insulating local Russian relief staff and the general population from political contamination by foreigners.[91] Given the disturbed local conditions, and keen memories of American, British, and other intervention in the Civil War, this suspicious approach was not entirely unwarranted, particularly with regard to the cities of the Middle Volga. They contained a large middle class, which together with dissatisfied refugees and war workers from the fighting zone in the World War, had often expressed dislike of central intervention, and had even encouraged local autonomy.[92]

Moving for the first time in this book to Moscow and central administration, we find that from 18 July 1921, the Central Commission for the Relief of the Starving (Pomgol) was in charge of the Famine programme. Although its decisions were intended to have 'military urgency' for the rest of the government,[93] Pomgol had an independent apparatus, since its staff was drawn from many Commissariats and departments. To put teeth into it, Pomgol was chaired by M. I. Kalinin, who was to become president of the newly formed USSR in December 1922. He was supported by three well-known figures, L. B. Kamenev, A. Rykov, and P. G. Smidovich, who took a prominent part in the suppression of the Tambov revolt according to the *Great Soviet Encyclopaedia*. Pomgol's activities extended to the purchase and distribution of foodstuffs, medicine, and other supplies; help to the starving to get work; and collecting donations. That it was not always successful, even in

Voznesensk guberniia, for example, clothes that had been collected in Oct. 1921 had still not been dispatched. At volost' levels several resolutions had been issued, but then nothing had been done in practice to gather in foodstuffs and other resources. See *Izvestiia Raboche-Krestianskoi Inspeksii*, 20 Apr. 1922, p. 19.

[91] Fisher, op. cit., pp. 217–19.
[92] See J. L. H. Keep, *The Russian Revolution: A Study in Mass Mobilisation* (London, 1976), p. 368.
[93] *Sobranie uzakonenii*, 55 (1921).

its own backyard, so to speak, can be gleaned from critical Rabkrin reports. In April 1922, Moscow collectors of valuables were not making proper valuations, and foodstuffs were being left to rot in warehouses.[94] Rabkrin was less perspicacious in its investigations of distant *pomgolgub* committees. It claimed that there were not enough members on them; yet we have seen that in Tsaritsyn at least there was a superfluity of ineffective plenary members.[95]

As with the guberniia committees, the small Pomgol presidium conducted nearly all the business, and in considerable secrecy. Only its formal subdivisions are known, despite the fact that the press was admitted to its open sessions.[96] Mystery also surrounds the brief existence of a rival non-governmental body, the All-Russian Famine Relief Committee, set up in July and dismantled at the end of August 1921. Besides Maxim Gorky and a daughter of L. Tolstoy, it included the President of the Second Duma and even S. N. Prokopovich, the Minister of Food in the Provisional Government of 1917, who was neither a Bolshevik nor a Menshevik. The official reason given for the committee's demise was that it had indulged in counter-revolution and illicit dealings with foreign powers.[97] Certainly suspect committee members had attempted to go abroad, but the real reason was probably that the committee had served its purpose by acting as a bait to attract foreign relief organizations (the ARA drew up an agreement on 20 August). Alternatively the committee could have served as a scapegoat if Pomgol activities had failed completely.

Since all foreign relief organizations dealt with Pomgol and with Eiduk as chief plenipotentiary, subsequent non-Russian scholars have tended to over-concentrate on the workings of Pomgol and its guberniia equivalents. Yet Pomgol was little more than a conglomerate made up of other relevant state departments. The Commissariat of Agriculture was the key element within Pomgol.[98] Light can be thrown on the adminis-

[94] *Izvestiia RKI*, 20 Apr. 1922.
[95] Ibid., Sept. 1922.
[96] *Itogi bor'by s golodom*, pp. 59–67.
[97] *Izvestiia*, 30 Aug. 1921.
[98] Weissman, op. cit., never mentions the Commissariat of Agriculture. Fisher, op. cit., mentions it once only, quoting a letter sent by the Commissar to the ARA on 4 Nov. 1922. 'The data at the disposal of the People's Commissariat of Agriculture

trative efficiency of this Commissariat (*Narkomzem*) by looking into the account of an inspection of it in early 1922. The Commissariat was found to be 'exceptionally developed' and full of 'a series of purely academic-parliamentary institutions'. Staffing had increased by 189 per cent between 1 January 1921 and 1 March 1922. Both large and small versions of many sections coexisted, but did not communicate with one another, or even know of one another's presence. There were chronic reshuffles of all organs. Central–local ties were weaker still. Provincial branches of Narkomzem only contacted Moscow when in need of salaries and funds—otherwise they led independent lives. When Narkomzem handed out a questionnaire with 226 questions at an All-Russian Congress of Agricultural Organizations, a single reply was returned. Central officials were ignorant of the number and location of their own local agencies. They gave out huge cash advances without checking: each local branch had its own accountants. If even only some of these criticisms were true, then national leadership in the agricultural sphere, and above all the subjugation of the Famine, was in precarious hands.[99] Another report from Rabkrin accused *Tsentroevak*, the Central Refugee Evacuation Commission, of behaving in a very complacent fashion over the number of migrants piling up in the cities of Samara, Penza and Voronezh.[100]

The administration of the Famine was divided into two distinct parts by VTsIK. On 12 September 1922 it issued a decree abolishing Pomgol and replacing it with *Posledgol* (the Committee for the Struggle Against the Consequences of the Famine). It was announced that 'the impact of the Famine had disappeared'.[101] Substantial foreign aid had helped; weather conditions seemed likely to give good crop yields, and the early

---

regarding the size of the seeded spring, as well as winter area in 1922, permit the assertion that all seed dispatched to the hunger-stricken districts was completely utilized for planting.'

[99] *Izvestiia RKI*, May 1922. From other sources it is clear that most of Narkomzem activity in 1922 was devoted to the Famine. See e.g. *Otchet narkomzemledeliia: X vserossiiskogo s'ezda sovetov za 1922 god* (Moscow, 1923), pp. 12–13.

[100] *Izvestiia RKI*, May 1922.

[101] *Izvestiia*, 4 Sept. 1922. This evaluation is taken at its face value by E. H. Carr: see *A History of Soviet Russia: The Bolshevik Revolution in 1919–1923*, 2 (London, 1952), p. 287.

returns of the spring harvest had provided a new supply of food. Gosplan and other central economic organs from 1921 on had accumulated on paper a number of plans for reconstruction which they were now eager to realize. As in the recent past, and as was to be the case with much greater frequency after the start of the Five-Year Plans, planners in Moscow drew up neat and rather abstract formulations that did not match up closely with local realities and timings. Foreign relief organizations and subsequent students of their work have tended to exaggerate this dichotomy with regard to the Famine, but internal Soviet sources lend credence to the view that the sudden withdrawal of many kinds of domestic relief was premature. In 1922 it was not so easy to predict crop yields as it is today. In that sense the shift in policy contained an element of chance. More important in human terms, *Izvestiia* and other papers in early October recorded many instances of further starvation. Local correspondents were 'warning every day that the events which we saw last winter may occur again'.[102] As late as January 1923 *Pravda* reported that in some villages in the Saratov guberniia 80 to 85 per cent of the population were still starving.[103]

The abolition of Pomgol was greeted with so many protests from the affected areas of Russia that Kalinin had to issue two statements in which he tried to show the stricken population that it had not been abandoned by the government. At first this was hard to prove, since local authorities were now given many new relief duties: at the same time a number of extensive taxation rights were transferred away from them to the Centre.[104] This move at least gave greater financial stability. Between 15 October 1922 and 1 August 1923, for example, it received 719,502 gold roubles from the tax in kind (its highest source of income was 1,344,639 roubles from church treasures).[105] When in September 1922 the ARA discovered that the Soviet government intended to export grain in considerable quantities, most foreign relief organizations joined in the hue and cry. The government gave a series of reasons for its

[102] *Izvestiia*, 5 Oct. 1922.
[103] *Pravda*, 28 Jan. 1923.
[104] *Itogi posledgol s 15. X 1922 g.–1. VIII 1923 g.* (Moscow, 1923), pp. 7, 92.
[105] Ibid., pp. 156–7.

decision, some of them more plausible than others;[106] but the main aim seemed to be to acquire cash or foreign credit for the rehabilitation of its industries. More grain than expected had to be exported due to the precipitous fall in the grain price in the middle of the winter of 1922–3. The fact that the price fell so steeply indicated that the gamble on the harvest had paid off, but due to delays and maladministration peasants were still starving, as we have seen.

It is clear that there were disagreements at the highest levels on the timing of the abolition of Pomgol and the export of grain. The correspondent of *The Times* in Riga, with access to both current Western and Soviet sources, picked up the discrepant views of M. Litvinov at the Hague and L. Krasin, the Commissar for Trade in Moscow. At the start of August the former was telling the outside world of Russia's quick recovery, just when the latter was still being very pessimistic.[107] Lenin's attitude, in so far as it is discernible, will be looked at in a moment, but by this time he was more cut off through illness from daily supervision of affairs. That there were divisions within the Politburo was indicated by the absence of Stalin, Trotsky, Bukharin, Tomsky, and Zinoviev from the friendly farewell ceremonies for the ARA.[108] The administration of the Famine was remarkable for the absence of nearly all leading Bolsheviks, apart from a few speeches from one or two of them. Kamenev and Rykov served on Pomgol, but the extent of their participation is unclear. Alone of all the top Bolsheviks, Kalinin visited some of the stricken areas by train, a peasant among peasants.[109]

Lenin knew the Middle Volga better than any other leader, for he was born in Simbirsk, not far up river from Samara, had studied at Kazan' university, and been a barrister in Samara. Traditionally it was an area of peasant insurrectionists,

[106] Edmondson, op. cit., pp. 316–17.

[107] *The Times*, 9 Aug., 1922. The correspondent also noted that an article in *Ekonomicheskaia zhizn'* blamed the 'over-optimism of the provincial Soviets'. This was a nice instance of the central pot calling the provincial kettle black.

[108] Weissman, op. cit., p. 193.

[109] Between 1921 and 1923 Kalinin visited the Volga region, the Ukraine, the Crimea, and other regions. See E. P. Murav'eva, 'Agitatsionno-propagandistkaia deiatel'nost' M. I. Kalinina sredi rabochikh i krest'ian v period vosstanovleniia narodnogo khoziaistva strany (1921–1923 gg.)', *Vestnik Moskovskogo universiteta*, No. 3 (1967), p. 18.

schismatics, and sectarians whose acerbic style was reflected in Lenin's own. Did he have any political motives for apparently dealing with the Volga population almost as harshly and coldly as with starving Ukrainians or the Tambov peasantry? What follows must be speculative in nature until the Cheka archives for 1921–2 are opened up, since matters are involved which would never have been aired publicly. Certainly from the spring of 1918 Lenin was almost obsessed by the need to get grain to the cities of the north-west, for it was their turn to starve at that time. He named the food supply crisis as the most important question of all, and called for a great 'crusade' against speculators and the '*kulak*', that recurring bogeyman of the regime until 1928. Conceivably he may have thought in 1921–2 that previous peasant intransigence was now receiving its just reward. Beyond this, it is quite clear that the Middle Volga still contained strong pockets of potential political resistance to the centre—the tradition of revolt died hard. At the Left Socialist Revolutionary trial in Moscow in 1922 it was revealed that the Left Socialist Revolutionary Central Committee had sent emissaries to Tambov and other nearby gubernii.[110] One of them was probably the Samara guberniia, where since July 1920 a Left Socialist Revolutionary peasant called Sapozhkov had led an insurrection in the Buzuluk uezd. After his death the standard was taken up by Serov, who still commanded 3,000 men as late as January 1922.[111] The threat to supply lines between Moscow and the Volga provinces was obvious. Lenin decreed the taking of hostages from villages along the rebels' line of march and instructed local party leaders to 'cut down at the root' any evidence of sympathy with the rebels on the part of the population.[112]

Repercussions of these disturbances came to the attention of foreign relief workers. In April 1922 an ARA representative complained to Eiduk that the local Soviet plenipotentiary's assistant had arrested five of his Russian employees in the Pugachev district of the Samara guberniia. Eiduk's reply was

[110] Radkey, op. cit., p. 128.
[111] I. Ya. Trifonov, *Klassy i klassovaia bor'ba v nachale nepa (1921–1923 gg.)*, Part I (Leningrad, 1964), p. 262. The Volga provinces also seethed with bandits in 1922; see p. 156.
[112] V. I. Lenin, *Polnoe sobranie sochinenii*, vol. 51 (5th edn., Moscow, 1958–65), pp. 347–8, and app. 23.

swift: 'all active members of the Socialist Revolutionary Party were being arrested and the ARA happened to have employed them.'[113] In Samara city another hostile faction, the Workers' Opposition, had been very strongly entrenched up to March 1921. One authority on nation-wide local party activity in this period states that of all provinces Samara was the most troubled by wrangles inside the party in 1921. The wounds were still visible in 1922.[114] May not Lenin have reacted in private in a way not so dissimilar from Stalin's overt and more violent reaction to political opposition in Georgia in the same year? Both men no doubt were vexed by the unorthodoxy of their own birthplaces.

Whatever was in Lenin's mind, it is certain that the great Famine of 1921–2 wiped out any likelihood of peasant resistance. Until 1921 some elements among the peasantry had kept a certain independence of outlook. The Revolution had impinged on their consciousness only in so far as it provided them with land, or took away foodstuffs during War Communism. It is usually said that the introduction of NEP pacified the peasants, but the Famine had a quicker effect in this respect. Agricultural resources had been reduced drastically. In the course of eight months 20 per cent of all horses in the country had been killed. Thirty-five per cent of all draught animals were lost, if Civil War casualties are included. Although the provinces round Petrograd and Moscow and on the Upper Volga recovered fast economically and were probably better treated, since they had stayed faithful to the Bolsheviks from 1917, they were relatively unimportant as agricultural producers. The fact that the government thought it vital to supplement the economic incentives of NEP by a new Agrarian Code, brought out at the end of 1922, showed how far the Famine had altered previous calculations. Rural areas were now allowed more freedom of choice as to farming methods, and the peasants' propensity to more individualistic action was encouraged.

The main consequence of the Famine, after human loss of life and suffering, was continuing economic and social

[113] Quoted in Weissman, op. cit., p. 111.
[114] See R. Service, *The Bolshevik Party in Revolution: A Study in Organizational Changes 1921–1923* (London, 1979), pp. 165, 170.

instability. At the conclusion of the survey of tax and other fiscal arrangements in the Smolensk guberniia[115] it was noted that the financial framework of NEP was shaky from the outset. When the disruptions caused by the Famine are added to this scenario, the situation appears more grave. Discounting loss of human and animal lives and equipment, the dislocation in revenue alone was enormous. The tax in kind for 1921–2 realized only 150 million pudy, half of the total collection for 1920–1. The estimate had been 240 million pudy.[116] This was not for lack of punitive methods. One uezd in Simbirsk guberniia, just to the west of Samara and nearly as badly affected, had been assessed for tax at 470,000 pudy in 1919 on a good crop, of which 350,000 had been collected. In 1922 the tax was 698,000 pudy on an indifferent crop.[117]

The chief symptom of continuing instability was the 'scissors crisis' which began to affect Smolensk and all other gubernii in 1922, as has been seen,[118] and reached a climax in 1923 when the scissors opened too widely in favour of manufactured goods. Industrial prices by then had risen two to three times more quickly than agricultural ones. The huge slump in the grain price on the Volga and elsewhere in the winter of 1922, and the lesser slide in the price of flax from Belorussia, were but two of the contributing factors, though grain played a basic role. As a result the rural population of all Russia would need four years, until 1926, to recover from the combined disasters of the Famine and crude central fiscal and administrative measures. There was little hope that it would weigh for much in the balance of political life until then. One of the main reasons for the introduction of NEP had been the peasants' ability to throttle the industrial towns of European Russia by withholding food supplies. The cities and the regime survived this temporary threat, but the boomerang effect of the Famine on the countryside had more lasting influence.

[115] See above, p. 47.
[116] *Piat' let vlasti sovetov* (Moscow, 1922), p. 373.
[117] Fisher, op. cit., pp. 309–10.
[118] See above, p. 47.

# 4. *Communications**

PROVINCIAL life as such is now left behind as we turn to various types of connections between it and the political and cultural centres of Russia. Some nationwide systems of Bolshevik political control are examined in the next chapter, whereas here more neutral communications networks are studied. However, since the accent in this book lies on social and political affairs, the railways and the press will be considered from this angle. In fact both networks were subject to heavy political intervention. The first carried goods and people, the second ideas and information. Within their own spheres, they were of overriding importance. Road, air, and even river transport were of little significance by comparison with the railways. The public relied to a minimal extent on what were by modern standards vestigial radio, telephone, and film-distribution systems.

Lenin and the Bolsheviks had grasped the supreme political importance of the railways and the press as instruments for turning their domination of some cities of European Russia in 1917 into an all-Russian revolution.[1] This lesson had been reinforced as far as the railways were concerned each spring from 1918 to 1920, when urgent orders went out from the highest level to rehabilitate them in order to cope with the influx of vital foodstuffs and fuel to the towns. In addition the strategic significance of the railways had impressed itself on the Bolsheviks. Through their hold over the nine main lines fanning out from Moscow to all points of the compass they had succeeded in cutting off one White force from another in the Civil War. Lenin took a personal interest in railway and

* Parts of this chapter were published as an article in *Soviet Studies*, Apr. 1986.
[1] See R. Pethybridge, *The Spread of the Russian Revolution: Essays on 1917* (London, 1972).

electricity technology for another reason. Both networks fed energy (light, and food, fuel, human agents) round the ex-Empire. Both were subject to easily measured norms, time-tables and co-ordinated planning: therefore of all systems they seemed to be the most suitable for the immediate application of Taylorism and what Lenin called 'the precision of clockwork'.[2] He also realized that if large-scale economic and social organ-ization on Marxist lines was ever to replace the small-scale realities of early Soviet life and improve the volume of exchange of goods between manufacturing plants and the villages, then efficient railways would serve as the thin edge of the wedge. The ex-peasant Sergei Esenin viewed them in a more suspicious way in a poem published in 1922:

> With what blind fear in snow-chaos
> The changing terror rocked and swayed.
> Good day to you, black Nemesis!
> I come out to meet you half way.[3]

The railway system continued to figure largely in high political planning in 1922. As Tomsky put it at the Fifth Congress of Trade Unions on 2 October 1922: 'Without the strengthening and support of transport there can be no con-struction of socialism.'[4] In reality, as opposed to the somewhat utopian visions of Lenin, the railways in 1922 were an unlikely candidate for Taylorist methods. Although the government placed 'the political and economic backbone of the Republic in heavy industry and in transport', Trotsky observed at the Twelfth Party Congress that they actually formed the rear-guard.[5] During the Civil War 1,885 km. of railway track had been destroyed;[6] 8.6 million pudy of metal were required to repair them, but only 5.3 million could be produced.[7] Of the 19,067 engines in stock in 1921–2, 64 per cent were unusable

[2] V. I. Lenin, *Collected Works*, vol. 27 (London, 1965), p. 211.

[3] From S. Esenin, *Wolf Nemesis*, in *Stikhotvorenia* (Moscow, 1987).

[4] M. P. Tomsky, *Stat'i i rechi*, vol. 4 (Moscow, 1928), p. 8.

[5] I. Smilga, *Vosstanovitel'nyi protsess. Piat' let Novoi Ekonomicheskoi Politiki. Stat'i i rechi* (Moscow, 1927), p. 71; and L. Trotsky, *Osnovnye voprosy promyshlennosti* (Moscow, 1923), p. 11.

[6] *Sovetskoe narodnoe khoziaistvo v 1921–25 gg.* (Moscow, 1960), p. 357.

[7] *Narodnoe i gosudarstvennoe khoziaistvo SSSRk seredine 1922–3 g.* (Moscow, 1923), p. 433.

according to official estimates.[8] Not until 1926 did servicing catch up with urgent repair needs. In 1922–3 32 per cent of all wagons lay idle for lack of maintenance. *Gudok*, the railway newspaper, reported on 22 September 1922 that the Moscow workshops on the Kursk line were full of rusting machinery, since rain came through the roof.[9] Railway stock sent from Black Sea ports to another area, the Middle Volga, was not sent back for more grain, but for the most part ended up in Siberia.[10] In Smolensk guberniia a long list of bridges, points, and crossings had been blown up in military action.[11] In the chapter on Smolensk guberniia it was noted how peasants were bludgeoned into hauling wood to engine fuel-dumps, although they were not paid for it. In January 1922 the Smolensk party committee estimated that there was only enough fuel of all kinds left for seven to eight days' consumption.[12] This was a nation-wide phenomenon. In Kharkov and Poltava lack of fuel was cited as the worst problem of all.[13] Three times as much unsuitable wood, which ruined engine-boilers, was being used throughout Russia than in 1913. It comprised 38 per cent of all fuel, as opposed to 13.1 per cent in 1913.[14]

The layman usually thinks of passenger traffic first, and freight second, but the latter is usually of far greater importance, and Russia was no exception. The level of truck loadings for 1922 was under one-third of what it had been in 1913,[15] although there was a fast improvement towards the end of the year. The carriage of private goods accelerated most. Despite Gosplan's Marxist ideal of trying to stop uneven economic development, by the end of NEP the position had changed very little from the old Tsarist need to move commodities from the south and east to the more heavily populated north and west of European Russia. That is why the Moscow–Kursk and Moscow–Volga lines were so sensitive, amongst others. In industry

[8] S. Strumilin, *Statistichesko-ekonomicheskie ocherki* (Moscow, 1958), p. 658.

[9] *Gudok*, 22 Sept. 1922.

[10] H. H. Fisher, *The Famine in Soviet Russia 1919–1923: The Operation of the American Relief Administration* (New York, 1927), p. 187.

[11] *Razvitie ekonomiki Belorussii v 1921–7 gg.* (Minsk, 1973), p. 139.

[12] Smolensk Archive, file WKP 273/32.

[13] *Narodnoe khoziaistvo Ukrainy v 1921–2 gg.* (Kharkov, 1923), p. 16.

[14] *Narodnoe i gosadarstvennoe khoziaistvo SSSR*, p. 432.

[15] *Transport i sviaz' SSSR* (Moscow, 1957), p. 32.

machines are stable and raw materials are mobile. On the other hand agricultural land is fixed so that beasts and tools have to be taken to the fields and then off them. Russian agriculture in early NEP was an involuntary small-scale transport industry which for the most part lay far away from the railway lines. Remember how our peasant woman made her way painstakingly on foot, then by boat and cart to the uezd centre of Roslavl' in Belorussia. The railways, like rivers, fertilized only a very narrow strip along their course, leaving nearly untouched the rhythm of life in the rural hinterland. A Soviet propaganda film showing a map of Russia lights up the rays of the 1917 Revolution spreading round the country. It is not fortuitous that they follow the railway lines from Petrograd and Moscow. Both the Provisional Government and the Bolsheviks were aware of this in 1917.[16] The position had not changed by early NEP. The more remote the locality from the main network of political and other communications, the more likelihood there was of unorthodox behaviour, whether of a passive kind, as in the recesses of the gubernii of Smolensk or Kursk, or of a more menacing nature, as with the Tambov and Siberian peasant revolts. As late as 1926 this general pattern, though subject to some exceptions, is clearly observable, as will be seen in the case-studies of Tver guberniia and Kazakhstan.

The number of passengers on Russian railways in 1922 was calculated to be 91.1 million, as opposed to 184.8 million in 1913. This huge decline was soon to be reversed in NEP, for by 1926 the figure was 259.9 million.[17] Some allowance must be made for the large number of passengers without tickets in 1922. In one incident alone near Smolensk, seventy-four persons were arrested for not paying for their journey.[18] The different categories of traveller are very hard to assess at all precisely. Before 1914 they would have been mainly peasant-workers commuting twice a year to the cities, gentry and their numerous domestic servants moving from their estates to town, kustari with their wares for sale, government servants, and the military, etc. By 1922 the first three types had either disappeared completely (the gentry) or were at a very low ebb. The

[16] See Pethybridge, op. cit., pp. 15–16, for more evidence on this subject.
[17] *Transport i sviaz' SSSR; statisticheskii sbornik* (Moscow, 1972), p. 91.
[18] Smolensk Archive, file WKP 273.

'Nepmen' had not yet prospered sufficiently to replace the 'bagmen', those petty speculators of War Communism. Demobilization was drawing to an end, and many of the suffering migrants like the Famine refugees and the wandering hordes of orphans and youths could not often afford to take a train. Travel went at a very slow pace. The average commercial speed was 12.8 km. per hour at the start of 1923. When ARA famine officials went from Kazan' to Simbirsk in the autumn of 1921, it took them four days to cover 150 miles.[19]

In July 1921 the new statutes of the Commissariat of Ways and Communications had been issued, putting the railways on a peacetime basis. In the spring of 1922 their management was decentralized to some extent and subjected to khozraschet (strict accounting principles). It was hoped that this would result in better co-operation from local administrators and party members in the supply of labour and fuel, etc. The reorganization was recommended by an engineer in the pages of a leading Petrograd journal, since he thought it would lead to the dissemination of experts.[20] At the local level, too, there were calls for the maximum amount of latitude in self-administration.[21] However, tension arose between the need for decentralization in order to ensure more technical efficiency and political fears of too much independence. It was not long before the chairman of each local railway-board was compelled to become a representative of the central Commissariat.

Railway construction, together with textiles, had provided the impetus for large-scale industrial products in Russia. For long-distance hauls the public, the economy, and virtually all messages in the form of letters, newspapers, telephone, and telegraph, continued to rely heavily on railway communications in the 1920s. Railways are a type of transport that fall easily under central control, and whose construction may even intensify political centralism, because of the rationality of disposing lines so as to converge at a central point. Like the absence of useful maritime peripheries, however, they can only serve as a secondary reinforcement of pre-existing leanings to

[19] Fisher, op. cit., p. 85.
[20] *Pechat' i revoliutsiia*, 7 (1922), p. 224.
[21] See e.g. A. Chaschikhin, *Kratkie ocherki po istorii professional'n ogo soiuza po permskoi zheleznoi dorogi* (Sverdlovsk, 1927), p. 105.

political centralism. Canada similarly depends greatly on railways, has widely separated confines and high latitudes, but possesses a very different socio-economic and political system.

Sea, inland waterway, and road transport came under the control of the Commissariat as well as the railways. For long hauls the rivers still remained more important than roads in NEP, despite the fact that many of them flow to the Arctic and are frozen for long periods. Long- and cheap-haul facilities were vital in a poor country occupying 17 per cent of the inhabited surface of the earth. Natural resources were scattered over vast areas. The faster Russia modernized, the more she needed her population dispersed in order to extract newly developed wealth. The massive preponderance of peasants up to the end of NEP and beyond also ensured a widely disseminated population. River traffic suffered in the Revolution as the railways had done. In 1913 there had been 59,400 km. of navigable internal waterways, but this was reduced to 53,900 by 1922, a relatively small decline compared with the railways. It is not so easy to destroy a waterway. The number of passengers carried was 11.5 million in 1913, 7 million in 1920, and 12 million by 1924:[22] the productivity of river transport rose much faster after 1921 than that of the railways,[23] although many problems had to be overcome, as was seen with regard to the Volga fleet in Chapter 3.

The length of metalled roads in the country was well under half that of navigable rivers in 1913—24,300 km. This remained steady at 25,000 km. in 1920, but actually dropped in the more prosperous years after 1922 to 23,100 in 1924.[24] Roads much traversed in the Civil War or in the invasion of Poland, like those of Belorussia, deteriorated from use by military vehicles.[25] Even less important than long-distance

---

[22] *Transport i sviaz' SSSR*, pp. 163, 175.

[23] e.g. in the north-western region river transport productivity was 3.4 times better in 1923 than it had been in 1921. The tonnage passing through the port of Petrograd rose by 240% over the same period; Iu. Klimov, *V surovye gody dvadsatye: Bol'sheviki severozapada v bor'be za provedenie NEPa v 1921–35* (Murmansk, 1968), p. 108.

[24] *Transport i sviaz' SSSR*, p. 262.

[25] *Razvitie ekonomiki Belorussii*, p. 153. After the agreement between the ostensibly separate governments of the Russian and Belorussian governments, all Belorussian communications and transport were brought directly under the control of the RSFSR Commissariat on 7 Sept. 1922. See *Organy gosudarstvennogo upravitel'stva BSSR 1919–67 gg.* (Minsk, 1968), p. 207.

roads were air routes. The first regular civil flight opened up in May 1922 between Moscow and Königsberg. A new service began between Moscow and Nizhnii Novgorod in 1923.[26]

Nearly all messages in the form of letters, newspapers, telephone, and telegraph went along the railway lines. Telecommunications were easier to build, service, and tap in this way. In 1913 there were 11,000 post and telecommunications offices, of which only 3,000 were in rural localities. The figures for 1924 were 9,000 and 2,700, showing yet another decline in facilities.[27] On 9 February 1922 a letter of complaint to the press from postmen headed 'The uncommunicative Commissariat' stated that the Moscow post office, with 4,000 employees, was frozen up for lack of snow-cleaners. Letters had to be sent in bulk to Smolensk to be sorted and distributed.[28] It took fifteen days for telegrams to get from Moscow to Tsaritsyn during the Famine.[29] In Smolensk guberniia 350 telegraph-workers went on strike for better pay and conditions on 29 April. On 5 May telegraph-wires were cut down near Bykhov. The party authorities ascribed this to sabotage by peasants objecting to tax assessments.[30]

Even by 1926 links remained feeble. In Kursk guberniia the telephone system was a subject for derision. Frequent administrative changes 'created conditions for its progressive (*sic*) decline and to a kustar' development of communications'[31] (it is interesting to note that 'kustar'' had by then followed '*kulak*' as a term of abuse). In the Tver guberniia conditions in 1926 were as good as anywhere outside a few industrial regions. Letters were delivered twice a week only. The inhabitants of Goritskaia volost' near Tver received fewer letters towards the end of 1926 than they had done in 1913. There were single telephones in one or two villages. It was too expensive for most private individuals there to send telegrams; the network was used almost exclusively by the authorities. Whereas 577

[26] L. Symons and C. White (eds.), *Russian Transport: An Historical and Geographical Survey* (London, 1975), p. 143.
[27] *Transport i sviaz' SSSR*, p. 271.
[28] *Trud*, 9 Feb. 1972.
[29] Fisher, op. cit., p. 105.
[30] Smolensk Archive, file WKP 273.
[31] *Otchet XIII-mu gubernskomu s'ezdu sovetov: Kurskii gubernskii ispolnytel'nyi komitet* (Kursk, 1926), p. 222.

telegrams had been sent off and 1,158 received in the volost' in
1913, the figures for 1926 were 672 and 785 respectively.[32] The
overwhelming majority of peasant communications were oral
in nature in a society that was still largely illiterate. The range
of information was thus short, though the art of rumour
sometimes had widespread effects.[33] The radio was a useful
political and social tool in a society of this kind, but its impact
did not hit even Britain until the 1920s. In Russia there were
almost no major broadcasts until 1922.[34]

The retarded development of all the means of communication mentioned above had certain economic, social, and political consequences throughout NEP. Not until the years of fast
industrialization and construction were these defects to be
remedied. The lack of an efficient railway system was a major
contributing factor to the stagnant economy. Since the railways and the cables alongside them carried most of the nation's
newspapers, letters, and long-distance oral messages, little
stimulus could be given towards the social and ethnic unification of a country that was notorious for the gap between town
and country living conditions. Together with Germany in the
1930s, Russia since 1917 has had the most penetrating system
of political propaganda, but it was severely hampered at first
by inefficient technical means for dissemination over vast
spaces and many minority nationalities.

In order to show how acute the problems were, let us return
to the government's handling of the railway network in 1922.
On the last day of 1921 the Party Central Committee
appointed Feliks Dzerzhinsky, the head of the Cheka and
Commissar for Transport, to the commission for the dispatch
of food supplies and grain seed from Siberia and the Ukraine.
On 5 January he went to Siberia. Three motives lay behind
this. The first was as stated in the conditions of his appointment; but there were two other political reasons which will be
examined later. One-fifth of all Russian victuals came from

---

[32] M. Bol'shakov, *Derevnia 1917–27* (Moscow, 1927), pp. 299, 303. For more detail
on the state of post and telecommunications in the Revolution itself, see Pethybridge,
op. cit., pp. 57–82.

[33] See Pethybridge, op. cit., pp. 170–5 for information on nation-wide rumours in
1917 on Rasputin and other topics.

[34] See *Bol'shaia sovetskaia entsiklopediia*, vol. 36, p. 557.

Siberia at this time according to local estimates.[35] Dzerzhinsky discovered 2,583 unused railway-trucks there (some of them sent on from the Volga and dumped, as has been seen). Over two thousand telegrams, mainly concerning the supply of the Famine areas, had been held up inside Siberia. Railway workers had gone without pay, proper food, and clothes for months. Dzerzhinsky at once put his programme on a military footing in nineteen rail-centres. The central authorities were instructed to send 100 million roubles to pay the railwaymen.[36] As a result loading went up in volume by four times within a month. Yet by the end of the year the fuel supply was still critical. *Gudok* reckoned that there would be only two to three days' reserve for the railways as a whole. This newspaper also criticized Dzerzhinsky for neglecting water transport and port facilities,[37] though no doubt his great energies were stretched in Siberia where he stayed until March. He did in fact inspect the port of Petrograd in late June.

Although politically a centralist, Dzerzhinsky was pragmatic enough on the spot. Once in Siberia he realized that estimates made on paper in Moscow for the dispatch of 250 wagons a day to the Volga were completely unrealistic. Only seventy could be handled.[38] In a letter sent later to the central authorities he advised that transport problems should be viewed in organic conjunction with local economic needs. Gosplan was still demanding central control.[39] Dzerzhinsky was also a strong advocate for the application of khozraschet, although he understood the peculiar difficulties of nation-wide utilities in this respect. In a report to a plenary meeting of *Tsektran* in June, he said that trains should stop acting like droshkys, carrying people and goods where they wished for little or no pay.[40] The tariff for goods carriage now stood at

[35] *Rabochii put'* (Omsk), 14 Jan. 1922.
[36] N. Zubov, *F. E. Dzerzhinskii: biografiia* (Moscow, 1965), pp. 297–9. See also A. V. Tishkov, *Pervyi chekist* (Moscow, 1968); A. A. Khaletskaia, *Ekspeditsiia F. E. Dzerzhinskogo v Sibir (1922 g.)* (Omsk, 1963); S. S. Khromov, *Po zadaniiu Lenina: deiatelnost' F. E. Dzerzhinskogo v Sibiri* (Moscow, 1964).
[37] *Gudok*, 4 Oct. 1922.
[38] Ibid., 3 Oct. 1922.
[39] *Istoricheskii arkhiv*, 2 (1960).
[40] *Gudok*, 17 June 1922.

20,000 times previous rates, but this still fell far below the cost-of-living index due to astronomical inflation.[41]

The second reason for the dispatch of Dzerzhinsky to Siberia was to clear up the situation after the Civil War, and to deal with Siberian peasant revolts. These aims are admitted to in Soviet sources, but we as yet know very little from any source about the nature and extent of peasant disturbances. White forces had intended to blow up more railway lines and workshops. Explosives were found in nearly all of the latter and there had been twenty fires in them between 1 November and 26 December 1921.[42] Dzerzhinsky had been made Commissar for Transport in the first place to deal with internal troubles among the railwaymen, many of whom had opposed the Bolsheviks in 1917 and nearly brought Lenin's government to its knees after the October Revolution.[43] Lingering resistance was not confined to Siberia. The railway secret police were active throughout 1922 in Smolensk guberniia: in their February report, they noted the presence in one section of the railways of six active Mensheviks, one SR, and an ex-Tsarist secret police agent.[44] Equal ruthlessness was applied to those who misused the railways and were brought before 'the revolutionary tribunal, whose avenging hammer will fall with all its crushing might and wrath'.[45] In September 211 speculators in railway tickets were arrested at Moscow stations. In October the secret police were permitted by the Central Committee to start shooting railway bandits on the spot without legal proceedings.[46] Yet another suspect category were the many *spetsy* (bourgeois specialists) who worked for the Commissariat. Dzerzhinsky stressed that local authorities should collaborate with them, but at the centre he was adamant that they should take no part in transport decisions that had any political implications.[47]

[41]  F. E. Dzerzhinsky, *Izbrannye proizvedeniia*, vol. 1 (Moscow, 1967), p. 312.
[42]  Zubov, op. cit., p. 297.
[43]  See Pethybridge, op. cit., pp. 33–56.
[44]  Smolensk Archive, file WKP 273/32.
[45]  Dzerzhinsky, op. cit., p. 309.
[46]  Tishkov, op. cit., pp. 118–19.
[47]  *Gudok*, 9 July 1922; *Istoricheskii arkhiv*, 2 (1960). More information on the role of the spetsy in the Commissariat will be provided when the Professor G. V. Lomonosov archive is open for examination at Leeds University Library. The author could not gain access to it.

The third reason why Dzerzhinsky was sent off to distant Siberia was purely political, and had little to do with the railways. At the Ninth All-Russian Congress of Soviets on 22 December 1921, Lenin called for the reform of the Cheka. since NEP required more 'revolutionary legality'.[48] In Dzerzhinsky's absence the Cheka was replaced by the GPU (*Gosudarstvennoe politicheskoe upravlenie*), which was now to be integrated within the Commissariat for Internal Affairs. No doubt it was easier to reform it with Dzerzhinsky out of Moscow, although he retained his post as head. In fact its effectiveness was hardly diminished, although its staff was reduced, like those of all Commissariats at this time. The new secret police swiftly recovered many of the powers of its predecessor.[49] It was one of those Bolshevik instruments of nation-wide control which will be studied in the next chapter. Dzerzhinsky frequently thought of the railway network in very similar terms. For lack of adequate progress in the improvement of central–local party and social ties in general, he and others, including Lenin, diverted their energies into the immediate practical tasks of rehabilitating the transport system. Dzerzhinsky wrote that the swifter exchange of goods would help to reduce taxes levied on the peasants and so mollify them and speed up the realization of smychka between town and country;[50] but towards the end of the year he admitted in a resigned tone: 'Can such a huge enterprise like transport really change in a moment, can people really be regenerated at once? It is done slowly, step by step.'[51] He was to die in 1926 with his vision still unfulfilled, although the Turkestan–Siberian railway, that considerable economic, social, and ethnic unifier, was on the drawing-boards. It was opened in 1931.

What type and number of men did Dzerzhinsky control on the railways? For the first time in this book we shall take a closer look at one branch of the proletariat. It was a very special branch in many ways. In the first place it comprised by far the largest number of workers in one industry. In 1922 there were no less than 983,045 of them, though the number

---

[48] *Deviatyi vsesoiuznyi s'ezd Sovetov* (Moscow, 1922), pp. 21–2.
[49] See G. Leggett, *The Cheka: Lenin's Political Police* (London, 1981), Ch. 15.
[50] Dzerzhinsky, op. cit., p. 397.
[51] *Gudok*, 4 Oct. 1922.

was reduced to 793,000 by 1923–4. Their trade union was instructed to find jobs for those thrown out of work.[52] Some had already left because pay was so far in arrears. Others with more initiative from the administrative ranks had taken up farming.[53] Whereas there had been 12.8 workers for every verst of line in 1913 there were 10.4 in 1922.[54] This was still overmanning to a considerable degree by world standards. The labour code of 1922 made labour productivity worse by introducing an eight-hour day for engine crews. Under the previous rules fourteen hours had been the maximum shift allowed.

The railway industry was huge in both size and geographical extent. At the top of the hierarchy were the civil service employees in the administration headquarters of the different branches and in Moscow. Next came the engineers, planners, statisticians, and less important office-workers. None of these could be classified strictly as proletarians, even by the loose and ideologically biased definitions of the early Soviet period. In 1917 this group had comprised between 16 and 17 per cent of all railway employees.[55] The gamut then descended from skilled engine-drivers and railway telegraph workers, conductors, points men, couplers, etc., to depot-workers and porters. At the bottom end of the scale we leave the proletariat altogether with the track-maintenance men, who were usually recruited from the local peasantry. In less industrial areas of the country there were more railway-workers than any other kind. In Belorussia in October 1922 there was a labour force of 23,438 on the railway network, as against 12,323 other workers in all Belorussian industry.[56]

Numbers alone did not mean automatic economic and political strength. The geographical and social distribution of railway-workers meant that they were not as cohesive a force as

[52] *Sovetskii transport 1917–27 gg.* (Moscow, 1927); Strumilin, op. cit., pp. 670–1; *Gudok*, 25 Oct. 1922.
[53] Smolensk Archive, file WKP 273/32.
[54] *Gudok*, 3 Oct. 1922.
[55] Compare A. Taniaev, *Ocherki po istorii dvizheniia zheleznodorozhnikov v revoliutsii 1917 goda* (Moscow, 1925), p. 3, who gives the figure as 16.8%, and I. Pushkareva, in *Lenin i oktiabrskoe vooruzhennoe vosstanie v Petrograde* (Moscow, 1964), p. 261, who puts the ratio at 'about 16%'.
[56] *Razvitie ekonomiki Belorussii*, p. 143.

other industrial groups like the steel- or textile-workers. These weaknesses were exploited by the Bolsheviks in 1917 when *Vikzhel*, the old railway trade union, threatened to cut off the capital and the government from the rest of Russia unless Lenin listened to its political demands. A rival trade union was formed which drew much more heavily on the lower social strata in the labour force and on the Moscow railway work-shops and other industrial centres. Never again was there to be a nation-wide intervention by the railway-workers, although those social tensions persisted which had helped the Bolsheviks to divide and rule in 1912. In March 1922 'snobbish clerks' on the Moscow–Kursk line, which had been one of the most revolutionary in 1905 and 1917, were refusing to attend meetings where common signalmen and the like were to be found.[57] Other lines showed more solidarity and local initi-ative. In the Gomel'sk workshops in Belorussia 450 railway staff collected one and a half million roubles in order to start up their own social insurance scheme for lack of an adequate state system. A training-school with forty students was opened.[58]

Like all other workers in 1922, Belorussian railwaymen complained about their pay. In May 200 struck on the Orlov–Vitebsk line on this account, declaring that instead of devoting its energy to extracting gold from the churches, the govern-ment should find ways of paying them better. The rank and file pointed out that even skilled workshop men earned only 12 million roubles, but administrative heads got 45 million: 'it's like the old monarchical structure.'[59] On the Moscow–Petro-grad line workers reported in the middle of February that they had not been paid for all January; in the Caucasus the backlog in August stretched back to October 1921.[60] When forty-two railway-workers who defected from Syzran' station were put on trial, their sentence was alleviated because they had not been paid. Railwaymen were encouraged to start up kitchen gardens near the stations in order to survive.[61] *Gudok* ran frequent articles on the wage demands of badly paid German railwaymen.[62]

The severe military tribunals of War Communism for

[57] *Gudok*, 14 Mar. 1922.
[59] Smolensk Archive, file WKP 273.
[61] Ibid., 4 Jan. and 1 Feb.
[58] Ibid., 13 Aug. and 18 Oct. 1922.
[60] *Gudok*, 19 Feb. and 13 Aug. 1922.
[62] Ibid., 1 Jan.

railway discipline were not disbanded until 1923, so potential strikers could be discouraged by the threat of what amounted to a court martial. Civil War conditions lingered on in other ways. In January an armoured car of the type that had proved so useful to Trotsky's campaign blocked the Tashkent–Moscow line and held up a locomotive that had been seized by an armed gang. In April a complete armoured train was sent in pursuit of bandits on the Vladikavkazskaia line. *Gudok* pointed out that such an exploit could not be repeated all over Russia, so staff on individual railway lines would have to keep their eyes skinned for military or criminal activity.[63] From the start of the year until 20 October there were thirty major railway crashes in contrast to none for all of 1913.[64] The bad state of the tracks and the huge shortage of sleepers were mainly to blame. Railway officials, like their political bosses in Moscow, were apt to muse on the brilliant future in order to escape from pressing current problems. The electrification of the network, a topic close to Lenin's heart, was discussed in the pages of *Gudok*. It was hoped that soon the lines to the Don basin and Nizhnii Novgorod would be electrified, followed quickly by the whole of the Siberian network. The railways were seen as 'colonization [*sic*] pioneers' for a huge agricultural country with vast mineral and other resources waiting to be exploited.[65]

In reality the system was caught between the stringencies of the Civil War and the burgeoning petty corruption of NEP. Bureaucratic wrangles were conspicuous at every level. Other Commissariats were accused of holding on to rolling-stock that should be handed back now the war was over. The Commissariat for War still hung on to 752 coaches; the Commissariat for Health had no fewer than 2,718, and was even demanding a further 1,200.[66] From a reading of *Gudok* for the whole year the impression is received of workers indulging in an endless series of meetings on a range of subjects from pay to culture, the Famine, technical improvement, national and international politics, usually during work hours. One sector pilfered from another, causing havoc. When the Vladikavkazskaia line stole the only shunting locomotive from Mozdok station, camels and bullocks were harnessed to trucks which had to be moved. A

[63] *Gudok*, 6 Jan. and 14 Apr.      [64] Ibid., 20 Oct.
[65] Ibid., 4 Feb. and 2 July.        [66] Ibid., 12 Feb.

cartoon shows them being supervised by an ass in uniform.[67]
'Uncultured' workers loaded manure on to a passenger train
bound for Ekaterinburg, so that not even 'hares' (passengers
without tickets) would board it.[68] Corruption flourished in the
wake of galloping inflation and the relaxed conditions of NEP.
Hens pecked at unwanted rouble notes from piles of sacks
dumped on the railway lines for no clear reason. One enterprising station-master frequently told all passengers that their
trains would not leave for a long time. When the trains left at
once, those stranded were invited to eat at the buffet, heated by
fuel filched from locomotives and run by the master and his
cronies. As trade picked up slowly towards the end of the year,
genuine Nepmen started to make their presence felt. Railway
employees, or 'Nepo-idols' as they were called, queued for
hours for scarce tickets for the Nepmen who tipped them for
their service. Other Nepmen used Pomgol labels on their goods
in order to avoid paying the railway tariffs.[69]

Compared with the railways, the press network suffered very
little from corruption or abuse. In this sphere Lenin had an
ever stronger interest than in the railways. His mainstream
career prior to 1917 had been that of a journalist. The
imposition of a severe censorship and the sacking of all hostile
editors (there were almost no spetsy in the press) immediately
upon the seizure of power in October 1917 had ensured its
smooth running from the political and administrative point of
view. The key to any understanding of the prime importance
of the Soviet press is contained in Lenin's remarks on its
function. For him a paper was much more than a published
news-sheet. It had to be a collective propagandist, agitator,
and organizer as well. He compared the press to a scaffold-
ing, surrounding a building under construction (the worker's
state), which marked the outlines of the structure, facilitated
communication among the builders, enhanced the effective
assignment of tasks, and made possible a clear view of the
achievements of the builders.[70]

In its role as the chief purveyor of propaganda and

[67] Ibid., 17 Sept.
[68] Ibid., 16 Aug.
[69] Ibid., 10 Aug., 26 Feb., 2 June, and 13 Oct.
[70] Lenin, *Collected Works*, vol. 4 (London, 1927), p. 114.

agitation, the press had shifted its accent at the start of NEP. The years 1917–21 had been devoted chiefly to the legitimization of the regime, whereas the stress from 1922 until 1926 lay on the urgent need to raise the cultural level of the population. After 1926 the accent was to lie on the development of technical education. Three levels of consciousness were involved in creating a sense of political and cultural unity in the largest country in the world. The first level was concerned with the stamping out of political regionalism and other local attitudes that limited central authority. This had been accomplished in the main by 1921, thanks to the combined application of brute force in the Civil War and the persuasive methods of the press and other media. Pockets of resistance still remained in 1922, in Tambov, Siberia, Georgia, and Central Asia: seemingly safe areas, like the Smolensk and Kursk gubernii, were not as stable as they seemed to be on the surface. Yet the general position had improved enough for the government to proceed to its second-level campaign—the creation of nation-wide cultural uniformity through mass education as the chief instrument of modernization in a period when technical means and financial resources were not as yet adequate for fast modernization through industrialization. The problems confronting the Bolsheviks in early NEP were formidable. The difficulty of undermining traditional ways and beliefs has been noted again and again, in the continuing hold of religion in Smolensk, the educational crisis in Kursk, the peculiar problems in Makarenko's colony. The cultural conquest of the countryside by the towns and of oral by literate culture was the prime aim of the press, and we shall examine this role in more detail. The third and most sophisticated level of consciousness comprised those intellectuals who were faithful to Bolshevik goals. They played a significant role in initiating cultural ideas at the centre for subsequent vulgarization and dissemination throughout Russia, at first through the 'fat' specialized journals and then later via the popular press. Their activities at the start of NEP are studied in the chapter devoted to the cultural capital, which was still Petrograd rather than Moscow in 1922. As will be seen, there was a serious lack of cohesion within the cultural élite itself. Furthermore their activities at the rarefied levels of Petrograd and Moscow often had very little impact, either at the time or subsequently, on the masses and on provincial life. The low circulation and poor distribution of leading literary journals provide clear evidence of the élitist character of the cultured few. *Young Guard*, one of the most popular of this type of journal, had a circulation of only 9,000 in 1922, and dropped to between 5,000 and 6,000 an issue by 1926.[71]

As the son of a school-inspector and a typical representative of the pre-Soviet intelligentsia, Lenin was torn between the conflicting needs of creating a politically and culturally conscious nation as fast as possible, yet at the same time ensuring that vulgarized, superficial agitation did not become a substitute for thoroughgoing education on a broad base.[72] The second alternative would take a long time to achieve. Neither alternative was anywhere near implemented by 1926, let alone in 1922. Prevailing conditions in the organization and distribution of the popular press were partly responsible for this. Two factors at the start of 1922 had an inhibiting influence. In January all newspapers were transferred to khozraschet. The initial deleterious effects of cost accounting struck the press as badly as they upset the railways, education, local Soviet administration, and trade. The Agitprop section of the Central Committee of the party worked out a blueprint for all the central and local press networks in January. Papers under the control of the gubispolkomy should be curtailed drastically, whilst central organs directed at mass party propaganda would expand quickly in numbers and influence. Party committees at every level should supervise local editorial boards more closely.[73] As a small sop to regional differences, special networks were to be set up in the Ukraine, the Caucasus, and the other national minority areas. Moscow and Petrograd papers were allowed to continue at the same volume but the rest of the press was to be reduced eventually to 232 papers, 158 of them guberniia and 74 uezd.[74]

[71] R. A. Maguire, *Red Virgin Soil: Soviet Literature in the 1920s* (Princeton, 1968), p. 366.

[72] The problem teased Lenin's mind with great frequency. For examples of his interest, see his *Collected Works* (4th edn.), vol. 28, pp. 94, 461; vol. 30, p. 298; vol. 31, pp. 177–9; vol. 32, pp. 121, 127–32, 272, 505.

[73] *Izvestiia Tsk* (Jan. 1922), pp. 18–20 and 42–3.

[74] *Partiinaia i sovetskaia pechat' v bor'be za postroenie sotsializma i kommunizma*, pt. 1 (Moscow, 1961), pp. 60–1.

The combined result of khozraschet and the over-centralized and ill-informed onslaught on the local press by Agitprop was a fast decline at guberniia and lower levels: of the 802 papers in existence on 1 January 1922, a mere 313 remained by 1 July. Some of the casualties had small circulations, but by the spring papers with an average circulation of about 50,000 copies were also going to the wall.[75] The total number picked up to 423 by 1 December. This situation was hardly conducive to the unification of the country through the medium of the press. Journalists themselves as well as the party seemed almost oblivious of the harm being wrought. The third congress of journalists which met at the end of January simply stressed the importance of party leadership of the press and made no practical survey of what was actually happening. Only a few delegates sensed that pressing problems had been shelved.[76] The situation had become so severe by the spring, however, that the Eleventh Party Congress took time off other matters to discuss it. The debate was opened by none other than our party visitor to Kursk, Ia. Yakovlev, the head of Agitprop and one of the chief architects of the cut-back in provincial newspapers in January. Yet he appeared surprised to find in Kursk guberniia near the end of 1922 that even villages near to the Moscow railway line had received their last single copies some months earlier.[77]

The Congress was told that journalists had been registered in only fifty of ninety guberniia committees. Editors were instructed to mould their articles far more to the educational levels of workers and peasants. Prime costs for newspaper production were rising fast as supporting industries and services demanded real payment under khozraschet conditions. Thus subscription prices were shooting up and cutting off thousands of readers who could no longer afford them. The Congress made several resolutions. Party members were now obliged to subscribe to at least one party newspaper. Such a basic prescription indicated how low the readership was sinking. The output of private presses, which was growing much faster than that of the party and the state, had to be monitored, and surpassed in quality by party organs. 'The rising gutter

[75] I. V. Vardin, *Sovetskaia pechat': sbornik statei* (Moscow, 1924), p. 54.
[76] *Pravda Gruzii*, 16 Feb. 1922.
[77] See Ch. 2, p. 68.

literature', as the private press was called, appealed especially to wayward youth. In this connection the whole of the local Komsomol press was ordered to put itself under the leadership of the party guberniia committees. In view of the unorthodox behaviour of the Komsomol that we have noted in the provinces, such a move was overdue. Finally, guberniia executive committees were charged with the resurrection of village reading-rooms, most of which had gone under in the changed economic conditions of NEP.[78]

Mere words could do little in the short term to reverse the chaotic situation. Saratov guberniia, admittedly a troubled area, reduced its press network from twenty-five organs in mid-1921 to two by the spring of 1922.[79] Petrograd, still the cultural centre of the whole country, had been spared the cut-back of January 1922, but due to financial pressures four papers merged into two in order to save costs. By the spring a single copy of *Krasnaia gazeta* in the city cost 100,000 roubles.[80] Only at the close of the summer did things improve at the central, though not yet at the local level. In August the Agitprop section of the Twelfth Party Conference had set up a commission to start a state subsidy for the politically reliable press.[81] Private journals continued to burgeon, as will be seen in Chapter 6, but the state press could henceforth stand better on its own feet financially.

A glance at the pages of *Gudok*, the organ of the railwaymen, will show the style and problems of a central newspaper at this time. A long puff of printed steam trailed over the title of the paper, and this popular touch prevailed through its pages. The language used was simpler and chattier than that of *Pravda* or even of *Trud*, the main labour organ. The format was smaller. Cartoons for semi-literate railwaymen studded the pages, and the back page was nearly full of capitalist-style advertisements of all kinds. This novel source of income was not available to papers in the stagnant agricultural hinterland. Despite the huge number of potential customers (just short of a million)

[78] *Resolutions and Decisions of the CPSU*, vol. 2 (Toronto, 1974), pp. 169–72.

[79] *Pravda*, 30 June 1922.

[80] M. L. Rappeport, *Desiat' let na boievom postu: istoriia 'Krasnoi gazety' 1918–1928* (Leningrad, 1928), pp. 66–72.

[81] Vardin, op. cit., p. 53.

and the fact that all copies of *Gudok* were delivered free on the railways, the circulation was a paltry 30,000 in June. A campaign was started to raise this figure to 100,000 by 1923.[82]

The military was more crucial in terms of political control than the railwaymen. As early as March 1918 the Bolsheviks had merged military and peasant newspapers into the single organ *Bednota* (Poverty) under the direct supervision of the Central Committee. The largest army in the world was recruited mainly from the peasantry, and, as has been seen in the provinces, the party still relied heavily in 1922 on ex-army men to act as leaven among the 'dark people'. *Bednota* up until 1923 was not a successful paper, however. It cost too much, its intellectual standard was far too high, and its distribution was inefficient. The independent Red Army press was rather better adapted to its readership. In 1922 it received a shot in the arm through a large subsidy from the Central Committee. The end of the Civil War, the transition to khozraschet, and its inability to use advertisements, had put all the military press in jeopardy. The Commissariat for War stressed that the new funds should be concentrated on papers produced for distant units which would not otherwise get any press organ.[83] In his writings on the military press, Trotsky made it quite clear that party interests came first and the military second.[84] Despite good intentions and solid backing, the military published only fourteen papers with a circulation of about 70,000 copies, or little more than double that of *Gudok* alone.[85]

Another vital area in terms of sensitive political control were the national minorities. Their press network, built up from 1917 on, had fluctuated in extent with the fortunes of the Civil War, but at its end nearly sixty papers in various national languages had been set up. Most of them had been due to efforts on the spot by units of the Red Army.[86] At the start of NEP many of these papers collapsed for the same reasons that affected others. It is strange that the party gave priority, not only to central and military organs, but also the guberniia- and

[82] *Gudok*, 8 June 1922.
[83] I. A. Portiankin, *Sovetskaia voennaia pechat': istoricheskii ocherk* (Moscow, 1960), p. 101.
[84] L. Trotsky, *Sochineniia*, vol. 21 (Moscow, 1925–7), pp. 219–34.
[85] Portiankin, op. cit., p. 120.
[86] *Partiinaia i sovetskaia pechat'*, p. 13.

uezd-level papers in 1922, before intervening in the national minority sector in 1923. Non-Russian papers were left to local military supervision until the end of Civil War, and largely to their own devices throughout 1922, unless they exhibited blatant defiance of high political directives, as in the case of Georgia. This did not necessarily mean that all local party chiefs in the minorities were also lethargic during 1922. We know from the Smolensk archive that the guberniia committee in the winter of 1922–3 convened meetings of many local organizations, compelling their members to subscribe to various Belorussian and Great-Russian newspapers. Particular stress was laid on subscriptions to *Rabochii put'*, the guberniia party and Soviet organ.[87] The local peasant press was in a lamentable condition still. *Bednota* was read very rarely in the villages and hardly ever subscribed to, because, as the peasants themselves recounted, it never printed real peasant articles but presented the countryside as some kind of fairyland.[88] Even *Smolenskaia derevnia*, an organ specifically designed for local peasant consumption and far better attuned to Belorussian interests than *Bednota*, was criticized in 1923 for insufficient contact with village life.[89]

At the start of NEP experienced Bolsheviks were not at the editorial helm of central and especially local newspapers. Frequent orders from Moscow to appoint them indicate that until after the Twelfth Party Congress party editors were the exception rather than the rule in the regions. Only by 1926–7 were 94.3 per cent of provincial editors party members.[90] In the early days of Soviet rule it was not unheard of for remote journals to attack *Izvestiia* and the Central Committee.[91] Below the editorial level the real contact between the masses and the press was intended to be the worker-peasant correspondents (*Rabselkor*). Until the beginning of NEP they constituted a disparate group of individuals to whom the party appealed for letters on local affairs, but in 1922 they acquired their official title and were subject to much more pressure from the centre.

---

[87] Smolensk Archive, file WKP 9, Jan.–Feb. 1923.
[88] R. Shafir, *Gazeta i derevniia* (Moscow, 1924), p. 5 ff.
[89] Smolensk Archive, file WKP 518, 1923.
[90] *Krasnaia pechat'*, 14–15 (1927), p. 6.
[91] For an example, see *Perepiska sekretariata Tsk RSDRP(b) s mestnymi partiinymi organizatsiiami*, vol. 3 (Moscow, 1952 ff.), pp. 86–7.

This change took place for three reasons. The fast growth of private trading and corruption associated with it could best be checked by individuals familiar with their localities. Secondly, the switch to khozraschet meant that the press had to attract paying subscribers, who wanted to read about their own regions and not be submitted to generalized and boring directives from Moscow all the time. In the third place peasant correspondents in particular looked as if they would be a useful source of information for the central authorities on dissatisfaction in the countryside and on the rising influence of peasant types not in favour with the party.

As with most initiatives, however, strength flowed from the centre first. In 1922 formal circles of worker correspondents sprang up in Moscow and Petrograd, and then in Rostov-on-Don and Baku. After the murder in April of one of *Pravda*'s rabkory who had reported abuses in a Moscow factory, the whole movement was galvanized into greater activity,[92] and was to spread round the provinces by 1923. By that year *Bednota* had a circulation of roughly 100,000, with a network of about 4,000 peasant correspondents.[93] From January 1922 on, Lenin received a report every two months from the *Bednota* editor on the contents and tenor of letters from peasant correspondents. Since the majority of them were neither party members, nor teachers or agronomists, they represented a valuable addition to the ranks of those who might be able to promote smychka in the countryside.[94] The hopes with regard to smychka that were current in this period were proved utopian once again. By 1923 there were frequent reports in the press of murders of peasant correspondents by fellow muzhiks. This only incited the centre to renewed activity. In November 1923 a new peasant paper, *Krest'ianskaia gazeta*, was to appear, with a circulation of 125,000 by March 1924.[95]

Many correspondents complained that their constructive advice, as opposed to their prying, fell on stony ground, since most peasants lacked the means to put technical advice on agriculture into effect.[96] There were other reasons. The

[92] *Pravda*, 29 July 1922; *Bednota*, 28 July 1922.

[93] *Krest'ianskii korrespondent. Ego rol'. Ego rabota* (Moscow, 1924), p. 111.

[94] Ibid., pp. 177, 127–73.

[95] 'Krest'ianskaia gazeta': article in the 1st edn. of the *Great Soviet Encyclopaedia*.

[96] *Krest'ianskii korrespondent*, p. 181.

peasants did not fail to note that the correspondents were often ex-clerks of the Tsarist regime, and so extremely bureaucratic and long used to writing what their employers wanted to read.[97] We can in fact penetrate beyond the officialese of the correspondents, thanks to the investigations conducted by R. Shafir at this time into the peasants' own view of the press. His main conclusion, after long travels round the countryside, was that among the peasants 'there are no subscribers, no readers'.[98] He found that most of them relied for information on their nearest educated contacts, the priests and the Nepmen, or else fell back on rumour, which still loomed large in their news lives. Most of the gossip was about taxation. It was thought that anyone subscribing to a newspaper would have to pay a special tax. Among the wilder rumours in strong circulation were that Lenin was dead, that the French had chosen Nicholas as their Tsar, and that England had declared war on Russia, so there would be wholesale peasant mobilization once again.[99]

The distribution speed of oral rumour was much quicker than that of newspapers, which from the guberniia capital of Voronezh' Shafir calculated to be one verst for every four and a half hours.[100] The chief stumbling block to a wider newspaper audience remained the high illiteracy rate. Shafir made a detailed study of comprehension levels by the supposedly literate. A 27-year-old party member and ex-Red Army man had read the press regularly since 1917, but did not know the meaning of words such as 'class enemy', occupation, period, or most abbreviations, including the USSR. Words of foreign origin defeated many readers, and place-names of remote areas like Georgia had no meaning at all.[101] From 1923 onwards the party was to single out key categories of the rural population for education: these included ex-Red Army men, Komsomol members, and women deputies to the local Soviets. In 1922 the number of literacy centres and those attending them fell to one-tenth of what they had risen to by 1921. Menshevik critics of the regime claimed that compared with the pre-revolutionary period Russia in 1922 had 30 per cent

---

[97] Shafir, op. cit., p. 134.
[98] Ibid., p. 5.
[99] Ibid., pp. 50, 99–114.
[100] Ibid., p. 96.
[101] Ibid., pp. 33–43.

fewer schools overall and that 70 per cent of all children between 8 and 11 years of age were illiterate.[102]

The burden of Russia's social backwardness could not be thrown off as quickly as the threat of political counter-revolution had been by the end of the Civil War. It lingered on well into the 1930s. Illiteracy was but one of its multiple facets. Military victory in the Civil War had been achieved by a heavy emphasis on combined political and military control from the centre, and this successful method was broadly reapplied in NEP to social life, despite the relaxation on the economic front. Insensitivity to local needs and aspirations was the result. The Tsarist system had suffered from a similar defect. Students of Russia who hail from much smaller and less heterogeneous countries might pause to ask themselves whether democratic rule under any kind of government is possible in a country as awesome in its administrative complexity as this one. The example of the United States may be cited in order to refute such a fatalistic approach, but the American colonies were the progeny of the most sophisticated democratic country in the world, and in any case the American republic expanded from a near *tabula rasa*, politically and geographically speaking. The Bolsheviks inherited a long tradition of centralist rule from which they had suffered, but whose methods they had imbibed only too deeply. So had the provinces, which scarcely knew how to struggle for local political and cultural rights.

This is not to deny that the Bolsheviks' intentions for future political, social and national minority devolution were genuine, but at the close of the Civil War they governed a financially exhausted country. Sufficient funds did not exist for the fast rehabilitation of the railways, for the immediate implementation of mass education. In the long run the central-ist traditions were to win the race against all hopes for some measure of local autonomy.

[102] *Nasha zhizn'*, Nov. 1922.

# 5. *Bolshevik Controls*

IT was seen in the previous chapter that there were initial attempts in early NEP to adopt a less centralist approach to the railways and to the press for technical and cultural reasons respectively. Thus Dzerzhinsky on the spot in Siberia discarded faulty theoretical calculations made in Moscow, and in the spring of 1922 railway administration in general was partly decentralized. Yet soon thereafter political fear led to the chairman of each local board becoming a direct representative of the central Commissariat. It was the same with the local press. The Eleventh Party Congress instructed editors to adapt their articles to local needs and educational levels, but by 1923 most peasant correspondents were expected to toe the line on central directives and were discovering how unpopular they were in the countryside as a result.

In this chapter some Bolshevik systems of nation-wide control are examined. They depended heavily for the efficient dissemination and harvesting of personnel and information on the more technical communications that have just been considered.

We shall see that centralist trends in Bolshevik instruments of control which were apparent in 1922, and were in marked contrast to attempts at economic decentralization, were as much due to geographical and socio-economic pressures from below and from the past as to ideological, administrative and personal pressures from on high. Take the influence of technical communications again before we leave them finally. Great powers of the imagination are needed to encompass the size, scale, and complexities of Soviet space. Every province had its peculiar problems, and reference has been made in particular only to our three chosen regions and briefly to Siberia, which is a multifarious continent in itself. All regimes in Russian history have felt the need to wage war on distance, widely varied climates, and thinly populated vastnesses. Not a few of the deficiencies and delays which are frequently attributed to a tradition of centralized bureaucracy were almost inevitable in 1922 as in earlier periods due to the hesitant flow of emissaries, goods, and information. The economic costs were crippling, and the movement of money and bills of exchange sluggish at the best of times. These problems were especially underes- timated in a non-capitalist society where time did not equal money.

Bolshevik networks of control attempted to cover every single corner of Russia, each nationality, and all classes, from Brest-Litovsk to Vladivostok, from Jews to gypsies and Buryat Mongols, from ex-noblemen to the igloo-bound Samoyeds of the frozen north. The wide arc by international standards that has been chosen in this book, from Smolensk to Tver and Kursk, and on to the Middle Volga and Kazakhstan, is like a galaxy in the night sky in terms of what it reveals in the course of one year against this huge backdrop. It was found impossible to gather enough local sources together for 1922 to make any sense beyond the Urals, so for that we shall have to wait until 1926 and northern Kazakhstan. Yet it is hoped that the method employed and the facts revealed will slowly begin to throw new light on certain aspects of society and politics by the time central viewpoints have been juxtaposed with what has gone before. At this stage we have reached a crucial divide, not only in terms of topics treated, but also of method. So far the author has acted like the hedgehog in Isaiah Berlin's essay,[1] paying attention most of the time to the very specific and the detailed. Now the fox enters on the scene as our vision broadens and we resort to occasional generalizations. That is why, for the first time, the broader problems involved in Bolshevik controls are now set out before proceeding to details. There is a need for a proper balance between low-level factual accounts and schematic surveys. This is the hardest connection to make in the study of human behaviour. The mental effort required in the case of a country the size of Russia renders not just the

---

[1] I. Berlin, *The Hedgehog and the Fox: an Essay on Tolstoy's view of History* (London, 1953). It is perhaps not a coincidence that the historical novelist who has given most thought to the dichotomy involved is a Russian.

historian, but also any ruler of that country, almost schizo-phrenic. As a result historians of Russia and her governors alike have tended to play down or ignore the spatial aspect in relation to central concerns. Difficulties in interpretation are rendered even more acute in the wake of a nation-wide revolution and civil war. Intellectuals, whether they be Bol-shevik theorists or historians of whatever political hue, have a nearly uncontrollable desire to cast the world in a more rational mould than the shapes into which it is thrown by the crude order, or rather disorder, of revolutionary experience. The conspiracy theory of history as applied to the Bolsheviks has made it easier for historians to regulate and distort the chaotic subject-matter of a multinational ex-Empire.

Despite strident Bolshevik denials for ideological reasons of any need for central bureaucratic hierarchies, they reappeared in a new guise, and sometimes not so new, after 1917. This was not due to pure Machiavellism on the part of the Soviet leaders. Other external factors besides faulty communications systems were at work. They are merely summarized here, since they are outlined at greater length elsewhere.[2] The continuing size and complexity of Russia after 1917 entailed the survival of large bureaucratic structures. In a predominantly illiterate yet multilingual society throughout the 1920s there was still a need for central scribes to co-ordinate and record its activities. The Revolution of 1917 ousted what remained of paternal local administration by the gentry. The Civil War cut the periphery off from the centre, enhancing the vacuum at provincial levels which took a long time to be replenished with reliable party, let alone Soviet, administrators. Military tradi-tions within the government dated back as far as the reigns of Alexander I and Nicholas I: they were reinforced strongly by the experience of the First World War and, for the Bolsheviks, by their successful merging of civilian and military methods in the Civil War. The considerable degree of military interven-tion in local administration in Smolensk guberniia and the Volga provinces *after* the end of the Civil War has been noted. As conditions improved during NEP this connection receded, but the military mentality at higher levels did not, and it was to

[2] For a more detailed analysis, see R. W. Pethybridge, *The Social Prelude to Stalinism* (London, 1974), in particular ch. 6.

prevail clearly again in the period of the Five-Year Plans. Fresh reasons for the maintenance or even expansion of administrative networks arose as a result of the Bolsheviks' progressive aims. Unlike the largely passive and repressive Tsarist regime, the new leaders wished to eliminate poverty, overhaul the class and educational systems, introduce a national health and social security system, and so on. Both Lenin and the Webbs underestimated the extent to which their plans involved an increase in administrative personnel.

Once it had become obvious that large-scale bureaucratic structures would long survive the Revolution (and it was crystal clear to Lenin by 1922, as we know from his criticism of them), further problems arose. Only the first of them was directly due to Bolshevik policy. Lenin's notion that untrained and inexperienced workers and even peasants were at once capable of running the new modes of administration had been shattered before NEP by the débâcle of workers' control. *A fortiori* the same home truth applied to the even larger hierarchies that it was hoped these two classes would soon manage. The few who were efficient quickly rose to the top. This trend was already visible in the Kursk guberniia hierarchy in 1922.[3] The élite became alienated from the rank and file in every sphere.[4] Thus hopes for administration by the proletariat, let alone by the peasantry, receded almost as fast as for the dictatorship of the proletariat.

Other problems were a common function of very large-scale organizations in most societies, although they were all exacerbated by specific Russian conditions. Since each person's and group's mental capacity is limited (especially with little training and in the novel situation after 1917), detailed control over organizations becomes weaker as they enlarge. The longer efforts are made by central officials to delve into the conduct of subordinate and local staff, the more the latter are tempted to take evasive action. This behaviour is easy to discern in the relations between the Smolensk party and Moscow, not just in 1922 and 1926, but throughout the 1920s and 1930s, as Merle Fainsod found.[5] Indeed he concludes that such evasion was one

[3] See p. 76 above.
[4] See Pethybridge, op. cit., pp. 275 ff.
[5] M. Fainsod, *Smolensk under Soviet Rule* (New York, 1963).

of the prime reasons why the Soviet system survived, since it watered down fanatical central directives and so staved off local insurrections.

In order to monitor burgeoning hierarchies, new supervisory organizations are often created, and in Soviet as in Tsarist Russia they played an exceptionally important role. Unfortunately they served to swell the bureaucratic ranks, and their areas of operation were nearly always ill-defined. This was true of the secret police, and also of the Workers' and Peasants' Inspectorate (Rabkrin) which will be examined presently for 1922, and of the Central Control Commission, to be put under the microscope in 1926. Some monitoring agencies became so large that they in turn required to be inspected, as Lenin urged with regard to Rabkrin in 1922–3. Finally, the mainline hierarchies were apt to enter into collusion with the monitoring organs that were supposed to be inspecting them. In 1922 Lenin tried to stop an example of this tendency when he argued that legal procurators should not be subordinated to central and local authorities alike. Such a suggestion was, he observed, 'an expression of the interests and prejudices of local bureaucrats and local influences, that is, the most pernicious wall that stands between the working people and the local and central Soviet authorities, as well as the central authority of the Russian Communist Party.'[6]

At the grass-roots level all the bureaucracies failed to create a workable relationship with the masses. Instances of this are scattered through the chapters of this book that are devoted to the regions. Smychka between town and countryside, between the lower tentacles of the bureaucracies and the peasant masses, remained at the level of a hopeful theory throughout NEP. This has been seen most clearly so far in the Nikol'skaia volost' of the Kursk guberniia. Neither the party cell, the Komsomol, the village Soviets, teachers, nor the ex-military managed to act as successful linking agents. The indigenous peasants from the start of NEP had more confidence in their richer brethren, that is in incipient '*kulaks*' and Nepmen, and even in the local priests.

The blame for the lack of an efficient command structure at

[6] V. I. Lenin, ' "Dual" Subordination and Observation of the Law', *Collected Works*, vol. 33 (London, 1960–70), pp. 363–7.

the rural level may indeed be put on the Bolsheviks as much as
on any 'objective' features. Their ideological neglect of the
peasantry in the past could not be remedied overnight. The
fact that most leading party members were townsmen by origin
raised major difficulties. Even if any of the bureaucratic
hierarchies had functioned reasonably well in early NEP—that
is with sensitive directives from the centre and with equally
sensitive feedback in the opposite direction—the Bolshevik
leaders would probably have rejected them in any case for the
following reasons. Above all, bureaucracy in their Marxist eyes
was an unnecessary encumbrance from the past. It also
entailed the sacrifice of revolutionary dash. If all the thousands
of intricate signals that arrived at the nerve-centre of Moscow
from the biggest body politic in the world had in fact been
studied in laborious detail, the Party would have become
swamped and lost in detail. This frame of mind persisted into
the calmer period of mid-NEP. The experience of 1917 had
conditioned the leadership in another way. Trotsky had then
pointed out that it did not matter if Petrograd and Moscow
were out of line with provincial sentiment, since as centres of
the proletariat they represented the only true dynamo of the
future.[7] Throughout NEP most Bolsheviks remained unwilling
to delegate authority to local officials, since they feared that
unenlightened regional autonomy would hamper their own
plans for socialist construction. They had endured too much
local physical resistance in the course of the Civil War for them
to remain patient thereafter with mental opposition.

Foxes tend to become intoxicated by the abstract internal
logic of their own theories, so now the hedgehog will take over
again in order to correlate some of the general points made
above with the detailed working of several instruments of
control in 1922. The most vital and the one most studied will be
taken first—the party structure. After that rather more attention than has usually been the case will be focused, first on local
government, then on its monitor, Rabkrin, and finally on
administrative and legal reforms working downwards from the
highest levels.

Let us start at the grass roots, as in previous chapters.
Although many thousands of peasants had entered the Com-

[7] See L. Trotsky, *The History of the Russian Revolution* (Ann Arbor, 1957).

munist Party in the Civil War, mainly through the ranks of the
Red Army, between January and August 1922 working
peasants comprised 14 per cent of those who left the party
compared with 5 per cent of those who joined it.[8] By the start of
1925 the actual proportion of party members who worked in
agriculture on a permanent basis was as low as 2 or 3 per cent,
or one person in three or four thousand of the adult population. Ex-military men sensed increasingly that they cut themselves off from their neighbours, as we saw in Nikol'skaia
volost', and above all from the new chances for private self-
enrichment offered by NEP, so long as they remained within
the party. Instead of pursuing the chimeras of state farms or
Lenin's co-operative system, they soon melted away into the
more traditional ocean of small-scale private farms. By 1922
only 7.5 per cent of those still serving in the Red Army were
party members.[9] The proportion of rurally situated party
members of any class was actually at its maximum in 1922, and
never approached the same level again, even by the 1960s.
Whereas in 1922 there were 314,000 urban as against 201,000
rural communists (155 per 10,000 persons in the towns and 18
per 10,000 in the countryside), by 1927 the numbers were
respectively 840,000 and 307,000. There were still only 26 rural
members per 10,000 population in 1927.[10] At the beginning of
NEP peasant members' contribution to the party was weak
qualitatively as well as quantitatively—70 per cent of them
were declared to be politically illiterate in 1922.[11]

The sparse numbers and low calibre of party workers in
rural areas was reflected in their extremely tenuous organizational hold over the grass roots. At the time of the October
Revolution there had been thirty-five uezd party committees
spread over forty-eight gubernii, less than one per ten uezdy.[12]
In 1922 Zinoviev declared that lack of activity at the uezd level
remained 'a current scourge and disaster'.[13] V. A. Antonov-

[8] *Izvestiia tsentral'nogo komiteta*, 10 (Oct. 1922).
[9] T. H. Rigby, *Communist Party Membership in the USSR 1917–1967* (Princeton, 1968), p. 135; Strumilin, *Statistichesko-economicheskie ocherki*, vol. 1 (Moscow, 1960), pp. 229 ff.
[10] Ibid., p. 491.
[11] *XI s'ezd RKP(b), stenograficheskii otchet, mart–aprel'* (1922), pp. 167, 235, 402–4.
[12] F. G. Zaikina, 'Organizatsionnaia perestroika kommunisticheskoi partii posle pobedy Oktiabria', *Voprosy Istorii KPSS*, 11 (1966), p. 56.
[13] *XI s'ezd*, p. 402.

Ovseenko put it in another way: 'Our party had laid down no solid roots in the countryside and easily loses its ties with it at the very first outbreak of revolt':[14] he had in mind the Tambov insurrection, but his words could have applied equally to any of the areas studied in previous chapters.

Because so few party members actually worked on a full-time basis in agriculture, their influence on peasant affairs was often restricted to negative, theoretical criticism, as opposed to useful constructive advice. An observer of party members in action at Ilino volost' in Smolensk guberniia noted: 'they strive to criticize, to command, but they do not . . . explain practically how it is necessary to work . . . [They] lashed into everything, saying, in general, that the sections are not working, that the work is not set up as it should be, etc., dictating vague trite phrases, but not getting down to concrete cases.'[15]

Party organization was more secure at the guberniia level. By 1921 there were almost 30,000 party cadres in seventy gubernii.[16] In the second half of that year they had carried out on average seventeen to eighteen propaganda campaigns in their areas.[17] Yet even in Smolensk, a relatively secure region by all-Russian standards, 30 per cent of the party had been eliminated in the 1921 purge, leaving 7,425 members, a total that declined further during 1922 to 5,925.[18] In recently liberated areas, such as Siberia, party control was far more tenuous. Dzerzhinsky's mission there revealed this much. The same went for Tambov guberniia, and for many of the national minorities. Belorussian nationalism was a weak flame in 1922, as has been seen, but the same could not be said of the Ukraine. Great Russian guberniia cadres near Moscow had considerable advantages in the form of a solid nucleus of Old Bolsheviks, a reasonably numerous proletarian base, and a long pre-Soviet tradition of pro-Moscow centralism. Yet Kursk guberniia, although ethnically Great Russian, lacked all these props. In the national minorities as a whole in 1922, two-thirds of all Communists did not hail from the local nationality, a

[14] *The Trotsky Papers, 1917–1922*, vol. 2 (The Hague, 1971), p. 557.
[15] Smolensk Archive, file WKP 331, pp. 108–36.
[16] Zaikina, op. cit., p. 56.
[17] *XI s'ezd*, pp. 42, 63, 156–7.
[18] *Izvestiia TsK*, 4 (Mar. 1922), pp. 20ff; 3 (Mar. 1923), pp. 162–4.

fact which revealed both the disinterest of non-Russians and the determination of the Russians to consolidate the gains of the Civil War and to hold on to the minorities. Scarcely one in 1,500 people in nationality areas was a native Communist.[19] The largest increases between 1922 and 1926 were made by the Belorussians and Ukrainians. Gains among the non-Slav minorities were to be far more modest, in spite of active campaigns to recruit members. This discrepancy will be out-lined in more detail with the investigation of Smolensk and northern Kazakhstan in 1926. Within the party organizations of almost all non-Russian areas, including the Ukraine and Belorussia, local nationals were much more likely than Rus-sians to be farmers and not workers, thus militating against their status in party eyes.[20]

Another debilitating factor that affected all gubernii irres-pective of national make-up was the extremely high turnover of party membership. By 1922 only 12.4 per cent of those who had been in the party in 1917 and 36.8 per cent of recruits between 1918 and 1920 remained in the ranks. Military mobilization, violent death, purges, demobilized soldiers push-ing others out of party jobs at a later stage, and a host of other reasons lay behind these startling figures. On this subject the central party leadership in 1922 takes its first bow in this book. We find Molotov at the Eleventh Party Congress actually welcoming the situation, since it helped to thwart the growth of local cliques which could block directives emanating from on high.[21]

The truth was that by 1922 much local initiative had already drained away from guberniia, let alone lower levels. The reasons for this between 1917 and 1922 are manifold, and still in dispute. They also lie beyond the scope of this book, and so are merely adumbrated here. Non-Bolsheviks like Y. Martov, F. Dan, and R. Abramovich accused the leading Bolsheviks of exercising unbridled authoritarian control, not influenced by any 'objective' pressures. This line was later adopted by non-socialist Western historians. Trotsky on the other hand

---

[19] I. N. Iudin, *Sotsial'naia baza rosta KPSS* (Moscow, 1973), p. 206.
[20] See Rigby, op. cit., pp. 366–8, for percentages of the national composition of the CPSU 1922–7.
[21] *XI s'ezd*, pp. 45–59.

stressed extraneous factors created by the turmoil inside Russia. Some Western scholars have taken up this theme, and yet others have also pointed out that the Bolshevik party was not centralized even in 1917, on account of the technical difficulties involved.[22] More recently it has been shown that local officials themselves clamoured between 1917 and 1921 for greater centralization in the search for better communication lines, more efficient staff, and better access to resources.[23] In the present author's opinion, none of these interpretations will have sole dominion in the long term, but an amalgam of them all.

What is not in dispute is that by 1922 the symptoms of local party decay were clearly visible and irreversible. Election processes had been ousted nearly everywhere by direct appointment from above, although the outward symbols of democratic procedure were still maintained. Genuine discussions at party meetings were stifled. Agendas were no longer announced in advance, and sessions were dominated by the secretary's report, as can be seen, amongst many examples from our three provincial areas, in the account of a Samara meeting in the spring of 1922.[24] The Saratov committee had advised Moscow on every conceivable topic after 1917, but by 1922 it was far more subservient and modest in its aims.[25] Most guberniia committees contented themselves by acting as conveyor belts for Moscow directives. They had taken to issuing uniform instructions to party organs at all lower levels, thus exacerbating the insensitive nature of their control over the grass roots. Such procedures sometimes bordered on the ludicrous, as was seen with regard to the local celebrations for the Paris Commune of 1871 and the fifth anniversary of the October Revolution in Roslavl'.[26]

From the guberniia level we now pass to the party summit, located in the Politburo and the Central Committee, in order

[22] This author has written in this vein. See Pethybridge, *The Spread of the Russian Revolution: Essays on 1917* (London, 1972).

[23] R. Service, *The Bolshevik Party in Revolution: A Study in Organisational Change, 1917–1923* (London, 1979).

[24] See *Kommuna* (Samara), 1010 (Apr. 1923). For a detailed substantiation of the general points made in this paragraph, see Service, op. cit., pp. 168–83.

[25] *Saratovskaia Izvestiia*, 155 (11 July 1922).

[26] Ibid. and p. 53 above.

to see how controls were manipulated from above. By 1922 a large number of strings were being pulled, and some of them got twisted administratively with each other. Investigations by the secret police remained rigidly segregated, and so are omitted here, though they should not be forgotten, and have been alluded to earlier in connection with Dzerzhinsky's mission to Siberia.[27] One of the most important links between central and guberniia levels has been neglected by both Soviet and Western scholars. The number of inspectors sent out from the Central Committee to inspect gubkomy jumped from five at the time of the Eleventh Party Congress of 1922 to seventeen in 1923, by which time seventy-six thorough investigations of local apparaty had taken place. Some of them entailed one month's stay in the province concerned.[28] In addition, between the Eleventh and Twelfth Congresses Central Committee members themselves visited sixty-six guberniia party organizations and attended ninety-eight local party conferences: only fifteen areas had been visited by them between the Tenth and Eleventh Congresses.[29] Personal visits to Moscow by local party secretaries were also stepped up considerably. Forty were summoned to the capital in 1922–3, as against sixteen in 1921–2.[30] In April 1922, that is immediately after Stalin had taken over as General Secretary of the Central Committee, an order was issued that written reports from local secretaries, which had been sporadic up till then, should be sent by the fifth of each month to Stalin personally.[31] It was no coincidence either that the inspectors on their return to Moscow reported back to the Organizational Bureau, also headed by Stalin.[32] From 1922 onwards, Stalin was the only Bolshevik leader who was a member of the Orgburo, the Secretariat, the Central Committee, and the Politburo. No doubt he listened in silent pleasure to a report at the Twelfth Party Congress which revealed that, unlike previously, information from local bodies was now

---

[27] For a recent scholarly account of secret police activity in this period, see G. Leggett, *The Cheka* (Oxford, 1981).

[28] *Itogi partiinoi raboty za god 1922–1923* (Moscow, 1923), pp. 131–7.

[29] *XII s'ezd*, p. 790.

[30] *Itogi*, pp. 139–41.

[31] *Spravochnik partiinogo rabotnika*, 3 (1922), p. 122.

[32] *Itogi*, p. 133.

flowing in, 'not in an unorganized way, but systematically and according to a precisely worked out plan'.[33]

After Stalin's appointment as General Secretary, special 'informers' drew up reports every two months on the work of the most important local party committees.[34] In addition the number of nation-wide telephone links in the Secretariat nearly doubled, from 267 to 500 between the Twelfth and Thirteenth Party Congresses.[35] Stalin also kept a careful watch over the regional bureaux, set up between 1920 and 1921. They served as supplementary checking organs for distant and difficult areas like Siberia and the national minorities. A glance at the news-sheet of the Central Committee for March 1922 shows how many of them were headed by Stalin's present and future accomplices.[36] In this same crucial month another instrument, the Central Control Commission, was allowed to intervene far more vigorously in the work of the local commissions. Originally intended as an external and therefore independent check on party bureaucracy, it was now transformed rapidly into an integral part of the centralized hierarchy. Thus separate administrative strings became intertwined and soon entered into collusion. This is precisely what Lenin feared with regard to the legal system at the same time, and what was also occurring between the state administration and its external investigator, Rabkrin, as we shall see shortly. In the spring of 1922 only one of the members of the Central Control Commission as it stood in 1921 was re-elected. Of the seven elected in 1922, four were to remain at their posts for many years to come, faithful to Stalin's wishes. Although most of the Commission's accusations concerning party workers were at first sight non-political, they were increasingly used as covers for the dismissal of local party leaders of an independent cast of mind.[37]

The overall results of these diverse methods of tightening up seemed impressive, at least on paper. By the Twelfth Party Congress in 1923 it was noted that every single guberniia was

[33] *XII s'ezd*, p. 71.
[34] *Itogi*, pp. 142–4.
[35] *XIII s'ezd*, p. 128.
[36] See *Izvestiia TsK*, Mar. 1922, p. 14.
[37] L. Schapiro, *The Communist Party of the Soviet Union* (London, 1960), p. 257.

being inspected on a regular basis, as opposed to forty-five in 1922 and twenty-two in 1921.[38] In reality several new and pejorative influences were at work. Collusion was but one of them. Another was the great ocean of undigested and uncorrelated detail that now flooded into Moscow party offices, clogging up what was left of any democratic processes at the centre. As E. Preobrazhensky observed, the Politburo now indulged in long debates about settling local prices for jam and other such trivia.[39] Worse than this, guberniia authorities began to retreat into the usual reaction to all top-heavy and prying bureaucracies. They produced increasingly optimistic reports in the hope of staving off further inspections. In this they were merely wholesaling for consumption at the national level what was being handed in to them in retail from so many sources—those ex-Tsarist scribes turned peasant correspondents, fearful party hacks in Roslavl' and Nikol'skaia, party officials involved in the Famine who agreed for the sake of peace and quiet with the central theory that the Famine was over in the spring of 1922, although they were well aware that it was not, since it still engulfed them in the localities.

At all levels party men had to contend with another administrative problem, that of the huge Soviet government hierarchy parallel with them on every rung of the ladder. The distribution of power between the two bureaucracies was a confused issue. In the Famine area in 1922 foreign helpers found that local party workers were 'fearful men, jumpy, flying off into violence on very slight provocation, and so insecure had been their hold on power that they were suspicious of the most innocent acts. They could not, and would not, tolerate any initiative in public affairs by non-party men.'[40] Such a reaction was to be found very frequently in Party–government relations. The theoretical foundation of Bolshevik legislation on the Soviets was ambiguous from the start with regard to the character and extent of their duties and powers. At the lower levels it is not surprising that all through NEP no one was clear as to whether the Soviets were just another branch of

---

[38] *XII s'ezd*, p. 790.
[39] Ibid., pp. 84–5.
[40] See H. H. Fisher, *The Famine in Soviet Russia 1919–1923* (New York, 1927), ch. 5, on these uneasy relationships.

Communist administration, or more like local councils on the lines of the Tsarist zemstvos or of West European local government, dealing with humdrum subjects such as housing, utilities, transport facilities, health matters, etc.[41]

At least the question of who owned whom was clear-cut. After the Civil War, elections to Soviets at every level went virtually uncontested, and the choice of candidates was closely controlled by the Party. Despite the scarcity of party members in village Soviets in 1922 (6.1 per cent), they had little difficulty, with help from higher Soviets, in arranging elections. In any case, the apathy of the public at all levels was apparent from the voting turnout in the 1922 Soviet elections of 22.3 per cent.[42] Yet it must not be imagined that the Party succeeded in eliminating politically or socially undesirable village chairmen at a stroke. One only has to recall the dubious backgrounds of the characters in Nikol'skaia who stayed in power in 1922. Rural government had been set up in many areas in the period from January to March 1918 when there were almost no party cells beside them. Job-holders had received little or no salary; as a result in Nikol'skaia it was seen that even by 1922 local chairmen had to rely on private means, and also used their positions to indulge in petty corruption. They had survived the austerities of War Communism and the kombedy. Here, as in most other Great-Russian gubernii, they were nurturing socio-economic trends right at the start of NEP that were to create a political crisis at the highest level after 1926. Instead of concentrating on improving the lot of the local peasants, many village chairmen lined their own nests, spent an inordinate time on tax-collecting like their Party counterparts, and also continued to exclude women. Ninety-nine per cent of all village Soviets in 1922 were composed of men, and only 14 per cent of all eligible women voted in the elections. A closer grip was taken by the Party over national minority areas from the start of NEP. The average of 6.1 per cent Party members in all village Soviets in fact masked a wide discrepancy: 11 to 25 per cent was the range for the minority area, as against 0.3 to 1.8 in

---

[41] For a detailed list of the duties of a uezd town Soviet such as Roslavl', see S. P. Margunskii, *Gosudarstvennoe stroitel'stvo BSSR v gody vosstanovleniia narodnogo khoziaistva 1921–1925* (Minsk, 1966), pp. 117–20.

[42] *Sovety, s'ezdy sovetov i ispolkomy* (Moscow, 1924), p. 12.

the Russian gubernii.[43] This imbalance mirrored the situation in the Party, where, as has been seen, two-thirds of all communists hailed from outside national minority area cadres.

The number of village Soviets for the whole territory of the RSFSR in 1922 was approximately 120,000 with over 484,000 members.[44] Given an average of just over four members per Soviet, and keeping in mind their crippling inadequacies, these seemingly impressive overall figures hid certain harsh realities. Important nationality interests of nearly half the population of the ex-Empire could not be articulated, let alone defended. Even in the relatively sophisticated Smolensk guberniia, one village deputy had to represent five village Soviets at uezd Soviet congresses for lack of time or expertise.[45] Neither could conditions of life at the grass roots in Russian gubernii possibly be described by rural Soviets and transmitted efficiently to higher levels for scrutiny and action. Increasingly the decision-making process became restricted to the now streamlined Party hierarchy.

As we climb through the volost' Soviet level to the uezd and guberniia organs, expected changes occur. Party membership almost doubled in volost' compared with village Soviets. The number of woman members went up from 1 to 1.2 per cent. Educational standards also improved slightly. But a truly remarkable change in style came at uezd level (Roslavl'): 5.2 per cent of their executive committee members had higher education, 18.3 secondary education, and 76.5 primary education, while 44.1 per cent in uezd ispolkomy were classified as officials, 31.5 per cent as workers (mainly in the urban uezd centres) and 24.4 per cent as peasants. No less than 81.2 per cent of members were in the Party. This figure shows a determination at the highest level to keep firm control over local government at the uezd level and above (the corresponding percentage in gubispolkomy was even higher—89 per cent).[46] Other considerations also emerge. We have already noted the tendency of Party members in the countryside to rise quickly to uezd and higher centres in pursuit of their careers. Again, 76 per cent of the Communists in uezd Soviets had joined the Party between 1917 and 1919. Taken together with

[43] Ibid.
[45] Margunskii, op. cit., p. 121 fn.
[44] Ibid.
[46] Ibid., p. 29.

the fact that 42 per cent of all uezdispolkom members had been serving for over three years by 1922, it looks likely, although it cannot be proved, that a great number of Tsarist zemstvo employees were still in office and had joined the Party band-wagon. Since former Tsarist employees still made up over 90 per cent of the staff of the vitally important State Control Commissariat after 1917,[47] it is not particularly surprising that at less sensitive levels officials from the past should be allowed to process routine administrative matters. There may be more to Lenin's statement of February 1922 than meets the eye: 'We have taken over from Tsarist Russia the poorest bureaucratism and Oblomovism from which we are literally choking.'[48]

As the Soviet executive committees in the 1920s became larger and more stable at uezd and guberniia levels, average party membership in them declined. The same change took place in the All-Russian Congress of Soviets and the Central Executive Committee of the USSR. In all these bodies the presidia, which had probably been Party preserves from the beginning, came to control more and more of the vital de-cisions. Once the Party's hold was secure at the essential points in these key organs, the constitutional fiction that they were independent from and coequal with the Party could be upheld more easily if non-Party officials figured prominently once again. At levels below the uezd Soviets, where the party's grip remained very weak, the opposite trend was to prevail between 1922 and 1926. Party membership rose quite fast, though by 1927 non-party officials still held half the chairmanships of volost' executive committees and three-quarters of village Soviet chairmanships.[49] The need to infiltrate was as urgent as ever. Party membership in those central Commissariats that had most to do with local administration was also very low— 4.6 per cent alike for the Commissariats of Ways and Communications and Health in 1922, and 7.9 per cent in the Commissariat of Agriculture. The reason was that the real power-houses that drove these large but passive administrative

[47] N. A. Voskresenskaia, *V. I. Lenin—Organizator sotsialisticheskogo kontrolia* (Moscow, 1970), p. 99.

[48] Lenin, *Polnoe sobranie sochineniia*, vol. 38 (Moscow, 1969), p. 287.

[49] *XV s'ezd*, vol. 1, pp. 448–9. See T. Seibert, *Red Russia* (London, 1932), pp. 89–95 for an analysis of party membership in the Soviets during NEP.

organs lay outside them, in the highest executive body, Sovnarkom, and in the Party Central Committee. Only the secret police in 1922, and to some extent Rabkrin, could act independently of the Party, and their party memberships were the highest of all the Commissariats, 38.7 and 13.6 per cent respectively, apart from the Commissariat for the Nationalities, which had 18.4 per cent (this high proportion mirrored those we have seen in the local national minority Soviets and Party committees).[50]

Let us now leave the Party and state hierarchies and turn to Rabkrin itself. It had been set up in February 1920 in order to monitor 'all the organs of state administration', as well as 'the economy and social organizations'. It ran the Bureau of Complaints and was supposed to suggest reforms for the government's administrative machinery as a whole.[51] Separate Party control organs had been created in September 1920. The functions and history of these bodies have been somewhat neglected, although they cast light on relationships between politics and society, and between the centre and the periphery. Monitoring agencies for both the Tsarist and early Soviet bureaucracies flourished to such an extent that the phenomenon became a specific Russian peculiarity, unrivalled in other countries. Since they are not a category easily identifiable elsewhere, except conceivably for the more recent Ombudsman system, they have in the past escaped classification and detailed analysis by non-Russians (the same may be said for other unique Soviet phenomena such as the kustari and the Nepmen).

The ideological intent that inspired the creation of Rabkrin differed greatly from Tsarist motives for running monitoring agencies. Initially Rabkrin was meant to be a mass organization. It was to engage in aggressive socialist reform rather than act as a suffocating tool of repression on Tsarist lines. 'Enter Rabkrin and learn to govern the state' was the slogan in the first elections for membership in September 1920. 'Several tens of thousands' of workers and peasants were said to have taken part in mass investigations during the first year.[52] Another

[50] Strumilin, op. cit., p. 246.
[51] *Sobranie uzakonenii RSFSR*, 16 (7 Feb. 1920), item 94.
[52] S. N. Ikonnikov, *Organizatsiia i deiatel'nost' RKI v 1920–25 gg.* (Moscow, 1960), pp. 32, 42.

source states euphorically that over 200,000 workers and peasants participated in 1921–2.[53] At first the government tried to merge all trade-union organizations with Rabkrin, but this failed since neither side wished to give up its rights of control. The ultimate aim behind this merger was the abolition of the separation of state and society so as to reunite the producer with the citizen.

These heady plans were suddenly cut short in March 1922 when all local control organs were brought under the direct supervision of the Party's Central Control Commission.[54] Since the latter had already been bound very closely to Party organs, this meant in fact that Stalin came to dominate the whole control mechanism. Yet the rapid decline of Rabkrin as a democratic agency cannot be ascribed, as has often been done, simply to Stalin's authoritarian methods from on high. The number of Rabkrin-delegated members was reduced between 1921 and 1922 by 90 per cent mainly because enterprises were no longer willing to pay the salaries of absent delegates now that they had to make a profit in NEP conditions. In any case nearly all state administrative agencies suffered a large staff reduction in 1922 (a significant exception was the NKVD, which increased its staff by 91 per cent between January 1921 and March 1922). As a result, by December 1922 72.3 per cent of Rabkrin's central apparatus was still staffed by employees who had joined control bodies in 1919 or even before 1917. Only 12.5 per cent of them claimed to be workers or peasants.[55] So much for hopes for a popular mass organization. Neither was it a particularly skilled one. A survey of twenty-seven gubernii in January 1922 showed that a mere 7 per cent of local inspectors were industrial specialists; only 6 per cent had received higher education.[56]

Already by the middle of 1921 Lenin had realized that the gap was widening fast between his somewhat utopian plans for

[53] *Istoriia kommunisticheskoi partii Sovetskogo Soiuza*, vol. 4 (Moscow, 1970), bk. 1, p. 128.

[54] *VKP(b) v rezoliutsiiakh*, vol. 1 (4th edn., Moscow, 1932), p. 523.

[55] See P. S. Spoerry, 'The Central Rabkrin Apparatus 1917–25', Ph.D. dissertation, Harvard 1968, pp. 138, 148. The source for the increase in NKVD staff is *Izvestiia raboche-krest'ianskoi inspektsii*, Apr. 1922, p. 3.

[56] A. I. Chugunov, *Organy sotsialisticheskogo kontrolia RSFSR 1923–1934 gg.* (Moscow, 1972), pp. 29–30.

Rabkrin and the reality under Stalin, its Commissar. In September 1921 Lenin criticized Stalin, stressing that the task of Rabkrin was to know how 'to put things right in good time' (umet' popravit' . . . vovremia), rather than to 'catch' and 'expose' (lovit' and izoblichat').[57] Early in 1922 Trotsky re-echoed Lenin's ideas, though more out of personal rivalry with Stalin. Yet Stalin continued to defy both of them. A leading anonymous article entitled 'Control or Inspection?' in the house journal of Rabkrin on 28 March 1922 still came down heavily on the side of rigorous inspection. It was claimed that discipline was even more essential in NEP conditions, which were producing a multitude of economic irregularities, more illegality, and quick, destabilizing changes in government institutions.[58] This article was in all probability intended as Stalin's parting salvo before giving up his job as Commissar of Rabkrin on 25 April.

Despite his illness and increasing isolation, it seemed on the surface of things as if Lenin had the final word in this debate. The last article he ever wrote was finished on 10 February 1923, but appeared in *Pravda* on 4 March only, due probably to delaying tactics by Stalin. In 'Better Fewer, but Better' Lenin recognized the cultural backwardness of the masses, and advocated a streamlined Rabkrin staffed with relatively few skilled and politically safe officials. In a proposal to the Twelfth Party Congress, Lenin suggested that the central Rabkrin apparatus be reduced to 300–400 persons and that it should be merged with the Central Control Commission. Lenin agreed that some might think that there was 'something improper in this suggestion', but he swept aside any possibility of collusion between Party and Soviet institutions. This was a strange oversight from the statesman who had so recently fought, as we have seen, against the subordination of legal officials to central authorities. He hoped that the new Central Control Commission would be allowed to 'systematically examine all the papers and documents of the Political Bureau'. Here is the dying spark of that dangerously naïve idealism that had sometimes affected Lenin's thought: 'These are the lofty

[57] Lenin, *Polnoe sobranie sochinenii*, vol. 44, pp. 127–32.
[58] *Izvestiia raboche-krest'ianskoi inspektsii*, 28 Mar. 1922.

tasks that I dream of for our Workers' and Peasants' Inspection' were nearly the last words he ever wrote.

As on so many other subjects, Lenin had of necessity turned élitist once again. Although he had claimed to gain power in October 1917 through the Soviets, he did so in fact through the disciplined ranks of his small party. He had once championed workers' control, but soon despaired of its anarchistic traits, as he was subsequently to be wary even of trade-union capabilities and attempts at independence from the Party. What hope then was there for the Central Control Commission as late as 1922–3? Strangely he continued to underestimate until the end the spider-like capacity of the party to suck in and devour all rivals for power. Furthermore, like so many leaders since his time, Lenin could not envisage the huge influence of the bureaucracy in a country that nationalized the chief sectors of the economy. Although acutely aware in 'Better Fewer, but Better' of the educational and other defects of the proletariat and the peasantry, he had never done a social analysis of administrative structures. He restricted himself to organizational scrutiny, and that at the highest levels only. One wonders if Lenin knew, for instance, that the pre-existing Siberian state-control apparatus did not even start to remould itself on the lines of Rabkrin until as late as November 1922, that is, thirty-four months after the latter's inception. In many other gubernii links between central and local inspectorates were established by March 1921 only.[59] These facts were symptomatic of two general trends in early NEP. First, the Rabkrin journal was certainly justified in claiming that administrative bodies were in a state of flux. We shall see more of this later in the chapter. Second, centrally inspired directives took so long to penetrate to the provinces that they were superseded before they could be implemented. In many Bolshevik control systems in the 1920s this lag through time and space is frequently apparent.

The future of the new Central Control Commission from 1923 onwards was to be quite different from what Lenin envisaged, but it was already a predictable fate. His hopes for its independence remained on paper. Since its members were

[59] Chugunov, op. cit., p. 27.

not elected, but appointed by the Orgburo, Stalin was to place
four of his closest associates one after the other at its head—
V. V. Kuibyshev (1923–6), G. K. Ordzhonikidze (1928–30),
A. A. Andreev (1930–1), and Ia. E. Rudzutak (1931–4). The
Politburo controlled it from the start, rather than vice versa. As
time went by, the packing of Rabkrin with Party members
favoured by Stalin and his kind actually led to a progressive
decline in the educational levels of its staff.[60] Lenin's fears on
the cultural front were more than justified.

The potential strengths and actual weaknesses of Rabkrin in
1922 were so typical of the control relationship between the
political centre and the rest of the country that it is worth
examining them in a little more detail at this point. Less than a
month after its defiance of Lenin's criticism, Rabkrin's journal
continued to vaunt its powers, despite the fact that Stalin now
ceased to be its Commissar. It interpreted the general call of
the Eleventh Party Congress 'not to retreat' as a personal
invitation to 'draw up the front line—dig in and fortify, in
general to set up new positions'.[61] The aggressive language of
the Civil War still lingered in the memory. Just before Stalin's
departure Rabkrin had decided to 'collect materials to serve as
a basis for the further regulation of the economic life of the
Republic'. This grandiose project was given teeth by a directive
to inspect documentation inside all kinds of government organs, rather than ask them to send copies to Rabkrin. The
prying nature of Stalin lurks behind this instruction. Rabkrin
inspectors in Orlov guberniia had already initiated on the spot
inspections of this kind, so the centre was consciously imitating
its more aggressive subordinates as it recognized in its journal.
Thus pressure from above for tighter discipline found a ready
echo from below. This had already proved to be a typical and
recurrent feature of central–local Party relations in the years
1918–21. Constant local conflicts between unorthodox and
more conventional Party groups had led to the call by some
provincial bodies for much greater discipline to be exercised

[60] Ibid., pp. 73–4, quoted in an interesting article by M. Perrins, '*Rabkrin* and
workers' control in Russia 1917–34', *European Studies Review* (1980), pp. 225–46. The
low educational levels of Rabkrin staff in the mid-1920s must have been a cause for
lament by its Deputy Commissar after 1926—Ia. Yakovlev, the author of the survey on
Kursk guberniia.

[61] *Izvestiia*, 20 Apr. 1922, p. 1.

from the centre.[62] This was a pattern that was to become familiar again at the very end of NEP, when Stalin once more used local fanaticism to fuel the fires of collectivization and industrialization.

The range of Rabkrin work in 1922 was very ambitious and varied from the important to the ridiculous. In this way it reflected Party intervention in all spheres of life, which made Party members become jacks of all trades. On a single page in the journal of Rabkrin reference is made in March to the need for inspections of the navy, Crimean resorts, and the nation's vineyards.[63] Many of the topics studied in previous chapters came in for real or anticipated scrutiny. Methods of fuel collection by Smolensk and other peasants for hungry railway-engines were to be reviewed. On the Lower Volga Rabkrin inspectors criticized the lack of accounts at the state fishery which might have been expected to help with the Famine.[64] The whole of Kursk guberniia, a huge area by West European standards, had only thirty Rabkrin members as late as 1925, yet they were instructed 'to know the work of other apparatuses better than they do themselves.'[65] In the majority of gubernii of European Russia the numbers of full-time workers varied between forty and seventy, but the large and partly industrial Urals region had a staff of 120 by 1924. Non-industrial and lesser-populated gubernii like Kursk, Riazan', and Kostroma had between ten and thirty-five.[66]

Rabkrin did not flinch from intervening at much higher levels. We have already noted how the powerful Commissariat of Agriculture was subjected to withering criticism by Rabkrin at the height of the Famine.[67] Another instance is the cultural and political life of Petrograd, which will be studied in the next chapter. The Commissariat of Enlightenment was pulled over the coals by Rabkrin for allowing Gosizdat, the beleaguered, infant state publishing house, to publish its journal on rival

[62] See Service, op. cit. The Orlov guberniia episode is recounted in the Rabkrin *Izvestiia*, 4 Apr. 1922.

[63] Ibid., 4 Mar.

[64] Ibid., 4 Apr.

[65] *Otchet XIII-mu gubernskomu s'ezdu sovetov. Kurskii gubernskii ispolnitel'nyi komitet* (Kursk, 1926), p. 393.

[66] Chugunov, op. cit., pp. 61–2.

[67] See p. 115 above.

private presses. Rabkrin officials also put pressure on Narkompros to devote more time and money to state film organizations
in Petrograd in order to compete with their more popular
private equivalents.[68]

Rabkrin wielded powers of prosecution, although they were
not formally granted to it.[69] Its inspectors felt they needed
these powers in order to deal with the widespread abuses they
uncovered. At the local level most of these were concerned with
private property, an abiding interest of the masses despite all
Bolshevik attempts to play down this fact of life. In the second
half of 1922 Rabkrin answered over 6,000 questions relating to
price and currency changes.[70] Its Central Bureau for Complaints dealt largely with property abuses dating back to the
Civil War period. Persons 'who have suffered from the previous
policies of Soviet power' were handed back requisitioned
houses and businesses.[71] In Kursk guberniia it was found that
most complaints to local Rabkrin officials referred to tax
miscalculations.[72]

On occasion Rabkrin did inspect itself in a half-hearted way.
It discovered that there was no proper check on its own
expenditure, but gave the reason or excuse that rapid inflation
made this a very difficult operation. By November 1922 it was
reported that those local inspectorates that had actually been
set up were already far too dependent on Moscow.[73] Yet in the
following month guberniia inspectorates were being advised to
regard gubispolkomy as part of their own organs and to avoid
any quarrels with them.[74] Thus collusion of the closest and
most naked sort was encouraged at local levels before the seal
was put on this kind of approach at the highest level with the
merging of Rabkrin and the Central Control Commission in
1923. By way of contrast, in the uezdy Rabkrin officials were
warned sternly against becoming engulfed in the swamp of
local corruption and nepotism in society at large.[75] The old

[68] *Izvestiia,* 4 Mar. and 28 Mar. 1922.
[69] Ikonnikov, op. cit., pp. 47–54. See also G. A. Dorokhova, *Raboche-kresti'anskaia inspektsiia v 1920–1923 gg.* (Moscow, 1959), p. 59.
[70] Ikonnikov, op. cit., p. 79.
[71] *Izvestiia,* 4 Mar. 1922.
[72] *Otchet,* pp. 407–8.
[73] *Izvestiia,* 1 Nov. 1922.
[74] Ibid., 1 Dec. 1922.
[75] Ibid., 9 May 1922.

artificial Tsarist gulf between state and society was opening up
again. It did not cross the Moscow-based mind that corruption
might equally flourish inside the gubispolkomy or in the
Central Control Commission itself.

It was noted earlier that Rabkrin wielded powers of prosecution. A decree of 8 February 1920 had expanded its rights to
supervise the execution of laws.[76] Even under the more relaxed
conditions of NEP the top layers of the legal system remained
firmly under central political control, although the lowest levels
continued to evade standardization. The legal system may
therefore be studied here as yet another aspect of almost direct
Bolshevik control. There was nothing new in this close relationship. Until the judiciary reform of 1864, the legal system had
been largely a branch of political administration, and
remained so in some ways until 1917. International and then
Civil War from 1914 to 1921 also permitted martial law and
Cheka courts to 'act on the internal front', as M. Latsis put it;[77]
that is, to intervene heavily in civil laws. Although the authority of the secret police was curbed in some respects in
February 1922, the new GPU kept all the powers of the old
Cheka to arrest, to carry out unrestricted searches and to
banish without trial to the forced-labour camps.

The year 1922 witnessed a great surge of activity in the legal
realm. A new system of civil and criminal courts was set up,
and Soviet codes of law were promulgated for the first time.
The first number of a new legal journal, *Pravo i zhizn'*, declared
an end to the spontaneity (*stikhiia*) of revolutionary consciousness, which had been 'motley, unsteady, and always subjective'
in legal matters. The Revolution was conceived of as a river
which had overflowed its banks, but was now about to flow
along the channel of legality with the introduction of the
codes.[78] It was in fact the case that in 1922 the judicial system
was regularized, but the new formal arrangements did not
change the power of the Party to control legal organs. Its
agents like Rabkrin and the secret police continued to intervene. The old revolutionary tribunals were to be replaced by

[76] *Sobranie uzakonenii RSFSR*, 16 (7 Feb. 1920), item 94.
[77] M. Latsis, *Chrezvychainye kommissii po bor'be s kontr-revoliutsiei* (Moscow, 1921), p. 8.
For more detail see Pethybridge, *The Social Prelude to Stalinism*, pp. 91–6.
[78] *Pravo i zhizn'*, 1 (June 1922), p. 8.

the people's courts, of which almost half the members were non-Communists by 1923.[79] Nevertheless the Party still managed to supervise their activities down to the guberniia level through its own newly disciplined hierarchy. The Party apparatus controlled the Commissariat of Justice in Moscow through appointments, and the Commissariat supervised the election and recall of judges at every level. However, the main way in which the Party continued to control the courts was through the state procurators.

Thus legal arrangements were formalized and centralized at the same time in 1922. It was still disputable whether they now flowed along a narrow channel of legality unpolluted by external sources. Only two weeks before the editor of *Pravo i zhizn'* offered this metaphor to the legal world, Lenin was still stressing that in the new criminal code 'the paragraph on terror must be formulated in as wide terms as possible, since only revolutionary consciousness of justice and revolutionary conscience can determine the conditions of its application in practice.'[80] There was no sudden hiatus or separation of politics from law in 1922. The abiding influence of the Russian past and the recent Revolution and Civil War lingered on. It was still there by the end of NEP, and may be encapsulated in the story of Leonid Leonov's *The Thief*, published in 1927. The outlaw group of the novel's hero stands for the whole of NEP society, which has but a weak grasp on the rule of justice or of law. This particular thief realizes that he has drifted into a life of crime as a result of an experience in the Civil War, when as a soldier in the Red Army he executed a White officer for shooting his horse from under him. Only later, during NEP, does our hero realize that the punishment he meted out in the name of revolutionary justice was in fact revenge veneered by principle. His relations with all others remain corrupted as a result.

The legal reforms of 1922 had no curative effect on the confusing, overlapping nature of the various institutions dealing with the administration of the law, but in other areas the arbitrariness of the period between 1917 and 1921 diminished

[79] See M. V. Kozhevnikov, *Istoriia sovetskogo suda* (Moscow, 1948), pp. 130, 143, cited in L. Schapiro, *The Communist Party of the Soviet Union* (London, 1960), p. 264.
[80] Quoted in Schapiro, op. cit., p. 265.

considerably. Legally trained Bolshevik politicians like
N. V. Krylenko had tired of the turbulent situation by 1921.
When he proposed in that year to audit all the work of the
revolutionary tribunals at a single central place, he lamented
that an attempt to do this in 1920 had failed 'because under the
conditions of the period it is extremely hard to establish courts
characterized by stability'.[81] By 1922 more professionally
trained legal experts were available to administer the new
codes. The presence of spetsy in their ranks also helped to
temper revolutionary ardour.

The main shift in emphasis, however, occurred for the
reason proclaimed by Lenin at the Ninth All-Russia Congress
of Soviets in December 1921: 'before us lies the task of
developing private exchange—this is required by the new
economic policy—and this requires more revolutionary legality'.[82] The infant Soviet Union could only recover and defend
itself if it could pull out of economic chaos, so that private
property and the creation of wealth had to be encouraged in
stable legal conditions. As late as 1931 the influential Soviet
jurist P. Stuchka was still describing the civil code of 1922 as
'nothing but the formulae of bourgeois civil law, repeating in
general the formulae of Roman law framed about 2,000 years
ago'.[83] This statement might not have shocked Marx, who
wrote that in the initial stage of the transition to socialism the
legal system would remain bourgeois in essence. Trotsky in
1922 was to put forward a similar argument for economic
planning on semi-capitalist lines. A leading expert on Soviet
civil law states that 'the appearance of the Code indicates that
it was framed after the pattern of the most advanced West
European codes, the German and the Swiss.'[84] This view is
corroborated in the pages of *Pravo i zhizn'*, where much interest
was taken in these same foreign codes in 1922.[85] Virtually the

---

[81] From a speech by N. V. Krylenko recorded in *VTsIK VIII sozyva, stenograficheskii
otchet* (Moscow, 1922), p. 185. Leading positions in criminology were still held by pre-
revolutionary professors like S. V. Poznyshev and A. A. Zhizhilenko. See S. S. Ostroumov, *Prestupnost' i ee prichiny v dorevoliutsionnoi Rossii* (Moscow, 1960).

[82] *VKP(B) v rezoliutskiakh*, vol. 1 (Moscow, 1941), p. 410.

[83] P. Stuchka, *13 let bor'by za revoliutsionno-marksistkuiu teoriiu prava* (Moscow, 1931),
p. 121.

[84] V. Gsovski, *Soviet Civil Law*, vol. 1 (Ann Arbor, 1948), p. 24.

[85] *Pravo i zhizn'*, 3 (1922), p. 19 ff.

only new general aspects of Soviet as opposed to Tsarist property law were the law of housing tenancy, and more significantly, the use of land. From 1922 on there was a complete prohibition of alienation of use of agricultural land. The trained draughtsmen of the 1922 criminal code were fully aware in their turn of its 1903 Imperial Russian equivalent. A detailed inspection of the 1922 code shows that there is nothing more revolutionary in it than in its predecessor, apart from the Soviet application of criminal law by analogy.[86]

The Bolshevik leadership made no mistake in predicting the urgent need for codification in the sphere of property. Whereas crimes of violence had predominated in the years 1917–21, an era of 'economic counter-revolution', as it was called, was ushered in under NEP conditions. Cases of embezzlement, sabotage, pilfering of state property, counterfeiting, and trade in contraband flooded the courts from 1921 to 1926, when they began to subside. In 1923, the first year for which figures are precise, 575,761 persons were convicted.[87] This is the sleazy ambience reflected in subsequent works of literature such as *The Twelve Chairs* by Il'f and Petrov. Instances of fuel pilfering in Smolensk guberniia, grain thefts in the Famine areas, and the illegal antics of Makarenko's pupils, have cropped up in our tour of the provinces, breathing life into these dead statistics. Dealers of the slicker sort now graduated to the big cities. An article in *Trud* on 23 March 1922 observed how the courts were 'mirrors of life'. A Nepman by the name of Gal'bershtein (doubly suspicious for being a Jew who had worked for the Provisional Government in the localities in 1917) had brought thirty-four villagers with him to Moscow, and was now exploiting their labour in a wholesale-retail business. He was fined 2,000 *gold* roubles and sentenced to heavy labour for two years.

The paradox of introducing a virtually capitalist civil code into a society struggling to achieve socialism did not escape keen minds like Krylenko. He could muster the Marxist argument, cited earlier, in his support. He also claimed that

---

[86] See J. N. Hazard, 'The Courts and the Legal System', in C. E. Black (ed.), *The Transformation of Russian Society: Aspects of Social Change since 1861* (Cambridge, Mass., 1960), pp. 157–8.

[87] *Statistika osuzhdennykh v SSSR za 1923–1924 gg.* (Moscow, 1927), pp. 8–9.

'NEP provided only the atmosphere, facilitating it is true and hastening the exposure of this inescapable phase of development of our court work, but it never did more than that. It never foreordained the content of our work.'[88] In two senses, however, he was wrong. The 'phase' has continued to this day, still based mainly on the 1922 codes, which were without doubt heavily conditioned by NEP. Stalin after 1928 merely built up a parallel system of terror alongside the pre-existing codes. The ultimate irony came in 1938, when Krylenko, E. B. Pashukanis, and their less famous legal colleagues were purged. The reason given for their demise was that in 1922 they had created a legal system based on models from the past. This was true, but Stalin was still making use of them in the 1930s.

The Soviet procuracy was created in May 1922. Soviet historians and some Western scholars state baldly that this was due to Lenin's letter to Stalin of that month. In fact the main architect was Krylenko, but as he was purged in 1937 and only rehabilitated in 1957, his leading role is omitted in Soviet accounts. In order to understand the discussion on the draft decree of the procuracy in the spring of 1922, it is necessary to recall some features of central–local legal controls over the years 1917–21. There was considerable delay in the establishment of new courts in the localities, many of which became engulfed in the Civil War. Not until the end of December 1917 had the Samara guberniia Soviet set up a local 'Commissariat of Justice', and at lower levels in this area delays were even more protracted.[89] Pre-revolutionary local and national peculiarities survived in many ways until the end of NEP. In Belorussia, including Smolensk and Roslavl', peasant women continued to have equal property rights with men, which was not the case until 1929 in many other parts of the Soviet Union. Around Roslavl', it was not legal edicts from on high which delineated farm boundaries, but family rituals immersed in the deep ethnic past.[90] Bolshevik defeats in the Civil War freed the party to concentrate its legal activities on the preservation

[88] Quoted in J. N. Hazard, *Settling Disputes in Soviet Society* (New York, 1960), p. 486.

[89] N. N. Lotov, 'Deiatel'nost' Samarskogo gubernskogo kommissariata iustitsii', *Proletarskaia revoliutsiia i pravo* (Moscow, Feb.–Apr. 1919).

[90] N. P. Vakar, *Belorussia: The Making of a Nation* (Cambridge, Mass., 1956), p. 21. Prior to 1917 virtually no written legal system was applicable in Belorussia, see pp. 24–5.

of the state, so that the record of how disputes between individuals were settled nearly disappeared from the legal literature.[91] A plethora of partly overlapping courts grew up, often quite independent from the centre in the case of the local revolutionary tribunals. It was not clear what fell under their jurisdiction or under that of the new military tribunals, established in February 1919, or else under that of the secret police courts.

Centralized supervision over the activity of all the courts by state procurators finally came into being in May 1922. As with the party and state control systems, there were social and administrative pressures from below as well as political ones from above for this move. Both elements were apparent in the VTsIK debate on the draft decree. In view of the tenuous central hold over the multifarious forms of legal life between 1917 and 1921, it comes as a surprise to find anyone left so bold as to oppose the procuracy for old-fashioned democratic, anti-centralist reasons: 'We must first of all improve the judicial apparatus from top to bottom, improve the people's courts. . . . There is your path to preserve and strengthen revolutionary legality, and not by putting controllers from above over the guberniia executive committees.'[92] Another objector pointed out prophetically that there were not enough qualified lawyers in the provinces to provide adequate staff for the local procuracy: 'We are not Belgium and not Germany, but Russia, a vast country, a country in which there are no cultural forces, even simply literate people, not even to speak of lawyers.'[93] As late as 1925 there were still frequent complaints about 'clearly illegal decrees . . . issued by the agencies of the lower apparatus as a result of legal ignorance . . .'.[94] M. I. Kalinin, the chairman of the VTsIK, and one of the very few top Bolshevik leaders of the time who travelled widely round his own country,[95] came

---

[91] Hazard, op. cit., p. 79.

[92] *Biulleten'. III sessiia vserossiiskogo tsentral'nogo ispolnitel'nogo komiteta, IX sozyva* (Moscow), 3 (17 May 1922), p. 16.

[93] Ibid., pp. 11–12.

[94] *Otchet prokuratury RSFSR prezidiumu VTsIK za 1925 g.* (Moscow, 1925), p. 106. In 1925 various local decrees prohibited, among other things, the drying of manure in front of houses, the gift of buns to priests at funeral banquets, but encouraged the confiscation of samovars and ploughs from citizens not attending meetings, ibid., pp. 87–8.

[95] See p. 117 above.

back at this objector, turning the point round in favour of the procuracy: 'The vastness of the Soviet Republic necessitates sending a person from the centre who would not administer a local area, but who would look after the legality of the administration. The larger the territory, the more supervision of the centre over legality is required.'[96] Kalinin's last sentence could stand as an epithet for the dilemma of Bolshevik controls in early NEP. Hence the proliferation in 1922 of agencies, all of them clearly subservient to the Party, but often crossing one another's administrative wires and becoming rapidly centralized and bureaucratically top-heavy. This goes equally for Rabkrin, the TsKK, the Soviet hierarchy, the secret police, and the procuracy.

Lenin backed up Krylenko, Kalinin, and the other centralizers. He based his view partly on the socio-cultural background, referring to the 'sea of lawlessness' in which the state was immersed. At the same time he retained his keen sense of the renewed need for close political control from above, as the country slipped into the economic quagmire of NEP. The central procuracy was to consist of about ten reliable Communists who would work under the close supervision of the Orgburo, the Political Bureau, and the TsKK, as well as the party congress. All these bodies were shortly to be submitted to the ruthless control of Stalin in the Secretariat.

Although the new procuracy proved to be professionally efficient from the start at the higher levels, its difficulties below the guberniia level mirrored those we have already observed in the lower party and state apparatuses. With the return to private enterprise, one of the main duties of the procurators was to protect private rights. Taxation at once loomed large in their business, and early provisions for challenging ordinances in the financial sphere were sent out to all gubernii and oblasti of the RSFSR. Some agencies proved to be recalcitrant at the lower levels. The Belgorod uezd congress of Soviets in Kursk guberniia exacted its own additional tax in kind. The gubispolkom approved, noting that 'the congress is the boss of the uezd', and so it overruled the local procurator's objections, but a referral to the central procuracy killed off any further

[96] *Biulleten'*, p. 16.

opposition.[97] Administrative wires got crossed on tax affairs too. In November 1922 we find V. Molotov acting in the name of the Central Committee: he rebuked the Smolensk gubispolkom for doing exactly the same thing—allowing subordinates to impose taxes beyond those laid down in the All-Union list.[98]

Below the guberniia level the influence of the procurators was even more slight than that of the Party. The delays in dealing with cases at and below this level were so severe that Krylenko advised the guberniia procurators to inform their Republic equivalents, who should take the cases to the presidium of the VTsIK.[99] By early 1923 in the uezdy 'the work of general supervision is not exercised or is exercised weakly'. In most local towns the procurators' penetration remained as hopes expressed on paper only.[100]

The attitude of the peasants to the workings of the central law, which in modern times is generally supposed to be applicable throughout the state for which it holds, may serve as another illustration of their parochial mental view. Before the Revolution very few cases were transferred from the local volost' courts to the towns.[101] In fact before 1917 and throughout NEP the mir usually did not feel bound by legal procedure nor even by the mir's own informal precedents. Local justice was utilitarian and practical, directed to the maintenance of ordained relations within a restricted circle of peasants with scant regard for external pressures. Thus Soviet writers on NEP have noted the considerable discrepancy between sentences passed for several types of crime in town and country. Very few court sessions were held away from the towns, which served large agricultural hinterlands. In 1923 it could still take fifteen days for legal documents to be sent by post from a volost' court to the nearest higher legal authority.[102] Despite

---

[97] 'Prokuratura i revoliutsionnaia zakonnost'', *Ezhenedel'nik sovetskoi iustitsii*, 51–2 (31 Dec. 1923), p. 1,200.

[98] Smolensk Archive, file WKP 125. See Fainsod, op. cit., pp. 174–5, for a description of the general supervision exercised by the Roslavl' assistant procurator in mid-NEP over the uezd executive committee.

[99] *Ezhenedel'nik sovetskoi iustitsii*, circular 134, 18 Nov. 1922.

[100] V. Zenkovich, 'Itogi i zadachi raboty obshchego nadzora', *Ezhenedel'nik sovetskoi iustitsii*, 18 (10 May 1923), p. 417.

[101] D. Kurskii, *Izbrannye stat'i i rechi* (Moscow, 1948), p. 78. Volost' courts were said to punish theft seven times more severely than city courts.

[102] Bol'shakov, *Derevnia 1917–27* (Moscow, 1927), p. 313.

the fact that even by 1926 the procurators failed to hold sway at the lower levels, Krylenko noted that some of them wished to 'embrace the unembraceable'. In other words, they got caught up in what Lenin referred to in the Sovnarkom as 'vermicelli'. All bureaucrats new to the job in the largest and most varied country in the world were an easy prey to this. Krylenko observed that there were procurators who demanded to know from a volost' executive committee on what occasion and on what legal basis there was a puddle outside the executive committee building.[103]

Walter Duranty, who reported on Russia for twelve years in the *New York Times*, wrote in 1922 that henceforth the procedure of the Soviet courts would be a sort of combination of West European and American systems. In this view he was merely repeating that of Soviet jurists at the time, as we have seen. He also believed that the GPU was being 'assimilated like . . . the English Scotland Yard under control of the Home Office'.[104] Other contemporary Soviet jurists with a better knowledge of recent Russian history were already speculating privately on the resurgence of terror.[105] Perhaps on balance, and in the broadest terms, Catherine had put through more secure and lasting legal reforms in the localities than her counterparts in 1922. She had firmly separated the powers of the procurators from those of the provincial governors, the rough equivalent of the Party. She had carried through the reforms in a slow, careful fashion over the 1760s and 1770s, and had toured the provinces extensively on inspections. Only Kalinin toured in the early Soviet period, and he was a figurehead and no jurist. The Soviet codes were introduced wholesale at enormous speed, and, as befitted aspects of the Marxist superstructure, they were originally intended as passing reflections of the twilight capitalist world they administered. Both the Tsarist and the early Soviet systems regarded crimes carried out by one private person against another or even of an official against a private person as matters of scant public concern. Justice was there above all, as in the Civil War period, in order to enforce

[103] N. V. Krylenko, *Osnovy sudoustroistva SSSR i soiuznykh respublik* (Moscow, 1927), p. 40.
[104] W. Duranty, *Russia Reported* (New York, 1934), pp. 119, 123.
[105] Hazard, op. cit., p. 480.

the government's will and to protect its interests. The monopoly of the party by 1922 over the law was tighter than that of
the Emperor after 1906, for he had to contend with the parties
in the Duma. The masses in NEP were as willing to tolerate
arbitrariness as much as in the Tsarist past, since the humaniz-
ing notion of an independent judiciary did not have a deep
hold on the Russian people. Furthermore the Soviet government claimed that it had replaced the absolutist state with a
state of the people, so any hint that the masses needed to be
protected against the arbitrary action of a judge by being
represented directly in the courts through free laymen on the
bench could be seen as a slur on the good faith of the
Communist Party.

At the close of this chapter we shall look at the performance
in 1922 of the Sovnarkom, the supreme organ that in the last
resort was supposed to control nearly all the central and
provincial tentacles examined so far, although some aspects of
the party and the secret police systems had already evaded its
grasp before 1922. But first mention should be made of the
sweeping territorial reforms of the period in conjunction with
the formulation of economic plans for the future.

The introduction of NEP did not lead to the abandonment
of long-term planning. Psychologically it tended to have the
reverse effect. The postponement of the millennium at first
nurtured a variety of somewhat theoretical, hothouse schemes.
These schemes were rendered even more theoretical, that is,
out of line with the small-scale socio-economic realities of life
in the 1920s, because they were based on large-scale Marxist
tenets. I have dwelt at some length on this dichotomy elsewhere, so I will not repeat myself here.[106] Other reasons for
difficulties in building bridges between government and society
have been referred to earlier. They appeared to be perennial in
Russia. This assessment by an expert on the Stolypin reforms of
the Duma period could apply word for word to the situation in
early NEP: 'the entire enterprise continued to be plagued by
arbitrariness, lack of consistency at the local level, conflict
between representatives of different government departments

---

[106] See Pethybridge, *The Social Prelude to Stalinism*, ch. 5.

who often worked at cross purposes, not to mention a frequent lack of co-ordination between centre and periphery.'[107]

At least the Bolsheviks were not troubled in 1922 by a gamut of conflicting political parties, as was the late Tsarist government by the various parties in the Duma. On the other hand they were confronted by gigantic dislocations that threatened to obscure all attempts at realistic economic planning. The Civil War and the Famine were the main causes of this. We have seen, just from the few areas treated, how Belorussia's boundaries shifted enormously as armies marched backwards and forwards over her territory. Rebellion rumbled on just to the east of Kursk guberniia. Social chaos still prevailed in much of the Ukraine in 1922, as is clear from the position in Makarenko's neck of the woods and known from many other sources. Widespread military action and famine resulted in migrations on an unprecedented scale.[108] Even if there had been an adequate legacy of social statistics from the pre-1917 period, they would have been rendered useless as a result of these disturbances. To cap it all, the administrative hub of Russia was suddenly shifted from Petrograd to Moscow after the Revolution. The disorientation caused by this move has never been calculated, even in broad terms, by either Soviet or Western historians. (It will be noted in the next chapter how Petrograd was in many ways still the cultural capital of Russia in 1922.) Lenin had a much harder task than Mao did later, for the Chinese leader gained invaluable experience over some years of how to run a large enclave (Yenan) on socialist lines. The Bolsheviks were plunged into macro-administration overnight.

Let us look in a little more detail at the dimensions of early Soviet administrative reforms. Between 1917 and the end of 1921 no less than 31 per cent more gubernii, 19 per cent more

---

[107] D. A. J. Macey, 'Bureaucratic Solutions to the Peasant Problem: Before and After Stolypin', unpublished paper presented at the Second World Congress on Soviet and East European Studies, Garmisch, Oct. 1980, p. 42.

[108] In an earlier draft of this book I devoted a complete chapter to the phenomenon of internal and external (by emigrés) migration in early NEP, so impressed have I been by its social and political significance. In the final draft I have scattered its impact over various themes and chapters (the role of the mobile Red Army men, fugitives from the Famine, the orphans, the comings and goings to Western Europe of Petrograd-based 'fellow-travellers', etc.).

uezdy, and 30 per cent new volosti were established on the lands of the former Empire minus the western territories lost in the Great War, Transcaucasia, and the Far East.[109] As late as September 1922 the Administrative Commission set up in February 1920 under the VTsIK was still asking its guberniia staff to send up information relating to the years 1917 to 1921 on local border and place-name changes 'whose precise date and nature are at present in large part hardly known or not at all' to the central authorities.[110] In June 1924 local gubispolkomy were still making local changes without telling Moscow.[111]

What were the motives behind these huge shifts? The old regime until well after the emancipation of the serfs had been attuned to the vision of a largely agrarian society, passive and sedentary, yielding peasant conscripts for military needs and sufficient taxes to support the central bureaucracy and the gentry at all levels. The Bolsheviks were intent on speeding up the change in emphasis between agriculture and industry. New territorial divisions were created with an eye to the future development of urban nexuses more closely related to the railways, material resources, and skilled populations which could be more quickly converted into full-blown proletarians. The agglomeration of small localities into larger centres would, it was hoped, be hastened during NEP by the penetration of a free-market economy into sleepy, self-sufficient hinterlands with low population densities. It remained a problem throughout the 1920s to find industrial and trade centres of enough significance to be awarded the status of a guberniia capital. Railway development was virtually stagnant over the same period. Another problem concerned the national minorities. Their boundaries were determined for the most part in 1920–1, that is, prior to Gosplan's scheme for economic regions. In a

[109] See K. Egorov, 'Administrativnoe delenie RSFSR v primenenii k ekonomicheskomu raionirovaniiu', *Vlast' sovetov*, 3 (1922), p. 28.

[110] *Biulleten' NKVD*, 37, circular 305, 26 Sept. 1922, p. 145. The administrative commission's mandate was ambitious. It intended to collect materials on the history of Russian territorial administration from the thirteenth century onwards, see Egorov, op. cit., p. 25. In spatial terms, a Russian geographer once calculated that it would take more than 12,000 years to map his country, using the British Ordnance Survey smallscale method, see C. Piazzi Smyth, *Three Cities in Russia*, vol. 1 (London, 1862), pp. 150–1.

[111] *Sobranie uzakonenii*, 51 (6 June 1924), art. 492.

period still fraught with political fears concerning the weak hold on the peripheries, where most of the minorities lay, the government in 1922 prudently sacrificed economic rationale to national sensibilities and made economic zones coincide with minorities rather than vice versa.[112] On the rare occasion where the reverse was tried, Moscow ran into strong opposition. The ethnic borders of the Ukrainian Republic and the Crimean Autonomous Republic were at first ignored in Gosplan's 1921 project for a south-west zone and a southern metallurgical oblast'. The plan was highly unpopular in the Ukraine. The Ukrainian Gosplan blandly ignored it, and the project was eventually shelved.[113] Jealousy could also erupt between old Great-Russian guberniia capitals, as when Kursk objected in 1922 to being subjected to Voronezh', which had been designated the capital of a new oblast' in which Kursk lay.[114]

It was self-evident that the creation of clearly defined economic regions was a *sine qua non* for national economic planning. In the course of the pre-revolutionary debate on territorial reorganization, politicians and administrators had wanted to set up a new unit larger than the volost' in order to concentrate nearer the grass roots the benefits of the guberniia towns—education, medicine, agronomic aid, etc. From their differing point of view, Tsarist economists and geographers tended to dismiss the pre-industrial divisions set up originally by Catherine. They wanted to divide the Empire into larger zones better adjusted to economic resources. A similar tussle took place in the years 1920–2. The Administrative Commission referred to previously which was set up in 1920 devoted most of its energies to political and social problems.[115] However on 22 February 1921 a rival State Planning Commission (Gosplan) was created with the aim of preparing a single national economic plan. Centralist economic theorizing was soon to prevail over the more sensitive, devolutionary ideas of

---

[112] See 'Tezisy doklada prezidiuma ocherednoi sessii VTsIK deviatogo sozyva po voprosu o ekonomicheskom raionirovanii Rossii', *Vlast' sovetov*, 3 (Mar. 1922), p. 35; and also 'Praktika raionirovaniia', *Ekonomicheskaia zhizn'*, 84 (18 Apr. 1923), p. 1.

[113] A. Volkov, 'Itogi raionirovaniia Ukrainy', *Ekonomicheskaia zhizn'*, 204 (11 Sept. 1923), p. 3.

[114] G. Pletnev, 'Sredne-chernozemnaia polosa', *Ekonomicheskaia zhizn'*, 245 (29 Oct. 1922), p. 5.

[115] P. M. Alampiev, *Ekonomicheskoe raionirovanie SSSR* (Moscow, 1959), p. 65.

the Administrative Commission, which was succeeded in November 1921 by a new commission whose initial subservient task was to comment (within a space of two weeks!) on Gosplan's first draft for economic regionalization.[116] At the end of 1921 the Ninth Congress of Soviets established yet another commission, since delegates were worried by the proliferation of new territorial units.[117] The elimination of twenty-six gubernii was proposed, but the notion was soon swept aside by nearly all the Commissariats consulted.[118] The administrative upheaval involved would have been appalling. From this point onwards Gosplan's pre-eminence among the various commissions was assured, and the scheme for the mechanical strengthening of the gubernii was dropped.[119]

Gosplan's economic regions were finally drawn up in 1923, but they remained highly abstract for several reasons. Confusion arising from the previous multiple agencies had not died down by the end of 1922. Lenin himself lamented that the 4,700 Communist executive workers in Moscow engaged in administrative planning were inefficient due to lack of training. So much for his vision of 1917 in *State and Revolution* of any worker or even peasant helping to run the country. The targets of planning were as problematic as the nature of the planners. The many dislocations cited earlier made it hard to get to grips with the regions. The location and extent of the raw material resources of most of Siberia and Central Asia were still unknown in NEP, thus making it impossible to calculate whether to concentrate future development on the old Muscovite heartland or whether to shift the emphasis further east. It comes as no surprise to find that the first All-Russian Economic Plan for Electrification (*GOELRO*), contained many utopian elements.[120]

Soon after the start of NEP several leading Bolsheviks and ex-Mensheviks began to stress the need for devolution in order to cope. A. I. Rykov was putting it this way by April 1923: 'Six

---

[116] Ibid., pp. 106–7.

[117] *Deviatyi vserossiiskii s'ezd sovetov . . ., stenograficheskii otchet* (Moscow, 1922), pp. 259, 300.

[118] Egorov, op. cit., p. 29.

[119] S. Chugunov, 'Etapy raionirovaniia', *Vlast' sovetov*, 28–29 (1928), p. 3.

[120] For a fuller discussion of this point, see Pethybridge, *The Social Prelude to Stalinism*, pp. 35–8.

years' experience has convinced us of the utter impossibility of having a systematic planned management for the country, and especially of a management based on the present system. . . . I ask you: can one bind to the centre an economy in which the kustar' industry has an enormous importance, where one-third of heavy industry relies on local organs and another third on oblast' organs?'[121] Rykov found an echo of his views in the writings of V. Bazarov, an ex-Menshevik who was induced to join Gosplan in 1922. He encouraged the restoration of a market system because in his view it alone made it possible to draw up general plans for socialist development. Otherwise prices which failed to reflect relative scarcities and costs would lead to the wrong allocation of resources. Trotsky too was nearly of the same opinion, although his enemies inside the Soviet Union and abroad subsequently depicted him as a super-industrializer of the same stamp as E. Preobrazhensky. In *The New Course*, conceived in 1922 and published in 1923, Trotsky argued that industrial costs should be reduced, not by suppressing the market, but on the basis of the market: 'success in economic organization will largely depend on how far we succeed, through precise knowledge of market conditions and correct economic forecasts, in harmonizing state industry with agriculture in accordance with a plan.'[122] As in the realm of law, so in economics, considerable reliance was now being put by a wide political variety of planners on capitalist precepts in order to suit passing organizational needs. The ideas of the Administrative Commission appear to have been based to some extent on the work of the nineteenth-century capitalist German economist J. K. von Thünen.[123]

The years between 1922 and 1926 threw up many modifications to the arrangement of the economic regions first proposed in 1921. Arbitrary drafts and redrafts from Gosplan incurred

[121] K. D. Egorova (ed.), *Raionirovanie SSSR, sbornik materialov po raionirovaniiu s 1917–1925 gg.* (Moscow, 1926), p. 57.

[122] Trotsky, *Novyi Kurs* (Moscow, 1923). The author is indebted to Dr Robert Bideleux for this unusual, but surely correct, estimation of Trotsky's aims in 1922.

[123] J. H. von Thünen, *Der isolierte Staat in Beziehung auf Landwirtschaft und Nationalökonomie* (Hamburg, 1826). This author's work had been the object of attention of Russian planners long before 1917. See H. Chambre, *L'Aménagement du territoire en URSSS: L'introduction à l'étude des régions économiques soviétiques* (Paris, 1959), p. 33. For a discussion of other non-Marxist German ideas which had a ready reception in the Soviet Union in these years, see Pethybridge, *The Social Prelude to Stalinism*, p. 43.

frequent criticisms at both local and central levels. Gosplan itself was fully aware of the precarious and theoretical character of its decisions, as it admitted at the start of 1926.[124] Yet Gosplan found increasingly that it had to centralize more and more as clashes arose between localities which it had to resolve. It is significant that by the end of 1926 Belorussia, the Ukraine, the North Caucasus, the Uzbek Republic, the Urals, and Siberia had all completed their regional administrative reforms, whereas European Russia had scarcely been affected. The strategically sensitive edges of the country and the national minorities had been dealt with first, despite the fact that the economic dynamo of Russia still lay in the old European heartland.[125] There was little hope that Gosplan would have the time, the staff, or the money to sift through the niceties of those economic problems that concerned our chosen regions—the decline of the flax industry in Smolensk, the realignment of the beet crop round Poltava for lack of a foreign market, the need for economic rehabilitation in the areas of the Volga devastated by the Famine. In the largest country in the world, so conscious of its relative backwardness, planning was seen by Gosplan as it had been viewed also in the late Tsarist period, as a race against time which could not allow for compromises with the regions: 'Planning must not spare the use of force.'[126]

NEP has been depicted almost universally in and outside the Soviet Union as a period of relaxed controls, at least in its initial stages. One apparently incontrovertible sign of this was the ending of the Civil War. Another was the apparent liberalization of cultural restraints, and a third the abandonment of War Communism and the adoption of semi-capitalist methods in certain aspects of the economy. The third reason is patently true in many spheres of the economy, although they are not listed or discussed in this book, which is devoted primarily to political attitudes and social situations. However, a sufficient number of socio-economic examples have cropped

[124] 'Ot redaktsii', *Planovoe khoziaistvo*, 1 (1926).
[125] L. Krzhizhanovsky (ed.), *Voprosy ekonomicheskogo raionirovaniia SSSR* (Moscow, 1957), pp. 309, 319.
[126] M. I. Bogolepov, *O putiakh buduschchego k voprosu ob ekonomicheskom plane* (Petrograd, 1916), p. 45.

up in the course of the foregoing chapters to show that NEP was by no means a one-way process in this area. Gosplan's long-term aims may have been little more than a ghost at the banquet in 1922, but they persisted and proliferated and were eventually to triumph. The coming of peace and hence slightly better party and Soviet penetration into the localities meant more fiscal control, and above all more taxes than before NEP. The drastic effects of this have been noted in every single guberniia treated here, from Smolensk to the Volga. More rigid controls affected peasants, tradespeople, and the Church alike. The introduction of the principle of khozraschet sent one economic sector after another to the wall in 1921–2, thus putting them at the mercy of the state. This has been noted with regard to a whole series of disparate concerns, from the timber industry in Belorussia to the nation-wide rail network. It was so powerful an agent that it sometimes succeeded involuntarily in crushing vital party institutions like the ideological journals that were started up in Petrograd in 1922.

The thesis concerning overall cultural relaxation must also be qualified very heavily, as the next chapter will attempt to show, by dealing with the phenomenon of heightened political controls over vital areas of the central intellectual press. We have already seen how the national press organizations were at first loosened up in some ways, only to be submitted almost at once to tighter curbs than ever. The life of the spirit also came in for a new wave of vigorous attacks, with the onslaught on church property and rights which were noted in the famine-stricken provinces, and in Smolensk guberniia. Finally, military controls by no means disappeared overnight. Apart from the fact that the Civil War dragged on into the mid-1920s in Central Asia and elsewhere, there were several substantial peasant uprisings going on in 1922, of which the Tambov revolt is merely the best documented to date. Lawlessness did not abate. The conditions of near-anarchy and brigandage which surrounded Makarenko and his pupils near Poltava were probably more the rule than the exception in much of the country, necessitating frequent military intervention. The party called directly on the army for aid in Smolensk and the Lower Volga, as has been seen. Ex-military men were often the leading lights in rural party and Soviet structures as was the case in Kursk guberniia. Dzerzhinsky applied straightforward military measures to bring the railways into some form of order, using legal institutions that did not lose their confusing overlapping traits (between civil, martial, and secret police courts) with the end of the Civil War.

Most of the underlying reasons for the apparent paradox of proclaimed liberalization resulting in greater stringencies in actual practice have already been teased out in earlier chapters. In part they form a perennial problem for a country unversed in a long historical growth of democracy and confronted by the largest spaces in the world, full of the most bewildering diversity of climates, peoples, and customs. During the Civil War the Bolsheviks at least were rid of the problems involved in administering much of the country, since it lay outside their grasp. When they began the vigorous penetration of the localities in peacetime, new difficulties quickly arose. For lack of insufficient trained party members, they were compelled to rely on ill-prepared provincial agents in all the spheres that we have examined, from the Soviet structure to the law. There was a high turnover of personnel, and the few who excelled graduated swiftly to more central rungs on the administrative ladder, as was seen in Kursk guberniia. Adding to the general lack of reliable information and control at the grass roots was the question of politically or socially unreliable agents, such as the village teachers, the profiteers from War Communism turned tax-collectors, or energetic but money-minded peasants who dominated local Soviets. To cap it all, genuinely efficient party members were often highly unpopular because they hailed from 'the Centre' and were prominent as tax-collectors.

The result of so many blocked lines of information-flow was central ignorance of the rapidly changing subtleties of local life. Even the limited amount of reliable detail that did arrive could not be properly digested and understood, for lack of time and experts in Moscow. Determined efforts were certainly made in 1922 to remedy these defects, but they turned out to be counter-productive. The Central Control Commission, Rabkrin, the procuracy, amongst other centrally inspired bodies, were encouraged to probe more deeply into local affairs. At the outset of NEP they were intended, in theory not least, as external and independent checks on the party and state lines of control, but they were rapidly converted into an integral part of the over-centralized system. Worse than that, their several powers soon overlapped, causing administrative confusion, waste of valuable experts' time, and, worst of all, the powerful reinforcement of a one-party monolithic political system. Lenin was quite aware of the dangers and warned against them in 1922, despite his long-standing preference for subordinating all power hierarchies to the Party. Nevertheless, Lenin's diatribes in 1922 against 'bureaucratism' as a malaise left over from the methods of the Tsarist system were self-deluding. As T. H. Rigby has pointed out, the real causes lay in the existing structure of authority in early NEP, and in particular in the party apparatus and the Vecheka. In turn they corrupted all the other administrative institutions listed above, since party apparatchiki were appointed to dominate them.

One of the prime aims of the preceding chapters has been to search out the socio-cultural reasons for renewed centralism at the start of NEP. Recent scholarship on the political scene in 1921–2 has clearly revealed a sharp reinforcement in that sphere as well in 1922. T. H. Rigby has shown that Soviet power until Lenin's illness in 1922 was exercised by the Sovnarkom under Lenin's chairmanship, and not by party government. Robert Service has pointed out that an efficient centralized party apparatus only finally emerged at the same time, as much due to local party antagonism as to confused local authority and poor links with the centre as the central initiative itself.[127] The Party had streamlined its hierarchy just in time to take advantage of Lenin's departure from the political stage. In 1922 it took over state authority just when the Sovnarkom could be pushed into ceding it. This fundamental shift was facilitated by the existence of the increasingly powerful Orgburo and Secretariat, which were responses to local calls for efficient control as well as being tools of Stalin's central ambition.

These two scholars' interpretations interlock and make excellent sense, although they tend to shove a little too far into the background the role of pre-existing ideology drawing on

[127] T. H. Rigby, *Lenin's Government: Sovnarkom 1917–1922* (Cambridge, England, 1979), p. 238; R. Service, op. cit.

centralist political theory. They also underestimate the power of Lenin's personality. Just because he was the legitimizing principle of the Soviet regime, there was no need during his heyday to stipulate that any particular party body should be the centre of the decision-making process. His preference for the Sovnarkom ensured its pre-eminence which faded together with his health in 1922. T. M. Rigby also occasionally underestimates the extent to which party and state apparatuses overlapped each other before 1922. At the local levels examined in previous chapters we have discovered this feature at every turn.

None of the social causes which reinforced political centralism in 1922 was to disappear fast. Indeed some of them, such as the fear of the wrong ideological agent at work in the localities, were to be even more prevalent by 1926. This fact meant that there was little hope for any softening of the highly centralized *party* government that finally emerged in 1922. The rising personality of Stalin was another nail in the coffin. Theory had preceded the harsh organizational facts of 1922. The Tenth Party Congress in 1921 had already institutionalized monolithism by barring factions within the Party. Paradoxically this measure had been passed in the hope on the part of some for more democracy. Karl Radek and others had voted for it because they wished to preserve democracy rather than wipe it out.

The second broad policy measure of the Tenth Congress had been the institution of the New Economic Policy, a move which was intended on the face of things to liberalize the economy and society as a whole. Yet its initial impact in 1922 contained many aspects that were the reverse of this. This paradox was not so extreme as the one concerning the Party, nor was nearly so much hypocrisy involved. The combined aim of these two measures was to restore the economic and social health of a nation exhausted by constant warfare since 1914, whilst reinforcing the ideological purity and strength of its political heart—a kind of socialism in one part of the country. The overall intent seemed to be eminently sensible and in everyone's best interests. Only Lenin and a few others foresaw grave dangers for the future. Indeed, things could have been worse. If Lenin had died abruptly in 1921 or 1922, rather than linger on as a great stabilizing shadow until 1924, it is not inconceivable that Russia might have experienced a kind of Thermidor in the way revolutionary France had done. The immediate result of that volte-face was the Directory, a little-studied period which entailed above all the devolution of power locally on to the *départements*. In the light of what we know about guberniia life and administration in early NEP, it seems likely that the result of such a shift of power in Russia would have been anarchy, separatism, and a worse fate than that which she actually experienced during NEP.

So far we have been looking first at life at the grass roots, and then at political methods of control over it. The next two chapters will be chiefly concerned with the life of the mind in the areas where it flourished freely still, which was above all in the twin capitals. The first of these chapters deals with cultural affairs in Petrograd. The second will try to show the relationships, or lack of them, between political and social theories on the one hand as they appeared from 1922 to 1926, and the concrete conditions of Soviet society on the other.

# 6. Cultural Crossroads in Petrograd

THE fate of Petrograd as the supreme source of high political action for over two hundred years had been sealed from the moment when the Bolsheviks took the decision to move the government to Moscow in March 1918. The party leaders and their infant administrative machine were far from being the only drain on the city's human resources. Most of the aristocracy and all the Tsarist bureaucracy had vanished, and with them had gone the large number of foreigners whose money and connections had permeated the economic life of the city for so long. The labour vacuum created by the swift departure of the political, social, and economic élites was enormous. In 1910 about 200,000 people had been employed by government offices or private persons alone, that is roughly as many as were then working in the city's factories.[1] Scholarly accounts of the depopulation of Petrograd in the years 1917–21 have paid scant attention to the factors just mentioned. Much more has been made of the exodus to the countryside by all classes due to the shortage of food and fuel and to disease. Driven back into their former peasant way of life, or enticed in their thousands to the decimation that awaited them in the ranks of the Red Army, the city's factory workers had lost much of their political cohesion so painfully won in 1905 and 1917.

The vision of a doomed city that had dominated A. Bely's *St Petersburg* and many other pre-revolutionary prognostications seemed to have turned into a reality by the end of the Civil War. The Baltic experienced its worst winter for fifteen years in 1921–2. The perennial lack of market gardening and other agricultural activity in the city's hinterland, a phenomenon that had never been remedied throughout the nineteenth

[1] E. E. Kruze, 'Rabochie v Peterburge v gody novogo revoliutsion nogo podëma', in S. N. Valk (ed.), *Istoriia rabochikh Leningrada*, vol. 1 (Leningrad, 1972), p. 390.

century,[2] meant that famine would continue to threaten daily life even in peacetime. The highly artificial location of the Petrine dream, however beautifully wreathed in its architecture, became even more starkly clear as the outside world put up boards against its blank window.[3]

Yet for all this it is simply not possible to give an integrated account of politics and society in the early Soviet period without reference to Petrograd. Once any civilization sets up a new metropolis, however recent its origin, the tremendous effort involved nearly always leads to subsequent inertia, often for hundreds of years, despite all the odds. Russia's twin capital was to survive and flourish again. Even in the realm of high politics the influence of Petrograd was to be felt in Moscow on at least three occasions in the Soviet future—in 1926, then again at the time of Kirov's assassination in December 1934 which touched off the purges, and finally during the 'Leningrad affair' of 1949. Economic revival was to be slow but sure. At the close of the summer of 1921 the city's port had at last been reopened. By 1923 the volume of shipping tonnage entering and leaving Petrograd had increased by 240 per cent over the very low 1921 level.[4] River transport in the north-west *oblast'* went up by 3.4 times over the same period.[5] Nearly one and a half thousand *subbotniki* had helped regular workers to restore the local railway network in 1921.[6] Given the opportunity to move manufactured goods again, light industry was being resurrected in 1922. In the latter half of 1921 the old Skorokhod shoe-factory, the largest enterprise of the All-Russian Leather Trust, started full-time production once more.[7] It maintains its supremacy to this day, as any visitor to Tsarskoe Selo can see as he passes its impressive but decrepit length on the road to the south-west. Between November 1921 and March 1922 twenty textile plants set their looms going

[2] James H. Bater, *St Petersburg: Industrialisation and Change* (London, 1976).

[3] For an explanation of the artificiality of Petrograd's location with regard to the rest of Russia in political, economic, and geographical terms in 1917, Pethybridge, 'Petrograd and the Provinces', in *The Spread of the Russian Revolution: Essays on 1917* (London, 1972).

[4] Iu. Klimov, *V surovye gody dvadtsatye—Bolshevisci severo-zapada v bor'be za provedenie nepa v 1921–1925* (Murmansk, 1968).

[5] Ibid.

[6] Ibid., pp. 67–8.

[7] *Ocherki istorii Leningrada*, vol. 4 (Moscow, 1964), p. 232.

again.[8] For 1922–3 the volume of production in the city reached a quarter of its prewar level at 1913 prices.[9]

One cannot measure cultural production and dissemination precisely, but a primary aim of this chapter is to demonstrate that in several ways Petrograd remained at least the cultural equal of Moscow at the start of NEP, and still surpassed its rival in some fields. The balance of cultural power was to swing more decisively towards Moscow only in the latter part of the 1920s.

How are we to define the culture of Petrograd in 1922? Prosper Mérimée's Slav soul or the concept of the *Zeitgeist* are far too vague and Hegelian. Intellectuals and statesmen have all too often put together jigsaw puzzles of the artistic or political culture of their own or of past time which are nicely constructed myths, not realities. Mérimée should have known better. When he went down the Rhône to visit Provence for the first time, he announced that he felt as though he was landing in a foreign country.[10] Most sophisticated Parisians at the start of this century still divided France culturally speaking between Paris, Provence, Brittany, and the rest. Their ideal view was not the sum total of French regions, nor a reconciliation of them, but a crude reification. If this was the case, it is easy to see why we must beware of a monolithic interpretation in the vast Russian context. The infant Soviet Union was in the process of reincorporating nearly all those diverse minority nationalities that had formed part of the Empire. Its internal means of communication were roughly as effective as those of half a century earlier in France. Its external cultural persona was far less sharply defined in the rest of the world.

It was a French historian, Lucien Febvre, who first brought into sharper focus what he called the '*mentalité*' of a specific time and place. Even if the temporal aspect is narrowed to the span of NEP, the diversity of the spatial aspect in Russia is all but overwhelming. In this book only three Great-Russian provincial areas, Kursk, the Lower Volga, and Tver, and three non-Russian areas, Belorussia, the East Ukraine, and northern Kazakhstan, are covered. Some discrepancies between literary

---

[8] Ibid.
[9] Ibid., p. 244.
[10] P. Mérimée, *Notes d'un voyage dans le Midi de la France* (1835), p. 131.

culture in Petrograd and Moscow are taken up here, and the political culture of Moscow is treated in the next chapter. Even within Petrograd itself the picture is complex. Periods of social unrest leading to political revolution throw up newly articulate layers and mixed strata of cultural life, so that before 1917 two youths, the proletarian Gorky and the peasant Esenin, both from the provinces, had made an impression on the city. They were drawn from much lower-moving backwaters into the fast vortex of artistic and political events, leaving behind them a semi-literate older generation surrounded by an ocean of illiteracy.

Although the cultural periphery paid court to the centre, which still meant Petrograd rather than Moscow in 1922, it was not wholly a one-way process, nor had it been in the nineteenth century. That embodiment of local Russian folk-life, the *baian* (accordion),[11] was used extensively by Tchaikovsky in his second orchestral suite. At the heart of imperial Petersburg stands the Russian Museum. On view are *prianniki* (gingerbreads) and *lubki* (woodcuts) hailing from all parts of the country. Their designs inspired the Primitivist painters M. Larionov and N. Goncharova, who in turn influenced the abstract works of K. Malevich. In a myriad ways, of which these are just two examples, the remote cultural hinterland could invigorate the most *outré* cosmopolitan ventures. Petrograd culture, particularly at this time of revolutionary ferment, was like a sand-dune shifting under the influence of near and far-off pressures.

Engels in his correspondence with Russian political figures had noticed this feature, which was as prominent in political as in artistic culture: 'in a country like yours, where modern large-scale industry has been grafted on to the primitive peasant commune and where, at the same time, all the intermediate stages of civilisation coexist with each other . . . in the case of such a country one should not wonder at the emergence of the most incredible and bizarre combinations of ideas.'[12]

In political terms the far edges of the country remained

[11] To this day 1.2 million accordions are made annually in the Soviet Union: none of them is for export, and large numbers are imported.
[12] Engels in *Perepiska Marksa i Engelsa s russkimi politicheskimi deiatelami* (Moscow, 1951), p. 341.

oddly nonconformist compared to Moscow and Petrograd, despite the fact that the Civil War was officially over. Thus on 23 July 1922, at a meeting of the Vladivostok *Zemskii Sobor*, it was agreed by 207 votes to 23 that the Romanovs were the supreme power in the land: a delegation was chosen to go to negotiate with the Dowager Empress Maria and Grand Duke Nicholas.[13]

Artistic and political culture frequently overlap, and nowhere more often and incestuously than in Russia from the nineteenth century to the present day. No other literature of world stature has been so socially and politically involved, nor has any other censor been so active for so long. In the immediate post-revolutionary period the symbiotic relationship was even clearer than previously. In a frenzy of mutual utopian enthusiasm political and cultural leaders alike heralded the end of the old order and the swift arrival of the new. On several fronts their ideas temporarily interlocked, as in the Futurists' veneration for technology or V. Tatlin's well-known utopian monument to the Third International.[14] Both camps in 1922 still tended to underestimate nation-wide economic and geographical limits on conscious human actions, as opposed to theories. True, the wilder aspects of economic theory had been shelved with the abandonment of War Communism, but some of the examples of Petrograd cultural life in 1922 that will be discussed in a moment also reveal a precarious detachment from the roots of culture in its widest sense, which include the whole nation, its economy, and its soil. We have seen how the agricultural modes of Belorussia and particularly the Volga region vitally affected the local social and political culture, and the very political stability of the regime itself in the latter case. A sea of unrest spread through gubernii as far away from the Volga as Smolensk and lapped against the Kremlin walls themselves.

The following examples of cultural activity will now be treated—the literary group known as the Serapion Brothers; film production; political control over the life of the mind through the journals *Pechat' i revoliutsiia* (Press and Revolution)

[13] *Vladivostok Daily News*, 12 Aug. 1922.

[14] For a treatment of socio-political visions in the years prior to 1922 see 'Social Visions 1917–21', in Pethybridge, *The Social Prelude to Stalinism* (London, 1974).

and *Pod znamenem Marksizma* (Under the Banner of Marxism); and events at Petrograd University in 1922. All are cultural phenomena pervaded to a greater or lesser extent by political influences.

Culture is a slow-growing plant, so it would be highly artificial to examine any of its aspects in 1922 which omitted immersion in past culture as a variable. All of these case studies are redolent with the fragrance of the past. Changing official political attitudes may best be assessed at the theoretical and behavioural levels respectively through the prism of the journals and university life, but the Serapion Brothers provide the clearest example of the interaction between dying and nascent cultural patterns. In 1922 E. Zamiatin, who helped to form the group, wrote a *Story about the Most Important Thing* in which the present is sensed as a kaleidoscope of swiftly changing values. One significant school of thought, Proletkul't, had receded, but not until 1923 did another clearly orientated group arise, when Maiakovsky's Left Front of Art began publishing the magazine *Lef*. In terms of publications by individuals, 1922 was likewise a year of hiatus. Great writers from the past, including Gorky, predominated in the public's reading lists, together with a few contemporary lyrical poets from Petrograd like A. Akhmatova and O. Mandelstam (their respective collections *Anno Domini* and *Tristia* both appeared in 1922). Although three of the Serapion Brothers, V. Ivanov, N. Nikitia, and M. Slonimsky, produced stories in 1922, longer novels were at a premium. Lack of paper, publishing houses, sustained comfort and energy, and of a sufficient interval in which to take in the significance of the Revolution and the Civil War, meant that there was only one swallow of the literary revival of the 1920s, B. Pilniak's *The Naked Year*.

Of the Serapion Brothers themselves, however, it may be said that 1922 in Petrograd represented the apogee of their collective fame. Their first Almanac appeared in May, and their manifesto in August.[15] This was written by one member only, as if to stress their belief that '*Each* of us has his own ideology, his own political convictions; each one paints his home his own colour.' However, they were unanimous on two

---

[15] Lev Lunts, *Why We are the Serapion Brothers* (Petrograd, 1922).

points. They wished to remain free from political utilitarianism, and they admired the artistic fantasies of the hermit Serapion as described in E. T. A. Hoffmann's stories. These good intentions were to go sadly awry in the subsequent careers of most of them, and even at the start of NEP their diverse social and geographical origins together with their personal inclinations threw up differing political attitudes to Petrograd, Moscow, and the provinces, to the demands of the Bolshevik censor, and to the past and the future. Let us therefore stand at this particular cultural crossroads and look down these alternative approaches.

The Serapion Brothers included the prose writers K. Fedin, M. Zoshchenko, V. Kaverin, V. Ivanov, M. Slonimskii, and N. Nikitin; the poets N. Tikhorov and E. Polonskaia; the critics I. Gruzdev and V. Pozner; and the dramatist, critic, and short-story writer L. Lunts. All of them except V. Ivanov came from an intellectual milieu and had either been to St Petersburg University or high school in the city. K. Fedin, it is true, spent his childhood in the provinces (Saratov). E. Polonskaia and V. Pozner were not born in the capital, but at least they came from foreign capitals, having been born in Warsaw and Paris respectively. This strikingly close affiliation with St Petersburg culture was echoed in the social background of the Formalist literary group which exerted considerable influence on the Serapions, and which came in for political criticism in 1922 from Trotsky.[16] V. Ivanov on the other hand was born in a Siberian village and ran away from home at the age of 15 to join a circus. Subsequently he fought on both sides in the Civil War, and when he turned up in Petrograd in 1921 he repeated this feat in literary terms by joining both the Serapion Brothers and the Cosmists, a group of proletarian poets. The latter soon expelled him.

Fedin too fitted somewhat uneasily into the Serapion brotherhood. The son of a merchant, he had gone to Bavaria in 1914 to improve his command of German, but was kept there as a civilian war prisoner until 1918. In the tug of war that began in the summer of 1921 between the Brothers as to the respective merits of St Petersburg and Muscovite culture, and

---

[16] L. Trotsky, 'Formal'naia shkola poezii i marksizm', in *Literatura i revoliutsiia* (Moscow, 1923), pp. 119–35.

of the West and the East, Fedin at first appeared to side with the Eastern or Scythian wing, but in 1922 and for long afterwards he adopted a unique stance somewhere in the middle. In his later work he pondered on the relationship between Europe and Russia and on the fate of the old St Petersburg and the Russian intelligentsia. The issue of the orientation of past and future culture had come to a head at a lively meeting of the Brothers in December 1922. Lunts, a St Petersburg Jew who in this year entered the philological faculty of the University in order to teach West European literature, declared 'we need not defend Russian prose, it is great enough not to need defence, but to block it from its Western neighbour means to doom it to repeat what has already passed. . . . Therefore our motto is "Go West!"'[17] Fedin disagreed, and Ivanov and Nikitin also. These three wished to reflect the ideals of the Revolution in the content of their writings, whereas the Petersburg set were more interested in form and in the preoccupations of the Formalists. The dichotomies of East versus West and of art versus ideology were to reverberate through the minds of many other fellow-travellers writing in prose throughout NEP.[18]

In the Russian élitist mentality since the foundation of St Petersburg, the West had usually been associated with the banks of the Neva and the East with Moscow. During the nineteenth century this over-neat intellectual equation had been reinforced by the Westernizers and the Slavophils. In 1922 the perennial theme cropped up again in a new guise. The Serapion Brothers were suspicious of the increasing influence of Moscow in cultural affairs. It was the home of *Krasnaia nov'* (Red Virgin Soil), the first 'fat' journal that hoped to convert fellow-travellers to the Marxist viewpoint. It was also the centre of action for Maiakovsky, who a year later was to found *Lef*. Significantly the first Brothers to drift away towards Moscow, both spiritually and physically, were Fedin and Ivanov. With Nikitin they now linked up with A. Voronsky (the editor of *Red Virgin Soil*) and B. Pilniak to establish a new

[17] K. Fedin, *Gor'kii sredi nas* (revd. edn., Moscow, 1967), p. 72.
[18] See e.g. Iu. Olesha's difficulty in reconciling what he called 'artistic vision' and 'proper theme', I. Ilf and E. Petrov's mixture of *skaz* and adventure, and Babel's equal penchant for Russian ornamental and French literary styles.

Moscow publishing house, *Krug* (The Circle). Nikitin made things worse by inviting the Scythian Pilniak to the Brothers' weekly meetings in Petrograd. Pilniak's highly successful novel *The Naked Year* no doubt created envy. Its emphasis on the survival of Russian life far away from both Petrograd and Moscow, together with its preference for anti-European Bolshevik organizers set against a degenerate cultural aristocracy, must have touched a sensitive nerve in the old capital.

Ivanov and Nikitin began to publish stories in *Red Virgin Soil*. Nikitin belied his St Petersburg origins by filling his prose with provincialisms and neologisms. His head was turned by the fame of his work in Moscow circles. Ivanov, often in Moscow, absented himself increasingly from the meetings of the Brothers, and in the mid-1920s moved to the new capital for good. The seepage to Moscow was not confined to the Serapions, nor to the literary sphere alone. Although 1922 represented a kind of vacuum with regard to clearly defined literary groups, it did witness the foundation of the Constructivists, who included artists as well as writers. They were the newest and most 'progressive' of three overlapping artistic strata and generations in 1922. The oldest stratum were aesthetes of the stamp of A. Lunacharsky, who had been much impressed by West European cultural ideas in the pre-revolutionary period. Next came the Futurist poets, painters like Larionov and Goncharova, and several rank-and-file Bolsheviks. Many of the early publications of the Futurist writers had been illustrated by these two artists. The Constructivists were drawn to a far greater extent than the two other strata from provincial and lower-class backgrounds. Their first artistic manifesto was published in 1922, not in Petrograd nor in Moscow, but in Tver. Its author, A. Gan, proclaimed that 'Art is dead!' Mastery of urban technology was to be the key to the new cultural life, with the working man of Moscow as its new master. In 1925 the literary Constructivists were to publish a symposium of their works entitled *Gosplan literatury* (The State Plan of Literature). There was nothing new in the notion of Moscow as the centre for the most avant-garde art movements in the whole of Europe. It had already fulfilled this role between 1907 and 1910. Already in 1918 most 'leftist' Petrograd artists had gone to Moscow, which in May 1922 witnessed an exhibition, in aid of famine relief, of paintings staged by the newly founded Association of Artists Studying Revolutionary Life.

Small wonder then, that Lunts envisaged the Serapion Brothers as being threatened by 'Muscovite glory, Muscovite criticism, Muscovite loyalties'.[19] He also, by implication, castigated Pilniak and all non-metropolitan creativity in his speech given to Brothers on 2 December 1922: 'The misfortune is that the majority of our prose writers proceeded to the very place we had abandoned. To Populism! You are Populists, typical Russian provincials, and *boring, boring* writers.'[20]

Even as of 1922, let alone later, the Serapion Brothers were far from being a cohesive group. Rather they were a third alternative which existed for those who were neither Futurists nor in Proletkul't. At first they were indeed all *poputchiki* (fellow-travellers), but then Trotsky, who coined the phrase, listed Pilniak as a typical poputchik[21] as well. The Brothers were so amorphous that Fedin, an ex-party member, oddly believed himself to be on its 'right wing'.[22] They came together because they thought it would be easier to publish as a group and to stay free from political pressures. In this they were sadly mistaken. Their main patron was Maxim Gorky, who continued to write to many of them and send them parcels of food and clothes after he left Russia on 16 October 1921. Gorky from 1917 to 1924 was a staunch upholder of the educated classes and of culture, a term which often took on a disparaging meaning at this time. He was careful to steer his protégés through the political rapids. He advised Fedin to associate with the House of the Arts on the Moika canal, founded with Gorky's help on 19 December 1919. Most of the other Serapions followed suit, abandoning the rival Writers' House on Vasil'evskii Island. Gorky referred to the members of the latter institution as remnants of the past.[23] However this judicious

[19] 'Posledniaia stat'ia L'va Luntsa', *Novyi zhurnal*, 81 (Dec. 1976), p. 101.

[20] From a speech by L. Lunts delivered on 2 Dec. 1922 entitled 'Go West!', subsequently published in the Berlin émigré journal *Beseda*.

[21] Trotsky, op. cit., p. 41.

[22] Fedin, 'V poriadke ankety', *Sobranie sochinenii*, vol. 9 (Moscow, 1962), pp. 546–7.

[23] Fedin, *Gor'kii sredi nas*, p. 26. Quoted in an article by B. Scherr, 'Notes on Literary Life in Petrograd, 1918–1922: A Tale of Three Houses', *Slavic Review*, 36 (1977), p. 263.

move did not pay off. At the end of 1922 both clubs were suddenly closed down. The official reason given in the case of the House of the Arts was financial maladministration, but most observers believed that Grigorii Zinoviev, head of the Leningrad party organization, had taken the decision. Political interference did not stop there. Zamiatin, the Serapions' other main patron, was put in prison for a brief period. V. Shklovsky, a prominent Serapion, felt it necessary to flee abroad to avoid arrest, and from Berlin he wrote: 'I lived with them [the Serapions] in one house. And I think that the GPU [the secret police] will not get angry at them for the fact that I drank tea with them.'[24]

In his history of Soviet Russia, E. H. Carr notes that in 1924 only did non-political literature become the subject of a resolution at a party congress. This is correct, but not so his other claim that literary controversies in general did not take on a political contour until 1923.[25] From the moment in the middle of 1918 when the Bolsheviks ordered the closing of all opposition journals, authors of all hues had been extremely limited as to where they could publish. In the year 1922 there are many examples in Petrograd alone of political intervention. One has merely to read through the journal *Pechat' i Revoliutsiia* in order to realize this. An article on the law and publishing asserts that 'All theoretical jurists ... stress the right of the state power ... to restrict citizens' liberties, not only in the interest of preserving these freedoms, but also in order to protect the basis of a law-abiding society.'[26] The author does not hesitate to cite a Tsarist article of 1909 by G. Meyer which maintains that the subjective rights of the citizen should not prevail over the state interest. From another 1922 article we learn of the actual censorship of literary and technical items. Between January and May alone, 41.6 per cent of all technical manuscripts in Petrograd were censored.[27] The Serapions themselves came under heavy fire. When S. Gorodetsky, ex-poet and now a

[24] V. Shklovsky, *Sentimental'noe puteshestvie, Vospominaniia 1917–1922* (Berlin, 1923), pp. 377–81.

[25] E. H. Carr, *A History of Soviet Russia*, vol. 6 (London, 1959), pp. 82 and 76 respectively.

[26] M. Shchelkunov, 'Zakonodatel'stvo o pechati za piat' let', *Pechat' i revoliutsiia* (Aug.–Sept. 1922), p. 173. See also pp. 185–7 for other arguments.

[27] *Pechat' i revoliutsiia* (July–Aug. 1922), pp. 131–2.

party member, found the Brothers' stories 'ideologically empty', Lunts cheekily counter-attacked, but was subdued by another broadside from V. Poliansky, the head of the censorship board, who pronounced ominously: 'Outside of ideology there is no salvation. Emptiness and grimacing, death and withering await its opponents.'[28]

The Brothers had hailed the Revolution as a licence for the fantastic imagination of the hermit Serapion as well as the liberation of the toiling masses. By the end of 1922 neither goal seemed to be remotely in sight. As late as March 1923 Gorky still held out great hopes for the Serapions *as a group*,[29] but he was abroad and out of touch. In fact, as we have seen, some of them had already defected to Moscow and safer political pastures. Most of those left in Petrograd had transferred their allegiance from the two clubs closed down to the Scholars' House near by. This institution had also been set up by the tireless Gorky in his role as head of the Petrograd division of the Commission to Improve Scholars' Living Conditions (*Kubu*). When they were still at the House of the Arts the Serapions had gone over to the Scholars' House to collect the free Kubu food ration[30] and to chat with some of the academicians and professors encountered later in this chapter. The Scholars' House survives to the present day in the same location, and in a later chapter we shall look at the careers of some of the scientists who passed through its doors in 1926. The Soviet world of culture was still a tiny and somewhat claustrophobic élite during NEP, reminiscent in this way of its Tsarist predecessor.

As the years went by, one after the other most of the surviving Serapions turned into subservient party hacks. One endearing trait, their brotherly friendship, survived for a long time. Through the terrifying 1930s some of them continued to meet on 1 February each year, and they comforted Zosh-

[28] See S. Gorodetskii, 'Zelen' pod plesen'fu', *Izvestiia*, 22 Feb. 1933; S. Lunts, 'Ob ideologii i publistike' (Leningrad, Oct. 1922); V. Polianskii, 'Ob ideologii v literature', in I. Oksënov (ed.), *Sovremennaia russkaia kritika* (Leningrad, 1925), pp. 98–107.

[29] 'Je suis le développement et les progrès spirituels des "Serapions" avec de grands espoirs. Il me semble que ces jeunes gens sont capables do fonder une nouvelle littérature en Russie ...' Letter of M. Gorky, published in *Le Disque Vert* (Brussels, 1923), p. 63.

[30] See M. L. Slonimskii, *Sobranie sochinenii*, vol. 4 (Leningrad, 1970), p. 401.

chenko in his political troubles. When Zoshchenko was expelled from the Writers' Union in August 1946, his fellow brother Tikhonov was simultaneously removed as Secretary of its Executive Board. In January 1968 Kaverin broke the long truce between brothers when he reproved Fedin in an open letter for his role in the suppression of *Doctor Zhivago*. The grim prophecy of V. Poliansky, the 1922 censor, had finally been fulfilled by one of the Serapions themselves: 'Outside of ideology there is no salvation.'

As far as the nascent Soviet cinema industry was concerned, the limits of what was ideologically permissible in 1922 were as hazy, or even more vague in some respects, than they appeared to the Serapions at that time. Despite Lenin's famous *mot* in 1922 on the political usefulness of the cinema as propaganda,[31] experimental groups independent of the Bolsheviks flourished,[32] and particularly in Petrograd, which was undoubtedly still the Soviet capital of film-making in 1922. In 1921 a 'laboratory' had been set up by FEKS (the Factory of the Eccentric Actor), and in 1922 it published an artistic manifesto in which the group turned its back on the old culture of Europe, but looked to American jazz, dance, and technology for inspiration. At its first exhibition in September 1922, held on the premises of Proletkul't, another wayward cultural phenomenon that came more closely under Lenin's scrutiny than FEKS ever did, further emphasis was put on the dynamic optimism and efficient industrial rhythm of the United States. A poster proclaimed that Gogol would soon be electrified.[33] Now it is interesting to note that in the following year Lenin was so enthused by an American film showing the production of tractors at the Ford factory that he had it slowed down for closer inspection.[34] This interest in another American idea,

---

[31] 'Of all the arts the cinema is the most important for us', *Lenin o kul'ture i isskustve* (Moscow, 1956), p. 529.
[32] Private firms had not ceased to produce films throughout the Civil War. See the article on the early Soviet cinema by K. Betz in N. A. Nilsson, *Art, Society, Revolution: Russia 1917–1921* (Stockholm, 1979).
[33] Presumably this was finally achieved much later in the USA itself with the monstrous distortion of Gogol's *The Government Inspector* in the film starring Danny Kaye.
[34] Cited in *Gudok*, 22 Apr. 1957.

Taylorism,[35] helps us to realize that as of 1922 there was no great political danger involved for lesser mortals who were likewise partial to capitalist modes of thought. Members of FEKS maintained close connections with the Serapions Shklovsky and Tikhonov. Another eminent individualist joined the ranks of FEKS in 1922—Sergei Eisenstein. It was evident, however, that some distinctions had to be drawn in order to stay on the right side of the censor. An interview with Leonid Trauberg, one of the leading FEKS film producers, elicited his detestation of American racist and sexual films.[36]

Although, as we shall see, no definitive curbs had been put on private enterprise in the film industry by the end of 1922, governmental attitudes were hardening in this year. Most film activity centred on Petrograd rather than Moscow. Indeed this had been the case since the Revolution. On 30 April 1918, the first Soviet cinema organization, the forerunner of *Lenfilm*,[37] was established in Petrograd. In the following year two schools were set up in the city for training technical experts and artistic producers.[38] From September 1920 onwards more attention was paid to the needs of all the north-west and even, in theory at least, to the purchase and sale of films abroad. This initiative bore fruit in 1922 with the formal organization of *Sevzapkino* (the north-western regional cinema administration), which at the time was the nation's chief co-ordinator of film distribution.

Lenin himself devoted a considerable portion of his energies to the cinema in 1922. He kept an open mind on the extent to which the industry would have to be centrally controlled. On 17 January he instructed the Commissariat for Enlightenment (*Narkompros*) to compile a film index which would distinguish carefully between propaganda and more frivolous material. He believed there was a particular need for the dissemination of the right kind of film (politically speaking) amongst the peasants in the localities. In February Lenin quizzed Luna-

[35] For more on Lenin's interest in Taylorism and his other utopian enthusiasms of this period, see Pethybridge, *The Social Prelude to Stalinism* (London, 1974), pp. 38–40.

[36] M. Verdone and B. Amengual, *La Feks* (Lyons, 1970), p. 35. In his Jan. directive, Lenin had inveighed against obscenity in entertainment films. See *Kino-Nedeliia*, 21 Jan. 1925, p. 6.

[37] *Iz istorii Lenfilma. Stat'i, vospominaniia, dokumenty* (3rd edn., Leningrad, 1971), p. 80.

[38] *Ocherki istorii Leningrada*, vol. 4 (Leningrad, 1964), p. 816.

charsky, the head of Narkompros, in person. He was told that few 'reliable' producers existed, and that funds for buying scarce film and for productions were lacking. Financial stringency in 1922, combined with capitalist competition in the cultural sphere as a result of NEP conditions, presented a frequent threat to Bolshevik predominance. Lenin contended that Bolshevik-inspired films could in the future bring in an excellent income, though he thought that the time was not yet ripe for propaganda material based on current events.[39]

He did not go on to give reasons for his diffidence, but it probably had to do with the confused and disillusioned state of the country at the outset of NEP. Lenin's repeated refusal to be filmed himself for the record and for propaganda purposes brought to light some other interesting reasons. After shooting a mere 20 m. of Lenin in action in November 1921, one producer was told curtly: 'There's no point in wasting film. It will be needed for more serious things.'[40] In February 1922 Lenin rejected an offer from P. I. Voevodin, the chairman of *Glavpolitprosvet*, who had been ordered by Krupskaia in 1921 to organize the film industry,[41] to make a film of his life and work. The hireling appeared to be a more rigid Marxist than his master and mistress. Voevodin insisted that 'correct attention to the historical process and the correct interpretation of the role and personality of the leader of the proletariat is of overriding importance to me.'[42] Krupskaia, replying for Lenin on 18 February 1922, wrote that Soviet film technique was 'very bad' and too expensive. Her husband's biographical details were incorrectly given, and the result would look like an inferior popular woodcut (*lubok*). Thus the subject of so many subsequent filmed hagiographies refused to be embalmed in life. The only moving pictures of Lenin known to me for 1922, and the last shots ever taken, are of him 'approaching . . . with his usual rapid gait' at the fourth Comintern Congress on 13 November.[43] Instead Lenin concentrated on the economic

[39] See G. M. Boltiansky (ed.), *Lenin i kino* (Moscow, 1925), pp. 16–19.

[40] Reported by the film-maker A. Levitsky in 'Moi vospominaniia', *Kino*, 4 (22 Jan. 1933).

[41] P. I. Voevodin, 'Tak uchil Il'ich', in *Don*, 4 (1960), pp. 29–31.

[42] *Samoe vazhnoe iz vsekh iskusstv: Lenin i kino* (Moscow, 1973), p. 100.

[43] A. M. Gak (ed.), *Lenin. Sobranie fotografii i kinokadrov*, vol. 2 (Moscow, 1972), p. 466.

substructure rather than on the role of the individual in the superstructure. Impatient letters in June and July issuing from the Sovnarkom but instigated by Lenin complained that a film ordered in 1921 on turf-extraction for the instruction of the peasantry had still not been made.[44]

The Party aimed at strict control of the cinema as early as 1922, but was thwarted on various fronts. Lenfilm, its very core, was saturated with aristocratic trainees who sold off their elegant clothes and precious objects in order to survive. A commoner who gained entry in 1922 was interviewed initially by Count Bibikov, a dandy with fine manners.[45]

Sevzapkino was more orthodox in its personnel, but it was hindered by financial difficulties. Film was a scarce commodity, expensive, and it took time to obtain abroad. In 1921 there had been a money surplus, but this had arisen since no account had been taken of vital forward expenditure for 1922 on film, equipment, publicity, and administration costs.[46] The change-over to khozraschet in NEP obscured the position further. Thirteen Petrograd cinemas were restored in 1922, but it was costly to heat them properly. No doubt the majority of the 3,254,520 visits during 1922 to the city's eighty-eight cinemas[47] were made to the private-sector houses which showed *Tarzan* and *Lady Hamilton* (a German film!) and were better heated from their greater profits. Lenin had shrewdly realized this trend in January. He advised that state receipts could be improved by showing entertainment and propaganda films together, and that private-building rentals should be heavily taxed. In October he received Charles Recht, an American lawyer, who told him that twenty million Americans went to the cinema every day. Lenin seriously considered his offer of capital to develop the Soviet film industry. Joseph Schenk, a Russian exile, offered to return to give advice.[48] Lenin pondered. At the start of NEP it was assumed that foreign capital could be widely and safely used to restore the economy. This

[44] Boltiansky, op. cit., p. 90.

[45] *Iz istorii Lenfil'ma*, vol. 2, pp. 111–13.

[46] S. Bratoluibov, *Na zare sovetskoi kinematografii* (Leningrad, 1976), p. 45.

[47] *XV let diktatury proletariata. Ekonomiko-statisticheskii sbornik po Leningrada i Leningradskoi oblasti* (Leningrad, 1932), tables, pp. 160–1. The figures for 1921 and 1926 respectively were 2,706,625 and 10,957,720.

[48] *Samoe vazhnoe*, pp. 105–7.

was to be a vain hope in all spheres including the cinema. Perhaps piqued by Krupskaia's strictures, Voevodin had already protested in February that a huge wave of old foreign films would overwhelm official productions unless more equipment could be imported at once from Berlin.[49] Indeed no Soviet feature film was made until 1923, and even FEKS did not produce a single item in 1922. Sevzapkino only managed to release five films of any length in 1922.[50]

Late in 1922 *Kinosever*, the distributive arm of Sevzapkino, was formed. It hastily spent 52,000 gold roubles on enlarging four city cinemas. It also ordered 75,000 metres of film from abroad, outbidding in price its Moscow-based equivalent. One of the main reasons for the establishment of the nation-wide *Goskino* in 1923 was to prevent cultural rivalry between the twin capitals and to try to centralize culture, propaganda, and government for good in Moscow. In 1922 Kinosever extended its influence, not just to the vicinity of Petrograd and the Karelian SSR, but to Belorussia, Saratov, and Samara, and even to Yaroslavl and Vladimir, which were not so far from Moscow.[51] Lunacharsky admitted late in 1922 that the centralized censorship advocated by Lenin in January was not yet effective.[52] By 1925 he still had to allow for the continued predominance of purely entertainment films: 'Vladimir Ilyich's idea of a proportional composition for each programme has not been realized to this day. To make up for this, we have, of course, progressed somewhat as far as film production is concerned, but only recently . . . even now we are more inclined to place hope in the future than to demonstrate the achievements of the present.'[53]

Sentiments like these provided the leitmotiv for so many cultural sectors, especially at the start of NEP, from utopian architectural plans which remained on the drawing-board to the gigantic unrealized projects of the Constructivists. Nevertheless two industrious film-makers were active as of 1922, both of them in Petrograd. One of them, D. Vertov, was

[49] Ibid., pp. 86–7.
[50] Z. V. Stepanov, *Kul'turnaia zhizn' Leningrada 20-x–nachala 30-x godov* (Leningrad, 1976), p. 133.
[51] Bratoliubov, op. cit., p. 48.
[52] *Lunacharskii o kino* (Moscow, 1965), p. 222.
[53] Boltiansky, op. cit., pp. 16–19.

a near genius. In his plan of action he shied away from 'the sweet embraces of romance' in older films: 'Our path is from the turgid citizen through the poetry of the machine to the complete electric man.'[54] Back to electrification. Lenin's rather utopian vision of its benefits[55] affected many contemporaries, but at least Vertov converted ideas into realities, since his second documentary in 1922 depicted the opening of the Kashir hydroelectric station. He was convinced that due to widespread illiteracy, chaotic statistics, and lack of time for writing weighty histories, the only way future students could understand early NEP would be by watching his documentary films from the series *Kinopravda*. Five of them appeared in 1922. There is some truth, although exaggerated, in this view. So much evidence from a mainly oral society slips through the net of recorded memory. Unfortunately, when one looks at the total list of films brought out in 1922, more of them have been lost for ever than have been preserved.[56]

Vertov was to announce in 1923 that 'I am a mechanical eye',[57] but despite the fact that his documentaries were influenced by the unorthodox Proletkul't, and included entirely neutral material on Caucasian spas and the Red Derby horse-race, he had to toe the political line on more serious matters. His film on the staged trial of the Social Revolutionaries focused on workers demonstrating in favour of punishing the defendants even before the trial had proved them to be supposedly guilty. At the same time he accused FEKS of planning 'art' films that would distort reality.[58] However by the 1930s his idiosyncratic and highly original techniques annoyed the authorities so much that he eventually ran foul of the censor.

The other prolific film-maker in 1922 was A. Panteleev, less gifted but more malleable than Vertov. He had made romantic melodramas, of the kind despised by Vertov, for Tsarist audiences since 1915. In 1922 he satisfied Lenin with *The Miracle Maker* (since lost), a mildly anti-religious film. In *No*

[54] D. Vertov, 'My. Variant manifesta', *Kino-Fot*, 1 (1922).
[55] See the list in *Sovetskie khudozhestvennye fil'my. Annotirovannyi katalog. Nemye fil'my, 1918–1935*, vol. 1 (Moscow, 1961), pp. 32–7.
[56] 'Kinoki. Perevorot', *Lef*, 3 (1923).
[57] See N. P. Abramov, *Dziga Vertov* (Moscow, 1962), p. 42.
[58] *Nizhegorodskaia kommuna*, 18 Mar. 1924.

*Happiness on Earth* he warns of the nascent economic and sexual vices of NEP, whilst adopting an ambivalent attitude to America and to Russian émigrés. The wife of an impecunious employee sells home-made food in the streets and is seduced by an 'American', who turns out to be an émigré friend of her husband. Her spouse kills himself, she loses her reason. This odd combination of pre-revolutionary 'bourgeois' sentimentality and doctrinaire propaganda is repeated in his *Infinite Sadness*. The wife and son of a Petrograd medical student sent to relatives on the Volga for health reasons flee from the 1921 famine. The son is chopped up and relished by famished peasants. The mother loses her reason (again). The penitent student organizes a medical group to go to the Volga to help in the famine. This moral tale on the need for town and country mutual aid (smychka) played to nearly full houses in Petrograd and was even recommended to W. Münzenberg in Germany as a fund-raiser abroad for famine relief in Russia. Doubtless the romantic blood and thunder appealed more than the gloss on Marxist teaching. In a bizarre exchange, Lenin ordered that a documentary film on the 'famine' in Berlin should be distributed round Russia, presumably in order to show the starving that they did not suffer alone.[59]

Clearly by the end of 1922 no governmental monopoly existed over film production, and even the officially inspired cinema still contained many traits derived from the pre-revolutionary era. On 24 December Lunacharsky told the Tenth All-Russian Congress of Soviets that some films would serve the Bolsheviks as a source of revenue rather than as propaganda material. He still looked to private and foreign capital investment in order to resuscitate the Soviet cinema.[60]

To judge by the Serapion Brothers and the cinema alone, one might conclude that the regime was making no headway at the start of NEP in its practical efforts to monitor culture from a political point of view. Indeed subsequent observers have frequently maintained that NEP entailed a climate of general relaxation in all spheres, political, economic, and social as well as cultural. However, when one comes to examine high-level

[59] *Kino-Nedelia*, 21 Jan. 1925, p. 6.    [60] *Lunacharskii o Kino*, p. 222.

Bolshevik ideological thinking in 1922, it is clear that an urgent need was felt already that cultural weapons must be manufactured and prepared for action precisely because the regime would soon find itself like a besieged fortress surrounded by economic and social unorthodoxy. Nowhere is this trend more easily discernible than in the sudden efflorescence of the official cultural journals that sprang up in 1922, many of them in Petrograd. We can proceed from general Bolshevik theories to organizational particulars by looking first at *Pod znamenem Marksizma*, which was set up to clarify the Marxist attitude to friends and foe alike. *Pechat'i revoliutsiia* laid down the more detailed rules by which the new orthodox press media would be guided.

The first editorial of *Pod znamenem Marksizma* claimed that the journal had 'arisen from the legitimate desire of the young proletarian intelligentsia to reflect on the present time', and was to act as a 'tribune for the broad working-masses'. A letter of 27 February 1922 from Trotsky is cited, in which he stresses that younger workers would have to acquire through books and governmental work the kind of experience that had been actually lived out by older generations.[61] Subsequently the editor of the Moscow journal *Rabochaia Moskva* wrote to his fellow editor asking for regular annotated lists of recently published Marxist literature which would be of more use to factory workers than the highbrow articles that had appeared so far in *Pod znamenem Marksizma*.[62] In an earlier article Lenin himself had suggested that the masses should be given a varied diet of eighteenth-century tracts to digest.[63] This was a case of handing caviare to the general, as had been hinted in the first number of the journal, where it was noted that in April 1917

[61] The two journals analysed here were but the spearhead of a phalanx of new journals intended to marshal cultural life in the Bolshevik interest. *Kommunisticheskaia revoliutsiia*, originating in 1920, was the organ of the *Agitprop* department of the Party Central Committee. On 13 Feb. 1922 *Trud* announced the start of *Novyi Mir*, a new literary journal which was 'to struggle with the old, rotten inheritance'. Education was covered by *Na Putiakh k novoi shkole*, founded in 1922 and soon to be monitored by the Society of Marxist Pedagogues of the Communist Academy. The Academy initiated its own organ, the *Vestnik Kommunisticheskoi Akademii* in 1922. An ideological counterblast came from Russian exiles in Prague in 1923 with the title *Russkaia shkola za rubezham* (the Russian school abroad).

[62] *Pod znamenem Marksizma*, 1 (1922).

[63] Ibid., 3 (1922), pp. 120–1.

P. Maslov had written to the Petrograd Soviet pointing out that political revolution unaccompanied by the development of productive forces or of industry would lead to more unemployment and the destruction of the proletariat as it existed in 1917.[64] The huge reduction that actually took place in the numbers of the Petrograd proletariat between 1917 and 1922 was referred to at the start of this chapter. It was a phenomenon that occurred on a lesser scale throughout the cities of European Russia.

There is a contradiction in Bolshevik attitudes here. Lenin had recently attacked Proletkul't on orthodox Marxist grounds for trying to introduce the superstructure of proletarian culture before the new socialist substructure had been given time to evolve, but now he was trying to force exotic ideological food down unreceptive or non-existent throats. He showed more perspicacity in advocating a mixed diet for the cinema. It was not that he was ignorant of the true state of affairs, as is shown by his comment on the provisional census of 1920 which showed that under 300 out of every 1,000 Soviet citizens could read and write: 'This shows how much urgent, laborious work we have to do in order to reach the level of a normal, civilized West European state.'[65] We have noted that Trotsky also assumed that factory workers would pore avidly over Marxist texts, yet he was just then composing his *Literature and Revolution*, in which he inveighed against Proletkul't's naïve assumptions. Other leading members of the pro-Bolshevik intelligentsia— M. N. Pokrovsky, P. F. Preobrazhensky, D. Riazanov—contributed to *Pod znamenem Marksizma* in 1922 and all took the same over-optimistic view. There is no clear explanation for such a contradiction, but it was probably motivated by a sense of urgency. It was less important that the proletariat should at once produce the right kind of literary work or watch correct films than that its political views should not be adulterated by the corrosive economic and social climate of NEP.

In fact the great bulk of the articles and reviews in *Pod znamenem Marksizma* were to be aimed not at the proletariat nor even less so at the peasantry, but at ideological foes subsisting at the same rarefied intellectual level as the contributors. Apart

[64] Ibid., 2 (1922), p. 7.
[65] Lenin, *O narodnom obrazovanii. Stat'i i rechi* (Moscow, 1957), pp. 414 ff.

from occasional rallies against the continuing hold of religion over the masses,[66] the problem of disseminating and vulgarizing high-level propaganda was left to *Pechat' i revoliutsiia*, as we shall see.

Many of the ideological foes now lived abroad, but the authors of *Pod znamenem Marksizma* did not leave them in peace. Indeed a large proportion of articles was devoted to this sector. The Civil War was hardly over, and the cultural battle dragged on. Some military opponents were dead, but the great majority of the political adversaries, on the left as well as on the right, flourished in Berlin, Prague, Paris, and London, and dispatched their counter-arguments in prolific journals of their own which still penetrated the inexperienced Soviet censor. The competing forces of the pre-1917 progressive intelligentsia were still locked in debate although scattered geographically. Until the end of NEP hundreds of the most eminent representatives of the external diaspora drifted in and out of Russia, undecided as to their final geographical and ideological resting-place.

It is too often assumed that from the magic moment of October 1917 Bolshevik ideology bore no resemblance whatsoever to Menshevik, Anarchist, Socialist Revolutionary, or to Russian Idealist thinking. Certainly Lenin abandoned all connections with the Anarchists when he came into power, but the subsequent bitter recriminations from the side of the Anarchists and the over-careful and repeated Bolshevik assertion reflected in many articles in *Pod znamenem Marksizma*, that they had never been near to each other, not even concerning tactics during 1917, belies the fact that both factions were then obsessed with creating disorder.[67] As late as 1922 many social groups remote from the main political and ideological powerhouses of Petrograd and Moscow still confused Bolshevik with Anarchist and Socialist Revolutionary doctrines. Contributors to the journal in 1922 frequently pointed out also that one of the main reasons for the promotion of class struggle among the

---

[66] See e.g. *Pod znamenem Marksizma*, 2, pp. 5 ff; 8, pp. 184 ff.

[67] For an example of the Bolsheviks' continuing concern to distinguish themselves from Anarchism, see the article 'Anarkhizm i Marksizm v massovom dvizhenii', in *Pod znamenem Marksizma*, 3, pp. 86 ff. For the whole of 1917, no *Times* leader article distinguished between the two, so it is not surprising that some elements in the Soviet masses still required clarification in 1922.

peasantry was to show the latter how the Bolsheviks differed from the Socialist Revolutionaries.[68]

During 1922, however, by far the greater bulk of the articles and reviews in *Pod znamenem Marksizma* dealt with the identification of the multifarious political attitudes of the Russian intelligentsia resident within and outside the country. The peasantry had been placated by the introduction of NEP, whilst the decimated proletariat was supposed to be the meek audience for the journal, as its first editorial had pointed out. Presumably the workers did not wish or were not intended to read about their own sorry state as their trade unions continued to lose influence. It was no easy task to categorize the intelligentsia, as is clear from the kaleidoscopic social, cultural, and political divergences even in the microcosmic world of the Serapion Brothers. Moreover, like the proletariat, the old intelligentsia had modified its political views considerably since the October Revolution. Like the Kadet party, most of the pre-1917 intelligentsia had non-partisanship written into their programme, and like the Kadets most of them became increasingly identified in 1917 with the bourgeoisie, despite the fact that this was incorrect from a sociological point of view. The intellectual isolation that had led to the distinctive features of the Russian intelligentsia in the nineteenth century was now reinforced, but instead of strengthening internal ties as in the past, it now weakened them. Whilst some groups of intellectuals were strongly opposed to governmental interference in their cultural mission, others welcomed it. When Gorky set up the society 'Culture and Freedom' in Petrograd in April 1918 with the aim of uniting socialist intellectuals, younger elements within it resisted, and some of them entered Proletkul't circles. At the end of March 1918 the Petrograd Union of Russian Writers recorded its disillusionment with the ignorant and savage masses.[69]

It came as no surprise, therefore, that Lenin opposed as 'nonsensical' Lunacharsky's statement, also made at the end of March 1918, that the regime had 'nothing against a *modus vivendi* with the most intelligent and creative strata of the

[68] See e.g. *Pod znamenem Marksizma*, 3, p. 106.
[69] *Vechernye ogni* (Petrograd) 1 Apr. 1918. In my interpretation of the schisms within the 'new' intelligentsia I have been influenced by the valuable article by C. Rougle in N. Å. Nilsson (ed.), *Art, Society, Revolution in Russia 1917–1921* (Stockholm, 1979), pp. 54–105.

bourgeoisie'.[70] The unpopularity of the intelligentsia and its own disarray made it possible for Lenin to divide and rule at leisure. After 1918 Proletkul't had borne the first onslaught from the Party. When that internal heresy had been suppressed, it appears by 1922 that the main adversary had become the so-called 'Idealists'. The term sometimes degenerated into an umbrella term of abuse in the pages of *Pod znamenem Marksizma*. The new 'Library of Materialism' series of publications was introduced with a fanfare against 'the idealist twaddle' of all West European socialist doctrines.[71] A critic of A. A. Bogdanov's theory of class more accurately labelled that theory as 'essentially idealist',[72] but the real targets by 1922 were not the genuine idealists of the left but of the right, both inside and outside Russia.

Control rather than suppression was the aim, as Professor Pokrovsky declared in his review of an internally published idealist critique of Marxism. That such a work could still appear was for him 'proof of the freedom of the press and of thought'.[73] In a survey of the first number of *Russkaia mysl'*, the organ of the Russian Idealists, their religious and capricious tendencies were exaggerated and then contrasted with the iron constancy of Marxist scientific laws.[74] Elsewhere it was maintained that religious idealism was the last card of the Russian 'bourgeoisie', a card that had been played by foreign idealists in 1789 and 1848 without success.[75] When an author wrote in *Russkaia mysl'* on the freedom opened up by religion, a Bolshevik critic recalled the acts of suppression carried out in the name of the obscurantist Tsarist Church. In another place the reader was reminded how the masses had decisively rejected religion in the course of the preceding year under the impact of Bolshevik teaching, the new school system, the evident decadence of the Church, and its reluctance to give financial aid in

[70] *Novaia zhizn'*, 29 Mar. 1918.
[71] *Pod znamenem Marksizma*, 3 (1922), p. 124.
[72] Ibid., 7, p. 100.
[73] Review of R. Vipper, *Krizis istoricheskoi nauki* (Kazan', 1921), in ibid., 3, p. 37.
[74] *Pod znamenem Marksizma*, 3, p. 122.
[75] Ibid., 5, pp. 82 ff, and pp. 94–5.

the great famine.[76] Thus the rather nebulous naïvety of the Idealists was easily rivalled by Bolshevik crudity of thought: 'How can science exist, where a god is seated on a throne, in the form of an "absolute being", who does not submit to any objective laws?'[77]

No doubt some of the more abstract flights of Idealist fancy, both at home and in Berlin, Prague, or elsewhere were reactions to the sad realities of post-revolutionary Russian life. Much effort was put into prophetic visions of the future, away from what one Idealist writer called 'the world of habitual reality'.[78] Yet were the leading Bolsheviks, most of whom were heirs of the same amorphous intelligentsia as the Idealists, all that different in some ways? When P. Struve in *Russkaia mysl'* praised the 'metaphysical people' and its great Russian spirit, a reviewer in *Pod znamenem Marksizma* replied that this concept did not 'include a single concrete person, it is not the people of Russian workers, peasants, artisans, etc.'[79] Neither, perhaps, did the increasingly influential Bolshevik reifications of the proletariat, nor of the supposedly three clearly separable peasant strata—'*kulak*', middle, and poor. As for predictions of the future, many Bolshevik ideologists could outdo the Idealists, and their more utopian representatives were no less oblivious of recalcitrant contemporary conditions.[80] As for the supposed dichotomy between Bolshevik reliance on science versus Idealist religion, one could point to a strong attack in *Pod znamenem Marksizma* in this year on Einstein for being an idealist.[81] Prestigious Soviet scientists like V. I. Vernadsky were already being attacked for not agreeing entirely with Bolshevik notions of materialism.[82] The campaign against so-called 'reactionary science schools' was initiated in the pages of the journal in 1922.[83] The open clash between Bolshevik ideology and

[76] Ibid., 8, p. 184.
[77] Ibid., 3, p. 122.
[78] Ibid., 4, p. 94.
[79] Ibid., 5, pp. 92–3.
[80] For a discussion of the more utopian interests of the Bolsheviks in the early Soviet period see Pethybridge, op. cit., pp. 22–8, 31–3, 63–5.
[81] *Pod znamenem Marksizma*, 7–8, p. 124.
[82] Ibid., pp. 119, 165.
[83] Ibid., 3, p. 9.

science, which will form our cultural case study for 1926, obviously had deep roots.

In 1922 the campaign for Bolshevik purity of thought, uncontaminated by all other sources, already began to take a sinister turn. The authors and reviewers not only believed implicitly that all outsiders were suspect; they also began to believe that within this ideological fortress only one correct line was permissible. In the first issue it was contended that even veterans like Bukharin and Trotsky were making philosophical 'errors'.[84] An anonymous reviewer of Bukharin's *Historical Materialism* who signed himself as 'a Plekhanovite' attacked Bukharin's innovations in sociology. They reminded him significantly of A. A. Bogdanov's developments of Marxism: 'Old Plekhanov taught us to react with especial care to all "developers".'[85] Soviet ideological conservatism was going through its birth pangs.

The subject-matter of *Pechat' i revoliutsiia* was far more down to earth but no less essential for the preservation of Bolshevik cultural and political dominance in the climate of NEP. In the first number for 1922 N. L. Meshcheriakov, the chairman of the editorial commission of Gosizdat, the state publishing-house, summed up the organizational problems of all the state press media.[86] Above all there was insufficient paper. When the first eight numbers of *Voprosy truda* for 1921 were published all together in 1922, a reviewer of them observed that until 1922 the whole basis for proper Bolshevik control of the press and the reconstruction of society had been purely theoretical.[87] The demand for paper in 1919 had been 5,270 pudy. None could be imported in 1919, and domestic production (much of it from Belorussia) had amounted to 2,630 pudy. Needs for paper shrank to 3,400 pudy for 1922, and supply eventually topped demand by the end of the year, although over half of it came from abroad,[88] which is not surprising when one recalls the state of the timber and pulp industry in Belorussia.

Other organizational problems included the very low fees for articles sent to the state press, and the fact that governmental agencies ordered huge editions of books and brochures

[84] *Pod znamenem Marksizma*, 1–2, p. 69.  [85] Ibid., 11–12, pp. 171–2.
[86] *Pechat' i revoliutsiia*, 1, pp. 163 ff.  [87] Ibid., 2, p. 224.
[88] *Bolezni nashego pechatnogo dela* (Moscow, 1924).

which were never distributed nor sold subsequently. These two difficulties melted away as khozraschet slowly penetrated into the world of publishing, but the Party still found in 1922 that it had to order its members to produce articles which had to be written in their spare time. Safe Bolshevik intellectuals were at a premium, given the very low educational levels of the Party as a whole.

The final problem cited by Meshcheriakov was the poor distribution levels of all central journals to the provinces. At this point we begin to see the nature of Bolshevik local controls through the other end of the telescope. The central agency for all RSFSR state-controlled publications was supposed to register and distribute all materials, but many never came to it in the first place. It lacked enough local agents in Kazan', Rostov, Tomsk, and Minsk, and ties with the Ukraine and the Caucasus were extremely tenuous.[89] Even by the end of 1922, when Petrograd and Moscow published between them only 30 per cent of all the journals in the Soviet Union, they nevertheless had 90 per cent of the circulation.[90] There were many other signs of the isolated hothouse atmosphere of the culture in the twin capitals. An article in a journal noted that central bibliographies on local questions were very scanty, despite the fact that efforts had been made since the 1860s to compile them.[91] From a total of 226 books sent for review for the months of July and August, 1922, only seven came from beyond Petrograd and Moscow.[92] Very little information from any province appeared in the regular chronicle of events published in *Pechat' i revoliutsiia*.

During 1922 the state publishing-houses by no means predominated in the rapidly growing tide of private enterprise. Much of the energies of the editors of our journal were devoted to the political dangers involved. By the end of May 1922 there were ninety-nine private publishers in Petrograd alone, although twenty-one of them had just one manuscript on hand.

---

[89] *Pechat' i revoliutsiia*, 1, pp. 168–71. This statement concerning the Ukraine and the Caucasus ties up with the fact, already mentioned on p. 137 above, that the central party reorganization of the press network of Jan. 1922 had not included these two areas.

[90] B. Lebedev, 'Zhurnaly SSSR', in *Zhurnalist*, 7 (1923), pp. 35–6.

[91] *Pechat' i revoliutsiia*, 1, p. 172.

[92] Ibid., 6, list of books sent for review and given at the end of the journal.

Moscow on the surface of things seemed to be experiencing a galloping boom. From 150 houses in February, the number rose to 220 by the end of May, yet 133 of these still had no manuscripts to process by July, and the lucky ones were dealing mainly in brochures, not books.[93] The future cultural capital was still too big for its boots. Despite the boom in the private sphere, party editors were not too alarmed. It would be hard to make a profit. Large numbers of the reading public had fled the country, or were now impoverished. Most private book-shops had closed down. Some trends were noted among the new 'bourgeois' authors. Religious mysticism was put at the top of the list, probably as a sop to current party directives to editors, since publications inside Russia showed little evidence of this trend. More convincing were references to depictions of the harmful effects of the Revolution, and bizarre attempts by city-dwellers and richer peasants to start up an anti-Bolshevik alliance.

More alarm was expressed over the new 'unprincipled, boulevard' newspapers that were springing up and attracting the younger generation. This fear was also voiced at the Eleventh Party Congress in March. The gutter press was said to be attracting party members, who were advised to subscribe to party newspapers only.[94] With the gift of hindsight we can see that the private sector was never going to swamp the state. At the time of Lenin's death in 1924 two-fifths of all publishing was still in private hands, but by the end of 1926 the proportion had sunk to one-tenth.[95] Even in 1922 the Soviet censor was not overworked. Between January and the end of May only 5.3 per cent of literary manuscripts were stopped in Petrograd, and 3.8 per cent in Moscow. However 41.6 per cent of Petrograd technical texts were cut back, compared with only 64 out of 813 Moscow texts.[96] As was noted with regard to the Serapion Brothers, Petrograd remained the suspected refuge of the Old Guard intellectuals, whilst Moscow now attracted the new left and the more technically inspired.

[93] *Pechat' i revoliutsiia*, 6, pp. 129 ff. The figure of 150 Moscow publishers in Feb. 1922 is cited in A. Ya. Viatkin, *Razgrom knig partiei trotskizma i drugikh antileninskikh grupp 1920–1925 gg.* (Leningrad, 1966), p. 61.

[94] *Resolutions and Decisions of the CPSU*, 2 (Toronto, 1974), p. 170.

[95] A. I. Nazarov, *Ocherki istorii sovetskogo knigoizdatel'stva* (Moscow, 1962).

[96] *Pechat' i revoliutsiia*, 6 (1922), pp. 131–2.

Commenting on the censor, one author repeated Lenin's argument of October 1917 to the effect that bourgeois societies are class censors even though there is no officially designated censorship.[97] The opening number of *Pechat' i revoliutsiia* in 1922 stressed that, unlike some elements in the disgraced Proletkul't movement, the Soviet authorities did not wish to burn books and pictures, but to create new ones. Another author admitted later that the Bolshevik view was also founded on a class basis, and could not be called objective.[98] Krupskaia in her role as pedagogue compiled a somewhat quirky list of proscribed books in 1922, but Gorky railed at it, and she later rejected it. The list included the works of Plato and Kant (yet another link with the contemporary obsession with Idealists) and Samuel Smiles's *Duty, Character, Self-Help*. From the sublime to the ridiculous. More serious were requests in September from party officials to halt the flow of anti-Soviet literature coming in through the port of Petrograd.[99] Some harmless foreign tracts were let in intentionally, like Viscount J. Bryce's *Contemporary Democracies*. The reviewer explained how the noble lord equated Russia with three other 'similar' regimes, Mexico, China, and Egypt, where the peasantry had created the same anarchy. Russian democracy should be restored by the League of Nations: 'such is the "objective" science of his practical deductions'.[100] Even more serious for the future were the 'errors' now being ascribed to Trotsky and others. A Leningrad historian writing in 1966 may not have been as anachronistic as he thought he should be to placate the censor of his time when he asserted that foes of the censor in 1922 included Trotskyites and Zinovievites.[101]

The general impression that emerges from the perusal of *Pod znamenem Marksizma* and *Pechat' i revoliutsiia* in 1922 is rather surprisingly that of a none-too-confident regime trying to sort out its own distinctive ideological viewpoint and to distance itself from all possible rivals. The physical civil war had been won, but the war of words raged more fiercely than before in the more relaxed though still nervous atmosphere of NEP. Intellectual foes remained to the right and to the left, inside as

---

[97] Ibid., 7, pp. 173, 186–7.   [98] Ibid., 1, p. 66, and 6, p. 245.
[99] Viatkin, op. cit., p. 62.   [100] *Pechat' i revoliutsiia*, 2 (1922), p. 297.
[101] Viatkin, op. cit., p. 62.

well as outside Russia. Already incipient was the tendency to criticize in the harshest terms any signs of new and original thought within the Bolshevik Party itself.

For the most part each topic discussed so far in this chapter has been concerned with mere perceptions and observations, whether cultural or political in nature. Actual political intervention remained minimal, despite the fact that for the first time in 1922 censorship methods were formalized with the creation of *Glavlit*. The arrest and exile of over a hundred professors and intellectuals in August 1922, many of the former connected with Petrograd University, marked a watershed which has attracted little attention, although it entailed the expulsion of one of the most brilliant groups ever to be deported.[102] Nor was it an isolated event. In the realm of high politics, the last twist of the knife towards one-party rule occurred with the public trial of the Socialist Revolutionaries. In the sphere of the arts the rising school of realists were now encouraged to attack abstract art with venom. V. Tatlin's studio was closed down. Kandinsky and Chagall fled to Western Europe. A new wave of intellectuals of all kinds hit Berlin.

Many of the non-academic deportees were Idealists and included men of great distinction like N. A. Berdiaev and S. L. Frank, both of whom had held university posts.[103] In 1920 a school of philosophical idealists had been set up in Petrograd, and the year 1921 had witnessed a great outburst of privately published books by this type of member of the old intelligentsia. The selection of those to be expelled was not as random as has been maintained.[104] We have already seen evidence of and reasons for the mounting campaign against Idealists. To sum up, their philosophy was an affront to Marxism, they were non-utilitarian, and they reminded Lenin uncomfortably of some of A. A. Bogdanov's views. They also included several theologians in their ranks, which was a dangerous thing to be in a

---

[102] The background to the deportation, though not the actual event, is well covered in a doctoral thesis by J. C. McClelland, 'Bolsheviks, Professors, and the Reform of Higher Education in Soviet Russia, 1917–1921' (University Microfilms, Ann Arbor, 1971).

[103] See P. Sorokin, *The Long Journey* (New Haven, 1953), p. 192. Frank was attacked in 1922 for believing in the objective existence of the spirit, in the pages of *Pechat' i revoliutsiia*, July–Aug., p. 238.

[104] S. Fitzpatrick, *Educational and Social Mobility in the Soviet Union 1921–1934* (Cambridge, 1979).

year when fifty-four priests and laymen went on trial for their convictions.[105] Those Idealists who had university connections fought harder than most academics for autonomy from the state.

The 1922 charter for higher education brought this sector directly under the control of the Commissariat of Enlightenment which could now appoint rectors and approve professorial appointments.[106] This move was the culminating point of a three-pronged attempt by Bolshevik groups to control education from 1917 on. Lunacharsky and others had sought to intervene in order to improve the cultural level of the population with all speed so as to prop up the Bolshevik regime. They had manœuvred with some tact, except for the deputy Commissar of Education, who was the same Professor Pokrovsky we have already seen writing critical reviews of Idealist works and extolling the cultural aims of the proletariat. He adopted a far more strident polemical approach against fellow academics. The second main line of attack had come from the Economic Left, which wished to harness education totally to material improvement. Lenin, as always, subordinated all other considerations to secure political control, resulting in the 1921 and 1922 charters for higher education and subsequent deportations.

The earliest issues of *Pod znamenem Marksizma* contained frequent forewarnings of what was to come in August 1922. Courses in Marxism and the social sciences were criticized for being disordered and overloaded. More ominous still were references to poor course-leaders and their loose diversity of approach.[107] The nervous atmosphere clearly affected student stability, disrupted by the opening and closing of faculty sections at Petrograd University.[108] Some of the difficulties with the curricula had plainly been induced by the left rather than by the right. In the law faculty all students had to take an extremely wide variety of 'foundation' courses, including

---

[105] See p. 212 above. Perhaps the most distinguished among the theologians was A. V. Florovsky.

[106] *Sobranie uzakonenii i rasporiazhenii rabochego i krestianskogo pravitel'stva RSFSR*, 43 (1922), art. 518.

[107] *Pod znamenem Marksizma*, 1–2, pp. 66 ff.

[108] Student unrest is revealed in the pages of *Istoriia Leningradskogo Universiteta* (Leningrad, 1969), p. 253 ff. In July 1922 there were 9,074 students. Many of them went hungry and had to take on jobs doing hard labour. When they did find time to study, they shivered in freezing lecture-rooms and laboratories for half of the year.

socialist prediction and retrodiction. Engels's notion of the polytechnic man, capable of imbibing all forms of knowledge, had been applied in an extreme form.[109] The cultural upheaval also appeared to affect membership of the local Komsomols dramatically. From a total of 21,100 in January 1922, the figure for the guberniia dropped to 12,860 in October, but rose quickly again in more settled conditions to 21,300 by April 1923.[110]

The exiled Petrograd academics were quickly replaced by new men more favourable to the Bolsheviks. By February 1923 a nucleus of twenty had swollen to 131, of whom thirty-five were party members.[111] It was noticeable that virtually no technical and scientific specialists had suffered expulsion in Petrograd or in other universities.[112] In this regard Lenin did pay attention to the arguments of the Economic Left. He needed the best advisers he could get for the State Planning Commission (Gosplan), set up in 1921 at his instigation. Nor did the rump of the old professoriate as a whole lose all its privileges, although their exiled colleagues naturally claimed that this was the case. In Petrograd and Moscow at least, professional appointments continued to be made in fact by the departments themselves until their final loss of independence in 1928–9. An authority on NEP education has pointed out that a division of spheres of influence emerged between the 'old' professors and the 'new' Communist students. The Commissariat for Enlightenment and the sectors appointed by it played a mediating role.[113] Nevertheless there was no doubt after 1922 as to the Bolshevik monopoly of education.

Did increasing political intervention in many intellectual spheres in 1921–2 point towards a radical change of direction for the party and the country? We have observed that Petrograd stood at some kind of cultural crossroads. Was this to be a long-standing state of hesitation, or were several Bolshevik

---

[109]  Ibid., pp. 272–3.
[110]  *Statisticheskii sbornik o sostoianii RLKSM za period s 1 okt. 1922 g. po 1 ianv. 1924 g.* (Moscow, 1924), pp. 15–18.
[111]  *Istoriia Leningradskogo Universiteta*, p. 248.
[112]  See S. A. Fediukin, *Velikii Oktiabr' i intelligentsiia* (Moscow, 1972), pp. 325–9, and T. M. Smirnova, *Reforma vysshei shkoly RSFSP 1917g–okt. 1922 g.* (Moscow, 1968), pp. 230–1.
[113]  S. Fitzpatrick, op. cit., pp. 66–7.

groups moving at varied but deliberate rates down a definite new and irretraceable path?

Certainly one tired Soviet onlooker in 1922 thought the latter supposition to be the case. He had been putting forth his views for many years. He was to die in 1926, but his posthumous fame was to grow continuously. Between 1898 and 1911 J. Machajski had elaborated the idea that the left-wing intelligentsia including the Bolsheviks were not genuine allies of the workers. Instead they were a new type of potential rulers, since they could and did exploit knowledge and culture with as much success as bourgeois capitalists wielding the means of production.[114] After 1917 he added to his criticism, claiming that a 'people's bureaucracy' was emerging after the October 'counter-revolution of the intellectuals'. He called for a second revolution leading to universal equality of incomes, including the intelligentsia.[115] This line was taken up in 1922 and 1923 by the dissident left in the shape of the Workers' Group led by G. Miasnikov. In its manifesto the Soviet government was depicted as 'a high-handed bunch of intelligenty' who had usurped the right to speak in the name of the proletariat.[116] These accusations were anathema for the Bolsheviks. Their supposed monopoly of ideas divorced from the material productive labour of the proletariat made them look very like Idealists of a sort. Indeed Machajski's views bore some resemblance to Bogdanov's, as the left pointed out. Here we have yet another reason for Bolshevik intransigence towards the group formally known as Idealists in 1922.

Since Marx had integrated the structure of social life chiefly on the basis of material production, he had failed to pin-point the position and influence of the intelligentsia, and especially its more rootless Russian version.[117] Likewise Bolshevik intellectuals neglected, inadvertently or deliberately, their own role in this respect. In a similar manner they ignored the true social and political influence of other *raznochintsy* besides

---

[114] See J. W. Machajski, *Burzhuaznaia revoliutsiia i rabochee delo* (St Petersburg, 1906), p. 86; and also by the same author, *Bankrotstvo sotzializma XIX stoletiia* (Geneva, 1905), p. 28.

[115] *Rabochaia revoliutsiia*, 1 (June–July 1918), pp. 4 ff.

[116] V. Sorin, *Rabochaia gruppa* (Moscow, 1924), pp. 63–4.

[117] This view was argued persuasively before Machajski by A. S. Izgoev in his article 'Intelligentsia, kak sotsial'naia gruppa', *Obrazovanie*, 1 (1904), sect. 2, pp. 79–81.

themselves—the kustary, the Nepmen, and the millions involved in the internal and external diaspora since 1914. The Russian intelligentsia was rootless in the sense that its Westernized education since the founding of St Petersburg had cut it off even further from the masses and particularly from the peasantry which in some ways still lived during NEP according to Muscovite traditions. The intellectual concerns of Petrograd in 1922 were a world apart from the provincial hinterland investigated earlier. Some leading Bolsheviks realized the possible future consequences of this dichotomy. The pedagogical expert Krupskaia had spent 1917 trying to inculcate a genuinely critical political awareness among the workers and worker-peasants of the industrial suburb of Vyborg, elements that were intended to form the imminent dictatorship of the proletariat.[118]

Machajski's fears appeared to have some substance as of 1922. Lenin had urged the need for cultural revolution soon after his political revolution. He was backed up aggressively at the start of NEP by real intellectuals like Pokrovsky. Neither of these men, nor their like, paid sufficient practical attention to the dangerous gap between cultural *dirigisme* on the one hand and the ignorant masses on the other. The situation was to change in the future. After Lenin's death the party leadership was to be taken over increasingly by Moscow-based philistines in the Stalinist mould. Moreover the literacy and educational campaigns initiated by Lenin, though often remaining in the realm of theory, were eventually to bear fruit in the 1930s. *Vydvizhenchestvo*, or promotion from the ranks, also became more of a reality than it had been in the 1920s. The pre-revolutionary dividing line between the educated and the dark masses at last became blurred.

Were the Bolsheviks intending to start a cultural revolution in 1922? If one compares the start of NEP with the revolution from above of 1928–31, then the answer is decisively in the negative. In that second period there was an abrupt acceleration in all cultural spheres which entailed a clear break with the past. To judge by our case-study of Petrograd culture, the party was fighting a rearguard action in the ideological fog of

[118] See Pethybridge, 'Spontaneity and Illiteracy in 1917', in R. C. Elwood (ed.), *Reconsiderations on the Russian Revolution* (Cambridge, Mass., 1976), pp. 81–99.

NEP in order to keep its position clear. Action was also needed urgently, since on many subjects no stance had been adopted at all due to the pressures of the Civil War. However action differed greatly according to the specific problem. Trotsky in *Literature and Revolution* laid down three broad approaches for the party to adopt for *all* its problems. In some areas it was necessary for the party to decide 'with authority' what was permissible, and it should then intervene heavily. This was the case with regard to the Idealists and to university reform. The second approach consisted in general supervision. The cinema and the press fell under this heading. Trotsky's third area was one in which 'the party is not called on to command'. This applied to *belles-lettres*, and is typified by the situation of the Serapions in 1922. The irony in the categorization given here is that Trotsky himself thought that all *cultural* affairs should come exclusively within the third area. This great guardian of Russia's cultural heritage did not realize that his advice was already out of date in some ways by the time his book was published in 1923. Indeed it only held good for literature. A Politburo commission in 1922 proposed an independent association of writers, to include such disparate and unorthodox members as Briusov, Zoshchenko, the Serapions, and even Proletkul't writers. Yet even such a liberal association was intended to include a communist fraction which would give it a 'secure profile'. In fact the association never came about, but a decade later a similar procedure was followed when the various literary groups were moved into a single Writers' Union.[119]

Before moving on to Moscow and all-Russian politics, let us consider again in the light of the case studies examined above why a separate chapter has been devoted to Petrograd. Russia at the start of NEP still maintained two genuine capitals, one cultural and the other political. This has been forgotten or ignored in Soviet and Western accounts alike. Yet although in a sense Petrograd may serve as a convenient geographical hold-all for any discussion of political influences over cultural matters, we must not fall into the trap to which scholars are so vulnerable, of trying to impose more order and precision than actually existed. Petrograd was not a watertight compartment,

---

[119] The notion of a writers' association in 1922 is discussed in A. Kemp-Welch, 'NEP in Culture', *Journal of Contemporary History*, 13 (1978), p. 452.

but more like Peter the Great's image of a window through which many influences flowed or came to a head. From the provinces came all those artefacts in the Russian Museum that had such a deep influence on Petersburg culture. From the hinterland flocked in rising cultural figures, from Esenin and Gorky, to V. Ivanov and K. Fedin among the Serapions. Out through the same window were now seeping away to Moscow important elements from all the sectors treated in this chapter. Like a window also, Petrograd threw a distorted reflection, through the two more political of the four case studies, of what was happening at the same time in the spheres of ideological control and education at the lower levels of the Smolensk guberniia.

There are genuine connections between the case studies, but again they should not be exaggerated for the sake of an unreal coherence. The protagonists in all of them were musing on the recent past and at the same time facing up to the future, in particular to the extent of political intervention in their affairs. They formed part of a confined and still highly élitist world, whose personnel overlapped between one sphere and another. Even *Pod znamenem Marksizma* was almost as much a purely cultural journal as a political weapon, though the ideological content was soon to become suffocating. It was clear that as late as 1922 the intellectual side of the Bolshevik political mind still led a double locational life in Petrograd and Moscow. This was not the position towards the end of NEP, by which time Petrograd had also quite clearly lost all pretensions to cultural supremacy over Moscow. In the long run only its ballet, post-Muscovite architecture, and the accumulated and mainly foreign artistic heritage of its museums and palaces continued to outshine its rival.[120]

---

[120] Political rivalry between the two capitals still simmered in 1925, when the struggle within the triumvirate in the Bolshevik leadership took on a geographical aspect. See E. H. Carr, *A History of Soviet Russia: Socialism in One Country 1924–1926*, vol. 2 (London, 1959), pp. 53–7.

# 7. *Political Reflections on Society 1922–1926*

ALTHOUGH Moscow did not have a monopoly over cultural controls at the start of NEP, it was certainly all-powerful with regard to political and economic decisions. Moreover the balance in the cultural sphere was tilting away from Petrograd, marked by the move to Moscow of several groups of intellectuals. The old capital was therefore of supreme importance on account of the interaction of its political, economic, and cultural élites which constantly brought out new ideas on how to manage society at large. Far too often in previous histories of the early Soviet period these ideas have been considered in a geographical vacuum. Theories were formulated by Soviet leaders with insufficient regard to realities outside Moscow. All the more reason, then, to investigate this dichotomy and the reasons for it. There was even a lack of precise knowledge about areas under the politicians' noses, as will be seen in the next chapter, dealing with the changing conditions of the Moscow working class between 1922 and 1926.

As late as 1926 the centre of Moscow still remained pockmarked by the shelling of 1917, as any foreign visitor to the old Metropol Hotel would notice as he approached its external walls. The main thoroughfare off the Red Square, now called Gorky street, was still called Tverskaia, since it pointed north towards Tver guberniia, the subject of one of our three local analyses for 1926. According to the All-Union census for this year, four out of five citizens of the USSR still lived in the countryside. The population of Moscow was given as 2,026,000 as against 1,854,000 in 1917. Between 1917 and 1920 about half a million workers were resettled from older quarters in the inner ring into housing that had previously belonged to the upper classes within the Sadovoe Ring. When Lenin entered his new government offices in the Kremlin for the first time on 12 March 1918, he said to his secretary: 'Worker-peasant power should be completely consolidated here.'[1] Certainly a capital city is the clearest example of rapid social change, but it is far from being a paradigm of change in any nation taken as a whole, and in Russia above all. Lenin only had to look out of his office windows any morning near dawn in 1926 to see the overwhelming influence on Moscow of slower-moving areas, both near and far. Most agricultural goods for sale in the city were carried in by a modern-sounding acronym VSLS, with a very old-fashioned technique—*Vremennaia Spomog'atel'naia Loshadinaia Sila*, or Temporary Auxiliary Horse-Power. In 1925 the whole of the Soviet Union contained only 5,500 lorries.

Like Petrograd's cultural life, Moscow's social and economic life must be examined in relationship to its vast hinterland. In some ways there were historical parallels with Berlin. Both cities were set among forests and lakes on the poor soils of plains, in a northerly climate with no significant resources of any kind near by: but both had been transformed by man into a state-unifying force. Moscow's nine railway stations, controlling the country like a spider's web, were one indication of this strength. Trotsky's armoured trains running out and back on those lines had saved the Bolsheviks in the Civil War. Yet in other ways Moscow was completely different from Berlin. In 1926 she was subject to increasing immigration on a scale which far surpassed that of the German capital. This was to become a torrent after the end of NEP. Moscow looked more like New Delhi than Berlin in mid-NEP as far as living-standards were concerned. It was a quiet, semi-rural capital, still retaining the air of a bastion set in an ocean of peasants, whose silent flood percolated into the centre in every way. Moscow, like modern Delhi, was also heir to a semi-colonial continent consisting of a bewildering variety of ethnic and religious minorities.

As the 1920s advanced, fewer top Bolsheviks seemed to spend as much time outside Moscow as they had done in early NEP. Consequently they gained less and less firsthand know-

---

[1] V. Bronch-Bruevich, *Pereezed sovetskogo pravitel'stva iz Petrograda v Moskvu* (Moscow, 1926), p. 19.

ledge of the intricacies of the vast hinterland they governed. In 1922 Lenin had spent time in Gorky, convalescing. Only the peasant Kalinin of all the high leaders had actually travelled round the famine-stricken areas, though Dzerzhinsky, as has been seen, spent a period in Siberia looking into the situation on the railways. Ordzhonikidze and Rykov were in Georgia (disobeying instructions from Moscow), and Trotsky went on duck-shooting holidays, leaving Stalin to get on with his dangerous intrigues in the capital.

These individuals engaged in the creation of high political decisions give us the illusion of having been eyewitnesses to the universal spectacle of all Russia in the process of change. In fact they were more myopic than most national leaders. Some of the reasons for this have been given in the preface to this book. More will be examined shortly. It is undeniable that they possessed enormous powers to control the central decision-making process and the party in the localities, but that is not the same thing as being aware of the complexities of their country or even being willing or able to change society through their decisions. They were powerful, in theory, since they had pushed through the October Revolution and remained *dirigiste* and authoritarian afterwards. Russia stayed as centralized as ever, if not more so. We have noted how scant were the horizontal connections between Kursk and Tambov gubernii at the time of the Tambov revolt. The administration of the famine was notoriously over-regulated from Moscow with scant reference to changing local conditions, or to the relations between the different provinces that were afflicted in varying degrees. We shall see again in 1926 that horizontal communications of any kind between the areas of Smolensk and Tver were almost entirely lacking, although a glance at the map will show that by Russian standards they lay very close to one another. All command routes led on a bilateral vertical basis to Moscow and back. Yet even these were often blocked, as we have seen in previous chapters.

Observers of NEP have become mesmerized by the danger-ously captivating world of Moscow politics, dominated from 1922 to 1926 by Lenin's potential heirs struggling amongst themselves for supremacy after the demise of their *primus inter pares*. In the course of their battle they resorted to theoretical analyses of Russian society and economics that often had little to do with reality. Over these years perhaps only one socio-economic large-scale influence was diagnosed swiftly and correctly by central politicians. That was the 'scissors crisis' of 1923, a highly obvious phenomenon. For the rest, the leaders were locked in a claustrophic struggle like 'spiders in a jar', as *The Times* put it in 1926.[2] True, high political events did not cease to take place in mid-NEP. Some of them seemed important to those living at the time, like the death of Lenin in 1924, although the most crucial decisions about who controlled what at the apex of politics had already been sorted out by the close of 1922, as was seen at the end of the chapter on Bolshevik controls. Lenin's first stroke in May 1922 was more important than his death.

Many apparently significant events in Moscow were soon to be consigned to the dustbin as headlines of the past. But some events, like Lenin's illness, were to have far-reaching consequences over a long period of time. Of course the critical decision to embark upon NEP in 1921 had been one such. Another embryonic move that did not attract so much attention at the time was the appointment of Stalin as General Secretary in 1922. The decision to strengthen state planning in April 1926 was a more obvious turning-point, though the specific ways in which to do this, and to industrialize, remained unclarified by the end of 1926.

During the years of national convalescence between 1921 and 1926 it was after all a central tenet of NEP that the hinterland should be relatively free of economic and social commands from above. The main aim was to allow a backward society shattered by war from 1914 to 1921 to recover quietly. Because of this salient feature of early NEP, it is imperative to see in what ways the political centre, which had changed beyond recognition after October 1917, was out of joint with the rest of the country, which had suffered great turbulence but had not altered radically in its ways. It is necessary to examine simultaneously, as though in transparent layers, all the different histories that coexisted in NEP. The greatest absurdity is to imagine some kind of synchrony of

<hr>

[2] *The Times*, 2 Jan. 1926.

events at all levels. The fast-moving political hub of Moscow was surrounded by strata moving at widely differing speeds through political and social time. There was no direct correlation between distance from the capital and backwardness. Neither Smolensk nor Tver gubernii were very far away, but the daily life of the peasant woman making her way to Roslavl' in the first chapter of this book was as backward in many respects as that of her Siberian equivalent. In fact Siberian peasants had been more sophisticated politically in the Duma period than their equivalents in Kursk guberniia.[3] Tver guberniia, as will be seen, contained some amazingly primitive forest areas, considering their relative proximity to Moscow. True, remote Kazakhstan was at another, lower level of development, apart from pockets of Great Russian settlements, but this was due largely to two incidental factors—the near-desert climate and the social constraints imposed over a long time by Islam.

Slower-moving social and cultural influences were nearly always relegated to the provinces, although there are always exceptions to the rule. Moscow's Old Believers still clung on to pre-seventeenth-century forms of Orthodox practice. In general, though, echoes from the distant past were easier to detect elsewhere. They were usually dying forms, like the pagan rites the Belorussian peasant woman confused with her Christian imagery in her hut. The rising, new forms of thought usually sprang up in the large cities. The latest scientific ideas, which will be looked at in this chapter, were one obvious example of this.

Even slower-moving than provincial mores were Russia's geographical features, which at first sight appear to be eternal and unchanging. They exerted their due influence on local economies and social attitudes, as we have seen in our surveys of Smolensk, Kursk, and the Volga gubernii. In turn these attitudes had political reverberations. Yet it is not true to say that the effect of geographical aspects are always unalterable. Although Russia was to suffer famines in the early 1930s, they were not on the scale of the Great Famine of 1921–2, due to improvements in human management of natural factors.

---

[3] See Ch. 2, p. 62 above.

Stalin aspired, unsuccessfully, to dam the Behring Straits so as to warm up eastern Siberia, but he and his successors did manage to investigate large tracts of Soviet Central Asia.

No strict hierarchy of causation can be enforced in the study of history. The notion of either geographical, social, or political imperialism is untenable. Everything affects everything else in infinitely varying degrees. What does seem to have been the case in early NEP is that after extending stringent political control over the rest of Russia in the aftermath of the Civil War, Bolshevik leaders debated the socio-economic future of their country in unusual isolation from real conditions in Russia at large. This picture is reflected very clearly in virtually all the history textbooks on the period. If, say, one reads through the relevant chapters, on politics in D. Treadgold's *Twentieth Century Russia*, on economic trends in A. Nove's *An Economic History of the U.S.S.R.*, and on social developments in P. Sorlin's *The Soviet People and Their Society*, one has the distinct impression of reading about three entirely different spheres of life. There is scant interconnection, even between the social and economic areas. There are great dangers in such an approach, however. The very lack of synchronization which certainly did exist was fated in the end to throw up problems of immense difficulty which were in fact dealt with after 1927 by Stalin's brutal personal acts of political imperialism from above. Not even the closest observer at the Fifteenth Party Congress in December 1927 could have guessed that the USSR was on the eve of social revolution, although Stalin had probably taken the relevant decisions in secret by this time. It was just because NEP was lived throughout in widely diverging spheres that it came to such a catastrophic close, involving swift and violent interraction between Moscow and the hinterland.

For all the reasons given above, this book has been given the form of a reversible sand hourglass. The neck between political perceptions and socio-economic realities was a narrow one, allowing for limited passage. The flow was never one-way in the years 1922–6. That is why from some chapters to others the hourglass is turned upside down, in order to observe in alternation the slowly accumulating evidence on either side of the communicating link. This particular chapter is entirely taken up with central political perceptions of society between 1922 and 1926.

The inevitable chronological gap caused by the method adopted here may be remedied in a perfunctory way by referring the reader to the chronology given at the beginning of this book. Unlike most given chronologies of the period, it attempts to list both high political events and crescive socio-economic changes. Beyond this, the reader is referred to a considerable body of scholarship which covers the period in more conventional ways.[4] Before turning to look at other aspects of politicians' views of the period, let us survey one of its opening events, the Eleventh Party Congress of March 1922.

The elimination of the market in economic production and distribution had been a theoretical goal in the years of War Communism, and was to become a reality after the collapse of NEP. Such a move entails the end of distinctions between state and civil society, so that socio-economic relationships become directly politicized. It might be imagined, therefore, that the first NEP Party Congress would deliberately steer away from *dirigisme* of this kind. In fact, the opposite was the case. Some delegates, including Preobrazhensky, who was destined to be the economic architect of the principles underlying the first Five-Year Plan, went so far as to attack the whole idea of NEP, maintaining that 'state capitalism' under NEP was far too similar to plain capitalism. Most of the business of the Congress reflected a vigorous majority will to control society as closely as the exhausted body politic was able. An attempt by the rump of the oppositionists to curtail the fierce powers of the Control Commissions over party discipline, both at the central and local levels, was thwarted by a rigged vote. It was at this time

---

[4] In addition to the three textbooks referred to earlier in this chapter, other works include: E. H. Carr, *A History of Soviet Russia* (7 vols.) (London, 1950 onwards); H. Carrere d'Encausse, *Lenin: Revolution and Power* (London, 1982); R. V. Daniels, *The Conscience of the Revolution* (Cambridge, Mass., 1960); I. Deutscher, *Stalin, a Political Biography* (London, 1967); A. B. Ulam, *Lenin and the Bolsheviks, the Intellectual and Political History of the Triumph of Communism in Russia* (London, 1966); L. Schapiro, *The Communist Party of the Soviet Union* (London, 1970); A. Erlich, *The Soviet Industrialisation Debate 1924–1928* (Cambridge, Mass., 1960); and M. Lewin, *Russian Peasants and Soviet Power* (London, 1968).

that the GPU was set up, reinforcing some aspects of secret-police control. The trade unions were brought more firmly under direct political supervision in the theses drafted by Lenin for the Congress on their role and tasks.

All these moves expressed a clear intent to offer no relaxation whatsoever in those areas of society that could actually be manipulated from on high. Yet, as in the case of the new cultural controls being established at the same time in Petrograd, there was an enormous gap between the will and the capacity to dominate. As has been seen time and again in preceding chapters, for lack of personnel, time, and financial resources, numerous spheres of socio-economic life remained poorly supervised, whether it was the railways, the press, education, or other areas. The best that the Central Committee could do was to hold on tight to the political summit and all that directly affected its freedom to manœuvre. In the remote provinces this only meant acute crises like the Famine and the Georgian question. The result for most of NEP until 1926 was that a combination of thwarted intent and creeping semi-capitalism did indeed produce, against the wishes of most, but not all, Bolshevik leaders, a weakening of *dirigisme*. By 1926 the economy had recovered to its pre-World War level, allowing the party more financial punch; and Stalin was already getting a clearer idea of how to direct these new assets.

In 1922 clear foresight was at a premium, however, although this did not prevent party leaders from viewing history as a convenient scheme rather than as a blurred reality. Not for nothing were they Marxists. It is vital to place ourselves before the bewildering alternatives that faced the Bolsheviks at the start of NEP. These alternatives derived from their rather abstract scenarios and tended to disorientate them and prevent them from making well-judged analyses of the state of the country.

The first alternative was the lingering vision of permanent revolution, on which, for Trotsky at least, all domestic progress still depended. This was a fading dream, but one which persisted until at least 1924 and overlapped bizarrely with other visions. Another alternative was that of capitalist aid. Lenin and others devoted a great deal of energy to this subject in 1921–3. It was intended as more than a passing fancy, judging by the scale and timing of the projects entered into. A British bank director arranged for huge concessions of Belorussian timber. Lenin corresponded with Rykov on the large-scale immigration of American workers into Russia. An agreement was drawn up with Krupp for the German exploitation of 50,000 desiatiny of land on the Don. Lenin went so far as to claim that capitalist regimes had to trade widely with Russia in order to prevent their own economic collapse.

An essential component of this scenario was its duration. The general supposition among Bolshevik leaders in 1922 was that foreign aid, and therefore NEP with it, would last for anything up to fifty years or so. The arrangement with Krupp, for instance, was entered into for twenty-four years.[5] Lenin's opinion of peasant co-operatives acting as the slow vehicle leading from small-scale production to state capitalism, and only thereafter to socialism and communism, was inevitably long-term in its implications, Gosplan in early NEP restricted itself largely to grandiose plans for state control in the distant future. The fact that all these vivid hopes for the long-term were to fade within a few years should not cause us to forget that they formed the theoretical basis of party planning for society at the start of NEP. The problem was that they conflicted with one another and brought about acute disorientation and confusion in the leaders' grasp of actualities.

There was another basic, albeit coincidental, reason for the inability of the leaders to fathom the true depths of society in early NEP. Lenin's fatal decline at an early age had enormous repercussions. His absence from the Eleventh Party Congress led to very unruly behaviour among all the delegates present. The struggle for his succession engaged most of the energies of his colleagues over the next five years. Preoccupied with internal party strife, the leaders debated the needs and problems of the social sector through the narrow and distorting prism of their particular personal interests. Every modern politician does this, of course, but the situation was acute in the 1920s. Personal power meant more in a country where democracy had never existed. As after the death of Stalin, so with

[5] The details regarding capitalist aid are taken from M. I. Trush, *Vneshnepoliticheskaia deiatel'nost V. I. Lenina 1921–1923 den' za dnem* (Moscow, 1967), pp. 298, 311, 319–22, 335.

the demise of Lenin, there were no rules for succession procedures, and no obvious heir apparent. But whereas it took Khrushchev a mere seventeen months after the Twentieth Party Congress to assert his primacy, Stalin did not gain a firm hold over the Politburo for five and a half more years after the Thirteenth Congress, although his control over the party apparatus dated from that Congress. It was inconceivable to imagine Malenkov in the 1950s issuing a public defence of his cause, as Trotsky did in his *Lessons of October*. The intervening years of harsh authoritarian government in the 1930s and 1940s made all the difference between the political climate of the 1920s and the 1950s.

When Marx was in a relaxed, philosophical frame of mind, he refined his theories on social structure, allowing for subtleties that on other occasions were swept aside by Marx the engaged revolutionary, who blunted his tools in his passion to win an argument. His Bolshevik disciples did likewise with a vengeance in the debates of NEP. Most of the top Bolsheviks were gifted intellectuals, unlike the following generation. Emerging from the gross *Unordnung* of revolution and war, and trying to keep their heads above the ocean of obscurantism that Russia still represented for the most part, they would have agreed with another intellectual, William James, on 'our indomitable desire to cast the world into a more rational shape in our minds than the shape into which it is thrown there by the crude order of experience'.[6]

It was easier to impose a pattern from above when time and data were lacking. Bolshevik leaders were condemned to be jacks of all trades in early NEP for lack of expertise due to the social upheaval caused by the Revolution. They were extremely busy, and administrative changes were taking place at lightning speed. Statistics were initially unobtainable on any social topic: instead, politicians were condemned to deal with the daily flood of unsorted 'vermicelli' that swept into their offices and committees from all levels of society.[7] A veritable Domesday Book would have been needed in order for them to apply their Marxist social engineering with any precision.

Of course many deviations from this general picture oc-

[6] W. James, *Essays on Faith and Morals* (Cleveland, Ohio, 1962), p. 147.
[7] See Ch. 5, p. 157 on the activities of the Sovnarkom.

curred amongst the Bolshevik leaders. At least three of them descended on occasion from their abstract heights and took a good dose of reality. Due to his grave illness, Lenin was allowed to escape from overwork and vermicelli into his study in 1922. He could still indulge in flights of fancy as he did on the future of peasant co-operatives, but at the same time he pin-pointed with uncanny accuracy the practical problems associated with bureaucracy that were already showing and which were to increase during NEP. He was close to the evils of bureaucracy, and distant from the realities of peasant communal life.

Bukharin, too, could be in two minds, though not at the same time, as Lenin was in 1922. In his earlier career Bukharin had been as abstract and unrealistic as many other Bolsheviks, but later he had rather more leisure to ponder and then to write out his changing ideas of society, in his *ABC of Communism* and other works. His views during NEP fitted squarely within the framework of the fifty-year alternative, giving his notions more apparent credibility than those of other leaders. He was perceptive enough to realize the psychological truth that any developing society must have a minimal amount of harmony between its class components in order to make progress. He abhorred the sharp class conflict that some of his colleagues wished to keep up, even in NEP. Yet when it came to practical details in his campaign for sending the workers among the peasantry in order to unite the two classes,[8] Bukharin's proposals remained as naïve in conception and projected execution as the similar attempts of the 1870s.

It is a notorious fact that intellectuals construct too many reifications out of reality. Stalin was lucky in this respect, since he was an intellectual *manqué*. The only theories he gave to the world were either a hotchpotch, like his nationality theory, or absurd, like the notion of the sharpening of class conflict as Russia entered communism at the height of the Great Purges. He preferred the apparent drudgery of his job as General Secretary from 1922 onwards, which gave him the practical advantage of being able to remould the party apparatus in his own image. The power struggle at the top also took up much of his energy, leaving him time merely to demolish the abstract

---

[8] N. Bukharin, *ABC of Communism* (London, 1969), pp. 187–8.

constructs of others—above all Trotsky's pet theory of permanent revolution.

However, one cannot deny the significance of colligatory concepts in history. Developments may not be connected externally by a logical series of empirical events, but they may be by the long-term speculations of a group of agents, like the Bolsheviks during NEP. And when historical developments become distorted, confused, and even degenerate in the eyes of the beholders, then ideas are taken all the more as being primary, and more valuable than any precise diagnosis of events. This is what happened in the 1920s. By 1923 even that pragmatic plodder, Molotov, was arguing that theory was needed more than practice in party circles. He accused the ninety-five Marxist circles in Moscow of not meriting their name, since they indulged wholly in political organization and jettisoned what he called '*ideinyi bagazh*' ('the luggage of ideas').[9]

Having now looked in general at the blinkers, either imposed or self-inflicted, on the Party's views of society in mid-NEP, it is proposed to focus in particular on three problem areas which continued to attract a lot of attention between 1922 and 1926—the administrative supervision of the economy, the nationalities, and cultural backwardness.

Soviet historiography on economic management in the 1920s has been keen to demonstrate that the prevailing idea of NEP held by what are termed 'bourgeois falsifiers' of history is erroneous. NEP was not, as the latter maintain, a contradiction of those Marxist theories held by the Bolsheviks prior to 1921. Neither was it introduced in a hurried and unexpected manner, nor abandoned suddenly in 1928 contrary to Lenin's intentions and prognostications concerning NEP which he expressed before his death in 1924. Lenin himself stressed that NEP was the outcome of purely practical circumstances, but since Marx asserted that only the general direction of the revolutionary transformation of capitalist into socialist society could be foreseen, this did not lead to a dichotomy between concrete circumstances and theory. Soviet historians see NEP as merely one stage, or rather a series of stages, standing in the chrono-

⁹ V. Molotov, *Na shestoi god. Kitogam i perspektivam partiinoi raboty* (Moscow, 1923), pp. 37–8.

logical middle of a logically planned continuum which spans Bolshevik thought and action between the years before 1917 and the end of the second Five-Year Plan. In support of this thesis they concentrate on four selected topics, two of which significantly fall outside the NEP period.[10] They hold, in the first place, that Lenin's unwavering determination to develop the economy on the basis of large-scale industrial production could allow him nevertheless to introduce an economic breathing-space in the spring of 1918 which was similar to NEP in many ways. One feature which was lacking in 1918, however, was the later admission during NEP of private trade under the control of the Soviet government. Thus NEP was not an unpremeditated nor an untried experiment in 1921. Secondly, Lenin never ceased to view NEP as an indispensable transitional period to be used for the dynamic change from small-scale production to state capitalism and thence to socialism. His pre-1917 analysis of imperialism as the highest and most concentrated stage of capitalism led him in *State and Revolution* to point out the close parallels between state capitalism of this kind and socialist organization, which could employ monopolistic combines and banks in a similar way. When neither domestic large-scale private enterprise nor foreign private capital had become adequate in the opening years of NEP (1921–2) to act as a basis for state capitalism which would draw within its beneficial influence and transform small-scale, reactionary peasant economic life, Lenin effected a major turning-point in his ideas, expressed in his article on co-operation written in January 1923. All forms of economic co-operation, including purely trading co-operatives, he now envisaged as belonging to the socialist, and not as formerly to the state capitalist, sector. They were collective and so anti-capitalist in nature, and were veering to the socialist sector since the land, on which the great majority of co-operatives were based, belonged to the state under the control of the working class. Thus already in 1923 socialist economic organization was beginning to occupy a dominating position *vis-à-vis* declining state capitalism.

[10] For a typical example of the kind of analysis which follows, see V. I. Kuz'min, 'Lenin's Ideas of NEP and their Practical Realization in the USSR', in *Voprosy Istorii* (Apr. 1970). This conventional Soviet interpretation of NEP is being slowly superseded in the light of historiographical *glasnost'* since Gorbachev's accession to power.

The third line of argument is that as early as 1924–5 the economic balance was tilted in the direction of the modification that took place at the close of NEP. By 1924–5 figures showed that under the stimulus of the peasant market industrial production was beginning to take precedence over trading activities. Large-scale socialist organization arising out of the mixed economy of NEP was preparing to move into a dominant position. The economic changes that took place at the end of NEP were regulated according to the principles worked out by Lenin before his death, although their timing and stringency were to some extent governed by circumstances arising after 1924–5. For instance, it became clear that agricultural production and small-scale peasant-exchange could not produce the required tempo of socialization in industry. Larger sown areas increased agricultural production more than improved machinery, and in industry itself the accumulation of worn-out machinery inherited from the past began to have a stronger effect. An accelerated population movement from the rural areas to the towns towards the end of NEP led to an increased demand for consumer goods. New social problems included rising unemployment and above all the '*kulaks*', who formed the main obstacle to the flow of economic wealth from the village to large-scale urban production.

Two alternatives were open to the government, according to Soviet historians. Either industrial production could be developed in order to meet the pressing demands made on it by worker and peasant alike, or the country could stagnate, submitting to '*kulak*' pressures. The first alternative was the more rational in economic terms, and the movement of the peasantry into the collective farms had been prepared for by the closer ties forged between state industry and small-scale peasant production between 1925 and 1927. Collectivization expressed the economic interests of the poor and middle peasants. It released millions of agricultural workers for industry and in time allowed for the production of agricultural machinery vital to peasant prosperity. The first Five-Year Plan incorporated the pre-existing peasant machinery co-operatives, thus saving them from the grip of the '*kulaks*'.

In the fourth place Soviet scholars point to the evolutionary ties which bound NEP to the period of the Five-Year Plans. Individual farming methods were squeezed out, but only gradually in several ways, and the situation was not fundamentally opposed to that which prevailed in NEP when free private trade had also been controlled in part. As late as June 1930, Stalin actually claimed at the Sixteenth Party Congress: 'In going over to the offensive along the whole front, we are not yet abolishing NEP, for private trade and capitalist elements still remain, commodity turnover and the money economy still remain. But we are certainly abolishing the initial stage of NEP, and developing its following stage, the present stage of NEP, which is the last stage.'[11] In the first two Five-Year Plans individual peasants were geared into the development of the economy, unlike the period of War Communism, when they had been totally excluded. Lenin said that the basis for a socialist economy would be laid in Russia when the peasantry was economically satisfied. This should be interpreted as meaning being satisfied not with consumer goods, but with the necessary agricultural machinery for socialist production.

In conclusion, Soviet authors show how Lenin and the Soviet government constantly adapted the economic structure to new circumstances through the linked stages that preceded, covered, and followed NEP. As the government came to master the workings of trade relationships, so it was able to merge the activities of state industry and small-scale peasant economic organization. The rise of a socialized industrial process in 1924–5 called for collectivization in order to ensure its continued development beyond the bounds of NEP. NEP did not alter ultimate Bolshevik objectives one bit, 'it only changed the approach to the resolution of those objectives'. Kuz'min epitomizes the period of the first two Five-Year Plans as 'NEP without capitalists, NEP withering away'.[12]

To anyone at all familiar with Soviet history as viewed by non-Soviet scholars, the discrepancies in interpretation between the two camps are very wide. It is difficult to analyse a general Soviet exposition of this kind which is bound together by a unifying hypothesis, but rather than reject the hypothesis

[11] *XVI s'ezd VKP(b)* (1931), p. 37.
[12] Ibid., pp. 78, 86.

*in toto* it would perhaps be more constructive to dwell in detail on a few sections of it. These will be considered in chronological sequence.

Any attempt to liberate historiography from the accepted watertight compartments of time in which it so often becomes imprisoned must be welcomed. With NEP, as with the periods before and after 1917, both Soviet and Western scholars have tended to underplay the extent of forces which overflowed the strict time-spans involved. Yet it remains incontrovertible on the basis of the evidence that NEP was in fact introduced in a hurried and unexpected manner. While it is true that the peasants' stranglehold on the grain supply to the towns had a cumulative effect which dated back at least to the summer of 1917, the Bolsheviks had until 1921 applied completely different methods to deal with the problem than those which were ushered in with NEP. Yet in 1918 itself there was no suggestion that the breathing-space might be repeated and prolonged in the future. Moreover, the parallel between the two periods is too loose to warrant serious consideration. The 1918 episode was too fleeting to be characterized. It took place at a chaotic moment when most economic measures were carried out through uncoordinated local initiative. The admission that private trade 'under the control of the Soviet government'[13] marked a difference between 1918 and NEP quite destroys the case for a comparison. When the analogy was drawn, at the Eleventh Party Conference in December 1921, the long-term effect of private trading could not be predicted. The real essence of NEP lies in its changing nature. By 1926–7 the overwhelming influence of the peasantry and of private trade placed them beyond the milder forms of social and economic control envisaged by Lenin. Political intervention on a massive scale was another kind of control. This was needed because socio-economic influences from below had gone so far as to endanger even the general direction of Marxist development in the Soviet Union. Thus Soviet assertions that the idiosyncrasies of NEP could be contained within the fluid frontiers of progressive Marxist theory may be valid for the early 1920s, but not for the latter part of NEP; nor, it may be added, for

13 *XVI s'ezd VKP(b)* (1931), p. 37.

NEP taken as an evolutionary whole. When some Bolsheviks realized this in the late 1920s—a realization which Soviet scholars do not concede—they executed under pressure a political and economic volte-face which bears little or no resemblance to a comparatively smooth transition.

The second argument concerning Lenin's progressive use of state capitalism and then the co-operative system as tools with which to push NEP into a large-scale socialist mould reflects the way in which both Lenin and Soviet historians take refuge in very broad theoretical assumptions which are subsequently belied by concrete socio-economic circumstances. Lenin himself discarded some of the more utopian strands of *State and Revolution* concerning the ease with which state capitalism could be transformed into socialism. Lenin's highly theoretical reasons for claiming in 1923 that the co-operative system was henceforth in the socialist sector are said to have changed the balance of the whole economy. This instant strength of mind over matter is staggering to contemplate, even for a non-Marxist. Quite apart from this, the increasing unsuitability of the co-operatives after Lenin's death to serve as a vehicle for uniting small-scale and large-scale sectors of the economy is ignored. Their social and economic role became increasingly limited in scope. The higher administrative levels were clogged by bureaucratic overstaffing, while business at the grass roots tended increasingly to favour the richer and more enterprising peasants. The most authentic groups in the late 1920s, which still preserved something of the genuine spirit of co-operation, were the 'wild' ones, evading the control of the state co-operatives. Soviet scholars agree that Lenin needed to change horses once with the decline of the potential influence of state capitalism in 1921–2, but they do not agree that Lenin then backed another loser. Given the great discrepancy between the Bolsheviks' large-scale projects and the small-scale realities at work in NEP, it is debatable whether any existing economic institution could gradually bridge the gap between the two without the use of wide-ranging political coercion. The whole weight of the peasants' psychological and social prejudices, which Lenin recognized but underrated in his optimistic view of the future, told against the possibility. The Soviets' purely economic reasoning ignores the mentality which is nowhere better expressed than in Maxim Gorky's *On The Russian Peasantry*. Countrymen saw the Soviet town workers as 'restless when they are in a big heap. They should be split up into small arteli, with a few hundreds here and a few hundreds there.' Diminutive, self-sufficient factories should be set up in every guberniia with lots of space between them.[14]

The third argument, that the years 1924–5 witnessed a decisive shift towards a socialized economy, is based on the slimmest statistical evidence, although Soviet scholars vary in their dating of this shift. Contemporary sources from the 1920s are used sparingly by present-day Soviet scholars apart from Lenin's generalizations. This method results in an abstract, theoretical approach, akin to the Whig tradition. Not only are the crucial later years of NEP observed through the filter of far more recent events and judgements rather than in paying attention to the facts and opinions on them as they emerged in the years 1925–7: Lenin's inadequate foresight before 1924 is also assumed to be sufficient in principle for the diagnosis of the close of NEP.

There is another basic internal contradiction in Soviet reasoning. If 1924–5 heralded the approach of a healthy socialist outcome for the mixed economy of NEP and the co-operative system continued to act thereafter as a socialist agent for the smychka between town and country, between large-scale and small-scale organization, why did economic problems—let alone a host of other administrative, political, and social sores—crop up so quickly and on so many fronts in the two years before collectivization? Western scholars like E. H. Carr, R. W. Davies, and Moshe Lewin point to an inseparable amalgam of political, social, and economic difficulties which reached a crescendo in 1926–7 but whose roots must be traced back to the origins of NEP and in some cases to far earlier periods. The collapse of NEP was surely a watershed and an acute crisis whose dimensions some Soviet authors cut down almost beyond recognition.

The usual official Soviet interpretation of NEP as given above shows clearly how subsequent Russian historians have failed to fathom its true organic, or rather inorganic develop-

---

[14] M. Gorky, *O russkom krestian'stve* (Berlin, 1922), pp. 39–40.

ment and collapse. Indeed, although they have the benefit of hindsight, their views are even more schematic and bald than the reifications of those who administered the economy and society at the time. Not only did the far from monolithic party leadership have no clearly agreed viewpoint: there were also at least three distinct levels at or near the peak of the Party. Each level had its own reasons for examining economic administration in a different light.

At the top level, Bolshevik titans like Stalin, Trotsky, Zinoviev, Kamenev, and others wrestled with one another in open political debate. In the course of this they tossed about changing economic arguments which had a great deal to do with their relative position at any given time in the kaleidoscopic personal coalitions of the mid-1920s, and little to do with realities in actual socio-economic life. Trotsky remained dangerously aloof from the in-fighting, and to this extent less interested in the instant propaganda value of his ideas. He was more faithful to untainted intellectual values and in particular to the force of rational dialectics. Unfortunately this led him by a different route to despise what he called 'dull empiricism, . . . cringing worship of the fact'.[15] His views on economic administration through NEP were pretty abstract, deriving from a continuing obsession with the progressive internal logic of his own brilliant debate with himself. It is not correct to say, as has often been the case, that he came down heavily and finally from 1922 onwards on the side of domestic heavy industry and primitive socialist accumulation as it actually came about in its later form.[16] In a speech to the Comintern Congress in November 1922 he argued that factories, like railway lines, should be judged in terms of efficiency 'only through the medium of the market'. He also asserted that 'private capital now operating in Russia is backed up by world capital'.[17] As late as the autumn of 1926 he was still advocating the deeper integration of the USSR in the world economy,[18]

[15] Quoted in B. Wolfe, *Three Who Made a Revolution* (New York, 1948), p. 193.
[16] See e.g. I. Deutscher, *The Prophet Unarmed: Trotsky 1921–1929* (London, 1959), pp. 40–4.
[17] Trotsky, *First Five Years of the Communist International*, vol. 2 (New York, 1953), pp. 234, 242.
[18] Trotsky, articles in *Pravda*, 1, 2, 16, 17, 20, and 22 Sept. 1926. The author is indebted to Dr R. Bideleux for advice on Trotsky's attitude to economic problems in NEP.

two years after Stalin's introduction of the theory of socialism in one country. Besides being foolhardy in terms of political tactics, Trotsky's obsession with the permanent reinvigoration of Russian trade and foreign aid had lost touch with the grim reality of increasing Soviet isolation by this time.

Stalin, quite contrary to both Trotsky and Bukharin, merely echoed Marxist notions on the very general outline of the future without going into any detail until 1926–9. In his acrobatic about-turns on the management of the economy in mid-NEP with the aim above all of dividing and ruling the other party leaders, he protected himself by mouthing vague orthodoxies. In 1926 when he was clearly in the ascendancy, he began to work out firmer ideas which he then stuck to, and acted upon in 1929. He never adopted Trotsky's supposed 1922 views on primitive socialist accumulation. However, he did add Preobrazhensky's *revised* views on this method, together with some detailed advice from S. G. Strumilin. For the rest, his strategy was based on the past practice of War Communism and on the much earlier programme of Arakcheev. Typically, he relied on pragmatic examples drawn from real history.

At the level just below the summit of the ruthless political struggle for Lenin's succession very different motives from those of Stalin can be detected. Bukharin was in the main a political loner until 1925. He was regarded as their junior in age and tenure by the senior members of the Politburo, of which he remained only a candidate member until 1924. His ambitions centred entirely on the fulfilment of his social and economic plans. It was his fervent belief in them rather than a lust for power that persuaded him in the first part of 1925 to join with Stalin as co-leader of the majority in the Central Committee. Having made one major volte-face, he pursued the steady elaboration of his new soft line towards the peasantry throughout NEP, with no sudden deviations in order to secure a firmer personal hold in the Politburo. Bukharin was the nearest of its members to what would nowadays be called a professional sociologist. His call for a genuine socio-economic balance and harmony between worker and peasant was based on a firmer grasp of the realities of NEP society. His notion of social change through evolution also appeared at first sight to correspond more closely with the general aims of the NEP economy, although Lenin had inaugurated it with the idea of social change by successive assaults: and in this way NEP was to be ended by Stalin. Above all, Bukharin tended to treat his fellow-countrymen of all classes as human beings, putting them before abstract principles. In this he was highly unusual among the Bolshevik leaders. Yet his very optimism and warmth led him into naïveties. He could not at first see how his backing of the peasant sector might antagonize unemployed urban workers, who numbered around two million between 1925 and 1929. He also allowed Stalin to adopt his theories, which were popular in 1925, in order to win a stable majority, and then to abandon him and his principles when it suited him later.

Another planner who got entangled in politics at the highest level at the end of NEP was E. Preobrazhensky. Like Bukharin he stuck to his theories, particularly to his famous definition of primitive socialist accumulation, which he elaborated slowly, starting with his 1922 book, *From NEP to Socialism*. This work also anticipated Stalin's theory of socialism in a separate country,[19] yet it had no obvious influence on Stalin or other top-level leaders at the time it was published. It was too deeply embedded in the ethos of War Communism to have any impact. Real economic authority in administrative, though hardly in political terms, remained in the Finance Commissariat and Gosbank until 1925. In fact the decisively pro-industrial shift in Preobrazhensky's writings did not take place before the end of 1922. Until then he saw loans in kind to the peasantry as an essential prerequisite of economic growth. He altered his stance, not because of any political machinations, but after the prospects for an excellent 1922 harvest were clear.

Bukharin's and Preobrazhensky's final reward for integrity and attention to detail in their forward planning was their own lives, in 1938 and 1937 respectively. They both refused to modify their own theories to save their political skins. At the third and lowest level of planning the participants were the playthings of high politics from the start of NEP and never achieved any independent status, as Bukharin and Preobrazhensky did for brief periods from 1925 onwards. An early

[19] For an excellent interpretation of Preobrazhensky's views, see R. B. Day, 'Preobrazhensky and the Theory of the Transition Period', in *Soviet Studies* (Apr. 1975), pp. 196–219.

example of this was the way in which the economic administrators in the Finance Commissariat and Gosplan were pushed around in 1922 as the result of a political wrangle between Trotsky and Lenin. Trotsky insisted on the vital need for a centralized economic plan and industrial development, and so campaigned to strengthen Gosplan and alter its membership. He succeeded in getting Gosplan consulted on drafts of important economic decrees passing through Sovnarkom,[20] but Lenin was able, before his stroke in May 1922, to stop Gosplan encroaching further on the powers of the Commissariat. Trotsky's enemies suspected him of aiming to become the head of Gosplan, but Lenin wanted an educated technician rather than a political visionary in charge, and vigorously defended his loyal friend G. I. Krzhizhanovsky, who remained in his post.

Large numbers of the Tsarist technical intelligentsia held on to their jobs after 1917, often due to personal ties of this kind. L. B. Krasin, one of the leaders of Bolshevik military organization in 1905, was an engineer who intervened during NEP in disputes between economic or technical administrators and left-wing party activists. Lenin's personal secretary, N. P. Gorbunov, was another engineer who protected non-party administrators. Thus even those whose political affinities were not clear could, until 1926, initiate and discuss plans among themselves, and forward them to the top level in the real hope that their voices would be heard. There was a high proportion of 'specialists' until the end of 1923 in leading posts. In 1922 73 per cent of the directors of the largest factories in the area round Moscow were still 'specialists'.[21] The Supreme Council of the National Economy itself was strongly under their influence from 1921 on. A surprisingly large number of ex-Mensheviks also survived in positions of some influence.[22] Their previous political views enabled them to mould their economic thought more closely than most to the contours of NEP, which many Mensheviks abroad claimed was the breathing-space they had been looking forward to in 1917.

Advisers in these categories simply did not have to grind any

[20] See *Sobranie Uzakonenii*, 40 (1922), art. 468.

[21] S. A. Fediukin, *Sovetskaia vlast' i burzhuaznye spetsialisty* (Moscow, 1965), p. 139.

[22] See Naum Jasny, *Great Soviet Economist of the 1920s* (Cambridge, England, 1972).

political axe, nor were the 'specialists' inclined by temperament to do so. They produced a large number of cool objective reports on many aspects of the economy in so far as obtainable data permitted. The great majority of these were not digested by Soviet and foreign scholars until quite recently. Occasionally Stalin profited from the subtle wisdom and wide knowledge of someone like Strumilin, but he, above all the other leaders, was averse to the 'specialists'. He spoke out against the 'Change of Landmarks' movement, run by 'specialists', at each party congress between 1923 and 1925. By the spring of 1928 he came out completely against this type of adviser. After 1926, as before 1921, Bolshevik politicians relied much more heavily on their own abstract rhetoric. In November 1922 N. Valentinov (Vol'skii) had penned a letter to Lenin, asking him whether he seriously believed that the Party could make economic progress on the basis of utopian ideas, and on books like those of A. Bebel, who, like Thomas More, wished to build society on a moneyless basis. Valentinov never received a reply from the paralysed invalid.[23]

The Bolsheviks as a whole were faced with the dilemma of trying to apply Marx's aim of creating large-scale economic and social structures to virtually the only major developing country in the world that abounded in practice in small-scale entities—the family farm, the kustari, etc.—spread out thinly through the largest country on earth, with poor communications and an atrocious climate in most regions. The author has dwelt on this problem at length elsewhere, so he refers the reader to the arguments given there.[24] During NEP most politicians could not, or did not want to bridge this gulf. Even the new Leninist glosses on Marxist theories, such as smychka and sheftsvo, failed to relate theory to practice. This was seen clearly in the chapter on Kursk guberniia in 1922. We shall see in the chapter on agents of the centre in the countryside in 1926 that the situation did not improve on 1922: indeed it deteriorated in some respects.

Apart from Bukharin and a considerable number of

[23] N. Valentinov, *Novaia ekonomicheskaia politika i krizis partii posle smerti Lenina* (Stanford, 1971), pp. 34–6.
[24] R. W. Pethybridge, 'Large-Scale Theories versus Small-Scale Realities', in *The Social Prelude to Stalinism* (London, 1974).

third-level thinkers, including scholars like A. V. Chaianov, highly placed administrators concentrated too much in good Marxist fashion on economic mainsprings, to the neglect of social criteria. Because the '*kulaks*' showed visible signs of accumulating private property in late NEP, they were picked out as the greatest threat to socialism. In reality the 25 million or so peasant households, all of them relatively impoverished, had not the slightest prospect of 'restoring capitalism'. Far more insidious in their long-term influence were in fact the Nepmen and the kustari, as will be shown later. Given their economic roles respectively as wholesale traders and small-scale producers, they showed fewer external signs of tangible property than the richest peasants. Moreover neither category had been discussed by Marx, who had spent much energy on diatribes against the peasantry as an economic phenomenon.

This over-concentration on purely economic criteria also led to a neglect of the relationship between socio-economic progress and free political discussion. It was left to Mensheviks in exile like Martov to argue in 1922 that only genuinely democratic government could turn the 'bourgeois' phase that was NEP into a truly radical and humane episode. Martov found Bolshevism by early NEP to be a historical absurdity—a Red dictatorship lulled by the New Economic Policy whose contradictions ate away its roots.[25]

It is doubtful whether any regime of any political cast could have made precise economic plans on the basis of the available data. Every subsequent historian of the early Soviet period has bewailed the lack of statistical evidence. Trotsky in his intellectual arrogance dismissed the need for it, as has been noted. On these occasions he produced mystifying mumbo-jumbo to deal with the lacunae.

I do not provide statistical data about differentiation in the village, because no figures have been collected which would make a general estimate of this process possible. This absence must be explained not so much by the defects of our statistics as by the peculiarities of the social process itself, which embraces the 'molecular' alterations of 22 million peasant establishments.[26]

---

[25] Y. I. Martov, 'Nasha Platforma', in *Sotsialisticheskii Vestnik*, 19 (4 Oct. 1922).
[26] Trotsky, *Pravda*, Sept. 1926.

In the chapter devoted to Smolensk in 1922 it was noted how the whole network of early Soviet fiscal control had to be vague. The rouble was fluctuating immensely at the start of NEP. It was impossible to estimate revenue from new taxes. Even by 1924 peasant mirs were still imposing self-taxation, unknown to the local authorities, who were supposed to receive it all through the rural Soviets. Near the end of NEP, standardization for timber lengths and treatment had been laid down in Moscow, on paper, but Belorussia and Tver gubernii were still not adhering to it.[27]

Vagueness abounded with regard to the all-important political concept of the '*kulak*'. It was indeed a polemical definition, since in retrospect it possesses no credibility as a social category. As early as 1922 Chaianov was pointing out that the behaviour of nearly all Russian peasants was impossible to account for in terms of the standard theories regarding the four main factors of production.[28] By 1926 the position was even more confused. The Commissar of Agriculture, A. P. Smirnov, now claimed that the '*kulak*' had almost vanished from peasant life.[29] In the same year Bukharin declared that the '*kulak*' was a type quite different from 'the strong farmer hiring some *batraki*'.[30] Yet this bogy was to be portrayed as the chief threat to the whole of the social and political structure of the Soviet Union. There is no better example than this in the whole of Soviet history of a social abstraction run riot.

To conclude, there were two further major barriers against the efficient administration of NEP. The first was geographical and structural dislocation brought about by the World War, the Civil War, and the Famine, all of which entailed huge alterations of boundaries and migrations of populations and industrial enterprises. The change of the capital city caused another vast disorientation in central supervision of the peripheries. The bitter fruits of dislocation have already been treated at length in the chapter on Bolshevik controls.[31] Economic regional planning remained unclear as a result

[27] A. P. Serebrovsky, *Ratsionalizatsiia proizvodstva i novoe promyshlennoe stroitel'stvo SSSR* (Moscow, 1927), pp. 43–9.

[28] A. V. Chaianov, *Theory of Peasant Economy* (London, 1966), p. xiv.

[29] Quoted in *Na agrarnom fronte*, 9 (1930), pp. 20–1.

[30] Bukharin, *Put' k sotsializmu i raboche-krest'ianskii blok* (Moscow, 1926), p. 13.

[31] See Ch. 5 above.

throughout NEP, leading to unresolved clashes over the need for devolution from the centre[32] and to rivalry between the needs of the minority nationalities on the one hand, and economic rationality on the other. In turn these structural uncertainties led to a proliferation of overlapping bureaucracies, both amongst those that rearranged the localities, like the Administrative Commission and Gosplan, and those that governed the central decision-making processes. The clashes between the Commissariats, the Central Control Commission, and the Moscow offices of Rabkrin were noted earlier.[33]

The final hazard was in part a self-inflicted one. Speed was of the essence for a regime in a hurry to overcome relative economic backwardness in order to fulfil its political promises to the proletariat, and now in NEP, to the peasantry as well. In 1922, the same year that the first Constitution of the USSR was drawn up, the whole of the legal system revised, the federal and nationality network established, Gosplan required the successor to the Administrative Commission to comment within the space of two weeks on its draft for the economic regionalization of the largest country on earth. Small wonder that NEP was a house built on sand.

Let us now turn to our second problem area, that of the national minorities. This question worried the Soviet leadership on frequent occasions and fronts between 1922 and 1926. I have already touched upon the subject briefly in the treatment of Belorussia, and the eastern Ukraine (Kharkov and Poltava). It will be a central theme of the final chapter concerning Kazahkhstan in mid-NEP. In order to relate these necessarily fragmented sections to a conceptual whole, the leading Bolsheviks' views on the national problem are discussed at this point. Particular attention is paid to the largest minority nationality (the Ukraine) and the most troublesome one (Georgia) between 1922 and 1926.

The vast expanse of the Union of Soviet Socialist Republics contained by 1926 69 millions of its 147 million inhabitants who were not Great Russians.[34] Stalin told the First Congress

[32] The arguments of A. I. Rykov in 1923 for devolution were thwarted, as were also the plans for decentralization in the transport administration. See p. 125 above.
[33] See p. 186 above.
[34] *Vsesoiuznaia perepis' naseleniia 1926 g.*

of the Soviets of the new Union on 30 December 1922 that it represented 'the victory of the new Russia over the old Russia, over the policeman of Europe and the butcher of Asia'. He hit at foreign scapegoats to the west and the east in order to avert attention from the fact that within a few years after the Revolution the Bolshevik government, despite its fiercely anti-imperialist views, had recouped by far the greater part of the former Empire. By the end of 1922 the RSFSR took charge of the few remaining semi-independent states—the Ukraine, Belorussia, and Transcaucasia. Their prerogatives had been progressively curtailed, and in the case of Georgia, taken by force. Opposition to these moves had taken three main forms. Straightforward nationalist opposition was most clearly represented by the Basmachis, and by the Turk, Enver Pasha, who wished to liberate the whole of Turkestan from Soviet rule. More complicated were the nationalist-communist objections of the Tartar communist, Sultan-Galiev. He claimed that the industrial proletariat of the Soviet heartland was more interested in exploiting the nationalities than in liberating them. The third and more lasting type of opposition came entirely from within the ranks of communism, and was directed primarily against Stalin in 1922.

After 1921 Lenin concentrated more on the establishment of the NEP, leaving Stalin discretionary powers over the nationalities. On 10 August 1922, a commission was set up to prepare the paperwork for the forthcoming federation. Stalin himself drafted the proposal for the statute. This was based on the structure of the RSFSR, which already embraced national groups within a statute of autonomy. In the new federation the larger national minorities would be included with the status of autonomous republics, like the groups already included in the RSFSR. Stalin's proposals met with complete rejection from the Georgians, and many reservations from the Ukrainians. Centralist control over these two nationalities and Belorussia between 1922 and 1926 will be examined shortly, but at this point the political and socio-economic motives of Stalin and Lenin in 1922 require clarification.

Due to his illness, Lenin only became aware of Stalin's draft in September 1922. He then opposed it completely, and drew up quite a different version. He proposed a federation of equal republics rather than a system dominated by the RSFSR.

Stalin openly criticized this in the Politburo, but yielded to Lenin by revising his document. Yet subject to reservations on the part of Georgia and the Ukraine, all the national parties were prepared to accept Stalin's projected federation of the USSR. The Constitution which was eventually adopted on 31 January 1924 by the Second Congress of the Soviets of the Union put the seal on Stalin's version. The powerful federal organs were those of the RSFSR, which dominated the nationalities. The Congress was due to meet once a year, but until 1931 it met every two years only. All the most important matters were dealt with by the central authorities in Moscow: cultural affairs alone remained essentially diverse.

Stalin's triumph over the dying Lenin was not as overwhelming nor as clear-cut as it might seem in the light of the final outcome. Lenin never really gave up his firm opinion that all national movements were reactionary and harmful to the Revolution, since they played down the class question and thus hampered the development of unity among the proletariat of separate countries (and among nationalities within the same country). However, he always distinguished between the smaller Soviet nationalities and Great-Russian nationalism: the harmful aspects of the former's views could be negated by the gradual and careful elimination of suspicion, whereas the latter factor was far more formidable.[35] Lenin reiterated this view even more forcefully in the winter of 1922–3 in the light of Stalin's head-on clash with Georgian Communists. Lenin saw this quarrel as symptomatic of the chauvinism and bureaucratic centralism of the old Great-Russian regime. Bureaucratism was preying on his mind at the time with regard to other Bolshevik control systems, as was seen in Chapter 5. Great-Russian heavy-handed ways were just another facet of this all-pervading evil. In his attack on the Georgian Stalin for exploiting Russian nationalism, Lenin was dealing with the perennial case of a marginal man overstressing his loyalty as a result of his minority complex. Many other empire-builders before Stalin came from areas that were marginal to great cultural hubs: Alexander from Macedonia, Tamerlane from Mongolia, Napoleon from Corsica, and Hitler from Austria.

[35] Lenin, *Sochineniia*, vol. 20 (4th edn., Moscow 1941–51), pp. 383–4.

Nevertheless Lenin was not concerned for the minority rights of the nationalities *per se*. He was afraid of aggravating relations between the Soviet nationalities: this would weaken their diplomatic unity against hostile capitalist countries. The unsuccessful experience of Bolshevik leaders in the Ukraine in 1919 had convinced him for good that only the most conciliatory attitude would succeed in the border areas, so long as Moscow remained a weak force in the world. Thus Lenin disagreed with Stalin on tactics and timing, not on fundamental issues. He accused Stalin of being in too much of a hurry over the Georgian question. Once again, as on the subject of the growth of bureaucracy, he was being prescient. We shall see in a later chapter how in 1926 Stalin looked upon the speedy transformation of Kazakh society and its economy as a precursor of what was to happen to the whole of the Union after the collapse of NEP.

For his part, Stalin ceded temporarily to Lenin's point of view in 1922 because he judged with cold realism that the pre-existing situation in the Tsarist Empire would endure through the sheer weight of history and human apathy, and so perpetuate the leading role of the RSFSR within the new federation. It seemed to him inevitable, and he was to be proved right, that since Russia had lost a large portion of its people, good agricultural land, and industrial resources in the west, it would recoup these losses in the south and the east. The birth-rate was higher in these areas and emigration eastwards started up again from 1921 on.

There were ideological as well as socio-economic reasons why both Lenin and Stalin wished to exert closer control over the regions concerned. Their frontier-type conditions, drought, and other hazards necessitated a high degree of peasant collaboration. The only profitable examples of Lenin's favourite bridge to larger-scale farming, the co-operatives, were to be found in Siberia and Turkestan. There were also flourishing state and collective farms in the Caucasus, forerunners of what were to become a universal type after NEP. Quite soon in NEP the Central Asian areas were exporting vital crops like cotton at low cost to the Great Russians. Perhaps there was something after all in Sultan-Galiev's thesis that the industrial Russian heartland was exploiting the minority areas.

The fate of Georgia in 1921–2 was indicative of the way things would go in the future for other minority nationalities after 1926. In February 1921 the Red Army invaded Georgia in order to oust the Menshevik government there. Lenin had rejected union by force, but it was he who gave the order to attack Georgia. Then in March 1922 the economic unification of a wider area was created by the federation of all the Soviet Socialist Republics of Transcaucasia. The Bolshevik Georgians objected strongly to this move, since they realized that a Soviet federal state would follow quickly in the wake of the Transcaucasian Republic. Stalin dealt with them swiftly and ruthlessly, so that by December 1922 the new Republic was set up.

Ideological thoughts on the nationality problem in the abstract had little to do with the brutal take-over of Georgia. Other, more compelling motives were at work. Perhaps the most deep-seated, as in the Anglo-Irish relationship, was the subconscious envy on the part of a newer but powerful civilization of a small culture over three thousand years old with an extensive literary and artistic tradition. Peter the Great was still trying to persuade the rest of the world in the eighteenth century that the Russians were no longer barbarians. An equally sore point, but one of very recent creation, was the Menshevik domination of Georgia until 1921. Internecine hatred on the left of politics has always been especially bitter, and the Russian Social Democrats were no exception. The Menshevik and Georgian perversion of the only true way haunted the Bolsheviks. The Mensheviks' aim of self-government by the Georgian people had percolated through several levels of society well before the fall of the autocracy, to an extent that the Bolsheviks did not achieve in Russia.[36] Georgian Mensheviks (Chkeidze, Tsereteli, and Chenkeli) had dominated the first Petrograd Soviet in 1917. In defeating the Georgian Menshevik state in 1921, Lenin and Stalin were taking revenge on the many Mensheviks in West European exile whose propaganda vehicles could not be so easily silenced.

Another reason why it was thought impossible to allow Georgia any freedom was its status as 'an advance post of the Entente'. It had well-established diplomatic links with several

[36] See G. Uratadze, *Vospominaniia gruzinskogo sotsial-demokrata* (Stanford, 1968).

Western powers, and lay on the edges of the ex-Empire, accessible by sea from the west. As a Red Army man in Georgia put it in a letter to Lenin in October 1922: 'We are daily preparing ourselves for the time when the enemies of the workers' and peasants' Republic attempt fresh armed attacks.'[37] Last, but not least, the Caucasus had provided pre-revolutionary Russia with two-thirds of its oil, three-quarters of its manganese, and a quarter of its copper.[38] Georgia held the key of access to these resources, and during Menshevik rule large amounts of oil had been sold to agents of Wrangel, the White general.[39]

In the Georgian affair significant positions on nationalism were taken up by other Bolshevik leaders. In spite of, or because of his Polish blood and his marriages to Jewesses, Dzerzhinsky proved to be as ruthless as Stalin. 'I fear', wrote Lenin, 'that Dzerzhinsky too . . . has distinguished himself here by his truly Russian attitude (it is well known that Russified aliens always overdo things in trying to show themselves to be authentic Russians).'[40] We have seen how Dzerzhinsky brought Siberian communications to heel in 1922. The same mentality was applied to Georgia. Trotsky foolishly stayed on the sidelines in the Lenin–Stalin debate. Although instructed by Lenin to attack Stalin's policy in public, he connived with it and remained silent. Many years later he confessed that he might have defeated Stalin for good at the Twelfth Congress if he had spoken up with the backing of Lenin's authority. For the first time in the history of the Bolshevik Party Stalin was applying open repression to its members in the persons of the Georgian leaders B. Mdivani and G. Makharadze. Trotsky was to suffer the same fate five years later.

Only Bukharin broke the silence and defended Georgia and the small nationalities. He pointed out what Sultan-Galiev had already dwelt on, that the minorities were basically peasant areas which were being alienated by centralist, proletarian domination. The whole notion of smychka was under threat.

[37] *Pis'ma trudiashchikhsia k V. I. Leninu, 1917–1924* (Moscow, 1960), p. 316.
[38] See R. Arskii, *Kavkaz i lgo znachenie dlia sovetskoi Rossii* (Petrograd, 1921).
[39] See a book review by N. Meshcheriakov, in *Pechat' i revoliutskiia* (Petrograd, July–Aug. 1923), pp. 176–7.
[40] Lenin, *Polnoe sobranie sochinenii*, vol. 45 (Moscow 1958–66), p. 358.

Bukharin also warned that the new Soviet Union would not be able to attract other colonial populations round the world if it was seen to be treating Georgia arbitrarily. He maintained this point of view throughout NEP, thus finding himself in a dwindling minority as time went by.

At the end of August 1924 rebellion against the Bolsheviks broke out again in Georgia. It was put down within a month. At least 20,000 people were deported to Siberia, and between 7,000 and 10,000 killed. The revolt had a strong anti-Russian emphasis. Tsereteli in exile considered the event disastrous both for the future of social democracy and of Georgia.[41] This was probably the case, but there is no doubt that the Georgian economy flourished in mid- and late NEP. Native skill in trading allowed the specialized agricultural sector to profit in the spirit of free enterprise. An extensive hydroelectric scheme was also completed. There was substance in the later claim of official Soviet historiography that 'the creation of a Federal Union . . . resulted in a significant improvement in the economic . . . position of the Soviet republics of the Transcaucasus.'[42]

There were important differences between Georgia and the Ukraine, the other most vociferous opponent of Great-Russian domination. The most obvious was sheer size of territory and population. Georgia's small estimated population of 2,600,400 in 1913[43] actually shrank to 2,410,500 by 1921.[44] Another less obvious difference lay in the cultural sphere. Georgia's ancient and completely distinctive civilization had no parallel in the Ukraine, where Great-Russian elements were deeply intermingled with local ethnic influences. Gogol wrote in Russian only, but he was born in the Ukraine, and some of his work is devoted to his homeland. Significant migrations from the densely inhabited Ukraine into Russia had been going on since at least the end of the nineteenth century. Great Russians and Jews predominated in the major Ukrainian cities. Finally, the large expanses of land towards the Black Sea that had been

[41] In a letter to Aksel'rod of 27 July 1924, in the International Institute of Social History, Amsterdam.

[42] D. A. Chugaev (ed.), *Natsional'no-gosudarstvennoe stroitel'stvo v SSSR v perekhodnyi period ot kapitalizma k sotsializmu (1917–1936 gg)* (Moscow, 1968), p. 353.

[43] *Itogi vsesoiuznoi perepisi naseleniia 1959 goda gruzinskogo SSR* (Moscow, 1963).

[44] *Narodnoe khoziaistvo gruzinskogo SSR v 1961 godu: statisticheskii ezhegodnik.*

incorporated into the Russian Empire, mostly in the reign of Catherine the Great, formed part of the modern Ukraine, yet were an ethnic melting-pot on the American scale, including many other nationalities besides Great Russians and Ukrainians.

From the time that the Bolsheviks came to a climax in their negotiations with the Ukraine during the Civil War, before the confrontation with Georgia, they had to use a softer glove, since their own position at the centre was that much weaker during the Civil War. In the section of this book devoted to Makarenko's orphanage near Poltava, it was observed how chaotic and uncontrolled the situation was in the eastern Ukraine, even as late as 1922. For long periods between 1917 and 1921 portions of the Ukraine were entirely out of Bolshevik control, and under foreign influences. Well into the 1920s the Bolsheviks feared that Western capitalist powers would support Polish intervention in the Ukraine. In 1917 optimistic delegates from the Ukrainian *Rada* were even trying to detach the greater parts of the gubernii of Kursk and Voronezh from Great-Russian control.

Nevertheless, the mainsprings of political nationalism were relatively weak in the Ukraine. The urban middle classes and the proletariat were the most Russianized sectors of Ukrainian society. In the Revolution the Donbass and the industrial cities had become the Bolsheviks' basis of support in their struggle against the Ukrainian national socialists. Within the local Communist Party itself, Great-Russian members were usually in a large majority: in fact they were often less sympathetic on the minority question than were Bolsheviks hailing from the RSFSR.[45] By 1923 less than 35 per cent of all government employees were ethnic Ukrainians, and only 24 per cent of the party membership were Ukrainians.

There existed one realistic basis for political nationalism—agrarian populism. Lenin noted the victory of the Ukrainian populists in the Constituent Assembly election, and warned his colleagues that they had to be reckoned with. Unfortunately

[45] At the Twelfth Party Congress in Moscow, Ukrainians complained of the negative attitude on the national problem displayed at the Seventh All-Ukrainian Party Conference. See *XII s'ezd Rossiiskoi Kommunisticheskoi Partii (b), 17–25 aprelia 1923 g; stenograficheskii otchet* (Moscow, 1923), pp. 459–60.

this movement was to suffer from all the usual political drawbacks associated with the peasantry. Although massive in numbers, and relatively well-off by Great-Russian standards, they were unable to co-ordinate their activities over the largest minority area in Russia. They did not have sufficient material resources to back their aspirations, nor above all did they wield any influence over the major population centres. Their connections with the small but energetic group of political and cultural nationalist intellectuals were poor.[46] This was a universal phenomenon throughout the ex-Empire. The lack of any *rapport* between the peasantry and the local intelligentsia was observed already with regard to Kursk guberniia in 1922.

Even at the very hub of vociferous Ukrainian opposition to Stalin in 1922 there was a certain ambivalence. Its main spokesman was K. Rakovsky. Yet he was a Bulgarian by birth, and until 1920, before changing his views, he had gone so far as to oppose Lenin's concessions to the nationalities.[47] From 1922 onwards, as has been seen, Moscow took firm control of political channels, while at the same time allowing considerable latitude in cultural affairs, on which Ukrainian nationalists now lavished all their energies. The Russian authorities were to discover by 1925 that cultural nationalism was bound to lead to a resurgence of political nationalism. As plans for highly centralized industrialization made progress from 1926 onwards, it also became obvious that clashes could soon arise on the economic front as well.

Following on a decree of August 1923, 'Ukrainization' of many aspects of life was pursued so long as it did not conflict with the political settlement of 1922. The Ukrainian language was introduced in all schools and in many more newspapers. Nationalist literary groups flourished, and the Ukrainian Church took on a new lease of life.[48] By 1925 a few intellectuals were crossing the sensitive borderline between culture and politics. M. Khvylovy urged that Ukrainian literature should

---

[46] See N. N. Popov, *Narys istorii komunistychnoi Partii (b) Ukrainy* (Kharkov, 1928), pp. 523–5.

[47] See Lenin, *Sochineniia*, vol. 24 (3rd edn., Moscow, 1928–36), pp. 818–19.

[48] For a detailed survey of the Ukrainian cultural revival during NEP, see an unpublished paper by A. Joukovsky, presented to the Second World Congress of Soviet and East European Studies at Garmisch, Oct. 1980: 'Ukrainisation, aspect de la question nationale en Ukraine soviétique dans les années 1920.'

develop independently of Russian influence and orientate itself towards Western Europe.[49] By April 1926 Stalin was writing to Lazar Kaganovich, now the Secretary-General of the Ukrainian Party: 'It is certain that on no account should it [Ukrainian cultural life] be allowed to fall into the hands of elements that are hostile to us.'[50]

Kaganovich was a protégé of Stalin, appointed explicitly in order to oust Ukrainian opposition groups from the Central Party. Stalin's new sterner line was easier for him to impose, because his main political opponents at that time supported him on this issue. Trotsky had no sympathy for local autonomy in any quarter. Zinoviev was attacking Ukrainian Bolsheviks for failing to safeguard the rights of their own resident minorities—Germans, Poles, Jews, and Moldavians. By 1927 Stalin was even more firmly in the saddle. Moreover, his notion of 'socialism in one country' had by now diminished interest in nationalist movements abroad. As so often with Stalin, his so-called principles changed markedly according to his personal political strength at the time.

Compared to Ukrainian and Georgian nationalist pretensions, the Belorussian claim was definitely lightweight. These three minorities formed the main opposition to federation on Stalinist lines in 1922, but the Belorussians only made up 1.1 per cent of the First Congress of Soviets of the Union. The Russians had already shown scant regard for Belorussia when they drew up the borders of the Belorussian SSR in January 1921. It was confined to a small border strip of 20,000 square miles and 1,500,000 inhabitants, encompassing Smolensk, but excluding important districts centred on Vitebsk, Gomel, and Mogilov. These were incorporated into the USSR.

In the course of the warring that raged backwards and forwards through Belorussia between 1914 and 1921, 480 industrial enterprises were wiped out in an area that was predominantly agricultural in any case. A minute local intelligentsia was set apart, as usual, from peasants with the highest illiteracy rate in European Russia. They were farmers on a much smaller scale than most Ukrainians, and many of those with any initiative had emigrated to Siberia before 1917.

[49] M. Khvylowy, *Kamo hryadeshy* (Kharkov, 1925).
[50] J. Stalin, *Sochineniia*, Vol. 8 (Moscow, 1948), pp. 149–54.

In the Belorussian towns after 1922 the Jews continued to be more disliked than the Russians. Seventy-two per cent of all party members were Russian, yet, as was seen in the chapter on Smolensk guberniia in 1922, they managed to conduct their business without any nationalist backlash. Most of the grumbling was about taxes and imposed work-loads.[51] As in the Ukraine, cultural freedom was allowed to flourish during NEP, but it cast little light. The Belorussian language was declared the official idiom, although it had not been in common usage since the sixteenth century. Cultural nationalists declared that their version of Slav civilization was purer and freer. Quite a number of Belorussian intellectuals returned from abroad, mainly from Prague. They were impressed by the relative liberalism of NEP. It was not until 1933, some time after the Ukraine, that Belorussia was brought firmly to heel in every way. The Russians could afford to wait longer where the potential opposition was so weak.

The subject of Belorussia is not dropped at this point for good, since the Smolensk area will be surveyed again for 1926, as will Kazakhstan, for the first time. Views from Moscow on the nationalities have been surveyed here in order to depict the problem from above as well as from below. Scholars usually devote a single, carefully circumscribed section of a general survey to the nationality problem, or zoom in close on a case-study, like that of Georgia, but only when it impinges momentarily on high politics. Yet there is obviously a slow continuum of relations both from above and below, over long periods. In a country with as many minority nationalities as Russia, their interrelationship presents nearly insoluble organizational problems in a conventionally arranged study. By returning to Smolensk as a kind of leitmotiv, the continuum will not go unheeded. So often observers of Russia still treat her in the way they used to deal with the USA. Just as they restricted their attention to the white Anglo-Saxon Protestant eastern seaboard, so they over-concentrate on the Great-Russian heartland round Moscow.

During early NEP most of the national minorities were allowed to develop their own cultural consciousness, free from

[51] *XIII s'ezd RKP(b)*, pp. 253–4.

direct political control by Moscow. The most obvious difference between NEP and the 1930s was the large degree of
autonomy inside three main levels of existence, and the striking
variations in the methods of control over them. The level of
high *politics* was always considered in the 1920s as an unshakeable ideological island surrounded by an increasingly polluted
sea. Right from the start of NEP this level was obsessed by
questions of internal discipline and control. These concerns
sharpened as NEP progressed. The *economic* level was only
partially controlled throughout, so that when central, large-
scale intervention finally arrived after 1928, it was swift,
draconic, and all-embracing. At the third level, *social* and
*cultural* life was usually permitted to go its own sweet way until
at least 1926.

Unfortunately for the Bolsheviks, these three levels were by
no means watertight, so that ideological heresies at the two
lower levels increasingly troubled the purity and stability of the
political summit. For example, the intellectual élite of the
Ukraine, the largest national minority, gaily extended its
cultural independence with great freedom during NEP, only to
find after a certain point, when it was deemed by Moscow to be
impinging on Great-Russian political hegemony, that it was
slowly suppressed. It should have kept in mind the fate of
Georgia as early as 1922.

The leading Bolsheviks' thoughts on the connections
between politics and economics on the one hand, and culture
on the other, are often studied as a footnote to the analysis of
NEP, yet they were absolutely crucial determinants in the
increasing distortions which led to the collapse of the system.
Let us now turn to our third problem area, that of cultural
backwardness.

Lenin, Trotsky, Bukharin, and other leaders who devoted much
thought to cultural problems all agreed on their definition of
*kul'tura*: this differed in several respects from the traditional
Western approach. In the first place, *kul'tura* for them meant the
material, technological, as well as the spiritual achievements of a
society at a certain stage of development of its productive forces.
Lenin, as the son of a school-inspector, usually had in mind
European civilization. It was a ready-made model, long admired

by Russian Westernizers, to which the Soviet Union should also conform, so long as it could be purged of its capitalist purse-strings and adapted to the political mould of the proletarian regime. For Lenin, as for Trotsky, there was no such thing as instantaneous, completely underivative proletarian culture. Hence their entrenched opposition to the Proletkul't movement, already alluded to in Chapter 6.

In the second place, Lenin equated culture with knowledge, meaning scientific and practical expertise as much as literary, artistic, or historical knowledge. The sole source of this knowledge in its most advanced stage was to be found in the hands of a privileged minority in the countries of high capitalism. This learning had to be transplanted as fast as possible on to the Soviet masses under the safe ideological supervision of the Communist Party, which represented the temporary dictatorship of the proletariat (and the peasantry). In 1922 in particular Lenin was obsessed by the cultural backwardness of his country and the political distortions to which this could lead. Even within the top ranks of the Bolsheviks he now detected an individual example of this—Stalin's uncivilized behaviour towards his fellow Georgians. The third rather unusual Soviet definition of kul'tura was exactly that—civilized manners and refinement. As Trotsky put it in 1922, most Soviet citizens lacked 'the most elementary habits and notions of culture (in regard to tidiness, instruction, punctuality, etc.)'.[52]

Serious political complications arose from Lenin's view that bourgeois culture could be imposed soon in a somewhat mechanistic way on the masses. At the start of NEP Trotsky wrote that 'politics are flexible, but custom is unyielding and obdurate'.[53] In his more reflective moments Lenin reluctantly agreed. Thus in the campaign against illiteracy he warned against the fast use of agitational methods and promoted genuine, long-term education.[54] It was harder to effect cultural revolution from above than its political, or even its economic equivalent. The year 1917 marked the political upheaval, 1928–9 the economic one, but inherited cultural backwardness continued to plague both political and economic progress until

[52] See Ch. 1.
[53] Ibid., p. 26.
[54] See Pethybridge, op. cit., pp. 144–7.

the present day. Bukharin in the last years of NEP continually pointed to ways in which cultural sloth damaged economic progress: for instance, lack of scientific culture militated against the effective exploitation of Russia's enormous mineral resources. By the middle of NEP it began to look to the Bolshevik leaders who survived Lenin as if continuing cultural backwardness might wash over the political bastion and submerge it. Revolution is fast, true education very slow.

Another problem lay in the artificial and passive way in which the masses were expected to imbibe ex-bourgeois culture. A. A. Bogdanov, the main theoretical opponent of Proletkul't, viewed the attainment of literacy and education by the people as an easy, spontaneous process which would be self-regulating. This was anathema to Lenin, who believed that consciousness (*soznatel'nost'*) and not spontaneity (*stikhiia*) should be the basis of mass culture. As early as December 1920 Proletkul't had been placed under the strict supervision of the Commissariat of Education. At this juncture the normally autonomous spheres in NEP of politics and socio-cultural life were locked together like tight cog-wheels, since consciousness could only come from the Bolshevik intellectual élite and from no other unorthodox source. In the long run this was to lead to the suppression of individual creativity, the spread of indifference, apathy, and conformism in society at large. Worse than that, as J. Machajski maintained, the Bolshevik élite was imposing its own 'counter-revolution of the intellectuals'.[55] The Party's growing monopoly over culture was as restrictive as the monopoly of the means of production in capitalist society.

Lenin was fully aware of the gigantic nature of the task ahead. Not for nothing did he hail originally from a sleepy provincial city, and had Tartar blood in his veins. In April 1921 he wrote:

Look at the map of the RSFSR. There is room for dozens of large civilized states in those vast areas which lie to the north of Vologda, the south-east of Rostov-on-Don and Saratov, the south of Orenburg and Omsk, and the north of Tomsk. They are a realm of patriarchalism and semi- and downright barbarism. And what about the peasant backwoods of the rest of Russia, where scores of versts of

[55] *Rabochaia revoliutsiia*, 1 (June–July 1918), p. 4 ff.

country track, or rather of trackless country, lie between the villages and the railways, i.e. the material link with the big cities, large-scale industry, capitalism and culture? Isn't that also an area of wholesale patriarchalism, and semi-barbarism?[56]

The huge gulf between Petrograd and Moscow culture in 1922 and the remote areas of Russia that was noted in Chapter 6 scarcely narrowed at all during NEP. If it is not possible to talk glibly of a nation-wide, unified culture for a country like modern France, then it is out of the question with regard to Russia in the 1920s. There were endless subcultures coexisting at the same time. Lenin was describing the RSFSR alone in the quotation above, to the exclusion of over seventy other national subcultures, some of which were both remote in space and embedded in deep time, like the semi-nomads of Central Asia. If they were able to read, which was highly unlikely in NEP, these Muslims used the Arabic script and were firmly fixed in the tradition of the Koran. We shall come across them in all their cultural, socio-economic, and even political diversity, in Chapter 12.

Several concrete examples, as opposed to Bolshevik theorizing, of the difficulties involved in spreading culture and knowledge downwards throughout society have already been examined in some detail in earlier chapters. It was a losing battle in the western *oblast'* of Smolensk guberniia in 1922 to inculcate the correct minimum standard of political culture, which was merely the prelude to broader realms of knowledge.[57] It will be seen when we return to the same area in 1926 that this initial prerequisite was far from being solved. In the Kursk guberniia in 1922 there were virtually no reliable cultural agents of any kind to spread the gospel to the backwaters. Neither the Komsomols, the teachers, nor the ex-military, amongst others, could succeed.[58] In neighbouring Poltava, Makarenko's somewhat naïve theories on the education of underprivileged youth were later to be taken up and distorted by Stalin in the 1930s. Makarenko's emphasis on strict military-type discipline was to appeal to a dictator who

---

[56] Lenin, *Collected Works*, vol. 32 (4th edn.), pp. 349–50.
[57] See Ch. 1, pp. 56–58.
[58] Ch. 2, pp. 77–9.

imposed culture from above as rigidly as he imposed agricultural collectivization.

As late as mid-NEP, Maxim Gorky, that great but ambivalent symbol of new-style Soviet culture, was still complaining that 'the fundamental obstacle on the path of Russia to Europeanization and culture is the fact of the overwhelming predominance of the illiterate village over the city'.[59] The Bolsheviks lived in constant apprehension of the unpredictable effects of this vast hinterland. Their anxieties reached fever pitch in 1926 and after. On three economic fronts they expected their commanding heights to be submerged in due course—by the '*kulaks*', the Nepmen, and the kustari. As will be seen in Chapter 9, they tended to exaggerate the purely economic and political potential of these three groups taken separately, or even in combination. Yet there was another dimension, that of cultural submersion as well. Not that the three groups remotely represented any peaks of enlightenment; but they did include in their ranks many of those with more initiative and native intelligence than the rest of the rural masses. They could in the long run have enormous nefarious cultural influence over the still 'dark people'.

One way for the Party and society to throw off the restricting influences from the past was to invest heavily in the future through the promotion of science, which, as we have seen, lay squarely at the centre of the official Soviet concept of culture.

At first after the Revolution the study of science was pursued, as in Tsarist times, in Peter the Great's Academy of Sciences and at institutions of higher education. During the period 1917 to 1921 four quite different views on higher education were promoted, and in part put into effect. Non-Bolshevik liberals continued to do scientific research free from any political motive or intervention. The Bolsheviks were split into three camps which agreed on little apart from their common dislike of the liberals.[60] Although this scenario led to considerable disorganization, it happened to prolong comparative freedom in the ways in which science was handled. As late as 1927, the Academy of Sciences remained the most

[59] Gorky, 'V. I. Lenin', in *Russkii sovremennik*, 1 (Moscow, 1924).
[60] See J. C. McLelland, 'Bolsheviks, Professors and the Reform of Higher Education in Soviet Russia, 1917–1921', unpublished doctoral thesis (Ann Arbor, 1971).

significant unreformed Tsarist institution. Not one academician had become a party member. For theoretical reasons also there was less pressure at first to subject the sciences to strict political control. Marx had asserted that the more developed any branch of science became, the more difficult it was to relate its connection to the modes of production. For this and another coincidental reason (A. A. Bogdanov was a medical doctor), Proletkul't did not call for a basic transformation of science, as it did for the arts.[61] Some Marxist scholars thought that Soviet science would be less of a handmaiden to commercial interests than in the capitalist West. In any case, until the expansion of Russia's industrial base in the 1930s, scientists were under no real obligation to become more applied, and so submit to closer political scrutiny.

Nevertheless the will to industrialize at a much faster pace was already a clearly declared intent in the programme adopted by the Fourteenth Party Congress in December 1925. More applied scientific institutions were raising the proportion of party members in their ranks. By 1925 the Moscow Agricultural Academy claimed that 20 per cent of its students were party members, whereas the University of Moscow had only crept up to 18 per cent.[62] The increasing ratio of politically safe students encouraged the Party to relax its organizational controls in another way in 1926. The quota system for overall student numbers based on class origin was replaced by a system founded on academic merit.[63]

When one looks in detail at the actual teaching methods used in science and related areas between 1922 and 1926, there is very little evidence of political intervention. Take the example of the teaching of mathematics, which has been the subject of meticulous research.[64] The professional teachers in the schools continued to rely on the textbooks dating from the Tsarist regime.

[61] See A. A. Malinovskii, *Tektologiia, vseobshchaia organizatsionnaia nauka* (Moscow, 1922).

[62] S. A. Fediukin, *Bol'shaia oktiabrskaia revoliutsiia i intelligentsia* (Moscow, 1975), p. 179.

[63] V. V. Ukraintsev, *KPSS-organizator revoliutsionnogo preobrazovaniia vysshei shkoly* (Moscow, 1963), p. 188.

[64] See H. Jahn, 'The Development of Soviet Educational Policy during 1917–1936: A Case Study of Mathematics Education at the Elementary and Secondary Levels', unpublished doctoral dissertation (Ann Arbor, 1968).

Efforts to thwart them by polemical, radical activists, like Krupskaia and Blonsky, were unavailing. Pre-revolutionary textbooks were being introduced into the secondary school curriculum as late as 1928. Due to lack of funds, and the rather chaotic federal organization by the People's Commissariat of Education in Moscow, local initiative intensified during NEP. This naturally led in many cases to the reinstatement of more traditional educational theory and practice in the provinces.[65]

Only after 1926 did stricter organizational control over science begin to permeate, slowly at first, from the summit downwards. In 1927 the Academy of Sciences was given a new charter which showed evidence of increasing political interest in this prestigious institution. It now came directly under the jurisdiction of the Council of People's Commissars.[66] The preponderance of the humanities was rectified, shifting more power to the natural sciences and soon thereafter to technology. Academicians in the humanities were more prone to cause trouble in the realm of political propaganda than mathematicians or astronomers. The new charter allowed for a large increase in the number of Academicians, some of whom could be appointed by politically influenced bodies outside the Academy's own ranks. As late as 1928 the Academy was still able to direct its own activities, but a swift change occurred in 1929. From then until 1932 the body was swamped by safe applied scientists appointed through party influence. In 1929 Lunacharsky said of himself and the government 'we waited, we were patient . . . hoping scientists would come over to the Bolsheviks, but they did not, and so the need arose to pull down completely the edifice of the past and to build it up anew according to an absolutely new plan.'[67]

We have seen that by 1926 controls over cultural life were still subtle, and the draconic measures that were to appear from 1928 onwards were nowhere in sight. Yet although the concrete, 'substructural' level was barely affected, the mental intent was already present in 1926, and there was already a determination to take future action in this sphere. In the

[65] Ibid., p. 359.
[66] See the authoritative monograph on this subject by L. R. Graham, *The Soviet Academy of Sciences and the Communist Party, 1927–1932* (Princeton, 1967), esp. pp. 85 ff.
[67] *Izvestiia*, Feb. 1929.

scientific realm this was clearly apparent in the debates over Einstein's theory of relativity. In 1925 a leading Soviet physicist, A. Timirazev, dismissed relativity theory.[68] When relativist equations are applied to cosmology, they result in finite conceptions of the universe. This conclusion conflicts with the assertion of dialectical materialism that the universe is infinite and eternal. Timirazev's views were not endorsed at the time by a mathematician, G. A. Khazarov, who implied that there was no direct connection between the philosophy of dialectical materialism and scientific discoveries.[69]

Nevertheless, a general trend towards future practical efforts to tighten political supervision over the intelligentsia was becoming apparent by 1926, under Stalin's protection. Already in January 1925 the first All-Union Congress of Proletarian Writers had passed a resolution attacking fellow-travellers, but this was partly rebuffed in July when Bukharin got the Party Central Committee to issue a warning against a 'frivolous and disdainful attitude toward the old cultural heritage and toward literary specialists'. Stalin could rely increasingly on groups in society that were not interested in safeguarding the past. It will be noted in the next chapter how certain elements in the working class, impatient with their unimproved standards by mid-NEP, were prepared to be as iconoclastic as Stalin. They were echoed in the provinces in 1926 by the Komsomol, as will be seen in Chapter 10. As yet Stalin was not sufficiently strong on his own initiative to translate his 'progressive' ideas into realities, though he and others like him were already tinkering with the economy in distant areas of the Soviet Union. Although the declared official intent of December 1925 to industrialize first was to remain largely on paper for some time thereafter, Stalin was already experimenting in a remote area with the quick transformation of small-scale economic enterprise into huge amalgamated and state-controlled units. That particular initiative is investigated in the final chapter of this book, which is concerned with Kazakhstan in 1926.

[68] A. Timiriazov, 'Otvet tov. Semkovskomu', *Pod znamenen marksizma*, 8–9 (Moscow, 1925), pp. 170 ff.
[69] G. A. Khazarov, 'Malyi printsip otnositel'nosti', *Vestnik kommunisticheskoi akademii*, 10 (1925).

# 8. *The Proletariat in Theory and in Practice*

THIS is the last of four consecutive chapters devoted to the political heights of Soviet society in NEP. In Bolshevik theory and aspiration the party should have been joined by the proletariat, its favoured class, in the deliberations and man-œuvres surveyed in these pages, but in reality it has scarcely merited any attention so far. It would be inconceivable, however, to neglect the changing condition of the working class up until 1926, since it still remained the social springboard from which the plunge into heavy industrialization was to be taken. This future was heralded by the programme adopted at the Fourteenth Party Congress in December 1925. Yet as of 1926 only approximately one out of every thirty citizens of the Soviet Union could be classified as a worker of any kind. Thus the allotment of even one chapter out of seven (the other six being concerned with peasant-dominated localities) is out of all proportion to the proletariat's *numerical* strength in NEP. It was only from 1927 onwards that its political weight was to have more impact on the party than the crushing burden of the peasantry. What follows here focuses mainly on the influential Moscow proletariat in 1926, though its ramifications in time and space are also considered in order to highlight its special political significance in the overall working-class scene around mid-NEP.

The longing for a strong, articulate working class preceded Marxism in Russia. In Dostoevsky's novel *The Possessed*, Ver-khovensky exclaims: 'Oh, what a pity there's no proletariat! But there will be—that's the way things are going.' After the turn of the century no less than four left-wing political parties were competing for the leadership of the nascent working class, but after the coup of October 1917 there could only be one monopolizing protector, the Bolsheviks. As Zinoviev put it in 1922: 'Although there are several workers' parties, there is only one proletarian party. A party can be a workers' party in its composition and yet not be proletarian in its orientation, programme and policy.'[1] At the start of NEP the Communist Party did not feel secure on either point with regard to the proletariat, since it was not yet predominantly working class in structure,[2] nor did it have a complete monopoly over the orientation of that class. Although no other political party now remained as a rival, Proletkul't's insistence on its role as the only authentic driving-force of the workers' cultural movement still threatened the autonomy of the Bolsheviks. That is why Lenin singled out Proletkul't for administrative persecution; none of the many other unorthodox intellectual movements of the time directly challenged the Party's hold over the workers.

A similar spirit permeated party policy towards the workers from 1917 to the start of NEP. Lenin's near obsession with total control over all sectors of the nation that could possibly threaten Bolshevik hegemony included even the party's co-heir to Russia's future. The Party could not permit its inevitable dependence upon labour for its survival to turn into a bargaining-point for political or even economic demands by the workers. Therefore right from the start workers' control and the trade unions had been curtailed. Work was made compulsory. Although the worst prospects as envisaged in Trotsky's militarized units were shunned by Lenin and other leaders, the dragooning of unskilled labour in the period 1917–22 virtually forced the dwindling ranks[3] of skilled workers into taking work in Soviet-controlled enterprises where conditions were rather better. Once there, they received less pay in return for more productivity. Admittedly, given Russia's impoverished re-

---

[1] G. Zinoviev, *History of the Bolshevik Party—A Popular Outline* (Moscow, 1923), p. 10.

[2] Only 44.4% of party members were working class by origin in 1922. See *Partiinoe stroitel'stvo*, 17 (Sept. 1931), p. 35.

[3] The large decline in the number of skilled workers in the years before NEP, due to lack of work, death, and disease in the Civil War, and the flight from the industrial cities, is not a figment of foreign propaganda. See the resolutions of the Third All-Russian Congress of Trade Unions (Moscow, 1920), p. 21, where delegates pointed out the decrease and even the obliteration in some sectors of skilled workers.

sources, this was the only way to rehabilitate the country, but it also suited the party politically. Political consolidation took precedence over the needs of the proletariat. Things were to remain this way until 1926–7, when, as we shall see, the interests of the workers and those of the party coincided, leading to relatively free bargaining powers for the former.

The practical consequences of such policies, which spilled over into the first unsettled years of NEP, have been noted in earlier chapters. To cite just one instance, the head of the secret police, Felix Dzerzhinsky, was applying ruthless pressures with which he was only too familiar to the railwaymen of Siberia in 1922. Military tribunals set up during War Communism for regulating railway discipline were not disbanded until 1923.[4] Quite apart and independent from any high-level directives, skilled labour tended to diminish radically in size and competence into early NEP, as has been observed for example in the city of Smolensk by 1922.[5]

This decline prompted a significant revision of leading Bolsheviks' assessment of the proletariat. Lenin was merely pointing out the sad facts concerning the decline of labour in the Ukraine when he commented on industrial resources in that area (it was noted in Chapter 2 how Kharkov's factories were depleted by 1922).[6] In his report to the Eleventh Party Congress in March 1922, he elaborated on the situation:

There we have to deal with workers. Very often the word 'workers' is taken to mean the factory proletariat. But it does not mean that at all. During the war people who were by no means proletarians went into the factories; they went into the factories to dodge the war. Are the social and economic conditions in our country today such as to induce real proletarians to go into the factories? No. It would be true according to Marx; but Marx did not write about Russia; he wrote about capitalism as a whole, beginning with the fifteenth century. It held true over a period of six hundred years, but it is not true for present-day Russia. Very often those who go into the factories are not proletarians; they are casual elements of every description.[7]

The logical deduction from this statement is that not all

---

[4] See p. 130 above.
[5] See p. 28 above.
[6] See pp. 81–2 above.
[7] V. I. Lenin, *Collected Works*, vol. 33 (London, 1966), p. 299.

workers in industrial production by early NEP are to be classified as the proletariat envisaged by Marx. In the Soviet context the 'proletariat' was rapidly becoming a reified and idealized concept. This process was speeded up in 1922 by another of Lenin's current concerns—the need to fight the inefficient and unprogressive bureaucracy. For Lenin the solution lay in the mass recruitment of the best elements in the proletariat to the state apparatus.[8] This only served to increase the dilution of the real proletariat in the ranks of those remaining at the work-bench. Lenin's wishes became a growing reality in the years after 1922.

Other high-ranking Bolsheviks took a line similar to that of Lenin and upheld it after his death. At the start of 1925 Zinoviev recalled Lenin's special respect for the 'proletarian' characteristics of the Leningrad workers. Zinoviev called them 'the vanguard of the vanguard' and separated them, not only from the rural influences that still hindered workers from other areas (including Moscow, as will be seen shortly), but also from the 'riff-raff'[9] that Lenin had alluded to in 1922.

The enfeebled condition and multiple layers of the working class until at least 1926 had two other side-effects besides the Party's flight into idealist theorizing in order to forget realities. Work discipline became an authoritarian method rigidly imposed from above by the Party through its submissive tools, which included the trade unions. Given the unreliable nature of the workers, both as to class solidarity and to sheer native efficiency, they could not be left to elaborate their own modes of operation with any latitude whatsoever. This situation persisted until the arguments of 1926–7, centred mainly on the Moscow production committees, which saw the partial rehabilitation of the skilled workers' point of view.

The other main consequence was a prolonged and agonized debate through the rest of NEP on the meaning of the 'dictatorship of the proletariat' and the exact nature of the workers' relationship to the ruling party. The actual living-conditions of the proletariat became even more neglected by self-styled party theorists as a result of this debate, since the protagonists used this class in the abstract as a cudgel with

    [8] *Collected Works*, p. 288.
    [9] Zinoviev, 'Lenin i Leningradskie rabochie', *Leningradskaia Pravda*, 21 Jan. 1925.

which to beat their changing opponents. Their theories altered with remarkable hypocrisy. Stalin was the worst culprit in this respect. At the Thirteenth Party Congress, in May 1924, he and his temporary supporters aimed to increase the proportion of workers from the bench to 50 per cent of the total party membership within a year (in fact this objective was never to be achieved). Yet as soon as Stalin had severed himself from Zinoviev and Kamenev (by April 1925), the proportion of workers among new recruits dropped by nearly 20 per cent.[10] A huge switch had been made in favour of peasant enrolment. This was the direct consequence of Stalin's temporary realignment with Bukharin and the 'right' in the period 1925–6. In the long run Stalin was to jettison the 'right' and refocus his interest on worker participation in the Party under his personal control. There is no clearer instance in NEP, apart from the debate over the political role of the '*kulaks*', of the wilful distortion of class realities for the sake of personal political gain.

So far no attempt has been made to define with any subtlety the precise structure and subdivisions of the working class in NEP. Apart from simplistic divisions of the proletariat into a few strata, no Bolshevik leader except for Bukharin on rare occasions, descended from the abstractions exemplified above into realistic diagnoses.

To some extent, this can never be done, for lack of precise statistics, particularly in the years 1917 to 1921 and during early NEP. For this reason also, scholarly debates—as to the detailed changes or constancy in the composition of the proletariat and its ongoing political consciousness or lack of it through these years—are academic in the bad sense of the word, since neither side can ever completely win or lose the arguments, which tend to become as abstract and polemical as those of the Bolshevik leaders at the time. Nevertheless in some areas progress on definitions can be made.

For the purposes of the rest of this chapter, which will concentrate on the atypical Moscow proletariat in 1926, the working class is taken to mean manual wage-workers directly involved in material production or in the provision of basic

[10] *Izvestiia Tsentral'nogo Komiteta*, 41 (26 Oct. 1925), quoted in T. H. Rigby, *Communist Party Membership in the USSR, 1917–1967* (Princeton, 1968), p. 142.

services. This definition includes workers (both male and female with their widely differing circumstances) in large and small-scale industry; transport workers (a very large proportion overall, as was noted in Chapter 4); miners, builders, and those in consumer services (including the huge numbers of ex-household servants).[11] The only statistics which appear to be reasonably reliable for both 1922 and 1926 refer to large-scale industry alone. In 1922 the number was 1,096,200, representing 42.2 per cent of the 1917 equivalent. By 1926 the figure had risen to 2,261,700, or 87.1 per cent of 1917. There had been an especially large rise in 1925, when half a million workers entered or re-entered the large-scale industrial labour force.[12] The numbers in transport and building on the other hand were considerably lower than in 1917, though the figures are less reliable in these areas.[13]

The geographical and social origins of NEP workers are even harder to fathom. Social origin was a delicate matter and therefore often veiled in secrecy. Localities did not keep statistics of any value on migration to factory jobs in the cities, and hundreds of thousands of peasant-workers and even some of Zinoviev's proletarian aristocrats, went in and out of the cities according to the prospects of employment, housing, disease, inheritances from peasant relatives, or simply on a seasonal basis. What is certain is that the normal West European hierarchy of foreman, skilled, semi skilled, and unskilled worker was extended down the ladder in early Soviet Russia to seasonal, itinerant, and tramp-workers (including miners, some kustari, and consumer-services workers for Nepmen). They were often lumped under one subcategory and called *brodiachie*. They included the despised *derevenshchina*, or those who had come in, perhaps on a permanent basis, from the rural hinterland. Up until 1925, the slow increase in the working class as a whole stemmed from a combination of both former workers and new ones. But from 1926 the immigration of derevenshchina flooded the market, which was also swelled by a greater recruitment of urban youth.

[11] See p. 189 above for the larger numbers employed in this manner in Petrograd up until 1917.

[12] See *Itogi desiatiletia sovetskoi vlasti v tsifrakh 1917–1927 gg.* (Moscow, 1927), p. 230.

[13] See L. S. Gaponenko, *Rabochii klass Rossii v 1917 godu* (Moscow, 1970), pp. 56–8.

In past scholarly studies the scrutiny of the working class in NEP has been obscured by many factors. The first is the acute reification of this class by party leaders, a tendency often copied by Soviet and non-Soviet researchers alike. The second is the sheer lack of information, compensated for by polemics, on a topic of such crucial importance to a Marxist regime. The third is the over-concentration on atypical aspects or locations, again for lack of concrete statistics. Thus employees in large-scale industry, for whom there is by far the most evidence, have been highlighted too much, and regarded as the norm. Again, as in every topic, the geographical centre is known and studied, to the neglect of the proletariat in the provinces. This study pleads guilty to this latter bias, though other provincial centres (Smolensk, Tver) will be examined in later chapters; and the last part of this chapter will be devoted to the town–country nexus. Moreover, there is a special reason for concentrating on the Moscow working class, since an investigation is being made into the nascent political relationship between the metropolitan party leaders and their city's proletariat in 1926, with its implications for the eventual demise of NEP.

Some pioneering monographs have already been written on history within the factory gates, concentrating on socio-economic relations at the bench.[14] Yet so far there have been few attempts to link up workers' internal problems and their political views with external pressures from the party.

Between 1923 and 1926 the rate of population growth in Moscow was 31 per cent, or the tenth highest of all urban areas in the Soviet Union.[15] Petrograd, the focus of interest in Chapter 6, grew by 49 per cent over the same period, from a more depleted base, due to greater disturbance there in the Revolution. At the start of NEP even the élite of Moscow workers, let alone those in other cities, was less conscious of its distinctive interests and role than it had been in 1917. The proletariat as a whole by 1922 had lost many of its leaders, been altered radically in composition, and plunged into a

---

[14] For an example of the detail that can be obtained on the more centrally located cotton mills in NEP, see an unpublished paper by C. Ward, 'Capitalism's Bequest: The Labour Process on Selfacting Mules in NEP Russia', Discussion Paper Series, University of Essex, 6.

[15] NKVD, *Goroda soiuza SSR* (Moscow, 1927), p. 17.

narrow struggle for food and survival based on individual need which was too pressing to permit the luxury of pursuing general class interests.

Between 1922 and 1924–5 the revolutionary programmes of the working class and that of the Party remained in the doldrums. Their historical origins had not been identical, despite Bolshevik assertions to the contrary. After 1917 the gap had widened again in practice, though aspirations towards unity of purpose lived on in the Party, and at some vital points on the pragmatic level the interests of labour and the politicians never ceased to intermesh; but not until 1925–8 did Bolshevik theories again merge in fruitful collaboration with workers' practical needs. In the intervening years the proletariat remained divided within itself on many issues, though as the years passed elements of unity began to reappear.

Internal schisms were the result of many factors. The extended hierarchy of different types of workers became even more outstretched, with one rung pitted against the other, as all were made to work more intensively. The economy regained its pre-war level by 1926, but at considerable cost in human terms. Industries had been concentrated, factory forces reduced, wages tied to productivity, and subsidies withdrawn. Contemporary observers noted that increasing periods of illegal leave were being taken by 1925 just in order to escape such pressures. Strikes were now held in protest against administrative oppression, and not out of sheer hunger, as had been the case in 1922.[16]

In his final speech to the Seventh Trade Union Congress in December 1926, M. P. Tomsky did not make a single reference to domestic strikes, although five pages of his script were devoted to the general strike in Britain.[17] Tomsky's speech is a good example of party official theory hovering in a hypocritical cloud above the realities of working-class life. Unemployment had risen from 976,400 in 1924–5 to 1,015,600 by 1925–6,[18] yet Tomsky did all he could to play it down, since its occurrence was anathema to party propaganda. He accused factories of juggling their statistics so as to highlight unemployment

[16] N. Valentinov, *Doktrina pravogo kommunizma* (Munich, 1960), pp. 68, 83.
[17] M. P. Tomsky, *Izbrannye stat'i i rechi* (Moscow, 1928), pp. 396–400.
[18] L. Guinsburg, *Sostoianie rabochego klassa SSSR* (Moscow, 1927), p. 82.

figures. He berated metallurgical workers for pretending to be unemployed and then flitting to another labour exchange in order to change their job location.[19] In the same year F. Dzerzhinsky (who we saw disciplining railwaymen in 1922) accused superfluous workers in Moscow factories of disorganizing discipline.[20] Women, and especially the young, came increasingly under the euphemistic heading of superfluous labour.[21] Tensions and divisions mounted within the ranks.

More and more rural inhabitants moved into city jobs through NEP, creating new problems. Older, more skilled Muscovites hated the greater exploitation and division of labour which came about. Piece-work increased rapidly, so that by 1926 66.5 per cent of all metallurgical workers and 83.8 per cent of food workers laboured on this basis.[22] Ex-peasant workers had no labour discipline, and thus annoyed and endangered their more experienced workmates. Tomsky had observed some years previously that accounts done by newly recruited workers were so bad that it looked as though the factories were being sabotaged. He added, 'I do not think it is sabotage, only Russian illiteracy'.[23]

If those conditions which led to divisiveness were bad in Moscow, they were worse in a provincial industrial centre like Kharkov, through which the reader passed from Kursk to Poltava in 1922. By 1926 a visiting American journalist in Kharkov noted that there were 160,000 trade union members out of a total population of 450,000. Unlike Moscow, but like many other provincial cities in European Russia, Kharkov had changed hands many times (no less than thirteen) in the Civil War. By 1926 there was a modest building boom, but little else of note. Local managers did not try to hide the backwardness of their foundry methods from a capitalist foreigner. Here even the metallurgical workers, the cream of the cream, were

[19] Tomsky, op. cit., pp. 406–8.
[20] F. Dzerzhinsky, *Osnovnye voprosy khoziaistvennogo stroitel'stva SSSR*, vol. 1 (Moscow, 1928), p. 96.
[21] Even if women could find factory work, they were paid on average 63.4% of male wages in 1926, see Guinsburg, op. cit., p. 73. By Apr. 1926 only 25.3% of trade-union members were women, see A. Dogadov, *Sostoianie professional'nogo dvizheniia v SSSR* (Moscow, 1927), p. 73.
[22] Guinsburg, op. cit., pp. 29–30.
[23] *Pervy s'ezd profsoiuzov* (Jan. 1918), p. 119.

disgruntled. The main electrical plant had been German-owned before the Revolution, another cause for division among the city's workers. Some of those employed at the electrical works still spoke German, regretted the much lower efficiency of their plant since the transfer to Russian ownership, and felt themselves in a different class from their fellows in other factories. The manager of the electrical works put in his oar about women workers, claiming that they would never be efficient mechanics.[24]

As NEP progressed, various emerging trends enhanced unity among workers and began to predominate in some instances over elements of disunity. Widespread resentment against factory managers of the type encountered by the American journalist in Kharkov tended to throw workers back in the arms of the Party. In traditional Russian fashion, the underdog took against his nearest, most visible oppressor, and so through false logic exonerated the party bosses who in their turn put pressure on the factory managers. The latter were compelled from above to cut costs, reduce staff, and slow down improvements through lack of funds. The very slow increase in wages until 1925 irritated all types of workers in Moscow, as witnessed by a proliferation of wild-cat strikes and disputes. The number of very young, and therefore very impatient workers grew. By 1926 25,000 workers in Moscow industries were under the age of 15.[25]

Class unity among all Moscow workers also deepened as the housing crisis worsened. Between 1923 and 1928 from 260,000 to 270,000 more people were housed in Moscow, but over the same period 880,000 persons immigrated into the city. In 1926 each Moscow inhabitant had on average a mere 5.8 sq. m for his accommodation.[26] Far above the average were specialists, professional employees, and the now-hated Nepmen. The general rising standard of living of these social categories caused widespread envy among Moscow workers in the lushest years of consumer NEP.

It was probably the Lenin levy of 1924 that tipped the

[24] W. Z. Foster, *Russian Workers and Workshops in 1926* (Chicago, 1926), pp. 27–32.
[25] K. Strievskii, *Material'noe i kul'turnoe polozhenie moskovskikh rabochikh* (Moscow, 1929), p. 7
[26] Ibid., p. 19.

balance in favour of better worker–Party relations. Urban workers, particularly in Moscow and Leningrad, took advantage of this easy opportunity to join the party. Only through the medium of the Party could the most ambitious workers influence high policy. They began to realize that it was no use continuing to batter away at the plant managers, who were merely middlemen. The reconciliation between Party and proletariat was to be a slow process, and was not solid until 1928–9. As living-conditions became less harsh, so some workers' horizons enlarged to an extent where they could take in the significance of the party's calls for quicker socialist industrialization and large-scale construction projects which became more clear-cut and vociferous in 1925–6. At the Seventh Trade Union Congress in December 1926, V. Kuibyshev stated that the growth of production of heavy industry had at last outstripped that of light industry. He also announced that real wages had almost reached the level of 1913.[27]

By 1926 party and proletarian interests began to converge on the need for greater productivity. Fast economic development was to become the corner-stone of official policy once Stalin had settled into his final line of argument. The manner in which this was to be achieved concerned the day-to-day conditions and needs of industrial workers at the more élitist end of their hierarchy, the apex of which was concentrated in Moscow, in geographical contact with the party summit. The more radical elements among the Moscow élite slowly realized that greater productivity on their part could be used as a bargaining-point for the democratization of production.

In the spring of 1926 the Council of Labour and Defence issued a long series of instructions on the need to improve labour productivity in industry and transport by at least 10 per cent. In June 1926 TsIK (the Central Executive Committee of the Soviet of Workers' and Soldiers' Deputies) and the Council of People's Commissars ordered the establishment of a 'regime of the strictest economy', and the end of abuses and waste in both state and co-operative establishments. To keep a check over employees and specialists alike, individual record-cards

[27] *Sedmoj S'ezd Professional'nykh Soiuzov SSSR, 10–24 dekabria 1928 g.* (Moscow, 1929), pp. 497–519, 746–9.

were introduced, to be handed over to the new employer with every change of job.

Factory and shop production meetings and conferences had become commonplace from 1924 onwards. Until 1926 the low numbers of workers who attended had seen them as just another lever with which their bosses tried to exert pressure on them. This changed in the second half of 1926, partly as a result of the decrees mentioned above. Worker participation mounted most swiftly in Moscow, especially in larger plants when there were many worker-Communists and trade-union organizers. Metalworkers were prominent. At first, however, overall attendance rates by workers was only 10 to 15 per cent.[28] Production meetings gained in legitimacy with the Party's growing campaign against managerial inefficiency. Rabkrin's increasing attacks on the same type of factory manager encouraged radical worker-participants to express their pent-up dislike of those who had whipped them along in earlier NEP. The Party's order of April 1927 to curtail the size of all administrative organs by 20 per cent added fuel to the flames. At last the party and skilled workers had found a common enemy over whose body they could find many points of agreement.

By the end of 1926 the old kind of party productivist who had tried to use meetings with workers for 'Economist'-type technical changes was being swept aside by worker-Communist radicals who were egged on by a new brand of party activist to voice their specific demands, and even to object to the outlines of NEP as a whole. This trend was not confined to production meetings, nor to Moscow. At the close of 1926 in the Dinamo factory in the capital there began the programme for *udarnik* workers who would surpass their colleagues in both output and revolutionary zeal.[29] In September and October 1926, on the eve of the Fifteenth Party Conference, militant members of the Workers' New Opposition sallied out to factory meetings in Leningrad and other cities besides Moscow, demanding

[28] L. S. Rogachevskaia, 'Rabota proizvodstvennykh soveshchanii v pervye gody industrializatsii (1926–1927)', *Istoricheskie zapiski*, vol. 57 (Moscow, 1956), pp. 255–75. By the same author see also *Iz istorii rabochego klassa SSSR v pervye gody industrializatzii 1926–1927 gg.* (Moscow, 1959).

[29] *Moskovskaia organizatsiia komsomola na stroike sotsialisticheskoi promyshlennosti. Informatsionnyi obzor* (Moscow, 1927), p. 50.

changes in their working conditions, and no longer fearing immediate reprisals from their managers.[30] At the same time Stalin was encouraging the faster recruitment to the party of young workers, who looked for prerequisites in return for their loyalty. Shades of the future were already beginning to lengthen. The climax of these particular trends came in 1928 with the staged *Shakhty* trials of specialists. The notion that Stalin's regime was imposed entirely by a revolution 'from above' has been shown to be inaccurate. Although more concrete evidence is needed to establish the actual links between Stalin's personal administration and workers' revolution 'from below', enough has been done by scholars to prove the general point.[31]

By 1927 roughly one in ten industrial workers in the Soviet Union was a party member or a candidate.[32] There was a high proportion in their ranks of skilled men in their twenties and thirties, and worker-Communist links with village life were more tenuous than the general rule amongst workers. According to the national census of 1926, approximately four out of every five persons at that time were living in rural communities.[33]

At this point in the narrative we begin to be pulled down again from the élitist urban heights of the largest country on earth, back into the enormous, all-pervasive hinterland that was still the crucial social factor in high politics in 1926. In 1924 Trotsky wrote that in the cities 'Communist life will not be formed blindly, like coral islands, but will be built consciously, will be tested by thought, will be directed and corrected'.[34] Yet in many ways the cities remained uncontrolled accretions, pounded senselessly by an enormous peasant ocean.

So far in this book there has been a tendency to treat urban and rural worlds as dichotomous, but after the chaos and

---

[30] *Rabochaia Moskva*, 6 Oct. 1926.

[31] See the essays in S. Fitzpatrick (ed.), *Cultural Revolution 1928–1931* (London, 1978).

[32] See *Industrializatsiia SSSR 1926–1928. Dokumenty i materialy* (Moscow, 1969), p. 348, and also A. G. Rashin, 'Dinamika promyshlennykh kadrov SSSR za 1917–1958 gg.', in *Izmeneniia v chislennosti i sostave sovetskogo rabochego klassa* (Moscow, 1961), p. 9.

[33] *Vsesoiuznaia perepis' naseleniia 1926 g.* (Moscow, 1927).

[34] L. Trotsky, *Literatura i revoliutsiia* (Moscow, 1924), pp. 191–2.

divisions of revolution, the Civil War, and the first years of
NEP are passed, it is more useful to think in terms of a slow
continuum between the two spheres. The significance of rural–
urban migration is realized when it is remembered that an
excess of deaths over births has often prevailed in cities (as was
the case in Moscow and Leningrad in the years 1914–21, on top
of the huge exodus over the same period). Thus the movement
of people from rural areas not only determines how fast cities
will expand, but also whether they will grow at all. Since cities
are concentrations of people who do not grow their own food
for the most part, they depend upon the agricultural sector for
survival, and peasants depend on them in turn for their
market. In the early stages of urbanization in history, cities
were parasitical to an extreme degree, in the sense that they
depended heavily on peasants for support but offered little
economically in return. This is exactly what happened in
modern conditions of near-chaos in Russia after 1917.

By 1926 the atrocious condition of transport, particularly
on the all-important railway network, had improved considerably over the situation described in Chapter 4. With this
amelioration, together with a rising rural standard of living,
the social and economic opportunities of Moscow and other
cities became more accessible to the rural population. Lenin
had already posited that the city was beginning to move to the
country because of its need for pure water and fresh lands.[35]
Up until his death in 1924 he continued to stress the connection
between electrification and better communications. He
claimed that the population at large would eventually be
spread more or less evenly over the whole of Russia. He
predicted that cities, as concentrations of wealth and industry,
would be dispersed for productive reasons, and the gulf
between town and country would disappear. This vision has
never been achieved to date in any country in the world.

It is interesting to note that whereas in 1923 the geographical
origins of the party Politburo members in Moscow were as
follows: villagers 3, urbanites 2, Muscovites and Leningraders
3, the relative number of urban-born members dropped
rapidly thereafter. In 1925 the three categories numbered 6, 1,

[35] Lenin, *The Agrarian Question and the Critics of Marx*, Selected Works, vol. 12, pp. 97–9.
Lenin was following Engels's argument on this subject.

and 2 respectively, and by 1929 they were 7, 2, and 0.[36] Thus Stalin's new men from the countryside conquered the gulf between town and country in themselves, but they were to do little to heal the general wound, splitting it open again in the collectivization campaign. The unglamorous, ruthless years of the 1930s found it hard to accommodate city-bred sophisticates like Bukharin and Zinoviev. Ex-peasant administrators of a duller, more plodding type were often in greater demand.

The somewhat nebulous Marxist–Leninist theory of town and country alliance was promoted in slightly more concrete forms during NEP through the twin movements of smychka (linking of town and country) and shefstvo (patronage societies). The uphill struggle to introduce smychka has already been examined in one case-study of the Kursk guberniia in 1922. Shefstvo was much more of a city-inspired campaign, since active patrons were extremely thin on the ground in the localities throughout NEP. Even in Moscow the movement was not a great success. Its tribulations provide one of the best pieces of evidence for the increasing strains between Moscow workers and the influx of migrants in the 1920s.

The first shefstvo committees were set up in the capital during the Famine of 1921–2 in order to collect funds for stricken rural regions. Permanent shefstvo societies were created in January 1923, according to Lenin's wishes. By 1925, at the peak of their influence, about 150,000 members were involved in the Moscow societies. Workers made up 60 per cent of the total, and were expected, like other members, to pay five kopeks a month towards funding. Practical aid to rural inhabitants hardly ever ranged beyond the immediate hinterland of Moscow. Peasants found their visitors over-patronizing, or more interested in looking for mushrooms or getting drunk than in giving advice. Sometimes, on the other hand, peasants managed to exploit naïve workers by getting them to scrub floors or do some other manual work.[37] From Lenin's sublime thoughts to the ridiculous.

---

[36] These numbers are worked out in G. K. Schueller, 'The Politburo', in H. D. Laswell and D. Lerner (eds.), *World Revolutionary Elites* (Cambridge, Mass.), 1965, pp. 109–10.

[37] See S. N. Harper, *Civic Training in Soviet Russia* (Chicago, 1929), pp. 190–4. Harper visited Russia in 1926.

By January 1926 there were said to be one million shefstvo members in the Soviet Union, of whom nearly 60 per cent were workers. Most members lived in big cities (Leningrad had 350,000 members, far more than Moscow for some reason). However, these large numbers did not reflect realities in a society where to be a member of a group that would promote one's career in some important ways was highly desirable.[38] In Moscow only 4.5 per cent of all members were activists.[39] The great majority paid their subscriptions and then did no more. By 1926 trade-union members, comprising the more skilled elements among the Moscow proletariat, not only were not attending shefstvo meetings, but were obstructing their meeting-times and meeting-places. Already by the autumn of 1926 the notion of abolishing shefstvo societies in Moscow was being discussed.[40] By 1927, as unemployment in Moscow reached nearly 20 per cent, largely due to immigration, membership in the societies dropped sharply. Workers were naturally reluctant to train peasants when the battle for urban jobs was getting worse.

The position in Moscow, as the largest and most industrialized of Soviet cities, was of course the most acute. When we come to look at workers' attitudes in Smolensk and Tver, towards the Smolensk party and the Tver rural hinterland respectively, it will be noted that the situation was not so tense, nor, more significantly, did they have any influence on high policy in Moscow. The only way in which this could be done, consciously or unconsciously, was for workers to emigrate to Moscow. In the 1920s, as at the end of the previous century, Tver and Smolensk did in fact provide a large number of migrants to the capital, together with the provinces of Moscow, Iaroslavl', Vladimir, Riazan, Kaluga, and Tula.

The impact of migration on Moscow was enormous. By 1926 only one-third of the population had been born in the city. A mere one-fifth of the workers were native residents. In late 1926, just under half of the city's migrant population (not including temporary residents) had moved in after 1920.[41]

---

[38] See Rogachevskaia, *Iz istorii rabochego klassa*, p. 187.

[39] *Voprosy shefstva*, 1 (1926), p. 12.

[40] Ibid., 10, p. 3.

[41] *Vsesoiuznaia Perepis'*, vol. 36, table IV, pp. 142, 174–83.

Newly arrived migrants went for help to *zemliaki* (fellow villagers) who tried to find them jobs and accommodation. Of course the great majority of them could not simply jump into a 'worker's' job, under the definition of 'worker' given earlier in this chapter. Bolshevik and Western scholars have concentrated too much in previous studies on the highly skilled worker-aristocrats, giving the impression that a city like Moscow possessed little else by way of a manual working population. In fact, in 1926 the population of the capital included only 28.2 per cent of factory workers of all kinds. They were outnumbered by *sluzhashchie* (employees of other kinds). The percentage of those unemployed was given as a further 12 per cent.[42] Soviet statistics usually leave out the considerable numbers of shopkeepers, Nepmen, kustari, and domestic servants, amongst others. An attempt to remedy two of these lacunae will be made in the next chapter, where Nepmen and kustari are singled out for examination.

Another strong link between the capital and the rural hinterland was the large number of *otkhodniki* (seasonal workers) who returned to their villages each year. Their numbers actually increased during NEP. In 1926, over 200,000 of them came into Moscow.[43] Amongst them were carpenters and masons from the Tver region.

Peasants migrated to Moscow for a number of reasons. They wished to leave their villages due to shortages of liquid cash or of agricultural implements. The 'scissors' crisis of 1923 had led them to expect a lack of consumer items as well. Often the land in their area was overcrowded, or their small plots were no longer economically viable. The big city attracted them with hopes of better wages, release from family domination and cultural backwardness. Yet many Muscovites continued to hold on to their ownership of land outside the capital. It should not be deduced that there was a direct tie between landholding and backwardness. The possession of land was often seen as a useful insurance against the renewal of economic misfortunes of the type experienced between 1917 and 1922. Additional

---

[42] *Vsia Moskva v karmane* (Moscow, 1976), p. 8.

[43] L. D. Mints, Agrarnoe perenaselenie i rynok trud SSSR (Moscow, 1929), pp. 408–15.

income for those who felt insecure in the capital was another motive for keeping up ties with their peasant background.

In view of the many different links which still bound much of the Soviet working class to the countryside during NEP, it is more fruitful to think of it in Asian rather than European terms, since it was more akin to its equivalent in Turkey, Japan, or even India in the 1920s. It was only after the first waves of the industrialization campaign which succeeded NEP that any such comparison swiftly becomes meaningless.

Turning from the Moscow labouring classes to the All-Russian situation in 1926, a few statistics culled from the first All-Union Soviet census, held in 1926, can give a general impression of the preponderance of connections between urban and rural workers. These figures refer to large-scale industry alone, the sector in which ties were fading faster than in the small-scale manufacturing, kustar, wholesale, and retail trade sectors.

Out of a total of 1,831,295 urban workers nation-wide, 857,544, or 49.8 per cent, had been born outside towns; 148,662 households from this total still held land in some form. Family holdings made up a further 64,959, and solitary holders another 83,703. The figures from these three categories that still actively worked on their land in 1926 were respectively 82,122, 37,775, and 46,347.[44]

Migration within European Russia was largely a movement to cities by 1926. The towns and cities of the Central Industrial Region now held 650,000 persons born in other regions. By 1926 there were twelve cities with more than 200,000 inhabitants, including Moscow with 2,029,000 and Leningrad with 1,690,000. Some of Moscow's suburbs were to increase threefold over the period 1926–39.[45] Yet in 1926 the larger cities had only 4 per cent more people than in 1917, reflecting the ongoing influence of the huge exodus between 1917 and 1921. Thus the more urban, literate, and industrialized gubernii of European Russia had experienced considerable out-migration as well as more in-migration prior to 1926. Moreover, emigration from rural areas in the Central Industrial Region into

[44] *Vsesoiuznaia Perepis'*, vol. 51, table III (V), and vol. 55, table I.

[45] O. A. Konstantinov, 'Geograficheskie razlichiia v dinamike gorodskogo naseleniia SSSR', *Izvestiia vsesoiuznogo geograficheskogo obshchestva*, 76/6 (1943), pp. 11–24.

other areas of Russia, plus emigration from cities in the Region to Leningrad, the Ukraine, etc. outweighed the influx into the Region. A scholar who examined the 1926 census in great detail for migratory movements identified at least nine complicated streams of population redistribution in 1926.[46] It should not be assumed that peasants from the Smolensk, Kursk, and Ukrainian gubernii, treated in Chapters 1–3, migrated automatically to their own nearby urban centres. Belorussians spread throughout Siberia, Great Russians from Kursk were to be found all over European Russia, Siberia, and the Far East. Ukrainians moved to other Black-Earth areas, to the north Caucasus, and to the Asiatic steppes.[47] Only the Kazakhs, of all the ethnic groups surveyed in this book, scarcely left their territory of origin, but it should be recalled that they were nomads within their own vast lands at the time, and only 7.1 per cent of them were able to read their own language.[48] The very notion of their forming a 'proletariat' of any kind would be beyond their comprehension in 1926. Yet it will be seen in the final chapter that in northern Kazakhstan a few Kazakhs had in fact settled down as labourers in mines run by Great Russians. There are always exceptions to general rules in the study of Russia's enormous variety. That is why the subject is so absorbing, hard to interpret, and full of pitfalls.

In 1924, L. Kritsman pronounced that due to the lack of a sufficiently strong proletariat in Marxist terms, there had occurred a smychka of proletarian and peasant revolutions, and the two classes were now marching triumphantly together towards an industrial future.[49] Even by 1926 there was no sign of this happening in reality. The ties that held the working class to the rural hinterland were the opposite of progressive in this sense. Yet at least it was already clear that, unlike India in the 1920s for example, there was no doubt as to which sector was in the ascendancy. There was no real danger, apart from Bolshevik fears (rather than objective circumstances) concerning the '*kulaks*', that the urban areas would be submerged by

[46] See F. Lorimer, *The Population of the Soviet Union* (Geneva, 1946), p. 49.
[47] Ibid., p. 55.
[48] Ibid., p. 57.
[49] L. Kritsman, *Tri goda novoi ekonomicheskoi politiki proletariata SSSR* (Moscow, 1924), p. 5.

peasant influences, as they nearly might have been towards the end of the Civil War. In Moscow, and to a lesser extent in Leningrad, the more articulate and better-organized elements of the working class, for the first time in Russian history, actually began to obtain some political leverage on the rising Bolshevik leaders. This influence was to prove temporary, but it enabled Stalin to move out of NEP and into the first period of fast industrialization.

# 9. *Lack of Improvement in Control over the Localities*

BEFORE turning to examine in later chapters the individual characteristics of three localities in 1926, a more general survey is given here of ideological theories, institutions, and human agents that were manipulated by the central authorities in their efforts to keep the later years of NEP on an even political and social keel in the provinces. The institutions singled out are the rural Soviets and the Central Control Commission and its branches. The agents will be divided into those who facilitated control and those who increasingly hampered it. The ideas and topics treated in this chapter should be related to the subjects discussed for 1922 in Chapter 5, as is implied by the similarity in the titles of the two chapters.

A theoretical concept which kept cropping up in the minds of leading Bolsheviks throughout NEP was smychka, the notion of town and country alliance. It has just featured in the previous chapter, for instance. Between 1921 and 1923 Lenin had moved towards an alliance with what were termed the middle peasants, who were considered by most central party leaders to be in the majority in the countryside. The practical effects of this line, or rather lack of them in 1922, were reviewed earlier in the case-study of the Kursk guberniia. By 1924 it was clear that smychka was having little or no impact on the realities of rural life. Even Stalin now devoted some thought to the problem of alliance in his role as temporary ally of Kamenev and Zinoviev. In October 1924 he was concerned with abandoning Lenin's policy and establishing a new alliance between the proletariat and what he called the 'toiling peasants', in particular the rural poor, who could be set against the more prosperous in the countryside.

Stalin attributed the weakness of party cells in the localities to the absence of a wide 'non-party active' who could work as a link between the cells and the local population. The fragile network as of 1924 'often breaks down, and instead of a connecting bridge, a blank wall sometimes arises between the Party and the non-Party masses in the countryside'.[1] A contemporary event which indicated the instability of the rural party cell as an institution capable of establishing a respected leading role was the murder of a correspondent in the village of Dymovka in March 1924. The victim had written to *Rabochii korrespondent* about corruption in a party cell, and was killed for his revelations. By the end of 1925 there were to be a further twenty-four murders of correspondents.[2] In an article published in January 1925, entitled 'Dymovka', Stalin wrote that the main point raised by that particular murder was not the death of a correspondent, but 'that here and there in the countryside, in the volosti, in the districts in the *okruga*, our local responsible workers look only toward Moscow and refuse to turn toward the peasantry'.[3] This was a tacit admission that proletarian workers in the localities regarded themselves first and foremost as agents of Moscow.

In the same period, September to November 1924, evidence from the elections to the local Soviets showed how the latter were becoming alienated from most of the peasantry. The role of the Soviets will be discussed later, but at this point Stalin's views in the autumn of 1924 may be recorded: 'We must take all measures to ensure that the peasants are drawn into the Soviets, that the Soviets are revitalized and put on their feet, that the peasantry find an outlet for their political activity, by participating unfailingly in the administration of the country.'[4] That same autumn, due to drought in the Volga basin and south-east European Russia, the last thing in the thoughts of many peasants was the administration of the country. It was to be another partial harvest failure at the close of NEP that would lead to the final rift between state and society and the collapse of NEP as a whole.

[1] J. Stalin, 'The Party's Tasks in the Countryside' (26 Oct. 1924), in *Collected Works* (Moscow, 1953), p. 319.

[2] See S. N. Harper, *Civic Training in Soviet Russia* (Chicago, 1929), pp. 98–9.

[3] Stalin, 'Dymovka' (26 Jan. 1925), *Collected Works* (Moscow, 1954), p. 20.

[4] Stalin, 'The Party's Tasks in the Countryside', op. cit., p. 320.

A close associate of Stalin, V. M. Molotov, did what he could in 1924 to bolster the practical side of the smychka theory. This was the system of shefstvo (patronage) which had got off to a slow start in 1923. After visiting Kursk among other regions, Molotov set out in an article 'the fundamental propositions of cultural patronage work'. He said the first task of cultural patronage work was, 'the establishment of comradely contact between the workers and rural workers with a view to strengthening the worker–peasant alliance and with a view to strengthening the union of the local organizations with the broad peasant masses'. He insisted that the work should take the form of (*a*) cultural and political instructive work in the village through the village reading-house, peasant houses in the towns, the schools, the meetings of women; and (*b*) help in the work of the Soviets, committees, co-operatives, and other local organizations. He defined a patron as a collective of workers or office-workers or an enterprise or an establishment. Candidates, party and non-party members, were selected by a general meeting of workers to take part in a committee. The committee was responsible for its work to that meeting. Party cells directed the work of party members on the committee though they were to avoid any kind of tutelage over the committee. The financial means of the committee were to come from voluntary wage deduction from the workers. When a committee became sufficiently large a society of cultural patronage was formed. In this way it was hoped that the urban workers could assist directly in the creation of an alliance between the peasant and proletariat.[5]

The grandiose schemes of Stalin and Molotov remained almost entirely in the realm of speculative ideas. For practical proof of this we may turn to a contemporary survey of proletarian agencies at work in the localities. In a book published in 1926, but relating to the period October 1924 to April 1925, N. Rosnitsky covered 28 volosti in Penza guberniia.[6] The area lay in the Middle Volga region, where drought occurred in 1924. The gubernii of Saratov and Samara, which were treated in Chapter 2, lay nearby, to the south and east. No doubt the peasants of Penza guberniia were somewhat

[5] *Izvestiia tsentral'nogo komiteta R.K.P (b)*, 9/14 (1 Dec. 1924).
[6] N. Rosnitsky, *Litso derevni* (Leningrad, 1926).

distracted by local hardships at the time, but there is little doubt that some of the general problems underlying the details of the study had much more than local significance.

Rosnitsky's researchers found that patronage in action was either sparse, or created more trouble than it was worth. Patrons adopted a domineering manner: peasants complained to the investigators of the way in which they were tormented by orders from patrons to transport them by cart from one place to another.[7] An excursion arranged by a Komsomol patron was characterized by drunkenness and hooliganism.[8] Other patrons had no idea of how to adapt themselves to peasant ways. At their first encounter with the locals in Olenevskii volost' they recited thousands of miles from the ocean a history of the glorious Soviet Baltic Fleet.[9]

As for evidence of Stalin's theory and hope that poor peasants could be attracted rapidly into collaboration with proletarian elements and with party-controlled organizations in the countryside, Rosnitsky's researchers were unable to produce any, despite the fact that they were bound to be biased in an optimistic way: of the forty-four investigators, seven were members of the guberniia party committee, six were on the guberniia executive committee, and the remainder were leaders of other guberniia institutions. They could not find any concrete evidence of the extent to which the so-called 'poor' peasantry (*bednota*) had become a solid group with identifiable economic interests. What was clear was that poorer peasant elements had not been drawn to the rural Soviets. Indeed, the opposite was occurring. The so-called '*kulaks*' were taking them over. In any case, as non-Soviet scholars[10] have subsequently corroborated, Rosnitsky found that 'the political climate in the villages is set not by the rural Soviets but by the *skhod*.'[11] The party cells in Penza guberniia were often 'invisible' to the rural population. In the village of Valiaevka the locals 'resolutely denied the existence of any cell there', although one had

---

[7] *Litso derevni*, p. 108.

[8] Ibid., p. 107.

[9] Ibid., p. 108.

[10] See D. J. Male, *Russian Peasant Organization Before Collectivization* (Cambridge, England, 1971), and Y. Taniuchi, *The Village Gathering in Russia in the Mid-1920s* (Birmingham, 1968).

[11] Rosnitsky, op. cit., p. 33.

existed for five years.[12] The rural Soviets were created 'solely for the execution of orders from above',[13] according to the peasants. As in Kursk guberniia in 1922, the nearest authorities were considered to be nothing but tax-collectors, and so best avoided.

Looking down from the apex of Soviet society, Bukharin had a different view in 1925, though it should be remembered that the following quotation was addressed as propaganda material for foreign consumption. Unlike Stalin, he took a genuine interest in the lower Soviets until 1929. 'The peasant has become far more active than before. His political horizon has broadened; his independence has increased; he feels the need to take part more energetically in political life, in the organs of administration, in the village Soviets, the co-operatives, etc.'[14]

The first part of Bukharin's assertion was certainly true. One of the main differences between peasant life in 1922 and 1925–6 was the increased standard of living for those with more initiative or luck after three years of relative calm and prosperity. At least some peasants were acquiring broader horizons. But were they directed wholeheartedly towards the Soviets?

That all was not perfect in this sphere was clear even at the highest level when a conference on the revitalization of the Soviets was convened for two sessions in January and April 1925. Its decisions provided the basis of policy in local administration for the rest of NEP.[15] As a result, the enquiries of the Central Control Commission revealed that the average number of deputies to town Soviets increased from eighty-seven to 117 from 1925 to 1926. Over 100,000 new members were appointed to village Soviets in the same period.[16] Unfortunately these figures meant little in terms of greater vigour or expertise. Two-thirds of all those elected in the RSFSR to village or town Soviets between 1918 and 1927 served for one year and were never re-elected.[17] In the rural Soviets repeat elections often turned out to have a smaller attendance than

---

[12] Ibid., p. 75.

[13] Ibid., p. 31.

[14] *Rasshirennyi Plenum Ispolkoma Kommunisticheskogo Internatsionala 1925* (Moscow, 1925), p. 370.

[15] *Soveshchanie po voprosam sovetskogo stroitel'stva, 1925 g.* (Moscow, 1925).

[16] *Vtoroi plenum TsKK. Sozyva XIV s'ezda VkP(b)* (Moscow, 1926), p. 118.

[17] L. Kaganovich, *Partiia i sovety* (Moscow, 1928), pp. 60–1.

the original one. Election meetings were irregular, and there were not enough lists available of disfranchised persons. Due to the frequent and continuing geographical reorganizations discussed in Chapter 5, Soviet numbers and administration fluctuated unpredictably as the old Tsarist four-tier system of local government was slowly replaced.

The conference on revitalization, and all subsequent central accounts of the rural Soviets during the rest of NEP, were obsessed with the alleged take-over of the Soviets by richer peasants. Broad class generalizations were made which obscured what was really going on in the provinces. As usual it is necessary to delve into local case studies in order to see what was really taking place.

On the whole, local materials show that not enough funds, skilled staff and time were dispensed by central authorities on the problems revealed by the 1926 conference. Let us return briefly to the Penza guberniia for our first case study. Rosnitsky's researchers reported that 'the initiative of the rural Soviet is nil'.[18] The number of Communist Party members in the rural Soviets was very low.[19] According to the local peasants, the Soviet chairman and secretary were the only activists, leaving all other members, who were deemed to be *seredniaki* ('middle' peasants) completely in the shade. Contrary to the generalizations of the Moscow conference on revitalization, even the local chairmen were not rich peasants, but normally seredniaki with a wooden plough: the secretaries were drawn from all economic categories of peasants.[20]

Orders arrived from higher authorities in a 'raw form', just as they had left the guberniia office. They were not often understood and so ignored. Ties with the volost' executive committee were minimal anyway, and rural Soviet chairmen had little idea of what kind of work went on up there.[21] The combination of poor literacy standards and the increasing flow of *bumazhnyi potop* (paper floods of bureaucratic instructions) militated against proper comprehension. The moral attainments of many rural Soviet executives were also low. Hard drinking, embezzlement, and bribing were rife. Before a woman was appointed to the post of schoolmistress in the

[18] Rosnitsky, op. cit., p. 31.　　[19] Ibid., p. 46.
[20] Ibid., pp. 30–2.　　[21] Ibid., p. 41.

village of Altarskii, her father was approached by the chairman of the Soviet for a bribe—either money or home-brew
would do.[22] In the same village tax exemptions went myster-
iously not to the local poor peasants but to the same chairman,
to his deputy, to his secretary, and to the chairman of the
mutual aid committee.[23]

Things were no better in the winter of 1925–6 in Tver
guberniia, to the north-west of Moscow. This province will
concern us as a whole for 1926 in a later chapter, but a
spotlight may now be turned on the local Soviets there.

Following on orders from the capital, a campaign to revive
the rural Soviets was duly organized. The guberniia executive
committee tried to ensure that Soviet reports coming up to it
from below should not be 'in a rosy light'.[24] Potemkin village
life of a supposedly efficient and idyllic kind remained a
perpetual problem for diagnosing superiors, whether at guberniia or all-Russian levels. What was ascertainable was that
participation in elections to Tver Soviets of all kinds was
improving. In 1924 the percentage of those eligible who had
voted was 35 per cent. By 1926 it had risen to 51.1 per cent,
though it was to drop again to 48.3 per cent in 1927.[25] It is clear
from the guberniia committee's deliberations that it had a far
more realistic and detailed view of life in the rural Soviets than
did the Moscow authorities. The committee, from its bitter
experience of the recent past, urged all members of the Soviets
to meet, and not just the chairman and his secretary. Meetings
should not be arranged in the open air at a vague time of day,
but convened precisely in a specific building. When a committee member objected that most Soviet members were too
ignorant to participate in the revitalization campaign, it was
decided to give all rural Soviets twenty days in order to draw
up their replies, so that relative enlightenment would have time
to spread its bright glow.[26]

Another speaker commented that for 1926 the best that
could be hoped for would be one voter from each household,

[22] Ibid., p. 32.
[23] Ibid., p. 34.
[24] *Stenograficheskii otchet III sessii Tverskogo gubispolkoma XIII-ogo sozyva 9–14 noiabriia
1925 goda* (Tver, 1926), pp. 140–2.
[25] Ibid., pp. 140, 261.
[26] Ibid., pp. 147–8.

and that would be the master of course.[27] In 1924 only 5 per cent of eligible women had voted for the Soviets. Yet between 1926 and 1927 there was to be a substantial improvement in this area at least. The percentage of women voting for the town Soviets rose from 39.5 to 51.2.[28] In less sophisticated areas, far away from the towns, it was much harder to drum up interest. Another speaker pointed out that it would need twenty separate statements from forest sectors on twenty different days, so that the rural Soviet executive could gather in views from this widely scattered population. Soviet chairmen were already used to claiming lower taxes or free firewood in return for having to travel 15 versts once a month in order to meet peasants in remote woodland areas.[29]

Lack of adequate finances was a perennial problem in Tver guberniia. In 1926 the People's Commissariat of Finance planned to introduce properly regulated rural Soviet budgets but the relief came too late to secure their independence. A speaker from Kashinskii uezd said in November 1925 at the guberniia committee meeting that his Soviet executive members were so badly paid that they were being 'illegally' financed by local peasants. He added sarcastically, 'As yet we don't conduct English-style elections because we don't have the means.'[30] It was pointed out that poor and middle peasants could never be got to work for the good of the people until they had enough money in their own pockets. At the other economic extreme in the countryside, support was given for upholding the voting rights of rich mill-owners and heads of *kustar'* nests. As for the so-called '*kulaks*', how could a peasant with one horse and three cows who neither traded nor exploited others be given such an artificial label? One delegate at the guberniia meeting declared that 'when I was a prisoner-of-war in Germany and Austria, efficient peasants weren't dubbed *kulaks*. The result here is that you don't want to elect him to a Soviet because he is a good *khoziain*.'[31] There was far greater tolerance of rich and poor at local levels than in Moscow, where class war was being whipped up once again.

For rural Soviets throughout the country, links to higher-level Soviets and up to Moscow were via the volost' executive

[27] *Stenograficheskii otchet III*, p. 144.    [28] Ibid., p. 262.    [29] Ibid., pp. 147, 153.
[30] Ibid., p. 152.    [31] Ibid., pp. 144, 155.

committee. The latter spent more time than rural Soviets on tax and conscription matters, and had a virtual monopoly over police affairs. Roughly 90 per cent of administration work of all types in rural Soviets came from higher organs.[32] The few ideas on amendments to legislation submitted by lower Soviet levels to higher ones often took as long as six months to reach the right office.[33] Rural Soviets in 1926 preferred their personal agents to hand up their views orally (*zhivaia sviaz'*), but in fact the written form of communication had to prevail for lack of agents with time on their hands. Written reports predominated by three to four times over oral ones in the first half of 1926.[34] Communications of all kinds and at all levels creaked along very slowly. In Tambov guberniia, which we visited during the Famine in 1922, six Soviet staff spent a total of 1,430 days in 1926 travelling round on their work. They had to work overtime for the short periods when they were settled in one location.[35] If conditions were like this in an European setting, they must have been atrocious in Siberia and Central Asia.

Soviet administration had to cover many remote areas that remained very poorly covered by party cells in 1926. In late 1925 only one out of every twenty-five or thirty villages contained a party cell.[36] So long as Stalin stayed in league with Bukharin, with the slogan 'Look to the Countryside', contacts of a relatively benign kind continued, so that by 1927 there were 217,400 peasant party members in 17,500 rural cells.[37] On the other hand in the same year non-party officials still occupied half the chairmanships of volost' executive committees and as much as three-quarters of the rural Soviet chairmanships.[38]

Even if the Party had had closer control over local Soviets through greater membership in 1926, it is doubtful whether the Soviets would have exercised more influence since they had a

[32] *Soveshchanie*, pp. 68–9.
[33] I. Muranov, *Apparat nizovykh sovetskikh organov. Po materialam obsledovaniia* (Moscow, 1926), pp. 95, 103.
[34] *VI S'ezd sovetov* (Moscow), 1 (1927), p. 23.
[35] Ibid., 41 (1927), p. 1.
[36] *Bol'shevik*, 23–4 (30 Dec. 1925), p. 44.
[37] G. S. Konyukhov, *KPSS v bor'be s khlebnymi zatrudneniyami v strane 1928–9* (Moscow, 1960).
[38] *XV s'ezd VkP(b), dekabr' 1927 goda: stenograficheskii otchet*, vol. 1 (Moscow, 1962), pp. 448–9.

strong administrative rival on their very doorstep. The local peasant assembly (*skhod*) of the local commune (*mir*) normally had more sway over the local population. In 1926 a full-scale debate developed on the comparative roles of the rural Soviet and the commune. Central organs could not agree on the subject. The Commissariat of Agriculture assumed that under the provisions of the Land Code the rural Soviets had no power over the commune.[39] Yet the Commissariat of Internal Affairs asserted that the commune, as a survivor from Tsarist times, had no official status: the Soviets clearly predominated.[40]

The *de facto* position, as opposed to the airy hypotheses of Muscovite bureaucrats, was more complex. As a Japanese scholar has shown,[41] village life had three administrative aspects. Local agricultural matters were almost entirely self-enclosed, and governed by the skhod even after 1926. Public services also had to be dealt with largely by the commune, since for lack of funds the Party could not achieve its ambition of taking over in this sphere. Only in the commune's administrative relations with the wider world was it easier for the Communists to dominate. Of these links by far the most important was taxation. This unpopular connection, as we have seen, warned the peasant and the skhod to keep as far apart from the 'Centre' as it could on all other matters. The few links that did exist between rural Soviets and the commune were vitiated in other ways as well. Since Soviet chairmen received such inadequate salaries for their services, they were tempted into corrupt and so subordinate liaisons with richer members of the skhod.[42] Even if they kept their hands clean, they were compelled to spend so much of their time studying bureaucratic orders from above that they had scant time for influencing local life or for farming, the basic occupation that had previously cemented them to their fellow peasants.

The question may well be posed whether the Party should have shifted its sympathies to the skhod as its spearhead in the localities. There were several reasons why this could never be contemplated. The mir was redolent of the Tsarist inheritance

[39] I. Kozhikov, 'Sel'skie sovety i zemel'nye obshchestva', *Na agrarnom fronte*, 5 (1928), p. 68.
[40] *Vlast' sovetov*, 15 Aug. 1926.
[41] Taniuchi, op. cit., pp. 24–5.
[42] Ibid., pp. 35–6.

that was anathema to the Bolsheviks. Although there were approximately 319,000 peasant assemblies in the Soviet Union at the end of 1925, covering 92 per cent of her land mass, they could attract a mere 25 per cent of the local population to vote in them.[43] No doubt some conscientious skhod elders existed in 1926. In the village of Chentsovo, near Smolensk, the skhod *starshye* took it in one-month turns to act as alternating head of the assembly and then member of the local Soviet.[44] Women were still not welcome at many assemblies, and frequent quarrels there put them off from taking an interest. Even many male peasants were unaware of meeting-times, so bells were used to attract attention. Often the local *izba-chital'nye* (reading-huts for illiterates) were used for assemblies, or some other small building that could not accommodate even those who did put in an attendance.[45] For once the central authorities conjectured rightly when they imagined that the skhod, like the rural Soviet, was apt to be taken over by peasants with more initiative, with a slightly wider view of the world beyond their remote fastnesses in the largest country in the world. This conjuncture of private initiative and private money began to frighten the Party in 1926. The strongest personal link between centre and periphery was precisely the one that went most against the ideological grain.

At the end of 1926 Rabkrin carried out a survey of the efficiency of the lower Soviet levels. It was perturbed to discover that the rural Soviets were still playing a very minor role in the localities. The communes, on the other hand, were handling most of the economic and cultural needs of the villages. Some even went further, electing the chairman of the rural Soviet and discussing and approving its work programme.[46] One local study of the period showed that although many communes met at least once a week, the rural Soviet assembled only five to eight times a year.[47] In 1926 the commune's activities covered nearly all aspects of local life, as the eagle eye of Rabkrin revealed. The largest number of

[43] M. D. Rezunov, *Sel'skie sovety i zemel'nye obshchestva* (Moscow, 1928), p. 42.
[44] *Bednota* (Moscow), 13 Nov. 1926.
[45] Rezunov, op. cit., pp. 44–5.
[46] Kozhikov, op. cit., p. 67.
[47] F. Kretov, *Derevnia posle revoliutsii* (Moscow, 1925), pp. 77–8.

questions naturally dealt with land. Then came in descending order of importance, finance, administration (local roads, repairs, etc.), cultural matters, public welfare (health care of orphans, etc.), and other concerns.[48]

A final effort during NEP to clarify the muddy relationship between the commune and the rural Soviet was made with the adoption on 14 March 1927 of a new law intended to set up a new type of village meeting. There were to be two kinds—general assemblies of the local population as well as the traditional gatherings of the commune.[49] The new assembly was to be open to landless residents who were not members of the commune, and was to meet under the aegis of the rural Soviet. This law was universally ignored. Practical peasants could see no profit in having to attend two meetings instead of one. They remained faithful to the commune system until its abolition after the end of NEP. Thus, as in so many social spheres, long and unsuccessful cajolement by distant authorities to reform led finally to swift and brutal action from the centre, with even less heed than before to local realities and interests.

In the middle of 1926 a Central Committee report on the campaign to revitalize the Soviets gave a pessimistic survey. Although 6,000 party and Komsomol workers had been sent to the localities, they had spent far too much time trying unsuccessfully to organize the poor peasants into isolated political battalions with which to assault the Soviets. On the contrary it was vital to integrate them into the Soviets and the cooperatives, working for the party within those institutions.[50] Party policy was moving away from Bukharin's soft line towards the '*kulaks*', and was becoming increasingly obsessed by class stratification among the peasantry. No one in the Central Committee heeded the sentiments echoed in the information from Tver and elsewhere that at the grass-roots level this perception of sharp socio-economic differentiation and antagonism simply did not exist. Not that Moscow panjandra were likely to know about or acknowledge obscure, detailed truths of this kind; but neither did they pay any attention to

---

[48] Regunov, op. cit., pp. 27–9.
[49] *Sobranie uzakonenii*, 51 (1927), art. 33.
[50] *Izvestiia tsentral'nogo komiteta kommunisticheskoi partii (b)*, 23/144 (14 June 1926), p. 1; 26/147 (30 June 1926), p. 3; 29–30/150–1 (26 July 1926), pp. 1–2.

their own sponsored researchers like Rezanov, who had told
them that it was not possible to define what was meant by the
'poor peasant'. Instead, central authorities began to resort to
wilder abstractions. In July 1926 the Central Committee and
the Central Control Commission resolved that the Soviet
campaign was now intended 'finally to explode the remains of
the influence of bourgeois elements (Nepmen, '*kulaks*', and
bourgeois intelligentsia) on the toiling masses'.[51]

The failure by the Party in late NEP to make the Soviet
hierarchy into a genuine conveyor belt for participation from
below and above had deeper roots than the events of 1925–6.
The whole of the Soviet network had been built up from the
apex downwards, and not vice versa. The principle of democratic centralism had always prevailed. The Party had controlled Soviets at all levels through appointments and control
of funds. The peasantry by and large never ceased to distrust
the Soviets, since they were manned, especially at the higher
levels, by party factions which prepared all the agendas before
meetings took place.

The Soviets were intended to have a twin organizational
role—as participating agencies, in order to make the government and the Party aware of the needs and demands of the
general population, and as mobilizing organs, to make the
localities aware of political instructions from above. As NEP
progressed, and neither ideal was taking shape, more accent
was put on the mobilizing aspect. The stronger Stalin became,
the more all linking agencies were treated as mere funnels
down which orders could be shovelled with increasing urgency.
By 1926–7, the only hopeful signs on the participatory front
were the slowly increasing *yavki* (voting turn-outs) and the
greater involvement of women and younger men in the rural
Soviets. On the dark side, these encouraging signs were to be
obscured by severe problems in late NEP in the Party's
agricultural procurements policy. These were to lead after
1926 to unpredictable changes and general lack of stability in
the countryside.

Let us now turn, or rather return, to two crucial supervisory institutions at the top end of the scale of political and

[51] *VKP(b) v rezoliutsiiakh*, vol. 2 (1941), pp. 103–11.

geographical influence, in deep contrast to the local Soviets. The activities of the People's Commissariat of Workers' and Peasants' Inspection (Rabkrin) in 1922 have already been examined in Chapter 5. It was noted then that in April 1923 it was merged with the Central Control Commission. The former checked on state administration at all levels, the latter on party affairs.

Supervisory organs of a similar kind have existed in Russia for two and a half centuries, since Peter the Great's creation of the *fiskaly*, yet they have been widely ignored by foreign scholars. The main reason for this seems to be that their equivalents have not existed in west European politics, where the chief checks over the rulers and the ruled stem from the three main branches of government—the executive, legislature, and judiciary. The need for supervisory organs of the Russian type actually grew as NEP progressed, precisely for lack of efficient communications along the formal channels of Party and government. This problem has loomed large in Chapters 4 and 5, and again with relation to the Soviet structure in this chapter.

The combined organ of Rabkrin and the Control Commission was a unique experiment that was dubious from the outset since it attempted to unite the masses with party and state administrators in one gigantic supervisory institution. Mass participation, including peasants as well as other groups, was never a reality after 1917, as has been seen. It was observed in Chapter 5 how attempts to establish it in Rabkrin were a dead letter by 1922 already. Both organs were partly modelled on the workers' control movement of 1917 and the administrative methods of War Communism, as some Bolsheviks noted in 1923.[52] Workers' control was both ephemeral and a failure, and War Communism methods were not supervisory checks, but brutal interference. The history of neither augured well. As Trotsky was to put it at a later date: 'Only fools and the blind can believe that socialism can be introduced from above, that it can be introduced bureaucratically.'[53]

There were other reasons why the joint supervisory organ was doomed as a body independent from the Party. It had to

[52] e.g. L. B. Krasin. See *Pravda*, 24 Mar. 1923.
[53] L. Trotsky, *Writings* (New York, 1963), p. 51.

be as multi-tentacled and expert as the institutions (i.e. all party and state organs) that it sought to supervise in order to deal with them properly. This was naturally out of the question. Secondly, who was to control the controller? In some cases it came to be the secret police, which defeated the independent aims of the supervisor. In general, however, and under Stalin's guidance in particular, it was to be the Party that refused to be interfered with.

Looking back in 1925 at the early period of Rabkrin before he had become head of the new joint body in 1923, V. V. Kuibyshev was realistic enough to notice a trend that had plagued Sovnarkom also in 1921–2—both organs soon became so entangled in the enormous detailed and complicated problems that flowed in from every quarter and from each remote province that they were in danger of becoming suffocated by what Lenin aptly called 'vermicelli'.[54] Kuibyshev observed how Rabkrin, on discovering that it was incapable of auditing all the state's books, so to speak, had gone to the other extreme, trying to supervise all state administration in a vague, generalized manner. This had only served to increase the gap between its aspirations and its capabilities.

The shift of emphasis had also led to endless clashes and overlaps with other institutions. Overlaps of this kind, as has been seen in previous chapters, were a perennial problem in most administrations in NEP. The vague boundaries between the rural party cells, the rural Soviet, and the peasant skhod have just been surveyed here. The Central Control Commission had suffered from exactly the same problem since its establishment in 1920. The line between its jurisdiction and that of the Party was unclear from the outset.[55] By the start of 1926, however, it became quite clear which of the two was to be boss. The Party, under Stalin's hand, was now supervising the supervisor to such an extent that the joint Central Control Commission and Rabkrin were being manipulated as a mere tool for political ends.

This was proved by an incident that created an uproar at the

---

[54] V. V. Kuibyshev, quoted in K. V. Gusev, *Kratkii ocherk istorii organov partiino-gosudarstvennogo kontrolia v SSSR* (Moscow, 1965), pp. 18–19. On Lenin's reference to 'vermicelli', see Ch. 5, p. 176.

[55] See L. Schapiro, *The Communist Party of the Soviet Union* (London, 1960), p. 256.

highest Party levels. In November 1928 Rabkrin was instructed to examine the work of the Central Statistical Board on the grain harvest and the peasantry. Rabkrin's findings turned into a savage campaign against the Kamenev–Zinoviev bloc. It accused the Board of exaggerating the power of the '*kulak*' and ignoring the place of the bedniak in the harvest.[56] It thus endorsed by implication the Stalin–Bukharin line at that time. The attack was patently set up by the Party Secretariat, now firmly under Stalin's control. Kamenev's oral counter-attack on Stalin was a brilliant prophecy of the near future, both in terms of personalities and of administrative irregularities:

We are against creating the theory of a 'leader'; we are against making a leader. We are against having the Secretariat combine in practice both politics and organization and placing itself above the political organ. We cannot regard it as normal; and we think it harmful to the party, to prolong a situation in which the Secretariat combines politics and organisation, and in fact decides policies in advance.[57]

This was the most damaging overlap of all, entailing the obliteration of the lines between Party and state. It was also an example of wilfully ignoring the data that could be procured by one of the best-equipped bodies in the land. Accurate facts on the 'dark people' were hard enough to come by at the best of times in the 1920s. Stalin was obviously fudging them in order to suit his own immediate personal and political ends. It was the most ominous sign of the future that cropped up in Party–state–society relations in 1925–6. Not only was the supervisor being misused. The whole of peasant society was reduced to an abstract cipher for personal advancement. Social engineering was proceeding on the basis of distorted calculations.

The local fieldwork of the combined supervisory organ was not as yet so completely under the thumb of the Party Secretariat. In 1926 the scope of the TsKK-NKRKI (unwieldy acronyms fell like autumn leaves from the tree of bureaucracy in the early Soviet period) was so wide as to be scarcely

[56] *Ekonomicheskaia zhizn'*, 12 Dec. 1925.
[57] Kamenev speaking at the Fourteenth Party Congress, quoted in E. A. Rees, *State Control in Soviet Russia: The Rise and Fall of the Workers' and Peasants' Inspectorate, 1920–34*, p. 130. Rees's book is a rare example of taking the supervisory organs seriously in scholarship.

compassed by any conference in Moscow, yet its plenums of that year struggled manfully, not only with central work, but with the extended tiers of local control commissions and representatives of Rabkrin throughout the Soviet Union. At least the effort was being made to keep in focus the almost infinite variety of administrative and social life.

The October plenum discussed the work-plan for 1926–7. One member took a stab at defining the overblown bureaucracy they were fighting against at all levels as being entirely the result of the splintering of small-scale economic producers of all kinds.[58] The *reductio ad absurdum* of all phenomena to economics was typical of the naïve Marxist of the time. It was also a case of the pot calling the kettle black. At another part of its proceedings plenum members noted fragmentation and what they called 'parallelism' in its own overlapping committees. There were too many staff members, cumbersome structures, and too much red tape.[59] A call was made for 'rationalization', and we know from separate later evidence that this duly took place.[60] In a book published in 1929, G. K. Ordzhonikidze, chairman of the institutions from November 1926 to November 1930, noted how Rabkrin units went down from 27,432 in 1925–6 to 21,246 by 1927–8.[61] A plenum member in 1926 congratulated his colleagues on the fact that of 3,619 members of local Control Commissions, 70 per cent were workers, and only 17.1 per cent peasants. It was thought better to have the proletariat tackle bureaucracy than the 'dark people'.[62]

Although the TsKK-NKRKI managed to discipline and trim its own ranks in June 1926, it had to backtrack when it tried to introduce a 'Regime of Economy' in the state administration.[63] The campaign angered the workers and the trade unions in particular. Already in August 1926 the Central

---

[58] *IV Plenum TsKK sozyva XIV s"ezda VKP(b), 21–22 oktiabria 1926g.* (Moscow, 1926), p. 117.

[59] Ibid., p. 123.

[60] Ibid., p. 4.

[61] G. K. Ordzhonikidze, *RkI v bor'be za uluchshenie sovetskogo apparata* (Moscow, 1929), p. 4.

[62] *IV Plenum*, p. 117.

[63] *Direktivy KPSS i sovetskogo pravitel'stva po khoziaistvennym voprosam*, vol. 1 (Moscow, 1957), p. 232.

Control Commission started to retreat. It was unwise to antagonize the proletariat just when some sections of it, especially in Moscow, were beginning to strike political and economic bargains with the party on other fronts.[64]

The plenum of April 1926 dwelt at length on work on the lower rungs of the administrative ladder. E. Yaroslavsky, one of Stalin's associates, gave a long account of local control commission checks on village party cells. He began 'as always, . . . the collation of materials in the localities has been delayed'.[65] In Belorussia later in the year a reporter noted that Rabkrin was having similar trouble. Between September 1926 and March 1927 only 55 per cent of the complaints sent into the local office had been processed.[66] Yaroslavsky cited examples of the age-old tendency of provincials subjected to the central microscope to say what the authorities wanted to hear, and to avoid trouble. Some party members over-rehearsed their answers to questions that were likely to be put to them by Control Commissions, others quit the Party just prior to an inspection.[67] Non-party peasants had the habit of crying out their complaints in unison at meetings with Commissioners in order to avoid being detected individually.[68] Commissions themselves were criticized for meeting non-party villagers before they inspected party cells, so they got a biased preview. One group of Commissioners arranged a drinking bout with local Socialist Revolutionaries the night before meeting Communist Party men.[69]

The behaviour of party cell members was no better. Many of them were 'absent', at weddings and the like, when Commissioners called in, and some were found to be drunk.[70] The further one got away from the capital, the worse the unorthodoxies. This was a rule that could often be detected throughout political and social life. In the Omsk *okrug* in Siberia the party cell was so corrupt that even an equally suspect *church* Soviet

[64] See Ch. 8.

[65] *Vtoroi plenum . . . 2–4 aprelia 1926 g.* (Moscow, 1926), p. 77.

[66] M. I. Zlotnik, *Deiatel'nost' organov partiino-gosudarstvennogo kontrolia BSSR v gosudarstvennom stroitel'stve* (Minsk, 1969), p. 404.

[67] *Vtoroi plenum TsKK*, p. 83.

[68] Ibid., p. 86.

[69] Ibid., pp. 82, 84.

[70] Ibid., p. 83.

made complaints about it to Commissioners. Local Komsomols lit their cigarettes from oil-lamps in church and let loose pigeons during the services. The peasants agreed that only careerists and card-players were to be found in the party cell. In another Siberian cell party members dabbled in spiritualism and tried to call up the spirit of Karl Marx. The October plenum of the Central Control Commission struck a brighter note with regard to inspections of local Soviets. In the industrial city of Kharkov, which we passed through in 1922, the numbers of worker members of the Soviet had risen from 790 in 1924 to 1,076 in 1926. Such proletarian dominance was a good thing, but the figures also happened to show the swelling numbers engaged in and impeding each other in administration. By the time of the Fourteenth Party Congress it was reported that nearly ten million persons were engaged in local committees apart from the Party and the Soviets.[71]

If neither the Central Control Commission, nor its local branches, nor the local Soviet and Party hierarchy was capable of galvanizing the peasantry into active collaboration with the wider aims of the Party by 1926, was it possible for other local agents nearer the grass roots to promote smychka?

The group with the most hope of achieving this aim were ex-military servicemen of peasant origin. In 1922 in Kursk guberniia and elsewhere survivors of the Civil War were seen to play an important role in introducing new ideas and organizational efficiency into the depths of the countryside. The huge exodus from the armed forces after 1921 had dried up, but during the mid-1920s about 260,000 young men were drafted annually into the peacetime ranks: roughly 70 per cent of these were of peasant origin.[72] Some of them returned to their villages after their service, but in 1926 they often tended to disassociate themselves from the local party cells and Soviets, as they had done in 1922.[73] In this way they kept their popularity among their less sophisticated fellow peasants in the commune, but in the eyes of the Party authorities they had fallen victim to the widespread disease of *vrastanie* (absorption into the peasantry, or, in their case, reabsorption).

[71] Ibid., pp. 88, 94.
[72] B. Tal', *Istoriia krasnoi armii* (Moscow, 1929), p. 190.
[73] See p. 77 above.

Quite a large proportion of returning ex-servicemen, however, did in fact enlist for rural administrative or party work. In 1925-6, 70 per cent of all chairmen of volost' executive committees had been Red Army men.[74] On the surface, this was a very encouraging omen, but the trouble was that due to their talents and ambition they returned to their grass-roots origins. Without doubt by 1926 the volost' towns and villages were the local power-houses through which central directives were channelled to the countryside at large. They housed the two chief nation-wide hierarchies—the state and the Party. Leading local members of the volost' executive committee, the Party, the judiciary, the militia, the medical and educational services, the agronomists, and the Komsomol usually resided in them. These categories overlapped to a considerable degree in their personnel, due to the continuing lack of enough intelligenty in the localities. To these diminutive centres flocked local inspectors of the Control Commission, Rabkrin, all other central Commissariats, together with the chairmen of the rural Soviets.

Various influences tended by 1926 to cement the interlocking relationships between these groups of employees and to cut them off from the only other power-house at the lower levels, the local commune. Most of them were underpaid, and nearly all of them were subject to enormous pressures via the guberniia centres from their superiors. Except for the medical staff and occasionally the agronomists, they were normally seen by the peasants in the hinterland as extractors of taxes and disciplined work.[75] Such behaviour acted as a brake on the slightly better relations by 1926 between *fel'dshers* (semi-trained doctors), agronomists, Komsomol workers and teachers on the one hand and the peasantry on the other.[76] The benign influence of these latter agents had improved *vis-à-vis* 1922 partly because there were just rather more of them by 1926.[77]

---

[74] *Perevybory v sovety RSKSR v 1925–26 g.* (Moscow, 1926), p. 35.

[75] D. Rogit, *Proverka raboty nizogo apparata v derevne* (Moscow, 1926), pp. 55–7.

[76] See L. Kritsman, P. Popov, and Ia. Yakovlev (eds.), *Sel'skoe khoziaistvo na putiakh vostanovleniia* (Moscow, 1925), pp. 777, 812.

[77] *Vsesoiuznaia Perepis'*, vol. 34, pp. 142–60. There were 3,228 agronomists in rural institutions in 1926, together with 2,306 land administrators and topographers (excluding instructors, professors, and academics).

Agronomists were virtually non-existent in 1922. By 1928 the number of doctors had only reached 63,200.[78]

The growing role of the Komsomol will be investigated in more detail when we arrive at Smolensk province in 1926. Rural teachers had their drawbacks as agents for smychka in 1922, as was noted in Kursk guberniia.[79] By 1926 they had shaken off some of these problems, but had now acquired new ones. They were becoming better educated in politics, and suffered less competition from the declining priesthood in the localities, but they were now in far greater demand for their services from the more relaxed peasantry of mid-NEP.[80] Their enormous teaching loads prevented most of them from playing a leading role in the villages. Those who did had often to neglect their schoolwork. Rosnitsky in Penza guberniia concluded that teachers should put the education of the rising generation first, and extra-mural political and cultural work second.[81]

In his great work on French society in the nineteenth century, Theodore Zeldin concluded that as early as the 1890s most of those living at or near the grass roots in the French provinces were witnessing the steep decline of a deep historical sense of belonging to a local community, with its own individual spirit.[82] Durkheim characterized the phenomenon with the single word 'anomie'. Although Russia had experienced a fundamental political revolution in 1917, hardly a whiff of anomie had penetrated from above to commune level by the end of NEP. Yet by 1926 it was true that ex-peasants now in state or party pay in the volost' settlements felt deeply alienated in their rural bastions, surrounded by a still largely hostile or at best uncomprehending population.

One of the major social causes, if not the *main* cause, of the collapse of NEP is said to have been, by both Soviet and foreign scholars, the socio-economic rise and possible political threat of the '*kulaks*'. This view should be modified in various

[78] *Vsesoiuznaia Perepis'*, vol. 36, p. 160. This was the number for fully trained doctors. Semi-trained *fel'dshers* far outnumbered them, amounting to 28,700.

[79] The 1926 census gave 170,900 full-time teachers in the countryside. They comprised half of the rural intelligentsia. See *Vsesoiuznaia Perepis'*, vol. 34, p. 160.

[80] See p. 76 above.

[81] Rosnitsky, op. cit., pp. 96–9.

[82] T. Zeldin, *France 1848–1945*, vol. 2 (Oxford, 1977), pp. 26–7.

ways. It is now time to turn to those independent agents, including the so-called '*kulaks*', who by their greater initiative in mid-NEP and later set up more pervasive links, mainly economic in nature, between the grass roots and higher levels of society than were being forged by Party, Soviet, or other state agents.

The most formidable linking agents were not in fact the '*kulaks*', but the Nepmen and the kustari. Both these groups have been neglected and underestimated in historical scholarship. Neither of them fit into Marxist socio-economic categories, and both became embarrassments to the regime in later NEP. This has given Soviet observers two good reasons for leaving them in the shade, yet the same may be said of non-Soviet historiography. It took until 1987 for a scholarly account of Nepmen[83] to appear, and the kustari remain unconsidered in a full-length study.

The definition of all words which became terms of abuse is notoriously difficult, and Nepman and '*kulak*' fall into this category. When they were not hounding them with political propaganda, the Soviet authorities in calmer mood divided Nepmen into three subgroups—labour-owners with wage labour, owners with family or artel' labour, and the self-employed. The main problem of definition lies in what to include or exclude. Large-scale urban traders, private manufacturers, financiers, speculators, and small-scale merchants and artisans whose businesses were their primary occupations clearly fall within the definition. Part-time petty vendors may or may not be included, according to the reporter. Some kustari certainly indulged in Nepmen-type trading on occasion, and richer peasants who sometimes sold produce in local markets might also be included, but since kustari and '*kulaks*' are about to be examined in their own right, the extent to which the three categories overlapped will be left aside at this point.

Although not all those who could be classified as Nepmen took out private trade licences, the number issued showed a marked rise from 496,454 in the second half of the tax year 1923–4 to a peak of 608,280 by the second half of 1925–6.[84]

[83] A. M. Ball, *Russia's Last Capitalists: The Nepmen, 1921–1929* (Berkeley, 1987). This is an important monograph.

[84] *Finansy i narodnoe khoziaistvo*, 4 (1928), p. 27.

The extent to which Nepmen dominated the trading stage by 1926 can be seen from the fact that in the same tax period only 119,700 co-operatives were issued licences, and a mere 38,600 to state organizations.[85] The rise and decline of the Nepmen was butterfly-like compared to that of the kustari and richer peasants, who had been active long before the turn of the century. True, some Nepmen had been small-scale producers or shopkeepers before the Revolution.[86] Others, but not all of them, as Soviet historians would like to think, had been bagmen, speculators, and black marketeers in the Civil War years.[87] Some had even been vigorous supporters of War Communism techniques for the Party.[88]

The year 1925 witnessed two contradictory political opinions at work on the subject of Nepmen. On the one hand, due to the state's inability by that year to replace the private sector, Nepmen had to be encouraged, since traders of any kind were better than none.[89] At the same time Bukharin was emerging as co-leader with Stalin to suit the latter's convenience in his struggle against Zinoviev and Kamenev. Bukharin was inclined to tolerate private traders, richer peasants, and kustari alike. On the other hand, sentiment against Nepmen abounded at the Fourteenth Party Congress in 1925. Delegates passed resolutions calling for systematic restrictions on private entrepreneurs. The fact that the Congress approved a policy of imminent socialist industrialization made the Nepmen's eventual elimination a virtual political obligation. From 1926 to 1927 taxes on Nepmen were raised, and their access to credit lowered. Following on a decision of the Fifteenth Party Congress in 1927, these measures were stepped up.[90]

Given the Nepmen's obvious capitalist techniques, it is not surprising that the Bolsheviks never lowered their sights against this particular target. Near the end of NEP, with increasing intensity from 1926 onwards, the Party claimed that although

---

[85] See an article by J. Reingold in *Soviet Policy in Public Finances* (Stanford, 1931), pp. 175 ff.

[86] See the example of D. A. D'iakov cited in the survey of Kursk guberniia in 1922, p. 70 above.

[87] Trifonov, op. cit., pp. 31–2, 71–4.

[88] See p. 70 above.

[89] L. F. Morozov, *Reshaiushchii etap bor'by s NEPmanskoi burzhuaziei (1926–1929 gg.)* (Moscow, 1960), p. 27.

[90] *Vsesoiuznaia Perepis'*, vol. 19, table IV, pp. 376–409.

the '*kulaks*' represented the greatest threat to society and the state, the Nepmen also figured somewhere in this dramatic scenario. What then were the strengths and weaknesses of the private traders as a socio-economic and possibly as a political force?

Although the average private undertaking was small, the number of Nepmen was impressive, and probably far exceeded those registered officially through licensing. They were widely disseminated all over the Soviet Union by 1926, so that their 'bourgeois' habits made a considerable impact on everyday life, particularly because they travelled more than most. Their activities cut across class barriers, from high finance to street peddling, from manufacturing to negotiating with local kustari. Neither could they be assigned to any single social class. Nepmen were influential since they predominated in the towns and particularly in the new and old capitals. In 1923 they controlled about two-thirds of the goods circulated within Moscow.[91] They tapped their *zemliaki* (fellow-countrymen) for hired labour from the localities to work in the capitals. They also made urban populations heavily dependent on them. Muscovites had to buy much of their clothing and roughly 70 per cent of their bread from private traders in 1924. It had been the shortage of the second of these two basic necessities that had sparked off the outbreak of the February Revolution in Petrograd.

Beyond the capitals Nepmen dominated the supply of certain essential goods. Even near the end of NEP 80 per cent of total retail sales of eggs, meat, fruit, vegetables, and dairy products were in their hands in the regional towns and cities.[92] In January 1926 it was estimated that all state organs had thirty-one times fewer personnel at work in the countryside than the swarms of private traders.[93] The present author has attempted in another book to point out the crucial strategic and political significance of supply control in a backward country the size of Russia in the first decades of this century.[94] Besides material goods, private traders distributed ideas. By

[91] Trifonov, op. cit., p. 52.
[92] *Torgovo-promyshlennaia gazeta*, 249 (30 Oct. 1927), p. 3.
[93] I. S. Kondurushkin, *Chastnyi kapital pered sovetskim sudom* (Moscow, 1927), p. 209.
[94] R. W. Pethybridge, *The Spread of the Russian Revolution: Essays on 1917* (London, 1972).

the start of 1923 they were responsible for the publication and dissemination of a third of all Soviet titles on philosophy, and for over 40 per cent in the sphere of poetry, *belles-lettres*, and literary criticism.[95] The unorthodoxies of the Petrograd publishing houses at this time have already been investigated in an earlier chapter.

Beyond these spheres of sophistication, Nepmen represented an even greater threat as time went by, as four-fifths of the Russian population employed in agriculture seemed to be getting more entrenched in private production. Trading networks dug deep into the hinterland. Nearly half of all private exchange took place in the central industrial region and the Ukraine. National minority problems compounded the threat of collusion between Nepmen, kustari, and richer peasants. In 1927 almost two-thirds of the private traders in Belorussia and over half in the Ukraine had pre-1917 trading experience.[96] This was primarily due to the resumption by many Jews of their former jobs. In the first half of 1925–6 the Nepmen's share of all trading was 80 per cent in the Belorussian Republic and 81 per cent in the Ukraine. In Central Asia, where we shall end our tour of the provinces for 1926, Nepmen controlled 97 per cent of all trade in the Uzbek Republic, and 93 per cent in the Turkmen Republic.[97] It was hard to set up state stores and co-operatives in these remote areas that had only recently been reconquered by the Bolsheviks.

Nepmen also congregated at points of crucial interchange for supplies, persons, news, and rumours. They controlled many cafés, restaurants, and bath-houses (whose social importance we know of through M. Zoshchenko's delightful stories). They were influential on the all-important railway network, often in a detrimental way. Widespread embezzlement occurred from train wagons, through the syphoning off of loads by private traders. For a period of nearly four years Nepmen were involved in bribes on the north-west railway system.[98]

[95] A. I. Nazarov, *Oktiabr' i kniga* (Moscow, 1968), p. 255.

[96] *Voprosy torgovli*, no. 15 (1929), p. 61.

[97] A. Zalkind (ed.), *Chastnaia torgovlia SSR* (Moscow, 1927), p. 8.

[98] Kondurushkin, op. cit., pp. 190–2. 1925 and 1926, together with 1923, were the 3 years during NEP to show substantial increases in railway freight traffic over the preceding year (30, 31.2, and 36.1% respectively). See *Transport i sviaz' SSSR, statisticheskii sbornik* (Moscow, 1957), p. 32.

Other Nepmen ran fleets on the inland waterways,[99] commandeered trucks and carts, and even ran a private airline based in
the Ukraine which served Moscow.

The reality of 1926 was that some Nepmen were overreach-
ing themselves and thus sowing the seeds of their doom.
Economic managers in the party slowly began to notice with
increasing concern and disapproval how the co-operatives, one
of Lenin's devices in 1922 for galvanizing the peasantry into
larger-scale organization and better links with the towns, were
being corrupted through infiltration by Nepmen. *Pravda*
reported on 20 April 1926 that it was becoming apparent how
many false co-operatives had been formed from 1923 on: as a
result state reductions in prices had led to the enrichment of the
Nepmen who controlled them. By June 1926 the co-operatives
as a whole remained an endangered species. There were 5.5 co-
operatives per 10,000 rural inhabitants as against 31 private
trading organizations.[100] A foreign observer in Russia in 1926
corroborated party evidence, observing how Nepmen in the
localities were paying admission fees for peasants, then buying
up their shares in co-operatives. They then had access to many
goods at rates reduced by the state, which they resold on the
private market at higher prices, unhindered by the 'Dead Soul'
co-operative members they had bought out.[101] A party poster
intent on counter-propaganda showed a peasant using a book
entitled *The Co-operative* to wipe at two insects labelled 'private
trade' and '*kulak*' gnawing at the roots of his grain crop.[102]

The Bolsheviks had some success in their efforts to turn the
Nepmen into the object of widespread envy. In 1925 there was
a new type of 'scissors' crisis, this time in fast-rising wholesale
prices. Nepmen were now speculating in 'trade deserts' (items
in short supply).[103] Retail prices in forty cities had surpassed
previous prices by 2.7 times in 1926, whereas wages had only
risen to pre-war levels. Nepmen looked for disproportionately
high profits as a compensation for what even they realized was

[99] A. M. Ginzburg (ed.), *Chastnyi kapital v narodnom khoziaistve SSSR. Materialy
kommissii VSNKh SSSR* (Moscow–Leningrad, 1927), pp. 268–9.
[100] Kondurushkin, op. cit., p. 209.
[101] S. N. Harper, *Civic Training in Soviet Russia* (Chicago, 1929), p. 176.
[102] Ibid., p. 183.
[103] Kondurushkin, op. cit., pp. 142–4.

going to be a short heyday and existence. Their pre-1913 equivalents had been painted, and whitewashed, in the pretty paintings of B. M. Kustodiev,[104] but they were soon to be anathema. They were manipulating bottle-necks in supplies to the towns, and at volost' level they had a near monopoly in liquid cash with which to trade, bribe, and corrupt. Contemporary satirists aided and abetted the party. A. Averchenko portrayed them as dealing in husbands, and even in diabetes, in his *Odessity v Petrograde*. Nepmen were the target of *chastushki* (folk-verse); in Belorussia and the Ukraine the fact that so many of them were Jews added another reason for their unpopularity.

Although there is scarcely any evidence that the Party tried to stir up envy and mistrust between Nepmen and kustari, it would have been a shrewd move, in order to divide and rule between these two organizers of small-scale handicrafts. Tax reforms of 1925 had already put roughly 200,000 large-scale private urban traders out of business;[105] before this the volume of Nepman business dealings in the towns had gone down by 30 per cent in 1923/4–1924/5.[106] Yet by 1926 their trading was still expanding in the localities, and competing more heavily with the kustari, except when they were sometimes one and the same person. Kustari are harder to trace than Nepmen since they did not appear in tax figures for businesses and often operated without state licences. Increasing reductions of state supplies of raw materials to the private sector as a whole actually had an adverse affect in that they brought Nepmen and kustari into harmonious collusion.

Locked together in *zamknutye krugi* (closed circles), kustari got raw materials from peasants, who might well have come under the party label of '*kulaks*'. These kustari would then sell their finished articles to Nepmen who retailed them to private customers. Thus all concerned avoided both raw-material supply shortages and state taxes. Nevertheless on other fronts Nepmen and kustari remained at loggerheads. Forced out of

---

[104] See V. Lebedeva, *B. M. Kustodiev* (Moscow, 1961), for reproductions of paintings of pre-revolutionary private traders and their buxom wives.

[105] Ginzburg, op. cit., p. 201.

[106] L. F. Morozov, 'Kooperatsiia i periodizatsiia istorii bor'by s nepmanskoi burzhuaziei', *Voprosy istorii*, 12 (1964).

the more conspicuous forms of large-scale production by 1926, some Nepmen disguised their factories as arteli (producers' co-operatives).[107] Independent kustari were not in a position to take advantage of these organs which were privileged since they formed part of the socialist sector.

If the weaknesses of the Nepmen are balanced against their strengths, it can be seen that the former outweighed the latter, and with increasing effect from 1925 onwards. Bolshevik propaganda exaggerated Nepmen's capacity to corrupt society, the economy, and even political life, but there was indeed more to fear from them than from that even greater butt of party criticism, the '*kulak*'. Nepmen were far more influential in urban centres and in their capacity to control or block supplies, communications, and other agents between town and country. Yet it should not be imagined that in the capital they held much sway beyond the confines of the great outdoor markets like the Sukharevka. Only 17 per cent of them were native Muscovites, according to the national census of 1926. After domestic servants, they had the lowest literacy rate of all occupational groups in the capital.[108] Their insecure status was reflected in their work methods. Over 70 per cent of all private traders did not operate from permanent business premises. The number of Nepmen in any given locality fluctuated widely. Seasonal changes, the lack of goods to sell, increasing levels of taxation and rents saw to this.

On the other hand, in one crucial sphere the activities of the Nepmen continued to worry some leading Bolsheviks. The Party realized that private help was needed during NEP to acquire food and raw materials from the peasantry, but the Nepmen's share of the *zagotovka* remained alarmingly high. It came to between 30 and 40 per cent in 1925–6, and around 30 per cent over the next two tax years.[109] The Party insisted in NEP on building up a large grain surplus, and saw it as a symbol of the state's smychka with the peasantry. When *Pravda* noted in the late summer of 1926 that Nepmen were blocking grain collection by the state by means of their offers of higher

---

[107] Ginzburg, op. cit., pp. 226–45.
[108] See *Vsesoiuznaia Perepis'*, vol. 19, table I, p. 118; table II, pp. 144–55; table IV, pp. 376–409.
[109] *Torgovo-promyshlennaia gazeta*, 31 (1927), p. 3; 283 (1928), p. 4.

prices to peasants and commandeering freight trains, the authorities began to deprive private zagotovka movements of all credit. This tactic worked for a time, but by 1928–9 Nepmen had more than recouped their position, controlling just under a quarter of the grain zagotovka.[110] Up until 1927, Stalin rarely mentioned the Nepmen in public, but by the winter of that year he was paying far more attention to their activities. He was parting company with Bukharin, whose views, together with the opinions of Rykov and Tomsky, were far more relaxed on this subject. Stalin had no trouble in finding allies in the Party against the Nepmen by this time. The rebound of the Nepmen into the grain-procurement campaign of 1928–9 was quite clearly one of the factors that caused Stalin to embark on the collectivization of the peasantry and to abolish all free trade in grain.

Another important candidate for the implementation of smychka as of 1926 were the kustari. This group differed fundamentally from the Nepmen in Bolshevik eyes, since from time to time, like the co-operative system, they were viewed as allies rather than rivals of the Party in the smychka campaign. The importance of this sector of society can be seen at a glance from the population figures for the first all-Union census of 1926. The rural–urban break in population was shown to correspond pretty rigidly between those dependent on agriculture and related occupations, and those dependent on industry, trade, and administration. The sole category that was clearly spread over urban and rural areas apart from Nepmen consisted of persons chiefly dependent on small-scale handicraft industry, i.e the kustari. This branch of the population seemed admirably placed to act as a link between town and country, poised as it was geographically between the two and economically serving and employing both peasants and town-dwellers alike. Viewed in this way, the kustari were an advance on agricultural co-operation, which, in the 1920s at least, only helped to unite peasants alone in larger social and economic groups.

Since the kustarnyi system, like the mir, was a direct

[110] G. A. Dikhtiar, *Sovetskaia torgovlia v period postroeniia sotsializma* (Moscow, 1961), p. 271.

inheritance from Tsarist Russia, its development before 1917 must be examined in order to understand its character and tenacity in NEP. Capitalist industry in Russia had started out in the 1830s and 1840s on the basis of handicrafts, but the relationship between the two diverged from the British prototype thereafter. Kustarnyi industries survived for a much longer period in Russia. Most of the peasants engaged in them remained attached to the villages because of restrictions on their movements and on the sale of land by a peasant household, despite the Emancipation of the Serfs in 1861. Even by 1917 Russian capitalists still resorted widely to the 'putting-out' system, by which part-time work was handed out to domestic artisans or to small subcontractors. The immense size of Russia also contributed to the prolonged vitality of handicraft work, which could prosper while huge distances and poor means of transport separated one industrial centre from another. The kustari fell into two main types. The first consisted of producers such as blacksmiths and shoemakers who provided for a small, local market and carried out orders for individual customers; the second concentrated on the output of specific items for a far wider market and was centred in particular regions, each region being known for the high quality of the goods it specialized in. These nexi were called 'nests' (*gnezda*). Articles produced by the kustari of the second type were sold throughout the Empire and were also exported. Kustari were active not only in Russian Central Asia, Siberia, and the Caucasus, but above all in the northern central zone of European Russia, the hub of the large-scale factory network. The traditional artisan areas of the Moscow region were injected with renewed vigour after the Emancipation, since peasants were forced to seek means of supplementing their earnings. Redemption payments were heavy relatively to the productivity of the land in this region, and the relationship of arable earth to meadows was adversely affected.

Let us now compare Bolshevik hypotheses on the kustari with their actual strengths and weaknesses by 1926. Why did such an apparently old-fashioned system survive in such strength until the end of NEP? Its equivalent had dropped out of the socio-economic spectrum in Britain shortly after the early period of the Industrial Revolution.

Some reasons for the survival of the kustar' network pre-dated the Revolution, but still held true in the 1920s. The highly seasonal character of agriculture, given the Russian climate, allowed peasants to supplement their meagre income on a part-time winter basis by making handicrafts. Overheads were low, taxes at first almost non-existent. Right through NEP factory industry produced different items and worked for different markets. After 1917 the chaos in communications that continued until 1922 and beyond, as we have seen, made the population even more reliant on local producers than in the pre-revolutionary period. The sheer size of the country as well as lack of transport made for price differentials between regions and times of year, to the profit of the kustari. The famine of 1920–1 had forced many industrial workers back to the countryside, together with their skills. During the 'scissors' crisis kustari were able to compete with state-armed factories, since the price-level was rising faster for items produced by state-operated factories than for rural products. Finally, the peasants still made up by far the largest consumer market, and they grew steadily more prosperous until nearly the end of NEP.

Before 1926–7 it was impossible to assess with much accuracy the actual numbers of kustari. Many never took out licences to trade. It was hard to distinguish between a peasant's agricultural activities, which were not covered by the first reliable census of 1927 (covering the year 1926–7), and his industrial activities as a kustar'. Over one hundred traders were covered by the census, though not all of them were listed separately. The total of kustari, in actual numbers, not full-time equivalents, came to 4,895,000.[111] This compares with the figure of 608,280 Nepmen at the same period. In terms of crude numbers, after allowing for part-timers, the kustari far outweighed Nepmen by their pervasive ubiquity.

After a sharp drop in production during the Civil War, kustarnyi industry recovered fast from 1922 onwards, approaching its pre-1917 level by 1926–7. No fundamental changes occurred in the economic and technical characteristics of those handicrafts and industries between the Revolution

[111] A. Debiuk, 'Udel'nyi ves melkoi promyshlennosti SSSR v obshchem promyshlennom proizvodstve', *Statisticheskoe obozrenie*, 2 (1929), pp. 28–32.

and 1926. They remained concentrated in consumer goods areas and were the main suppliers of many types of items as varied as shoes, bread, vegetable oil, and spinning-wheels. Nevertheless, significant shifts took place within and between the two main kustar′ sectors. From 1922 the smaller-scale local handicrafts recovered quicker than the nest centres and urban kustari. As time passed, the reorganization of small producers into producer co-operatives brought many of them into the category of nests.

Of the two main kinds of kustar′ systems, the nests represented the greatest long-term economic and social threat to the Party. They brought together much larger groups of workers in one area. Their tentacles moved into broad mass markets, into the cities, and even abroad. They were more organized into co-operatives, setting up entirely capitalist examples of the institution that the Party wished to tame and socialize. They specialized in commodities like carpets and instruments which would have saturated local markets too fast.[112] For instance by 1927 the Kaluga region was sending off hand-turned spinning-wheels via 700 railway stations all round Russia. The system had built up gradually again through NEP. Nest-masters sent off their wheels by slow train from Kaluga, then followed after them, selling twenty to thirty items at a time to local merchants. In the first years of NEP they would condescend to sell and repair individual wheels by peddling on the streets.[113] By 1928 in the Vologda area five employers had built up a substantial lace industry, with up to 800 kustari working for each of them.[114] The sheer weight of kustar′ numbers impinged heavily in the region round the capital. In 1924–5 there were 131,000 of them at work in Moscow guberniia. This figure swelled rapidly to 194,000 by 1926–7, and was scheduled to grow to at least 217,000 by 1927–8. By 1926–7 they were sending off 86 per cent of their goods to state and co-operative institutions. This flow almost drove out socialist competition entirely in some sectors.[115]

---

[112] *Melkaia promyshlennost′ SSSR po dannym vseosoiuznoi perepisi* (Moscow, 1933), p. 18.

[113] N. A. and M. E. Sheremeteva, *Samoprialochnyi promysel v piatovskom kustarnom raione* (Kaluga, 1929), pp. 58–9.

[114] K. Sokolov, *Klassovaia bor′ba v promkooperatsii* (Moscow, 1930), pp. 6–7.

[115] *Moskovskii sovet za 10 let raboty* (Moscow, 1927), p. 14.

As late as 1928 some provincial observers of the kustari were still hoping that they could be converted into good socialists, two years after the central authorities had taken steps to curb the activities of large-scale nests. Noting the rising prosperity of small-scale kustari in Belorussia, one writer exclaimed: 'All these circumstances create favourable conditions for the further development of kustar' industry in Belorussia, and its organization into co-operatives.'[116] This was a typical example of the lack of a political sense at the regional levels of just how fast central policies were changing at the end of NEP. It was indeed the case that in the rural areas round Smolensk, Mogilev, and Vitebsk kustari were still expanding their activities. This part of the Soviet Union had always had high kustar' numbers, who were mainly engaged in articles made from wood, flax, and leather. In July 1925 a new organizational bureau for the kustar' industry was set up in Belorussia. Between November 1926 and November 1927 the numbers of arteli grew in Belorussia by 51 per cent, and the number of workers in them by 117 per cent. Kustar' turnover went up by 62 per cent from 1925–6 to 1926–7. Woodworkers in remote areas did the best of all. Their average property worth increased by 114 per cent from 1926 to 1927. These signs of boom were taking place far away from the towns and large-scale nests. In Belorussia, woodworkers, brick-makers, and preparers of lime were all still based in tiny localities.[117]

This was also the case in the heavily forested Tver guberniia. In 1886 3.4 per cent of the total population of this area had been engaged in large-scale kustar' industry. By 1925, after initial attempts to suppress it entirely between 1919 and 1921, it had shrunk slightly to 2.9 per cent. On the other hand, kustari of all kinds had increased from 12.8 per cent of the overall population to 25 per cent by 1925.[118] These figures showed that Tver was similar to Belorussia in that its smaller-scale networks did better than the nests. Yet one can never generalize on Russian localities, even when only two are

---

[116] A. M. Enbaeva (ed.), *Kustarnaia promyshlennost' i promyslovaia kooperatsiia v natsional'noi respublike i oblastiach Belorusskoi SSR* (Moscow, 1928), p. 142.

[117] Ibid., pp. 135–40.

[118] *Verkhne-Molozhskaia ekspeditsiia: Izvestiia Tverskogo pedagogicheskogo instituta* (Tver, 1927), p. 105.

involved. A list of the largest nests for the whole of the country in 1926–7 included two shoe-factories in Tver guberniia. They were outstripped only by the famous metal workshops of Tula that had flourished since the nineteenth century.[119]

Among the Bolshevik leaders, there were those who persisted into late NEP in seeing the continuing strengths of the kustar' systems as possible grist to the socialist mill, rather than as a threat. The Bolsheviks' view of the kustarnyi industry, particularly the 'nest' system, as a possible social and economic link that could convert itself and its workers to large-scale methods and promote smychka, changed considerably during the years 1917–28. A pattern that should by now be familiar to the reader emerged. During War Communism the notion that such a traditional and semi-capitalist institution could be harnessed to Soviet idealism was completely discounted. After all since the 1890s 'kulaks' had begun to control the kustarnyi industries by employing casual peasant wage-labour in them. The Bolshevik left was especially vociferous in its condemnation of the handicraft system. A. Bogdanov claimed that it was quite impossible to create an atmosphere of what he called 'collective collaboration' on the basis of the master–apprentice relationship of the kustari. Trotsky concurred at this time. In a speech to the Eighth Party Congress in March 1919, he drew an interesting analogy between the militia and the kustarnyi systems, two small-scale social structures which he rejected with equal vigour: 'To preach partisan warfare as a military programme is just the same as recommending a return to handicrafts from large-scale industry.'[120]

Typically, it was Bukharin who converted himself and some of his colleagues to taking a different view. He foresaw with percipience that the kustari would probably increase in power and in numbers after the end of the Civil War. Instead of jettisoning such a formidable and potentially dangerous organization, he thought that his party would be wiser to incorporate the kustarnyi industry in their own plans for the future.[121]

[119] D. Shapiro, *Kustarnaia promnyshlennost' i narodnoe khoziaistvo SSSR* (Moscow, 1928), p. 22.

[120] Trotsky, *Kak vooruzhalas' revoliutsiia*, vol. 1 (Moscow, 1923), p. 188.

[121] Baron von Haxthausen, *The Russian Empire, Its People, Institutions, and Resources*, vol. 1 (London, 1856), p. 160.

Bukharin found himself in strange company with others who had adopted this view before his time. Baron von Haxthausen, the German admirer of the mir in the 1850s, also praised Russian handicrafts and wanted the Tsarist government to promote their 'natural' virtues in preference to artificial, capitalist large-scale industries copied from Western Europe.[122] Economic experts in the last decade of Tsarist rule no longer wanted to do away with these established heavy industries, but they agreed that 'the success of large-scale industry in many of its sectors feeds on the talents of the handicraft workers'.[123]

Lenin upheld Bukharin's view that the kustarnyi industry should not be smashed. Like agricultural co-operation, it wavered in his estimation between semi-capitalist and proto-socialist methods. Under the careful guidance of the Bolshevik Party it could be persuaded without coercion into the right path. In the words of the official resolution, the party would 'paralyse the efforts of the kustari to turn themselves into petty industrialists and effect a painless transition of these outdated forms of production into a higher type of large-scale machine industry'. There was also a sound practical reason for encouraging handicrafts at the close of the Civil War, as Lenin realized. Since they did not rely on large machines, they could help to set the economy on its feet before large-scale industry was in a position to do so.[124] It appeared to be relatively easy during NEP for the political centre to control the kustarnyi industry, for most of the privately run handicrafts were largely dependent on supplies of materials from state industry, and the majority of their workshops were leased from the state. Furthermore, relatively concentrated 'nests' of kustari, possessing strong economic ties with the nearby industrial cities of northern central Russia, proved to be of considerable use in reviving the hub of the economy. Although the kustarnyi tail still wagged the dog of large-scale consumer industry by the end of NEP, a partial *rapprochement* process did appear to be at work in the Moscow region.[125]

[122] *Kustarnaia promyshlennost' Rossii*, vol. 3, p. iii.
[123] *KPSS v rezoliutsiiakh i resheniiakh s'ezdov, konferentsii i plenumov Tsk*, vol. 1 (Moscow, 1953), p. 422.
[124] Lenin, *Sochineniia*, vol. 24, pp. 332–3.
[125] A. Buzlaeva, *Leninskii plan kooperirovaniia melkoi promyshlennosti SSSR* (Moscow, 1969), p. 70.

In his enthusiasm for handicrafts, Bukharin suggested four practical ways of harnessing them to progressive methods. They should be requested to gather fuel and raw materials for large-scale factories. The state should hand out credit to them, as well as placing large orders for goods from them. Most important of all, the kustari should be invited to join trade unions and slowly come into line with the factory proletariat. None of these aims materialized to any extent. The private sector remained dominant, and the overwhelming preponderance of single family units rendered negotiations of the kind suggested by Bukharin totally unsuitable. Like the co-operatives, the kustarnyi industry slipped from the Bolsheviks' tenuous grasp. It too became infiltrated by an increasing number of semi-capitalist manipulators in the guise of '*kulaks*' and Nepmen. Profiting from the gradual improvement of trade and financial liquidity in NEP, these agents began to monopolize the distribution of handicraft products. They could run individual craftsmen into debt, since the kustari were still cut off by the nature of small-scale society both from the market for their products and from personal access to the raw materials they needed. The evils of Tsarist semi-capitalist methods in the countryside returned once again.

The failure of the kustarnyi industry to link up on a healthy socialist basis with large-scale industry coincided with the similar lack of success on the part of the agricultural co-operatives. Both systems belonged mainly to the peasant social world, and they resisted Bolshevik blandishments for similar reasons. Bukharin was telling the truth better than he knew when he wrote in *Historical Materialism*, 'Is it possible that the technological system of society should be based on machines, while the productive relation, the actual labour relation, should be based on petty industry working with hand tools? Of course, this is an impossibility; wherever a society exists, there must be a certain equilibrium between its technology and its economy.'[126] Soviet society, on his own evidence, did not exist as a unified whole by the end of NEP. Both types of technology did in fact coexist in a strained relationship, or rather lack of one, which was only to be solved by violent socio-economic revolution.

[126] N. Bukharin, *Historical Materialism* (London, 1926), p. 136.

If one looks at the practical details of kustar' affairs in 1926, further internal weaknesses in both the small and large-scale networks were becoming apparent. Although small-scale ventures were still flourishing in Belorussia, Tver, and indeed all over the country, including remote Kazakhstan (which will be treated in the final chapter), they suffered increasingly from exploitation by the very agent that could conceivably have toppled the state system if it had worked in harmony with the kustari—the Nepman. The main Nepman antidote to higher taxes and more restrictions from the state sector in late NEP was heavier reliance on the small-scale kustari in the deep countryside. Between 80 and 90 per cent of the output from private manufacturers was now finding its way to consumers through Nepmen.[127] The problem was that the kustari were being badly exploited in the process. Full-time kustari in 1926 were earning an average of 25 to 40 roubles a year, as opposed to Moscow factory workers who were getting on average 31 a month. Pre-1914 a kustar's working day had varied from between 13 to 20 hours, but in 1926 it fluctuated between 15 and 21 hours.[128] They worked so hard for so little mainly because the fruits of their labour were being picked off by local Nepmen. Kustari were paying between 40 to 200 per cent more for raw materials to the Nepmen than the latter had paid for them in the first place. Nepmen later rejected from 5 to 15 per cent of the finished products as below standard.[129] In Belorussia Nepmen were making between 40 and 80 per cent profit on their resale of kustar' goods, whilst often charging kustari from 75 to 150 per cent interest annually on the credit they often could not do without.[130]

Naturally personal enmity flared up between Nepmen and kustari, even when they were not competing directly as salesmen within the same area. The large-scale nests in or near the towns certainly represented a greater threat, both to Nepmen and to Party and state, but as they grew larger in mid-NEP they became classified as 'census' industries. They thus fell under much closer scrutiny from above, and with that came

[127] Ginzburg, op. cit., p. 240.
[128] V. Feigin, *Kustarno-remyslennaia promyshlennost' SSSB* (Moscow, 1927), pp. 60–1.
[129] Ibid., p. 62.
[130] Ibid., p. 121.

higher taxes, restrictions on supplies, and increasingly, complete absorption into state-controlled large-scale industry even before the era of the Five-Year Plan. Roughly half of the 1927 employment in small-scale industry was shifted into large-scale industry between 1927 and 1931. The move was further precipitated by the severe shortage of industrial raw materials, which compelled the government to reduce their supply to the kustari. Although this displacement of small-scale industry was undoubtedly massive, part of it may have been illusory because there were changes in the definition of large-scale production which led to incorporation in that sphere of what was formerly treated as small-scale production. In the course of the First Five-Year Plan over 1,600,000 kustari of all types were forced into state-controlled co-operative unions. During the same period the output of small-scale industry fell to one-tenth of total production.[131] The demise of this long-entrenched sector of Russian manufacture and distribution, which had become for a brief period a potential linking agent in some Bolsheviks' eyes, was swift and terminal, though the collapse of the Nepmen and the '*kulaks*' was even more dramatic at the close of NEP.

This swift dissolution was one of the main signs that all three had been in part paper tigers in the first place, propaganda issues wielded by Stalin and his allies with increasing energy from 1927 on. Yet if any of them was a real menace to the regime, it was the Nepmen first, the kustari second, and the '*kulaks*' well in third place. The reasons for the potential strengths of the first two have been mentioned already. What of the '*kulaks*'?

In a transitional, unstable era like NEP, it was virtually impossible to draw hard-and-fast class lines. The revolutionary turmoil had thrown up new subtleties like the spetsy, but even more enduring social categories were often spuriously labelled. Class differentiation among the peasantry was notoriously confusing. The '*kulak*', who was partly the product of the Stolypin reforms of 1906, appeared to be relatively easy to detect, but in fact this was not the case. In a generally impoverished rural society the material goods which set him

---

[131] A. Malikova, 'O sotsialisticheskom preobrazovanii melkotovarnogo uklada v promyshlennosti SSSR', in *Istoriia SSSR*, 4 (1963), p. 23.

apart from the so-called *seredniak*, or middle peasant, were so negligible that they could be swept away by a slight change in fortune, such as bad weather, the loss of one labourer or even a horse. Strangely enough, the most reliable defining rule had nothing to do with agriculture, since a '*kulak*'s' small capital acquired through a trade or craft, or the sale of liquor, was what often set him apart from the seredniak.

There is almost no internal evidence of the subjective views of the peasants themselves with regard to their own prestige and status. We are left with the arbitrary categories imposed on them by the Bolshevik leaders and their advisers, most of whom during NEP had originated from towns and remained in them. Their tool was Marxist doctrine. It is true, though astonishing, that the role of the class concept is nowhere exposed in the works of either Marx or Engels, despite the fact that the notion is used very frequently. It is virtually an undefined concept of which the meaning is explained contextually, yet in highly abstract terms. The Bolsheviks adopted the very broad class divisions discussed by Marx and tried to apply them to a society in which Marx had taken no particular interest. As far as the proletariat was concerned, Lenin eventually divorced its 'class-consciousness', which became embodied in the authority of the Communist Party, from the empirically observed thoughts of real Soviet proletarians. To a slightly lesser degree the same thing happened with the peasantry. The reified Bolshevik concept of the '*kulak*' had little to do with the infinite subtleties of the actual class position of the richer peasant. Thus the *batraks*, men usually living solely from paid agricultural labour, were naïvely and confusingly held to be like proletarians by the Bolsheviks, who thought (wrongly) that official aid to the batraki and the bedniaky ('poor peasants') would encourage the 'middle' peasants to side with them against the '*kulaks*'.

The whole issue of class was clouded further by the changing party-line during NEP, which meant that the diagnosis of peasant stratification altered according to the shifting arguments of political theorists. Finally, it is doubtful whether Marx's economic postulates were of much use in a largely non-monetized peasant world, where barter prevailed in casual exchanges between acquaintances on a basis of goodwill. This was a far cry from the impersonal forces of the market as seen by Marx. The Russian peasant was not often interested in maximizing output, and the family unit could not be described by applying standard theories of the main factors of production.

In the middle of the decade, a predominantly pro-peasant group led by Bukharin faced an 'opposition' made up of the Trotsky–Preobrazhensky bloc, which was swept aside at the Fourteenth Party Congress at the end of 1925. Although it was joined by Kamenev and Zinoviev in 1928, it still lost out in the political battle that followed. The various party views on the peasantry now became more complicated. There were supposed to be growing 'deviations' (from Stalin's standpoint). The defeated opposition's exaggerated fear of all peasants was now counterbalanced by an equally mistaken tendency to underestimate the '*kulak*' menace. The odd thing was that only after the old opposition had been vanquished did the campaign against the '*kulak*' really take off.

What was the reality with regard to the numbers and influence of the richer peasantry? It was obscured by all these high-level manœuvres as Stalin moved into a commanding centralist position before inflicting lethal blows on the better-off sector of the peasantry with the close of NEP. The numerical importance of richer peasants, almost irrespective of the criteria with which they were classified, was indubitably four or five times less than before the First World War. They had lost much of their previous economic influence.[132] Renewed differentiation among the peasantry did of course take place after 1921, but it was at a much slower rate than before 1914. Nevertheless, due to general economic weakness, the lack of capital and the acute shortage of livestock at the start of NEP, those peasants with a slight edge on their neighbours did have greater pull than prior to 1914.[133] Yet in 1925 the official state Central Statistic Board calculated '*kulak*' households as roughly 3 per cent of the total peasantry. There was little change on this through the rest of NEP. Both high-level politicians and agrarian scholars agreed in their more sober moments, that 'middle' peasants formed an overwhelm-

---

[132] A. M. Bol'shakov, *Derevnia 1917–27* (Moscow, 1927), p. 243.
[133] Ibid., pp. 65 ff.

ing majority. Soviet scholars then and now have tried to modify this stark fact by trying to link up the rich peasants with a wider group of those who were well off (*zazhitochnye*). In a way this was an admission in the midst of their abstract theorizing that differentiation was indeed very blurred. But it was not capitalist farming-methods nor the exploitation of wage-workers that distinguished either of these groups, which in any case fluctuated widely in cyclical fashion according to passing influences. They were merely made up of larger households using more intensive methods in terms of capital per unit of land and per person.[134]

Since there were no generally acceptable criteria throughout NEP (nor indeed since) to determine exactly a peasant's socio-economic status, central investigators used what few reliable data they could lay their hands on. At the highest official theoretical level it was admitted that the term '*kulak*' was so vague that an article in *Bolshevik* proposed to jettison it completely.[135] Agrarian Marxist scholars agreed. A. Gaister admitted in the autumn of 1926 that he was continually led into 'blind alleys' in his efforts to classify the peasantry. He was also acutely aware that the whole question 'arouses powerful political debates'.[136]

The truth was that the better-off peasants, however they were comprised, were not a credible *political* danger. The leading agrarian Marxist, L. N. Kritsman, whose work was more scholarly than that of most in 1926, pointed out that richer peasants were frequently beneficiaries of party policy in many ways, even if this was fortuitous. Some of them were actually party members. Neither were they ever a serious *economic* threat, due to the strength of the state sector in agriculture. The differentiation that had got off to a slow start in 1921 had not gone far enough to impede any policies that might be imposed from above. Looked at in their *social* context, the richer peasants could never compete in influence with the kustari, let alone the Nepmen. All peasants, including the top stratum, were far more static than most kustari, except for

---

[134] See T. Shanin, *The Awkward Class: Political Sociology of Peasantry in a Developing Society: Russia 1910–1925* (Oxford, 1972), p. 173.
[135] See *Bol'shevik*, 19–20 (30 Oct. 1925), pp. 26–46.
[136] A. Gaister, *Rassloenie sovetskoi derevni* (Moscow, 1928), pp. 1, 104.

types like a remotely located wood-carver in the forests of Tver guberniia. They were even less educated and more illiterate and innumerate. By dint of being so individualist in their farming practices, they could gain no strength by combining in groups with others, as kustari had to do as a vital part of their livelihood. Some kustari travelled far and wide, met all sorts and conditions of men, and had connections in the big cities. '*Kulaks*' rarely encountered anyone more influential than non-party functionaries in the rural Soviets and other such uninspiring forms of local life.

The only significant way in which richer peasants could hold the government up to ransom was by echoing the threat that had frightened the Party into NEP in 1921—they could indulge in a total grain strike. It was this excuse that Stalin was to use in the autumn of 1927 when he resorted to 'extraordinary measures' against the peasantry. That it was a political excuse has since been proved by scholars.[137] In fact rich peasants sold grain in good quantities in the summer of 1927. It was the poor and middle peasants who were reluctant to deliver. With their vast numbers, they were the chief consumers of manufactured goods, and not the tiny proportion of '*kulaks*', as Kamenev imagined. In 1927 there were not enough commodities available to exchange against cereals. Stalin was not being totally perverse, nor were those who supported him in 1927. They were misled in their interpretation of events by Kamenev's previous wrong diagnosis of the cereal crisis of 1925, which he had also attributed to the '*kulaks*'' recalcitrance. In 1925 the terms of credit for poorer peasants worsened, so that farm tools were not delivered to them until it was too late. The figures on which Kamenev based his view of a '*kulak*' grain strike were challenged at the time by a government commission.[138]

[137] See, amongst others, S. Grosskopf, *L'alliance ouvrière et paysanne en URSS (1921–1928): Le probleme du blé* (Paris, 1976).

[138] Ibid., p. 140. V. P. Danilov has made clear the crucial significance of tools and machines in peasant life in mid-NEP. If they had been widely available, they would have turned the old-fashioned peasant economy, based on the commune and using mainly natural forces of production (land, labour, and animal draught energy) into one based more on those man-made forces (tools, machines) which predominate in capitalist agriculture. See his *Sovetskaia dokolkhoznaia derevnia: naselenie, zemlepol'zovanie, khoziaistvo* (Moscow, 1977).

Some scholars continue to argue whether NEP as a whole was compatible with a programme of industrialization. They still suppose that NEP meant a policy of concessions to the richer peasants which was *forced* on the government by the peasants' reaction to the compulsory grain requisitions of War Communism. Rather it was the neglect of the poorer peasants during NEP, especially in the years 1923 to 1925, that caused the worst problems, both in 1925 and 1927. What the poor badly needed, and got too late and too little of, was a favourable credit policy that would help them to buy implements and so ensure their eventual independence from richer peasants. They needed also a pricing policy on means of production so that they would be cheap enough for them to buy.

The '*kulaks*' were the most prominent of the class scapegoats that Stalin attacked in order to escape from the house built on sand that was NEP. The torrent of inaccurate propaganda that has issued from the Soviet government since the 1920s has obscured the fact that richer peasants were the least menacing of the three quasi-capitalist groups that were very slowly growing in wealth and confidence in mid-NEP. For this reason more space has been devoted here to the Nepmen and the kustari, whose producing and trading tentacles might indeed in the long run have overwhelmed the socialist sector. Stalin's moves at the close of NEP were motivated by a combination of reasons: the desire to score political points on his rivals in the Politburo: the fact that he was misinformed as to peasant realities through sheer lack of facts and previous misinterpretations, like that of Kamenev in 1925; and the justifiable need to take prophylactic measures against a future (though scarcely an actual) *malaise*.

# 10. *Smolensk Guberniia in 1926*

WE now plunge back into the mainstream of social life. We return to it via the same river we first entered into it in 1922. Yet, as with a river, some things are the same in the Smolensk area, others changed by the waters of time which move history on.

The territory of Smolensk guberniia in 1926 included the same area and had the same administrative arrangements as in 1922. This situation was to continue until 1929. However, the boundaries of the Belorussian Republic just to the west were only finally established in 1926. This delay was due to the upheavals of the Revolution and the Civil War which had split the Belorussians up and handed them out to differing nations. By 1926 11 per cent of all Belorussians lived outside the boundaries of the newly formed Republic. Quite a few of these lived in the Smolensk guberniia, though some were to be found as far away as Siberia.[1] Nearly 45 per cent of the national rate of increase of the rural population in Belorussia emigrated to towns in the Republic between 1923 and 1927.

The number of those moving into the cities throughout the Soviet Union was approximately 670,000 in 1924 and 900,000 by 1926.[2] Between 1925 and 1929 the rate of population growth in the cities doubled. In the mid-1920s over three-quarters of this growth was due to peasant immigration. The social and political effects of this demographic revolution were noted for Moscow in Chapter 8. Notwithstanding emigration on this scale, rural populations continued to increase on account of the huge number of children born between 1922 and 1926—19.2 million, or 16.1 per cent of the total rural

[1] A. A. Rakov, *Naselenie BSSR* (Minsk, 1969), p. 83.
[2] *Arkheograficheskii ezhegodnik za 1968 god* (Moscow, 1970), p. 253.

population.[3] Thus despite considerable emigration to Moscow, Leningrad, and other cities, the total population of Smolensk guberniia in 1926 at 2,292,589 was still 2.64 per cent up on 1920. The uezd of Roslavl', through which our Red Army man's mother travelled in 1922, had increased its population by no less than 14.95 per cent compared with the 1920 census. It contained 366,787 people, or 16 per cent of the total population of the guberniia.[4] Roslavl' uezd benefited from its position astride the important railway line from Smolensk to Kursk.

The urban population of the guberniia went up by only 9.8 per cent compared with 1923. This was slightly below the all-Russian average.[5] Taken together, all these figures gave evidence of certain trends over the years 1922–6. Rural prosperity had begun to take roots in the calmer atmosphere which had prevailed since the close of 1922. No warring armies tramped backwards and forwards, as they had done in the period 1914–21, and the economic concessions introduced in 1921 were starting to have their effect on the peasantry, whose relative security was reflected in the very high birth-rate. On the other hand the rather slow increase in the population of Smolensk city showed that its industrial base was still even more insecure than that of its giant neighbour to the north-east, Moscow.

Let us take a closer look at the peasantry, the urban workers, and the state of communications within the guberniia. The land was still covered with forests and marshes, and subject as always to severe winter weather. Some land-draining took place between 1922 and 1926 on a small scale. More dramatic were the transfers of additional land to the peasants. In Belorussia alone the Central Executive Committee authorized the transfer of 609,000 hectares of land to peasant communes from the start of 1925.[6] Within the Russian Federation as a whole peasants were granted 0.3 million hectares between 1923 and 1924, 1 million between 1924 and 1925, and 6.1 million hectares between 1925 and 1926. There was a significant

[3] *Vsesoiuznaia Perepis'*, vol. 17, pp. 46–9.
[4] *Predvaritel'nie itogi vseoiuznoi perepisi naselenii 1926 goda po Smolenskoi gubernii* (Smolensk, 1927), pp. 9–10.
[5] See *Arkeografcheskii ezhegodnik*, p. 251.
[6] *Kommunisticheskaia partiia Belorussii v rezoliutsiiakh i resheniakh s'edov i plenumov Tsk*, vol. 1 (Minsk, 1973), p. 329.

slowing down, for political reasons, as the future became clearer in Stalin's view; between 1926 and 1928 only 2.6 million hectares were handed over.[7]

Some Soviet, as well as Western scholars conclude that the main reason for attaining pre-war agricultural levels of production by 1925–6 lay in these huge land grants. The reallocation of what were called 'peasant woods' also had considerable significance for heavily forested areas like Smolensk and Tver gubernii. These regions were not merely a source of timber, but provided fungi and berries for food, bark for shoes and other kustar' goods, and in the two gubernii concerned they were used for grazing cattle. In 1925 the Third All Union Soviet Congress set up a timetable for the transfer of local woodlands to the peasantry.[8] Within the RSFSR the area of woods handed over to peasants by October 1926 reached 20,417,000 hectares.[9]

The population census of 1926 showed the continuing predominance of smallholding family production in the rural localities. 'Family members, working in the household economy' amounted to 64.6 per cent of the independent rural population; 99.6 per cent of these 'family members' worked in agriculture, relying on their combined muscle power rather than on sophisticated implements.[10] This was a purely peasant and kustar' phenomenon. Craft industries as an extra occupation employed 574,300 households with family labour.[11] There were no 'family members' at all among workers and white-collar employees in factories, in rail transport, and in social organizations.

A close investigation in 1924 of the volost' of Pochinok between Smolensk and Roslavl' revealed that most peasant households could be classified as 'middle' in terms of prosperity. There was not a single agronomist resident within the volost', in spite of the fact that it lay not far from the guberniia capital and on a main railway line. When the head of a local

[7] See *K voprosu ob ocherednykh zadachakh po rabote v derevne. Materialy k XY s'ezdu VKP (f)* (Moscow, 1928); *Materialy po perspektivomu planu razvitiia sel'skogo i lesnogo khoziaistva*, pt. I (Moscow, 1929), p. 3.

[8] *S'ezdy Sovetov v dokumentakh 1917–1936*, vol. 3 (Moscow, 1960), p. 85.

[9] *Sel'skokhoziaistvennaia zhizn'*, 39 (1926), pp. 33–4.

[10] *Vsesoiuznaia Perepis'*, vol. 34, pp. 2–3.

[11] Ibid., pp. 164–5.

group for the promotion of literacy took the initiative to invite an agronomist from another volost' to give a lecture, the agronomist demanded 100 eggs as a fee, which it was found impossible to extract from the peasants. Instead a circle was organized and led by a local teacher who was almost as ignorant of agricultural improvement methods as his pupils.[12]

These signs of continuing backwardness among the local peasantry, together with two bad grain harvests in 1926 and again in 1927, created problems for the Smolensk guberniia that were surprisingly reminiscent of 1922 in their siege mentality. The first secretary of the guberniia reported in 1926: 'Rumours of the possibility of war, [rumours] that the state was hoarding stocks for the satisfaction of the needs of the Red Army and others, created a mood of panic in the grain market. The population, drawing on the experience of the last war, tried to hoard grain, and the surpluses on hand were not put into the market.'[13] Things were even worse in Roslavl':

owing to insufficient supplies of flour in the Central Workers' Co-operative, the local populace and some of the peasants broke the doors and counters of two shops of the Central Workers' Co-operative. The interference of the police was necessary. In Smolensk in one of the meal shops of the Grain Products Organization up to 700 peasants assembled to buy oats, and all kinds of indignant outbursts and complaints were made against the employees of the meal shop . . . in connection with the rumors about war and the grain crisis the anti-Soviet elements of the city and the country became noticeably more active . . . There were completely inadmissible actions also on the part of individual farmers, for example, cases of refusal to deliver grain because of the disadvantageous selling conditions, which also made the situation worse.[14]

Throughout the Soviet Union the peasant commune was closely tied up with the communal system of land relations. A survey of October 1925 undertaken in Smolensk guberniia showed that only 2.6 per cent of all enclosed land use plots were to be found in communes.[15] In general by the close of NEP

---

[12] A. Gagarin, *Khoziaistvo, zhizn' i nastroenie derevni po itogam obsledovaniia Pochinkovskoi volosti Smolenskoi gubernii* (Moscow, 1925), pp. 7, 10.
[13] Smolensk Archive, file WKP 134, pp. 69–75.
[14] Ibid.
[15] V. P. Danilov, *Rural Russia under the New Regime* (London, 1988), p. 101.

significant collective elements had developed within the commune—its slow transformation into a sowing association, the execution of set agronomic programmes, and the introduction of new areas of collective cultivation. Yet by 1928–9 the commune was to become a victim and not a vehicle of socialist transformation. This was because in the eyes of the Party its overall conservative ways and traditions still outweighed its collective manners.

Smolensk was an exception to a general rule between the Revolution and the end of NEP. Although between 1918 and 1920 a broad trend against enclosed peasant holdings swept across the south-east, the south, and the centre of European Russia, in Smolensk guberniia and Belorussia the systems of *khutor* and *otrub* did not decline. If a peasant consolidated his field plots but kept his house and garden plot in the village, this was known as 'otrub'. The alternative was to transfer the homestead from the village to his consolidated field land; this created a farm called a 'khutor'. By 1925 33.5 per cent of peasant households in Smolensk guberniia were on otrub or khutor land, compared with only 16.9 per cent in 1916.[16] The motive here was to consolidate land in one piece and strengthen land use. This pull was so irresistible that it caused a deviation from standard party policy in the case of the Smolensk area. The party executive passed a land reorganization plan in November 1925 which allocated 69.9 per cent of the total for conversion into khutora and otruba.[17] The reason for these deviant methods was almost entirely due to the predominance of flax cultivation in the region. In 1925 93 per cent of all peasant households in Smolensk guberniia were cultivating this crop.[18] Due to favourable market prices, the area under flax cultivation grew fast in the mid-1920s. The production of flax fibre in communal households scarcely covered the costs.[19] On the other hand in khutor homesteads profits of about 45 per cent were possible, affording capital accumulation which in

[16] *Rural Russia under the New Regime*, p. 144.

[17] *Kollektivatsiia sel'skogo khoziaistva v zapadnom raione RSFSR (1927–1932 gg.): sbornik dokumentov* (Smolensk, 1968), p. 652.

[18] *Ocherki tovarnykh otraslei sel'skogo khoziaistva SSSR v sviazi s kreditovaniem* (Moscow, 1926), p. 41.

[19] *Sel'skoe khoziaistvo SSSR 1925–1928. Sbornik statisticheskikh svedenii* (Moscow, 1929), p. 454.

turn allowed the purchase of equipment essential to independent peasants. In his story *Transvaal'*, published in 1926, K. Fedin gives us a vivid portrait of a rich khutor peasant in the Dorogobuzhskii uezd. Otrub plots were not so rewarding, but still far more productive than the strip system in the communes.

The production of flax increased liquid cash income above all. The percentage of money income levied as agricultural tax did not overburden peasants in mid-NEP. In 1924–5 the tax amounted to 10.6 per cent of money income, and sank to 5.8 per cent in 1925–6 before rising slightly again to 7.1 per cent in 1926–7.[20] A small minority of flax producers could be said to be 'better off' by 1926, but the majority were 'middle' peasants. Two observers of Smolensk guberniia came to the same conclusion in 1924 and 1926 respectively. The proportions for 1924 were given as 'better-off' peasants, 12 per cent, 'middle' peasants 65 per cent, and poorer peasants 23 per cent.[21]

On the whole the area remained backward by 1926. Flax was one of the Soviet crops which failed to come up to pre-1914 harvest yields.[22] In the late 1920s it did recover to some extent. From 1922 to 1926 trade in the guberniia actually diminished. The small-scale nature of the three-field system was an inhibiting factor. The amount of land per household declined from 9.4 hectares in 1923 to 8.55 in 1926 (the number of households increased over the same period from 354,945 to 393,601.[23] In the whole of the country production for the market, which in the last analysis governed the real share of agriculture in economic life, came to only about half the proportion held by agriculture before 1914.[24] The development of agriculture in the second half of the 1920s increased at a slower rate than was necessary to meet the requirements of industrial growth, and just as vital but often neglected, of that larger surge in population noted previously. The increase in the marketable surplus of grain slowed down and then was reversed. Although four years had elapsed since the stormy political climate of

[20] G. Sokolnikov (ed.), *Soviet Policy in Public Finance* (Stanford, 1931), p. 167.
[21] *Nasha praktika v derevne* (Moscow, 1925), p. 31. For 1926, see A. Gaister, *Rassloenie sovetskoi derevni* (Moscow, 1928), pp. 47–52.
[22] *Sel'skoe khoziaistvo SSSR* (Moscow, 1971), p. 24.
[23] *Iz istorii Smolenskogo kraia* (Smolensk, 1958), p. 169.
[24] J. Stalin, *Sochineniia*, vol. 11, p. 85.

1922, better-off peasants in Smolensk guberniia and elsewhere still had no faith in the stability of the currency. They often stored their crop surpluses or used them for their own immediate consumption. Any rural accumulations of wealth did not go into wide circulation. V. P. Danilov, the distinguished Soviet expert on agriculture during NEP, concludes 'Ending poverty and exploitation was impossible on the traditional basis of peasant economy. Peasant participation in national economic development necessitated a colossal improvement in productivity, the transfer of millions of peasants into industry and enormous advances in technology and culture.'[25]

Another reason for the difficulties experienced in getting wealth to circulate was the continuing poor condition of communications by 1926. F. Dzerzhinsky noted with satisfaction in February 1926 a considerable increase in the output of funds for transport use,[26] yet the general situation remained highly unsatisfactory. All modes of transport were irregular, slow, and filthy. In *Bania* V. Maiakovsky portrays an urban bureaucrat praising the 'progress' made in the running of trams. Their paint was freshened up and changed colour, but fares doubled and the system remained unreliable.

In the provinces matters were worse. By 1926 Belorussia had twenty-eight towns of some size, but only twenty of them were on the railway system.[27] By April 1926 the Republic was still short of 2,500 railway wagons for sending off its timber harvest. A new line was projected in 1926 to run from Roslavl' to Mogilev and Osipovich, but it was slow in materializing. A campaign to build more roads had begun in 1924, but only one or two, and two bridges had been built by 1926. More urgent was the repair of the roads that did exist.[28] Priority was given throughout NEP in Smolensk guberniia to the improvement of fuel and energy resources. Of thirty-four new industrial enterprises set up between 1918 and 1928, half of them were in this sector (mainly turf-burning and electricity stations).[29]

[25] Danilov, op. cit., p. 304. On the fate of Smolensk guberniia during collectivization, see D. R. Brower, 'Collectivized Agriculture in Smolensk: The Party, the Peasantry, and the Crisis of 1932', *Russian Review*, 36 (1977), pp. 151–66.

[26] *Pravda*, 12 Feb. 1926.

[27] NKVD RSFSR, *Goroda soiuza SSR* (Moscow, 1927), p. 10.

[28] *Belorusskaia SSR* (Minsk, 1927), pp. 367–71.

[29] *Iz istorii Smolenskogo kraia*, p. 218.

We shall see later in the chapter that despite energetic attempts to inculcate political education into the local peasantry, the Party had scant success in 1926. Yet the crucial relationship for the future, as in Moscow, was the collaboration of Party with industrial workers in the guberniia, and vice versa.

In 1926 about 60,000 industrial workers, out of a total population in the guberniia of above 2 million, worked mainly in machine-building and metalworking plants, textiles, paper processing, and chemicals.[30] They were concentrated in relatively few plants in the main towns. From the start of NEP high-level policies sent down from Moscow often tended to impede the economic and political health of Party–worker smychka. In an interesting article on this subject, W. G. Rosenberg shows how the Kalinin ironworks, one of the largest industrial enterprises in Smolensk city, suffered from the introduction in 1923 of khozraschet (independent accounting).[31] The work-force had to be reduced, as demand fell sharply, since central organizations were no longer sending in orders as before. Industrial unemployment in the guberniia remained a problem throughout NEP.

The low living standards of workers in Smolensk in 1922 was noted in Chapter 1. Material welfare was important to them as proof that the Party cared for their lot. The voluminous verbal and written political propaganda to which they were subjected often had the opposite effect. Between 1922 and 1926 there was little improvement in their housing and food supplies, social and medical care. Conflicts between workers and management were severe enough in 1926 to form the subject of party investigations.[32] Increasing wage differentials in the semi-capitalist climate of NEP also aroused continuing resentment. Workers' complaints revealed a strange mixture of anger towards the management that was close to them, and deference

---

[30] *Fabrichno-zavodskaia promyshlennost' v period 1913–1918 gg.* (Moscow, 1926), pp. 404–13.

[31] W. G. Rosenberg, 'Smolensk in the 1920s: Party-Worker Relations and the "Vanguard" Problem', *Russian Review*, 36 (1977), pp. 127–50.

[32] For conditions amongst workers and factory cell work in 1926, see Smolensk Archive, files WKP 294, T87, roll 34, item 294, and WKP 369, T87, roll 42, item 369. The latter item records the proceedings and findings of a commission to investigate a conflict between workers and management at a local glass factory.

to the Party that stretched away from them up to Moscow levels. This was a Soviet proletarian version of the nineteenth-century peasants' unshakeable faith that the 'Tsar will give' (*tsar' dast*).[33] The favourite proverb still had some power—'the Tsar is gracious, but not his kennel-keeper.' Recruitment of Smolensk workers to party membership went ahead, but there were drawbacks. The Lenin Draft improved the situation, particularly between 1923 and 1925. New recruits had more respect and influence among non-party workers than their older comrades, and they brought new energies with them. On the other hand they sometimes provoked the jealousy of older party members, who gave them menial tasks which were disliked. Ambitious ex-workers in the Party therefore tended to look to higher levels for their personal advancement. This led to the neglect by local cadres of the promotion of Party–worker relations on the shop-floor. A Rabkrin report of March 1927 was still worrying over the low political consciousness of many Smolensk party members, and pointed to 'insufficient attention' to decisions of the Central Committee in the area of mass work.[34]

Further distrust in Party–worker relations was created by the gubkom's suspicion that many problems were due to the recent peasant origin of many workers, combined with their ongoing connections with their rural background. In fact rebellious attitudes and difficulties with labour discipline were more acute in the large industrial plants of Smolensk city. Smaller enterprises in other places, like those tied to kustar' industries, were more peaceful. In the autumn and winter of 1926–7 it was in larger plants that party cells were found to be passive and poorly organized. Some of them continued to exclude women, even in plants which employed female workers.[35]

By mid-NEP the general mood in Smolensk city factories was one of apathy towards the Party rather than outright rebelliousness. In 1926 there were no signs at all of that growing realization on the part of many Moscow party and

[33] See O. V. Aptekman, *Obshchestvo 'Zemlia i volia' 70-kh gg* (Petrograd, 1924), pp. 144–5.

[34] Rosenberg, op. cit., pp. 146–9.

[35] Smolensk Archive, file WKP 244, T87, roll 34. Also in Rosenberg, op. cit., pp. 138–9, 142–3.

non-party workers that an economic and political bargain could be made with the Party, to the benefit of both sides. Indeed, as late as 1928, when the industrialization drive was reaching Smolensk, there was still little evidence of a revolutionary Leninist vanguard among the city's workers, eager to co-operate with the Party in the smooth implementation of the campaign.[36] Thus Trotsky's view at the time of the 1917 Revolution still held good: at the hub of the proletarian movement there was a dynamo for change which was now humming again. His further deduction, that the provinces would soon be galvanized from the centre, had not materialized by the end of NEP, even in an industrial centre so close to Moscow as Smolensk.

Further evidence relating to the habitual practice in a country the size of Russia of the periphery frequently being out of step with the centre comes to light when party recruitment numbers for Smolensk workers and peasants are compared. The total numbers of party members and candidates went up in the countryside from 1,712 on 1 April 1924, to 2,672 by 1 January 1926. Of the 2,672, 1,291 were candidates of uncertain quality, as the *gubkom* in Smolensk noted.[37] Between January and October 1927 the number of peasant full members of the CPSU increased dramatically from 17 to 35 per cent; during the same period bench-workers diminished from 30 to 21 per cent. This peasant increase came above all from those who worked their own farms, mainly the new khutora and otruba run by flax producers. By October 1927 these individualistic entrepreneurs had moved from representing 7 to 22 per cent of all full party members in the guberniia as a whole. This now made them the most numerous occupational group after officials. Over the same months the proportion of new peasant candidate members easily surpassed the proportion of bench-workers enlisted.[38] The gubkom's deviance from central directives, noted earlier, in allowing the considerable expansion of non-communal farming in the area, was having a potentially dangerous political effect. Just when in Moscow Stalin was distancing himself from Bukharin and the Right on

---

[36] Rosenberg, op. cit., p. 149.
[37] Smolensk Archive, files WKP 29, pp. 42–3, and WKP 134, pp. 69–75.
[38] Ibid., WKP 33, *Protokol*, 13, p. 62.

the peasant question, Smolensk was still moving in the opposite direction. By the time of the Fifteenth Party Congress in December 1927, Stalin had already made up his mind to bring NEP to an end.

Let us now move to an overall examination of the local Party's strengths and weaknesses. When a survey of the guberniia Party was made in January 1924, it was found that only 128 members had joined the Party before 1917, and only 366 others became members during 1917.[39] In the course of the 1921 purge, over 30 per cent of all members lost their party cards, leaving a total of 7,425. By 1 April 1924 this number had dwindled again to 3,696 full members and 1,720 candidates; 3,704 lived in towns, and 1,712 in the rural areas, giving only 16 members for every 10,000 rural inhabitants of working age, or roughly one Communist for every ten villages. Ninety per cent of the population still lived in rural areas.[40] By October 1927 the total membership rose again to 9,076.[41] The national composition in the guberniia by mid-NEP reflected the huge predominance of Great Russians (78 per cent), and the somewhat surprising and possibly dangerous number of Jews (7.7 per cent), many of whom were involved with Nepmen in the area, as was noted in the previous chapter. Belorussians only accounted for 1.2 per cent. Even when the neighbouring Belorussian Republic's party members are taken into consideration as well, Belorussians everywhere only came to 1.5 per cent of all-Union party membership in 1922, rising to 3.2 per cent by 1927. Even Central Asians, including Kazakhs, formed 2.5 per cent in 1922 and 3.5 per cent in 1927. Allowance must be made, however, for the relative sizes of these national minorities. In 1926 Belorussians formed 3.2 per cent of the country's population, whilst Central Asians made up 7 per cent.[42]

The main reason for the decline in party membership in 1924–5 was the purging activity of the local Control Commis-

[39] Smolensk Archive, file WKP 275, p. 98.

[40] *Izvestiia TsK*, 4 (March 1922), pp. 20 ff; ibid. 3 (Mar. 1923), pp. 162–4; Smolensk Archive, file WKP 275, pp. 15–16.

[41] Smolensk Archive, file WKP 33, p. 60.

[42] *Izvestiia Tsentral'nogo Komiteta*, 7–8 (Aug.–Sept. 1923), p. 61; *Sotsial'nyi i natsional'-nyi sostav VKP(b): itogi vsesoiuznoi partiinoi perepisi 1927 g.*, p. 114; F. Lorimer, *The Population of the Soviet Union: History and Prospects* (Geneva, 1946), pp. 55–61.

sion at that period. Figures for Smolensk alone are not available, but 16,000 members were expelled nation-wide in 1924 and 20,000 in 1925.[43] Of 289 Communists dismissed in the guberniia in 1923, 117 went because of alcoholism, and 57 for criminal or administrative offences.[44]

The gubkom in Smolensk city was of course the linchpin between Moscow and lower party organs in the guberniia. The Central Committee of the CPSU observed in 1926: 'The question as to who controls our party organs in the localities is of overriding importance for the Party.'[45] In the same period, Smolensk Communists were filling in a long questionnaire with 86 queries. Question number 81 asked 'What, in your opinion, are the main defects which undermine the Party?' The answers included above all 'bureaucratism', followed by alcoholism, a surfeit of permanent posts which were hard to change, and last but not least, uncivil and mutually neglectful relations between party militants and the masses.[46] The meaning of 'bureaucratism' is quickly apparent to any assiduous reader of the Smolensk Archives, whether it be for 1922 or 1926. Indeed, the incessant flow of *bumazhnyi potop* increased as the NEP years went by. By 1926 the gubkom was collecting information once a week throughout the year on the following matters, amongst others: the rural economy, co-operatives, the growth and organization of the Party, women's participation in political life, Red Army needs, rural and urban party cells, agitation and propaganda work, etc. Extremely frequent meetings were being held in 1926 at all levels throughout the guberniia in order to obtain the correct interpretation of orders issued on a great range of subjects.[47] As if this was not enough, no less than five documents, one of which required four signatures, were needed in order to acquire galoshes from a co-operative in Briansk for Smolensk gubkom officials, all of whom had to be listed.[48] Gogol would have revelled in such details.

In view of the enormous, and sometimes unnecessary,

---

[43] E. Iaroslavskii, *Za bolshevistkuiu proverku i chistku riadov partii* (Moscow, 1933), p. 47.

[44] Smolensk Archive, file WKP 275, p. 20.

[45] *Partiinye, professional'nye i kooperativnye organy i gosapparat k XIV s'ezdu RKP(b)* (Moscow, 1926), p. 7.

[46] Smolensk Archive, file WKP 342, p. 81.

[47] Ibid., file WKP 287, roll 33, items 287, 288, 289.

[48] Ibid., file WKP 23.

work-load that weighed upon gubkom members, it is scarcely surprising that they had little time to devote to the complicated and kaleidoscopic shifts in party struggles in Moscow. According to M. Fainsod, who did a great service in his initial overview of all the Smolensk Archive, 'Judging by the discussions and types of questions put at local party meetings, the issues were far from clear to the party rank and file.'[49] This incomprehension through lack of time was mutual, in that at the highest level party leaders so often either expressed blanket opinions on the whole of provincial life, or descended into sentiments showing slight disdain. The latter characteristic is clearly discernible in the sarcastic descriptions of local party and Soviet activities by the Central Control Commission in 1926.[50]

A similar mixture of lack of time leading to over-generalization, exasperation, and lack of respect, is seen even more clearly in the gubkom's own view of lower organs in the guberniia. One is reminded of Chekhov's observation 'the pettiest official or clerk treats the peasants like tramps.'[51] We have already noted how highly placed interpreters of society erroneously accused party workers of lacking political sense on account of their proximity to peasant life. The universal phenomenon of those with initiative moving up and out of their milieu into higher party and Soviet organs has also been observed in Kursk as well as in Smolensk. By 1928 complaints were being made that successful gubkom party leaders were becoming more and more like government and economic managers. Those who still considered themselves as party militants accused them of becoming old-fashioned bureaucrats.[52] Even some militants had lost their cutting edge as early as 1922 in neighbouring Belorussia. They were accused at a local Party Congress of losing interest in active politics and in expressing independent opinions. This trend was ascribed to the fact that as early as 1922 militants were left no room by

[49] M. Fainsod, *Smolensk under Soviet Rule* (New York, 1963), p. 48.

[50] See p. 307 above. One can well imagine highly placed party members laughing in their sleeves at attempts to raise Marx from the dead at spiritualist party seances in distant Siberia.

[51] A. Chekhov, *Peasants*, in *Polnoe sobranie sochinenii* (Moscow, 1975).

[52] Smolensk Archive, file WKP 331, roll 15.

higher party organs for using their own initiative.[53] By 1926 this attitude was to have ominous consequences in Belorussia and throughout all the provinces. As a member of the Minsk party organ put it: 'We are all against opposition, all fractions, any discussion; we are against those who, through discussion, want to alter the teaching of Lenin. We are for the unity of the Party in action; we want to build socialism, to obey the Central Committee of our Party; we want to work and not lose time in discussions.'[54]

Nevertheless at the lowest party level sparks of independent energy could still fly in 1926. When the party leadership in the Belyi uezd was at first thwarted in its attempts to control the local Agricultural-Industrial Credit Union, it took measures that were deemed by the Smolensk gubkom to be high-handed and too authoritarian. When the uezd leaders were duly rebuked by Smolensk, they objected that the gubkom had misinterpreted the local situation. This was probably a justified point of view, in the light of endless examples of this tendency. Smolensk retaliated by deciding to remove both the first secretary of the Belyi uezd and the chairman of the Soviet. Once again the local party protested. The man who was later to become Belyi's first secretary dared to comment that 'the measures taken by the gubkom are extraordinarily extreme'. The harsh facts of the matter were that it was a case of dog eating dog. The uezd party had been heavy-handed with the Credit Union, and gubkom officials acted similarly in their dealings with the uezd leaders.[55] Even into the 1930s the Belyi uezd was to remain a source of worry for Smolensk bureaucrats. By 1935 only one-third of one per cent of the population there were party members.[56] In 1937 three first secretaries followed one another in quick succession.[57] The long tentacles of the Great Purge finally dug down to this obscure level.

Although the Belyi party organization remained a live wire in 1926, the same could not be said for the local Soviets in the area. V. Molotov hoped that the re-elections to the Soviets

[53] *VI s'ezd kommunisticheskoi partii Belorussii, stenograficheskii otchet* (Minsk, 1922), p. 114.
[54] *Zvezda*, 26 Nov. 1926.
[55] Smolensk Archive, file WKP 249, pp. 219–58.
[56] Ibid., file WKP 313, pp. 130–1.
[57] Ibid., file WKP 111, p. 117.

would end the party practice of 'putting candidates up for the Soviets, and even sometimes directly appointing them'.[58] In spite of this recommendation from on high, it was the uezd party committees that carried out the survey of village Soviets in Smolensk guberniia. They criticized the Soviets for their weak links with the rural depths.[59] Yet local party as well as Soviet administration could be censured for similar reasons. Directives in the elections arrived late in Belyi uezd, as did posters and report forms. There was not sufficient time to instruct those responsible in the Party and the Soviets about how to use documents; and at every level, from the lowest to the gubkom, there was a 'scornful, and what is more, careless' attitude to reporting on the campaign.[60]

In some ways the atmosphere in the political backwoods of Smolensk guberniia had altered little since 1922. The image of the Party as an army of occupation still lingered. Belyi party men in 1926 referred to surviving Socialist Revolutionaries with considerable influence over better-off peasants. On a market-day in April about fifty posters appeared on walls in Belyi town with the slogans 'Leninism leads to poverty. Down with Leninism. Down with taxes.'[61] Nearly a decade after the Revolution, the day-to-day life of the peasantry was little disturbed by higher authorities. Even after 1929, in contrast to many other parts of the country, Smolensk guberniia was at first slow in taking on collectivization and industrialization.

Like an army too, the Party deployed its still tiny personnel at strategic geographical and administrative points to procure maximal effects for minimum effort. This crucial lesson had been learnt during the course of 1917. The means by which the party network originally wove its fine web from Petrograd and Moscow outward has been the subject of a monograph by the present author.[62] This central lesson was applied to the peri-

---

[58] See V. M. Molotov, *Politika partii v derevne: stat'i i rechi* (Moscow, 1927), pp. 155–7.

[59] Smolensk Archive, file WKP 20. The period covered was from Oct. 1925 to 1 Apr. 1926.

[60] Ibid., file WKP 25, pp. 107–8. This is the report on the Belyi uezd for the period from Oct. 1925 to 1 Aug. 1926.

[61] Ibid., file WKP 249, p. 203.

[62] R. W. Pethybridge, *The Spread of the Russian Revolution: Essays on 1917* (London, 1972).

phery from 1917 on, and remained the master plan for strategy by the end of NEP.

In other ways, though, purely military influences had receded greatly since 1922. No longer did soldiers play a major role in tax-collecting in the area. Neither did they continue to keep a prominent profile in hospitals, automobile workshops, and on the railways. Their hold on mental communications had diminished in line with their withdrawal from physical lines of communication: in 1922 Red Army men had been prominent on committees for political education, but this was no longer the case in 1926. The chaos around Roslavl', or Poltava, or in the Famine areas in 1922, was not to be seen in any area of Russia by 1926. The minor cornucopia that was NEP had poured some balm into the system.

The military presence had certainly subsided, but the powers of the less obvious secret police remained intact, and its bureaucracy pervaded all levels. There is little specific evidence for 1926,[63] but for the next year guide-lists appeared on topics that had to be classified as secret. No less than twenty-five topics were listed as sensitive in the sole realm of trade union organizations.[64] By the close of NEP it was still clear that a large majority of secret policemen in the guberniia had previously served in the Red Army. Many of them were poor peasants by social origin. The Civil War generation still dominated the local OGPU apparatus. Their educational level was as low, or even lower, than that of the average party member.[65]

The Party's instruments of coercion had not disappeared, but merely gone underground and become more subtle. Military jargon continued to generate all political instructions. The Party was still fighting, as in the Civil War, 'on every front' in 'the struggle' to introduce 'shock tactics' against the 'class

---

[63] The only secret-police involvement that is properly recorded for 1926 concerns directives from the Smolensk party headquarters on, amongst many other topics, pre-election campaign procedures in local committees (how to select candidates); the general political situation of the whole guberniia; and the background of all rural police employees (the militia, which was closely watched by the secret police). See Smolensk Archive, file WKP 134, T87, 18, 134. Of course secret-police activity, by its very nature, was not often recorded on paper.

[64] Ibid., file WKP 138, pp. 7, 22–3.

[65] Ibid., files WKP 36 and 49.

enemy'. This somnolent militancy could be revived at any time, and was to be on a grand scale from 1929 onwards. In the meantime the Party survived in Smolensk, and elsewhere, through a paradoxical combination of its own and others' inefficiency, and a lack of personnel and expertise. If its ruthless aims expressed at every turn on paper in the Archives could have been implemented in full, attempts at counter-revolution might conceivably have followed at any date between 1921 and 1928. Merle Fainsod gives a further reason for Bolshevik supremacy—the creation of a new class of beneficiaries who were grateful and loyal to the new regime.[66] In this author's view Fainsod has exaggerated this motive somewhat, at least with regard to the 1920s. Our 1922 investigations of the localities showed that as many ex-Red Army men rejected their party affiliations as strengthened them on returning to their peasant roots, for fear of being spurned by their fellow villagers. We have just seen how relations were strained in 1926 between the Smolensk party and its favourite acolyte, the proletariat. In a moment we shall turn to look at the Komsomol: its path towards promotion and collaboration with senior party elements did not run smoothly either. The opportunities that were opened up by the tiny party membership in a still depressed economic situation were few and far between until after 1929. The small numbers who did profit from allegiance to the Party during NEP soon rose out of sight of the localities in the upward curve of their ambitious careers. Talent was scarce, and their elevation was often swift.

The general situation in 1926 was definitely calmer than in 1922. The fact that the archives for 1926 continued to dwell on problems rather than on successes merely shows the ongoing dynamism and conscientiousness of the party machine, although some of its zeal was due to endless pressure from Moscow. Yet by the winter of 1926–7 the party gubkom was reduced again to a mounting sense of insecurity in a largely hostile environment. By August 1927, when a confidential gubkom report, in liaison with the secret police, covered the overall situation in the province over the previous twelve months, the double burdens of national and local develop-

---

[66] Fainsod, op. cit., pp. 452–3.

ments had turned the tenor of the account into something approaching panic.[67] It did not take much to upset the ramshackle political architecture of NEP.

This report began with an alarmist survey of a new wave of international espionage bearing down upon the USSR in general, and on Smolensk guberniia and Belorussia in particular. This foreign scapegoat, unearthed in Moscow party circles for domestic agricultural and other failures, was being handed on via Smolensk to the localities. But nearer to hand lay a supposed threat from the Whites and the English in the shape of a 'terrorist group' led by a certain General Kutepov that had infiltrated into Belorussia and Smolensk and had been 'liquidated'. The English connection remained unsubstantiated and bizarre, but the reminder to the populace that this part of Russia lay close to disturbed international borders must have rung a bell in the minds of many who could recall the invasions here from the west and the east in the course of the Civil War. The Party now appealed for greater vigilance on the railways and other communication routes. The local militia was accused of 'extreme laxity and irresponsibility verging on criminality in a series of institutions' that were not properly guarded. Militiamen on duty had been found asleep at vital factories, and a fire at a sawmill had been due to negligence. Hints at sabotage were in the air.

Another, and no doubt real, cause for alarm was the insufficient grain supply in 1926–7. In Roslavl' employees in shops supposed to be selling flour, but now empty, had been assaulted, and in Smolensk city 700 peasants had assembled in a bid to get their hands on oatmeal by hook or by crook. Some co-operatives had let Nepmen (another scapegoat) have their grain, so its price immediately went up. The gubkom tried to reduce retail prices of grain and other goods by 10 per cent in the winter of 1926–7, but local party groups and co-operatives ignored the campaign, so that reductions varied from 3 to 9 per cent from one place to another, causing further grievances. Rumours were so rife that it was widely believed that grain was being siphoned off to the Red Army, since a war was brewing.

Anti-Soviet feeling was reported to be increasing, chiefly in

[67] Smolensk Archive, file WKP 134, T87, 18, 134.

the city of Smolensk, and also from '*kulaks*' and lessees of flour-mills in the countryside. This was obviously a crude adaptation to local uses of class reifications handed down from Moscow. So too was a campaign to bring the poor peasants swiftly to the side of the Party. Over a million roubles were given out in aid to them by the gubkom in 1926–7. Yet the report noted no movement of the poorer peasants into the very few collective farms. Only a small proportion of them had been touched by political propaganda, since the majority had been unimpressed due to the 'lack of practical measures' in solving their problems. Even party officials realized on occasions how often their piles of verbal exhortation remained on paper only. The final section of this illuminating report noted that there was much talk of getting rid of 'bureaucratism', but no concrete cases of it. Each sector accused other sectors. As the head of one enterprise in Smolensk city put it: 'bureaucratism only exists in Western Europe, not in the USSR.'[68]

One obvious way in which the Party could throw off its bureaucratic, centralized image and rejuvenate its connections with the geographical hinterland was through the Komsomol. In 1924–5 A. Gagarin singled it out as 'the liveliest force' in the countryside of the Smolensk guberniia. He gave it this accolade for its unceasing activity throughout the period.[69] By 1926 the rural population in Smolensk and elsewhere was very young. More than half of it (50.6 per cent) was under the age of 20 in the Soviet Union as a whole. A further 27.7 per cent was aged between 20 and 39. Those who had reached maturity after 1917 came to 59.3 per cent of the total population. This sector was by far the most literate, and was to stay young enough to be able to embark on a radically new way of life after collectivization. It was also more than usually receptive to influences emanating from young political activists working on them in 1926. Between 1924 and 1926 the Party's campaign to turn towards the village had resulted in a nation-wide increase in the proportion of peasants in the Komsomol, from 45.3 per cent in 1924 to 53.7 per cent in 1926.[70] The total numbers of

[68] Smolensk Archive, file WKP 134, T87, 18, 134.

[69] Gagarin, op. cit., pp. 50–1.

[70] *VII s'ezd vsesoiuznogo leninskogo kommunisticheskogo soiuza molodezhi: stenographicheskii otchet* (11–12 Mar. 1926), pp. 46–7.

rural Komsomol members grew fast, from 300,000 in July 1924 to 900,000 on 1 December 1925.[71] By 1926 there was still no party cell in many villages, so the Komsomol now represented the main agent of party influence. A delegate at the Seventh Komsomol Congress in March 1926 proposed that only party members should serve as secretaries of rural Komsomol cells, but this was scarcely feasible, since there were only 47,000 party members and candidates in all rural assignments to cover 41,000 village Komsomol cells.[72]

That the Komsomol's spread was superior to that of the Party can be seen in the case of Belyi uezd in Smolensk guberniia in late 1925. There were no less than fifty-two Komsomol cells, including 905 Komsomol members (of whom only 135 were young women), and 750 Pioneers (the junior branch of the Komsomol).[73] There were obvious incentives for the youth of Belyi uezd to enlist in the Komsomol. It gave them the sense of belonging to a wider, adult society when they engaged in courses of political lectures on broad-ranging topics. They released themselves from their parents' narrow grasp and looked towards chances for promotion and travel away from their drab surroundings. A survey in mid-Nep showed that a mere 3 per cent of Komsomol members in one province wanted to work in agriculture in the future, although 85 per cent of those interviewed were of peasant origin.[74]

The fact that for the time being most Komsomol members were better represented in peasant communities than the Party gave them a political advantage that was as vital to the Party as that crucial tie set up between iconoclastic members of the Moscow working class and central party leaders in 1926. If properly conducted, and managed from above, the Komsomol–peasant connection might have provided a smooth bridge towards socialization in the countryside. This was not to be, however. The aggressive manners of rural Komsomol members often had boomerang effects. The very low proportion of female members, attributed to parental pressure on this sex,[75]

[71] Ibid., p. 395.
[72] Ibid., pp. 430–1.
[73] Smolensk Archive, file WKP 25, T87, 4, 25.
[74] I. E. Liubimov, *Komsomol v sovetskom stroitel'stve 1917–27* (Moscow, 1928), p. 149.
[75] I. Taradin, *Sloboda Roven'ki. Voronezhskaia derevnia, vyposk 1* (Voronezh, 1926), p. 101.

was one of the reasons for latent hooliganism in the ranks.
Male activists were accused of treating the older generation
arrogantly,[76] and of creating disturbances in church services,
particularly at Easter time.[77] In Poltava guberniia, which had
been a violent area in 1922, as was seen in Chapter 2,
Komsomol groups remained under arms like military units into
mid-Nep in order to fight what they called 'criminal and
political banditry'.[78] Action of this type had been more typical
of the Komsomol during the Civil War, when the Party had
viewed it as an adjunct to its military forces, but in the more
humdrum climate of mid-Nep the Party was no longer looking
for a junior partner whose continuing militant idealism could
prove embarrassing in calmer times. It was noted earlier how
the Civil War ethos still affected the Komsomol in Kursk and
Smolensk gubernii in 1922. Even by 1926 this ardent flame had
not been properly tamed by Komsomol and party leaders
sitting in the volost' centres.

The Komsomol showed other weaknesses. It was less rigorously organized than the Party, and on account of its structure
prone to a large turnover of membership. The average peasant
married at a very early age, and often settled back into
apathy.[79] Other Komsomol members retreated into alcoholism,
debauchery,[80] or crime. By 1926 juvenile delinquency was at an
all-time high.[81] In a study of Soviet youth in this year, one
author found Komsomol members to be pessimistic with
regard to the future, individualistic to the point of adopting
'petty bourgeois' attitudes, and anti-Semitic into the bargain.[82]
Komsomol leaders in volost' and guberniia centres were often
city-based and were unable to deal with the hostile reception
they received at the hands of the peasants and even of the
members in their charge in the localities. Their pay was very
low, and their quality often poor as a consequence.[83] One

[76] M. Golubykh, *Ocherki glukhoi derevni* (Moscow, 1926), pp. 70–1.
[77] V. A. Murin, *Byt i nravy derevenskoi molodezhi* (Moscow, 1926), pp. 37–8.
[78] *VI s"ezd kommunisticheskoi partii Belorussi*, pp. 240–1.
[79] I. Pisarev, *Narodonaselenie SSSR* (Moscow, 1962), p. 178.
[80] See *Komsomolskaia pravda*, Apr.–June and Sept.–Oct. 1926 for articles on sexual problems amongst Soviet youth.
[81] See W. D. Connor, *Deviance in Soviet Society* (London, 1972), p. 24 ff.
[82] N. Bobryshev, *Melko-burzhuaznye vliania sredi molodezhi* (Moscow, 1926).
[83] *VII s'ezd*, pp. 184–5.

cannot deny, however, the greater success of the Komsomol in the villages themselves as compared with the Party. Their human contacts were far closer and on the whole more relaxed. They were also freer from the ideological preconceptions of party men. When asked about the activities of the '*kulaks*' in a Smolensk gubkom survey of December 1925, a Komsomol member asserted flatly: 'You won't find kulaks in the country: there are very few of them, and in my opinion they are not dangerous.'[84]

Turning now to other Komsomol activities in Smolensk guberniia, we find members in 1924 engaged in such varied activities as tax-collecting (which tended to make them unpopular), collaboration with village teachers in the schools, and the administration of rural 'reading-huts' for illiterates.[85] During 1925 the Komsomol in Belyi uezd was concentrating on political propaganda. It was advised to devote most of its efforts to workers in the only two factories in the area. Due to weak or non-existent party leadership in Belyi cells, Komsomol members had got bogged down in 'trivialities' (in fact the Party was not famous for freedom from this defect either). In 1925 thirty Komsomol members left the ranks in Belyi—eleven for drinking, seven for hooliganism, and twelve who quit voluntarily in order to get married or for some other reason.[86]

Youth cannot survive without levity, so in order to avoid alcoholism and hooliganism the head of the political education section of the Smolensk city Komsomol committee in 1926 ordered all uezd and volost' branches to arrange parties on certain lines: 'It is necessary to organize Red evenings, which should be just as lively as the old-fashioned ones. There should be dances, new songs, games, etc. The Komsomol should invite to the party all non-Party youth.' Humorous journals (which apart from *Krokodil* were in short supply) were to be read aloud. Young women should be attracted to parties by setting up knitting- and sewing-circles where they could discuss Leninism as they laboured.[87] These must have caught on in a big way, since by 1927 instructions were coming down from on

[84] See Smolensk Archive, file WKP 29, pp. 48–60.
[85] Gagarin, op. cit., p. 52.
[86] Smolensk Archive, file WKP 25, T87, 4, 25.
[87] Ibid., file WKP 403, 28.

354 Smolensk Guberniia in 1926

high to discourage dancing and to stop kissing games, which were said to spread venereal disease.[88] The sexual mores of NEP never ceased to be a strange compound of laxity and puritanism.[89]

There is little concrete evidence that the Komsomol in Smolensk or elsewhere had a radical effect on the local population in 1926, but at the least it gave its own members a sense of belonging and a certain status. They learnt how to speak and pass on a strange new political vocabulary. Their youthful enthusiasm lit up a new pattern of behaviour that must have helped thousands of still young peasants after 1928 to endure what they had to endure during collectivization.

If the Komsomol in particular and youth in general looked towards the future, however clouded that might be, there still appeared to be a preponderance of backward-looking and conservative social elements in the provinces. To conclude this chapter, attention is focused first on the status of women, and then on the role of religion by 1926.

With the aim of implementing Engels's and Lenin's aims with regard to the position of women in society, a Code for their protection was issued as early as 1918. In the same year the maternity insurance programme that had been planned by A. Kollontai was put into effect, although, as with so many other welfare plans, its scope was limited due to lack of funds and personnel. After an enthusiastic start, *Zhenotdel* (the womens' section in the Party Central Committee and its local branches), began to lose its verve. The central authorities were indifferent to it in practice, if not in theory. At lower levels Zhenotdel encountered resentment of its attempts to intrude into provincial party, factory, and village life. Between 1917 and 1926 family policy was designed to break up the age-old subservience of women, and with it family structure in general. A decree was issued in Vladimir in 1918 which made all women state property on attaining the age of 18. Such daring projects made little headway outside the sophisticated cities of Euro-

[88] Smolensk Archive, file WKP 126, 114.
[89] For an interesting discussion of sexual attitudes during NEP, see R. Stites, *The Women's Liberation Movement in Russia* (Princeton, 1978), ch. 11.

pean Russia: in Central Asia activist women were sometimes murdered.

By 1926 early signs that society was about to undergo great new upheavals in the throes of industrialization led to efforts to provide stabilizing counterweights. Stricter legislation in the 1926 Code of Common Law tightened up the obligations of couples irrespective of whether they were married under civil or common law. By late 1929 the Secretariat of the Central Committee, under Stalin's control, abolished the Women's Section and amalgamated it with the Mass Agitation Campaign. Throughout NEP, due to a general high rate of unemployment and competitive semi-capitalist conditions, the number of females without jobs did not decrease. In 1923 the female proportion of workers in large-scale industry was 29.8 per cent. By 1928 it was still only 28.7 per cent. In 1926 it was 28.4.[90] Lower wages for women persisted into the 1930s.

The absence of menfolk at the Front in the First World War and the Civil War had served to increase the influence of women, particularly in peasant households, but it was usually short-lived. Peasant women in Smolensk guberniia and elsewhere had to look after the *usad'ba* (the plot around the house), the domestic animals, and the garden in addition to their maternal duties, yet custom still allotted authority over the household to the men. Women until the end of NEP were often prevented by wagging male tongues and even brute force from seeking rights in the commune meetings. Rural Soviets were induced through pressure from above to increase the number of female members from one per cent in 1922 to 10 per cent by the end of 1925, but their heads were always men.[91] The proportion of women in the Party rose slowly from 8 per cent in 1922 to 10.5 per cent according to the party census of 1927.[92] More politically active women came from the ranks of the single, the divorced, and the widowed.[93] Numbers in all three categories had risen, due to war casualties, a higher divorce rate (12 per 100 marriages in the countryside in 1926), and the

---

[90] E. Orlikova, 'Sovetskaia zhenshchina v obshchestvennom proizvodstve', *Problemy ekonomiki*, 7 (Moscow, 1940), p. 114.
[91] *Perevybory v sovety RSFSR v 1925–6 g.* (Moscow, 1928), pp. 16, 20.
[92] *Sotsial'nyi i natsional'nyi sostav VKP(B)* (Moscow, 1928), pp. 138–9.
[93] Gagarin, op. cit., p. 58.

increasing tendency for women to marry later, partly due to a
law fixing the lowest legal age at 18.[94]

In many ways women were getting the worst of both
reforming and conservative worlds of thought in 1926. The
new Code of Common Law accidentally hemmed in some
women more than had been the case under the Land Code of
1922, which had stipulated that the property of the household
belonged to all its members. The 1926 Code gave a woman a
share only in her husband's property acquired after marriage.
The reforming legislation still appeared to weigh unfairly on
all peasants and most factory workers who could not afford to
pay alimony to the extent that Nepmen could. Most of the
legal changes applied to townspeople only. As E. Preobrazhensky put it somewhat cynically: 'Once we have, in the
towns, taken a firm stand for the Code, ... we cannot turn
back from it just because some peasant households are behind
with it.'[95]

The *belles-lettres* of the period pointed up women's dilemma.
They often became victims of progressive laws and modes of
thought. In Zoshchenko's short story *The Receipt*, a young spiv
induces a naïve girl-friend to sign a statement, prior to going to
bed with him, that he would bear no responsibility if a child
resulted. In P. Romanov's *Bez cheremukhi* one girl comments to
another that whilst external life created by Bolshevik power
may seem clear and sure, her inner life seemed to be dirty, since
all personal relations had been reduced to sex by the doctrine
of free love put about until 1926.[96] Such attitudes threw
potentially emancipated women back into the arms of conservative critics of Kollontai's policies like S. Smidovich, who
claimed that since the Soviet Union was still in a slow
transitional period from capitalism to socialism, Kollontai's
ideas were premature.[97]

One unfortunate consequence of reforming family law from
the Revolution to 1926 did seep down into the countryside,

[94] See *Taradin*, p. 70, and F. Zheleznov, *Bol'sheverezhskaia volost', Voronezhskaia derevnia* (Voronezh, 1926), p. 28.
[95] See R. Schlesinger (ed.), *The Family in the USSR: Documents and Readings* (London,
1949), pp. 145–6.
[96] P. Romanov, *Bez cheremukhi: sbornik rasskazov* (Moscow, 1927).
[97] S. Smidovich, 'Otmenit' li registratsiiu braka i sistemu alimentov', *Komsomol'skaia
Pravda*, 37/220 (1926), p. 2.

including Smolensk. Sly young men got married the easy way, for a working spring–summer season, then duly declared a unilateral divorce from the girls who had acted as their unpaid labourers. How had the daily mode of life changed for the peasant woman we encountered in 1922 on the way to find her soldier son at Roslavl' railway station? In truth, very little. If she was still, four years on, rearing young children, for herself as for her daughters, she would still be sole nurse in their infancy. They would be swinging in their *zybka*, birch-bark cradles hanging from a ceiling joist. The mother-in-law traditionally cared for the first-born grandson. As they grew up, boys would still move over to the supervision of their father, whilst girls remained with their mothers.

In summertime, as always, women would work as hard as the men in the fields, though forking remained a man's job. Women would take off instead to the marshy areas, which abounded in Smolensk guberniia. They skipped from tussock to tussock, raking up the long grass to take home to be dried. It was their job, too, to bind up the grass and pile it up artistically in bundles (*babki*) of twelve to fifteen, proof against rain and snow. The culture of flax, an all-important crop in the province, lay entirely in women's hands. In August they plucked it up by the root to lay it out to dry. In September they shook the heads to extract the grains which provided oil. The flower heads were laid out on the grass until the first snow fell. Then they were pounded, and the fibre tufts were combed twice. From November to Lent they spun the flax on a distaff or a spindle. Young girls still began their apprenticeship to this routine at the age of seven. They would help to thread the flax on to bobbins, then wove the stuff into all sorts of articles— long, brightly embroidered tablecloths, men's blouses and trousers, night curtains for protection against the mosquitoes which rose up from the marshes. Ninety long days of work were needed to produce seven pieces of flax between 11 m. and 12 m. in length.

Strict division of labour between men and women in northern Russia had certain results. It mattered less if from the purely economic point of view women were illiterate in a largely self-subsistent system, since the few clerical dealings with the wide world beyond could be handled by the men; and the women had financial control over the produce of their own labour—flax, dairy items, eggs, and down. As a rule, women in the north were freer than their counterparts in the south, where there were fewer varied types of household income. In the north families were better and cleaner housed, but worse fed, and the struggle against the winter was naturally more severe. In 1926 men and women still followed different routines and ways of life; in sum had different social histories. They went to different parts of the communal bath-house. Men drank and sweated in one part, women chatted and cleaned clothes as they scrubbed themselves in another part. They even walked apart in the evening stroll (*gulanie*) through the village. Three or four girls went one way hand in hand, throwing off ironic verses at the men going by on the other side. They in turn responded with tender-violent phrases.

Unfortunately this kind of divided life affected social and political progress in 1926. When elections were held in Roslavl' uezd for female delegates from local party cells to gubkom meetings in Smolensk city, 4,250 women turned out to vote, but only 1,568 men. All the organizational work for the elections fell completely on women's shoulders.[98] In the winter of 1925–6 200 women were drummed up to represent non-Communist organizations for the six regions of Moshchinsk volost'. They were given no less than sixty-five separate tasks to carry out in their spare time. No wonder single women figured more prominently in the ranks of activists. Near the top of the list came the education of illiterate females: according to the 1926 census, only about 25 per cent of women could read and write in rural areas (37 per cent was the highest estimate for the cities). Lecturing on politics and on the outcome of Party Congresses and Soviet meetings also figured high on this list.[99] Instruction was often more enthusiastically naïve than accurate. One delegate's summary of high politics went as follows: 'Previously there was Lenin, and all went well for poor peasants ... The 14th Party Congress has taken place, it split into two trends; the Leningrad trend, with Lenin's wife, which is for the poor peasants, and the Moscow trend, which is for middle peasants. We come under the zone of the Moscow trend, and that's why things are going so badly.'[100]

[98] Smolensk Archive, file WKP 287, T87, 33, 288.
[99] Ibid., file WKP 424, T87, 48, 425.
[100] Ibid., file WKP 211, 29 (referring to early 1927).

To supplement the sixty-five tasks, these women delegates were given a questionnaire with thirty-four questions they had to answer. As always, the Smolensk Archive reveals a frenzy of bureaucratic activity and energy, most of it dissipated on an apathetic society. Delegates' handwritten answers, in fading ink and hurried scrawl, reveal that in Moshchinsk women's organizations had only commenced in November 1925. There was no day-book nor checks on work done, no women were attending the local reading-huts, and only two females in the whole volost' were subscribing to journals. When asked what other voluntary work they themselves were doing, the hard-pressed delegates wrote that they were also on the local Komsomol committee, the Soviet, etc. One admitted to six other jobs.[101] Female activists deserved their appellation.

At gubkom level in Smolensk itself there was also a hive of activity. During the spring of 1926 weekly reports were issued on female participation in politics throughout the guberniia. Regular checks were made as to whether local delegates were 'poor', 'middle', or '*kulak*' peasant women. It was found that older women were having less and less influence over an increasingly young peasant society. Our woman from Roslavl' uezd with the son now in his mid-twenties would fall into this time trap by now, if she were an activist, which would be a chance of 1 in 10,000, or less. The gubkom even received reports that illiteracy among women was actually increasing.[102] The election campaign for delegates to Zhenotdel was 'especially unsatisfactory' in 1926.[103] In view of such backslidings, it is admirable to note that despair never creeps into the Archive for 1926, though sarcasm often rears its head.

Religion was a continuing cause for worry in party circles in the guberniia. It still permeated the minds of the older generation, and women in particular. Our peasant from Roslavl' uezd was crossing herself before her icon in the corner of the hut in 1922, and she would be sure to be repeating the daily custom four years on. The antics of the Komsomol had little effect on the likes of her. In some ways 1922 had been an exceptional year in the religious history of the area, due to the

---

[101] Ibid., file WKP 424, T87, 48, 425.
[102] Ibid., file WKP 249. This was a report from the Belzi uezd committee for Mar. 1926.
[103] Ibid., file WKP 424, T87, 48, 425.

Party's call for the sacrifice of church valuables to the cause of the Famine. The attempts to empty churches led to considerable opposition, as was noted in Chapter 1. The intervening years witnessed a return in the guberniia to the more usual policy of allowing religious institutions and belief to decay of their own accord. The death of V. Tikhon, the locum tenens of the patriarchate, in April 1925, and the publication of his call for loyalty to the Soviet government among his followers, led to a temporary truce between the authorities and the Orthodox Church, but the position very soon deteriorated. The League of Godless was set up in the same year.

The Smolensk Archive contains a long series of instructions drawn up by the local guberniia council of the League for the use of cell-organizers in the winter of 1925–6. There were only 2,500 guberniia members of the League, and numbers did not increase much in 1926.[104] Special efforts were made to bring in non-party people and above all women. The chief task of the cells was to organize a collective subscription for *Bezbozhnik*, the anti-religious journal. Lectures on atheism had to be given, and revolutionary ceremonies were to replace the ritualism of the Church. 'Komsomol Christmases' were to oust the Christian version. In the countryside activists were to avoid 'the worst aspect of anti-religious propaganda—the method of crude attacks against and ridicule of faith'.[105] Yet Komsomols did not always incline to this kind of sensitivity, as we saw earlier.

In Chapter 1 it was observed how the Smolensk party authorities in 1922 tried to divide and rule between Orthodox, Catholic, and Jewish believers in this province of several faiths. Similar tactics were used in 1926. Attention was directed towards the concentration of Old Believers in Smolensk and Gzhatsk uezdy, and to the twenty-seven evangelical communes in the guberniia. There were also about thirty synagogues and eleven prayer-houses for Jews. The latter faith was reported to be 'still strong, mainly among the petty bourgeoisie, the *déclassé* element, and the small producers'.[106] Another account, confined to a Jewish community in Smolensk uezd, claimed that the whole economy of the local population 'rested on two bases:

---

[104] Smolensk Archive, file WKP 458, 28–34.     [105] Ibid.     [106] Ibid.

flax and . . . the rabbi'.[107] The apparent tie between Judaism and the accumulation of private capital was a red rag to the party bull, as was the fact that Nepmen were often Jews in this guberniia.

The actual extent of religious belief is always hard to assess, since faith can burgeon without external evidence. We know from a survey undertaken in 1926 in another north-Russian guberniia that only 3 per cent of the peasantry were converted to atheism.[108] Another writer in 1926 did find that young men were becoming less religious.[109] One focus of atheist influence was the schools. Military service was another, although it was noted that peasants returning from the army still married in church and had their children baptized;[110] 59 per cent of young people and 46 per cent of schoolchildren still went to church regularly.[111] Writing specifically on Smolensk guberniia, one writer claimed that 'the priests' way of life and customs have become democratized'.[112] They had lost their plots of land since the Revolution, were much worse paid, and had often been reduced to becoming servants of the mir. According to the 1926 all-Soviet census there were 60,900 practitioners of religious faiths (51,600 of them were Orthodox) by their primary occupation, and another 27,000 (of whom 16,400 were Orthodox) by their secondary occupation. In the winter of 1925-6 there were still 548 Orthodox churches and 736 priests active in Smolensk guberniia alone.[113]

Despite these still relatively high figures, there was no doubt by 1926, in Smolensk and elsewhere, that with the dissolution of the old regime, much of the authority of the priesthood had suffered beyond repair. The external trappings of the Orthodox faith were crumbling fast, but not, to all appearances, the internal faith of the traditional peasant household. The Smolensk Archive gives us a vivid whiff, although a much distorted one, of the ongoing strength of what was still a prime ideological foe.

[107] Ibid., file WKP 14, pp. 120–4.
[108] Taradin, op. cit., p. 110.
[109] Murin, op. cit., p. 22.
[110] Ia. Yakovlev, *Derevnia kak ona est'*, p. 120.
[111] Taradin, op. cit., p. 110.
[112] Gagarin, op. cit., p. 83.
[113] Smolensk Archive, file WKP 458.

# 11.  *Tver Guberniia*

MOVING north-east from Smolensk guberniia, a travelling kustar in 1926 would cross into Tver guberniia. Both provinces abutted on Moscow guberniia. Whereas Smolensk connected the capital via the railway to Western Europe, the city of Tver lay on the line to Leningrad. The north and east of Tver guberniia were on the route to nowhere in particular, and the hinterland was so densely forested as to provide a natural barrier to good communications and enlightenment of all kinds.

The 1926 census shows the population of Tver guberniia to be 2,242,350, just 50,239 less than Smolensk. Nearly all of them were Great Russians (unlike Smolensk), though there was a small group of 140,567 Karelians. Those living in Tver city totalled 108,413, whilst the rest of the inhabitants were dispersed over a scattered firmament of small-scale settlements: no less than 263,503 of these existed in an area larger than the whole of Holland or Switzerland. Tver city lay near the more densely populated southern edge of the guberniia, looking towards Moscow. One-third of its inhabitants were employed in factories. A devastating fire in 1763 had destroyed most of the city's historical buildings, but in 1976 it could still claim to have a good historical museum and a pedagogical institute with 750 students.

The north-west part of the guberniia was a lake district. The rest consisted of dense forests, rivers, and land cleared slowly over the centuries. As in Smolensk guberniia, flax and timber products were predominant. Porcelain was an industry special to Tver. The source of the great Volga river lay in the province. It took between eight and ten days to go by steamer and railway from Rzhev in the south-west to Tver.[1] Great-

[1] *Dal'nie ekskursi po Tverskoi gubernii* (1928), p. 6 ff.

Russian traditions weighed far more heavily here than in Smolensk. Rzhev had been a fort and an estate of a junior line of princes of Muscovy since the fourteenth century. In the nineteenth century the nobility of Tver had made their presence felt by objecting to terms on which the serfs were emancipated. The Tsar had felt it necessary to exile them to Viatka.

Although the Soviet land mass constitutes one-sixth of the world's surface, only 40 per cent of it was fit for use in the mid-1920s. Yet most of this suitable area was covered by forests (551.9 million hectares). Arable land, including fallow parts, and garden areas, covering kitchen gardens, orchards, and vineyards, covered a mere 8 per cent of the total land surface.[2] In this respect Tver guberniia was typical, lying largely in a forest zone. An influential report of 1925 called for a general survey of the country's forests. It appealed for an end to indiscriminate wood-felling by individuals and to the frequent fires caused by carelessness. Laws on the use of the forest were to be tightened up, and methods of cutting and transporting timber improved.[3]

In 1926 the forest zone of European Russia–Muscovy and the area to the north of it—was surprisingly overpopulated in economic terms. Unlike Smolensk guberniia and much of the rest of the country, this part of Russia had escaped the ravages of the Civil War. Most households possessed a plot of land. The birth-rate had stayed high. The yearly growth of Tver guberniia was about 25 per thousand in 1926. As all the available land had been distributed, the young drifted in large numbers to Tver and Moscow, but the rural population still continued to increase rapidly.

The woodlands were not just a source of timber for the peasants, but the origin of many agricultural and non-agricultural occupations, from mushroom and berry gathering to the use of bark for shoes, baskets, and innumerable other items. In northern areas like Tver, forests were used for grazing cattle. These activities, and the problems associated with them, had been acknowledged in the 1923 Forestry Code which had

[2] *Mirovoe khoziaistvo. Sbornik statisticheskikh materialov za 1913–1922 gg.* (Moscow, 1928), pp. 116–17.

[3] S. G. Strumilin (ed.), *Lesnye bogatstva SSSR* (Moscow, 1925), pp. 74–5.

instructed the Commissariat of Agriculture to transfer local woods without significance for the forest economy to working land-users.[4] With typical administrative impatience, if not downright utopianism, the 1923 order had wanted compliance within two weeks; in August 1925 the Third Soviet Congress was still pondering on a strict timetable for the transfer to be carried out. In fact it went on until 1927, and even later in more remote areas than Tver. Reasons for such procrastination are not hard to find if one delves into local realities. When peasants from the Rzhev area made enquiries on forestry matters, it took over two years in mid-May to get an answer out of the authorities down the river in Tver.[5]

The guberniia's agricultural agents were themselves not clear on how much woodland there was in 1926. There were supposed to be 1,900,000 desiatini, but so much of it had been felled illegally that estimates became vague.[6] Neither was ownership or usage clear. Poorer peasants with only two or three desiatini for mowing would rent a hut in the woods from foresters at an exorbitant rate so that they could mow forest clearings.[7]

In open agricultural areas flax was an important crop, and Tver ranked in third or fourth place in all Russia. Lower prices for flax by 1926 hit the peasantry here, as in Smolensk. Taxes on it were lowered by 50 per cent to alleviate hardship.[8] Another important agricultural product in Tver guberniia was turf, derived from the bogs and lake areas. The model agricultural organizations for the future were of course collective and state farms, but in 1926 they were little more than a neglected and very small part of peasant life. The number of collective farms in the guberniia actually dropped from fifty-four in November 1927 to fifty in April 1928, before recording a sudden increase to 183 by 1 November 1928 with the onset of collectivization.[9] In 1926 state farms in these parts usually

[4] *Sbornik dokumentov po zemel'nomu zakonodatel'stvu SSSR i RSFSR, 1917–1954 gg.* (Moscow, 1954), p. 198.
[5] *Tverskaia guberniia v 1926–1928 gg. K otchetu gubispolkoma k XVI gub-s'ezdu sovetov* (Tver, 1929), p. 95.
[6] Ibid., p. 91.
[7] Ibid., p. 94.
[8] Ibid., p. 44.
[9] Ibid., pp. 98 ff.

existed on abandoned gentry estates, and were run down and inefficient. They were subsidized to the tune of twenty roubles a desiatin, but they were said to require sixty-one roubles if they were to work properly.[10] The idea was even raised of liquidating all state farms in the province, but the following reply came from a party authority: 'If we do away with state farms at once, then I'm sure that within a few years, as the material conditions of our gubernii improve, we will have to raise the question of organizing model farms, which will have to be state farms.'[11] In 1926 this was not a view universally held in the gubernii. State-farm chairmen were accused of acting 'just like a tsar, a king, a god—they make no approach of any kind to the workers and peasant masses; the result is not Soviet economics, but an unintelligible bastion.'[12]

All types of agricultural organization were being hampered in their development through poor distribution and supplies. Shortage of seed had naturally been a problem in 1922 after the Great Famine, but it remained a bugbear in 1926. Farmers complained that they had ploughed large areas that were still lacking seed.[13] The supply of human expertise was also poor. Agronomists without qualifications were sent down to volost' agricultural centres. In this guberniia, larger than Switzerland, there were only ninety-two veterinary doctors in 1926. As one commentator put it from Bezhetsk: 'In our volost' there are still no veterinary centres, no hospitals, no schools.'[14] In the rare event of backwoods peasants receiving up-to-date machinery, they often left it unused for lack of technical advice. There was much talk of the quantity of ploughs delivered, with no mention of their quality. Peasants were sent hammers without handles, etc.[15]

We shall return to peasant ways at the end of this chapter, as we sink into remote forest fastnesses, but now we shall ascend quickly to the relative sophistication of Tver city and its industries. The vewpoint of the Party is mainly avoided on

[10] Ibid.
[11] Ibid., pp. 101–2.
[12] Ibid., p. 97.
[13] Ibid., p. 90.
[14] Ibid., pp. 56, 88.
[15] Ibid., pp. 88, 91. For further details of peasant life in Tver guberniia in 1926, see *Vlast' sovetov*, 16 (1926).

purpose in this chapter, since it dominated and distorted our understanding of Smolensk guberniia in 1922 and 1926 (due to the overriding significance of the Smolensk Archive), and to a lesser extent of Kursk guberniia (the report of party member Yakovlev) and the famine-stricken areas in 1922. For Tver an attempt is being made to see society in its own right and light, or at least in its supplications to the body politic, rather than the latter's unceasing attempts to stir up local society.

Like all gubernii in European Russia, Tver had its fair share of kustari and Nepmen leaving the hinterland to go to the towns through their economic activities. A substantial increase in Tver trade can be gauged in late NEP from a study of trade licences (Table 2). The preponderance of private trade was not as alarming politically as might appear from the higher figures in this sector, since it was extremely small-scale compared to state and co-operative enterprises.[16]

TABLE 2.  Number of trade licences issued

|              | 1925–6 | 1926–7 | 1927–8 |
| ------------ | ------ | ------ | ------ |
| State        | 352    | 471    | 389    |
| Co-operative | 1467   | 1867   | 2138   |
| Private      | 8131   | 8630   | 6363   |

Attempts were made in mid-Nep to organize kustari into unions specializing in the production of particular items, so that they would fit better into the co-operative system and eventually become members of large-scale structures. In 1926–7 there were 95,313 kustar' groups of this kind in the guberniia, of which 18,640 were in co-operatives. The figures for 1927–8 were 97,431 and 22,167 respectively. Despite the encouraging though slow shift towards systems that could be brought into the socialist sphere more easily in the near future, there was still a great deal of dikost' ('wild', or independent kustari) in 1926.[17] Neither was all well in the co-operative sector. A delegate to a local Congress of Soviets stated that although co-operatives should be viewed as the 'nail' of all future agriculture, they were in fact taking 'a petty, mercenary line'.[18] Co-

[16] *Tverskaia guberniia*, p. 109.     [17] Ibid., p. 136.     [18] Ibid., p. 89.

operatives' efficiency suffered from machinery that broke down frequently because it was made by the less able kustari who had joined their ranks. The co-operatives had to rely on such goods on account of the defective distribution of factory products from Tver.[19] The more traditional type of individual craftsmen still pursued their trade in the localities in direct contact with their customers. In the remote northern Mologa river area of the guberniia 47 per cent of these kustari were woodcutters, 22 per cent wheelwrights, 11 per cent coal-tar processors, 9 per cent sledge-makers, etc.[20] Nearly all of them derived their living from the forests.

At least the highlights of political goings-on did reach down into these dark woods. As one woodsman put it in 1924, 'In such a grey corner of Tver guberniia as Okovetskaia volost', the news of the death of our Il'ich [Lenin] awoke dismay.'[21] The workers in Tver city electric-station were much bolder, electing Lenin as an honorary member of the city Soviet in his lifetime.[22] The number of workers in the guberniia as a whole went up from 43,100 in 1924–5 to 47,200 in 1925–6, 50,400 in 1926–7, and 51,500 by 1927–8. The biggest increase occurred at the start of these years. In 1926 just over 2 per cent of the province's inhabitants were workers. More cotton and brick-making factories were added to existing ones, and a new refrigerator plant was set up in Tver city. In 1927–8 three new electric stations were constructed, with the aim of meeting expected energy requirements after the full onset of industrialization.[23] The textile sector was long-established, and included 30,000 sophisticated workers, even though many of them were women, as was usually the case in this industry. Three of the textile factories had been set up as early as 1853, 1857, and 1866 respectively. By 1926 all the plants were united in a common textile trust.[24] Other important industries in the city included timber-processing and silicate.

---

[19] Ibid., p. 90. For more information on co-operatives in Tver guberniia, see I. E. Liubimov, *Dva napravleniia v kooperatsii* (Moscow, 1927), pp. 26 ff.

[20] *Dal'nie ekskursii*, p. 93.

[21] *Pis'ma tveriakov k Leninu* (Moscow, 1973), p. 267.

[22] *Lenin i tverskoi krai* (Moscow, 1969), p. 156.

[23] *Tverskaia guberniia*, pp. 4–6.

[24] S. Rogachevskaia, *Iz istorii rabochego klassa SSSR v pervye gody industrializatsii 1926–1927 gg.* (Moscow, 1959), p. 9; *Dal'nie ekskursii*, p. 50.

In spite of their relative sophistication, Tver workers were not as involved in crucial political activities and posts in 1926 as were their Moscow equivalents. Only 2.2 per cent of workers from the factory bench were on the plenary sessions of party committees in the guberniia.[25] Nevertheless at less exalted levels there was a good deal of political activism. In April 1926 the journal *Tverskaia Pravda* inspired workers to engage in a campaign for raising productivity (echoes of similar campaigns in Moscow at this time). In July a suggestions-box was set up in the largest tannery in Tver. Workers came up with forty-two worth-while suggestions on productivity and discipline. They also insisted on prolonging a conference that had been arranged by two days.[26] Out of a total of 2,000 workers from a porcelain factory 1,500 took part in another conference run by the newspaper. Later, in January 1927, the largest single factory in the guberniia, the 'Proletarka', agreed to be surveyed by the *Tverskaia Pravda*: 929 workers from it wrote letters to the paper, and even illiterate members were brought into discussions.[27] Yet there was not a wholesale conversion of all the local proletariat to the Party's course. Whereas one group of workers in late 1926 from a wood sawmill offered on their own initiative to have their wages fixed according to the 'growth of socialist production', and not on the basis of their own demands, opposing views were to be found in 1927 from the Koniaev plant. 'We, non-party workers, will not follow them.'[28]

Unemployment afflicted Tver as badly as Moscow at this time. The nationwide figure for the jobless in October 1925 was 920,000, rising to 1,041,000 in October 1927.[29] By 1 April 1928 in Tver guberniia the number was said to be 31,742, but it was easier to calculate figures for workers than for peasants. The numbers decreased greatly during the summer months. Indeed, the Tver Labour Office found it hard then to find enough unskilled workers to man building projects, kitchen gardens,

[25] S. L. Dmitrenko, 'Sostav mestnykh partiinykh komitetov v 1924–1927 gg.', in *Istoricheskie zapiski*, 79 (1966), p. 104.

[26] *Tverskaia Pravda*, 18 July to 6 Aug. 1926.

[27] Ibid., 19 Jan. 1927.

[28] Ibid., 6 Nov. 1926 and 16 Nov. 1927.

[29] *Rogachevskaia*, op. cit., p. 57.

and outdoor factory jobs; 102,833 peasants were engaged in part-time work in the towns, 37,012 of them in the construction business. Nevertheless, the nation-wide numbers of *otkhodniki* (peasants working part-time in non-agricultural employment) only rose from 15 per 1,000 in 1923–4 to 28 by the end of NEP. At the turn of the century it had been 80 per 1,000. In 1926 fifteen correspondent centres were established around the guberniia in order to assess unemployment figures more accurately.[30] In mid-NEP a spade was still called a spade. As yet no euphemistic phrases had been coined to tone down the shameful word 'unemployment' in a polity dedicated on Marx's instructions to get rid of this affliction completely and permanently.

The most active investigating agent in Tver factories was Rabkrin (the Peasants' and Workers' Inspectorate). Its influence at many levels of Soviet life in NEP was all-pervasive. It therefore provides later scholars with a mine of reasonably accurate information on local affairs. Although it was politically motivated, its ear was much closer to the ground than most other inquisitional political authorities. In this way it tended more towards concrete facts and less towards airy theorizing. Its counterpart at the highest level in Moscow was that third tier of more sober planners for Soviet society which was pin-pointed and categorized in Chapter 7. Like this tier, it was able on occasion to scent out coercive influences before they were spotted by top-tier party leaders. Thus we find Rabkrin coming across growing evidence in early NEP of the alcoholism and corruption in the Smolensk party machine that was to blow up eventually into the scandal of 1928. High Moscow authorities became aware of it much more slowly.[31] Back in Tver, Rabkrin did a good job of putting its finger on those administrative problems in local factory life that were leading in part to the eventual collapse of the NEP system. The trouble was that difficulties picked up at these levels were neither relayed clearly and fast enough to Moscow, nor were

---

[30] *Tverskaia guberniia*, pp. 101–5. For the numbers of *otkhodniki*, see M. Sonin, *Vosproizvodstvo rabochei sily v SSSR i balans truda* (Moscow, 1959), p. 180.

[31] In the winter of 1922–3 alone, Rabkrin representatives heard 180 cases in Smolensk guberniia of complaints against party officials; nearly one-third of them were for drunkenness. See Smolensk Archive, file WKP 368, 42.

they acted on in time when they did make an impact. Rabkrin
discovered in 1926 that 17 per cent of all industrial staff in Tver
guberniia were administrators. Their numbers had gone up by
22 per cent in 1925–6 alone, whilst the number of workers had
risen by only 15 per cent over the same period. For a repair in a
cotton factory costing a mere 230 roubles, the written agreement of *Glavtekstil* was needed. Documentation of transactions
of any kind had to be put on paper, often in triplicate or more.
Oral communications had no validity.[32]

One thing that Rabkrin continually failed to notice throughout NEP, on the other hand, was its own over-indulgence in
administrative and bureaucratic overloading. No less than
twenty-nine separate sections of Rabkrin were involved in
inspecting the textile industry in Tver. Within the space of ten
months they issued 45,506 documents to the local textile trust.
It was not surprising that 4,100 of these had not been processed
or delivered. The local leather board was another much-
bombarded target. On average it received 13,000 queries per
month from Rabkrin.[33]

The best paid sector of the proletariat in Tver in 1926 were
the metalworkers, as was the case throughout the Soviet Union.
They earned an average 74.38 roubles a month. The worst paid
were naturally women. Female process silk workers received
only 32.72 roubles per month on average.[34] Such minute wages
were not yet cushioned by widespread social insurance, one of
the prime aims of the Bolshevik government. Sheer lack of
sufficient liquid funds in the state sector hampered the achievement of welfare targets. A nation-wide survey conducted in
1925 claimed that 'we have secured significant gains in all the
activities of our insurance agencies', yet by 1 October 1926
only 8,494,000 people were covered by a minimal amount of
insurance.[35] The vast majority of the beneficiaries lived in the
big cities of European Russia.[36] The total funds available or
social insurance in Tver guberniia in 1926–7 amounted to

[32] *Tverskaia guberniia*, pp. 291–2.
[33] Ibid.
[34] *Statisticheskii spravochnik po Tverskoi gubernii* (Tver, 1929), p. 185.
[35] A. P. Shteinberg, *Oktiabr' i sotsialisticheskoe strakhovanie* (Moscow, 1925), p. 44;
*Pervye shagi industrializatsii SSSR 1926–7 gg.* (Moscow, 1959), p. 231.
[36] V. Basiubin, *Opyt raboty Moskovskogo strakhkassa 1925–1929* (Moscow, 1930), p. 6.

572,650 roubles. However there was an encouraging increase to 924,089 roubles by 1927–8. Vigorous attempts were made to distribute funds to the most deserving and needy. War pensioners got 329,025 roubles in 1926, and 567,042 in 1927; 5,000 roubles were distributed to the blind in 1926, 6,179 in 1927.[37]

In 1926 there was no provision for old-age pensioners, apart from disability pensions. On the tenth anniversary of the Revolution a promise was made to introduce a scheme. Payments to the fast-increasing number of unemployed workers in 1926 were strictly limited, partly for lack of money, but also due to the reluctance of the proletarian élite in the Moscow and other big city trade unions to cater for the ex-peasants flooding into the conurbations from areas like Tver and Smolensk gubernii. Yet by 1926, on account of the big rise in the jobless, 350,000 unemployed workers were getting an average of ten roubles a month for the unskilled and fifteen for the skilled.[38]

Living standards were often still atrocious for those who had a job. Housing remained the worst problem in the towns, as we know from the biting satire in Zoshchenko's short stories.[39] In its control figures for 1926–7, Gosplan confessed that the housing problem would not go away.[40] Living space was declining in the besieged industrial cities. The high number of temporary peasant labourers employed on building during the summer in Tver city was noted earlier, but they were poorly organized. The city's factories were not directly involved in housing development and allocation: instead inefficient building co-operatives were responsible.[41]

The general low standard of living had a major impact on health. Free medical care was only available to workers in 1926. It cost a total of 239.6 million roubles in 1926 for the nation as a whole.[42] During NEP there existed four main subsections for expenditure on the RSFSR health service. The

---

[37] *Tverskaia guberniia*, pp. 233–8.
[38] *Vos'moi s"ezd professional'nykh soiuzou SSSR* (Moscow, 1962), pp. 355–6.
[39] M. Zoshchenko, 'Houses and People', in *Scenes from the Bathhouse* (Ann Arbor, 1962).
[40] *Kontrol'nye tsifry narodnogo khoziaistva na 1926–7 god* (Moscow, 1926), p. 219.
[41] See *Piatnadsatyi s"ezd VKP(B)*, vol. 2 (Moscow, 1962), p. 922.
[42] *Kontrol'nye tsifry narodnogo khoziaistva SSSR na 1928–9 god* (1929), p. 162.

central state budget and the local budget (a consolidation of expenditures on health by the differing levels of local government, as in Tver) were supplemented by the social insurance fund of medical aid and by legal payments by individuals or organizations to medical institutions for services. In both 1925–6 and and 1926–7 per capita expenditure from state and local budgets in the RSFSR was lower than the all-Union average. The Belorussian SSR was also below the average, whereas the Uzbek SSR in Soviet Central Asia was well above the average in 1926–7. These figures, taken from areas under scrutiny in this book, together with the high figures for the generously treated areas like the Transcaucasus and Turkmenia,[43] show that a conscious effort was being made to bring the health standards of the least privileged areas of the continent into line with European Russia. Yet it should be remembered that not all western areas were better off. Health statistics for later NEP in the parts of the RSFSR and the Ukraine hit by the Great Famine show that they were still suffering from its after-effects.

There had certainly been a considerable improvement in some areas of medicine since the Revolution. The number of physicians more than tripled between 1913 and the end of NEP. There were 63,200 of them by 1928, backed up by 113,700 semi-professional medical staff.[44] The number of hospital beds increased from 93,200 to 168,500 in the cities.[45] These figures should be treated with caution, as the author knows from his personal experience of drawing up Soviet medical statistics.[46] Two surveys published in Tver gave differing figures for the number of hospitals in the guberniia in 1927. One claimed 79, with 2,081 beds, the other 86 with 3,038 beds.[47] Both estimates fall considerably short of the number of

---

[43] 'Finansirovanie zdravokhranenie po gosudarstvennomu biudzhetu u prochim istochnikam', *Biulleten' narodnogo kommissariata zdravokhraneniia RSFSR*, 21 (Moscow, 1927), p. 15.

[44] *Zdravokhranenie v SSSR: statisticheskii sbornik* (Moscow, 1960), p. 79; *Narodnoe khoziaistvo SSSR v 1961 g.*, p. 745.

[45] G. A. Miterev, *XXV let sovetskogo zdravokhraneniia* (Moscow, 1944), p. 81.

[46] In 1960 the author, under the direction of Sir John Charles, collected Soviet health statistics (amongst others) for the *Annual Report* of the WHO.

[47] These two sources are respectively *Tverskaia guberniia*, p. 221, and *Statisticheskii spravochnik po Tverskoi gubernii*, p. 61.

beds recorded for the same year (6,788) in the city of Kursk alone, excluding its guberniia hinterland.[48]

By 1926 there existed one hospital for mental illnesses in Tver city, with 650 places. There was also an institute with 20 beds for chronic alcoholics, those escapists from the evils of Tsarist and Soviet rule alike. Quite a lot of building took place for the health service between 1925 and 1927, but it was concentrated almost entirely on Tver itself. There had been no sanitary administration in the city prior to 1917, but by 1926 there were thirty qualified personnel. In spite of these improvements, it was clear that better provision in the guberniia capital did not necessarily imply better health throughout the province. In 1916 329,474 vaccinations were carried out, a remarkably high number which must have involved the hinterland to a great degree, since the population of Tver was only 108,413. Yet some diseases were on the increase. Typhus had jumped up from 1.6 per cent per 10,000 persons in 1913 to 4.4 per cent in 1926. Scarlet fever and other children's illnesses were spreading (there were eighteen paediatricians here in 1926). Dysentery was declining, but malaria, caused by mosquito infection in the widespread marshy areas, was on the increase.[49]

In 1913 no provision was made for doctors to visit private homes. Only the rich or privileged could pay for domestic calls. By 1926 twenty-nine doctors were engaged in this service, irrespective of their patients' status, but of course they rarely went outside Tver city or the other towns.[50] In theory, the villages were supposed to counteract the town–country divide by fitting up mutual aid societies for medical and other provision. An American who worked on Soviet 'reconstruction farms' at the time let out his optimistic thoughts on the subject :

Practically every village has its Mutual Aid Society for the purpose of aiding the poor, the aged, the crippled, and the orphaned members of the population. While the care of these classes is normally the function of the government, just as in the case of the society for raising funds for adult education to aid the Department of Education, so these local

[48] *Otchet o rabote Kurskogo goroda za 20 marta 1927 do 1 oktiabriia 1928 g.* (Kursk, 1928), p. 71.

[49] *Tverskaia guberniia*, pp. 223–30.

[50] *Statisticheskii spravochnik*, p. 61.

organizations, in view of the poverty of the government budgets, share in this social obligation. Graduated dues are provided according to the economic status of the member. Certain sections of land are set apart and cultivated for the fund, and occasional benefits of one sort or another are held. The resources of this fund may be used to make loans for seed, to give medicines to the poor, or food and clothing in cases of emergency, such as to families that have been ruined by fire or flood. In other words, that Mutual Aid Society is the Associated Charities and Red Cross of the Community on the healthier basis of a sort of social insurance, to which the person in need may appeal without the usual connotations of charity.[51]

Even if this idyllic vision could have been achieved in some altruistic community, it still could not have counterbalanced general inequality. In 1926 the urban population of the Soviet Union formed 17 per cent of the total, with rural inhabitants making up the other 83 per cent.[52] Per capita health expenditure on uninsured persons in the countryside rose from only 69 kopeks in 1924–5 to 1.05 roubles in 1926–7, as against 4.41 to 6.26 roubles for townspeople.[53] The number of hospital beds per head was still ten times lower in the RSFSR for rural than for town-dwellers in 1924. The average number of persons per doctor was 13,840.[54]

The health authorities in Tver city were told by their Moscow superiors in 1926: 'You have a big head and a little body.'[55] Using a proverb in typical Russian manner to soften the criticism with humour, Moscow meant that too many medical developments were concentrated on Tver. For once they were correct in their central analysis of detailed local conditions. Comments coming up from the uezd level to the guberniia capital accused local doctors of not forming part of rural society. They just 'sit in hospitals'.[56] Like their fellow intellectuals in the countryside, they hugged together in the volost' centres. Doctors in rural areas had been less well paid

---

[51] K. Borders, *Village Life under the Soviets* (New York, 1927), pp. 149–50.

[52] *Statisticheskii spravochnik za 1928* (Moscow, 1929).

[53] M. Donskoi, 'Kontrol'nye tsifry po zdravokhraneniiu na 1926–7 g.', *Biulleten' narodnogo kommissariata zdravokhraneniia RSFSR*, 19 (Moscow, 1926), p. 6.

[54] N. Nosov, 'Perspektivy razvitiia sel'skoi uchastkovoi seti', *Biulleten' narodnogo kommissariata zdravokhraneniia RSFSR*, 20 (Moscow, 1926) p.6.

[55] *Doklad gubzdrava* (Tver, 1926), p. 105.

[56] Ibid., p. 116.

than their urban counterparts since the introduction of khoz-raschet near the start of NEP. Medical centres often disintegrated completely in the backwoods of the guberniia since even *fel'dsheri* (semi-trained doctors) abandoned them. They went in for private work, and were paid by the peasants with sacks of flour and other items.[57] This was a disturbing picture, especially in view of the fact that the industry intake of peasants in the guberniia had only increased from a base of 100 in 1920 to 122.6 by 1926. The urban level had reached 142.4 by the same year.[58] These figures show that the peasants' stranglehold on food supply to the towns, which had led to NEP in the first place, was more than reversed by 1926.

When poorer peasants fell sick, they did not have a horse available to take them to a doctor. Doctors could not or would not go to them. The Tver medical authority urged locally trained staff to get out to women in childbirth. Women often 'give birth in their huts, and take on an old woman or a quack to help'.[59] Talking of quacks, the Tver authorities did claim to be freer of them than were other gubernii; yet there was the recent case of one who passed through Tver from the frozen north on his way to Moscow. He claimed that he could cure tuberculosis in a flash. When asked about his methods, he replied that he had to keep them a deadly secret to avoid patients flooding in from America to be healed.[60] Was this an atheist Soviet version of the 'holy fool'?

The reason why mountebanks of this kind could still flourish in the provinces was the continuing gullibility and low educational standards of the local people. The equitable distribution of public resources is crucial in a developing society. Marxist-Leninist theory on class equality ran into conflict with intransigent realities more strikingly in this sphere than in any other during NEP. The actual situation by 1926 was still one of gross inequality of provision and opportunity. This continuing disparity was of more crucial importance in Marxist eyes in the educational sector than in health or housing. The transfer of

---

[57] Ibid., p. 107.
[58] *Statisticheskii spravochnik*, p. 432.
[59] *Doklad gubzdrava*, p. 106.
[60] Ibid. For details of health conditions in one volost' in Tver guberniia in 1926, see Bol'shakov, *Derevnia 1917–27* (Moscow, 1927), pp. 288 ff.

privilege from one generation to the next through the provision of capital is most easily broken by putting the accent on education for the young as the greatest treasure of all.

Certainly some progress had been made nation-wide between early and mid-NEP. The pathetic naïvety and lack of acquaintance with the simplest terms of political jargon that was observed in Smolensk guberniia in 1922 was slowly receding. In 1921–2 local Soviets struggling with khozraschet were forced to reintroduce school fees. This system was given *de jure* recognition by the Congress of Soviets in 1922. We have noted how richer peasants could do better for their children's education in Kursk guberniia as early as 1922. By 1926 it was common knowledge that '*kulaks*', Nepmen, and kustari were profiting far more widely as NEP produced more prosperity from perquisites of this type, which meant that their offspring could become even more privileged in relative terms. It was not until August 1925 that a plan was drawn up to promote universal primary education. Only at the start of 1927 were fees abolished in primary schools.

The relatively small number of peasants' children who moved on to extended primary education in the towns were confronted with a maximum fee of sixty roubles. Compare this with the average health expenditure on Tver peasants of 1.05 roubles per head. One solution for clever peasant pupils was to enrol in Schools of Peasant Youth. They were set up on the initiative of the Komsomol in rural locations, yet they provided the equivalent of urban secondary grades 5 to 7. They gave classes on small-scale farming, and allowed for further upward educational mobility.[61]

Townspeople, in Tver and elsewhere, did far better than peasants out of improved access to secondary education. For instance, numbers in grades 5 to 7 (junior secondary level in ordinary urban schools) went up two and a half times between 1914–15 and 1927–8.[62] In 1926 the majority of urban children progressed through the four grades of primary school. Marxist-Leninist class principles were upheld in that working-class children were the biggest social group here, but only at the

[61] See A. Lunacharsky and A. Shokhin, *K edinoi sisteme narodnogo obrazovaniia* (Moscow, 1929), p. 17.
[62] *Kul'turnoe stroitel'stvo SSSR* (Moscow, 1956), pp. 122–3.

lower levels. From grade 5 on they were outnumbered by children of white-collar workers. This trend worsened in the higher grades of secondary education. Although workers were better paid than most peasants, they could not compete with higher social classes over long years of fee-paying for their children. Despite the great increase in the early Soviet period in the number of urban pupils entering grades 5 to 7, the overall figures for Tver guberniia as a whole show that for all types of children, amongst whom peasants predominated by a ratio of four to one, the position did not improve much between 1913–14 and 1926–7. The total number of pupils in the guberniia had gone up from 149,489 to 155,179, but educational institutions had shrunk slightly from 2,373 to 2,146 and there were slightly fewer teachers in 1927 than in 1914—3,970 as opposed to 4,067.[63] The nadir had occurred in the Civil War and at the start of NEP. Expenditure on education nearly tripled between 1923 and 1927. No less than sixty-five schools were rebuilt or newly built in 1926–7, despite problems encountered due to the distance of rural timber-yards from town sites.[64]

In 1926–7 the accent on higher-grade education was still heavily concentrated on the towns in the guberniia. Although there were 2,050 first-grade schools in the rural areas, with 141 in urban sites, the position altered increasingly for higher grades. Even at the second grade, urban schools outnumbered rural ones by forty-two to twenty-eight.[65] Yet things were improving even at the most deprived levels of rustic society. By 1926 90.4 per cent of children from all classes were receiving a minimal education of some sort.[66] In 1922 a shockingly high proportion of minors of school age had been vagrant orphans. One only has to recall Poltava and A. Makarenko's flourishing, but at that time exceptional special institution for the bezprizornye. Between 1922 and 1926 the number of orphans in Tver guberniia had declined from 3,271 to 2,135. More surprising was the continuing low number of party 'pioneers' in grade one schools, only 14.2 per cent of all pupils by 1927. In the countryside the amount of 'red corners' for political agitation increased, but the poorer peasants, the supposed new ally of the party, did not make use of them. Eight per cent of the 'corners'

[63] *Statisticheskii spravochnik*, p. 61.   [64] *Tverskaia guberniia*, pp. 191, 194.
[65] Ibid., p. 195.   [66] Ibid., p. 196.

had been set up by party workers, but the rest had been organized by the ubiquitous Komsomol (34.5 per cent) and non-party activists (57.5 per cent). This did not bode well for the faithful transmission of party propaganda from on high.[67]

As early as 1922 a *rabfak* had been set up in Tver city. This was one of a nation-wide network of secondary schools for adult workers who had missed out on conventional school education in the turmoil of the Revolution and the Civil War. Its intake grew from eighty pupils in 1922 to 256 in 1926. When the Soviet Union's peasant President, M. I. Kalinin, told the Commissar for Enlightenment, A. Lunacharsky, in 1925 that the peasantry was angry because there were no *krestfaks*, only rabfaky (no peasant, only worker faculties), the Commissar pointed out with some satisfaction that over 50 per cent of those studying in rabfaky were in fact peasants.[68]

There was a marked surge in the numbers of lower-grade professionals passing out of the Tver rabfak and the conventional secondary schools by 1926; 1,999 qualified in the province in that year, as opposed to 210 in 1913.[69] Some of them became village schoolteachers. Their lot was not much better than the situation described for Kursk guberniia in 1922. In a report issuing from Penza guberniia in 1925 (an area on the north-western edge of the Famine region surveyed in Chapter 3), rural teachers were said to possess no authority among the local population. They were seen as external administrators by the peasants. As members of the village Soviet, they were engaged in arresting drunkards, collecting taxes, and many other unpopular duties. Since there was on average one teacher for every 135 peasant pupils, it was not surprising that they found it hard to impress their authority and exact discipline.[70]

Given the continuing lack of success in instilling education or even a minimum of literacy in the rural depths, it is interesting to note a huge increase in the number of radio points installed in the province's villages. In the short space of time between 1926 and 1927–8 the number rose from 332 to 4,598.[71] The

[67] *Tverskaia guberniia*, pp. 199–202, 215.
[68] Lunacharsky and Shokhin, op. cit., pp. 28–9.
[69] *Tverskaia guberniia*, op. cit., p. 209.
[70] Rosnitsky, *Litso derevni* (Leningrad, 1926), pp. 93–8. For details of school life in 1926 in one volost' of Tver guberniia, see Bol'shakov, op. cit., pp. 227 ff.
[71] *Tverskaia guberniia*, p. 217.

countryside was being fitted out with instant oral communication so as to be indoctrinated on the ruthless and fundamental changes in agriculture that were by then being aimed at central and increasingly at middle party levels. Thus the lingering influence of illiteracy could be bypassed.

The need for improved communications networks at all levels was even more crucial now than at the start of NEP. Marxist-Leninist doctrine on economic and social organization had at its core the notion of the efficiency of large-scale structures. Only they could usher in the age of communism.[72] Meanwhile all forms of communication had not improved much on the situation described for 1922 in Chapter 4. The political authorities were well aware of the problem at both the national and local levels. In April 1925 the Second Conference of Soviet Construction passed a resolution intended to deal with snags in administrative communication,[73] but it was scarcely acted on in the years up to the end of NEP. M. Kalinin, the peasants' spokesman at the highest level, declared that the villages were cut off from the centre and left to their own devices.[74]

Let us look at some other aspects of communications in 1926. In 1922 our survey was pitched mainly at the nation-wide level, but here the internal guberniia network, from the volost' centre to the deep countryside, is examined in the context of Tver. But first let us take another glance at two crucial national services in 1926, the railways and water transport.

The fastest train from Moscow to Smolensk—the 'Key and the Gate of Russia' to Western Europe—averaged 25 mph in 1924 and ran only twice a week. By 1927 there was a daily service, but still at the same speed. It was not until 1926 that the backlog of repairs to locomotives began to be reduced to any great extent. In 1925–6 45 per cent of all locomotive stock was out of service. By the end of NEP engines and rolling-stock managed to regain the 1913 level, but the condition of the railway infrastructure in general was still below pre-war

[72] For a much fuller treatment of this theme, see Pethybridge, 'Large-scale Theories versus Small-scale Realities', in *The Social Prelude to Stalinism* (London, 1974), pp. 200–6.

[73] *Soveshchanie po voprosam sovetskogo stroitel'stva* (Moscow, 1925), pp. 175–80.

[74] Ibid., pp. 113–14.

standards. Light-weight trains remained a weakness. In 1925 roughly two-fifths of all sleepers were over age. At the start of 1926 one-tenth of bridges still needed to be renewed or replaced.[75]

If one compares Baedeker's *Russland* for 1914 with a Soviet guide issued in 1925, it appears that the express train from Kiev to Odessa which took twelve and a half hours in 1914 took 16 hours in 1925. Just before the First World War the following steamship lines called in at Odessa on a regular basis—North German Lloyd, Austrian Lloyd, Società Marittima Italiana, and Messageries Maritimes. In 1925 only a few Soviet coastal ships on the Black Sea routes called in.[76] The productivity of river transport rose faster after 1922 than that of the railways. In 1913 the number of persons carried had been 11.5 million. By 1924 it was 7 to 12 million.[77] Boat passengers making good use of river transport on the Volga from Rzhev to Tver in 1926, but the vital bridge across the river at Rzhev had not been improved at all since it was photographed in 1909 by S. M. Prokudin-Gorskii of the Tsarist Ministry of Ways and Communications. It consisted of a single-width, shaky pontoon with mud tracks approaching it at either side. Logs awaiting removal still lay strewn higgledy-piggledly over the road.

The impact of poor communications at the local level was felt all the more keenly when the volost' areas were enlarged after 1923–4. In 1925 some rural Soviets were still not aware of the laws concerning this.[78] The central authorities claimed that the changes could only be beneficial: whereas the Tsarist regime had been concerned solely with imposing control from above, they were intent on harnessing the economic and cultural needs of the local population to larger-scale administrative units. The average increase in population coverage under the new scheme rose from 7,218 to 21,698 persons per volost' in Tver guberniia between 1913 and 1926.[79] The

[75] See J. N. Westwood, *A History of Russian Railways* (London, 1964), pp. 209, 201–2.

[76] Compare K. Baedeker, *Russia* (London, 1914), p. 386, with *Führer durch die Sovjetunion* (Moscow, 1925), p. 347.

[77] *Transport i sviaz'* (Moscow, 1972), p. 262.

[78] *Voprosy ekonomicheskogo raionirovanii* (Moscow, 1957), p. 267.

[79] Bol'shakov, op. cit., pp. 185–8.

resulting dislocation in administrative terms over a whole range of subjects, from taxation to health and to education, must have been as disruptive at the microcosmic level as were those nation-wide administrative reorganizations discussed in Chapter 5.

Travellers by train on the Nicholas railway from St Petersburg via Tver to Moscow at the end of the old regime were advised by Baedeker that 'this journey may be advantageously performed at night, as little of interest is passed on the way'. So much for the present centre of our interest in the minds of the foreign tourist or the sybaritic inhabitants of the twin capitals. As the train approached Tver, forests gave place more and more to open meadows. The station, as so often in Russia, lay some distance outside the town. Visitors could put up at the London Hotel (renamed by 1926) where bed-linen cost sixty kopeks extra in 1914. This was not as grand as the Club of Noblesse where tourists could stay in Smolensk. A horse-drawn cab, in 1914 or 1926 alike, could take one instead to the steamboat pier on the Volga for the fastest way of going on into the depths of the guberniia. In spring and autumn the side roads were virtually impassable for motorized vehicles. In winter sledges were as fast or faster than river transport in summer.[80]

Beyond Tver travel facilities had not improved at all since 1914. In some ways they had deteriorated. If one studies the time and effort needed in 1926 for a peasant from the village of Blokhino, much lower down the same Volga river, to cover the 40 km. to the guberniia capital of Nizhnii Novgorod, 500 km. east of Tver, the conditions at once recall the slow progress of that Smolensk guberniia peasant woman on her way to Roslavl' in 1922. In 1926 it took from eight to ten hours to get to Nizhnii from Blokhino. Most of the way was undertaken at night, so as not to lose a day's work, and on foot, unless a goods cart not full to overflowing could give one an occasional lift. Much patience was needed on arrival at the bank of the Volga facing the city. Ferry boats were slow and scarce.

The greatest strides in modernization were to happen later, between the start of the Five-Year Plans and the 1950s. By the

[80] Baedeker, op. cit., pp. 266–7, 251.

1960s a double-tier bridge spanned the Volga at the old ferry site. Asphalt roads allowed thirty-three bus lines to run on a network of 1,200 km. through villages like Blokhino, which now bristled with radio and television aerials. By 1968 only nine illiterates survived in the village, old peasants who had refused to take lessons in the 1930s and later regretted it deeply. Only they did not have access to the good library in Blokhino with its 7,650 volumes.[81]

In 1926 villages like Blokhino still represented the deepest bite of Great-Russian colonization into the forest wilderness in this part of the land mass. It had been founded at the end of the eighteenth century. In mid-NEP Blokhino villagers had very little contact with Belkino, which lay a mere two kilometres away, but was separated by a marsh which had to be circumvented. Unlike Blokhino, Belkino possessed a church, the rural Soviet, a run-down school put up by the zemstvo in the later nineteenth century, and a fire-station. Yet to get in touch with the wider world, it was necessary to travel on from Belkino to Ostankino, which boasted a post and telegraph office. A telegram sent from Moscow in 1926 took five days to reach this office.[82]

The postal system varied considerably in efficiency according to which part of the country one lived in. In Tver guberniia it was as good as anywhere outside a few industrial regions. Before the Revolution letters arrived in Goritskaia volost' twice a week, although post could only be sent off and stamps obtained from the vain volost' community which was miles from some villages. By November 1927 the situation had not improved much. Letters were still delivered twice a week. They were handed direct to the addressees by means of one horse and two pedestrian circuits, which also sold stamps and took in letters *en route*.[83] Given the disruption of all communications by the Revolution, and continuing illiteracy, the figures for any year during NEP, had they been recorded, might not have been significantly higher than those for the year 1913, when it was found that on average each inhabitant of the Empire posted four letters, received 2.6 newspapers or journals of any

[81] P. Pascal, *Civilisation paysanne en Russie* (Lausanne, 1969), pp. 76–7, 104, 108.
[82] Ibid., pp. 77–8.
[83] Bol'shakov, op. cit., p. 299.

kind, and dispatched 0.26 telegrams.[84] Certainly in Goritskaia volost' people received fewer letters in 1926 than they had done in 1913. The number dropped drastically after 1920 when Soviet citizens were no longer allowed to send letters free of charge. Telephone connections did not exist in Goritskaia volost' before the Revolution, but by 1927 there were single instruments in one or two villages. It was too expensive for most private individuals to send telegrams, so the network was used almost entirely by the authorities. Whereas 577 telegrams had been sent off and 1,158 received in the volost' in 1913, the figures for 1926 were 672 and 785 respectively.[85]

Goritskaia volost' lay only 50 km. north-east of Tver city, yet it took twenty hours to cover the distance on horseback in 1926. Horses were still the most useful type of motive power outside the big towns. In Tver guberniia only 66.5 per cent of households possessed a horse, and a mere 0.8 per cent had two horses or more, thus leaving one free for travel during farming hours.[86] The slow postal system combined with the paucity of individual means of transport slowed up the whole course of Soviet and party administration. The results of these technical deficiencies have been observed in all the chapters devoted to local government. The penetration of the legal system into the hinterland was also affected. In mid-NEP it took fifteen days for legal documents to be sent from Goritskaia volost' to a neighbouring volost'. Before the Revolution each volost' centre had a court, but since 1928 one people's court served two volosti in Tver guberniia: 73 per cent of the rural population was now 15 or more versts away from the nearest court. They applied to the law even less than before as a result. It was expensive to leave work, and difficult to travel far.[87]

The flow of money into Goritskaia volost' was also more restricted than just before the World War. From 1913 to 1926 the volume went down in value about fourfold in real terms. NEP remained a stagnating or even a declining economic system at these levels. Fewer peasants were now that type of *otkhodnik* who still sent funds back to their villages. The number

---

[84] *Bol'shaia sovetskaia entsiklopediia*, vol. 35, p. 328.
[85] Bol'shakov, op. cit., pp. 299, 301–3.
[86] Ibid., p. 37.
[87] Ibid., pp. 306–13.

of shepherds on jobs in other parts remained at nearly the pre-war level (fifty to sixty men), but local dyers no longer took off to work in Vologda and Archangel gubernii. The only trades that were flourishing at home were distilling and woodcut-ting—both of them illegal.[88]

Only in the sphere of the press did communications register a significant improvement over the position recorded in Chapter 4 for 1922. When khozraschet was applied in Goritskaia volost' in 1921–2, the volost' executive committee, which had been receiving newspapers free up till then, cut down on the number ordered now they had to be paid for. In 1923 the committee was ordering 900 copies of *Tverskaia Pravda*, leaving only three to four other private subscribers. From 1924 peasant interest was catered for somewhat better, and more copies of *Krest'-ianskaia gazeta* and *Bednota* were being bought. By mid-NEP it was still the local traders, white-collar employees, and clergy who were the main readers of journals. By 1927 every third or fourth peasant household was occasionally buying a local paper. Hardly any one of any class ever looked at the nation-ally circulated *Pravda* and *Izvestiia*.[89]

Despite this encouraging increase in reading, oral rumour still prevailed, as it had done for centuries, as the chief means of communication of news and ideas of all kinds. Political notions usually spread into the villages via kustari, otkhodniki, or factory workers returning home.[90] Then the peasants would elaborate on them, weaving new concoctions which they added to the rhyming *chastushki* they threw at one another on their evening promenades. Thus couplets on the eternal theme of love were joined by jibes at the church, the taxmen, the Nepmen, or even the Party itself. A typical anti-religious rhyme flying round the volost' in 1926 went as follows:

> In the clouds the prophet Elijah
> Rides on a steed.
> Wouldn't it be interesting to know, friends
> What the steed is feeding on up there?[91]

Goritskaia volost' was only 50 km. away from Tver, in the most developed rural part of the guberniia which lay not far

[88] Bol'shakov, op. cit., pp. 303, 118.
[89] Ibid., pp. 301 ff.
[90] Pascal, op. cit., p. 80.
[91] Bol'shakov, op. cit., p. 385.

from the Moscow–Leningrad railway line. Greater isolation was to be found in the north of the guberniia, on the Mologa river. This was a left tributary of the Volga which meandered through forests and marshy plains, forming huge loops. It froze over in late October and stayed that way until April or May. Only a small part of it was navigable in summer. Nearly 70 per cent of the dry land was covered by conifers, birch, and aspen, with the occasional oak or linden tree. Through the peat bogs and woods roamed brown bears, roes, and wolves. Peasants could hunt for black grouse, capercaillies, and willow ptarmigans, or fish for bream, pike, and carp.

In 1926 members of the Tver pedagogical institute went up to survey the area and wrote a book on it called *Expedition to the Upper Mologa*.[92] For them it was indeed an adventure into the virtually unknown. They came across many ex-serfs among the older generation. Some of them had been dispatched there as children by a gentleman from Riazan' who had paid his debts at the card-table with them, handing them over to a Tver nobleman. In 1886 14 per cent of the local males had been literate. In 1926 about 50 per cent of them were still illiterate. Over 70 per cent of the women could not read or write. The chief source of income and food came from the forests, though little impression had been made on them by 1926. The railway was nowhere near, and it took a long time to float logs on the sinuous river to Rybinsk town. Income from lumber had nearly doubled between 1924 and 1926, nevertheless. Even in this remote area NEP was slowly having its effect on the peasants. A tiny housing boom was taking place, with many huts under construction. More children were being born and fathers were building huts for their eldest sons.[93]

Where open fields existed, the three-field system of cultivation was used by some Great-Russian peasants and by all those of Karelian origin who had arrived in the area in the seventeenth century. Some Russian peasants still applied agricultural methods that their Slav ancestors had brought with them when they settled the forests in the ninth and tenth centuries.[94]

---

[92] *Verkhne-Molozhskaia ekspeditsiia: izvestiia Tverskogo pedagogicheskogo instituta* (Tver, 1927).

[93] Ibid., pp. 12, 18, 23 ff., 112.

[94] Ibid., p. 43.

Most local artisans made and sold wooden articles inside the locality, including wheels, sledges, farm tools, and barrels, etc. In 1886 3.4 per cent of this group were engaged in selling their goods to outside areas, but by 1925 only 2.5 per cent were thus employed.[95] House-builders were virtually self-sufficient. They had no need of plaster, tiles, nor of nails. Wood sufficed. The izby they constructed would have been familiar to foreign travellers like Olearius or Mayerberg in the seventeenth century. The windows were slightly larger, and the chimneys had changed a little.

Only a third of the Upper Mologa peasants had ploughs. A samovar was a luxury. In any case, few could afford to buy tea, so they drank local apple or berry juice instead. In winter they kept themselves warm with an abundance of logs, cheap liquor, and the woollen clothes they made on their own looms. In winter, some children did not get to the distant school for lack of enough warm clothes or sturdy shoes. In summer they were sometimes kept back at home to help in the busy farming period.[96] The solitary teacher had to be paid for by the peasants. The schoolroom went unheated, and there were neither books nor discipline.[97]

Upper Mologa villages were not atypical. In another part of the guberniia in the village of Brylevo in Novotozhrskii uezd, the school was in a peasant's hut: seventy pupils were being crammed into it in 1925. The only object in the schoolroom cupboard was a whip. On rare occasions the local Komsomol would stage propaganda spectacles for the children.[98] There was no sign of the Komsomol in the Upper Mologa villages in 1926. There was a factory stationed 30 versts away from Brylevo, but none of the local peasants worked in it. There were only two winnowing machines in Brylevo, both of them owned by the same family. A rural Soviet did exist, but its energies were consumed in trying to extract taxes on orders from above.[99]

Life was not perpetually gloomy at the grass-roots level. In

---

[95] *Verkhne-Molozhskaia ekspeditsiia*, pp. 60, 93, 105.
[96] Ibid., p. 119.
[97] Ibid., p. 122.
[98] *Nasha praktika v derevne* (Moscow, 1925), p. 24.
[99] Ibid., p. 23.

Goritskaia volost' the peasantry could afford from four to six feast-days a year. Preparation began several days in advance. Huts were washed down, curtains ironed, and glad rags laid out for inspection. Home-made beer and *samogon* were brewed up in quantity. Early in the morning of the feast-day cooking began—meat soup, sweet soup, *kasha*. Women free from domestic duties put on their embroidered dresses and went to church. Guests trickled in from ten o'clock onwards to nibble *zakuski* and start drinking. After the church service the priest went round huts saying prayers, though by 1926 he was not welcome in all homes. At midday everyone sat down to eat until two o'clock. Children over five drank spirits with their elders. At three o'clock everyone began again, drinking tea, eating cow-heel jelly, rolls, and luxury pickled herrings. Then the young set began to dance quadrilles, or strut about, shooting off chastushki at the opposite sex. The proud possessor of an accordion would play into the night. Long, repetitive songs were chanted, and the men would start to brawl under the influence of drink. There were a lot of sore heads the following morning.[100]

Nearly four out of five of the total population of the Soviet Union in 1926 lived in similar general circumstances to those described in the last part of this chapter, although there were huge variations according to where one lived, and what one's ethnic origins were. What was general to all of them was the fact of still existing for the most part beyond the tentacles of the reforming Party and the cities, despite five years of NEP. These millions of people were to have no intimation of the sweeping policy changes that were to crash over them suddenly with devastating effects in 1928–9.

The massive social and economic centralization generated by the First Five-Year Plan was to be a direct, impatient reply to years of frustrated effort to use less violent means to bridge gaps. Instead of remaining largely in the realm of speculative theory, as was the case with the first utopian period during the Civil War, the typically Russian maximalist solution was firmly fixed in actuality, with devastating effects for the whole population. Some of the earlier utopian ideas lingered on in the

[100] Bol'shakov, op. cit., pp. 388–90.

second period, but they were now shorn of libertarian elements. The palimpsest of the writings of Marx and Engels was invoked again in order to advocate tight centralization.

Under Stalinism the effort to promote the gradual evolution of lower-level social organs for state purposes was to be abandoned. Rural culture was overrun by the towns with scant regard for indigenous traditions of long standing. The fact that town workers had to play the major role in the task of enforcing collectivization illustrates in social terms the complete failure of smychka in NEP. The buffers between town and country, the all-powerful centre and the masses, collapsed, revealing the clear outlines of an authoritarian political regime. Here was the classic social basis for a modern government of this type, as described by R. Aron, H. Arendt, and W. Kornhauser,[101] in which the atomized masses face their ruler without the protection of adequate intermediary institutions. Aron maintains that a kind of classless society existed in the Stalinist period. It was not the classless society envisaged by Marx, but one in which an élite controls a fragmented mass.

[101]  H. Arendt, *On Revolution* (London, 1963); R. Aron, 'Social Structure and Ruling Class', *British Journal of Sociology*, 1 (1950); W. Kornhauser, *The Politics of Mass Society* (London, 1960).

# 12. *Kazakhstan*

IF the learned members of the Tver pedagogical institute thought they were being adventurous in embarking upon an anthropological expedition to the Upper Mologa river, a mere 300 km. from Moscow, what would they have thought about doing a survey of Kazakhstan in 1926? Its western edges lay approximately 2,300 km. from the capital. Here was isolation indeed, though of a completely different geographical, socio-economic, and religious type from the solitudes of European Russia.

We have seen how agricultural and other local conditions had important effects on social and political life in Smolensk and above all in the Volga provinces in 1921–2. The area that became known as the Kazakh Autonomous Republic from 1924 onwards contained features which were completely different from any that we have encountered in other regions. These features were bound to have an enormous influence on political conduct. For this reason the geographical and ethnic contours of the area are surveyed first.

The borders of Kazakhstan continued to fluctuate after 1924, but in general outline it covered a territory of over 1,000,000 square miles stretching from the Volga delta to China. According to the 1926 census, out of a total population of 6,503,000, 91.7 per cent lived in rural areas and 8.3 per cent in towns.[1] Northern Kazakhstan is covered by vast steppes, beneath which lay one of the great mineral storehouses of the Soviet Union. Semi-desert or pure desert cover most of the rest of the Republic, apart from mountains in the south-east. The climate is continental, with hot summers and surprisingly cold winters. Precipitation is low throughout the Republic. The

---

[1] *Vsesoiuznaia perepis' naseleniia 1926 g.*, vol. 17 (Moscow, 1927), pp. 2–3.

steppe area with its good chestnut-coloured soil was dotted sparsely in the mid-1920s with villages surrounded by fields of wheat and stocks of sheep and cattle. Separated from each other by large distances were rough-hewn mining communities that still had a Wild East look about them in NEP. To the south of the steppe region aridity increases greatly. The south was very thinly inhabited, mainly by nomadic Muslim herdsmen of Kazakh origin. Administrative centres dominated by Great Russians lay like pins in a vast haystack over the region.

The ethnic situation was complicated. Great-Russian and Ukrainian administrators, peasants, and miners had colonized parts of northern and central Kazakhstan between the 1890s and the First World War. It was these groups, and not the Kazakhs, that had introduced settled agriculture. The colonial atmosphere was clearly indicated by the location of the first Soviet administrative capital, at Orenburg at the extreme north-western fringe. Only in 1925 was the capital of the newly formed Kazakh Autonomous SSR transferred to Kzyl-Orda in the centre of the steppes. This move separated the Volga Muslims from the Muslims of Central Asia and helped to stop once and for all the nationalist urge to unite Russia's Turkic peoples. In 1927 the capital was moved even further from Moscow, to Alma-Ata (formerly the Tsarist garrison of Verny) in the south-east corner of the Republic. Many Kazakhs lived beyond the borders of the new Republic in 1926, and vice versa many Kirghiz and other Central Asian nationalities wandered about the Republic. The Kazakhs and Kirghiz belong to the south-Siberian type formed as a result of the inbreeding of Central Asian Mongoloids with the ancient Caucasoid population of Kazakhstan.

How did the majority of Kazakhs live in 1926? Apart from occasional and rare photographs, the clearest indication can be gained by visiting the state museum of the ethnography of the peoples of the USSR.[2] In 1926 only 23 per cent of Kazakhs lived a settled life, though not all the nomadic majority travelled great distances any longer. Seven per cent of all Kazakhs migrated over 50 km. annually; 9.1 per cent over

---

[2] The author is indebted to the staff of this museum for their help during his visits to the section dealing with the Kazakhs.

25 km., 15.2 per cent over 10, and 34 per cent up to 10. Over a third of all Kazakhs dealt with livestock only. They were the ones most involved in the nomadic life: 24 per cent did agricultural field-work and 33.2 per cent mixed agriculture with livestock. The size of settled areas controlled by households varied greatly in 1926, from 28 to 328 desiatiny per person.[3]

It was a minority of the indigenous nationality, therefore, which lived permanently in conventional housing in the north. Larger numbers wintered in huts or round yourts made from clay, wood, or brick, then roamed south with portable yourts carried on pack-animals to grazing grounds for their livestock. During slack periods they fished (on Lake Balkash, in the Irtysh river), or made carpets and articles of felt and bone. Poorer families shared a simply furnished yourt, but richer households travelled in style. If you were invited to enter and drink tea in a summer tent, you would be served in a Chinese-style porcelain bowl filled from a Russian samovar. Tripping over the row of leather slippers inside the entry flap, you would be seated on a pile of silk cushions and blankets at a low round table covered with an embroidered cloth. At one side three or four carved wooden chests reared up against colourful hangings draped round the curving walls.

The most important organizational unit was the aul, or mobile village. The aul consisted of a number of tents whose occupants moved their herds along together. In winter an aul could reach 300 yourts, but in summer it declined to as little as fifteen tents on the move. In winter the larger conglomerations sheltered in the river-valleys against the wind and severe cold.[4] Since grazing areas were assigned by tradition to the individual aul, it was the most significant political unit, as will be seen later. Less fortunate Kazakhs in the north had been forced by Russian and Ukrainian settlers on to land marginal even for nomadic herding. Some Kazakhs worked as labourers for the incoming peasants, or for Cossacks. This had already led to deep resentment by the time of the Revolution.

European settlement in Kazakhstan was aggressive and

[3] G. F. Dakshleiger, *Sotsial'no-ekonomicheskaia preobrazovaniia v aule i derevne Kazakhstana 1921–1929* (Alma-Ata, 1965), pp. 229, 301, 309.
[4] According to the 1926 census, there were 70,000 winter auls in Kazakhstan.

eventually far-reaching in its effects. By 1916 Russification was a fact, although it was a thin spider's web suspended over the vast area. Caravan routes were slowly giving way to railways, and remote Cossack outposts were developing into towns and even small cities. One of the reasons for the tardy industrial development was the absence of an adequate transport system. In 1913 there was only half a mile of railway for every thousand square miles of territory. The vast expanse lying between the Orenburg–Tashkent Railway and the Russo-Chinese border had no rail communications whatever. Before the Revolution nineteen of Kazakhstan's twenty-eight towns were not connected by railway. Goods were transported chiefly by caravans of camels and carts. Camels were even used in taking coal to some of the factories. Road transport was practically unknown in pre-revolutionary days. Transportation of heavy equipment for hundreds of miles, using animals, was a difficult and, at times, an insoluble task.

In order to overcome these huge discrepancies between communications in European and Asiatic Russia, a large proportion of railway lines built during NEP were in Asia, or else connected Asia with Europe. In Central Asia a route was built from Djambul to Frunze, the capital of Kirghizia, and a line was constructed from Samsonovo to Termez. The route of the future Karaganda railway through Kazakhstan began to extend southwards from its starting point on the Trans-Siberian railway. The building of the Turksib railway was commemorated by a silent film, with captions like 'Civilization breaks through'. It is clear from its visual propaganda that culture came in the form of fit, muscular Russian workers standing out singly against hordes of stunted but beavering Asian labourers.

Where railways led the way into the vast interior of Kazakhstan, other facilities followed the same routes. In this part of the Soviet Union irrigation was more important than the telegraph lines which soon rose beside the tracks. In March 1926 a decree ordered irrigators to apply to the central authorities for permission to construct water-channels from navigable rivers and lakes. Far too many individual farmers were draining away public resources.[5] Not long afterwards the

[5] See *Postanovlenie soveta narodnogo kommissara KSSR* (Kzyl-Orda), 17 March 1926.

authorities called for much better irrigation near the railways, in order to service the steam locomotives and to exploit the bordering land. Water-tanks and soil advice were needed urgently. Only then would the local railways cease to be arrows piercing a barren hinterland. Settled communities would grow alongside, providing loads for the freight-wagons.[6] That water was the breath of life was fully realized by Moscow after 1925. The amount spent for irrigation in Kazakhstan rose from 1,017,000 roubles to 2,491,000 in 1926 and 6,755,000 by 1927.[7]

Obstacles to movement, and areas of rough terrain prohibiting settlement, were in fact remarkably few. Topographically, Kazakhstan is a huge lowland interrupted by only two regions of moderately high relief, the Mugodzhar hills and the Kazakh upland. The real mountains lie on the east and south-eastern boundaries. Despite this, modern road-building only got under way in 1924–5.[8] By 1928 there were a mere 22,559 km., including local dust tracks.[9] Navigable rivers were not plentiful. The Irtysh could take freight-boats for 1,642 km. and the Ural for 885. The Amur-Daria ran too swiftly, and its bed often changed course.[10] Air transport was non-existent until 1927–8, and thereafter vestigial for some time.[11] Over the vast area of Kazakhstan, there were only 110 post and telegraph offices by the end of NEP; 1,625 telephones spanned the void, whilst post was only delivered in a few settled areas.[12]

The development of communications, especially railways, was essential for the reorientation of the agricultural settlers in the area from a subsistence to a commercial basis. For example the turnover at an important annual *iarmarka*, or trading-fair, had gone up nearly three times between 1899 and 1913, simply because it was situated near Semipalatinsk, which had been linked to the railway system. Yet the 1899 volume of trade was only reached again by 1925. The reason for the renewed 'trade desert' was the lack of industrial and commercial goods to

[6] *Narodnoe khoziaistvo Kazakhstana*, 5 (Kzyl-Orda, 1927), p. 96.

[7] *10 let Kazakhstana 1920–1930* (Alma-Ata, 1930), p. 167.

[8] Ibid., p. 157.

[9] *Materialy k otchetu tsentral'nogo ispolitel'nogo komiteta KSSR na 3 sessii VTsIK 13 ogo sozyva* (Kzyl-Orda, 1928), p. 79.

[10] Ibid., p. 80.

[11] *10 let Kazakhstana*, p. 157.

[12] *Materialy*, p. 82.

exchange from the First World War until mid-NEP.[13] Even where railways existed in Central Asia, many transported goods were spoilt due to their extremely slow delivery.[14] Local technology was also wanting. To be exported to European Russia, Kazakh grain had to be in the form of flour, yet by the end of 1926 only 20 to 25 per cent of it could be milled in local plants.[15] By 1926–7 the only significant trading-nexuses in Kazakhstan remained the traditional iarmarki. The eight main ones had a turnover of 8 million roubles in 1925, jumping to 17.8 million by 1927. In contrast exports from the area to western Europe were worth a mere 28,000 roubles in 1927. Exports to China were valued at 27,000 roubles.[16]

Technical and economic communication systems may have been fragile in Kazakhstan in 1926, but human communications, particularly between the Kazakhs on the one hand and the Great Russians and Ukrainian settlers on the other, were even more tenuous and politically explosive. Traditional Kazakh mores combined with built-up resentment of their colonial masters that long predated 1917 and was not swept aside in any way by the Revolution. These were the greatest barriers against calm Soviet expansion into the hinterland. Oddly enough, it was not the Muslim faith of the Kazakhs that threw up the most daunting gulf. Kazakhs were not strict Muslims for the most part, and their womenfolk maintained a surprising amount of independence. A woman of outstanding personality who could run her aul and would be appointed as khan.[17]

We shall examine Kazakh political nationalism later on. Of course it was this that created the greatest barrier to Soviet infiltration. The rift was made wider by the discrepancies in educational levels between Kazakhs and Russians. In 1926 only one per cent of Kazakh women were literate, as opposed to 34 per cent of Russian females (the figures for males were 12 and 58 per cent respectively).[18] As late as 1929 only 11 per cent

---

[13] *Narodnoe khoziaistvo Kazakhstana*, 1, p. 82.

[14] Ibid., 2, p. 82.

[15] Ibid., 3, p. 7.

[16] *Materialy*, pp. 85–7.

[17] 'The Social Structure and Customs of the Kazakhs', *Central Asian Review*, 5/1 (1957).

[18] *Vsesouiznaia perepis'*, vol. 17, pp. 26–32.

of Kazakh girls were attending school. Nevertheless, the Soviet authorities did make enormous efforts from 1926 onwards to improve the situation. In 1926–7 no less than 1,545 new schools were opened in areas populated by Kazakhs. Until after 1927 illiterates were taught to read and write in the Arabic script. In that year 67,975 Kazakhs were struggling with this script, which had then to be followed up by a mastery of the Cyrillic alphabet. In 1928 only was a Latinized alphabet brought into common use. In 1922 there had existed fifty-two journals in the Kazakh language, with a total run of 18,400 copies. By 1926 fifty-six titles were being issued in 434,590 copies.[19]

Backwardness in education spelt traditionalism in agricultural methods. Whereas multi-field systems with crop rotation and ley farming had been adopted in parts of the RSFSR by mid-NEP, the fallow system remained far more common on land settled by Kazakhs. Peasants and semi-nomads cultivated a single crop—usually wheat—on one plot for several years in succession. After five to eight years, when the soil became exhausted, the plot was left to fallow for a similar period.[20] In other ways, however, as an expert on Kazakhstan has pointed out, Russians and Kazakhs alike were afflicted with similar problems from 1921 onwards. Most of them suffered from the after-effects of the Civil War, which raged in Central Asia as well as in European Russia. Both zones were hampered by lack of livestock, and both tried to extend their sown areas.

North-western Kazakhstan mirrored most closely the Lower Volga area in that both were hit by the famine of 1921–2. Forty per cent of Kazakh-owned lands were affected. The proportion of households without livestock rose from 3.5 per cent in 1920 to 27.8 per cent in 1923.[21] As in the Famine area of European Russia, this widened the gap between poorer and richer peasants. In the Kazakh auls, it was the bais who profited. Here the comparison stops. Although the Soviet authorities sitting in Moscow frequently put the bais (rich cattle-owners with up to 12,000 animals) into the same category as European '*kulaks*', the similarity was more apparent

[19] *10 let Kazakhstana*, pp. 292–8, 325–6.
[20] V. P. Danilov, *Rural Russia under the New Regime* (London, 1988), p. 271.
[21] Dakhshleiger, op. cit., p. 219.

than real, since different racial customs obliterated any genuine comparison.

In the distant future, Kazakh wheat-lands were to prove a blessing to All-Union agriculture, when Khrushchev embarked upon the Virgin Lands campaign in 1954. The spring crops of Kazakhstan were to provide an insurance against autumn crop failure in the Ukraine or the Lower Volga. Such a large-scale project was out of the question in the 1920s, mainly due to the lack of transport and technical infrastructure. Nevertheless, the eastern producer region of the USSR, including the Urals, Siberia, and the Far East as well as Kazakhstan, did improve far better than European Russia in the 1920s. The eastern region cropped about one to two million tons of surplus grain, as opposed to under one million before the Revolution.[22] This success resulted in part from investment policy in Kazakhstan. From 1924 to 1928 81.9 per cent of all investment went into agriculture, to the detriment of transport, which received only 6.5 per cent, and of industry, which got a paltry 6.7 per cent.[23]

Although grain production improved, the Kazakh way of life changed little, despite the fact that when the Bolsheviks came to power they made the settlement of the nomads an avowed goal. A decree of 1924 tried to enforce this,[24] but the campaign for the 'sovietization of the Kazakh aul' from 1925 to 1928 was unsuccessful. As we shall see in more detail, the local Kazakh authorities took over control of the rural Soviets and refused to introduce the policies sent down from Moscow. Unlike the situation in Smolensk or Tver, Kazakh party leaders in the area were reluctant to take strong measures against their co-nationals.

If agriculture was still backward in 1926, even by European Russian standards, then industry was almost non-existent compared to other parts of the USSR. By 1926 a mere 18,200 workers were in large-scale industry in Kazakhstan. A higher

---

[22] S. G. Wheatcroft, *Soviet Agricultural Production in the 1920s and 1930s*, paper presented to a *Table ronde* on the industrialization of the USSR in the 1930s (Paris, Dec. 1981).

[23] G. Chulanov, *Ocherki istorii narodnogo khoziaistva Kazakhskoi SSR* (Alma-Ata), pp. 50–1.

[24] H. Chambre, 'Le Kazakhstan: Tiers-monde soviétique?', in *Union soviétique et développement économique* (Paris, 1967), p. 261.

figure, 20,600, were employed in transport, and a further 4,800 laboured on construction sites. The 1913 level of employment was only regained in 1928, but it is interesting to note that Kazakhs were beginning to enlist as industrial workers at a faster rate than other ethnic groups in Kazakhstan.[25] By 1926 2.5 per cent of Kazakhs were occupied in industry and other manual labour inside Kazakhstan: this compares with 6.6 per cent of native Ukrainians similarly engaged within the Ukraine.[26] Local ethnic traditions, once again, presented a greater hurdle than ownership or class relations to the Party's policy of forming an advanced working class throughout the Soviet Union. For a Muslim nomad or semi-nomad to move to a town like Karaganda and adapt to industrial labour was far more difficult than for a peasant from Tver guberniia to commute, perhaps for the winter months only, to Tver city to work there. In the 1920s it was still more expensive to train native Kazakh workers than to import labour from the European zones. Just over half industrial workers of *all* types in Kazakhstan were to be found in three main mining regions. Most of them worked in the north and the north-eastern towns of the narrow mining belt, which was interspersed with fortresses and trading centres. This belt spanned Kazakhstan from Ural'sk on the river Ural in the north-west, to the river Irtysh in the north-west, and then southwards along it to the foothills of the Altai mountains and the oasis zones in the south-east mountainous area.

Kustari are included under this head. In 1925 they made up no less than 95 per cent of all types of workers, whose total came to 54,087.[27] Most kustari were employed in food industries (wheat, tobacco, oil-pressing, flour-milling), felt, metalwork, and woodwork. Others worked on a very small scale in mines near the surface and those with insignificant deposits. The biggest money turnover in the kustar sector was in flourmilling; it was noted earlier that demand did not meet the need in this process. The lowest turnover was for kustari who made

[25] See A. N. Nusupbekov, *Formirovanie i razvitie sovetskogo rabochego klassa v Kazakhstane (1917–1940) gg.* (Alma-Ata, 1966), pp. 36, 38, 147.
[26] Iu. V. Arutiunian, 'Izmenenie sotsial'noi struktury sovetskikh natsii', *Istoriia SSSR*, 4 (1972), p. 4.
[27] First Party Conference, Oct.–Nov. 1926, p. 17.

tents for nomads. The dominant type of kustar was far more like the near self-subsistent backwoodsman in Tver guberniia than the roving wholesaler with wide connections. The aspect of even a major mining-centre like Karaganda in 1926 revealed the continuing small-scale nature of Kazakh industry. Karaganda was more a widely strung-out series of settlements round individual mineshafts than a concentrated urban mass. The first systematic geological surveys did not begin here until 1928; a modern centre was constructed from 1936 on.[28] Photographs of the Karaganda area taken near the end of NEP show scattered shanty villages on a great rolling steppe, serviced by bullock-carts struggling along dust tracks.[29] The national and political aspirations of the Kazakhs were played out in the mid-1920s against the socio-economic background portrayed above, and to a great extent governed by it. In order to gauge local ethnic feeling in Kazakhstan around 1926, it is necessary to look first at some of the broader aspects of nationalist movements in the Soviet Union.

The general situation from 1922 onwards was given in Chapter 7.[30] It will be recalled that nationalist sentiment against the Great Russians took three main forms. Outright opposition was most clearly shown in Soviet Central Asia by the aim of the Turk, Enver Pasha, to liberate the whole of Turkestan from Soviet rule. This dream soon faded, as did also by early 1923, with the arrest of Sultan Galiev, the hope that the sovietization of non-Russian territories of the Union would mean freedom from Russian domination rather than its acceptance.

The third and more lasting type of opposition came from within the ranks of Soviet communism. In Kazakhstan this came in the form of the Alash Orda, whose members began to join the Party between February 1917 and the end of the Civil War. They were still active in 1926, though they were to be eliminated as a political force in 1928. Like other Muslim Bolsheviks, such as the Young Bukharians and the Young Khivians in Central Asia, they were attracted by Lenin's vague

---

[28] T. Ia. Barag, *Karaganda* (Moscow, 1950), pp. 11–12.

[29] A. A. Gapeev, *Karaganda i ee znachenie v industrializatsii SSSR* (Moscow, 1931), p. 23.

[30] Chapter 7, pp. 250–61 above.

promise in his 'April theses' to give Muslims the right of secession. They noted the incompetence of the White Armies, and lent an ear to Stalin's attempts to woo the radical elements in the national movements.[31] If members of the Bolshevik Party Central Committee could not sort out the ambiguities and caveats in Lenin's and Stalin's statements, *a fortiori* remote Kazakh intellectuals were apt to accept hopeful omens and turn a deaf ear to less encouraging signs for the future.

From the arrest of Sultan Galiev in 1923 until 1928 an uneasy truce existed between Bolshevik Muslim nationalists and the Party. Soviet official sources still claim, without going into the question in sufficient detail for scholarly corroboration, that Sultan Galiev left behind him a wide network of Soviet underground organizations in which the Alash Orda, among other groups, was involved with such outright opponents of all things Soviet as the counter-revolutionary Basmachis.[32]

The Soviet official view may or may not be believed. What is clearer is that Kazakh party members were not in as strong a position as some other Muslim activists to promote nationalist tendencies. The reasons for this are the following. The Alash Orda realized that on its own it was hardly likely to be in a position to exert much influence on the Party as a whole. Other national minorities in the mid-1920s entered into close relationships with each other in order to consolidate their claims. The Kazakhs' obvious partner in such a venture were the Uzbeks, but there were several snags in such an arrangement. Literate Kazakhs lived mainly at Russian headquarters like Orenburg, Akmolinsk, and Semipalatinsk. They outnumbered literate Uzbeks, who lived in Central Asia's ancient cities, in both absolute and relative numbers by 1926.[33] Unfortunately, although educated Kazakhs were better located in crucial places for influencing opinion, there were three times more Uzbeks than Kazakhs in all the professions apart from higher education in 1926.[34] This fact did not escape the Party's

[31] A. Bennigsen and M. Broxup, *The Islamic Threat to the Soviet State* (London, 1983), pp. 81–5.
[32] Ibid., p. 85.
[33] *Vsesoiuznaia perepis'*, vol. 8, pp. 15–16, 200–1; vol. 15, pp. 8–9.
[34] Ibid., vol. 25, pp. 70–2, 167–71, 243–51; vol. 32, pp. 76–83, 177–82.

attention. From 1925 on the possibility that the Uzbeks would be a strong partner for the Kazakhs was prevented by restrictions imposed on their movements inside the newly formed internal borders within Soviet Central Asia.

Two other nationalist symbols of the Kazakhs, their religion and their language, were also not as strongly deployed as they were in other ethnic cases. We have already observed that the Kazakhs were neither as orthodox nor as fanatical as other Muslim minorities in the Soviet Union. Thus they could not rely on the potent political fires ignited by religious fervour. The very high level of illiteracy among Kazakhs as late as 1926 made it that much easier for the Russians to indoctrinate whilst they taught. Many new Russian and international terms were introduced into the Kazakh language, particularly in areas of political significance, so that abstract political concepts could be given a Bolshevik slant. Thus Kazakh and other Muslim intellectuals gradually lost control over the minds and thoughts of their less well educated co-nationals.

The temporary balance of forces between Russian communists in Kazakhstan and the Alash Orda and its supporters is discernible in the careers of two eminent Kazakhs in the years 1925–6. The leading Kazakh poet at this time was Magjan Jumabay-uli. He was now losing his earlier hopes, expressed in lyrical lines, for an independent Central Asia. Instead he gave vent to his growing disillusionment in books of verse entitled *Olim—Ajal* (Death) and *Karkit* (The Camelskin Bag).[35] A Kazakh historian who ventured more directly into politics was Turar Ryskulov. Born into a rich nomadic family from the Semirechie region of Kazakhstan, he joined the national movement before the First World War. He joined the Soviet Communist Party in September 1917, and despite his continuing nationalist leanings went on up the political career ladder to become chairman of the Sovnarkom of the Turkestan Republic in 1923. Yet by mid-NEP his career, like the fate of all Kazakh nationalists in communist ranks, was in the balance, and soon on the decline. In 1925 he was holding an insignificant post as Comintern representative in Mongolia, away from his native land. By 1926 he was demoted further,

[35] G. Togzhanov, 'Kazakhskaia literatura', *Literaturnaia entsiklopediia*, vol. 5 (Moscow, 1931), pp. 20–1.

and still in exile, as head of the press department of the Caucasian Regional Commission of the Party. He was to be arrested in 1927, and executed in February 1938.

The vital Soviet blow against the Muslim Republics as a whole took place two years after 1926. It began in the Crimea, and in the same year, 1928, the Kazakh Alash Orda was eliminated. This political move coincided with the forced settlement of Kazakh nomads. The nomadic life, together with linguistic and religious separateness, had been the chief symbols of Kazakh independence from Russian ways of life. Its gradual extermination, and the imposition of collectivization, meant more in Central Asia than, say, in Tver or Smolensk. It spelt the final Russian victory over both nationalist cultural and political strivings in Kazakhstan.

Yet the fatal twist of the Russian knife was in fact a reaction to a final burst of independent nationalist energy. As late as 1927 a precarious majority of the party leadership in the Republic was still in the hands of the nationalists whose chief aim was to implement land reform at the expense of the Russian (and Ukrainian) agricultural settlers. A party conference went so far as to decree that Kazakhs should have precedence in matters of land distribution. As a result Russians and Ukrainians were ejected from their productive farms and resettled on poor ground. This was more than the central Soviet authorities could stomach. Nationalist elements were quickly removed from the Kazakhstan party, and another conference was held which agreed on the equality of all nationalities with regard to the distribution of land. These convulsions seemed an admirable opportunity to introduce socialist principles with the changes, but by 1928 less than 4 per cent of all livestock in Kazakhstan had changed hands, and a mere 200,000 hectares of land nationalized.[36]

In 1922 Bukharin had pointed out in the case of Georgia that the national minorities were peasant areas which were being alienated by Russian centralist, proletarian domination. For him the basic Marxist-Leninist notion of smychka, town and country alliance, was under threat. Bukharin's view was an exact echo of Sultan Galiev's view of the fate of the minorities.

---

[36] See M. B. Olcott, *Socio-economic Change and Political Development in Soviet Central Asia* (Chicago, 1978), pp. 251–7.

If smychka was hard to attain in Georgia in 1922, it was an utterly utopian ideal in Kazakhstan in 1926. However could Great-Russian miners and soldiers get together with Muslim nomads and semi-nomads? The Revolution had not changed the colonial juxtaposition one jot in this respect.

Although Kazakhstan was enormous in size, and Georgia relatively tiny, Georgia was more of a threat to Russian hegemony. Above all it had diplomatic links with several Western powers in 1922, and was accessible by sea from the west. The Kazakhs were still remote and isolated in 1926, even from their closest allies, the Uzbeks. The only danger for the Bolsheviks in Kazakhstan was that in a distant border area of this type ethnic differentials were better preserved and might acquire eccentric dynamics of their own. This is what happened at the first, nationalist-dominated conference of 1927. In an area where it was extremely difficult to bring two very disparate cultures into quick harmony, the temptation for the Russians was to impose a solution by force. This is precisely what took place from 1917 to 1928 apart from three years' uneasy truce between 1924 and 1927. The Civil War in Russian Central Asia raged from 1917 to 1924, and force was reapplied to Kazakh institutions from 1927 onwards.

Lenin was right in thinking that Great-Russian nationalism was far more formidable and ruthless than that of the minorities.[37] It was still natural in the 1920s for all colonial and other great powers to act in an authoritarian manner towards the least developed regions of the world under their sway. The Soviet Union was not alone in this. As late as 1937, in the Wajaristan war, the British were acting just as ruthlessly towards Pathan rebels in a part of the world not far from Kazakhstan. It has been estimated, however, that over one and a half million Kazakhs lost their lives in the decade of the 1930s.[38] Almost 80 per cent of their herds were annihilated in the years 1928–32.[39] At least the British Empire in India did not indulge in such large-scale atrocities.

Moving on now from the nationalist struggle to the practical

---

[37] Lenin, *Sochineniia*, vol. 20 (4th edn., Moscow, 1941–51), pp. 383–4.
[38] N. Jasny, *The Socialized Agriculture of the USSR* (Stanford, 1941), p. 323.
[39] *10 let Kazakhstana*, p. 209.

details of party and Soviet organization in Kazakhstan, the most surprising feature that confronts us is the fact that in 1927 there were enough activist Kazakhs in the Party to push through, albeit temporarily, that decree on land redistribution which favoured their rights over those of the Russian and Ukrainian settlers. By 1 October 1925, as T. R. Ryskulov tells us, only 68.5 per cent of all those involved in party organization in Kazakhstan were Russians. The total number from all ethnic groups was 30,447, but of these only 14,438 were party members. By 1 June 1926 there were 17,083 members, of whom 54.4 per cent were peasants, 25.6 workers and 15.4 officials. At this date Ryskulov claims that 37.3 per cent of all party members were Kazakhs.[40] Another source gives this percentage as 44.1, adding that in 1926 Kazakhs had the fourth highest guberniia committee representation of all the national minorities in the USSR.[41] According to the party census, in 1927 29 out of every 1,000 Kazakhs were communist.[42] On an All-Union basis, this was still a drop in the ocean: Kazakhs made up 1.05 per cent of all Soviet communists in 1927. In 1922 they had not been differentiated from the Kirgiz, and their combined proportion had been 1.3 per cent.[43]

It is necessary to look back briefly into the history of local party structure in order to find the reasons for the comparatively high number of Kazakhs which disguised their own eventual weakness and the shaky state of the Kazakhstan Party as a whole.

The distinctive political culture of the Kazakhs in their own history hardly trained them for their future role in the tight-knit Bolshevik Party. Their indigenous organizational units were very loosely defined and normally lacked authority except at the grass-roots level. The only large-scale political groupings were the hordes, which had been formed in the seventeenth century. They functioned independently of one another. Each horde was made up of a number of tribes which recognized a single khan. He was hardly ever powerful enough to unite the

[40] T. R. Ryskulov, *Kazakhstan* (Moscow, 1927), pp. 89–91.
[41] L. Dmitrenko, 'Sostav mestnykh partiinikh komitetov v 1924–1927 gg.', *Istoricheskie zapiski*, 79 (1966), p. 107.
[42] *Sotsial'nyi i natsional'nyi sostav VKP(b). Itogi vsesoiuznoi partiinoi perepisi* (Moscow, 1928), p. 114.
[43] Ibid.

different tribes in his horde. Far more significant as a strong organizational unit was the aul. This traditional localization of power did not shift to a more centralized system during the 1920s.

The immediate need for the Russian Bolsheviks after 1917, however, was to build up the Party from above. Yet the central apparatus itself remained badly split right up to 1926. There were serious divisions between leading Russian and Ukrainian party members up to 1925. These were self-caused by tough infighting between primitive ex-peasants and somewhat violent political bosses and mining workers in northern Kazakhstan towns. Nevertheless a naïvely propagandist 1936 history of the Party asserted that these splits were the result of 'bad bai-kulak influences in the Party'.[44] Party members were accused further of quarrelling among themselves yet again in 1926–7 when they were said to have got caught up in the 'Trotsky–Zinoviev opposition'. The local opposition was reviled as a 'counter-revolutionary group', trying to satisfy the demands of the aul bais and rejecting the proletarian line. Kazakh nationalism during NEP was ascribed neatly in the Stalinist diatribe of 1936 to the 'sharpness of the class struggle' fomented by the local 'bourgeois (*sic*) youth' in Kazakhstan![45]

This opposition bloc, which was a real one, even allowing for the naïve Stalinist interpretation, was removed from the Party after the sixth regional party conference in November 1927. The new local party leader, F. I. Goloshchekin, a Great Russian, ejected all the Kazakh leaders. Even he admitted that as late as November 1926 the party bureaucracy at the *kraikom* level had three different and uncoordinated heads.[46]

If disunity was rife at the top level, the situation was even worse down below. Goloshchekin had been exhorting the Party to build up from below rather than from above from 1925 onwards.[47] Yet he admitted in that year that originally 'healthy' Kazakh nationalists either became victims of intrigue due to local pressures, or else quit politics under the stress and became small-time bureaucrats.[48] In 1926 Goloshchekin

[44] *Iz istorii partiinogo stroitel'stva v Kazakhstane* (Alma-Ata, 1936), pp. 81–2.
[45] Ibid., pp. 83, 80.
[46] Ibid., p. 194.
[47] F. I. Goloshchekin, *Partiinoe stroitel'stvo v Kazakhstane* (Moscow, 1930), p. 65.
[48] Ibid., p. 10.

reported that 20 per cent of all party members were located in the auls (6,374 members), yet he declared in the same speech 'We may be able to create a large bureaucratic apparatus but there will still not be any proper social organization.'[49] He was referring obliquely to political problems at the aul level that were caused by social conditions.

In 1924 over 2,000 members of the Kazakh Party were illiterate, and most of these lived in the auls.[50] The bais were all-powerful in the auls, together with the mullahs and the *aksakals* (village elders), and it was usually they who decided on the distribution of party cards. In the Semipalatinsk region in 1926 they were even asked by the central authorities to suggest new party members.[51] Other local party auls were set up on the Kazakh kin principle. The custom became so widespread that already in 1925 608 bais were rounded up and exiled beyond the borders of Kazakhstan.[52] What the Russians saw as corruption, the Kazakh auls viewed as the continuance of their old political culture.

What hope then for smychka in the auls, let alone in the desert caravan? Apart from unreliable party members and the Komsomol, there were no agents of any kind, whether good or bad, for the Bolshevik cause, to confront the bais and the mullahs. In his more lucid moments, Goloshchekin realized the absurdity of applying European party methods to Central Asia: 'We are setting up Soviets in the auls as if we were in Kursk, Tver or the gubernii in Central Russia. This is the fundamental error.'[53] In the same speech, however, he insists in applying false European, pseudo-Marxist criteria to the Kazakh situation: 'In the auls there *must* be middle peasants between the bais and the poor peasants.'[54]

These quotations come from a speech made by Goloshchekin in 1926 to the sixth conference of the Kazakhstan Komsomol. He opened it with a self-condemnation: 'We carry within ourselves the traces and the inheritance of the damned past' (a

---

[49] Ibid., pp. 63, 58.
[50] 'Za sozdanie massovoi bolshevistkoi part-organizatsii v Kazakhstane', in Goloshchekin, op. cit., pp. 20–1.
[51] Goloshchekin, op. cit., p. 66.
[52] *Iz istorii*, p. 88.
[53] Goloshchekin, op. cit., p. 70.
[54] Ibid., p. 67.

reference to Great-Russian nationalism).[55] He went on to urge the Komsomol, the only plausible agent in the steppes, to gird itself for more effective action. He pointed out that as of 1926 the Komsomol was weakly based even in the towns, and consisted mainly of employees, bureaucrats, and 'even traders'. Goloshchekin showed a certain sensitivity to rural conditions. He told his youthful audience that they would have to behave more delicately than their equivalents in European Russia. It was no use leaving the towns for one day in order to survey aul elections. In areas where Komsomol members had to cover strung-out series of Kazakh winter huts, where there were no school buildings, but only semi-literate mullahs and no churches, more time and energy had to be expended than in a European Russian village of between 50 to 100 concentrated households.[56] After all, there were a mere 51,850 Komsomol members and candidates at the end of 1925 out of a population of over 6 million.[57] The number of women in the *Zhenotdel* for Kazakhstan was minimal in the same period—123 in all.[58] By 1927 there were 437 women party members, 307 of whom were candidates.[59] In 1928 only 11 per cent of Kazakh girls were attending schooling of any kind (contrasted with 33.7 per cent of Russian girls).[60]

If the party structure was still shaky in 1926, the hierarchy of the Soviets was even more vestigial. Before 1925 there were only nine town Soviets in Kazakhstan, although fourteen more were set up in 1925–6. They had no budgets of their own to administer until 1927. They also lacked influence due to the fact that they were made up almost entirely of Russians. In 1926 this situation was remedied slightly with the establishment of separate ethnic town Soviets. The ethnic and other complexities of Kazakhstan can be seen from the several varieties of Soviet that were set up—to mention only four of them, for Ukrainians, Tartars, Volga Germans, and Cossacks.[61]

At the aul level Soviets were usually non-existent in 1926. Where they survived weakly, they were often convened briefly

[55] Goloshchekin, op. cit., pp. 51–2.
[56] Ibid., pp. 53–4.
[57] Ryskulov, op. cit., p. 93.
[58] Ibid., p. 94.
[59] *Sotsial'nyi i natsional'nyi sostav*, p. 122.
[60] *10 let Kazakhstana*, pp. 71, 293.
[61] *Materialy*, pp. 26–7.

in order to elect a chairman (usually the richest bai) and then dispersed until the next election. Only in 1928 did they begin to resemble their European equivalents in any way.[62] What was dubbed as an 'illegal tribal administration' prevailed in the rural Soviets: it was so powerful that 'the bai and the *atkamyner* (chieftain) in fact rule the economic and social life of the aul'.[63] Another report dating from 1926 affirmed that local Soviets were 'a fiction'.[64] On the steppes Soviets occasionally existed in rather more settled 'villages' than the auls. These were the *kishlaks*, which were quite influential, since they had more funds and were trading-centres, besides being more permanent in character. The trouble was that they were dominated, not by Kazakhs, but by trading Uzbeks and Dungans who had more liquid cash. This led to more ethnic complexities at the local level.[65]

There were also considerable administrative changes. At the grass roots the 70,000 auls of Kazakhstan in 1926[66] were mostly nomadic outside the winter season. Each basic Soviet administrative area comprised twenty to thirty auls. The area was constantly changing in size according to shifting nomadic routes. There was also scant administrative stability at large-scale levels in the second half of NEP. In 1925 the capital of the Kazakh Autonomous SSR, as it was then called, was moved from Orenburg at the far north-western edge to Kzyl-Orda in the middle of the steppes. Orenburg was then separated from Kazakhstan. Within a mere two years the capital was shifted once again to Alma-Ata, which lay on the south-eastern frontier of Kazakhstan, 1,850 km. away from Orenburg. The Kazakh republic itself had only been founded in 1924.

These two large-scale administrative changes were introduced by the Bolsheviks in order respectively to penetrate the Kazakh steppes more easily, and to cut off one minority nationality from another and so divide and rule. There were two other broad reasons, both of which applied in European as well as in Asiatic Russia, and were discussed in Chapter 5.

[62] Ibid., p. 19.
[63] A. P. Kuchkin, *Sovetizatsiia kazakhskogo aula 1926–1928 gg.* (Moscow, 1962), p. 156.
[64] Goloshchekin, op. cit., p. 73.
[65] *Materialy*, p. 24.
[66] Ibid., p. 12.

Administrative changes were needed by a regime which had a dynamic rather than the Tsarist passive view of political and socio-economic organization. Both regimes maintained a rigidly centralized attitude towards administrative control, since both were authoritarian in character, and both were made more so by the virtually identical problems of size and complexity that faced them. These difficulties remained practically the same for the Bolsheviks, since the old Empire was all but re-formed as the Soviet Union. Relaxations in other spheres in early NEP did not lead to administrative decentralization.[67]

The second Bolshevik reason for so much administrative relocation was unique to them. They were intent on shifting quickly the balance between the agricultural and the industrial sectors in favour of the latter. There was an urgent need to set up new urban nexuses which would dominate their agricultural hinterlands and revitalize them. This was a special reason for setting up two new Kazakh capitals in so many years.

It was noted in Chapter 5 that Gosplan's new economic regions were established, if only on paper, as early as 1923.[68] By the end of 1925 many of the strategically and ethnically sensitive edges of the USSR had completed their administrative reforms, whereas European Russia had scarcely been affected.[69] Kazakhstan's turn came very shortly thereafter. The continuation of the Civil War until 1924 in Central Asia held up sweeping changes at first, but when they came, from 1925–6 onwards, they were more drastic and more ruthless than in other peripheral areas of the country.

Before looking in more detail at the practical changes that occurred, the reasons for their draconic nature must be sought out. Soviet Central Asia, and the newly formed Kazakhstan in particular, was a most suitable case for radical treatment, since it was a virtual *tabula rasa* on which it was easier to make a deep impression quickly. It was nearly a vacuum in terms of population, of previous industrialization, and of conventional European methods of agriculture. Its indigenous inhabitants either could not read or write, or else wrote in an alien language drawn from an alien culture. A second reason for a

[67] Above, p. 145.     [68] Above, p. 181.     [69] Above, p. 183.

show of strength was mounting Kazakh nationalism, both outside and within the Party, which culminated in the 1927 decree against the existing settlement provisions for Russians and Ukrainians in northern Kazakhstan. This was a far more palpable obstruction to Soviet aims than the so-called '*kulak*' threat in European Russia. The third reason was connected with that undercurrent of continued militarism which pervaded the management of European Russia in 1922, and had not quite died out by 1926. Kazakhstan experienced only two to three years' respite from warlike conditions, from 1924 to 1926–7, a much shorter lull than, say, in Kursk or Tver gubernii, both of which avoided the worst effects of the Civil War (and the famine), and were not to suffer such aggressive measures again until the collapse of NEP. In a region like Central Asia, highly unsettled conditions were the norm rather than the exception from 1917 to 1928.

A final reason lay in the political rise and personality of Stalin. The ex-Commissar for the Nationalities had already shown his ruthlessness and dispatch in dealing with his own nation, Georgia, in early NEP. It was hardly likely that he would be less aggressive in dealing with a weak, remote, and non-Christian nationality; Stalin's early career as a seminarist in Georgia should not be forgotten, nor his general aversion to most of the national minorities, such as the Jews, etc. In any case, a general clamp-down was about to occur in 1926–7 on the activities of all the national minorities, not excluding the largest of them—the Ukraine.[70]

Let us now turn to look at the practical results of such a policy. On 10 December 1925 the first trade-fair was opened at the new capital, Kzyl-Orda. Unlike trade in European Russia and Siberia, which was still strongly influenced by the Nepmen at this time, 88 per cent of the sellers in Kzyl-Orda were state-controlled, with only 9 per cent co-operative, and 3 per cent private. The wholesale sector here was now dominated by the state, and even in the retail sector private dealers could only compete in trade in shoes, leather goods, and cattle. Kazakhs flocked to the Kzyl-Orda fair in large numbers. They were traditionally attracted to the iarmarki, and the Soviet authorities

[70] Above, p. 259.

played on this in order to induce them to move over into state trading as fast as possible.[71]

By a decree of 2 June 1926, all trade and industrial institutions in Kazakhstan were ordered peremptorily to subscribe to a news-sheet on workers' and peasants' law. On the same day another decree proclaimed that all the necessary agricultural state farms (*sovkhozy*) would be established by 1927 at the latest.[72] In actual fact, 11.7 thousand hectares of sovkhoz land were sown in 1926; by the end of 1928 44.1 thousand hectares were covered, and the plan projected for 1929–30 looked for a total of 173.5.[73] By mid-1928 Kazakhstan also contained the third largest average individual kolkhoz (collective farm) land area in the Soviet Union (226.6 hectares).[74]

These measures were an omen of what was to happen soon in the rest of the Soviet Union. Kazakhstan was the guinea-pig. Besides being premature, swift, and large-scale in nature, these moves were bungled, as they were to be in the rest of the country later. The promulgation of the 1926 decree occurred in June, when the nomadic and semi-nomadic Kazakhs were away in their summer pastures, and thus out of touch with what was going on. That this was not intended maliciously was proved by the subsequent finding that local party and Soviet organizations were equally unaware of the campaign for some time.[75]

On the industrial front large-scale activities, as opposed to hopeful words, also began in 1926, earlier than in European Russia. One hundred extra candidates were trained to administer at a higher level in the government bureaucracy under a special scheme for the promotion of cadres (*vydvzhenstvo*). Later a census was carried out to find out how many employees in the government sector knew the Kazakh language.[76] Efforts were now made to boost the output of the local mineral wealth. By 1926 coal production in Kazakhstan had dropped to a mere

---

[71] *Narodnoe khoziaistvo Kazakhstana*, 1, pp. 91–2.
[72] Ibid., 2, p. 151.
[73] *10 let Kazakhstana*, pp. 166–7.
[74] Gosplan SSSR, *Sdvigi v sel'skom khoziaistve SSSR mezhdu 15 i 16 partiinymi s'ezdami. Statisticheskie svedeniia po sel'skomu khoziaistvu SSSR za 1927–1930 gg.* (Moscow, 1931), pp. 22–5.
[75] Dakhschleiger, op. cit., p. 315.
[76] *Materialy*, pp. 30–1.

16.51 per cent of pre-1914 output, partly due to the exit of British and French entrepreneurs after 1917. Oil production had only dropped 4 per cent over the same period.[77] The sown area of cotton for industrial use in the Republic jumped from 39,652 hectares in 1925 to 56,860 in 1926, and then sloped off to 67,482 by 1927.[78] In 1926 the construction of the Turksib railway also began. When finished, this line was intended to allow the movement southwards of cheap Siberian wood and wheat. It would also facilitate the expansion southwards of the cotton industry, together with the spread of tobacco and rice cultivation.[79]

Frequently predictions in 1926 of Kazakhstan's brilliant industrial, proletarian future smacked 'more than a little of extravagant utopianism thrown up in order to obfuscate painful, backward realities. A railway engineer estimated that when the Turksib was completed 'Kazakhstan will play a leading role on the world market for non-ferrous metals'. Since Semipalatinsk lay on the line, and was also connected with the Arctic and so the Atlantic via the Irtysh and Ob' rivers, the engineer imagined that Western Europe would soon provide a greedy market for all kinds of exports from Kazakhstan.[80] Other dreamers in the previous century, and not all of them Russian, had indulged in similar fantasies. Captain Joseph Wiggins is the only British trader who has ever tried to make a profit out of shipping English goods in the 1880s round the North Cape, along the Russian Arctic coast and up the great length of the Ob'.[81] An English Member of Parliament bought up tracts of land near the new railway line around Samara on the Volga before the turn of the century: he was sure that land prices would rise by the side of the track, as they had done in Britain.[82]

[77] Ibid., pp. 66–7.

[78] Ibid., p. 47.

[79] Ibid., p. 78.

[80] G. F. Prokopovich, 'Problemy zheleznodorozhnoi stroitel'stva v Kazakhstane', *Narodnoe khoziaistvo Kazakhstana*, 2 (Kzyl-Orda, 1926), pp. 95–107.

[81] See H. J. Johnson, *The Life and Voyages of Joseph Wiggins* (London, 1907), pp. 278, 375.

[82] F. Burnaby, *A Ride to Khiva: Travels and Adventures in Central Asia* (London, 1877), p. 57. A typical Russian utopian of this breed in the 19th was Count N. Muravev, Governor-General of Eastern Siberia. He had the vision of Russian exploitation of the western Pacific. See C. Vevier, *Siberian Journey Down the Amur to the Pacific 1856–57* (Madison, 1962).

Prognostications in 1926 for the future development of irrigation in Kazakhstan were just as naïvely grandiose as plans for trade promotion. An agricultural expert believed that by means of voluntary co-operatives most of the desert area of the region would be a green paradise within twenty years.[83] In the realm of electrification, a favourite focus for utopian notions since Lenin's concentration on the subject, another engineer in 1926 estimated blithely that several [Marxist] stages of economic development could be skipped over in Kazakhstan. The electrical 'skeleton' for future industrial centres could be constructed at once. If *'udarnost''* ('shock tactics') were applied, one gigantic and two more modest electric stations could be built within two years. They would go up near existing industrial centres like Karaganda. Other areas of human settlement would have to wait for electricity for a considerable time.[84]

These utopian visions were redolent of the climate that was soon to pervade the whole of the Soviet Union. Gigantism, ruthless shock tactics, unattainable economic plans, and above all complete disregard for human suffering were to be typical symptoms of Stalinism. As we have seen, Kazakhstan was perceived from Moscow to be a suitable case for early treatment. In a similar way Hitler, a refugee from his own ethnic origins like Stalin, was to single out the Ukraine as the German bread-basket of the future. Seen from Berlin, the Ukraine was remote, backward, alien, and inferior. Stalin's efforts in Kazakhstan came to grief for the most part in the early 1930s, although it is true that Khrushchev's plans for the Republic from 1954 were more realistic and better fulfilled. In 1926 it was simply too early to expect instant miracles. Moscow, and its living-standards and planners' visions, were still a world apart from Central Asia and Siberia. The viewpoint of the Siberian peasant who questioned Chekhov on his journey to Sakhalin in 1890 could scarcely have changed by 1926. 'Are you from Russia, your Honour?' 'Yes', replied Chekhov, the

[83]    M. M. Davydov, 'Obshchie predposylki k vodokhoziaistvennomu planu na blizhaishie 15–20 let do iuzhnoi chasti KASSR', *Narodnoe khoziaistvo Kazakhstana*, 4 (1929), p. 7.
[84]    L. E. Vitsman, 'Planovaia elektrifikatsiia Kazakhstana', *Narodnoe khoziaistvo Kazakhstana*, 4 (1926), pp. 62–5.

European *intelligent*. 'Never been there myself', replied the Siberian.

Let us leave Kazakhstan and this review of society and politics in NEP at the practical local level where we started. In the spring of 1922 a peasant woman from a village near Roslavl' in Smolensk guberniia rose at dawn, carried out her daily tasks and then took off to Roslavl' to see her soldier son. In the autumn of 1926 imagine one of the wives of a prosperous Kazakh nomad preparing one morning to take down the yourt for the last time that travelling season. The only visible connection between her life and that of the Belorussian peasant woman was the ubiquitous Russian samovar, made in Tula, that stood at one side of her tent as it would in the wooden hut of her northern counterpart. The only invisible thread that lay between them was the future and universal fate of all Soviet peasant women—collectivization, suffering, but with it enhanced rights against their menfolk and a far superior education for their children.

The Kazakh woman gathers up the cushions and blankets that litter the floor of the tent and packs them away in her carved wooden chests. At the same time she chants a *koshtasu*, or song of parting, handed down over centuries through oral tradition. She is recording in song her imminent separation from her favourite summer pasture steppes. And so we follow suit as we part from her and from all those human souls whose fates have flickered through this book.

# Conclusion

THERE has been no intention in this book to detect the essence of NEP, since there was none. The evaporations that float across to us through time derive from a multitude of scattered pot-pourris. Neither has it been possible to cover all aspects of society and politics. Russia is too large and too varied for that. An attempt has been made to cover most social classes, except for the upper strata of the Old Regime. They were well and truly off-stage politically and for the most part physically by 1922. Their presence has been felt in severed remains only, as in the more privileged members of the Serapion Brothers, or in the person of Felix Dzerzhinsky, a typical product of the minor Polish gentry. The absence of the old ruling class in the countryside was felt more keenly, however. The obliteration of their local administration, patronage, and haphazard compassion left a vacuum in European Russia that was not refilled at the lowest levels as late as 1926.

Some space has been devoted to the activities of the courts, the law, and the secret police. Only four of Russia's many national minorities have been treated in any detail. Many volumes would be needed to deal with them alone. Party and Soviet administration, together with communications in the widest sense of the word, have been a prime focus of interest. Their tentacles often became entwined and self-strangling. Their main social targets were the working classes and the peasantry. So much attention has been paid in previous scholarship to these two groups that other sectors have been neglected. That is why an effort has been made to diagnose the social, administrative, and political influence of the many other categories that determined the course of everyday life—kustari, Nepmen, the new professional classes, the priests, the ex-military, and so on.

None of these categories was homogeneous within itself. A world of sophistication separated the nearly self-subsistent kustar' of the Tver forests from the wide-roving craftsman who sold his specialized product all over European Russia. It is not possible to talk of a unified Soviet culture, or even of Great-Russian culture in NEP. The folk culture of Tver villages had only remote connections with the high culture of Leningrad, through, say the use of the accordion in popular and classical music alike, or in the verses of the ex-peasant Esenin, yearning for rural tranquillities that were soon to pass away.

The dichotomies as well as the links between social, intellectual, and political history at many levels have been explored in this book. In British scholarship there is still too wide a gap between the study of social, political, and intellectual history. Trotsky at least knew better when he declared that there could be no true democracy without cultured masses.

Any reader who is acquainted with my previous book, *The Social Prelude to Stalinism*, may be curious to know how I have modified my general views expressed there as a result of my research for the present study. This is quite a different kind of book. Whereas the earlier work was concerned mainly with high politics, I have been intent here on seeing how lower forms of life did or did not interact with the centre. The fact that they usually did not was one of the prime reasons for Stalin's unifying ruthlessness after NEP. I have also concentrated on the spatial rather than the temporal aspects of NEP. The passage of political time was perhaps too teleologically conceived in the earlier book, and I was looking above all beyond the 1920s to Stalinism. Although in the first book I dissected Bolshevik reifications of actual forms of life, I indulged in abstractions myself to a limited extent. Thus I discussed 'bureaucracy' without looking into its practical varieties and intricacies. I have tried to remedy this in Chapters 5 and 9 here. Although I attacked the socio-economic abstraction of the '*kulak*', I did not realize until now that the kustari were more insidious as a possible class enemy of Bolshevik aims by mid-NEP. Nor did I grasp the fact previously that at central levels there never was any real relaxation throughout NEP over political and especially over cultural activities (compare Chapter 6 with the section on science in Chapter 7). I did posit that military influences continued to be an influence in high politics, but had not guessed how pervasive and long-lasting they were to be at all levels (recall the continuing undertones of political violence into mid-NEP, whether in Smolensk or Kazakhstan). I viewed problems in Great-Russian terms, without seeing them from the point of view of the national minorities. Nor did I enter at all into the details of political and social life in the gubernii, whether Great Russian or not.

If the local and central chapters in this book appear to be scarcely attached to one another, then that is as it should be, since life was like that during NEP. From the Middle Ages in Western Europe until the seventeenth century, and in Russia from the Tartar invasions until the eighteenth century, high and low cultures agreed on their basic interpretation of the world. The onset of natural science and rationalism set up a separate culture of the literate, while the illiterate, still roughly 70 per cent of the Soviet population in the 1920s, clung on to old ways. Urban masses were quicker to assimilate rationalistic ideas, including, amongst many others, the notions of Marx. Popular wisdom in the rural localities remained in fragmented bits, consisting of a multitude of ceremonies and rituals on which the Orthodox faith struggled to impose a general pattern. The years 1917–21 reinforced local specificity. Chaos reigned, and there were no longer gentry, bureaucrats, merchants, nor capitalists from the Old Regime to uphold administrative networks. Richer peasants with co-ordinating skills went underground, and authority reverted almost entirely to the individual peasant commune.

Tsarist political and administrative control systems had been paternal, enforcing passivity through inertia and restriction of physical and social movement. The Bolsheviks could not throw off the authoritarian manners of their predecessors, but in other ways they were quite different. They were determined to be dynamic and active, wishing to penetrate to the depths of society and to shake it to its foundations. During NEP, as has been seen, this wish was not fulfilled. The commanding heights of politics and economics were taken over and transformed, but human and technical resources were not yet sufficient to make many further advances. This may have been a blessing in disguise for the leadership, since central ruthlessness could not be substantiated in local practice. To that extent counter-revolution was less likely during NEP.

It was only in the 1930s that all levels came under close and constant control from the political centre. Earlier aspirations became grim practicalities. The notion of historical inevitability is a seductive doctrine: both Western and Soviet, liberal and Marxist scholars have fallen prey to it in the interpretation of Soviet history, as has been pointed out at some length in the introduction to this book. Yet NEP above all was an unpredictable and ephemeral creature. It was intended from its inception to be doomed. As long as it lasted, it behaved like a slaughter-house animal, rushing wildly at a large number of possible exits from the cage. No one, not even the practical Stalin nor the visionary Trotsky, could tell the form of the final exit.

Nor was the outcome, via collectivization and industrialization, any more teleological in its implications for the future. The process of modernization in Russia did not imply, as has so often been assumed, a static millennium as a specific target to be aimed at. The goal has never been clear nor unchanging, least of all in Gorbachev's Russia. History and progress can never, as Herbert Butterfield wrote, assume a 'primitive and simple shape'. Many leading personalities in NEP apparently thought that it could, hence the interesting but naïve predictions from all sides, from men as diverse as Lenin, Gorky, Zamiatin, Maiakovsky, Stalin, the historian Pokrovsky, Trotsky, and the educationalist Makarenko. Their visions of the future have been discussed in earlier pages. The tragic reality, by contrast, was that Soviet officialdom did not recognize in time the nature of the crisis that was brewing by 1926, if not before. The reasons for this myopia have been investigated throughout this book, and need not be repeated here.

In 1926 and thereafter, until the close of NEP, there was not the slightest sign that the political hierarchy was going to loosen the strong central control systems that had been re-asserted with such vigour in 1921–2, despite some relaxation in other spheres. Yet control had not been translated into greater administrative efficiency by late NEP. One only has to look at frustrated efforts in Smolensk guberniia (in Party–worker relations for instance), in Tver province (the lack of penetration into the forest hinterland), or in the remote steppes of Kazakhstan to grasp this fact. By 1925–6 the economy had been restored to 1914 levels, but increasing prosperity brought with it politically undesirable and unorthodox agents in the countryside—richer peasants and, more significant, mobile Nepmen and kustari. At the geographical hub of power a new social problem was looming in the shape of a restless Moscow proletariat upset by poor pay and housing, and threatened by new recruits from the countryside. Stalin found ways of harnessing its energies to his political will. The harvest failures of 1927 and 1928 were merely the tip of a long time-fuse, and not, as has frequently been made out in Soviet and Western scholarship, the prime cause of the collapse of NEP.

Bolshevik hopes for genuine proletarian rule seeped away in the marsh of NEP. In 1927–8 the Party lost confidence and patience, and reverted to swift brutalities reminiscent of War Communism. The most crucial question of all now arises. Given her political past, her size, variety, climate, and relative political and economic backwardness, could Soviet Russia have become democratic quickly under any form of government whatsoever? The only other country in the world of comparable size and complexity that worked as a democracy in the 1920s was the USA. Russia suffered many objective disadvantages that did not permit her to compete, quite apart from the political inclinations of the Bolsheviks. Not many glimmers of democracy shone through from her pre-1917 inheritance. America was the progeny of the most sophisticated democracy in the world at the time of her revolution. Soviet Russia was a conglomeration of many nationalities *in situ*, some of which had longer cultural traditions than the Great Russians. The United States swiftly overran vast virgin territories, encountering here and there Indian tribes. The millions of non-Anglo-Saxons who flooded in from Europe later represented no threat to the entrenched political and social élite. It took Tsarist Russia three centuries to infiltrate into her enormous continental hinterland, encountering on the way the severest climate on the globe, mountains, deserts, land-locked seas, and great rivers that ran perversely into the Arctic. The easy plains of the Midwest led to nothing more alarming than the Rockies, with their amenable passes, and on to the sybaritic Pacific coast. Communications and administration were far simpler to deal with in the USA.

Even in a country the size of France, it took until the final years of the nineteenth century to build a nation-wide ideology and culture based on democracy. T. Zeldin describes the necessary prerequisites for such a unification:

Despite evidence to the contrary, inhabitants of the hexagon in 1870 generally knew themselves to be French subjects, but to many this status was no more than an abstraction. The people of whole regions felt little identity with the state or with people of other regions. Before this changed, before the inhabitants of France could come to feel a significant community, they had to share significant experiences with each other. Roads, railroads, schools, markets, military service, and the circulation of money, goods and printed matter provided those experiences, swept away old commitments, instilled a national view of things in regional minds, and confirmed the power of that view by offering advancement to those who adopted it. The national ideology was still diffuse and amorphous around the middle of the nineteenth century, French culture became truly national only in the last years of the century.

Very few of the prerequisites listed above existed in any strength in Russia by 1926. Major roads were few and far between, and the railway network was still in a chaotic state in 1922. Even by the end of NEP trains were mainly intended for the carriage of goods, not people. The wide circulation of printed matter did represent a great achievement in the early Soviet period, but it was censored and could not be read by roughly four out of five citizens, who were still illiterate. The proliferation and upkeep of Soviet schools was another laudable achievement, but many teachers were demoralized throughout NEP, quite unlike their respected French counterparts. Military service was a great national unifying force, in Russia as in France, but during NEP the previous massive army was pared down into a medium-sized force, thus decreasing somewhat the numbers and influence of ex-military men as time went by.

'The circulation of money and goods', apart from areas like Kazakhstan, was in fact speeding up by mid-NEP, but in Russia, as opposed to France, types inimical to central government were most involved—Nepmen, kustari, and the so-called '*kulaks*'. Another vital difference between the two countries lay in the fact that towards the end of the nineteenth century French peasants became convinced that they themselves were agents of change, helping to stamp out remaining elements of local isolation and backwardness. There were no signs at all of this among the Soviet peasantry by the end of NEP. Indeed only the Party, together with a few chosen intellectuals and a growing band of skilled workers in a few large cities in European Russia could act as agents of this kind. It was not just the peasantry that remained either passive or rejected in relationship to the centre—the same went for most professional groups, the suspected trading groups mentioned above, and even for local party and Soviet administrators.

These brief contrasts between Russia on the one hand and America and France on the other have been made in order to highlight the objective difficulties that faced the Bolshevik leaders in their dealings with early Soviet society. So often too much blame has been laid at the foot of the Party monolith, to the exclusion of the external pressures that would have hindered any regime of any political hue.

The effects of rapid industrialization in the 1930s were to be politically draconic for Soviet citizens, but at least they were starting out on the long road to a higher standard of living. For most of the population in NEP Chekhov's dream still seemed unattainable: 'And how lovely life on earth might be but for poverty—sheer, grinding poverty that you could not escape from.' Throughout the 1920s, and indeed from the 1930s until the present day, no political regime, not even Stalin's, has been able to extinguish the vital source of Russian life, which remains a love of humanity warmed by the deep compassion of a Dostoevsky. One can only hope that this inspiration will at last, in the 1990s, overflow into high politics and official administration. Modern technology and relative wealth are now dealing with most of the difficulties overcome by France a century ago but still assailing Russia until recently.

# Bibliography

A conventional, alphabetically arranged bibliography of all the works consulted for this book would be prohibitively long and of little help to anyone interested in pursuing research in the local aspects of the subjects treated in this book. Instead I have selected mainly primary sources that may be of most help to students and scholars of early Soviet history. The titles are arranged in groups that correspond to the chapters.

## CHAPTER I

Abetsedarskii, L. S. (ed.), *Istoriia BSSR*, vol. 2 (Minsk, 1961).

Afanasii, M., *Belorus' v istoricheskoi, gosudarstvennoi i tserkovnoi zhizni* (Buenos Aires, 1966).

*Arkhivnoe delo v BSSR, 1918–1968 Sbornik zakonodatel'nykh i rukovodiaishchykh dokumentov* (Minsk, 1972).

Bondarchik, V. K. (ed.), *Izmeneniia v bytu i kul'ture gorodskogo naseleniia Belorussii* (Minsk, 1976).

Bugaev, E., *Vozniknovenie bol'shevistskikh organizatsii i obrazovanie Kompartii Belorussii* (Moscow, 1959).

—— *Khronika vazhneishikh sobytii istorii KPB* (Minsk, 1962, 1970).

—— *Ocherki po istorii kommunisticheskoi partii Belorussii*, vol. 1 (Minsk, 1968).

Daiian, M., *Smolensk v revoliutsii 1917 goda*, Smolensk Izd. Smolenskogo istparta, 1927.

*Desiatyi Vserossiiskii S'ezd Sovetov* (1923).

*Dokymenty oblichaiut Reaktsionnaia rol'religii i tserkvi na territorii Belorussii* (Minsk, 1964).

Drujski, A., *Religious Life in Belorussia* (Chicago, 1976).

*Ekonomicheskii biuleten' koniunkturnogo instituta*, 7–8 (1923).

Fainsod, M., *Smolensk under Soviet Rule* (New York, 1963).

*Finansovaia politika za period s dekiabria 1920 g. po dekabr' 1921 g: otchet k IX vserossiiskomu s'ezdu sovetov* (Moscow, 1921).

Fridman, S. L., *Chastnyi kapital na denezhnom rynke* (Moscow, 1925).

Gal', V. I., *Zarozhdenie rabsel'korovskogo dvizheniia v Belorussii* (Minsk, 1977).

Glybinny, U., *Die Weissruthenische Kultur unter den Sovjets* (Munich, 1958).

Gorky, M., *O russkom krest'ianstve* (Berlin, 1922).

*Gosudarstvennye arkhivy Brestskoi Grodnenskoi oblastei, filial Gosudarstvennogo arkhiva Minskoi oblasti v Molodechno. Spravochnik po dokumentalnym materialam 1919–1939 gg.* (Minsk, 1969).

Govin, S. V., *Druk zakhodniai Belarusi 1921–1939 gg.* (Minsk, 1974).

Grevko, V. G., *Komsomol Belorussii v period grazhdanskoi voiny* (Minsk, 1958).

Hlebka, P. *et al.*, *Farmiravanne i razviccjo belaruskaj sacyjalistycnaj nacyi* (Minsk, 1958).

Il'uikhov, A., 'Iz istorii kul'turnogo stroitelstva na Smolenskchine v pervye gody Sov. Vlasti', in *Smolenskii krai v istorii russkoi kul'tury* (Smolensk, 1973).

*Istoriia gosudarstva i prava BSSR 1917–36 gg.* (Minsk).

Kamenskaja, N., *Utvarenne Belaruskaj Soveckaj Socyjalistyncnaj Respubliki* (Minsk, 1946).

—— *Belorussskii narod v bor'be za Sovetskuyu vlast* (Minsk, 1963).

*Khronika vazhneishikh sobytii istorii kommunisticheskoi partii Belorussii, 1919g–1941g.*, pt. 2 (Minsk, 1970).

Korzun, I. P., *Preodolenie razluchii mezhdu gorodom i derevnei v bytu i kul'ture. Istoriko-etnograficheskoe issledovanie po materialam BSSR* (Minsk, 1972).

Kreceuski, P., *Zameznaja Belarus'*, 1 (Prague, 1926).

Krekane, M., and Sakol'cyk, A., *Belarusi, Feadalizm i Kapitalizm* (Minsk, 1969).

Krutalevich, V., *Rozhdenie Belorusskoi Sovetskoi Respubliki* (Minsk, 1975).

Kykharev, B. E., *Sel'skoe khoziaistvo zapadnoi Belorussii 1919–1939 gg.* (Minsk, 1975).

Lezhnev-Finkovsky, P. Ya., *Kak zhivet derevniia* (Moscow, 1925), pp. 31–2.

Lubachko, I. S., *Belorussia under Soviet Rule 1917–1957* (Lexington, 1972).

Margunskii, S. V., *Sozdanie i uprochenie Belorusskoi gosudarstvennosti 1917–1922* (Moscow, 1958).

Markiianov, B. K., *Bor'ba kompartii Belorussii za ukrplenie edinvstva svoikh riadov v 1921–1925 gg.* (Minsk, 1961).

Martinevich, F. S., and Drits, V. I., *Razvitie ekonomiki Belorussii v 1921–27 gg.* (Minsk, 1973).

Martinovich, I. I., *Sudostroistvo i prokurorskii nadzor v BSSR v period vosstanovleniia narodnogo khoziaistva 1921–1925 gg.* (Minsk, 1960).

*Materialy mestnykh soveschanii oblastnykh konferentsii narodnogo kommissariata zemledeliia o vesennei kampanii 1922 goda* (Moscow, 1922).

Menski, J., 'The Establishment of the Belorussian SSR', *Belorussian Review*, 1 (1955), pp. 5–33.

Min'ko, L. I., *Sueveriia i primety. Istok i sushchnost'* (Minsk, 1975).

Mints, I. *et al.*, *Pobeda Sovetskoi vlasti v Belorussii* (Minsk, 1967).

*Narodnoe khoziaistvo BSSR za 40 let* (Minsk, 1957), p. 26.

Neiasek, N., *Bol'shevizm na putyakh k ustanovleniiu kontrolia nad Belorussiei* (Munich, 1954).

*Ocherki istorii marksistskoi–leninskoi filosofii v Belorussii, 1919–1968* (Minsk, 1968).

Oganovsky, N. P., *Narodnoe khoziaistvo SSSR 1923–24 gg.* (Moscow, 1925).

*Prakticheskoe razreshenie natsional'nogo voprosa v BSSR* (Minsk, 1927).

Petrikov, P. T., *Zabota sovetskoi vlasti o zdorove trudiashchikhsia. Na materialakh BSSR* (Minsk, 1976).

Picaida, G. de, *The Belorussian Church* (Chicago, 1976).

Radkey, O. H., *The Election to the Russian Constituent Assembly of 1917* (Cambridge, Mass., 1950).

Ragulia, V., *Uspaminy* (New York, 1957).

*Razvitie ekonomiki Belorussii v 1921–1927 gg.* (Minsk, 1973).

*Revoliutsionnye komitety BSSR i ikh deiatel'nost' po uprochneniu sovetskoi vlasti i organizatsii sotsialisticheskogo stroitel'stva iul'–detabr' 1920 g., sbornik dokumentov* (Minsk, 1957).

Rokashevich, V. K., *Pod znamenem bratstva 1917–1922* (Minsk, 1972).

Saladkov, N. I., *K voprosu o proniknovenii kapitala v ekonomiu do revoliutsinnoi Belorussii* (Moscow, 1967).

Savostenok, P., *Kritika antinauchnykh kontseptsii braka v sem'u Belorussii 1920–1930 gg.* (Minsk, 1975).

Seduro, V. I., 'Belorussian Culture and Totalitarianism', *Proceedings of the Conference of the Institute for the Study of the History and Culture of the USSR* (New York, 1953).

Shcharbakou, V. K., *Kastrychnitskaia revoliutsyia na Belarusi i belapol'skaia okupatsyia* (Minsk, 1975).

Smolensk Archive.

*Sotsialisticheskaia zakonnost' v deiatel'nosti mestnykh sovetov BSSR 1917–1958 gg.* (Minsk, 1960).

Stankevich, I., *Sovetskae khval'shavan'ne gistoryi Belarusi* (Munich, 1956).

*Sto god Beloruskae precy* (New York, 1978–9).

*Struktura sovetskoi intelligentsii po problemam BSSR* (Minsk, 1970).

Strumilin, S. G., *Biudzhet vremeni russkogo rabochego i krest'ianina v 1922–23 godu* (Moscow, 1924).

Szczebiot, G., 'Belusha and Struga in Belorussia', in *Newsletter* 14 of the Welsh Branch of the Great Britain–USSR Association (Nov. 1980), p. 8.

Vakar, N. P., *Belorussia: The Making of a Nation* (Cambridge, Mass., 1956).

Vakar, N., *A Bibliographical Guide to Belorussia* (Cambridge, Mass., 1956).

*Vbor'be i trude* (Minsk, 1970).

*Velikaia oktiabr'kaia sotsialisticheskaia revoliutsiia v Belorussii. Dokumenty i materialy* (Minsk, 1957).

Vinogradoff, E. D., 'The Russian Peasantry and the Elections to the Fourth State Duma', in L. H. Haimson, *The Politics of Rural Russia 1905–1914* (Bloomington, 1979), pp. 219–60.

*V nachale bol'shogo puti. Memuarnyi sbornik* (Minsk, 1975).

Volokhovich, L. I., *Partiinoe stroitel'stvo v Belorussii v pervye gody NEPa, 1921–1924 gg.* (Moscow, 1962).

*Voprosy arkhivovedeniia i istochnikovedeniia v BSSR posviaschchennoi 50-letiiu arkhivnogo stroitel'stva v SSSR* (Minsk, 1971).

*Vosstanovlenie narodnogo khoziaistva Gomel'skoi gubernii 1921–1925 gg. Sbornik dokomenty i materialov* (Gomel, 1960).

Zlotnik, M. I., *Deiatel'nost' organov partiino-gosudarstvennogo kontrolia BSSR v gosudarstvennom stroitel'stve, 1917–1934 gg.* (Minsk, 1969).

## CHAPTER 2

Allen, W. E. D., *The Ukraine: A History* (New York, 1963).

*Arkhivnyi otdel upravleniia a vnutrennykh del ispolkoma kurskogo oblsoveta deputatov trudiashchikhsia. Putevoditel'* (Kursk, 1958).

Boldyrev, M., *Sel'skoe khoziaistvo na putiakh vosstanovleniia* (Moscow, 1925).

Danilov, V. P., 'Zemel'nye otnosheniia v sovetskoi dokolkhoznoi derevne', *Istoriia SSSR*, 3 (Moscow, 1958).

Eklof, H., 'The Village and the Outsider: The Rural Teacher in Russia, 1864–1914', in *Slavic and European Education Review*, 1 (1979).

Gaister, A., *Rassloenie sovetskoi derevni* (Moscow, 1928).

Hillig, G., and Weitz, S., 'A. S. Makarenko—Leiter der Dzerzinskij-Kommune in Char'kov?', *Paedagogica Historica*, 10/3 (1970).

*Iz istorii kurskogo kraia. Sbornik dokumentov i materialov* (Voronezh, 1966).

Kaplan, D. A., *Kustarnaia promyshlennost' Ukrainy* (Kharkov, 1922).

Kolichevsky, I., 'Literatura ob oktiabrskoi revoliutsii', *Proletarskaia revoliutsiia*, 37 (1924).

*Komsomol Poltavshchini v bidbydovnii period 1921–1925 gg. Zbirnik documentiv i materialiv* (Poltava, 1962).

Kossior, S., *Die Ergebnisse und die nächsten Aufgaben der Nationalitätenpolitik in der Ukraine* (Moscow, 1934).

Kostelianets, B., *Makarenko (Kritiko-biograficheskii ocherk)* (Moscow, 1954).

Krupskaia, N. K., *Izbrannye pedagogicheskie proizvedeniia* (Moscow, 1955).

Kubanin, M., 'K istorii oktiabr'ia v derevne', *Istorik Marksist* (Moscow, 1928).

Kurman, M. V., and Lebensinsky, I. V., *Naselenie bol'shogo sotsialisticheskogo goroda* (Moscow, 1968).

*Kurskaia guberniia v gody inostrannoi voennoi interventsii i grazhdanskoi voiny 1918–1920* (Voronezh, 1966–7).

Makarenko, A., *The Road to Life* (London, 1936).

—— *Sochineniia v semi tomakh*, 2nd edn. (Moscow, 1957–8).

—— *Gesammelte Werke*, vol. 1 (Ravensburg, 1976).

Nezhinsky, N. P., *A. S. Makarenko i pedagogika shkoly* (Kiev, 1976).

Oganovsky, I., *Obshchina i zemel'noe tovarishchestvo* (Moscow, 1923).

Ogorodnikov, I. T., and Shimbirev, P. N., *Lehrbuch der Pädagokik* (Berlin, 1953).

'O sostave RKSM', in *Statisticheskii sbornik*, vol. 1 (Moscow, 1924).

*Podpol'naia pechat' kurskikh bol'shevikov 1901–1908 g. Sbornik dokumentov* (Kursk, 1962).

*Poltavi 800 pokiv, 1174–1974* (Kiev, 1974).

*Predvaritel'nye itogi perepisi po Kurskoi gubernii* (Kursk, 1927).

Radkey, O. K., *The Unknown Civil War in Soviet Russia: A Study of the Green Movement in the Tambov Region 1920–1921* (Stanford, 1976).

Shafir, Ya., *Gazeta i derevnia* (Moscow, 1924).

Shestskov, A., 'Iiul'skie dni v derevne', *Proletarskaia revoliutsiia*, 5 (Moscow, 1927).

Shlikher, A. G., 'Bor'ba za khleb na Ukraine v 1919 godu', *Litopys revoliutsii*, 2 (1928).

Shvartz, G., and Zaitsev, V., *Molodezh' SSSR v Tsifrakh* (Moscow, 1924).

Sullivant, R. S., *Soviet Politics and the Ukraine 1917–1957* (New York, 1962).

Trifonov, I. Ia., *Klassy i klassovaia bor'ba v SSSR v nachale NEPa* (Leningrad, 1964).

*Trud v SSSR: statistiko-ekonomicheskii obzor, oktiabr' 1922 do marta 1924* (Moscow, 1925).

Vinogradoff, E. D., 'The Russian Peasantry and the Elections to the Fourth State Duma', in L. H. Haimson (ed.), *The Politics of Rural Russia 1905–1914* (Bloomington, 1979), pp. 219–60.

Yakovlev, Ia., *Nasha derevnia Novoe v starom i staroe v novom* (Moscow, 1924).

—— *Derevnia kak ona est': ocherki Nikol'skoi volosti* (Moscow, 1923).

Zaitsev, V., *Polozhenie truda podrostkov i ego oplata v promyshlennosti, Molodaia gvardiia* (1924).

Zalkind, A. B., article in *Bol'shaia sovetskaia entsiklopediia*, vol. 5 (Moscow, 1927).

Zenzinov, V., *Les enfants abandonnés en Russie soviétique* (Paris, 1929).

*Znamiia kommunizma: organ Kurskogo gubkoma RKP(b)*, 4–5 (1922).

*Zolotye zvezdy trudovoi slavy (Sbornik dokumentov i materialov o kynianakh-Geroiakh Sotsialisticheskogo Truda)* (Kursk, 1976).

## CHAPTER 3

Antonov-Ovseenko, V. A., 'O banditskom dvizhenii v Tambovskoi gubernii', Trotsky Archive, Harvard University.

Asquith, M., *Famine: Quaker Work in Russia 1921–3* (London, 1943).

Bechhofer, C. E., *Through Starving Russia: Being the Record of a Journey to Moscow and the Volga Provinces in August and September, 1921* (London, 1921).

Beeuwkes, H., 'American Medical and Sanitary Relief in the Russian Famine 1921–23', *ARA Bulletin* (1922).

Blumenthal, Iosif Il'ich, *Revoliutsiia 1917–1918 gg. v Samarskoi gubernii (khronika sobytii)* (Samara, 1927).

De Tef'e, B. (ed.), *Chernaia godina: Sbornik o golode v Tsaritsynskoi gubernii i obzor deiatel'nosti gubkompomgola za 1921–1922 god* (Tsaritzyn, 1922).

*Die Hungersnot in der Ukraine* (Berlin, 1923).

Edmondson, C. M., 'Soviet Famine Relief Measures 1921–1923', unpublished doctoral thesis of the Florida State University, 1970.

Eiduck, A. V., *Die russische Hungersnot 1921–1922 und ihre Bekämpfung in Lichte der Tatsachen* (Berlin, 1922).

Eudin, Xenia Joukoff, and Fisher, Harold H., *Soviet Famine and the West, 1920–1927: A Documentary Survey* (Stanford, 1957).

Fisher, H. H., *The Famine in Soviet Russia 1919–1923: The Operations of the American Relief Administration* (New York, 1927).

Fox, R. W., *People of the Steppes* (New York, 1925).

Geraklitov, Aleksandr Aleksandrovich, *Kratkii istoricheskii ocherk* (Saratov, 1923).

Bibliography 427

Glavnyi politiko-prosvetitel'nyi komitet, *Chto govoriat tsifry o golode* (Moscow, 1923).

Gorev, Mikhail, *Otkuda neurozhai i golodovki* (Moscow, 1922).

Gurevich, M. B., *Golod i sel'skoe khoziaistvo Ukrainy: Ocherk* (Kharkov, 1923).

Harasymovych, I., 'Holod na Ukraini', *Ukrainskoe Slovo* (Berlin, 1922).

Ingersol, Jean M., *Historical Examples of Ecological Disaster: Famine in Russia 1921–1922; Famin in Bechuanaland 1965* (New York, 1965).

*Itogi posledgol s 15.10 1922 g.–1.8.1923 g.* (Moscow, 1923).

Ivanov, Sergei, *La famine en Russie Bolcheviste, avec vingt-huit dessins dans la texte et trois hors texte de l'auteur* (Paris, 1924).

Izvestiia RKI, *Otchet narkomzemledeliia: X vserossiiskogo s'ezda sovetov za 1923 god* (Moscow, 1923).

Kameneva, O. D., *Kak proletarii vzekh stran pomogaiut golodaiushchim Rossii* (Moscow, 1923).

Kellogg, Vernon, 'Russian-American Famine Region', *Annals of the American Academy of Political and Social Science* (March 1922).

Kotov, Grigorii Grigor'evich, *Rassloenie Sredne-Volzhskoi derevni; Samarskaia guberniia* (Samara, 1928).

Kovalevskii, A. G., *Ocherki po demografii Saratova (rozhdaemost' i smertnost' za 1914–1927 gg.)* (Saratov, 1928).

League of Nations, *Records of the Second Assembly, Plenary Meetings*, II (Geneva, 1921).

—— *Records of the Third Assembly, Plenary Meetings*, III (Geneva, 1922), p. 59.

—— *Report on Economic Conditions in Russia, with Special Reference to the Famine of 1921–22 and the State of Agriculture* (Geneva, 1922).

*Materialy mestnykh soveshchanii oblastnykh konferentsii narodnogo kommissariata zemledeliia o vesennoi kampanii 1922 goda* (Moscow, 1922).

*Na bor'by s golodom, sbornik statei i materialov* (Petrograd, 1921).

Nansen, Fridtjof, *Through the Caucasus to the Volga* (London, 1931).

National Information Bureau: Commission on Russian Relief, *The Russian Famines, 1921–22, 1922–23: Summary Report* (New York, 1923).

*Ocherki po demografii Saratova* (Saratov, 1928).

Payne, Muriel A., *Plague, Pestilence and Famine* (London, 1923).

Ponafidine, Emma, 'Famine and the Bolsheviki', *Yale Review*, 12 (1922).

*Povol'zhe, ekonomichesko-geograficheskai a kharakteristika* (Moscow, 1957).

Raleigh, D. (ed.), *A Russian Civil War Diary: Alexis Babine in Saratov, 1917–1922* (Duke University Press, 1988).

Robbins, R. G., 'Russia's System of Food Supply Relief on the Eve of the Famine of 1891–1892', *Agricultural History*, 45 (1981).

Russia *Chto govoriat tsifry o golode* (Moscow, 1922).

Russia *Itogi posledgol s 15/X–1922 g. 1/VIII–1923 g.* (Moscow, 1923).

Russia *Nakaz mestnym kommissiiam pomoshchi golodaiuschim* (Moscow, 1922).

Russia *Na bor'bu s posledstviiami goloda* (Moscow, 1922).

Russia (1917-RSFSR), Glavnyi politiko-prosvetitel'nyi komitet, *Golod i tserkovnye bogatstva* (Moscow, 1922).

Russia (1917-RSFSR), Tsentral'naia komissiia pomoshchi golodaiushchim, *Itogi bor'by s golodom v 1921–1922 gg. Sbornik statei i otchetov* (Moscow, 1922).

Russian Liberation Committee, *The Famine* (London, 1922).

Russian Trade Delegation, *The Famine in Russia: Documents and Statistics presented to the Brussels Conference on Famine Relief* (London, 1921).

Samara, Russia, *Gubernskii statisticheskii otdel. Naselenie Samarskoi gubernii po dannym Vsesoiuznoi perepisi 17 dekabria 1926 g.* (Samara, 1928).

Samara, Russia, *S"ezd sovetov, 1921. Diagrammy i organizatsionnye skhemy; materialy k istorii sovetskogo stroitel'stva v Samarskoi gobernii k 8-mu Gubernskomu s"ezdu sovetov rab., kr. i kr. deputatov, 18 iiunia 1921 g.* (Samara, 1922).

Saratov, Russia, *Gubernskii s"ezd sovetov. Tezisy i proekty . . .* (Saratov, 1923).

Saratov, Russia (Government) Gubernskoe statisticheskoe biuro, *Statisticheskii Sbornik po Saratovskoi Gubernii* (Saratov, 1923).

Simpson, M., 'L. N. Tolstoy and the Famine of 1891–2', *Melbourne Slavonic Studies*, 15 (1981).

Sorokin, Pitrim, *Leaves from a Russian Diary* (New York, 1924).

Trifonov, I. Ia., *Klassy i klassovaia bor'ba v SSSR v nachale NEPa (1921–1923)* (Leningrad, 1964).

*Trudy Zemplany*, vol. 1 (Moscow, 1924).

Tsybul'skii, V. A., 'Nalogovaia politika v derevne v pervye gody NEPa', *Voprosy Istorii*, 40 (1962).

Tulaikov, Nikolai Maksimovich, *Kratkii otchet o rabotakh Otdela polevodstva za 1923 i 1924 gg.* (Saratov, 1925).

US National Archives, *Records of the Department of State Relating to the Internal Affairs of Russia and the Soviet Union: 1910–29*, File No. 861.48/1562.

Wheatcroft, S. G., Three articles in *Soviet Industrialization Project Series* (Birmingham, 1977, 1981, and 1982).

Weissman, E. M., *Herbert Hoover and Famine Relief to Soviet Russia: 1921–1923* (Stanford, 1974).

Zubov, N., *F. E. Dzerzhinsky: Biografiia* (Moscow, 1965).

CHAPTER 4

Baedeker, K., *Russia* (New York, 1914).
*Bolezni nashego pechatnogo dela* (Moscow, 1924).
Bol'shakov, M., *Derevnia 1917–27* (Moscow, 1927).
Chaschikhin, A., *Kratkie ocherki po istorii professional'nogo soiuza na permskoi zheleznoi dorogi* (Sverdlovsk, 1927).
*Deviatyi vsesoiuznyi s'ezd Sovetov* (Moscow, 1922).
Dzerzhinsky, F., *Izbrannye proizvedeniia*, vol. 1 (Moscow, 1967).
Fomin, V. V., *Lenin i transport* (Moscow, 1973).
Fomin, V., *Piatiletii sovetskogo transporta 1917–1922 gg. i ego blizhaishie perspektivy* (Moscow, 1923).
*Gudok* (Moscow, 1922).
Khaletskaia, A. A., *Ekspeditsiia F. E. Dzerzhinskogo v Sibir (1922 g.)* (Omsk, 1963).
Khromov, S. S., *Po zadaniiu Lenina: deiatel'nost' F. E. Dzerzhinskogo v Sibiri* (Moscow, 1964).
Klimov, Iu., *V surovye gody dvadsatye: Bol'sheviki severo-zapada v bor'be za provedenie NEPa v 1921–35* (Murmansk, 1968)
*Krasnaia pechat'*, 14–15 (1927).
*Krest'ianskii korrespondent. Ego rol'. Ego rabota* (Moscow, 1924).
Lomonossov Collections, Leeds University Library (not as yet open to the author).
Mil'kov, F. N., *Srednee Povolzh'e* (Moscow, 1953).
*Narodnoe i gosudarstvennoe khoziaistvo SSSR k seredine 1922–3 g.* (Moscow, 1923).
Naiashkin, Y. Ka., *Ocherki iz istorii srednego Povolzh'ia* (Kuibyshev, 1955).
*Narodnoe khoziaistvo Ukrainy v 1921–2 gg.* (Kharkov, 1923).
*Organy gosudarstvennogo upravitel'stva BSSR 1919–67 gg.* (Minsk, 1968).
*Otchet XIII-mu gubernskomu s'ezdu sovetov: Kurskii gubernskii ispolnitel'nyi komitet* (Kursk, 1926).
*Partiinaia i sovetskaia pechat' v bor'be za postroenie sotsializma i kommunizma*, pt. 1 (Moscow, 1961).
*Pechat' i revoliutsiia*, 7 (1922).
*Perepiska sekretariata tsk RSDRP(b) s mestnymi partiinymi organizatsiiami*, vol. 3 (Moscow, 1952 onwards).
Pethybridge, R., *The Spread of the Russian Revolution: Essays on 1917* (London, 1972).
Portiankin, I. A., *Sovetskaia voennaia pechat': istoricheskii ocherk* (1960).
Rado, A., *Führer durch die Sowjetunion* (Moscow, 1925).
Rappeport, M. L., *Desiat' let na boievom posta: istoriia 'Krasnoi gazety' 1918–1928* (Leningrad, 1928).

Sergeev, I., *Vneshniaia torgovlia i vodnyi transport* (Moscow, 1921).
Shafir, R., *Gazeta i derevnia* (Moscow, 1924).
*Sovetskoe narodnoe khoziaistvo v 1921–25 gg.* (Moscow, 1969).
*Sovetskii transport 1917–27 gg.* (Moscow, 1927).
Strumilin, S., *Statistitesko-ekonomicheskie ocherki* (Moscow, 1958).
Symons, L., and White, C. (eds.), *Russian Transport: An Historical and Geographical Survey* (London, 1975).
Taniaev, A., *Ocherki po istorii dvizheniia zheleznodorozhnikov v revoliutsii 1917 goda* (Moscow, 1925).
Trotsky, M. P., *Stat'i i rechi*, vol. 4 (Moscow, 1928).
*Transport i sviaz' SSSR; statisticheskii sbornik* (Moscow, 1972).
Valedinskii, V., and Apollov, B., *Del'ta Volgi. Podannym izyskanii 1919–1925 gg.*, vol. 1 (Tiflis, 1928–30).
Vardin, I. V., *Sovetskaia pechat': sbornik statei* (Moscow, 1924).
Zubov, N., *F. E. Dzerzhinskii: Biografiia* (Moscow, 1965).

## CHAPTER 5

Alampiev, P. M., *Ekonomicheskoe raionirovanie SSSR* (Moscow, 1959).
*Biulleten' NKVD*, 37, circular 305 (Moscow, 1928).
Bogolepov, M. I., *O putiakh buduschchego k voprosu ob ekonomicheskom plane* (Petrograd, 1916).
Chambre, H., *L'Aménagement du territoire en URSSS: L'introduction à l'étude des régions économiques soviétiques* (Paris, 1959).
Chugunov, A. I., *Organy sotsialisticheskogo kontrolia RSFSR 1923–1934 gg.* (Moscow, 1972).
Chugunov, S., 'Etapy raionirovaniia', *Vlast' sovetov*, 28–9 (1928).
Dorokhova, G. A., *Raboche-krest'ianskaia inspektsiia v 1920–1923 gg.* (Moscow, 1959).
Egorova, K. D. (ed.), *Raionirovanie SSSR, sbornik materialov po raionirovaniiu s 1917–1925 gg.* (Moscow, 1926).
Egorov, K., 'Administrativnoe delenie RSFSR v primenenii k ekonomicheskomu raionirovaniiu', *Vlast' sovetov*, 3 (1922).
Gimpel'son, E., *Sovety v gody inostrannoi interventsii i grazhdanskoi voiny* (Moscow, n.d.).
Ikonnikov, S. N., *Organizatsiia i deiatel'nost' RKI v 1920–25 gg.* (Moscow, 1960).
*Istoriia kommunisticheskoi partii Sovetskogo Soiuza*, vol. 4, bk. 1 (Moscow, 1970).
*Itogi partiinoi raboty za god 1922–1923* (Moscow, 1923).
Iudin, I. N., *Sotsial'naia baza rosta KPSS* (Moscow, 1973).
*Izvestiia raboche-krest'ianskoi inspektsii*, 28 Mar. 1922.
Kim, M. P., *Sorok let sovetskoi kul'tury* (Moscow, 1957).

Kozhevnikov, M. V., *Istoriia sovetskogo suda* (Moscow, 1948).

Krylenko, N. V., *Osnovy sudoustroistva SSSR i soiuznykh respublik* (Moscow, 1927).

Krzhizhanovsky, L. (ed.), *Voprosy ekonomicheskogo raionirovaniia SSSR* (Moscow, 1957).

Kurskii, D., *Izbrannye stat'i i rechi* (Moscow, 1948).

Latsis, M., *Chrezvychainye kommissii po bor'be s kontr-revoliutsiei* (Moscow, 1921).

Lenin, V. I., '"Dual" subordination and observation of the law', *Collected Works*, vol. 33 (London, 1960–70), pp. 363–7.

Margunskii, S. P., *Gosudarstvennoe stroitel'stvo BSSR v gody vosstanovleniia narodnogo khoziaistva 1921–1925* (Minsk, 1966).

Morozov, L. F., and Portnov, V. P., *Organy TsKK—NK RKI v bor'ba za sovershenstvovanie sovetskogo gosudarstvennogo apparata (1923–1934), Iuridicheskaia Literatura* (Moscow, 1964).

Ostroumov, S. S., *Prestupnost' i ee prichiny v dorevoliutsionnoi Rossii* (Moscow, 1960).

*Otchet prokuratury RSFSR prezidiumu VTsIK za 1925 g.* (Moscow, 1925).

*Otchet XIII-mu gubernskomu s'ezdu sovetov. Kurskii gubernskii ispol'nitelnyi komitet* (Kursk, 1926).

Perrins, M., '*Rabkrin* and workers' control in Russia 1917–34', *European Studies Review* (1980).

Pethybridge, R. W., *The Social Prelude to Stalinism* (London, 1974), ch. 6.

Pletnev, G., 'Sredne-chernozemnaia polosa', *Ekonomicheskaia zhizn'*, 245 (29 Oct. 1922).

'Praktika raionirovaniia', *Ekonomicheskaia zhizn*, 84 (18 Apr. 1923).

*Pravo i zhizn'*, 3 (1922).

'Prokuratura i revoliutsionnaia zakonnost'', *Ezhenedel'nik sovetskoi iustitsii*, 51–2, 31 Dec. 1923.

Rigby, T. H., *Lenin's Government: Sovnarkom 1917–1922* (Cambridge, 1979).

Service, R., *The Bolshevik Party in Revolution: A Study in Organisational Change, 1917–1923* (London, 1979).

Seibert, T., *Red Russia* (London, 1932).

Smolensk Archive.

Sofinov, P. G., *Ocherki istorii vserossiiskoi chrezvychainoi komissii (1917–1922)* (Moscow, 1960).

*Sovety, s'ezdy sovetov i ispolkomy* (Moscow, 1924).

*Spravochnik partiinogo rabotnika*, 3 (1922).

*Statistika osuzhdennykh v SSSR za 1923–1924 gg.* (Moscow, 1927).

Stuchka, P., *13 let bor'by za revoliutsionno-marksistkuiu teoriiu prava* (Moscow, 1931).

'Tezisy doklada prezidiuma ocherednoi sessi VTsIK deviatogo sozyva po voprosu ob ekonomicheskom raionirovanii Rossii', *Vlast' sovetov*, 3 (Mar. 1922).

Von Thünen, J. H., *Der isolierte Staat in Beziehung auf Landwirtschaft und Nationalökonomie* (Hamburg, 1826).

Volkov, A., 'Itogi raionirovaniia Ukrainy', *Ekonomicheskaia zhizn'*, 204 (11 Sept. 1923).

*Vserossiiskaia perepis' chlenov RKP 1922 goda* (Moscow, 1923).

*XI S'ezd RKP(b)*, *stenograficheskii otchet, mart–aprel'* (1922).

Zaikina, F. G., 'Organizatsionnaia perestroika kommunisticheskoi partii posle pobedy Oktiabria', *Voprosy Istorii KPSS*, 11 (1966).

Zenkovich, V., 'Itogi i zadachi raboty obshchego nadzora', *Ezhenedelnik sovetskoi iustitsii*, 18 (10 May 1923).

CHAPTER 6

Alekseeva, G. D., *Oktiabr'skaia revoliutsiia i istoricheskie nauki v Rossii (1917–1923 gg.)* (Moscow, 1968).

Aleksinsky, M. A., *O reorganizatsii organov narodnogo obrazovaniia* (Moscow, 1930).

Anweiler, O., *Geschichte der Schule und Pädagogik in Russland vom Ende des Zarenreiches bis zum Beginn der Stalin-Ära* (Berlin, 1964).

Bater, J. H., *St Petersburg: Industrialisation and Change* (London, 1976).

Bogdanov, A. A., *Filosofiia zhivogo opyta: Populiarnye ocherki* (St Petersburg, 1913; 2nd edn., Moscow, 1920; 3rd edn., Moscow, and Petrograd, 1923).

Boltiansky, G. M. (ed.), *Lenin i kino* (Moscow, 1925).

Chanbarisov, Sh. Kh., *Formirovanie sovetskoi universitetskoi sistemy (1917–1938 gg.)* (Ufa, 1973).

Fediukin, S. A., *Velikii Oktiabr' i intelligentsiia* (Moscow, 1972).

Gorky, M., 'The Intelligentsia and the Revolution', *Manchester Guardian Commercial: Reconstruction in Europe*, 6 July 1922.

*Istoriia Leningradskogo Universiteta* (Leningrad, 1969).

*Iz istorii Lenfil'ma. Stat'i, vospominaniia, dokumenty* (3rd edn., Leningrad, 1971).

Kim, M. P., *Iz istorii sovetskoi intelligentsii* (Moscow, 1966).

Klimov, Iu. *V surovye gody dvadtsatye—Bol'shevikii severo-zapada v bor'be za provedenie nepa v 1921–1925* (Murmansk, 1968).

Klushin, V. I., *Pervye uchenye-marksisty Petrograda. Istoriko-sotsiologicheskie ocherki* (Leningrad, 1971).

*Kommunisty v sostave apparata gosuchrezhdenii i obshchestvennykh organizatsii. Itogi vsesoyuznoi partiinoi perepisi 1927 g.* (Moscow, Tsentral'nyi komitet VKP(b), Statisticheskii otdel, 1929).

Lunacharskii, A. V., *Intelligentsiia, v ee proshlom, nastoiashchem, i budush-chem* (Moscow, 1924).

*Lunacharskii o kino* (Moscow, 1965).

Lunacharsky, A. V. 'Culture in the Soviet Republic', *Manchester Guardian Commercial: Reconstruction in Europe*, 6 July 1922.

Lunts, L., *Why We are the Serapion Brothers* (Petrograd, 1922).

Machajski, J. W., *Bankrotstvo sotsializma XIX stoletiia* (Geneva, 1905).

—— *Burzhuaznaia revoliutsiia i rabochee delo* (St Petersburg, 1906).

Mandel', S. Z., 'Kul'turno-prosvetitel'naia deiatel'nost' uchenykh Petrogradskogo universiteta v pervye gody sovetskoi vlasti', *Ocherki po istorii Leningradskogo universiteta*, vol. 1 (Leningrad, 1962).

McLelland, J. *Bolsheviks, Professors, and the Reform of Higher Education in Soviet Russia, 1917–1921* (University Microfilms, Ann Arbor, 1971).

Meshcheriakov, N., 'Sovremennoe studenchestvo i ego nuzhdy', *Vysshaia shkola v RSFSR i novoe studenchestvo: Al'bom* (Moscow, 1923).

Novikov, M. M., 'Sud'ba rossiiskikh universitetov', *Russkaia shkola za rubezhom*, 5–6 (Prague, 1923).

*Pechat' i revoliutsiia* (Petrograd, 1922).

Pethybridge, R. W., 'Petrograd and the Provinces', in *The Spread of the Russian Revolution: Essays on 1917* (London, 1972).

*Pod znamenem Marksizma* (Petrograd, 1922).

Pokrovsky, M. N., 'What Lenin was for Our Higher Schools', *Pravda*, 22 (27 Jan. 1924).

Polianskii, V., 'Ob ideologii v literature', in I. Oksënov (ed.), *Sovremennaia russkaia kritika* (Leningrad, 1925).

*Samoe vazhnoe iz vsekh iskusstv: Lenin i kino* (Moscow, 1973).

Scheffer, P., 'University Life and the Press in Revolutionary Russia', *Manchester Guardian Commercial: Reconstruction in Europe*, 6 July 1922.

Shklovsky, V., *Sentimental'noe puteshestvie. Vospominaniia 1917–1922* (Berlin, 1923).

Smirnova, T. M., *Reforma vysshei shkoly RSFSR 1917 g.–okt. 1922 g.* (Moscow, 1968).

Sorokin, P., *The Long Journay* (New Haven, 1953).

Stepanov, Z. V., *Kul'turnaia zhizn' Leningrada 20-kh–nachala 30-kh godov* (Leningrad, 1976).

Suvorov, L. N., 'Iz istorii bor'by V. I. Lenina, partii bol'shevikov protiv bogdanovskoi "organizatsionnoi nauki"', *Filosofskie nauki*, 3 (1966).

Trotsky, L., *Literatura i revoliutsiia* (Moscow, 1923).

Ukraintsev, V. V., *KPSS—Organizator revoliutsionnogo preobrazovaniia vysshei shkoly* (Moscow, 1963).

Verdone, M., and Amengual, B., *La Feks* (Lyons, 1970).

Viatkin, A. Ia., *Razgrom knig partiei trotskimma i drugikh antileninskikh grupp 1920–1925 gg.* (Leningrad, 1966).
Zalkind, A. B., *Ocherki kul'tury revoliutsionnogo vremeni* (Moscow, 1922).


CHAPTER 7

Arskii, *Kavkaz i ego znachenie dlia sovetskoi Rossii* (Petrograd, 1921).
Averbakh, L., *Na putiakh kul'turnoi revoliutsii* (Moscow, 1929).
Bukharin, N. I., *Put' k sotsializmu i raboche-krest'ianskii blok* (Moscow, 1926).
—— *ABC of Communism* (London, 1969).
Carr, E. H., *A History of Soviet Russia*, 7 vols. (London, 1950 onwards).
Carrere d'Encausse, H., *Lenin: Revolution and Power* (London, 1982).
Chaianov, A. V., *Theory of Peasant Economy* (London, 1966).
Chugaev, D. A. (ed.), *Natsional'no-gosudarstvennoe stroitel'stve v SSSR v perekhodnyi period ot kapitalizma k sotsializmu (1917–1936 gg.)* (Moscow, 1968), p. 353.
Daniels, R. V., *The Conscience of the Revolution* (Cambridge, Mass., 1960).
Day, R. B., 'Preobrazhensky and the Theory of the Transition Period', in *Soviet Studies*, Apr. 1975.
Deutscher, I., *Stalin: a Political Biography* (London, 1967).
Erlich, A., *The Soviet Industrialization Debate, 1924–1928* (Cambridge, Mass., 1960).
Fediukin, S. A., *Sovetskaia vlast' i burzhuaznye spetsialisty* (Moscow, 1965).
Gorky, M., *O russkom krest'ianstve* (Berlin, 1922).
Jasny, N., *Great Soviet Economists of the 1920s* (Cambridge, 1972).
Kuz'min, V. I., 'Lenin's Ideas of NEP and their Practical Realization in the USSR', in *Voprosy Istorii*, Apr. 1970.
Lewin, M., *Russian Peasants and Soviet Power* (London, 1968).
Martov, Y. I., 'Nasha Platforma', in *Sotsialisticheskii Vestnik*, 19 (4 Oct. 1922).
Molotov, V., *Na shestoi god. K itogam i perspektivam partiinoi raboty* (Moscow, 1923).
Pethybridge, R. W., 'Large-Scale Theories versus Small-Scale Realities', in *The Social Prelude to Stalinism* (London, 1974).
Schapiro, L., *The Communist Party of the Soviet Union* (London, 1970).
Serebrovsky, A. P., *Ratsionalizatsiia proizvodstva i novoe promyshlennoe stroitel'stvo SSSR* (Moscow, 1927).
Strumilin, S. G., *Ocherki sovetskoi ekonomii* (Moscow, 1928).
Trotsky, L., *Pravda*, articles 1, 2, 16, 17, 20, 22 Sept. 1926.
Ulam, A. B., *Lenin and the Bolsheviks, the Intellectual and Political History of the Triumph of Communism in Russia* (London, 1966).

Uratadze, G., *Vospominaniia gruzinskogo sotsial-demokrata* (Stanford, 1968).
Valentinov, N., *Novaia ekonomicheskaia politika i krizis partii posle smerti Lenina* (Stanford, 1971).
*Vsesoiuznaia perepis' naseleniia 1926 g.* (Moscow, 1927).

CHAPTER 8

Bakhutov, A., 'Bezrabotitsa v SSSR i bor'ba s nei', *Vestnik truda*, 11 (1927).
*Dokumenty trudovoi slavy Moskvichei 1919–1965* (Moscow, 1967).
Dogadov, A., *Sostoianie professional'nogo dvizheniia v SSSR* (Moscow, 1927).
*Fabrichno-zavodskie sluzhashchie v SSSR (chislennost', sostav, zarabotnaia plata)* (Moscow, 1929).
Gaponenko, L. S., *Rabochii klass Rossii v 1917 godu* (Moscow, 1970).
Guinsburg, L., *Sostoianie rabochego klassa SSSR* (Moscow, 1927).
Il'inskii, V., *Biudzhet rabochikh SSSR v 1922–1926 godakh* (Moscow, 1928).
Ioffe, P., 'Proizvodstvennye soveshchaniia v 1-m polugodii 1926/7 khoz. goda', *Vestnik truda*, 12 (1927).
*Istoriia Moskvy*, 6 vols. (Moscow, 1957), vol. 1.
*Itogi desiatiletia sovetskoi vlasti v tsifrakh 1917–1927 gg.* (Moscow, 1927).
*Izvestiia tekstil'noi promyshlennosti i torgovli* (1926).
Kabo, E. O., *Ocherki rabochego byta* (Moscow, 1928).
Khriashchina, A. I., *Gruppy i klassy v krest'ianstve* (Moscow, 1926).
Kritsman, L., *Tri goda novoi ekonomicheskoi politiki proletariata SSSR* (Moscow, 1924).
Matiugin, A. A., *Moskva v period vosstanovleniia narodnogo khoziaistva (1921–1925)* (Moscow, 1947).
Mints, L. D., *Agrarnoe perenaselenie i rynok trud SSSR* (Moscow, 1929).
*Moskovskaia organizatsiia komsomola na stroike sotsialisticheskoi promyshlennosti. Informatsionnyi obzor* (Moscow, 1927).
*Moskovskie bol'sheviki v bor'be s pravym i 'levym' opportunizmom 1921–1928 gg.* (Moscow, 1969).
*Moskovskii proletarii*, 1926, 1927.
*Moskva za 50 let sovetskoi vlasti* (Moscow, 1968).
NKVD, *Goroda soiuza SSR* (Moscow, 1927).
*Ocherki istorii Moskovskoi organizatssii KPSS: 1883–1965* (Moscow, 1966).
Plotnikov, V. E., 'Krest'ianskaia obshchina piati uezdov moskovskoi gubernii', *Zemleustroitel'*, 7 (1925).
*Rabochaia Moskva*, 1926.
Rashin, A. G., *Zhenskii trud v SSSR* (Moscow, 1928).

Rashin, A. G., *Fabrichno-zavodskie sluzhashchie v SSSR (chislennost', sostav, zarabotnaia plata)* (Moscow, 1929).
Rodionova, N., *Gody napriazhennogo truda iz istorii Moskovskoi partiinoi organizatsii 1921–1925 gg.* (Moscow, 1963).
Rogachevskaia, L. S., 'Rabota proizvodstvennykh soveshchanii v pervye gody industrializatsii (1926–1927)', *Istoricheskie zapiski*, 57 (Moscow, 1956).
—— *Iz istorii rabochego klassa SSSR v pervye gody industrializatsii 1926–1927 gg.* (Moscow, 1959).
—— *Likvidatsiia bezrabotitsy v SSSR, 1917–1930gg.* (Moscow, 1973).
Serebrennikov, G. N., *Zhenskii trud v SSSR* (Moscow, and Leningrad, 1934).
*Sovet deputatov trudiashchikhsia. Massovaia rabota Moskovskogo i raionnykh sovetov* (Moscow, 1927).
*Statisticheskii ezhegodnik g. Moskvy i Moskovskoi gubernii, 1914–1925* (Moscow, 1927).
*Statisticheskii otdel. Ob"edinennoe biuro promyshlennoi statistiki. Fabrichno-zavodskaia promyshlennost' gor. Moskvy i Moskovskoi gubernii, 1917–1927 gg.* (Moscow, 1928).
*Statisticheskii otdel. Fabrichno-zavodskaia promyshlennost' gor. Moskvy i Moskovskoi gubernii 1917–1927 gg.* (Moscow, 1928).
*Statisticheskii spravochnik g. Moskvy u Moskovskoi gub., 1927g.* (Moscow, 1928).
Strievskii, K., *Material'noe i kul'turnoe polozhenie moskovskikh rabochikh* (Moscow, 1929).
Sulianov, A. S., 'Shefskaia pomoshch' rabochego klassa derevne v podgotovke sotsialisticheskogo preobrazovaniia sel'skogo khoziaistva (1925–1929 gg.)', in *Rol' rabochego klassa v sotsialisticheskom preobrazovanii derevnii v SSSR* (Moscow, 1968), pp. 5–60.
Suvorov, K. I., *Istoricheskii opyt KPSS po likvidatsii bezrabotitsy (1917–1930)* (Moscow, 1968).
Trifonov, I. Ia., *Klassy i klassovaia bor'ba v SSSR v nachale NEPa (1921–1925 gg.)* (Leningrad, 1969).
*Trud*, 1926.
*Voprosy shefstva*, 1 (1920).
*Voprosy truda*, 1926.
*Vsesoiuznaya perepis' naseleniya 1926 g.*, vol. 57 (Moscow, 1928–33).
*Vsia Moskva v karmane* (Moscow, 1976).
Vydro, M. Ia., *Naselenie Moskvy. Po materialam perepisei naseleniia 1871–1970 gg.* (Moscow, 1976).

CHAPTER 9

Angarov, A., *Klassovaia bor'ba v derevne i sel'sovet* (Moscow, 1929).
Arkhipov, V. A., and Morozov, L. F., *Bor'ba protiv kapitalisticheskikh elementov v promyshlennosti i torgovle 20-e–nachalo 30-kh godov* (Moscow, 1978).
Ball, A. M., *Russia's Last Capitalists: The Nepmen, 1921–1929* (Berkeley, 1987).
Bauer, O., *Bor'ba za zemliu* (Leningrad, 1926).
Belkin, G., *Rabochii vopros v chastnoi promyshlennosti* (Moscow, 1926).
Bukharin, N., *Put' k sotsializmu i raboche-krest'ianski soiuz* (Moscow, 1926).
Buzlaeva, A., *Leniniskii plan kooperirovaniia melkoi promyshlennosti SSSR* (Moscow, 1969).
Chernyshev, I. V., *Agrarnyi vopros v Rossii* (Kursk, 1927).
Chugunov, S. I., *Rabota sel'skikh sovetov* (Moscow, 1926).
—— *Chto pokazali poslednie perevybory sovetov* (Moscow, 1926).
Danilov, V. P., 'Izuchenie istorii sovetskogo krest'ianstva', in *Sovetskaia istoricheskaia nauka ot 20-ogo do 22-ogo S'ezda KPSS* (Moscow, 1962).
—— *Sovetskaia dokolkhoznaia derevnia: naselenie, zemlepol'zovanie, khoziaistvo* (Moscow, 1977).
Dikhtiar, G. A., *Sovetskaia torgovlia v period postroeniia sotsializma* (Moscow, 1961).
Enbaeva, A. M. (ed.), *Kustarnaia promyshlennost' i promyslovaia kooperatsiia v natsional'noi respublike i oblastiach Belorusskoi SSR* (Moscow, 1928).
Feigin, V., *Kustarno-remeslennaia promyshlennost' SSSR* (Moscow, 1927).
Fridman, S. L., *Chastnyi kapital na denezhnom rynke* (Moscow, 1925).
Gaister, A., *Rassloenie sovetskoi derevni* (Moscow, 1928).
Ginzburg, A. M. (ed.), *Chastnyi kapital v narodnom khoziaistve SSSR. Materialy kommissii VSNKh SSSR* (Moscow and Leningrad, 1927).
Kaganovich, L., *Partiia i sovety* (Moscow, 1928).
Karpinskii, V., 'Nekotorye techenii v nashei politike (k voprosu o rasshirenii kruga izbiratelei', *Bol'shevik*, 11 (1929).
Khryashcheva, A., *Gruppy i klassy v krest'ianstve* (Moscow, 1926).
*Klassovoe rassloenie v sovetskoi derevne* (Moscow, 1926).
Kondurushkin, I. S., *Chastnyi kapital pered sovetskom sudom* (Moscow, 1927).
Konyukhov, G. S., *KPSS v bor'be s khlebnymi zatrudneniami v strane 1928–9* (Moscow, 1960).
Kozhikov, I., 'Sel'skie sovety i zemel'nye obshchestva', *Na agrarnom fronte*, 5 (1928).

Kozlov, N. I., *O zemel'nom obshchestve* (Moscow, 1926).

Kretov, F., *Derevnia posle revoliutsii* (Moscow, 1925).

Kritsman, L., *Geroicheskii period velikoi russkoi revoliutsii* (Moscow, 1926).

——, Popov, P., and Yakovlev, Ia. (eds.), *Sel'skoe khoziaistvo na putiakh vostanovleniia* (Moscow, 1925).

Kukushkin, Iu., *Rol' sel'skikh sovetov v sotsialisticheskom preobrazovanii derevni* (Moscow, 1962).

*Kustarnaia promyshlennost' Rossii*, vol. 3 (Moscow, n.d.).

Lebedeva, V., *B. M. Kustodiev* (Moscow, 1961).

Luzhin, A., and Rezunov, M., *Nizovoi sovetskii apparat* (Moscow, 1929).

Malikova, A., 'O sotsialisticheskom preobrazovanii melkotovarnogo uklada v promyshlennosti SSSR', in *Istoriia SSSR*, 4 (1963).

Meerson, G. *Semeino-trudovaia teoriia i differentsiatsiia krest'ianstva v Rossii* (Moscow, 1926).

*Melkaia promyshlennost' SSSR po dannym vseosoiuznoi perepisi* (Moscow, 1933).

Morozov, L. F., 'Kooperatsiia i periodizatsiia istorii bor'by s nepmanskoi burzhuaziei', *Voprosy istorii*, 12 (1964).

Morozov, L. F., *Reshaiushchii etap bor'by s NEPmanskoi burzhuaziei (1926–1929 gg.)* (Moscow, 1960).

Muranov, I., *Apparat nizovykh sovetskikh organov. Po materialam obsledvaniia* (Moscow, 1926).

Ordzhonikidze, G. K., *RkI v bor'be za uluchshenie sovetskogo apparata* (Moscow, 1929).

*Perevybory v sovety RSKSR v 1925–26 g.* (Moscow, 1926).

Pershin, P., *Uchastkovoe zemlepol'zovanie v Rossii* (Moscow, 1922).

*Postroenie Fundamenta Sotsialisticheskoi Ekonomiki v SSSR, 1926–32* (Moscow, 1926).

Preobrazhenskii, E., *Novaia ekonomika* (1st edn., Moscow, 1926).

Rees, E. A., *State Control in Soviet Russia: The Rise and Fall of the Workers' and Peasants' Inspectorate, 1920–34* (London, 1987).

Rogit, D., *Proverka raboty nizogo apparata v derevne* (Moscow, 1926).

Rosnitsky, N., *Litso derevni* (Leningrad, 1926).

Shapiro, D., *Kustarnaia promyshlennost' i narodnoe khoziaistvo SSSR* (Moscow, 1928).

Sheremeteva, N. A., and Sheremeteva, M. E., *Samoprialochnyi promysel v piatovskom kustarnom raione* (Kaluga, 1929).

Sokolov, K., *Klassovaia bor'ba v promkooperatsii* (Moscow, 1930).

Spektor, G. V., 'Raspad mnogodvornykh obshchin v samarskoi gubernii', *VZP*, 1 (1929).

Stalin, J., 'Dymovka', 26 Jan. 1925, in *Collected Works* (Moscow, 1954).

*Stenograficheskii otchet tret'ego vserossiiskogo soveshchaniia zemorganov 28 fevralia–7 marta 1928 g.* (Moscow, 1926).
Tal', B., *Istoriia krasnoi armii* (Moscow, 1929).
*Verkhne-Molozhskaia ekspeditsiia: Izvestiia Tverskogo pedagogicheskogo instituta* (Tver, 1927).
*XV s'ezd VkP(b), dekabr' 1927 goda: stenograficheskii otchet* (Moscow).
Zalkind, A. (ed.), *Chastnaia torgovlia SSR* (Moscow, 1927).
Zhirmunskii, M. M., *Chastnyi torgovyi kapital v narodnom khoziaistve SSR* (Moscow, 1927).
Zlobin, A., *Gosudarstvennyi, kooperativnyi i chastnyi kapital v tovarooborote sibirskogo kraia* (Novosibirsk, 1927).
Zlotnik, M. I., *Deiatel'nost' organov partiino-gosudarstvennogo kontrolia BSSR v gosudarstvennom stroitelstve* (Minsk, 1969).
Zolotarev, A., *Regulirovanie tovarooborota* (Khar'kov, 1926).

CHAPTER 10

*Belorusskaia SSR* (Minsk, 1927).
Bobryshev, N., *Melko-burzhuazhnye vliania sredi molodezhi* (Moscow, 1926).
Danilov, V. P., *Rural Russia under the New Regime* (London, 1988).
*Fabrichno-zavodskaia promyshlennost' v period 1913–1918 gg.* (Moscow, 1926).
Fainsod, M., *Smolensk under Soviet Rule* (New York, 1963).
Gagarin, A., *Khoziaistvo, zhizn' i nastroenie derevni po itogam obsledovaniia Pochinkovskoi volosti Smolenskoi gubernii* (Moscow, 1925).
Golubykh, M., *Ocherki glukhoi derevni* (Moscow, 1926).
*Gubernskii statisticheskii otdel: predvaritel'nye itogi* (Smolensk, 1927).
*Iz istorii Smolenskogo kraia* (Smolensk, 1958).
*Izvestia TsK*, 4 (Mar. 1922).
*Kollektivatsiia sel'skogo khoziaistva v zapadnom raione RSFSR (1921–1932 gg.): sbornik dokumentov* (Smolensk, 1968).
*Kommunisticheskaia partiia Belorussii v rezoliutsiiakh i resheniakh s'ezdov i plenumov Tsk*, vol. 1 (Minsk, 1973).
*Komsomolskaia pravda*, Apr.–June and Sept.–Oct. 1926.
Liubimov, I. E., *Komsomol v sovetskom stroitel'stve 1917–27* (Moscow, 1928).
Molotov, V. M., *Politika partii v derevne: stat'l i rechi* (Moscow, 1927).
Murin, V. A., *Byt i nravy derevenskoi molodezhi* (Moscow, 1926).
*Nasha praktika v derevne* (Moscow, 1925).
NKVD RSFSR, *Goroda soiuza SSR* (Moscow, 1927).
*Ocherki tovarnykh otraslei sel'skogo khoziaistva SSSR v sviazi s kreditovaniem* (Moscow, 1926).

*Partiinye, professional'nye i kooperativnye organy i gosapparat k XIV s'ezdu RKP(b)* (Moscow, 1926).

*Perevybory v sovety RSFSR v 1925–6 g.* (Moscow, 1926).

*Predvaritel'nie itogi vseoiuznoi perepisi naselenii 1926 goda po Smolenskoi gubernii* (Smolensk, 1927).

Rakov, A. A., *Naselenie BSSR* (Minsk, 1969).

Rosenberg, W. G., 'Smolensk in the 1920s: Party-Worker Relations and the "Vanguard" Problem', *Russian Review*, 36 (1977), pp. 127–50.

Rudnev, A. G., *Biblioteka im. Lenina v g. Smolenske; opyt organizatsii, tekhnicheskogo oborudovaniia i deiatel'nost' za piat' let* (Smolensk, 1927).

*Sel'skoe khoziaistvo SSSR 1925–1928. Sbornik statisticheskikh svedenii* (Moscow, 1929).

Smidovich, S., 'Otmenit' li registratsiiu braka i sistemu alimentov', *Komsomol'skaia Pravda*, 37/220 (1926).

Smolensk Archive.

Sokolnikov, G. (ed.), *Soviet Policy in Public Finance* (Stanford, 1931).

*Sotsial'nyi i natsional'nyi sostav VKP(b): itogi vsesoiuznoi partiinoi perepisi 1927 g.* (Moscow, 1928).

*Sotsial'nyi i natsional'nyi sostav VKP(B)* (Moscow, 1928).

Taradin, I., *Sloboda Roven'ki, Voronezhskaia derevnia*, first issue (Voronezh, 1926).

*VI s'ezd kommunisticheskoi partii Belorussii, stenograficheskii otchet* (Minsk, 1922).

*VII s"ezd vsesoiuznogo leninskogo kommunisticheskogo soiuza molodezhi: stenographicheskii otchet*, 11–22 Mar. 1926.

Zheleznov, F., *Bol'sheverezhskaia volost', Voronezhskaia derevnia* (Voronezh, 1926).

CHAPTER 11

Baedeker, K., *Russia* (London, 1914).

Basiubin, V., *Opyt raboty Moskovskogo strakhkassa 1925–1929* (Moscow, 1930).

Bol'shakov, A., *Krest'ianskie biudzhety podgorodnoi derevni. Trudy Leningradskogo obshchestva izucheniia mestnogo kraia*, vol. 1 (Leningrad, 1927).

——— *Derevniia 1917–27* (Moscow, 1927).

Borders, K., *Village Life under the Soviets* (New York, 1927).

*Dal'nie ekskursii po Tverskoi gubernii* (Tver, 1928).

Dmitrenko, S. L., 'Sostav mestnykh partiinykh komitetov v 1924–1927 gg.', in *Istoricheskie zapiski*, 79 (1966).

*Doklad gubzdrava* (Tver, 1926).

Donskoi, M., 'Kontrol'nye tsifry po zdravokhraneniiu na 1926–7 g.', *Biulleten' narodnogo kommissariata zdravokhraneniia RSFSR*, 19 (Moscow, 1926).

'Finansirovanie zdravokhranenie po gosudarstvennomu biudzhetu u prochim istochnikam', *Biulleten' narodnogo kommissariata zdravokhraneniia RSFSR*, 21 (Moscow, 1927).

*Führer durch die Sovjetunion* (Moscow, 1925).

*Kontrol'nye tsifry narodnogo khoziaistva SSSR na 1928–9 god* (1929).

*Kontrol'nye tsifry narodnogo khoziaistva na 1926–7 god* (Moscow, 1926).

*Kul'turnoe stroitel'stvo SSSR* (Moscow, 1956).

*Lenin i Tverskoi krai* (Moscow, 1969).

Liubimov, I. E., *Dva napravleniia v kooperatsii* (Moscow, 1927).

Lunacharsky, A., and Shokhin, A., *K edinoi sisteme narodnogo obrazovaniia* (Moscow, 1929).

*Mirovoe khoziaistvo. Sbornik statisticheskikh materialov za 1913–1922 gg.* (Moscow, 1928).

Miterev, G. A., *XXV let sovetskogo zdravokhraneniia* (Moscow, 1944).

*Nasha praktika v derevne* (Moscow, 1925).

Nosov, N., 'Perspektivy razvitiia sel'skoi uchastkovoi seti', *Biulleten' narodnogo kommissariata zdravokhraneniia RSFSR*, 20 (1926).

*Otchet o rabote Kurskogo goroda za 20 marta 1927 do 1 oktobriia 1928 g.* (Kursk, 1928).

*Otchet XV Tverskomu uezdnomu s'ezdu sovetov rabochikh, krest'ianskikh i krasnoarmeiskikh deputatov ispolkomiteta xiv sozyva o rabote za period 1 oktiabria 1925 goda do 1 ianvariia 1927 goda* (Tver, 1928).

Pascal, P., *Civilisation paysanne en Russie* (Lausanne, 1969).

*Pervye shagi industrializatsii SSSR 1926–7 gg.* (Moscow, 1959).

Pethybridge, R. W., 'Large-Scale Theories versus Small-Scale Realities', in *The Social Prelude to Stalinism* (London, 1974).

*Piatnadsatyi s"ezd VKP(B)*, vol. 2 (Moscow, 1962).

*Pis'ma Tveriakov k Leninu* (Moscow, 1973).

Rogachevskaia, S., *Iz istorii rabochego klassa SSSR v pervye gody industrializatsii 1926–1927 gg.* (Moscow, 1959).

*Sbornik dekretov po rasshireniu prav mestnykh sovetov: ofitsial'noe izdanie Orgotdela Prezidiuma Tverskogo gubispolkoma* (Tver, 1928).

*Sbornik dokumentov po zemel'nomu zakonodatel'stvu SSSR i RSFSR, 1917–1954 gg.* (Moscow, 1954).

Sonin, M., *Vosproizvodstvo rabochei sily v SSSR i balans truda* (Moscow, 1959).

*Soveshchanie po voprosam sovetskogo stroitel'stva* (Moscow, 1925).

Shteinberg, A. P., *Oktiabr' i sotsialisticheskoe strakhovanie* (Moscow, 1925).

*Statisticheskii spravochnik po Tverskoi gubernii* (Tver, 1929).
*Statisticheskii spravochnik za 1928* (Moscow, 1929).
Strumilin, S. G. (ed.), *Lesnye bogatstva SSSR* (Moscow, 1925).
*Transport i sviaz'* (Moscow, 1972).
*Tverskaia guberniia v 1926–1928 gg. K otchetu gubispolkoma k XVI gubs'ezdu sovetov* (Tver, 1929).
*Tverskaia pravda* (1926).
*Verkhne-Molozhskaia ekspeditsiia: izvestiia Tverskogo pedagogicheskogo instituta* (Tver, 1927).
*Vlast' sovetov*, 16 (1926).
*Voprosy ekonomicheskogo raionirovanii* (Moscow, 1957).
*Vos'moi s"ezd professional'nykh soiuzov SSSR* (Moscow, 1929).
Westwood, J. N., *A History of Russian Railways* (London, 1964).
*Zdravokhranenie v SSSR: statisticheskii sbornik* (Moscow, 1960)

## Chapter 12

Abdykalykova, M., and Pankratova, A., *Istoriia kazakhskoi SSR* (Alma-Ata, 1943).
*Akademiia nauk kazakhskoi SSR: Izvestiia: seriia obschchestvennaia* (Alma-Ata, 1970).
Arutiunian, Iu. V., 'Izmenenie sotsial'noi struktury sovetskikh natsii', *Istoriia SSSR*, 4 (1972).
Barag, T. Ia., *Karaganda* (Moscow, 1950).
Baronov, S. F., Bukeikhan, A. N., and Rudenko, S. I., *Kazaki: Antropologicheskie ocherki* (Leningrad, 1927).
Bennigsen, A., and Broxup, M., *The Islamic Threat to the Soviet State* (London, 1983).
Chambre, H., 'Le Kazakhstan: Tiers-monde soviétique?', in *Union soviétique et développement économique* (Paris, 1967).
Chulanov, G., *Ocherki istorii narodnogo khoziaistva Kazakhskoi SSR* (Alma-Ata, 1962).
Dakshleiger, G. F., *Sotsial'no-ekonomicheskaia preobrazovaniia v aule i derevne Kazakhstana 1921–1929* (Alma-Ata, 1965).
Davydov, M. M., 'Obshchie predposylki k vodokhoziaistvennomu planu na blizhaishie 15–20 let do iuzhnoi chasti KASSR', *Narodnoe khoziaistvo Kazakhstana*, 4 (1926).
Dmitrenko, L., 'Sostav mestnykh partiinikh komitetov v 1924–1927 gg.', *Istoricheskie zapiski*, 79 (1966).
Gafurova, K. A., 'Ideologicheskaia bor'ba v Srednei Azii i Kazakhstane v pervye gody sovetskoi vlasti', *Voprosy istorii* (1973).
Gapeev, A. A., *Karaganda i ee znachenie v industrializatsii SSSR* (Moscow, 1931).

Goloshchekin, F. I., *Partiinoe stroitel'stvo v Kazakhstane* (Moscow, 1930).

Hostler, W., *Turkism and the Soviets*, (London, 1957).

Hudson, A. E., 'Kazakh Social Structure', *Yale University Publications on Anthropology*, 20 (Yale, 1938).

*Iz istorii partiinogo stroitel'stva v Kazakhstane* (Alma-Ata, 1936).

Kazakh SSR, Gosudarstvennaia planovaia komissiia. *10 let Kazakstana 1920–1930* (Alma-Ata, 1930).

Kazakh SSR, Tsentral'nyi ispolnitel'nyi komitet. *Materialy k otchetu na 3 sessii VTSIK 13-go sozyyva* (Kzyl-Orda, 1928).

Kazakhstanskaia ekspeditsiia, 1927, and Antropologicheskii otriad, *Kazaki: sbornik statei antropologicheskogo otriada Kazakhstanskoi ekspeditsii Akademii nauk SSSR. Issledovanie 1927 g.*

Kuchkin, A. P., *Sovetizatsiia kazakhskogo aula 1926–1928 gg.* (Moscow, 1962).

*Materialy k otchetu tsentral'nogo ispolitel'nogo komiteta KSSR na 3 sessii VTsIK 13-ogo sozyva* (Kzyl-Orda, 1928).

*Narodnoe khoziaistvo Kazakhstana*, 5 (Kzyl-Orda, 1927).

Nusupbekov, A. N., *Formirovanie i razvitie sovetskogo rabochego klassa v Kazakhstane (1917–1940 gg.)* (Alma-Ata, 1966).

Olcott, M. B., *The Kazakhs* (Indiana University Press, Bloomington, 1987).

Prokopovich, G. F., 'Problemy zheleznodorozhnoi stroitel'stva v Kazakhstane', *Narodnoe khoziaistvo Kazakhstana*, 2 (Kzyl-Orda, 1926).

Ryskulov, T. R., *Kazakhstan* (Moscow, 1927).

Shorish, M. M., 'Soviet Development Strategies in Central Asia', *Canadian Slavonic Papers*, 17/2 and 3 (1975).

Shvetsov, S. P. (ed.), *Kazakskoe khoziaistvo v ego estestvenno-istoricheskikh i bytovykh usloviiakh* (Leningrad, 1925).

'The Social Structure and Customs of the Kazakhs', *Central Asian Review*, 5/1 (1957).

Togzhanov, G., 'Kazakhskaia literatura', *Literaturnaia entsiklopediia*, vol. 5 (Moscow, 1931).

Vitsman, L. E. 'Planovaia elektrifikatsiia Kazakhstana', *Narodnoe khoziaistvo Kazakhstana*, 4 (1927).

Voshchinin, V. P., *Kazakstan* (Moscow, 1929).

Wheeler, G., *The Modern History of Soviet Central Asia* (London, 1964).

Zhdanko, T. A., 'Nomadizm v Srednei Azii i Kazakhstane', *Istoriia, arkheologiia i etnografiia srednei Azii* (Moscow, 1968).

# Index

Bolsheviks (*cont.*)
  and kustari 318–19, 322, 324
  and local party initiatives 153–4
  model of history 4–8
  and national minorities 250
  and nepmen 314–17
  party network and local
    communications 23–4
  party organization 152–4
  and peasants 327–30
  and political control 51–4, 56–7
  and Poltava, orphanage at 85–6
  and press 141–4
  and promotion of science 265–8
  and railways 121–2, 128–32
  and Red Army 54
  and Ukraine 257–8
Briusov, V. 223
Bryce, Viscount J. 217
Bukharin, N. I. 214, 283, 341, 401
  and administration of the
    economy 235, 244–5, 247, 249
  and attack on Georgia 255–6
  and cultural problems 261, 263
  and kustari 322–4, 328
  and proletariat 270–3
  and rural Soviets 297, 300
  and smychka 293
bureaucracy
  and Bolsheviks 11–12
  in Smolensk (1926) 343–5, 350
  in Soviet Union 149–50
Butterfield, Herbert 3, 417

Carr, E. H. 6–8, 13, 199, 242
Central Committee of Communist
    Party, control over local
    parties 154–6
Central Control Committee 289,
    293, 301
  and *Rabkrin* 162–4, 302–3, 306–7
central control from
    Moscow 228–35, 417
Chagall, M. 218
Chaianov, A. V. 248–9
Chekov, Anton 412, 420
cinema 201–7
  in Petrograd 202, 204–5, 207
class in Soviet Union 327
Commissariat of Ways and
    Communications 125–6, 127
communications 121–44
  air travel 126–7

and centralist attitudes of
    Bolsheviks 145–6
  in Middle Volga 101–3, 106
  and rivers 126
  roads 126
  to Tver 38–3
Communist party
  cells: in localities 290–1, 293–7;
    and *Rabkrin* 306
  coercion by 347–8
  in Kazakhstan 398–9;
    organization of 403–5
  membership 159–60; and
    committee control 160–1; and
    peasants 151–2; in Smolensk
    (1926) 341–2
  in Smolensk (1926) 342–6
  in Tver 368
  women in 354–9
courts 172–5
culture
  and ideology 208–14
  in Moscow 226
  and new economic policy:
    control 50–1;
    monitoring 207–8; problems
    of 261–8
  of Petrograd 192–201

Dan, F. 153
Danilov, V. P. 338
Davies, R. W. 242
determinism in history of Soviet
    Union 3–6
Deutscher, I. 16–17
D'iakov, D. A. 70, 72
disease and famine 106–7
Dostoevsky, F. 269
Duncan, Isadora 3
Duranty, Walter 176
Durkheim, E. 11, 309
Dzerzhinsky, Felix 103, 155, 185,
    227, 271, 277, 338
  and Georgia 255
  in Siberia 128–31, 145

economic regional planning 180–2
economy
  administration of 236–50
  of Kursk 69–71
education
  at Poltava 86–7
  and ideology 218–19

post and telecommunications 127
Pozner, V. 105
Preobrazhensky, E. 157, 182, 231,
    245, 356
Preobrazhensky, P. F. 209, 244
press 135–44
    and Bolsheviks 141–4
    and Eleventh Party Congress 138
    and national minorities 140–1
    and railway workers 139–40
    and Red Army 140
    in Tver 384
Prokopovich, S. N. 114
proletariat 269–88, 418
    in census 286
    decline in party 271–2
    differentiations of 273
    divisions of 276–7; in new
        economic policy 278
    and ideology 208–12
    of Moscow 273–88
    and party policy 270–1
    productivity in new economic
        policy 279–80
publications
    distribution of 215–16
    on ideology 208–11, 213–18
publishing
    and new economic policy 50
    in Petrograd 196–7, 216

*Rabkrin* 87, 115
    and Central Control
        Committee 302–3, 306–7
    decline 162
    operation of 165–8
    origins 161–2
    and rural Soviets 299–300
    as supervisory organization 149,
        150
    and Tver 369–70
Radek, Karl 187
radio 128
railways
    in 1926 379–80
    in Belorussia 132–3, 338
    and Bolshevik party 121–2,
        128–32
    freight transport 123–4
    and government 128–32
    in Kazakhstan 392–3
    passenger transport 124–5
    role of 125–6

workers in 131–3; and press 139
Rakovsky, K. 258
Ransome, Arthur 3
Recht, Charles 204
Red Army 54, 77
    and famine 99, 108
    and party membership 151
    and press 140
    in Smolensk (1926) 347–8
refugees from famine in Middle
        Volga 104
religion
    in Kazakhstan 400
    in Kursk 63–4, 67
    in Middle Volga 98, 107–8, 109
    in Smolensk (1926) 359–61
religion in Belorussia 35–9
Riazanov, D. 209
Rigby, T. H. 186, 187
rivers 126
roads 126
Romanov, P. 356
Rosenberg, W. G. 339
Rosnitsky, N. 291–2, 294, 309
Rudzutak, Ia. E. 165
rural–urban migration 277, 282
    to Moscow 284–6
Russell, Bertrand 2
Rykov, A. 15, 113, 181–2, 227, 233,
        317
Ryskulov, Turar 400, 403

Samara 91
    famine in 96–7, 99, 106
    *see also* Middle Volga
Saratov 91
    communications 101–2
    famine in 97, 101, 104, 106–7
    *see also* Middle Volga
Savrasov, A. K. 60
Schenk, Joseph 204
science, promotion of 265–8
Secret Police 128, 131, 168, 232
Serapion Brothers 193–8, 200–1
Service, Robert 186
Shafir, R. 143
Shanin, T. 11
*shefstvo* movement 55–6, 283–4
Shklovsky, V. 199, 202
Siberia
    agriculture in 62
    and Civil war 130
    railways in 128–31, 145